KU-242-929

FREEMASONRY
The Reality

Acknowledgements

I would like to thank the following for their help and
encouragement on the long and winding road
that led to this book:
Lord and Lady Northampton, my agent Fiona Spencer Thomas,
Philip Wilkinson, Julian Perry, Dr Christopher McIntosh,
Michael Embleton, Geraldine and Bali at the Atlantis Bookshop,
Professor Nicholas Goodrick-Clarke, David and Belinda Parsons-
Scott, Jim and Pattie Parsons, Helène and Andrew Symington,
Carol McGilvery, Julian Rees, Martin Faulks, Matthew Scanlan,
Michael Baigent, Geoffrey Baber, Tuvia Fogel, Ranald
McWilliam, The Mainwaring Arms (Whitmore), my mother
and father – Victor and Patricia Churton –
and, above all, my wife, Joanna.

This book is dedicated to all those who understand that
truth
and self-interest are identical.

Also by Tobias Churton

Miraval – A Quest (Weidenfeld & Nicolson, 1989)
The Fear of Vision (poetry; the Lichfield Press, 1995)
The Gnostics (Barnes & Noble, 1997)
The Golden Builders (Red Wheel-Weiser, 2004)
Gnostic Philosophy (Inner Traditions, 2005)
The Magus of Freemasonry (Inner Traditions, 2006)
Kiss of Death – the True History of the Gospel of Judas
(Watkins, 2008)
Invisibles (Lewis Masonic, 2009

FREEMASONRY
The Reality

Tobias Churton

Lewis Masonic

First published in hardback 2007
This paperback edition first published 2009

ISBN 978 0 85318 330 3

All rights reserved. No part of this book may be reproduced or transmitted
in any form or by any means, electronic or mechanical, including
photocopying, recording or by any information storage and retrieval system,
without permission from the Publisher in writing.

© Tobias Churton 2007/09

Published by Lewis Masonic

an imprint of Ian Allan Publishing Ltd,
Hersham, Surrey KT12 4RG.
Printed by CPI Mackays,
Chatham, Kent ME5 8TD

Contents

Contents

List of Illustrations

Figure 1. The 'son' accepts the secrets from the master; engraving by Robert Vaughan in Ashmole's *Theatrum Chemicum Britannicum*, 1652.

Figure 2. Presumed 'Master's chair', probably owned by Edward Minshull, dated 1595, now in the possession of Lord Northampton, Pro Grand Master, United Grand Lodge of England (photograph used by permission).

Figure 3. Unique carving on chair of 1597, in possession of Lord Northampton, – possibly one of a pair formerly owned by Edward Minshull (photograph used by permission).

Figure 4. Entrance to Stoke Hall (private), near Nantwich, once home to Edward Minshull, father to Ellen Mainwaring.

Figure 5. Stoke Hall (private), near Nantwich, formerly home of Edward Minshull, as it is today.

Figure 6. Tomb of Sir Philip Mainwaring (d.1647) and Ellen (*née* Minshull, d.1656), by John Stone, King's Master Mason.

Figure 7. Combined arms of Mainwaring (left) and Minshull families; tomb of Sir Philip and Lady Ellen Mainwaring, church of St Lawrence, Upper Peover, Cheshire, 1656, by John Stone, King's Master Mason, Windsor 1666–1667.

Figure 8. Acton church, near Nantwich, Cheshire.

Figure 9. Tomb of Sir William Mainwaring, of Baddiley and Peover, (d.1399), Acton church, near Nantwich, Cheshire.

Figure 10. Tomb of Sir Thomas and Lady Wilbraham, Acton, Cheshire, thought to be the work of Edward Marshall, King's Master Mason.

Figure 11. The octagonal tower of Nantwich church, Cheshire, once filled with monuments to the Mainwaring, Minshull and Wilbraham families.

Figure 12. 17th century brass plaque to Richard Minshull, Nantwich church, Cheshire.

Figure 29. Cloth from *Friendship* lodge No 100, Great Yarmouth (1809).

Figure 30. Cloth from *Friendship* lodge No 100, Great Yarmouth, originally meeting in Norwich (dated 1809).

Figure 31. Striking third degree cloth from *Friendship* lodge No 100, which used to meet in Norwich (dated 1809).

Figure 32. Tracing board found at Bristol (19th century).

Figure 33. Tracing board from Bristol (19th century).

Figure 33b. Unusual tracing board found at Bristol.

Figs.34-36. Unique circular boards (18 inch diameter) from lodge No 24, Newcastle on Tyne.

Figure 37. Board designed by Brother Jacobs of 3, Charles Street, Hatton Gardens, London.

Figure 38. Second degree board designed by Jacobs of Hatton Gardens; similar to a set in lodge *Freedom* No 77, Gravesend.Figure 39. Fascinating design for a third degree tracing board by Brother Jacobs of Hatton Gardens, London (mid 19th century).

Figure 40. First degree tracing board from *Royal Naval* lodge No 59.

Figure 41. Second degree tracing board from *Royal Naval* lodge No 59.

Figure 42. Interesting oriental style third degree tracing board from *Royal Naval* lodge No 59 (19th century).

Figure 43. Board from *All Souls* lodge No 170, Weymouth.

Figure 44. Second degree board from *All Souls* lodge No 170, Weymouth.

Figure 45. Striking board showing Hiram lying in state in the temple; *All Souls* lodge No 170, Weymouth.

Figure 46. Framed cloth from the *Loyal Cambrian* lodge No 110, Merthyr Tydvil, constituted 1810.

Figure 47. Framed cloth from the *Loyal Cambrian* lodge No 110, combining Royal Arch and craft Freemasonry.

Figure 64. The Rose gives her honey to the Bees, from *Summum Bonum*, Joachim Frizius (Robert Fludd), 1629. Masons are meant to be busy bees.

Figure 63. Man the Microcosm, from Robert Fludd's *Utriusque Cosmi…Historia*, 2nd volume, Johann Theodore de Bry, Oppenheim, 1619.

Figure 65. Amazing presentation of man as universal co-creator and Free Mason: 'At the centre of the circle, the Master Mason cannot err' – note the square at his feet; *Three Books of Occult Philosophy*, Henry Cornelius Agrippa, London, 1651.

Figure 66. Masons Avenue, off Basinghall Street, city of London – former home of the London Company of Masons.

Figure 67. Site of Masons' Hall, Masons Avenue, Basinghall Street, London.

Figure 68. Lifesize statue of Charles II, Lichfield cathedral, by Accepted Free Mason (1682), architect Sir William Wilson.

Figure 69. Title page, James Anderson's book of Free-Masons' *Constitutions*, 1723.

Figure 70. Frontispiece to Anderson's *Constitutions* (1723) showing the Duke of Montagu handing the constitutions to Philip, Duke of Wharton, watched (right) by Deputy Grand Master, JT Desaguliers.

Figure 71. Jacob Böhme, from Edward Taylor and Jacob Böhme's *Theosophick Philosophy Unfolded*, London, 1691.

Figure 72. Illustration from Jacob Böhme's 'theosophick' *Way to Christ* – the geometry of the Heart.

Figure. 73. Alchemical emblem from Malachias Geiger's *Microcosmus hypochondriacus sive de melancolia hypochondriaca*, Munich 1651, engraved by Jan Sadeler (1568–1665), *Bibliotheca Philosophica Hermetica*, Amsterdam.

Figure 74. Title page: *Narrative of a Journey through the Upper Provinces of India*, by Reginald Heber DD, bishop of Calcutta, John Murray, 1828.

Introduction

To be intelligible is to be found out.
(Oscar Wilde – Freemason)

Always read the small print. Things are revealed when the thought behind them is clear and true. Those who promise 'revelations' always seem to be holding something back; usually, it is ignorance.

There appear to be three types of book published on Freemasonry. First, those books that cater for lodge members – ritual books, inspiring stories from masonic history, any number of works on masonic medals, costume and memorabilia. Second, books that use elements of masonic lore to weave speculative stories - stories often couched in sensationalist terms. Fun to read, they tend to obscure more valid stories behind them. The road of excess leads to the palace of confusion.

On the whole, books written for practising Freemasons tend to play down symbolism, spirituality and esoteric content. The stress is usually on cementing community and relationships. In speculative books, however, the typical masonic experience – turning up for monthly meetings and raising funds for charity – seems to get lost altogether, such is the barrage of half-baked, pseudo-mystical titillation and conspiracy theory. The 'revelations' fail to satisfy the curiosity evoked; there is no revelation – only the hint of one.

These two classes of book are flatly opposed by a third class purporting to 'reveal the truth' behind Freemasonry. These books are usually hostile to the craft. Authors of these books tend to be influenced by the climate of conspiracy of the second class, but find in the mythic confusion nothing but dark intentions. It is not unknown for hostile authors – those who suppose Freemasons to be involved in immoral activities of covert influence and control – to be forced to invent a kind of super-class of 'men in black'/'gnomes of Zurich' or *éminences grises* to explain the obvious innocence and ordinariness of Freemasons.

The first known 'exposure' of the craft derives from religious fanaticism in the late 17th century. You might think there was nothing left to 'expose'!

Hostile exposures have been enormously influential. They have given Freemasonry the reputation of being a 'secret society'. Secrets are taken to be synonymous with conspiracy.

We all have secrets; are we all conspirators?

It is not unknown to hear that the three degrees of Freemasonry are perfectly OK (if you like that sort of thing), but the 'dodgy' stuff can be found among members of 'higher degrees'. These degrees – Knights Templar, Rose Croix, and so on – attract interest as a result – though not, I observe, huge influxes of new recruits who actually want to experience the real thing!

We like our fictions, but they do tend to colour our perception of everyday life. When a thing is magnified, its true proportion is distorted. Monsters were portrayed like medieval devils or hideously deformed people until the microscope gave us magnified images of spiders, beetles and microorganisms. Cinema completed the process, by magnifying the innocent and natural into the scary and supernatural. The invasion of the GIANT spiders! Magnification is a benefit to science, but when applied to popular culture, it changes our sense of the real.

Freemasonry has been magnified. It is persistently presented outside of its true proportions. To be sure, you will find more secrecy in the workings of elected governments (often with very serious implications for life, limb and pocket) than you will ever find in the running of masonic fraternities.

You get the idea.

Given the extent of so much dis-information and bad information, I thought it worthwhile to attempt an open look at the reality of Freemasonry. It has been a valuable experience to serve as lecturer on Freemasonry at Exeter University's

Department of Humanities and Social Sciences. Dealing with the interests of students who naturally want to know everything has helped me to take up the objective position so rarely, if ever, found among writers on the subject. Students, on the whole, want the facts. They demand objectivity, fairness, and a sense of humour.

There have been many defences of Freemasonry, attacks on Freemasonry, investigations of masonic history, analyses of masonic philosophy, and many useful detailed approaches to the evidence, mostly written by masons themselves. What I have been unable to find is an objective, standard account that yet has the courage to go beneath the surface of the 'official version'.

There are many reasons for this lack of a standard work, not the least of which is the fact that masons have themselves long been unable to satisfy questions put to them on any number of aspects of the craft. And if *they* cannot give you the answers, who can?

In Germany, under Hitler, the Nazi High Command decided that Freemasons were all part of a 'Masonic-Jewish conspiracy' to dominate the world – and fascists were not slow in publishing this propaganda wherever they could, especially in the Middle East, which still suffers from its effects. Everyone who wants to take over the world will tell you they're only trying to save you from a fate worse than them!

Nevertheless, in spite of being so absolutely certain of their imagined conspiracy, the Nazi SS still had to commission a serious study of the subject because it lacked hard information. Like so many bad historians, first they had the theory then they looked for the 'evidence' to try and back it up.

Across the English Channel, and in our own time, Chris Mullin MP launched a Commons Select Committee investigation of Freemasonry in Britain roughly co-incident with Tony Blair's ascension to power in 1997. Grand Secretary Michael Higham's videotaped interrogation by members of the committee stimulated some (non-mason) observers to write to the papers comparing the outrageous scenes with the anti-communist excesses of the House Un-American Activities Committee during the McCarthyite era.

When asked by journalist Doug Pickford what his chief source of information on Freemasonry was, Chris Mullin MP cited Martin Short's undeniably hostile exposé, *Inside the Brotherhood*. Whatever else its merits, Short's book was not an objective academic study.

It is often said that truth is stranger than fiction. We can try to aim at the truth, but sometimes the evidence is difficult to understand, or to interpret definitively. Facts alone may tell us very little; they do not stand in isolation. Motives are seldom easy to ascertain. We rarely have the facility of forensic evidence, and, to be sure, we do not always need it. After all, we are not attempting to nail a conviction before the evidence 'goes cold'. Most of the evidence for – or against – Freemasonry went cold a very long time ago, and we cannot, with the best will in the world, revivify corpses. Nor can a book of this size hope to include every fact or detail of the subject that some readers might want or expect to find.

My aim is to establish a standard overview of a vast, complex – and fascinating – subject that does not duck the most difficult questions. If I can convey some of that genuine fascination while at the same time giving interested readers a clear picture of the reality of Freemasonry, I shall hope to be acquitted of all crimes against either truth or prejudice.

Freemasonry and the Grand Lodge idea

Readers should be aware of an important distinction. There is a 'thing' called Freemasonry that has grown and changed over time. 'Freemasonry' consists of ideas, concepts, moral convictions, hybrid theologies and knowledge both practical and spiritual. The spiritual content – being spiritual – cannot change and has not changed. We do not know when this spiritual content first appeared; it certainly pre-dates the appearance of the word 'Freemasonry', the meaning of which we shall discuss in due course.

Then there are a number of organisations – the most significant of which is undoubtedly the United Grand Lodge of England – which hope to practise Freemasonry by inviting or permitting people to 'become Freemasons'. No organisation likes to believe that it is out of touch with significant aspects of the thing it claims to practise. However, it is a tendency of Grand Lodge to regard itself as the precise embodiment of what 'Freemasonry' is. By declaring itself to be the true home of 'regular Freemasonry', the United Grand Lodge of England suggests that anything within its field with which it does not agree is 'irregular' Freemasonry. It is a short step then to take 'irregular' Freemasonry as meaning a false or illegitimate version of the 'pure thing', presuming that is what you have.

As the Roman Church defines its authority in terms of its creeds and the canonical interpretation of those creeds, so does the United Grand Lodge of England define its authority in terms of its perception of 'regularity'. The nature, source and validity of this claim will be discussed in this book.

Regulated Freemasonry undoubtedly existed before the appearance of the first self-appointed 'Grand Lodge'.

The Problems of Modernism

The 19th century was an exciting time if you were in the right place with the right connections. This period has, however, left a number of frightful legacies. Nobody would deny that the typical Victorian go-getter, like *Sunny Jim*, leapt high o'er the fields in leaps and bounds, confident of his undoubted *Force*, both moral and military. Nevertheless, the power and extent of his leaping could prove highly destructive – and blindly optimistic – to those following his trail.

The widespread wrecking of many of our ancient churches and chapels through wanton acts of misguided renovation, profiteering and bad architectural concepts is just one of the Victorians' questionable legacies.

Another legacy of doubtful value lies in that period's confident embrace of scientific modes of analysis in areas unsuited to strict, unmodified scientific discipline. This embrace manifested itself in a mania for categorisation, noticeable today in the fields of anthropology, archaeology and history generally. Thus, we find that something called the 'middle ages' ended about the time of the battle of Bosworth in 1485, being replaced not with the 'later ages' – or even the 'last ages' – but various kinds of eras imagined to be the precursors of the 'modern era'.

The 'modern era' was of course the 19th century – supposed as the very summit of enlightenment and 'progress'. The conceit carried on – or 'progressed' – into the 20th century, where we see 'modern warfare' along with 'modern medicine', 'modern music', 'modern architecture' and so on.

Since the 'modern era' was generally identified with literacy, recognition of 'human rights', liberal emancipation in political society and other things regarded as indubitably *good*, there were always going to be problems with things like 'modern warfare'. Modern warfare was undoubtedly a shining example of applied science - think of all those bristling shells trundling off the *Krupp* assembly line. The results of their utility, however, more resembled 'medieval' depictions of hell than the promised utopias of the era.

Only a truly 'modern' fool could say the war had been fought to end all war. When 'modern warfare' really found its feet with Nazi Blitzkrieg tactics and the rationalised mass murder of civilians, the apostles of modernism were quick to point out that this sort of thing – when done by Germans – was nothing less than a throwback to the middle or dark ages! So much for 'modern warfare'!

The atrocities of modern war were not the work of medieval princes, but of modern men whose minds were formed in the crucible of 19th century science. Hitler's self-justification was a rigorously applied theory of the survival of the fittest – Nature's way, according to the science of Darwin.

The defining of the past in terms of the optimism and confidence of the present simply does not work.

One notable category in the assessment of civilisations, informed by contemporary ideas of the 'modern' and the 'enlightened', was the importance given to literacy and book learning. The 'scientific historians' of the 19th century defined culture largely in terms of developed literacy. If you could not read the writings of a particular civilisation, the chances were that that civilisation was not civilised! This must be so (it was held) since civilisation has been defined in terms of literacy and literature. This was good news for the Greeks and Romans, bad news for 'oral traditions'.

Even the Bible's former dignity would suffer mercilessly at the hands of German theologians who decided that the gospel records – indeed all religious records – depended heavily on 'oral tradition'. This could mean only one thing. These records did not conform to the needs of science. Therefore, they were questionable. The men of Jesus' era were often thus dismissed as 'illiterate peasants', and their beliefs as fantastical or superstitious.

Ancient spiritual traditions such as those residing in the bosom of the Yezidi people of Transcaucasia, for example, were generally dismissed as irrelevant to scholarship since they cleaved to no written tradition. The faith was passed over by word of mouth. This was not good enough for science or 'scientific history'. Once you could decide that the Yezidis' *religion* did not require much respect, you could soon reach the conclusion that the Yezidi *people* deserved no special respect.

In this atmosphere of scientific confidence, Freemasonry suffered particularly badly – at the hands, curiously enough, of its own 'educated' members. Not wishing to be consigned to the bin of superstition, modern Freemasons turned against their own traditions.

Until relatively recently, Freemasonry was an entirely *oral tradition*, passed on by word of mouth, by memory, and in mythic tales and legends of hoary antiquity. Its content was vouchsafed only to those deemed ready to share in it. To outsiders, it was secret. This is how the oral tradition was preserved. This is how most oral traditions are preserved to this day.

19th century historians of Freemasonry – they were nearly all members of masonic orders – had got used to the idea of documentation – paper work - as comprising the 'culture' of the subject. It's no good being a scholar if you've got nothing to read.

The first 'official' publication of Freemasons – as a defined order – dated from 1723. This was the *Book of Constitutions*, notably revised in 1738. Oh, happy eruption of literacy! In the revised edition, readers learned that the 'Grand Lodge' had been curiously re-activated at a meeting of four London lodges in 1716, receiving the additional dignity of a 'Grand Master' in 1717.

Masonry had a culture. That culture was written down, published openly, and approved by at least one aristocrat in good stead with the government of the day.

As far as the United Grand Lodge of England was concerned, the date of 1717 marked the beginning of 'properly regulated Freemasonry'. That means: properly regulated *the Grand Lodge way*. Its authority, however, had to come from somewhere. Cleverly, its authority was presumed from its being in direct continuity with the 'Antient Masonry' that preceded it.

You may not have known it but there had *always* been a grand lodge – and grand masters – right back through the ages. Grand Lodge claimed to be a revival of an ancient institution after a 'period of neglect'.

This paper ruse did get round the problem of authority, but it presented problems for the tidy minds of 19th and 20th century masonic historians, mindful of the shortfall of writings before the alleged 'revival'. How could they justify this supposed ancient lineage when there was very little written cultural material?

Maybe, they reasoned, it wasn't a revival in the ordinary sense of the word; maybe it was the creation of something *new*, if somehow derived from something older. This and other curious ambiguities have created many problems – mostly, if not mercilessly, confined to scholarship. For the no-nonsense mind, it was often safer simply to say that the origins of so-called 'Speculative Freemasonry' (the thing they were interested in) should be seen as being solidified in an orderly fashion in 1717. Before that, there was some kind of vague 'evolution'. The notion of evolution of course justifies the nature of that into which something is assumed to have evolved. Evolution was linked to progress – and progress was good.

Stonemasons had always believed that their craft went back to the beginnings of human civilisation, with some notable 'star-turns' along the way, such as the building of King Solomon's temple, which everybody knew about. Here was something masons could talk about that everyone would understand. The masons had been there *then*, and they were beloved of God! Without masons, no places of worship: no religion.

However, scientific history could not verify this claim; there was not enough documentation. Therefore, went the growing 'scientific' reappraisal of masonic history, the supposition of antiquity must have been a product of illiterate and superstitious times.

If you do not have the written records, you do not have the evidence. Without 'evidence', there is neither 'fact' nor truth. Science says so. Thus, the once forbidden practice of writing things down about Freemasonry became the very category for deciding whether 'real' Masonry was in fact taking place! Oral freemasonry was illiterate freemasonry. The freestone masons must have got anything of interest (like the science of architecture for example) from the monks!

It is, in fact, the literate or non-oral Freemasonry that was the innovation – and very late in the masonic day it came too.

The modern version of the old oral tradition lies in the practice of Freemasons reading books and then memorising what they have read. It is onerous, and not what was intended as an oral tradition. It involves a kind of fake level of secrecy. How many wives have helped their husbands learn their 'secrets'? Nor does Freemasonry then function as an oral tradition. It has become, effectively, a written tradition, tidied up for scholarship.

The oral tradition, as such, has been almost completely lost. But Freemasonry was once an oral tradition, and, as far as we can tell, always had been. Grand Lodge has been stuck with the dilemma of this situation ever since, though you would hardly notice, so comfortable it appears to be with the (not entirely tidy) science of its supposed origins.

The aforesaid dilemma is clearly illustrated by the continued uncertainty in using lower or upper case 'm's' or 'f's' for masons, masonry, freemasons, freemasonry – *or is it Masons, Masonry, Freemasons, Freemasonry?*

The convention observed in this book is as follows: lower case 'm's' and 'f's' for the trade practice of stonemasonry (exercised by freemasons or freestone masons), with upper case 'M's' and 'F's' when referring to the period of organised symbolic Masonry separated from the trade after *c*.1723.

When referring to Freemasons in general – and where the context supports it – a lower case 'm' for masons is to be preferred.

It should be noted that within masonic circles, an extraordinary number of words are given gilt-edged dignity by capital letters - words such as Lodge, Mason, Masonic, Craft, Grand, Grip, Token, Master, Third Degree, Deacon, Candidate, Globe, Chair, Apron and so on. This archaic practice continues to ensure that aspects of Freemasonry operate within an almost verbally sectarian atmosphere. It is ironic that what was once an oral tradition should be separated from mainstream society by use of peculiarities of written language.

So, having downgraded the significance of the tradition of oral transmission of the craft, it became 'scientifically' easier in the late 19th and 20th centuries to assert that *proper* Freemasonry was Grand Lodge Freemasonry, and *that* began (according to – and yet oddly against - its own record) in AD 1716-1717. Freemasonry was firmly identified with the 'Enlightenment'.

But what of all the masons who have been encouraged to believe that Freemasonry is truly ancient? Their beliefs have become akin to what the Church might call 'matters of personal belief', as contrasted with 'substantial matters of faith'. You can believe what you like about these sorts of things so long as you do not lose faith in the institution that guarantees these matters of belief!

So, while science can hardly deny that there is evidence for some kind of 'Freemasonry' existing before Grand Lodge, it is all 'very open to interpretation' – and therefore weak science with a tendency to drift into superstition and fantasy. This approach is typical of the mindset that a large number of mason-historians have adopted in conducting their researches into masonic origins. What they are looking for really are the origins of the grand lodge – since that institution has been identified so completely with 'Freemasonry' itself.

Grand Lodge Freemasonry represents the 'modern era' – the culmination of all that went before it, the yardstick and measure of all within its proper purview. If evidence does not conform to the general idea of what today is understood as Freemasonry, then masonic historians doubt whether such evidence is truly masonic at all.

'Medieval' evidence (pre-1485), for example, allegedly offers very little akin to what the modern masonic historian knows of Freemasonry today, so medieval evidence is frequently regarded as the province of another category – that is: OPERATIVE Freemasonry. This means that it is to do with stonemasons and their trade, which, while strangely relevant to 'Masonry', lacks the cultural credentials of so-called SPECULATIVE or symbolic Masonry.

Has science sent us a little mad here? Masonry is two distinct things? Operative and Speculative? What is this distinction all about?

We shall analyse what these two words 'operative' and 'speculative' have come to mean in the way that 'orthodox' Freemasonry defines itself. It is a bumpy ride, but I assure readers, a destination will be reached – and readers may count themselves more knowledgeable for the ride!

Freemasonry – The Reality demonstrates that Freemasonry as a body of knowledge, philosophy, practice and theory, is of ancient provenance. The old boys, it transpires, were right.

Freemasonry is full of genuine mysteries. But we need to be sure we know what we mean by 'mysteries'. A 'mystery' is something that you enter into, and the more you go into it, the more you find, while never reaching a complete, encompassing comprehension of the mystery itself. Science does not like mysteries, while yet being surrounded by them. Mysteries are there to be *solved*, goes the cry. Quite right, and why not? But real mysteries are not there for the solving but for the *experiencing*. The more you go in, the more you find. There is more to a mystery than a mere puzzle. There is no all-conquering code in a genuine mystery. There is no hidden formula, no *Da Vinci* or *Pyramid* Code.

Nevertheless, it should also be borne in mind that for many centuries before the establishment of the grand lodge idea the word 'mystery' was used simply for the peculiar technical knowledge of any particular craft.

Those in the 16th and 17th century who had received a 'Renaissance' intellectual education (with all that era's pleasure in classical and biblical mysteries and allegories) were prone to imagine that the 'mystery' of the trade of freemasons necessarily contained a mystical or esoteric element. It may be imagined that practising freemasons were not hasty to disabuse the wealthy curious of such an idea.

Furthermore, the master masons were themselves not ignorant of such knowledge: the carving of allegorical, symbolic and esoteric subject matter was in demand throughout the period. Indeed, to cross from the notion of initiation into a fraternity united by special technical knowledge to initiation into symbolic brotherhood with esoteric knowledge was not a difficult leap to make for the educated people of the time. Technical and symbolic knowledge had been in each other's pockets for as long as the liberal arts had been practised.

Having now made the case for a critique of 19th century modes of historical categorisation (ie: that such modes were prejudiced against oral traditions), I am not suggesting that the tools of scientific analysis cannot be applied to the history and philosophy (or philosophies) of masonic traditions.

Rational tools of analysis can and must be applied, in so far as they are helpful in the search for truth. Telepathy isn't going to help us. If our minds employ occult principles, we remain unconscious of it. There is much that can be learned, so long as we do not regard our learning as having reached some absolute culmination. God forbid that we should once again stray into the delusion of having entered the *Modern Era*!

Common Questions and Common Answers

Who was the first symbolic Freemason?

Where was the first lodge of Freemasons?

Why is the figure of St John so important in Freemasonry?

Who was Hiram Abif?

How do we account that something so peculiar has changed the world?

Whence came the attraction and fascination with Freemasonry?

Why did it spread so far and so fast?

Why is Freemasonry so opposed by certain kinds of government?

Why is the pentagram a symbol of health?

What is the Lost Word of Freemasonry?

Some of these questions have answers, and not every one of these questions is a genuine mystery. By the end of the book, you should be able to tell what is answerable, and what is a genuine mystery.

There are mysteries of origin, of meaning – and, yes, there are esoteric mysteries too. The book aims to show the reality – not the myth – of the world's oldest fraternal society. Along the way, archaeologists of human ideas should be delighted to see a number of historical problems and problems of interpretation solved as well. Yes, there are solutions to puzzles, but revelations remain strictly the responsibility of the reader.

The exact origins of Freemasonry cannot, I suspect, ever be

found. They are lost in the mists of time, with only myth to guide us. Masons have written very little directly about what drives them. I suspect the old masons were quite right to believe that their spiritual ancestors went back to the beginnings of human knowledge. There has always been something like 'Freemasonry' in the thinking, human world. Masons have been talking about it – to one another – literally for ages. This book gives us a rare opportunity to listen hard to their Lost Word.

'In the beginning was the Word and the Word was with God'
(*John* I.1)

Chapter One

The Degrees

*The most obscure poem is intended for
everybody.*
(Jacques Audiberti, 1899–1965)

Initiations can often be scary events for those about to
undergo them; they are supposed to be. The candidate is
entering into something new with very little guidance as to
what he may expect. The nervous system has had no training in
what may be required; there is a great deal of trust involved.
That means there is going to be a degree of letting go of normal
controls and defences – an acceptance, in the case of
Freemasonry, of the discipline of the lodge.

One must enter an initiation willingly, or else it won't be
initiation that is taking place, but the kind of exotic fearsome
experience sprung with devilish delight on the unwary in young
men's sodalities, whether in colleges, work-places or in
motorcycle-based subculture.

Masonic initiation has not been set up to try the courage – or
patience – of the candidate – though it might have begun that
way. Apprentices have often had to suffer before being admitted
into a group experience. Indeed, the one thing the group will all
share is the initiation experience; the shock becomes a bond. The
positive benefits of the bond make the unpleasantness worthwhile.

Suffering very quickly becomes a badge of honour in the
psychic life of the young man. He wants to be tried and found true
in the eyes of those whose respect and protection he seeks.
He needs self-respect too. Pain is not always a deterrent; nobody
would join the army if it were so. Initiation can make suffering
meaningful.

What is going on beyond the closed door? Many a candidate for masonic initiation has asked himself this question when waiting outside a lodge for the first time. There is the imagination of course – but this can often make the apprehension even more painful to bear. And yet, without the imagination of the candidate, the initiation is unlikely to be very enriching.

Rituals draw the outlines, but the deeper colouring can come only from the inner life and previous knowledge and experience of the candidate. The fact is that the experience, if experienced deeply, has the potential to bring forth a new consciousness in the candidate. That is what initiation is all about: starting a process. The purpose of masonic initiation is illumination – not total enlightenment, but the initiation of a gentle process, undertaken willingly. The first degree sets the potential master mason on the path.

Of what does it consist?

Emulation Ritual

Emulation Ritual is the name now given to the rituals as ratified and agreed after the union of the 'Moderns' and 'Antient' grand lodges in 1813. The deliberations (completed in 1816) were held in secret and we can seldom be sure of precisely what went on in lodges before that time. There had been, of course, 'exposures' from time to time, claiming to reveal what Freemasons were up to in their lodges, but practices varied nonetheless. On the continent and in other parts of the world, practices could vary greatly.

For example, the oldest printed first degree ritual in Germany included the terrifying prospect of the candidate being challenged verbally by a giant of a man (where such a big fellow could be found presumably). This scary man carried chains and made a crashing din with them, intimidating the candidate to conduct himself properly and honestly. (Perhaps he was intended to represent somehow the left hand pillar 'Boaz' – strength – which was decorated, according to the Bible, with chains).

This discomfiting drama went on while the candidate was waiting outside the lodge in what has become known as 'the chamber of reflection'. The peculiar practice of goading the candidate seems to have been a way of dramatising a common continental injunction, namely, that if you were in the chamber of reflection out of curiosity, you should depart at once. The French *VA-T-EN!* is even more emphatic, even rude; Shakespeare would have translated it as 'Get thee hence!' Today we might employ a more vulgar phrase.

The use of the chamber of reflection is generally known in the United Kingdom only in the Ancient & Accepted Rite (a trinitarian Christian order). The Ancient & Accepted Rite, administered from Duke Street, London, is chartered to work degrees from a 4th to a 33rd and does not come under the jurisdiction of any of the British Isles' grand lodges, though there is no objection to master masons joining this order.

On the continent, however, the chamber of reflection is frequently to be found as a preliminary experience for the candidate before entry into a lodge. Precise practices vary, again, but in the Grand Lodge of France, for example, the candidate will be left in a room to write his 'philosophical will', an account of the candidate's expectations and ideas of Freemasonry. This will be read out to the lodge later.

Isolated in the room, illuminated only by the light of a single candle, the candidate may just make out a human skull, some bones, a lump of bread, a flask of water, an hourglass, a saucer containing salt and another holding sulphur. Attached to the wall are sheets of paper, one showing a cockerel. On another, the letters V.I.T.R.I.O.L indicate an ancient alchemical injunction: *visita interiora terrae, rectificando invenies occultam lapidem*: visit the centre of the earth and by rectifying you will find the hidden stone.

We note the injunction to go to the centre and observe also that on the continent, the arrival of Freemasonry after about 1730 coincided with a revival of alchemical, Rosicrucian and Hermetic philosophy. This special context gave the masonic theme of transformation a more pronounced alchemical, psychological and spiritual ring than appears to have been the norm in the British Isles during the same period.

British Masonry rooted its ideas and imagery much more strongly in biblical territory. Its interest in classicism tended to be confined to orders of architecture and moral nobility, rather than pagan or Neoplatonic symbolism.

On the continent, on the other hand, the cockerel, for example, was associated with gnostic ideas of the appearance of the light, as well as with Mercury/Hermes who sets limits and helps neophytes to cross them.

There is simply more philosophy in the continental approach, as one might expect. In England, by contrast, the 'chamber of reflection' is really no more than a changing room for the candidate. There he is not prepared mentally, but physically, by the tyler (or outer guard) who stands outside with a sword to guard the lodge from intruders.

The task of the tyler before the 'entered apprentice' ceremony is to reduce the dress of the candidate to a desired minimum of artifice, suitable for a poor supplicant, in want of light and with nothing to offer but his heart, if he will. Thus the candidate is rendered somewhat foolish. He is to experience physically his inner state of un-enlightenment. The dress is not to induce mirth in the thoughts of the lodge members. However, taken out of context, the initiate's appearance has been used to cast a risible reputation on all Freemasons. It should be stressed that the initiate's initial appearance in the lodge is for his benefit alone – and occurs only once in his life.

These latter points indicate the importance of ritual. It is not enough to know intellectually that a thing is so; it is also important to *experience* this knowledge, if such is possible. Ritual and symbol make the bridge between idea and experience.

The special function of ritual to enable knowledge to come alive in the being of the recipient goes back to our remote ancestry and is vital to human psychological development and maturity. It is, if you like, the difference between sitting in the audience watching, and being on stage: a difference between pondering and being.

The First Degree – Entered Apprentice

Inside the lodge, the 'worshipful master' sits behind a pedestal, in the east of the lodge. From his chair, he sees the 'senior deacon' to his right in the north of the lodge, the 'junior warden' to his left in the south of the lodge. The 'junior deacon' is also in the south but nearer to the door in the west. The 'senior warden' is in the southwest, while the 'inner guard' is in the north of the lodge, close to the door. Outside the door, the presence of the tyler completes the seven principal officers of the lodge.

The tyler knocks the lodge door from the outside three times.

Inside, the inner guard rises from his chair to declare to the junior warden that 'there is a report', whereupon the worshipful master asks the junior warden to inquire as to whom seeks admission to the lodge. The inner guard is instructed to unlock the door and, without crossing the threshold, to check the work of the tyler while holding the door close to.

The inner guard asks the tyler 'Whom have you there?'

The tyler replies that he has a 'poor candidate in a state of darkness' whom of his own will and accord comes humbly to be admitted to the mysteries and privileges of Freemasonry. The inner guard reports his exchange with the tyler to the master who asks how the candidate hopes to obtain the privileges. The inner guard answers, 'By the help of God, being free and of good report.'

Satisfied that the candidate has been properly prepared, the inner guard is instructed by the master to admit the candidate. The inner guard, accompanied by the junior and senior deacons, returns to the door, carrying a poniard. The point of the blade is brought to touch the candidate's naked left breast.

'Do you feel anything?' asks the inner guard.

On hearing an affirmative, the junior deacon takes the candidate by the right hand and leads him to a kneeling stool. This gives the members of the lodge, who are seated to the north and south of the lodge (with 'past masters' in the east), a first opportunity of seeing the candidate in a state appropriate for initiation.

The candidate is blindfolded. His shirt is open to reveal the left breast. He has a cable tow around his neck. His trouser legs are rolled up in an ungainly manner around his knees and, as a result of being slipshod, that is, wearing a rough leather shoe on one of his feet, he is compelled to limp forwards, blindly (he knows not where) supported by the junior deacon. The junior deacon will prompt the candidate when he is questioned; the candidate will repeat the words he hears.

Being assured that the candidate is a free man and of full age (21 years), the master asks that the 'blessing of Heaven' be invoked on the proceedings. Then, the master and wardens make a knock with their gavels, consecutively, as the deacons cross their wands over the head of the candidate.

The prayer is addressed to the 'Almighty Father and Supreme Governor of the Universe'. It asks that the candidate be endued 'with a competency of Thy divine wisdom, that, assisted by the secrets of our Masonic art, he may the better be enabled to unfold the beauties of true godliness, to the honour and glory of Thy Holy Name'.

After a further three impressive knocks of the gavel, the candidate is gently instructed in stepping off from the kneeling stool on his left foot and is led up the north to the northeast corner of the lodge. He is then led towards the south, passing the master in the east, then on towards the junior warden's pedestal in the south. At each corner, the candidate must stop and then set off from the left foot in the correct direction. Thus the lodge is 'squared'.

Standing at a distance from the junior warden's pedestal the junior deacon takes the candidate's right hand and strikes the junior warden three times on the shoulder. The junior warden asks 'Whom have you there?' Assured the candidate has been properly proposed and recommended, with his hope placed in God, the candidate's hand is placed by the deacon into that of the junior warden.

The junior warden then takes the candidate to the south west corner of the lodge – which is squared – and then to the south of the senior warden's pedestal. The senior warden now receives the hand of the candidate striking his right shoulder, and the previous question is repeated.

The candidate's hand is now placed in the right hand of the senior warden, who returns it to the deacon. It should be remembered that the candidate is blindfolded.

The junior deacon takes him to the north of the senior warden's pedestal, turns anti-clockwise and places the candidate's hand in the left hand of the senior warden. The candidate is turned to face the east and presented to the master. The master will ask him more questions:

'Do you seriously declare on your honour that, unbiased by the improper solicitation of friends against your own inclination, and uninfluenced by mercenary or other unworthy motive, you freely and voluntarily offer yourself a Candidate for the mysteries and privileges of Freemasonry?'

The candidate is then asked if he has a 'general desire of knowledge' and a sincere wish to render himself 'more extensively serviceable' to his fellow creatures.' The master commands the junior deacon to advance the candidate to the master's pedestal.

Led off from the left foot, the candidate will be stopped and instructed to keep his left foot facing the east with his right foot forming a square. He thus 'squares' his way – square by square – towards the pedestal, each time leading off with the left foot, advancing a little more each time. His feet still in a square he comes before the master (unknown to himself). The master addresses the candidate, informing him that Freemasonry 'is founded on the purest principles of piety and virtue', its 'great and invaluable privileges' secured to worthy men alone by vows of fidelity. Understanding that 'there is nothing incompatible' with the candidate's 'civil, moral or religious duties' involved in the 'sacred oath', an invitation to take that oath freely is now made.

The candidate helps support a pair of compasses with his left hand while his right is placed on the VOSL (Volume of the Sacred Law). One point of the compass is presented to his naked left breast (the heart). Three knocks from the master and wardens follow, whereafter the candidate swears to keep inviolate the secrets and mysteries of the order, an oath sealed by kissing the VOSL.

The master addresses the candidate: 'Having been kept for a considerable time in a state of darkness, what, in your present situation, is the predominant wish of your heart?' – to which the answer is made: 'Light'.

As the master's gavel strikes the pedestal, every member of the lodge claps – a powerful sound, muffled by the white gloves the brethren are wearing. The blindfold is removed.

Restored to the 'blessing of material light' – thus in all likelihood indicating another *spiritual* light – simple explanations are provided for the 'three Great Lights' of Masonry: the VOSL, square and compasses. The master then takes the candidate's right hand: 'Rise, newly obligated Brother among Masons.'

After having referred to the 'three lesser lights' of the lodge (representing the sun, moon and the master), the master, who is 'to rule and direct the lodge', informs the candidate as to how he has escaped two great dangers already.

The poniard, presented to the left breast on entering, would have secured the candidate's own death by accessory had he rashly attempted to rush into the lodge.

The junior deacon now removes the cable tow from round the neck of the candidate and hands it to the master. The cable tow with the running noose 'would have rendered any attempt at retreat equally fatal' says the master.

However, the greatest danger avoided was the traditional penalty that would have greeted the 'Brother' who had 'improperly disclosed the secrets of Masonry', once contained in the obligation. Traditionally, betrayal of the craft would have entailed the penalty of having the throat cut and the body disposed unceremoniously. 'The inclusion of such a penalty is unnecessary, for the Obligation you have taken this evening is binding on you for so long as you shall live.'

The candidate is then shown how to stand erect as a mason, his feet in a square, in which position he is told of the 'grip' or 'token' of an entered apprentice Freemason, which demands a word from a brother mason.

The Mason Word

The idea of the 'Mason Word' is known from documents going back to the early to mid-17th century in Scotland. As far as we can tell, it was simply a mode of recognition to prove that the brother mason was an initiated mason, and not a *cowan*, that is, an unauthorised practitioner of the mason's trade – what we might today call a 'cowboy builder'. It was a simple means by which a mason might be automatically accepted into a lodge, combined with a 'grip' or handshake to prove his origin and full respect for the secrets of the craft.

Nowadays, people's suitability for entry to various kinds of specialised work is made good with certificates and CVs and so on. But in the old days, most people were illiterate. Furthermore, letters, indentures and so on can be forged. A secret sign therefore was an economical way of demonstrating skill and probity, without the need for verbal or literate ability. One can therefore see why – since livelihoods (and therefore lives) depended on it – the oaths bore the bloodcurdling character of the times. Such oaths were once common practice.

It should be said here that the idea of masons today greeting each other with 'funny handshakes' to seal or to initiate business relations makes no sense. First, if members meet in a lodge, then they already know who is a mason. Second, there is no point giving a handshake in ordinary circumstances if you cannot be sure the person to whom it is offered understands its special nature. Indeed, you would run the risk of giving away the nature of the exchange! Third, masons tend to have a knack for telling which person is a brother. Like attracts like perhaps, but nothing but peculiar intuition can explain what is a very common phenomenon.

Nowadays, if you wish to know if someone is a Freemason, feel free to ask: openness is nowadays the recommendation of masonic authority. In those parts of the world where Freemasons have been persecuted and even murdered for their membership, or are otherwise under threat, such openness would be harmful to Freemasons and their families. Totalitarian or fundamentalist religious states will not, given their current perceptions of life and history, tolerate Freemasonry.

In other countries, if a Freemason is invited to another lodge, there is on occasion a testing of the visitor's masonic knowledge. This is almost always a formality, since for masons it is not unknown to forget the odd word or sign under the pressure of being asked for them!

In the case of the 'word' or token of the entered apprentice degree, the word is now related to King Solomon's temple, but the words have been changed over time. They have no great meaning in themselves in the password context – and certainly no 'magic power'.

It has been a persistent error in assessing the essence of Freemasonry that the secret passwords have been related to esoteric contexts with which they properly have nothing to do. There is always around Freemasonry the suspicion of masons being privy to 'esoteric secrets', and that those secrets are embodied in hidden words – words of occult or revealing power and meaning. Such esoteric content as may be reflected in Freemasonry is not as banal as this.

It is also true, as we shall see when we consider the third degree, that the meaning of the masonic 'Word' has acquired more meaning than a mere password, but that is a special case and valid only in specific contexts.

It is true that among some communities of ancient Gnostics (2nd to 4th centuries AD) members were taught special passwords. These were to be given to angelic powers in order to break out of the constraints of the cosmos and ascend to the realm of pure spirit, the mysterious 'Depth' or infinite ocean of absolute divinity.

There is no evidence, however, in the oldest masonic material to suggest such a notion ever entered the thought or practice of lodges of masons. Every secret invites the creation of fantasy.

In fact, the passwords teach Freemasons nothing at all, except the virtue of keeping a secret when asked to do so – a rare enough thing, it must be said in an era when the temple of our common discourse seems mostly to be supported by gossip columns.

Masons consider it a duty connected to their obligations as an upright brother not to bandy the words about in public among persons for whom they cannot have any meaning. If you wish to know them, a mason will say, *join the order* – since that is the only possible environment in which the words have any value whatsoever.

No non-mason is deprived of any useful knowledge by not knowing them. For example, if a guild of carpenters had their own words for 'feet' and 'inches' as a mutual conceit among members, not knowing these words would not frustrate the ordinary user of rule and plane.

Many masons consider it simply a test of the ability to keep a promise that the words are not openly stated outside of the craft. Functioning as a kind of masonic 'pin number', it would cause confusion to Freemasons if the words became familiar to non-masons – and they would simply have to be altered again, thus proving the point that the sole value of a secret of this kind is when it is kept secret.

In due course, this book will reveal (not for the first time) the oldest known 'Mason Word', since it is useful knowledge. The word may offer clues as to the historic origins of aspects of the craft. Such a value could never be ascribed to the current passwords of the entered apprentice degree.

We return to our first degree ceremony. Following the reception of the grip or token, the candidate is taken to the junior warden who asks if he has anything to communicate. The junior deacon informing the warden that he was 'taught to be cautious' at his own initiation, the word is exchanged by halving it into two syllables.

The candidate continues his perambulation past the lodge members until he is brought once more to the senior warden. The candidate is encouraged to demonstrate the 'sign' of an entered apprentice Freemason. The sign is based on the square, though this time expressed by the hand. The grip or token is then demonstrated – which demands, once more, the word.

Knowing what the word means, in the context of King Solomon's temple, the Freemason is instructed to 'Pass'.

The apron

The 'worshipful master' now asks the senior warden to invest the candidate with 'the distinguishing badge of a Mason'. The warden explains that this badge 'is more ancient than the Golden Fleece or Roman Eagle, more honourable than the Garter or any other Order in existence, being the badge of innocence and the bond of friendship'. If the candidate undertakes never to disgrace the badge, the badge will never disgrace him.

The 'badge' is a simple white apron, not much bigger than a napkin.

In the old days, the custom was to wear a white lambskin; nowadays the apron is usually of simpler stuff. Its justification is in part in imitation of the 'craftsman', though we do not know whether lodges of 'operative masons' were compelled to wear their working aprons at the proceedings.

In the 18th century, Freemasons were able to decorate their aprons as they preferred, in appropriate masonic symbols and images. Madame de Lafayette was said to have sewn George Washington's apron symbols. There seems some psychological kinship here with the practice of girlfriends in motorcyclists' fraternities sewing striking badges on to the bikers' leathers and jeans.

This interesting practice was tidied up after the union of 'Antients' and 'Moderns' of 1813; one can think of all kinds of reasons why. However, the simple white apron – said in the degree lectures to reflect the dress of Adam and Eve in *Genesis* chapter III – is discarded in the third degree of *Emulation Ritual* for a more elaborate but standardised blue and white leather apron.

Masters and other senior ranks acquire even more elaborate aprons. The purpose of the simple apron – greater than any other order – seems to have thus been confused in time with the military practice of adding braid to the uniform.

Such is not the case throughout the world. In Germany, for example, the custom continues whereby the master wears the same, proud and simple apron as the entered apprentices and 'fellow crafts' (those who have been subjected to the 'second degree').

All classes are supposed to be levelled in the confines of masonic practice. But many masons are very fond of badges and medals and feel that their collecting interests reinforce their interest. It is worth noting that the 'aprons' worn by Adam and Eve in the authorised version of the Bible are hardly badges of innocence. They are hastily sewn together as the consciousness of shame emerges in the minds of the first human couple, after 'they knew that they were naked' and discovered there was no hiding place from the eye of the Lord. They had become morally conscious beings.

Aprons may have been an attempt to re-establish some kind of hoped-for innocence, but were in fact both to 'cover their shame' and, as such, are nothing less than symbols of innocence lost.

The 'badge of innocence' was nakedness.

If the Adam and Eve story did not convince, there was also the masonic explanation that the aprons in some way echo the 'ephod' worn by Jewish priests, said to be apron-like, and therefore suitable costume for the 'temple'. This, at least to the author of this book, sounds like another explanation made to cover some kind of problem, if you will pardon the pun. Perhaps gentlemen and aristocrats, joining the order after the inception of the grand lodge system, needed persuasion as to why they were going to have to dress like their tailors.

The entered apprentice, having been given his badge of innocence, is informed that wearing it he can never attend a lodge while in some kind of enmity or conflict with a brother mason. He should desist from attendance while such a situation persists, to preserve the lodge from the stain of disharmony.

The junior deacon is next instructed to 'place our new-made brother at the North East part of the Lodge', that is to say at the far corner of the lodge, to the master's right.

This part of the ceremony has great resonance for we can see the old mason's symbolic identification of his work with the work of God. He becomes a stone in the edifice of the temple and must square and perfect himself up for the job. He makes the temple with himself.

'It is customary,' explains the master, 'at the erection of all stately and superb edifices, to lay the first or foundation stone at the North East corner of the building. You, being newly admitted into Masonry, are placed at the North East part of the Lodge figuratively to represent that stone, and from the foundation laid this evening may you raise a superstructure perfect in its parts and honourable to the builder.'

Rather than continue with an explanation of the long, biblical tradition behind the symbolism of the 'stone', as might have proved useful and stimulating, the Emulation Ritual moves quickly along to test 'that virtue which may justly be denominated the distinguishing characteristic of a Freemason's heart – I mean Charity'. The entered apprentice is reminded that life being life, while some brethren across the globe are provided for, there are others who have hit on hard times. Is the entered apprentice willing to offer anything in the cause of charity?

To further his moral development, the newly admitted brother is introduced to the working tools of the entered apprentice, the 24-inch gauge, the common gavel – 'to knock off all superfluous knobs and excrescences', and the chisel. The chisel is 'to further smooth and prepare the stone and render it fit for the hands of the more expert workman. But, as we are not all operative Masons, but rather free and accepted, or speculative, we apply these tools to our morals.'

It should be observed that the word 'morals' was understood during the 18th century – when the 'modern' rituals were evolving – as more than a list of social rights and wrongs, but had to do with the total relationship of the human being to a transcendent judge of all human conduct. The morality of a person made them acceptable – or not – to the favour of the Lord. Goodness was an act of will, not only a state of grace. Charity meant giving, and was a divinely stimulated function of the heart, the mason's centre.

As an old Plymouth Brethren preacher used to say, 'Get right with God!'

Having been informed that dues are to be paid to the lodge, the authority to collect them is alluded to by the presence of the lodge's charter; a book of *Constitutions* and by-laws is handed to the candidate. The candidate may now retire to dress himself, or as the ritual has it, 'restore yourself to your personal comforts'. The candidate salutes the master as a mason with his right hand forming a square. The salute is repeated on his return to the lodge.

Returning, the master reads the 'Charge' to the initiated brother, while he stands with the junior deacon – his guide through all the proceedings – at the north of the south west pedestal.

The word 'Charge' comes from the freemasons' 'Old Charges'. These writings (usually learned by heart) contained a history of the craft and the rules to be observed by those privy to the craft's secrets. As we might say 'Charge your glasses!', so the 'Charges' of the Freemasons were intended to fill the attention of the initiated and 'charge him up'. The old police/military phrase, 'He's on a charge, sir' has the same origin, since the one so called has caused an infraction of the rules, or charges. By the charge, he should live, and by the charge he is condemned, should he fail to do so.

Perhaps it would be helpful today if young persons, new to society's rules, were first read the 'charges', before they hear the words, 'You are charged with…'

The old ritual seemed to know that the context – initiation – of hearing the charges, was vital to their effectiveness. Criminals today are more likely to be 'initiated' into crime than initiated into a bond of social goodness. Perhaps you cannot become good by 'osmosis'; it is an act of will.

The charge received by the newly admitted brother is intended to fill him with the dignity of what he has undertaken. Freemasonry, he is told, has 'subsisted from time immemorial', resting on the solid foundation of 'the practice of every moral and social virtue'. Monarchs have been promoters of the art, and have 'not thought it derogatory to their dignity to exchange the sceptre for the trowel'. There is some truth in this; King George VI was initiated into the craft by a Scottish postmaster.

The mason is recommended to contemplate seriously the 'Volume of the Sacred Law', 'the unerring standard of truth and justice'. In it are contained 'the important duties you owe to God, to your neighbour and to yourself'.

Masons are enjoined to do all in their power to preserve their mental and corporeal capacities 'in their fullest energy'. Perhaps the masons were the first to recommend the 'Keep Fit' regimes now ubiquitous in our image – if not morally – conscious times.

The mason is now addressed as 'a citizen of the world' – a striking phrase. He is forbidden to countenance any act 'to subvert the peace and good order of society, by paying due obedience to the laws of any State which may for a time become the place of your residence or afford you its protection, and above all, by never losing sight of the allegiance due to the Sovereign of your native land, ever remembering that nature has implanted in your breast a sacred and indissoluble attachment towards the country whence you derived your birth and infant nurture'.

In social matters, the brother is to be directed by Prudence, Temperance, Fortitude, Benevolence and Charity; it is perhaps strange that these virtues were traditionally personified by images of women!

As a Freemason, the brother is not to shout his membership from the rooftops but is enjoined to do his good work unnoticed and unheralded in the world. Thus he must value secrecy (with regard to his obligation), fidelity (to the *Constitutions*) and obedience. The latter is to be proved by strict observance of the laws and regulations and 'modest and correct demeanour in the Lodge'.

Furthermore – and importantly – brethren must abstain from 'every topic of political or religious discussion'. This latter charge needs some remark.

Political and religious discussion frequently leads to argument of an unedifying kind. The lodge must not be thrown into disharmony by exploiting the contentions that perennially divide humankind. The lodge works by rooting itself in the foundation principles common to all godly societies that follow the precepts of wisdom, of truth over fashion, of beauty over despoilation and destruction.

Political and religious argument can frequently be traced to a failure to see a transcending principle, a wilfulness to act on partial not absolute principle. Again, the lodge works on the principle of what disparate types have in common, or ought to have in common. It associates this principle with an absolute principle: divine wisdom. However, we shall see that this charge restraining discussion of religion or politics almost certainly appears in 'Accepted Freemasonry' at a particular point in history, when religious and political argument threatened civil war and social anarchy.

At the time of Grand Lodge's beginnings, there were still men alive who could remember the battle of Naseby and the ferocious destruction and waste of those awful, inconclusive years of struggle. These were the terrible times of rebellion when political and religious conflict was given full rein to render the country apart into armed camps, each claiming right and God as their patron.

When masonic chronicles tell us of the first mooting of some kind of a grand lodge (1716), barely a year had passed since the attempt of James Stuart to wrest the sovereignty of the nation from King George I (the Hanoverian monarch).

The cause of the Stuarts had been upheld (broadly) by one political party; another party upheld resistance to it. The fundamental issue was religion, and this issue split both parties even further. The apparently fragile circumstances seem to have encouraged the masonic formula whereby Freemasons agreed to adhere to 'that religion on which all men can agree', without further definition. It was perhaps a brave start to a new age where space would finally exist to side step the explosive cocktail of religious extremism.

Freemasonry may be credited with upholding a concept of a polity designed to free society from such miseries, without advocating atheism, nationalism, communism or the neglect of moral conscience.

Politico-religious fundamentalism 'naturally' rejects this polity; rebellion is in its interest. On the other hand, it may also be argued that the encouragement of pacific and latitudinarian principles essentially served the purposes of that party (the Whigs) for which trade was in practice more politically important than religion. The Whig Party was conscious that the religion of the Stuarts (Catholicism) would eventually inhibit their political, mercantile and social liberties. Was a new-style Freemasonry proposed to pacify a restive people? But who, on the other hand, would dare to argue that Freemasons should support rebellion? We shall see in chapter ten.

The master now closes the first degree charges to the entered apprentice, exhorting him to study 'such of the liberal Arts and Sciences as may lie within the compass of your attainment, and without neglecting the ordinary duties of your station, to endeavour to make a daily advancement in Masonic knowledge'.

The apprentice should indelibly imprint on his heart 'the sacred dictates of Truth, of Honour and of Virtue'.

So what is the first degree all about?

The first degree is an attempt to inculcate some 'first principles' into the masonic explorer. These are expressed as the obligations to practise brotherly love, relief (charity) and truth.

The first degree is traditionally the first part of the journey through the temple of Solomon.

The apprentice is divested of metal. This image not only suggests his poverty and deprivation with respect to the wisdom of the craft, but also the legend that the Solomonic temple, being of extraordinary holiness, was built in virtual silence on holy ground. According to the legend, all the components were cut and squared in a place apart from the building itself. There is a deep vein of allegorical symbolism in this legend.

Arriving in the lodge, the candidate is acquainted with his first obligations to his fellow man and mason and bound by loyalty and aspiration to the journey ahead. His thoughts are to be purified by virtue, so that his mind may be a fit receptacle for knowledge and, ultimately, inspiration and transformation. He is the rough stone from which the perfect stone may be drawn. This is a fine moral picture of masonic progress. But it may yet constitute a veil over a more profound process.

There is a more esoteric understanding of the initiation ceremony. This appears if we think of the candidate coming not so much into 'a masonic lodge' but as one entering into the *House of Wisdom* herself – namely, the cosmos: the projection in time and space of God's mind.

The entered apprentice, after a period of secluded darkness is about to enter the material world. The experience may be likened to a drama of birth – the soul's first entry. The knocking on the lodge door, signifying a new arrival, causes a disturbance in the lodge, a possible breach in the smooth, harmonious order of its universe.

The master sends a 'Guard' to inspect the cause of the disturbance. What kind of being is it? The candidate enters the 'lodge' (his temporary place of lodging) in a state of darkness; the darkness is his, not the lodge's.

According to this interpretation, the lodge is the projected imagination of the cosmos, 'as high as the heavens' as the old catechism has it. An embodied soul is entering the world. He limps; he can just about feel, but knows nothing except as his heart dictates. He must see first with his heart, before what William Blake called the operation of the 'vegetable eye'.

About him, like the planetary governors of old, are seven principals who will conduct and inspect the one who cannot stand straight, who is ignorant of his potential and blind to his obligations and dependencies.

It is noteworthy in this respect that the oldest known specifications of lodge membership require five, or six; seven becomes the later minimum. Someone at some stage, it seems, wanted there to be seven principal officers. Was this in conscious imitation of Mithraic and other ancient mystery systems wherein the candidate had to 'run the gauntlet' of zodiacal powers before reaching the 'Sun'?

Were the revisers of older practice at all conscious of the Carpocratian Gnostics, for example, who had grips, passwords and grades – and secret scenarios for re-ascent through the guardians of the created cosmos?

Someone it seems, by having the candidate perform a circumnambulation of the lodge was perhaps alluding to the universe – the planets, sun and moon of the old system, or even the seven steps of alchemy that might begin with a rough stone awaiting transformation.

A Platonist conception of birth – familiar to late antiquity – was that the soul (*psyche*) that enters the universe progressively loses its memory of its divine origin (it moves apart from its centre, we might say). In gnostic expressions of this myth, the tragedy of the soul occurs as it falls through the seven spheres of cosmic power, each governed by an angel who clothes the once spiritual soul in successive layers of darkness and sinfulness – cutting it off from vision of the divine *pneuma* (spirit).

In order to return 'home', the soul must give the angels of the spheres their 'due', with a special password or phrase that had the authority of a higher power.

There is no doubt that this picture makes a certain sense of the first degree ceremony as we know it today, at least if your *sensorium* is open to gnostic modes of thinking. If not, you have the moral interpretation that, admittedly, seems to satisfy most masons unaccustomed to esoteric thought and experience.

Returning to our indigent soul, entering the lodge, soon he will realise his darkness, as the blindfold is taken away. The darkness that once – in ignorance – stood as 'light', is made visible. You cannot 'see' darkness, until you have known light. Indeed, the master refers to the 'blessing of material light', thereby indicating a greater. On the other hand, there is also a loss – a loss that will have to be repaired.

Blindfolded, he had to see with the 'eyes of the heart' not his primary physical senses. Now he will be presented with a more sensory world – until he learns, at the end of his journey, to 'see through it'.

The candidate will be shown the square and compasses laid on the holy book. The square traditionally symbolises material things (its base being the earth); the compasses, tracing arcs and bounding spheres, symbolise heavenly things.

The square is derived from the circle, as we shall discuss in chapter four. Everything else the candidate sees supports a basic dualist symbolism: the chequered pavement of darkness and light (the creation), the seven stars that light the way (the lights of the lesser mysteries, the creative powers), the 'Blazing Star' of divine presence, the rough stone that must be squared and raised to righteous ashlar (perfectly finished stone) – the transforming power of the holy *logos*.

In this world is a confusion of light and darkness. It is, as the alchemists used to say, a *massa confusa*. How can he begin his search for the lost secrets of the master mason? The entered apprentice is going to be taught the rudiments of standing straight before the master, the cornerstone. If he cannot learn to stand straight with full respect for the laws of the universe, he will be neither ready for – nor able to withstand – the tremor of the final moment for which initiation is the first preparation.

The Second Degree – Fellow Craft

It should first be borne in mind that, as far as we can tell, there were originally only two principal ceremonies or 'degrees' (this word was not, as far as we can tell, an original word) in Freemasonry. It also appears to be the case that these ceremonies were most often in the earliest known practice worked on the same occasion. We do not know if these two ceremonies constituted the 'Acception' ceremony associated with the London Company of Masons, or whether something of the 'Acception' later became a component of the third degree (for which we have no certain reference until 1725).

We also do not know if some element or elements of the third used to exist in the first and second degrees, as they came in time to be called. It is possible, but we have no evidence to give us confidence in favouring any one hypothesis on this issue. There is the likelihood that 'fellowship' was accorded to non-masons in a single ceremony as early as 1646.

York has the earliest records of admission of non-masons into working men's lodges, as Neville Barker Cryer has recently shown in his fresh studies of York Masonry.

The 'arrival' of a master's degree some time before or around 1725 – though the conferring of the master's degree was not automatic for a very long time – did leave the 'fellowship' ceremony stuck rather in the middle, where once it might have been climactic.

When it became common practice to separate the ceremonies into three distinct parts, the fellow craft distinction became even more isolated. Even today, it is customary to think of the 'second' as a bit of a relaxation, even a kind of reward for having persevered in Masonry from initiation through maybe six months to a year.

We cannot then know much about the original fellow craft ritual, if, indeed, anything other than the fact it conferred fellowship. However, the significance given to the master's degree, or 'third', lessened the once proud status of fellowship. In short, the 'second degree' became somewhat transitory. This is a shame; it contains some interesting components.

It was perhaps an attempt to dignify it that led the creators of the modern second to seek inspiration in the Bible. They did not have to look very far. Indeed, there was a ready-made text just waiting for someone to come in and grasp its significance. Now that the fellow craft ritual was a middle ritual – stuck between two great masonic moments – what could better suit its refreshed symbolism than a reference to I *Kings* VI.8?

The text reads as follows: 'The door for the middle chamber was in the right side of the house: and they went up with winding stairs into the middle chamber, and out of the middle into the third.' It must have appeared God-given. There it was – a middle chamber reached by winding stairs (Jacob's ladder or alchemical initiatory symbolism again) that leads to 'the third'.

Readers will, I am sure, be grateful if they are spared the movement details of the Emulation Ritual 'Ceremony of Passing', except where something illuminates our understanding of the degree.

The first thing that happens is the master questions the candidate as to what he has learned about Freemasonry from his initiation. He must learn his lines this time and soon finds himself repeating William Preston's definition of Freemasonry as: 'a peculiar system of morality, veiled in allegory and illustrated by symbols'. This is not holy writ, but masons find it useful.

The candidate says the order has been founded on 'Brotherly love, relief and truth'. He is shown a 'pass grip' (handshake) and taught the password that takes the candidate from the first degree to the second, based on a Bible story.

This time the senior deacon is the candidate's guide and it is he who takes the candidate before the senior warden to demonstrate his newly acquired knowledge of grip and password. The candidate is then taken in a semi-circular movement, as if ascending stairs, towards the master in the east. The meaning of this is obvious.

Having sworn on the VOSL to keep the secrets of the degree inviolate, the candidate kisses it, and is shown the hand signs of the degree, which are private matters for masons. He is next given the word of the degree, again, like most essential parts of the modern degree, based on the architecture of Solomon's temple.

The temple is understood not just as the temple beloved to Jewish memory, but as the temple of the One God who has made Himself known through all religions. Solomon is an image of wisdom. His wisdom lies in his love of God, from which other gifts follow. There is no place for religious bigotry here; this is holy ground.

The fellow craft now demonstrates the grip and word of the degree to the junior and senior wardens. He will then be presented with the 'badge' of the Fellow Craft Freemason: a white lambskin apron with two pale blue rosettes. The master then points out to the candidate that he is 'expected to make the liberal Arts and Sciences your future study, that you may the better be enabled to discharge your duties as a Mason and estimate the wonderful works of the Almighty.'

For those who have not made the liberal arts and sciences their study (and that must include many masons), the traditional seven liberal arts (sometimes related to a seven stepped staircase) are Dialectics (or Logic), Rhetoric, Music, Geometry, Arithmetic, Grammar and Astrology (or Astronomy). What a learned craft there would be if all fellow crafts studied as the master enjoins them to do!

The master continues by observing 'that, as in the previous Degree you made yourself acquainted with the principles of

Moral Truth and Virtue, you are now permitted to extend your researches into the hidden mysteries of Nature and Science'. This latter phrase – 'the hidden mysteries of Nature and Science' – has a very interesting pedigree.

The Hidden Mysteries of Nature and Science

In 1486, the 24-year-old Giovanni Pico della Mirandola, put his pen to writing a preface that would serve as an introduction to 900 Theses to be debated publicly in Florence. The debate never happened; the Church smelt heresy and condemned a number of them. Pico's introductory *Oration on the Dignity of Man* was never delivered in public. Notwithstanding, the *Oratio*, as it is known, became, according to Italian scholar Ernesto Garin, the 'manifesto of the Renaissance' – no mean description.

Pico's magnificent estimation of man's hidden potential, his freedom to establish the limits of his nature, poised midway in the 'Great Chain of Being', able to sink or to ascend – gave an impetus of sublime confidence not entirely extinguished in continental life until the 20th century.

The *Oration* of Pico might as justly be called the 'manifesto of Freemasonry'. Much has been said of the debt owed by so-called 'speculative' or symbolic Freemasonry to the Renaissance. This was not only in matters of revived classicism in architecture; the philosophy may be found there too. In Pico it is intact, at its birth: perfect. It is surely noteworthy that Pico launches his heavenwards trajectory with a quotation from Hermes Trismegistus, patron of (at least) late medieval Freemasons: 'A great Miracle, O Asclepius, is man.'

Compare the following to the conception of the perfect lodge as a 'House of Wisdom':

'God the Father, the supreme Architect, had already built this cosmic house we behold, the most sacred temple of the godhead, by the laws of His mysterious wisdom.'

Pico has the fashioners of Adam address him thus:

'Thou shalt have the power, out of thy soul's judgement, to be reborn into the higher forms, which are divine.'

Man will find the means to ascend to the heavens, to work all sciences and arts of life, to plunge to the depths of the ocean. He may delve into the earth in search of fresh wonders, but, 'if, happy in the lot of no created thing, he withdraws into the centre of his own unity, his spirit; made one with God, in the solitary darkness of God, who is set above all things, he shall surpass them all.'

To my ears, this sounds like nothing so much as a lost peroration to the 'hidden' theme that later went by the name of the 'third degree'.

In the course of Pico's stunning review of human knowledge, he draws attention to the importance of 'natural philosophy', which he calls 'magia', the art of the holy magi. This might be well described as 'a holy science', a reverence for the works of God in Nature, coupled with the will to find the divine genius secreted in those 'hidden mysteries'.

Pico quotes the philosopher Plotinus who says that 'magus' is the name given to the wise man. Pico distinguishes between 'magia' and 'goetia', the latter the sinful evocation of demons that bind the fool to their power, 'a loathsome thing to be abhorred, so help me the God of truth', declares Pico.

Goetia means what we now call 'black magic'. Pico concludes that goetia 'can claim for itself the name of neither art nor science, while the latter [magia], abounding in the loftiest mysteries, embraces the deepest contemplation of the most secret things, and at last the knowledge of all nature'.

'The hidden mysteries of Nature and Science' may well today be taken to mean a course in biology, physics, chemistry and mathematics. However, the first Freemason to put the phrase into the ritual was using a Renaissance-style shorthand that had even found its way into Mary Shelley's *Frankenstein* (1818). In that novel, Victor Frankenstein goes to Ingolstadt University in search of the hidden mysteries of nature and science, described also as 'divine signatures'.

These marks and signs of the creator's nature and care had been left in Nature. In the fullness of time, they would offer clues to both His being and His methods: a potential revelation of what today we call, without reverence, 'science'.

The phrase 'divine signatures', relating to the hidden mysteries of nature and science was one favoured by the discoverer of 'laudanum' (the first effective painkiller). He was the first man to introduce chemistry systematically into medicine, and he called himself Paracelsus, born seven years after Pico's *Oratio* and the kind of 'magus' Pico was talking about.

Pico goes on to explain what he means by *magia*. We may legitimately suppose his kind of thinking to have been present in the mind of the one who first spoke of 'the hidden mysteries of nature and science' in Freemasonry:

> Magia, 'in calling forth into the light as if from their hiding places the powers scattered and sown in the world by the loving-kindness of God, does not so much work wonders as diligently serve a wonder-working nature. The latter [magia] having more searchingly examined into the harmony of the universe [a key Renaissance concept and central to Freemasonry], which the Greeks with greater significance call 'sympatheia', and having clearly perceived the reciprocal affinity of natures, and applying to each single thing the suitable and peculiar inducements (which are called the 'iunges' of the magicians) brings forth into the open the miracles concealed in the recesses of the world, in the depths of nature, and in the storehouses and mysteries of God, just as if she herself were their maker; and, as the farmer weds his elms to vines, even so does the magus wed earth to heaven, that is, he weds lower things to the endowments and powers of higher things.'

> Magia rouses man 'to the admiration of God's works which is the most certain condition of a willing faith, hope and love. For nothing moves one to religion and to the worship of God more than the diligent contemplation of the wonders of God; if we have thoroughly examined them by this natural magic we are considering, we shall be compelled to sing, more ardently inspired to the worship and love of the

Creator: 'The heavens and all the earth are full of the majesty of thy glory.' And this is enough about magic. I have said these things about it, for I know there are many who, just as dogs always bark at strangers, in the same way often condemn and hate what they do not understand.'

(*The Renaissance Philosophy of Man*, ed. Kristeller, Cassirer, Randall, Chicago, 1948)

The power of Pico's synthesis of spiritual humanism was felt throughout European intellectual circles for the next 200 years and beyond. We find it notably in J. Freake's first English translation of Henry Cornelius Agrippa's *Three Books of Occult Philosophy* (1651), (see chapter four in relation to the pentagram).

John Booker, one of two licensers of mathematical books at the time, contributed glowing verses to the publication in praise of Agrippa's survey of the three worlds, terrestrial (sublunary), celestial and supercelestial. Booker was an astrologer and a friend of Free Mason, Elias Ashmole.

What has the English version of Agrippa to say about the 'hidden mysteries of Nature and Science'?

Agrippa opens chapter two in praise of the nature and necessity of 'the philosophy of mathematics'. Mathematics, he says, is a discipline central to what he calls 'Magick', by which he means the same as Pico's *magia* :

Magick is a faculty of wonderful virtue, full of most high mysteries, containing the most profound Contemplation of most secret things [a virtual quotation from Pico], together with the nature, power, quality, substance and virtues [hidden powers] thereof, as also the knowledge of whole nature, and it doth instruct us concerning the differing and agreement of things amongst themselves, whence it produceth its wonderful effects, by uniting the virtues of things through the application of them one to the other, and to their inferior suitable subjects, joining and knitting them together thoroughly by the powers, and virtues of the superior bodies. This is the most perfect and chief Science, that sacred, and sublimer kind of Philosophy, and lastly the most excellent perfection of all most excellent Philosophy.

Also noteworthy in Agrippa's treatment is the way he links his division of the three worlds as involving an ascent by degrees:

Seeing there is a three-fold World, Elementary, Celestial, and Intellectual, and every inferior is governed by its superior, and receiveth the influence of the virtues thereof, so that the very original, and chief Worker of all doth by Angels, the Heavens, Stars, Elements, Animals, Plants, Metals and Stones convey from himself the virtues of his Omnipotency upon us, for whose service he made, and created all these things: Wise men conceive it no way irrational that it should be possible for us to ascend by the same degrees through each World, to the same very original World itself, the Maker of all things, the first Cause, from whence all things are, and proceed;

(*Three Books of Occult Philosophy*,
Trans. J. F. London, 1651, pp.2–3)

This concept of the three worlds, experienced by ascent by degrees surely has something to say to us about the three degrees of Freemasonry, even if the substance of that thought has, in our culture, been long forgotten or consciously discarded.

It seems something of a comedown to step from the three worlds of Agrippa back into our more prosaic-sounding 'ceremony of passing', as currently practised. The master – whether for the purposes of extending the candidate's researches into the hidden mysteries of nature and science is unclear – now introduces the fellow craft to the working tools of the degree. These are the square, the level and the plumb-rule.

The master's explanations seem prosaic and moralistic enough until we come to his peroration, which sounds somewhat Agrippan in its idealist, spiritual ascension:

...we apply these tools to our morals. In this sense, the Square teaches morality, the Level equality, and the Plumb-Rule justness and uprightness of life and actions. Thus by square conduct, level steps, and upright intentions we hope to ascend to those immortal mansions whence all goodness emanates.

(*Emulation Ritual, Second Degree*, p.138, Lewis Masonic)

The fellow craft is then permitted to retire, not to the immortal mansions, but to the changing room before being summoned back to the lodge for an explanation of the second degree 'tracing board'.

The Second Degree Tracing Board

Perhaps in an effort to make the ceremony of passing somewhat more interesting for the candidate, a brief lecture on the second degree tracing board has been adjoined to the ritual.

The candidate sees a beautifully painted design showing in the lower half, the porch of Solomon's temple with its mighty pillars (topped by globes), and in the upper portion, a design showing a side entrance to the temple.

Outside the entrance is a flowing river. A warden holding a staff waits at the entrance on a chequered pavement (squares at a zig-zag angle). A rather grand staircase leads up to the second or middle chamber, a floor above.

At the top of the staircase, at the end of the chamber, another warden waits with a plumb-rule and square. Above him is the 'glory' of the Lord, shown as a blazing golden light, in which the name of God in Hebrew letters is shown. This is the entrance to the third and holiest chamber. The lecture tells of how the fellow crafts building the structure were paid wages of corn, oil and wine for their pains; the allowance paid in the middle chamber. Corn, wine and oil are significant masonic objects and are related to consecrations of new structures.

The individual mason is a new structure in the making.

The fellow craft is enjoined to think of how his symbolic masonic ancestors could not gain entrance to the middle chamber for their reward without knowing the passwords and appropriate grip. He is told that a lodge is ruled by the master and two wardens; that the five who hold a lodge are the master, wardens and two fellow crafts (making five – the old minimum), but that the lodge is perfected by the addition of two entered apprentices – making the perfect seven.

An explanation of why 'three' rule a lodge is not very convincing. There were, the fellow craft is told, three grand masters: Solomon king of Israel, Hiram king of Tyre and Hiram Abif. Five hold a lodge because of the five noble orders of architecture – Corinthian, Doric and Ionic are rejoined by the Tuscan and Composite (otherwise of little symbolic interest to Freemasonry). Seven is apparently special because Solomon was seven years in the building of the temple. Seven also alludes, the master says, to the seven liberal arts.

This explanation has plainly been cobbled together to try and tidy up some loose ends with some innovations and anomalies. For example, one might ask why only the three orders of Corinthian, Doric and Ionic may represent Wisdom, Strength and Beauty. Here the other two orders of classical architecture are added for reasons of completeness. Masonic rituals should not be treated as holy writ, though the compilers did make an effort to include at some level anything inherited that they could understand – and even things that they could not.

The master closes the lecture with a tease that seems to have more to do with the third degree and which alludes, in part, to the 'Royal Arch' legend. He says that the fellow crafts' attention in the middle chamber was drawn to the Hebrew characters mentioned earlier (the sacred name of God) that are, the master continues, to be found in the lodge.

In the lodge the name of God is depicted in the form of a 'G' 'denoting God – the Grand Geometrician of the Universe, to whom we must all submit and whom we ought humbly to adore.'

The rediscovery of the name – or Word – (expressed in the Bible in the lost Book of Law) forms the symbolic basis of Royal Arch Freemasonry.

English Royal Arch Freemasonry is governed by a Grand Chapter. This is run in close association with craft Freemasonry (the three degrees). Royal Arch chapters, in the rest of the world, are governed by sovereign Grand Chapters.

Royal Arch Masonry seems to have originated around 1730, but whether from France, Scotland, Ireland or England is uncertain (see chapter fifteen). Ritual details differ – the USA and Scotland set the discovery of the temple's 'lost vault' in the period of King Josiah's reform, whereas in England the setting for the discovery of the lost law is after the return of Hebrew exiles from the Babylonian Captivity. The vault is discovered in the ruins of the old temple, as an attempt is made to rebuild the fallen wonder of old.

The recovery of the lost law and Name in a lost vault seems to this author to have been inspired (at least in part) by the mythical account in the *Fama Fraternitatis* (first published 1614). This famous 'manifesto' of 'Rosicrucian Enlightenment' tells of the rediscovery of the perfect body of Christian Rosenkreuz, founder of a secret fraternity dedicated to the spiritual and scientific reformation of Europe. (See my book, *The Golden Builders*.)

Opinions on this matter differ considerably, and we are getting ahead of ourselves.

However, it is significant that the term Royal Arch (with its suggestion of a completion keystone – masons talk of 'completing their third' with Royal Arch) may have been a misunderstanding for an 'Ark'.

In the Rosenkreuz narrative, the secrets of the brotherhood are held in an 'arca', or ark. As we move to the third degree, it is the idea of the Ark that should be borne in mind, for from it, according to the biblical account, the glory of God emanated.

The mason is moving towards his goal.

The Third Degree

As we have seen in our progression through the modern degrees of Freemasonry, there are many layers of understanding that have gone to make up the ritual we now know. One of the problems in sorting the layers out is that, from time to time, additions have been made. These additions have been accompanied by explanations (usually in the form of lectures) that seem to ill-fit the context originally established. The problem – if it is one – is that after that time, what was once novel becomes a 'landmark' for the craft: sacred territory never to be changed. The ritual-making process was basically put on ice during the early 19th century. It is still deep in cryogenic freeze.

The patchwork process by which the rituals have come together is particularly evident in the third degree. In that traditionally awesome degree it seems that there are basically two major but distinct thrusts of meaning that have been sewn together. Frankly, the joins show. The result has been confusion that some have taken for mystery. But there is no place for confusion in a mystic ritual; the point must be to take the imagination to a stage where meaning becomes apparent.

There are those today – and probably always have been – who are confident that the third degree was never intended to be a 'mystic ritual'; it was simply an allegory concerned with loyalty to the group, keeping secrets, bound together with a good stiff moral lesson ('how to die'). Readers must judge for themselves what kind of ritual the third degree is, and what it may once have been intended to be. For, sadly, we know nothing for certain about how it came to its present form or who was most deeply involved in its creation.

However, we can begin by saying that the two chief strands are almost certainly not contemporaneous. But again, there is a problem. It is fairly certain that the third degree, in anything like the form in which we now know it, did not exist even at the time of the founding of the grand lodge system. There may have been a separate ceremony for making 'masters'; there may not. If there was, there is no reason to think it has anything to do with the third, as we now know it.

There may have been elements of the 'Third' in some kind of proto-'Royal Arch' ceremony or there may not. The fellow craft might also once have contained a climactic element reminiscent of the third degree; it may not. Even the entered apprentice may have had to undergo something of an ordeal – as apprentices often did – more like the third than the relatively mild restraints of the modern first degree. We do not know.

Why cannot we be sure on any of these issues? Because, in the main, Freemasons have kept their obligations to keep their mouths shut and their pens perfectly still. Freemasonry in the 17th, 18th and 19th centuries was almost completely learned by memory; this gave it the capacity to go deeper within the psyche of the participant, and also allowed – before 1813 – for evolution, development and variation.

The 'evidence' for 'early' masonic ritual wording is mostly the result of printed 'exposures', the most famous and influential of which was probably *Masonry Dissected* by one Samuel Prichard (1730). Even the contents of that work show the presence of relatively recent ritual making (the verses are in the style of the period). Its success as a publication led to London's Grand Lodge changing some of the passwords, an act which upset many masons, who were not asked for their opinion and who resented tampering with time-honoured tradition.

Of course, by 1730, many of the newly admitted masons only knew such tradition as had been made available to them through the offices of the Grand Lodge, whose first *Book of Constitutions* had appeared as recently as 1723. They were told that what they received was of very ancient provenance. The scholar of comparative literature was a rare bird in those days. Many of the exposures were plainly invented by their authors from scraps of information, then re-worked and rendered, often in deliberately silly ways. They can be very entertaining, which was, presumably, their purpose.

In the meantime, old practices, customs, words and conceptions familiar to the older (pre-1720) 'Free and Accepted Masons' (many from the trade) were no longer understood by those who (in part) followed them. The rituals, as they now stand, were compiled to give a sheen of unity – often spurious as we have seen – to the scattered lines of masonic traditions that informed them. We can therefore say little with absolute confidence about the 'original meaning' of the rituals. On the other hand, some degree of illumination is yet possible from a careful attempt to locate the thrust of the ritual.

In the case of the third degree, we have, first, a certain velocity set up in the second degree. The fellow craft has come very close to the portal of the Holy of Holies, a sacred place, filled with the dark cloud of the Lord, through which men cannot ordinarily see. (There was of course a penalty of death for those who entered the sanctuary without authorisation).

The veil of the sanctuary was associated with death (the Old Testament) and with the death (and ultimate resurrection) of the 'Master' (in the Gospels).

So we have the veil, the sanctuary, the Ark (with its staves), the Presence of God, and the shadow of death. These are all, incidentally, key visual elements present on the oldest known chair of a distinctly masonic type (1595), as well as being key elements on the tracing boards that survive from the early 19th century, and from the painted cloths that have survived from the late 18th century.

The second thrust of the degree is that of the legendary murder of Hiram Abif. This story, which to the literary critic bears all the marks of being externally contrived in the shape of an allegory with a strained *mythos* attempting to galvanise it, dominates the modern degree. It has a strong residual aroma of having been cooked up from pre-existing and invented elements to suit an occasion; it creaks.

It is possible that the 'occasion' was the desire among some masons for an attractive new degree to give 'added value' to the craft and so to acquire new members in search of some genuine mystery. Also, one could, if fortunate, get to become a *master*, better surely than being a mere fellow! It may be presumed that the fellow craft and apprentice ceremonies – or ceremony – did not quite have sufficient 'whack' for those (like the antiquarian and 'Free Mason', William Stukeley) seeking the 'mysteries of the ancients'.

It is also possible that an original 'Acception' ceremony, practised at the London Company of Masons, was not in its fullness known to those who came to dominate the new grand lodge system. It is possible that some brethren 'got wind' that they were being denied something – something truly secret and mysterious – and the third degree was the best that could be concocted from what was known – and from what the governance of the craft wanted to be known.

This is not to say that the third degree, enacted today with precision, fervour and sincerity, is not an impressive or even meaningful experience to those that undergo it. After all, 'what you never had you never miss', but there has long been a deep feeling in the craft that members had touched on something – something very special – but never quite got *into* it.

Masons are rather left to try and sort it out for themselves. It is as though the brother had one night encountered a fabulous and mysterious woman in a strange part of town. He hungers for the kiss, but is given a phone number. When, next day, in the cold light, he fumbles in his trousers for the number and plucks up the courage to dial it, he finds the number reaches nowhere. He attempts to locate the part of town where the meeting took place, only to discover that he cannot find it. Was it a dream? And if it was, what did it mean?

In the second degree the mason comes to the portal of the third chamber. But does he get inside?

Let us see.

The candidate is first questioned on the nature of his passing to the second degree. He is asked the 'peculiar objects of research' in this degree. They are 'the hidden mysteries of Nature and Science'. The candidate is then asked if he will 'steadfastly persevere through the ceremony of being raised to the sublime degree of a master mason. He receives a pass grip and a password leading to the degree. He leaves the lodge and the door is locked behind him.

When the candidate returns to the lodge, all lights save that of the master have been extinguished. The candidate may dimly perceive the design of the third degree tracing board, placed in the centre of the lodge. On it is depicted a coffin. A vivid skull and crossbones rest upon it. A plumb-rule, level and maul rest upon it. Across the coffin a sheet is spread. It depicts a third chamber. A veil is partially drawn over the Holy of Holies at the far end. A figure approaches that place's golden glow. Within the light, the Ark may just be made out. From the top of the coffin, a sprig of acacia grows.

The candidate is led by the junior and senior wardens to a kneeling stool. The candidate kneels as the wardens cross their wands over his head. A prayer, addressed to the 'Great Architect of the Universe', is said:

'Endue him [the candidate] with such fortitude that in the hour of trial he fail not; but that, passing safely under Thy protection through the valley of the shadow of death, he may finally rise from the tomb of transgression, to shine as the stars for ever and ever.'

The candidate then advances to the junior warden and senior warden, giving the token and word of the first and second degrees respectively. He is permitted to pass. After more perambulation, the candidate demonstrates the pass grip to pass from the second to the third degree with the appropriate password. He then advances to the east (north side), to find the image of a grave – possibly a sheet spread on the carpet – around which a complicated series of steps is traced.

The candidate then makes an oath, kneeling before the VOSL to keep the secrets of the degree inviolate and to be ready always to offer succour and support to needy brethren. He also swears to 'most strictly respect the chastity of those nearest and dearest to him, in the person of his wife, his sister and his child'.

He is shown the compass points on the VOSL entire (in the first the points were obscured; in the second, one point was disclosed). He is told he is 'now at liberty to work with both these points in order to render the circle of your Masonic duties complete'.

There follows an impressive exhortation. He is told that his admission as an entered apprentice was 'an emblematical representation of the entrance of all men on this, their mortal existence'.

'Proceeding onwards, still guiding your progress by the principles of moral truth, you were led to the Second Degree to contemplate the intellectual faculty and to trace it from its development, through the paths of heavenly science [Note that term 'heavenly science'; it is another phrase for Pico's *magia*], even to the throne of God Himself [this is the knowledge that leads to awareness of divinity]. The secrets of Nature and the principle of intellectual truth were then unveiled to your view. To your mind, thus modelled by virtue and science, Nature, however, presents one great and useful lesson more. She prepares you, by contemplation, for the closing hour of existence; and when by means of that contemplation she has conducted you through the intricate windings of this mortal life, she finally instructs you how to die.'

The master then switches the theme from philosophical and mystical discourse to a moral object lesson. The candidate is informed that the virtue of Hiram Abif in his noble death shows that death has no terrors to compare with dishonour. Hiram Abif had rather die than give up his secrets to the unworthy. He is slain just before the completion of King Solomon's temple, at which construction he was, the candidate is told, the principal architect. Even, as it were, in the hour of triumph, something has been lost.

This theme of loss – an important one to the philosophical underpinning of the degree – is brought out more strongly in other degrees, composed to elucidate this and other themes that hover mysteriously about the third degree. It is the sense of loss – and imminent loss – that brings us to understanding.

One can just sense the lurking thought that the third degree involves a special kind of acceptance. The manner of Hiram Abif's death is then described. The story is told of how fifteen fellow crafts, anxious to obtain the secrets of the third degree (a somewhat tautological ambition since the third degree involves knowledge of this anxiety and its aftermath!) conspired to get said secrets through threat of violence.

We may wonder what the 'secrets of the Third Degree' were for Hiram Abif. Since the candidate will later hear that the degree now has 'substituted secrets' (Hiram took the originals with him to the grave), the search for the 'lost word' is on for the mason prepared to rise to the challenge of recovering what was lost and completing the spiritual temple.

The degree offers him the tools to begin his work. Becoming a master mason is not an end, but a beginning. There may also be secreted within this story the possibility that the framers of the degree really had 'lost' or been unable to obtain the 'secrets' of an older rite and chose to allegorise their very ignorance, transforming it into a virtue of sorts. If that is the case, the defence would be that they did the best they could with what they had.

Returning to the tale of the bullyboy fellow crafts – twelve of them recanted their folly, but three persist and place themselves at the east, north and south entrances to the temple. Attending to his devotions, Hiram Abif is accosted by the first ruffian demanding secrets that are denied him. He receives a violent blow to the head from a plumb-rule. The junior warden touches the candidate's right temple with a plumb-rule. The force is imaginary. Hiram is not killed; he falls to his left knee. The candidate follows this movement then stands again. Hiram makes for the north entrance. The same scene ensues. This time he's struck by the level and brought to his right knee. The candidate is touched on his left temple with a level.

Staggering, faint and bleeding, Hiram gropes his way to the east, where a ruffian with a maul hits him violently on his forehead – the candidate is similarly touched – and falls to his death.

The candidate is now lowered into the 'grave' by the wardens who are asked by the master to attempt to raise him by the entered apprentice and fellow craft grips; but these cannot raise him – a fairly obvious bit of allegorical suggestion.

The candidate can be raised from the grave only by means of the 'Five Points of Fellowship'. The 'Five Points of Fellowship' appear to be a development of the body to body embrace by which the master conveyed the 'word' in one of the earliest known English catechisms (*Sloane* MS. 3329), and which seems once to have been part of the fellow craft ceremony.

The onlooker might describe the 'Five Points of Fellowship' as a kind of geometrical hug or abstract embrace, whereby the knees, heels and hands of master and candidate are placed together in a way suggesting the operation of compass point and square in unison. The number 'five' may relate to the five-pointed star to be discussed in chapter four.

The master now addresses the candidate directly, delivering the *charge* – a marvellous piece of prose with a powerful, if elusive, mystical message.

Let me now beg you to observe that the Light of a Master Mason is darkness visible, serving only to express that gloom which rests on the prospect of futurity. It is that mysterious veil which the eye of human reason cannot penetrate, unless assisted by that Light which is from above. Yet, even by this glimmering ray, you may perceive that you stand on the very bottom of the grave into which you have just figuratively descended, and which, when this transitory life shall have passed away, will again receive you into its cold bosom. Let the emblems of mortality which lie before you lead you to contemplate on your inevitable destiny, and guide your reflections to that most interesting of all human studies, the knowledge of your self. Be careful to perform your allotted task while it is yet day. Continue to listen to the voice of Nature, which bears witness that even in this perishable frame resides a vital and immortal principle, which inspires a holy confidence that the Lord of Life will enable us to trample the King of Terrors beneath our feet, and lift our eyes to that bright Morning Star, whose rising brings peace and salvation to the faithful and obedient of the human race.

(*Third Degree, Emulation Ritual*, Lewis Masonic, p.183)

This charge is probably the most significant item of masonic prose to be found in the canon of masonic philosophising and lecturing. One could write a book on it, so dense and yet so lucid is this exhibition of an insight both radically realist and spiritually idealist. I can only draw attention in this book to some outstanding phrases.

The 'darkness visible' should be seen in the context, I think, of the Holy of Holies. The writer seems to be making a metaphorical link between the darkness of the cloud that is the expression of God's presence in the Holy of Holies and the fear that all people entertain at some time or another for their ultimate future. We are to confront this darkness.

There is even I think a slight pun on the word 'futurity' which may be taken either as our 'long (or short) term prospects of life (and judgement)' or as *eternity*, the life of the divine. The contrasting themes of light and darkness are brought out powerfully and cleverly interchanged. The dark cloud in which God manifests Himself is depicted on the tracing board as blazing light – unapproachable in its essence.

The light of the master mason is a 'mysterious veil which the eye of human reason cannot penetrate'. This is a remarkable phrase to come out of a movement that has often been considered to be central to the European Enlightenment, known also as the 'Age of Reason'.

Reason alone cannot take you to the core of self-knowledge, to the centre. Reason is understood as a gift of the spirit, not the other way around. Reason is a tool, but its scope is transcended. We need to look to the source of reason. Without the 'Light which is from above' reason is useless, helpless to cope with the darkness. Reason alone must surely lead us to materialism or some kind of grim existentialism – or the resigned stoicism of the brave, but ultimately subdued thinker. At its worst we might find ourselves agreeing with actor Robert Mitchum and his much-echoed phrase: 'Life is shit and then you die'. This is the cry from the bottom of the grave – its 'cold bosom' beckons.

Reason cannot provide us with the special light we need; it cannot grasp it. That light is not subjected to reason. Rather, an enlightened reason serves the light.

How might that light come to us? We must come to *It*. There is, the charge insists, a 'vital and immortal principle' that yet exists in the perishable frame; finding and becoming one with this principle is the 'knowledge of your self' that the charge gently and allusively advocates.

The raising of the man from the grave of darkness means letting go of our ordinary understanding, casting aside a false view of ourselves – that empty 'self' dominated by the 'King of Terrors' who nails us down in our fears.

In the context of the 'Tracing Board', the true rising seems to mean accepting within ourselves the Presence of God. Then is darkness visible for what it is.

We are to look to Nature. Nature provides signs for them that see – the hidden mysteries of heavenly science, expressed in geometry. Even from the grave, our earthly eyes can see the Morning Star rising – Venus, that is, *Love* – a sign of the gift of day and the light that raises life to flower and bloom. The stars then are indeed 'windows into heaven'; it is not them, but our 'eyes' that need cleaning.

Well, we may now ask whether the third degree has taken the candidate 'all the way'. That may depend on the candidate. The raw material is there, but it is most unlikely that the degree ceremony itself – or even an inspiring and mysterious speech – could work an immediate ontological transformation in the candidate. Such a radical shift in consciousness might in any case be unwise. The mysteries are not disclosed at once, as if the 'Answer' was '42'. The mysteries must be lived, according to the capacities of the candidate. Some may penetrate the darkness; some may not. Those that do not are most likely to deny that anyone could, or should.

It might surprise some non-masons reading this book to learn that there are many in the craft who believe that the craft has either no, or only incidental and accidental, spiritual content. For them, it is a fraternal society with some archaic rituals – a bit of fun that should not be taken too seriously. 'If it's spirituality you want', they say, 'then go to church!'

Who built the churches?

I sometimes wonder if at the gates of heaven there will be a noisy demonstration of angry people wielding placards declaring that Heaven does not exist.

After the magnificence of the third degree charge, it is again something of a 'comedown' to observe that this part of the degree is followed by more communications to the candidate of signs, tokens, words and promises to care for brethren. The raised brother salutes the master 'in the Three Degrees', then briefly retires from the lodge.

On his return, he is presented with his master mason's apron, which has silver tassles and blue lining, and obligates the master mason to give instruction and assistance to brethren in the 'inferior degrees'.

The master then delivers the 'Traditional History' of the degree. This largely consists of the legend of what happened in Jerusalem after the slaying of the master Hiram Abif.

The twelve who recanted of their intention to threaten the master inform King Solomon of what they had planned. Solomon is worried he might lose his premier artist and a search party is sent out of the city to find the culprits and, hopefully, save the master.

Resting for a moment, one of the fellow crafts pulls up a sprig of acacia. In the process, he discovers that the ground had been recently dug. Calling his colleagues, they uncover Hiram's body, hurriedly buried. They try to raise him but their grips are insufficient, until a third raises him on the five points of fellowship. Everyone is grief-stricken at the sight of the poor master. Such is the grief that the postures of shock and dismay become signs associated with the degree.

The culprits are found in the mouth of a cavern and are dispatched for execution in Jerusalem. Hiram is buried as close to the *Sanctum Sanctorum* as possible – nothing unclean being permitted therein. Even the high priest is only admitted once a year.

The master mason is informed by the master of the lodge that the ornaments of a master mason's lodge are the porch, square pavement, and dormer – the latter being a window for the *Sanctum Sanctorum*.

He is presented with the working tools of the degree, which are: the skirret, the pencil and the compasses. The skirret is an implement that works from a centre pin, is drawn out and enables the mason to mark out ground for a foundation. The tools are interpreted morally as the means of maintaining a straight and undeviating line of conduct, that the Almighty records all our actions and words – for which we shall be called to account – while the compasses delineate His unerring and impartial justice.

The master mason must follow the laws of the divine creator, that, when summoned 'from this sublunary abode', 'we may ascend to the Grand Lodge above, where the world's Great Architect lives and reigns for ever'. This pious hope concludes the ceremony.

Chapter Two
Hiram Abif

Our examination of the third degree has introduced us to the masonic legend of Hiram Abif. There is a good deal more to this essentially masonic figure than might first meet the eye. Freemasons have sometimes been referred to as the 'sons of the widow'. The 'widow's son' of the modern third degree, born of the tribe of Naphtali (in *Kings*), and of Dan (in II *Chronicles*), is the wise man, full of understanding and magnificent worker of brass, Hiram Abif.

This, in part, legendary figure has assumed a significance for Freemasonry that was apparently not recognised in the days before Grand Lodge established itself between 1716 and 1725. Even the choice of Hiram as one of the first grand masters does not fit with earlier traditional histories (which have no 'grand masters'), as we shall see more clearly in chapter five.

Investigating what was intended by raising Hiram to such heights may give us more idea about some of the thinking behind the famous third degree.

Like the strange biblical figures Melchizedek and Enoch, Hiram of Tyre has become something of a mythological figure, yet the record of I *Kings* and II *Chronicles* – as well as the record of Josephus, the first century Jewish historian (*Antiquities* VII.22) – seems straightforward enough.

Hiram's technical services were made available to King Solomon's temple project as a gift from the King of Tyre, also called Hiram (Huram in *Chronicles*). However, in masonic circles the oft-quoted reference in I *Kings* VII.13-14 is frequently conjoined to a reference to Hiram Abiff or Abif.

But nowhere in the Bible (as we know it) does the name appear in this form. This masonic name seems to be a corruption derived from II *Chronicles* II.13: 'And now I have sent a cunning man, endued with understanding, of Huram my father's.' (Authorised Version). The Geneva ('Breeches') Bible of 1607 has: 'Now therefore I have sent a wise man, of understanding of my father Hurams.'

The Hebrew phrase 'Huram abi' clearly has no certain translation in its context. The scribe concerned seems to be working from an ambiguous text (now lost to us). It is especially odd since *Chronicles* is generally regarded as having relied on *Kings* for some of its information – the textual ambiguity does not pertain to *Kings*. Furthermore, *Kings* says Hiram was of the tribe of Naphtali, whereas 'Huram' is of the tribe of Dan. Was there something significant in this distinction now lost to us?

The author of *Chronicles* appears to have another tradition before him and seems to be prepared to put an ambiguous phrase into his text, perhaps in fidelity to it – or perhaps problems may have occurred due to a later copyist's error. But why have the translators kept the distinction between Hiram and Huram, when it is plain that the same persons are being referred to? Was this merely another tradition? It is not enough to say simply 'Hiram (or Huram)', especially since the Phoenician king is plainly called Huram also in *Chronicles*.

Huram abi could once have been a single name, whose equivalent could be something like Huramson: the son of Huram (literally 'Huram of my father'). A case can be made for Huram being either the father or son of the King of Tyre – and either word may not necessarily imply a physical relation.

What is interesting is that in spite of all this, some masonic writer in, presumably, the early 18th century, seems to have chosen to confound the references and create a 'new figure' – essentially a *masonic* figure – Hiram Abif. It is reasonable to suppose that the composer of the ritual had older material to work on. If such material ever existed, then it – like the 'original secrets' – has also disappeared.

J. S. M. Ward's book, *Who was Hiram Abiff?* (Lewis Masonic

– first published in 1925) has been popular among masons seeking further elucidation on the subject but tends to be disparaged by masonic scholars for its over-reliance on J.G. Frazer's famous but mainly discredited study of ancient religion, *The Golden Bough*. However, in spite of the eccentricities of Ward's book, I believe it has a point of view worthy of consideration.

Ward tells us that the name 'Hiram' may mean 'Whiteness', 'Exaltation of Life', 'Their liberty' and, most interestingly, 'He that destroys'. The name is suggestive of the religious role associated with middle eastern kings who apparently enjoyed priestly functions bound to their deified status. (The epithets also correspond to the Hindu god Shiva, and to the Egyptian god, Seth).

Ward makes much of a relation (and identification) of god and king, filling his book with examples from primitive cultures involving the ritual and often actual physical sacrifice of kings once they had lost their powers of generation.

The theosophist Ward combines this idea with his knowledge of the Ishtar/Astarte-Tammuz/Adonis cult. The result of the combination is a theory accounting not only for the identity of 'Hiram Abiff' (who was, he thinks, the slain father of the king of Tyre, sacrificed at the foundation of the Solomonic temple) but also for key aspects of Masonry's third degree.

According to the theory, the slaying of the master artisan was originally an acceptable cult sacrifice, not the work of three 'villains', but of key officers of the cult. There can be little doubt that the third degree, read through the eyes of one acquainted with the Ishtar-Tammuz cult does bear striking striking similarities to this particular mystery. What is the essence of this ancient cult?

Ishtar and Tammuz

The cult legend (which the biblical prophets assert was very popular among Israelites) has many forms, but the basic scheme concerns the marriage of the fertility goddess from on high with the spirit of vegetation (Tammuz) who impregnates her. This act, like that of the bee in relation to its female counterpart, is his 'undoing' and (losing his phallic potential) he dies and (like the seed that falls when the corn is cut at harvest-time) enters the underworld.

Ishtar (Babylonian) or Astarte (Syrian) goes in search of him, being led (or perambulated) through the gates and guardians of the underworld (divested of her 'garments' as she goes) until she recovers Tammuz and ensures his 'resurrection' in Spring.

Astarte/Ishtar emerges in the eastern sky as the 'Morning Star' – our Venus. As goddess of 'love', she is the guarantor of the continuity of life and harbinger of the sun. Ishtar is of course 'the widow' (her husband having 'died') and Hiram is called 'a widow's son', as masons are also called 'sons of the widow'.

Ward also observes that the name Hiram is found in a number of biblical figures who were killed: 'Adoniram' for example, where 'Adon' means Lord (Adonai) – another name for Tammuz – and the apparent root of the Greek *Adonis*, the beautiful god who must suffer sacrifice.

Ward's implication is clear. The king of Tyre took it that Solomon was building a temple to 'the Lord' (the site of the building was an ancient threshing floor – significant in the destiny of Tammuz). King Hiram offered his old infertile father as a foundation sacrifice, ritually assuming the role of Tammuz, and giving his spirit to the enterprise. Solomon is well known as one who entertained the worship of gods derided by the Hebrew prophets. Ward offers many clues to his thesis, among them the ancient notion that the spirit of the sacrificial stand-in for Tammuz emerged as a tree, from which votive offerings (and sometimes the god himself) were hung. Witnesses to the third degree will think of the sprig of acacia at the grave.

All in all, Ward's main thesis is suggestive – especially perhaps to those readers familiar with the cult film *The Wicker Man*. Ward makes it more so by reminding his readers that forms of the Ishtar-Tammuz cult existed in Syria at the time of the crusades. It is known that during the crusading era, masons were brought thence to this country. Similar rites have existed among country-folk in this country since time immemorial – just think of 'John Barleycorn' and the making of corn-dollies. It is difficult to fail to identify a Tammuz-like figure with that of our familiar 'Green Man' who, like Nature herself, is sometimes seen in the role of 'one who destroys'.

Mainstream Christian writers have not been impressed by Frazer's presentation of the 'slain and resurrected god' as the underlying type or myth for the destiny and cultic significance of the 'Easter Jesus', condemning the idea that 'Christianity' might in fact be seen as a form of ethical paganism.

Those who have fixed critical dates of the Christian calendar in tune with the natural fertility cycle have recognised a connection, albeit understood symbolically, *viz*: the 'Morning Star' can represent Christ or the Virgin Mary (and in northern Iraq, Mary Magdalene). Ishtar, like the 'black madonnas' was black (see *The Song of Solomon*).

But if the rituals of Freemasonry can be seen to be derived from ancient, near-universally prevalent myths concerning death and rebirth, the presumably 17th or early 18th century formation of the Hiram Abif ritual is almost certainly Judaeo-Christian (if universalist) in orientation. How could this be?

The Breeches Bible

A copy of the *Breeches Bible* (Printed by Robert Barker in 1607), employed continually throughout the 17th century and beyond, may hold a clue. Therein is to be found a printed note to I *Kings* V.7. The *Kings* reference is as follows: 'And when [King] Hiram heard the words of Salomon [sic.], he rejoiced greatly, and sayd, Blessed be the Lord this day, which hath given unto David a wise son over this mighty people.' (cf. *Luke* I.68-69)

The 1607 notes also tell us that King Hiram had 'the true knowledge of God'.

The note-maker of the 1607 Bible is not slow to pick up the messianic (Son of David) reference (as he or his tradition saw it) within the text and wrote, startlingly: 'In Hiram is prefigurate the vocation of the Gentiles, who should help to build the spiritual Temple.'

Let's hear that again:

> *In Hiram is prefigurate the vocation of the Gentiles,*
> *who should help to build the spiritual Temple.*

It is not unreasonable to suppose that the wise man, full of understanding, who is sent to Solomon, may in fact be one of the *sons* of the King of Tyre or his surviving father: a wise son sent to a wise son in the bond of divine knowledge. (Hiram the worker of brass could have been the offspring of another marriage of the King's father – or himself – to a 'widow' or even a 'cult child', born from a female devotee or priestess of Astarte, dedicated to the service of the cult, embodying the spirit of the god/goddess). That is to say, Hiram the craftsman was an initiate.

Anyhow, the note above was certainly read by Freemasons and Accepted Free Masons in the 17th century and its implications would be astounding. It is the one who sent the craftsman, skilful and understanding, the legendary 'son of the widow', the 'Gentile', who will build the spiritual temple.

In fact, from the point of view of Masonry, it does not matter whether the builder was the father or the son. Either way, he was the instrument of the Most High. In the modern third degree King Hiram of Tyre gets equal grand master status with Solomon and Hiram Abif.

A hand-written copy of the traditional history of Masonry, appended to the masonic *Charges*, dated 1646, tells us that 'there was a King of an other Region yt men called Hyram and hee loved well Kinge Solomon; and gave him timber for his worke; And hee had a sonne that was named Aynon and he was Mr [Master] of Geometry; and hee was chiefe Mr of all his Masons,' (*Sloane* MS. 3848 –British Library).

While the provenance of the name 'Aynon' is obscure, it is clear that this very rare masonic document sees not 'Hiram Abif' as the key figure but instead the King of Tyre and, particularly his son, inheritor of his father's wisdom.

In this regard, it may be significant that there is a 13th century Jewish midrash on *Ezekiel* XXVIII.1-10, the *Yalkut Shimoni*, attributed to Simeon of Frankfurt, which describes the horrific murder of King Hiram of Tyre. According to Rabbi Michael Plaskow, the midrash contains themes of death, decay and resurrection. Perhaps the intention behind the first reference in a masonic context to 'Hiram Abif' was to force an identification of the master mason with the 'son of the father' (the *apprentice*). That 'father' might be understood as King Hiram, King Solomon (masons were known as 'Solomon's sons') or the King of Kings Himself.

The subtextual Hiramic messianic identification (Son of David/Christ/ Hiram) could have been made to preserve a hidden, mystical Christian element while the craft in England opened its doors to men holding 'that religion on which all men can agree' (see Anderson's *Constitutions*).

This religion of harmony may be seen as the universal temple of the Lord whose construction united Jews and Gentiles in common purpose. For Christians, the 'slain Master' can stand for Christ (a strong allusion in the *Rose Croix* ritual of the Ancient & Accepted Rite). The raising of the master is both reminiscent and suggestive of the resurrection of Christ or of the Christian mason in Christ, understood as the lost *Word* and 'rejected cornerstone', or, alchemically, the *Stone* (or *logos spermatikos*) that fell from heaven to make the 'bread of life'.

The tradition of seeing Christ as the *Master Mason* of all master masons is of course a long one. One need only look to I *Corinthians* III.10 to find Christ linked to the work of the master mason, save that He is not only the one who lays the stone but *is* the foundation stone of the spiritual temple itself.

St Paul writes: 'According to the grace of God which is given unto me, as a wise master-mason [Greek *architektōn* = master builder, origin of our inclusive term 'architect'], I have laid the foundation, and another buildeth thereon... For other foundation stone can no man lay than that is laid, which is Jesus

Christ.' (Jesus himself is described in the gospels as the son of a *tektōn*; usually translated as 'carpenter', the word means craftsman or builder, of stone or any other material.)

The 16th century English magus John Dee (much admired by 17th century initiate and adept Elias Ashmole) referred to Christ as 'our Heavenly Archemaster'.

The earliest known English masonic catechism (*c.*1700. *Sloane* MS 3329) asks, 'Who is that on earth that is greater than a Freemason? [Answer] He it was carried to ye highest pinnacle of the Temple of Jerusalem.'

The masonic figure of 'Hiram Abiff' is perhaps a gloss on a number of deep biblical traditions, and his death is tantalisingly conflated – but not necessarily equated with – the sacrifice of Christ. 'Huram abi' would be an ingenious choice for masonic progenitor: in him the believers in one Lord could all find an example or type of the divine builder.

His legend may then have been re-conflated by Freemasons with the masonic tradition of sworn secrecy: Hiram Abif dies to protect the 'secrets'. The resulting *mythos* is, of course, so rich that masons have been vouchsafed an endless trail of possible speculations, with the vital caveat that all this is to be understood as an allegory, so returning us to the spiritual temple, which all master masons must strive to build.

The name Hiram Abif in the Bible

There is evidence that the masonic figure of Hiram Abif was known to masons by that very name before the formation of the modern third degree. Furthermore, it is historically possible that the old Freemasons *did* have an independent tradition of some kind relating to a figure called Hiram Abif. Support for this hypothesis (which necessarily denies the idea that 18th century masons created a 'Hiram Abif' for their own purposes) comes from long since discarded translations of the Bible.

Since the translations cause problems, as we have seen, could it be that the name *Hiram Abif* was originally simply a proper name, kept alive in obscure circles, independent of the composition of the biblical texts? It seems far-fetched, but it is possible.

One possible translation of 'Ab' – normally 'father' – is 'master'. The original phrase might have been, 'my master Hiram'. In alchemy for example, the terms 'master' and 'father' are synonymous. When the master wishes to pass on his secrets, he chooses his 'son'. The master-pupil relationship was in matters of special knowledge a 'father-son' relationship.

In the 1520s Martin Luther's German translation of II *Chronicles* IV.16, gives us: '... und alle ire gefess macht Huram Abif dem Konige Solomo'. While his translation of II *Chronicles* II.13 refers to 'Huram Abi' – two separate parts of a name.

Escaping from persecution in England to Hamburg in 1528, Miles Coverdale worked with William Tyndale on an English translation of the Pentateuch. Coverdale made great strides, and by 1535, based on the Latin Vulgate – and Luther's German translation – he had finished a translation of the whole Bible. Published that year and in the following two years, Coverdale's translation of II *Chronicles* IV.16 gives us an unequivocal Hiram Abif (with Hiram Abi in his translation of II *Chronicles*.13).

As masonic writer Canon Richard Tydeman has written:

> Out of all this bewildering mass of material, one fact of great significance emerges clearly: that in England the name Hiram Abif had appeared in print but once, in a little known Bible of 1535, and nothing like it was used in Scripture for 400 years. Yet Freemasons in 1723 were apparently familiar with the name and did not find it necessary to explain it in any way. Can we really suppose that Anderson and his Brethren [Rev James Anderson, main author of the first Book of Constitutions] invented a legend, and took the trouble to dig out a name from a Bible of two centuries earlier to go with it? Is it not far more probable that the name Hiram Abif was in regular use among Masons even before Luther and Coverdale came across it, and that it has been in continuous use among Masons ever

since? Perhaps someone should do a little research on the relationship between Luther and the Craft, to see which way round the borrowing took place.

(*From the Canon's Mouth*, QC Correspondence
Circle Ltd, 1999, p.37)

The Rev James Anderson himself (author of the *Constitutions* of Free Masons, 1723, 1738) gives some confirmation of Canon Tydeman's view. On page 41 of the historical section of his *Constitutions* Anderson makes his position clear that the 'vulgar' translators have got it wrong, and that their textual problems would be solved if they had simply accepted – or known – that the Master's name was Hiram (or Huram) Abif:

> We read (2 Chron. ii.13.) HIRAM, King of Tyre (called there Huram) in his Letter to King SOLOMON, says, I have sent a cunning Man, ie Huram Abhi, not to be translated according to the vulgar Greek and Latin, Huram my Father, as if this Architect was King HIRAM's father; for his Description, ver. 14, refutes it, and the Original plainly imports, Huram of my Father's, viz. The Chief Master-Mason of my Father, King Abibalus (who enlarged and beautyfy'd the City of Tyre, as ancient Histories inform us, whereby the Tyrians at this time were most expert in Masonry) tho' some think HIRAM the King might call Hiram the Architect Father, as learned and skilful Men were wont to be call'd of old Times, or as Joseph was call'd the Father of PHARAOH; and as the same Hiram is call'd Solomon's FATHER, (2 Chron.iv.16.) where tis said 'Shelomoh lanimelech Abhif Churam ghnafa', [Hebrew] Did Huram, his Father, make to King Solomon.
> But the Difficulty is over at once, by allowing the word Abif to be the surname of Hiram the Mason, called also (Chap. ii.13.) Hiram Abi, as here Hiram Abif; for being so amply describ'd, (Chap.ii.14.) we

may easily suppose his Surname would not be conceal'd: And this Reading makes the Sense plain and compleat, viz. that HIRAM, King of Tyre, sent to King Solomon his Namesake HIRAM ABIF, the Prince of Architects, describ'd (I Kings vii 14.) to be a Widow's Son of the Tribe of Naphtali; and in (2 Chron.ii.14.) the said King of Tyre calls him the Son of a Woman of the Daughters of Dan; and in both Places, that his Father was a Man of Tyre; which Difficulty is remov'd, by supposing his Mother was either of the Tribe of Dan, or of the Daughters of the City called Dan in the Tribe of Naphtali, and his deceased Father had been a Naphtalite, whence his Mother was call'd a Widow of Naphtali; for his Father is not call'd a Tyrian by Descent, but a Man of Tyre by Habitation;

> (*The Constitutions of the FREE-MASONS*,
> London, 1723, pp.41-42)

Why Anderson was so emphatic about what he believed to be the true name of Hiram the architect is unknown. Anderson calls Hiram, 'or Huram, the most accomplish'd Mason upon Earth', but there is no recognition of Hiram Abif as one of the first grand masters of Masonry, as stated in the modern third degree.

A few pages earlier in Anderson's History of Masonry, Moses is called a *Grand Master*, while at the time of the building of the temple in Jerusalem, Anderson states that King Hiram was 'Grand Master' at the lodge in Tyre. At the same time, King Solomon was 'Grand Master' of the lodge in Jerusalem.

The 'inspired Hiram Abif was Master of Work'. Furthermore, Anderson says nothing of any murder of Hiram Abif. One would think such an event would have given him ample cause to dip his busy pen and relate the circumstances, but there is not the vaguest hint of anything untoward happening to Hiram at all.

According to the third degree legend, Hiram was dead before

the completion of the temple. In Anderson's account, he appears to be there to the end and beyond, a continual inspiration – and not even a grand master:

> So that after the Erection of Solomon's Temple, Masonry was improv'd in all the neighbouring Nations; for the many Artists employ'd about it, under Hiram Abif, after it was finish'd, dispers'd themselves into Syria, Mesopotamia, Assyria, Chaldea, Babylonia, Media, Persia, Arabia, Africa, Lesser Asia, Greece, and other parts of Europe, where they taught this liberal Art to the free born Sons of eminent Persons, by whose Dexterity the Kings, Princes and Potentates, built many glorious Piles, and became the GRAND MASTERS, each in his own Territory...
>
> (*Constitutions*, pp.44–45)

It seems difficult to avoid concluding that Anderson knew very little of what was supposed to have occurred to Hiram, as told in the third degree legend. While 'Hiram Abif' might have been a figure of Freemasons' oral tradition before Anderson, the peculiar importance given to him in the modern third degree seems to be for the most part at least, an innovation – like the degree itself.

The question then arises, if there ever had been in any Freemasonic ceremony a ritually significant slaying of a master – one who was raised afterwards – who could it have been? Since we cannot be sure if such a theme of 'the slain master' pre-dated the third degree, readers must judge for themselves whether such a theme might have been important, and, if so, who was the central figure, if it was not Hiram Abif.

Q.   As a Master Mason, whence come you?

A.   The East.

Q.   Whither directing your course?

A.   The West.

Q.   What inducement have you to leave the East and go to the West?

A.   To seek for that which was lost, which by your instruction and our own industry, we hope to find.

Q.   What is that which was lost?

A.   The genuine secrets of a Master Mason.

Q.   How came they lost?

A.   By the untimely death of our Master Hiram Abif.

(Emulation *Third Lecture*, First Section)

Chapter Three

As High as the Heavens – Entering the Lodge

A dispassionate observer of lodge furniture might conclude that he had entered upon the tidily arranged remnants of a cargo cult. In case you don't know, a 'cargo cult' refers to what has happened in remote parts of the world where a primitive culture has suddenly been left with artifacts which, being beyond their comprehension, are taken to be tokens of a higher or divine visitation. The flotsam and jetsam of the oceans, washed up by chance on the natives' shore, is taken to be a deliberate, miraculous intervention from on high.

Such is the awe induced by the objects' strangeness that the alien items are likely to be arranged as a totem and worshipped. Thus, a *Huntley & Palmers* biscuit tin may acquire a whole new theological or mythic meaning through the eyes of one who has never taken afternoon tea.

If you were to ask an unlearned Freemason about the meaning and origin of the peculiar trappings of the modern lodge, he will generally be at a loss to provide satisfaction, at least where some of the lodge furniture is concerned. If, on the other hand, you were to ask a learned Freemason about the origin and meaning of some of the items or images in a modern lodge, he would offer some tentative theory. He would, however, be careful to stress that there are a number of meanings and possible origins of the furniture and symbols to be found in the lodge. He might suggest you read some of the lectures that accompany the degrees worked in the lodges. Such explanations given therein, however, are often of a general or speculative nature. He may add that it is all explained in a book somewhere.

This is why I have compared the situation to a 'cargo cult'. It is as though some things have been washed into the lodge in the process of time, but no one is quite sure why. In the absence of certainty, members have projected their best ideas onto the objects in the search for some understanding.

The situation of vagueness, or if you like, polyvalence (things ascribed a number of values), is exacerbated by the fact that it has become the custom in Freemasonry to expect explanations to be provided by higher authority. Alas! The higher authority is also in a position of seeking a higher authority – often not found.

Perhaps the higher authority has sailed off elsewhere.

Freemasonry has been handed down, for much of its history, by word of mouth and in the spirit of hallowed custom. While everything encompassed by oral tradition, the tradition remained alive, spiritually vital. However, when some things came to be written down, and masonic orthodoxies entered the scene (after the 1720s), the disparity between authority and evolving tradition has left many members with the feeling that 'there must be more to it', if only one knew where to look.

A dispassionate observer, granting that he or she was a well-informed observer of symbols and mythology, should have little difficulty in finding meaning and tradition behind many of the features to be encountered within a lodge. The observer would not necessarily ascribe these meanings to Masonry. Struck by the variety of features derived from other disciplines, he or she might conclude that if these objects had not simply arrived together at random, then a process of syncretism was at work.

A syncretistic order is one made out of separate elements brought together from distinct contexts into a new framework.

The observer might have to try and work out what this relatively new framework really portended. Asking individual Freemasons might not always be very helpful. To give you one example, the author once attended a third degree ('raising') ceremony in Staffordshire. There was some commotion before the start of the ceremony as to where the 'Volume of the Sacred Law' (the Bible) should be opened before its resting on a little lectern near to the master's chair.

Now, every Freemason knows that the 'Three Great Lights' of Freemasonry (as they are called) are the 'Volume of the Sacred Law', the square, and the compasses. You would think then, that every mason would understand why this was so, and what every 'Great Light' was there for.

Well, these fellows knew that the VOSL had to be there – and opened, *but at which page*? As I was the only guest of the lodge present on the occasion, it was hazarded that I might be of some service. Happy to oblige, I suggested that John's Gospel, chapter one, verse one, would be a suitable place to open the Bible – especially for the third degree: 'In the beginning was the Word, and the Word was with God.'

Freemasons have long speculated that the real meaning of the 'Master's Word' in Freemasonry, or even the legend of the 'lost Word' of Freemasonry was in fact the creative *Word* (or Wisdom) of God, that became flesh (as *John* tells us) and was slain and raised.

This idea is quite explicit in the Ancient & Accepted Rite 18th degree, known as the *Rose Croix*. My suggestion was greeted by incomprehension combined with not a little anxious suspicion. Surely, I was told, John's Gospel was from the *New Testament* and, therefore, specifically Christian. Freemasonry was 'universal', was it not? So it was decided to open the VOSL somewhere in the Old Testament on the curious basis that *that* collection of sacred law was more universal, or, at least, more masonic, on account of the story of Solomon's temple being included within its pages!

That the third degree contained the legend of a slain master who is prepared to die rather than reveal his word (or secrets) to the unworthy (that does not itself occur in the Old Testament) cut no ice with these particular brethren. And so the Bible, which included the New Testament, was duly opened in that part of it known as the Hebrew scriptures – of universal significance, doubtless, to Christians and Jews.

There was no doubt that transgression into the latter part of the sacred law book could only be sanctioned by due authority from above. It was as though only half the original story had ever been washed to the shore of this particular lodge. The result was people doing things, but not really knowing why. Of course, in time, after repetition of the semi-mindful act, a new meaning appears with which members are more or less comfortable, while remaining more or less ignorant. This kind of confusion is endemic in the craft. Can we assuage its contagion by taking an objective itinerary of lodge furniture?

Inside the Lodge

This sounds simple enough – *inside the lodge*. The reader may now expect the author to offer a guided tour of a typical lodge. Except that... well, that would be to presume we knew what a *lodge* was.

What is a 'lodge'?

Surely, a lodge is a room in which Freemasons meet and do their rituals, is it not? It's a sort of temple, isn't it? If you ask a Freemason this question today, his first instinct would be to think of his lodge as being the community of men of which he is proud to be a part. When he talks of 'my lodge' he will be thinking in terms analogous to saying 'my club'. He won't be referring strictly to the lodge room. He might talk of the room or rooms where 'my lodge' meets. Undoubtedly, the core of the lodge is, for him, its members. The lodge is something of which he is a part.

It was not always quite like this. The first references to Freemasons and lodges, sometimes associated with the word 'chapters' (another name for a congregation of masons), occur before the 16th century (so-called) Reformation of the Church.

It seems reasonably clear that a lodge was once a name given to a craftsman's lean-to on a building site; a simple structure perhaps where tools were kept or which would serve as shelter in impossible weather. Examinations of masons might take place there and payment may also have been sorted there. There might have been a definite sense of 'lodging' in the word lodge, that is to say, the word may have referred to temporary living quarters –

as a hunting lodge gave nightly succour to those on a protracted hunt. Since such provision might vary from project to project, Freemasons might well have got used to personalising their otherwise impersonal accommodation by calling such places their lodge. It may be supposed they had traditional means of decorating such places, as workmen will, but further speculation on this theme is of little value in the absence of evidence. Lodges of whatever kind, being temporary, have not survived.

The itinerant nature of a travelling freemason's life might have added something of a universal character to his place of residence and meeting with fellows. That is to say, there might have been, even before the trade 'mystery' was sundered from the symbolic cult of Freemasonry, a tendency to think of the 'lodge' as being a universal projection on to any circumstances that gave freemasons shelter. A 'lodge' might be 'virtual' or imaginary, more of a concept than a building.

The lodge was the centre of freemasons' lives as freemasons. Wherever there was a lodge, the freemason was always somewhere, though he might be 'anywhere'. – far from his family, his native soil. As a freemason, he was a *someone*, even though, when alone, he might appear a nobody. We may suppose that coming to the lodge actualised the freemason's life as a freemason. There he might find succour, understanding, friendship as well as hard cash.

This existential aspect of freemasons' lives clearly had resonance for those who joined non-trade Masonry in the centuries that followed the great era of ecclesiastical building in the so-called middle ages. Lost or lonely in a cold and unfeeling world, there was always the fraternal embrace of lodge membership to light the nights and warm the days – possibly centred around an inn with its fires, drink and dining services.

However, we are in some difficulty in trying to locate the position and meaning of the word 'lodge' when we come to the post-Reformation period, though that is a difficult period to date precisely. (We can say that the key legal acts securing the English Reformation had been passed by the time of the accession of James VI of Scotland to the English throne in

1603. After that, the great politico-religious conflicts consisted of defending, attacking or attempting to expand the scope of the 16th century breach with Rome.)

Anyhow, we can hardly doubt that the Dissolution of the Monasteries (1530s) greatly affected the lives of English freemasons. The employers of freemasons would be more likely to be gentlemen rather than clergymen; the market in stone had changed – not to say that many a clergyman was not a gentleman.

By the end of the 17th century, at least, the lodge was already something of an imaginative space. As we have seen, from a late 17th century English masonic catechism, when asked the height of the candidate's lodge, the candidate was to reply that 'it reaches to heaven'. From the same catechism (*Sloane* Ms. 3329 – British Library), we learn that the lodge has a 'Door'. But as the keys to that door are symbolic, so might the door be, the keys being made of 'the tongue of a good report behind a Brother's back, as well as before his face'.

We learn from this rare early English catechism that a lodge has three 'Jewels': a square pavement, 'the blazing star' and a perpend ashlar – that is, a squared and finished stone, its length being, ideally perhaps, a double cube. The perpend ashlar served as a binding stone. It extended from one side of a wall to the other. This strikes me as rather a potent symbol.

The lodge has 'three Lights' – the sun, the master, and the square (compare with today's 'Three Great Lights'). We learn that the lodge stands east and west 'as all holy Temples stand'.

The eastern part of the lodge is 'the master's place', 'and the 'Jewel' resteth on him first, and he setteth men to work'. The jewel here is clearly intended to be the sun that rises in the east.

We are told what makes 'a just and perfect or just and Lawful Lodge'. It is the presence of two apprentices, two fellow crafts and two masters. If there is only one master, then 'five will serve'.

The lodge is to be situated 'on the highest hill or Lowest Valley of the world, without the crow of a Cock or the Bark of a Dog'. Again, we are in symbolic territory.

There is a biblical tradition that God is most present at the highest and lowest parts of the earth, but in one sense and interpretation, which is simply to say that God is everywhere. He is everywhere, but His *Presence* may yet be particularised; indeed, in a number of spiritual traditions, it must be. One thinks of the German mystic Meister Eckhart's aphorism, 'God is in everything from the angel to the spider' or the Hermetic axiom paraphrased by William Blake as 'God is in the lowest effects as well as in the highest causes'. This realisation may come to those who are truly 'centred'.

Masonic tradition gives a high value – both geometrical and symbolic – to the 'centre'. One appealing aphorism that brings together the unity of God's cosmos with the significance of the centre comes from the pen of 15th century philosopher, Nicholas of Cusa: 'God is an infinite sphere whose centre is everywhere, circumference nowhere.' I have seen these words embossed in gold in a kind of Hermetic temple in Amsterdam; they would be very suitable in a lodge.

The lodge is a centre whose centre is in the heart of the Freemason – when the chips have been knocked off it. Thus, the lodge is a kind of divine projection, drawn 'in the spirit' or imagination and projected into the lodge space, with the added living dimension of symbolic officers. It is like a multi-dimensional, cosmic 'chess-set', but unlike chess, which is set for imminent conflict, the lodge is poised, ideally, on an harmonic fulcrum; it is balanced. There is more to 'lodge harmony' than simply being well behaved and warmly sociable!

The properly appointed lodge is a three dimensional living allegory of the cosmos – and man's place within it.

The idea goes like this: when God 'thinks' creatively in three (or more) dimensions, geometry is manifested. Geometry involves a system of projections from a centre. To be a master freemason, you had to get into the creative mind of God – His *Word*, or creative wisdom. The master must give himself wholly and without reservation to the task. Egotism must be transcended: 'not my will, but Thine, O Lord'. A good workman and his tool are one.

Is it possible that apprentices were symbolically 'slain' at the start of the project? We know precious things have been buried in the foundations of special buildings. One can imagine a pious abbot lecturing an apprentice on such a theme while the youngster struggled to square the stubborn stone – but did he need the abbot – or clerk of works – to tell him? Would his master have not told him already?

This kind of insight ought to help us to understand the peculiar 'position' of the 'just and perfect Lodge'. The 'just and perfect Lodge' is an idea, a symbolic concept actualised by the formal presence of Freemasons – who themselves stand *in the presence*. What presence?

The presence of God.

This vital insight is reinforced by all masonic lore; it is not a speculation of the author's making. The Freemason is learning to stand in the *Presence*. That is the end of wisdom of which Wisdom is the means. 'At the centre of the circle,' the Freemason is taught today, 'the Master Mason cannot err.' This siting of the divine being within the centre or heart of the Freemason has gnostic and mystical antecedents, though this may have been quite unconscious. But then, the mysteries of the unconscious are the sources of *gnosis*.

Realising that by at least some time in the 17th century, the Freemason's lodge came to mean something emblematic and conceptual, we are in a better position to recognise why the 'lodges' of that period are apparently so various – from the point of view of external vision, that is.

The Oldest Known Lodges

The Lodge of St Mary's, Edinburgh, has minutes going back to July 1599, making those minutes the second oldest examples of masonic minutes in the world (those of Aitchison's Haven, also in Scotland, go back a year earlier to 1598).

The Edinburgh lodge (entirely concerned with the trade of stonemasonry in this period) met, after November 1613 (when the location is first mentioned), in Mary's Chapel on the east side of Niddry's Wynd. Dedicated to the Virgin, the chapel – demolished in 1787 – was built and endowed by Elizabeth,

Countess of Ross in 1504. In 1600 it came into the possession of James Chalmers, a macer before the Court of Session. Chalmers sold it to the Incorporation of Masons and Wrights in 1618 who converted it into a 'convening house'. The lodge – independent of the incorporation – paid rent to the owners. We know nothing of the lodge's appurtenances in this period.

When Robert Moray – first president of the Royal Society – was initiated into *St Mary's* lodge in May 1641, the meeting was held, uniquely (as far as records go), on English soil, at Newcastle, where Moray was 'Quartermaster General' to the Scottish army. It is noteworthy that a 'lodge' could travel.

Five years later, the English Hermetic philosopher Elias Ashmole was initiated in or near Warrington. It is quite possible that the lodge (which had one statutory skilled freemason) was convened at Sankey Manor, the home of the Sankey family. Richard Sankey was present at Ashmole's initiation and it is highly likely that his son Edward wrote the traditional account of the history and charges of Freemasons to be read on the day. A precious manuscript, bearing Edward Sankey's name and dated October 1646 (the date of Ashmole's initiation) still survives. Sankey Manor has been demolished but parts of its parkland may still be visited.

We have precious little indeed to go on in trying to ascertain what a lodge might have consisted of in this critical century of masonic development, the seventeenth. Our first certain indications of the contents of some lodges belong to the following century, when masonic practices differed widely.

Most lodges of which we have any knowledge met either at private homes or, mostly, in the upper rooms of public houses or coffee houses. Symbols might be chalked on the floor and washed away with a mop and pail after ceremonies. We know that there were special cloths and painted boards, covered in symbols and illustrations, which were discussed. We shall discuss these symbols in due course.

Freemasons convened around a table, a practice that has come to be known as 'the festive board'; it is, as it were, the other side of the elevated work of the 'tracing board', of which more in a moment. The shared meal and toasts were important. Ceremonies may have been conducted while brethren were seated at table, with an illustrated cloth draped over the table until meals were served. Otherwise, the cloth or board may have been put over the floor as a kind of carpet or 'pavement', around which the ceremonies took place.

One striking feature of the rare surviving cloths and boards is that they sometimes feature a chequered design of black and white squares. This simple design is now familiar to anyone who has ever visited a masonic lodge or who has seen the many published pictures of old masonic workings. It may have its origin in the 'square pavement' referred to in early masonic catechisms. It would seem to be a common sense proposition that this design must have been derived from an antecedent. Most persons presented with the question would, I think, suggest that this design was based on a marble flooring of alternating black and white squares – hardly uncommon.

Today, Freemasons are encouraged to see in this design the alternating vicissitudes of life – the good and the bad times that happen to everyone, binding the masonic community together in trust that one's brethren will help one through those bad times that they themselves have been helped through. Rather like chess or draughts, you can, in life, 'land on the wrong square'. Some poor souls never seem to come off them. For the masonic brother of course, being 'on the square' means that no dark square should induce panic. He is taught that there is an underlying harmony, a balance and symmetry in the laws of life and creation, and this is so for his, and our, own good. The universe has providence built into it, as it were. Freemasonry helps her practitioners to steer a better course through life's ups and downs.

There is also a more philosophical interpretation of the black and white squares. There is a dualistic character to the perceptible cosmos as a whole – light and darkness; good and evil; love and hate; sight and blindness; sound and silence; matter and spirit; earth and heaven. In order to live in right relation to the cosmic order as a whole, one needs wisdom – the highest wisdom being grounded, according to the Bible, in the 'fear and knowledge of the Lord'. As the Gospels, echoing the Book of *Proverbs*, say: 'Wisdom has been proved right by all her children.'

It is surely telling that as soon as lodges were able or felt inclined to establish permanent meeting-places, the 'floor cloths' of custom underwent a certain metamorphosis. The floor of the lodge was frequently covered with a carpet of alternate squares with tessellated indents at the edges, suggesting tiles.

The corners of the design included 'cable ropes' to secure the lodge through the storms of its life. It should be reflected upon that the old temporary lodges had no proper foundations, as would befit a lasting structure. The lodge, originally a temporary structure, is traditionally bound together by the moral uprightness of its members, in mutual interdependence.

Lodges have been compared to the tabernacles or tents erected in the wilderness by Moses in his quest for the Promised Land; they too were secured by cable ropes. The Ark of the Covenant was kept in such a structure during its wanderings, a biblical conception that does not seem to have passed masons by. The Ark came to symbolise or express the living presence of God. Cable ropes suggest a divine anchorage. One may think of Noah's Ark and the highest mountain on which it found rest.

Another use for ropes in the old days was for the extension from a centre to create either a circular structure or to lay out equidistant corners for a new structure. Allegorising the ropes as signifiers of the 'Four Cardinal Virtues' has obliterated their original meaning; this can happen when allegorical moralising goes too far, as undoubtedly occurred in the 18th and 19th centuries when lodge lectures came to resemble Sunday schools for bigger boys. This was the style of the times, no doubt, but it hasn't travelled well (in time) – though masons themselves never fail to appreciate and applaud the sheer hard work involved in attempting to memorise them. If you get the whole lot right, you get a prize – just like Sunday school.

This reflection is, of course, open to severe censure from today's stern moralist, if he can be found. The floor cloth having been turned into a more expansive carpet or floor design, the symbols that used to grace the cloths were, in the 18th and 19th centuries, placed around the lodge, on its walls or furniture, or contained within what have come to be called 'tracing boards'.

The phrase 'tracing board' probably derives from the heavy-duty boards the old mason-geometers used for the purpose of making, memorising and reproducing architectural plans and geometrical elevations. Every child has enjoyed 'tracing a picture' at some time or other.

This practice brings us to the all-important masonic interpretation of geometry, one of the seven liberal arts of classical education (they knew what to give 'em in those days!)

Geometry, the art and science of projections from points, used to be known as 'speculating', from the Latin *speculatio*, meaning spying out, exploration or observation, with a secondary meaning of a contemplation or speculation (as we know it). When this speculating in the craft of freemasonry finally acquired more symbolic meaning than practical usefulness (in the lodges of Accepted Freemasonry), the phrase 'Speculative Freemasonry' eventually emerged. In the 19th century particularly, this phrase became a convenient way of distinguishing symbolic Freemasonry from her one-time handmaid, the art, science and trade of freemasonry.

The distinction of 'speculative' from 'operative' freemasonry has not always been a helpful one, since it ignores the fact that practical freemasons had perforce been 'speculating' for centuries. Furthermore, the distinction too neatly dealt with the historic problem of how symbolic Freemasonry came to be severed from the art, science and trade of the same name.

Furthermore, no one speaks of 'operative plumbing' or 'operative architecture'. It strikes one, on deeper investigation, as an awkward distinction, an unnecessary qualification, as we shall see. There is no doubt that 'speculative' Freemasons thought of their discipline as being superior to – and indeed the parent of – the 'humble' builder, at least after the development of Grand Lodge. Calling a lodge 'Grand' may be a bit like knighting a fool; he remains the same, but thinks he's different.

This development has had some unpleasant consequences. One cannot help feeling that an Accepted Freemason pursuing his trade (in the 17th century) might have been expected to use the tradesman's entrance if he had slipped through time and come to advise a 'Provincial Grand Master' in times (hopefully) gone by!

It is noteworthy that both the words 'speculating' and 'projecting' are also words with definite meanings in the disciplines both of alchemy and of ritual magic. Indeed, the word 'projection' has now entered the argot of psychology.

So, having paved the modern lodge with a carpet of alternate squares, has the lodge evolved, or has it attempted, albeit unconsciously, to return to elements of an older tradition? It is possible that in trying to answer this question, we may find the missing link between the stonemasons' lodge or lodging, of old, and aspects of the modern conception of the masonic lodge.

The 17th Century Symbolic Lodge

In attempting to answer the question of evolution, we must needs return to the outstanding mystery (no esotericism intended) of what lodges might have been like in the 17th century – the critical century.

Why critical?

The 17th century is critical in masonic development because this is the first century when records reveal beyond doubt that there existed both lodges of working freemasons and (at least one) lodge made up principally of gentlemen – that in which Elias Ashmole was 'made a Free Mason' in October, 1646. These gentlemen (with one exception) were not engaged in the work of stone cutting, sculpture and architecture – though a number of them were almost certainly patrons of such activities. This does not mean though that what these gentlemen experienced was in the main different to what certain practical freemasons (especially high-ranking freemasons) experienced at the time.

Why do I say 'certain practical freemasons'?

There is written evidence to prove that in the 17th century, members of the London Masons Company hosted a ceremony of a special kind called an 'Accepcon' or 'Acception'. Some kind of ceremony took place at the premises of the company at Masons Avenue, off Basinghall Street, London.

Of those that were invited to it, most were senior members of the London Masons' Company (formerly the London Freemasons' Company). As we shall see in a later chapter, Elias Ashmole himself attended the premises for the admission 'into the Fellowship of Free Masons' of Sir William Wilson, an architect of Nottingham castle, along with five others, in 1682. Ashmole describes himself as the 'senior fellow' at the meeting, since his own initiation, in 1646, pre-dated that of any others attending.

That the meeting took place at the company premises, whereas the dinner that followed it was held at a tavern elsewhere, suggests the existence of a room set aside for a ceremony in Masons Avenue.

One may legitimately speculate about the contents of any such room, even if such a hypothetical place did not provide permanent accommodation for an Acception ceremony – if, indeed, such a ceremony ever existed.

Rational speculation may be enhanced by two surviving items of evidence that, at least to Freemasons, are powerfully suggestive. The link between the two items seems to be the seminal figure of Elias Ashmole, without whose records and published works we should be very much in the dark as regards Accepted Freemasonry in the 17th century.

The Lost Symbolic Lodge

In 1652, Elias Ashmole published an extraordinary collection of the works of English alchemists. It was called *Theatrum Chemicum Britannicum* and it would become one of Isaac Newton's favourite sources for alchemical studies when he experimented with alchemy towards the end of the 17th century.

The book is adorned with a series of very fine engravings by

Welsh engraver Robert Vaughan, who shared a number of Ashmole's interests. One of these engravings depicts the alchemical 'son' (disciple, pupil or heir) of an alchemist receiving a special book from his master. The master is seated while the 'son' kneels.

The master commands his seat in what an unbiased observer might think is a masonic lodge, or something very much like it. The floor is chequered. To the left and right of the men are two pillars, supporting an arch. Through the arch, the chequered floor continues to an edge, representing – or so it appears – a limit to earthly existence.

Above the edge is a blazing sun or star, from which there appears a dove, eagle or possibly phoenix, its wings outspread. These creatures are generally employed as symbols for the holy spirit. Below the blazing light are winged figures (presumably angels) in 17th century dress, commenting on the scene below them. The master gives the book to his alchemical 'son' who takes the book with the oath: 'I will keep secret [or set apart] the secrets [or sacred things] of Alchemy.' The words of the master eliciting the oath from his son are even more intriguing.

Urging him to dedicate himself by keeping the knowledge holy (or separate from worldly things), the master tells him to take this 'gift of God' to himself (*Accipe donum Dei*). The verb used is the Latin *Accipio*, which means to take a person or thing into oneself, to take possession of, or to take one's share in, or simply to accept. Seeing this word in this mystical and alchemical context suddenly makes one possible interpretation of the mysterious 'Accepcon' or 'Acception' ceremony make crystalline sense.

The Meaning of 'Acception'

The 18th century phrase 'Free and Accepted Mason' to designate a Freemason is still in use today. Most readers seeing the words will immediately imagine the word 'accepted' means that the person has been accepted within a community. This is the way masons today like to think of it. I've heard brethren sing heartily of how glad they are to have been accepted as Freemasons.

However, an alternative interpretation of the evidence not only makes this supposition less secure, but it also makes sense of one of the great conundra of the Acception phenomenon itself.

How could it have been that leading professional architects, long since initiated into freemasons' apprenticeships and redeemed therefrom, were prepared to pay good money to join the 'Fellowship of Free Masons' (as Ashmole styles the fraternity in 1682)?

The reason would be that they were going to *receive* something, or rather, and more specifically, they were going to have to *accept* something; they were going to have to *take something in*.

This acceptance was not simply a form of gain, but of giving also – perhaps, even, surrendering; something sacred is being suggested – the need to consecrate, keep separate, keep apart, to secrete.

This 'secret' was not to be a thing simply withheld from others but something to secrete in oneself. This was, perhaps, not a word, but an experience. The 'secret' is something holy, to be kept apart from the world: secreted in awe. In this context, we must try to stop thinking of 'secrets' as things you cannot tell, or want to find out, but as something you are could not utter even if you wanted to, something literally *unspeakable*.

If this interpretation is correct, we not only see why professional architects were prepared to go an extra mile in pursuing or confirming their identity (being perhaps profoundly intrigued), we also have some idea of where that confirmation could have taken place.

In Vaughan's engraving for Ashmole, the supplicant to the master is being asked to accept something: he is not the one being accepted. Again, it must be stressed, what he must 'take into himself' appears to be something sacred; hence the appearance of heavenly characters in the engraving at the moment the secret or secrets are accepted.

Now, of course, it is reasonable to object that the engraving for Ashmole's book is plainly a reference to that section of the book dealing with Sir Thomas Norton's *Ordinall of Alchemy*, a 15th century work which Ashmole wished to bring to the attention of his 17th century readers. In other words, the engraving has nothing to do with Freemasonry at all, in any context. It is to do with alchemy and only alchemy.

However, several other factors might give us pause before we too readily adopt a path of justifiable scepticism. First, in Norton's *Ordinall*, as published by Ashmole, the alchemist-author Norton makes the point that among other trades, freemasons have not been reluctant to take an interest in, and practical value from, alchemy. There was in the 15th century a recognised link between freemasons and the happy pursuit of alchemy. This link is attested in other alchemical works where the male and female figures depicting the alchemical *Sol* and *Luna* (sun and moon) are seen carrying compasses and a setsquare respectively (*viz*: Jamsthaler, *Viatorium spagyricum*, Frankfurt, 1625).

It is also the case that during the 1650s and afterwards, Ashmole was himself the alchemical 'son' of English gentleman-alchemist, Sir William Backhouse, as well as being an initiated Free Mason. The connection between Freemasonry and alchemy could hardly have passed Ashmole by.

Second, the appearance of the blazing star above the chequered floor in Vaughan's engraving to Ashmole's alchemical masterpiece is itself highly suggestive. The earliest known English catechism makes special mention of the 'blazing Star' as a 'Jewel' of the Lodge. The blazing star to this day is a significant symbolic image adorning most lodges throughout the world. It was the author of this book who discovered what appears to be the earliest reference to the blazing star in an almost certainly masonic context. Again, the link is within the life of Elias Ashmole.

The Blazing Star

In January 1652, the first copy of Ashmole's *Theatrum Chemicum Britannicum* was sold to Philip Herbert, 5th Earl of Pembroke, recently promoted to the presidency of the nation's Council of

State. This book was of significance to one of the most powerful men in Cromwell's England. Note – it was not a gift: Pembroke paid for it.

Eight months later, Ashmole made an extended journey to Staffordshire and Derbyshire. Near Buxton, Ashmole encountered a Mr Owlerinshaw who had studied at Cambridge. Ashmole noted in his diary that this man had given 'King James greate Satisfaction about the blazing Star'. It is a masonic tradition that King James I was an admitted Freemason.

Masonry in Scotland was re-organised during James' reign there by the King's Master Mason, William Schaw. Giving 'great satisfaction' on the subject – a most recondite subject – may have been obtained in the context of something like a question and answer scenario. Masons were familiar with question and answer scenarios when being tested on their masonic knowledge. These scenarios are called catechisms and are still in widespread use today in lodge work.

One of the earliest detailed accounts of the blazing star as a peculiarly masonic symbol occurs in John Browne's *Master Key*, published, in cipher, in 1790.

According to Browne: 'The Blazing Star, the Glory in the Centre, reminds us of that awful [awesome] period, when the Almighty delivered the two tables of stone containing the ten commandments [note the 'stone' inference], to his faithful servant, Moses, on Mount Sinai, when the Rays of His Divine Glory shone so bright, with such effulgent splendour and unparalleled lustre, that none could behold it without fear or trembling.'

It is interesting that the appearance of the blazing star, representing the presence of God, appears when something is being accepted from an awesome source. If we may use the phrase 'lodge of Acception' – with some caution – such an occasion would be realised when something sacred was taken within. Something special was to be held in sacred trust thereafter. If this interpretation is sound, then those who may have experienced such a thing surely kept the secret to themselves.

Not only do we know practically nothing about anything imparted at the Acception, but also it is quite possible that even the word itself has, through ignorance of its proper reference, come to mean something quite different from its original intent. This lack of knowledge may in part account for the reference today in the third degree ritual material to the newly made master mason receiving only the 'substituted secrets'. The originals, according to the legend, went to the grave with the master Hiram Abif at the building of the temple in Jerusalem. There is every good reason not to take this gloss in its apparent historical sense.

However, the allegorical death of masonic hero Hiram Abif may yet be significant with regard to trying to understand the 17th century lodge in which men experienced Acception. This significance may be highlighted if we take the Acception to be the particular point from which modern Freemasonry was projected, albeit unconsciously.

The World's Oldest Artifact of Symbolic Freemasonry?

The nearest iconographical cousin to Vaughan's engraving of the alchemical master and son of which I am aware is in the possession of Lord Northampton, currently 'Pro Grand Master' of the United Grand Lodge of England. It is in the form of a remarkable chair. One might reasonably suppose it to be a master's chair, but whether from a masonic context or some other symbolic context is uncertain. However, its contents blend so well with traditional masonic philosophy, even illuminating it, that it might seem churlish to doubt its masonic provenance. Nevertheless, that is not proof alone that Freemasonry was its original setting.

The back of the chair is decorated with rare marquetry. Two fat pillars support an archway. At the head of the pillars is a date, halved: 15 to the left, 95 to the right. The date of the chair appears to be 1595.

Passing through the arch, we find we are in a chamber with a chequered floor. Towards the end of the chamber and flanked by two upright structures is what appears to be a tabernacle of some kind with an arched opening. Within the opening floats a veil. Above it appear two figures, possibly cherubim or angels facing one another as we might imagine if we think of the ark in which the tablets of the law (the 10 commandments) were kept in Solomon's temple. Above the angelic figures is another arch. This might be the night sky or the limit to the light the arch encompasses, or, indeed, what masons have come to call the 'Royal Arch' (see chapter fifteen).

The truly extraordinary thing about the chair's marquetry is invisible until one moves to one side and examines the image from another angle. Then it becomes apparent that the levelling of the planes within the carving has been so cleverly executed that the effect of a change of light upon the design instantly reveals that at the far end of the chamber – the veil – is a *skull*.

Meditations on death were not uncommon in the 16th century. Ingenious ways of including the theme of the ubiquity of death (*Et in Arcadia Ego…*) are well known. For example, the skull painted at such an acute (and at first sight invisible) angle in a lower corner of Holbein's *The Ambassadors* still intrigues those to whom it has been brought to notice.

Nevertheless, the skull of death that is also the veil to – what? – the Holy of Holies, the Ark, the *Shekinah* or presence of God – at the end of the chequered floor of life is deeply suggestive from a masonic as well as from a mystical point-of-view.

That one must die to the world to be reborn in the spirit is a staple insight of mystical understanding. The 'burial' or sacrifice of the 'apprentice' at the foundation of a new building (the temple to-be) is part of old masonic mythology. 'Unless ye be born again, ye cannot inherit the kingdom of God.'

As we shall see, the masonic third degree contains an allegory built around a kindred conception of spiritual transformation. The symbolic slaying of both the *prima materia* and mercurial principle in alchemy is deeply analogous to the process of spiritual transformation. The theme of 'acceptance' is very powerful in traditional accounts of Christ's agony in the garden before crucifixion and, 'after three days', the climax of resurrection.

'Take this cup away from me,' says Christ, contemplating the reality of the cup of suffering from which He must drink. All that would be reborn must accept this cup. Those who seek this 'grail' had better understand what is involved; it is not for the unwary.

It should be added that there is another chair, also in the possession of Lord Northampton, very much like the first, but dated two years later, to 1597. Here the main pillars and archway are the same, but at the end of the chequered pavement, enclosed in a simple arch, is a simple cross. The cross is made of contrasting kinds of wood. There might be the implication that this stark and powerful image represents, as it were, the 'view from the other side'. That is to say, the image may depict what one might see if one were to have passed through the veil of the first chair to find a near identical chamber on the other side, then to walk to the great archway and turn around. Then, the two schemes would be literally two sides of a single experience. (In alchemy, the cross is a symbol of mercurial transformation.) Perhaps the second chair was commissioned as a companion to the first following some special realisation in the mind of the first chair's owner.

The Oldest Known Symbolic Freemason?

Who was the chairs' original owner?

Another detail of these chairs is intriguing. Above the archway of the first chair is a crest. The crest consists of a crescent moon beneath and embracing a blazing sun or star. It is the crest of the Minshull family, a very old Cheshire family. The first chair is initialled to the left and right in large capitals: E. M.

In the summer months before his initiation (October 1646) Ashmole was courting Elinor Minshull. Elinor was born on 7 September 1622, the second daughter of Captain Peter Minshull of Erdeswick (sometimes spelt Eardswick) Hall, Minshull Vernon, Cheshire.

Another lady of the family, Ellen Minshull, was married to Philip Mainwaring of Upper Peover, Cheshire, a relative of Ashmole's, both through his mother and Ashmole's first wife, Eleanor Mainwaring. When Ashmole was initiated at Warrington in October 1646, he was 'made a Free Mason' with Colonel Henry Mainwaring, a kinsman of Philip Mainwaring.

The tomb of Ellen (*née*) Minshull and Sir Philip Mainwaring was sculpted by one of the freemason sons of King James I's English Master Mason, Nicholas Stone – most probably John Stone (King's Master Mason at Windsor, 1660-1667).

Nicholas Stone received the 'Accepcon' at Masons' Hall, London, in 1638. Perhaps the Stones were well acquainted with the Mainwaring and Minshull families. Perhaps there were shared fraternal interests.

It is highly probable that the 'E. M.' inscribed above the Minshull crest marked the name of Edward Minshull. I have recently been able to verify this hypothesis to a high degree of probability.

In 1595 – the date on the chair – Edward and John Minshull were involved in a legal dispute over land in Clive and Waverton with Sir George Mainwaring (*Mainwaring Papers*, John Rylands Library, Manchester). This Edward Minshull was probably the Edward Minshull who was Ellen Minshull's father. Ellen Minshull's funerary monument, as we have seen, was carved by the son of Nicholas Stone, an Accepted Free Mason.

Edward Minshull lived at Stoke Hall, a couple of miles outside Nantwich, Cheshire.

Having identified Edward Minshull, the connections between the Mainwarings, Minshulls, and Elias Ashmole came thick and fast.

On 11 September 1663, Elias Ashmole and his friend Sir William Dugdale held an heraldic visitation 'at the signe of the Crowne' (inn) in Nantwich, Cheshire. There they invited local families to come and establish their arms and pedigrees (Ashmole was Windsor Herald; Dugdale was Norroy King-of-Arms). On that day, Sir Thomas Mainwaring of Peover Hall came and signed his pedigree. Ashmole, meanwhile, drew up a pedigree of the Nantwich branch of Mainwarings. He took extracts from the heraldic visitation of 1613 and made note of the fact that the visitations revealed that there had been no fewer than five alliances between the Mainwarings of Nantwich and the Minshulls of Nantwich, Stoke and Eardswick, Cheshire, in four consecutive generations.

Ashmole undoubtedly saw himself as part of the story. His first wife was Eleanor Mainwaring, his current wife was born Mary Mainwaring – and, seventeen years earlier, he had been 'made a Free Mason' in the company of Colonel Henry Mainwaring of Karincham (now Kermincham), Cheshire, his first wife's cousin.

There are many other highly suggestive links in the area between freemasons and the three dominant families of Nantwich in the period: the Mainwarings, the Minshulls, and the Wilbrahams. Ashmole and Dugdale recorded many of the monuments to be found in Nantwich church (St Mary's) and in that church's mother church, Acton, just outside Nantwich. Among several coats of arms of Mainwarings on tablets in Nantwich church were those of William Mainwaring of Wich-malbank – the old name for Nantwich – who died on 22 April 1637. There were also to be seen the tombstones of Elizabetha Minshull, wife of Richard Minshull who died on 17 February 1637. Elizabetha's maiden name was Wilbraham.

It was important for dominant families to maintain control and, if possible, extend their land-holdings. Thus we find the land interests of the Mainwarings, Minshulls and Wilbrahams closely entwined over many generations. And with the land interests came the relationship with the freemasons. The relationship derived from the land interests – buildings and entombments, and we may suppose that the relationship was long lasting. It almost certainly derived from the times of settlement of Norman families in Cheshire in the century after the Conquest.

The church at Acton (St Mary) was of ancient establishment. The church at Nantwich was originally a chapel of rest, connected to Acton. It was in existence by 1130, and was called the chapel of Wich Malbank. In the early 12th century, the second baron of Wich Malbank gave the church of Acton (along with the chapel of rest) and their lands to the Cistercian monks (the 'white monks') who were establishing themselves at Combermere, south of Nantwich, in the county Palatine of Chester. Along with these churches, the church of St Bartholomew, at Church Minshull, is also mentioned in a confirmation charter of Combermere abbey as an appendage chapel to Acton.

The local families took a very serious interest in the churches and lands about them – and in their privileges. These privileges were granted – for money – by the monks of Combermere. The families secured their control through the guild system, and it has been well established that this system was important to the development of freemasons' fraternities.

According to Raymond Richards (*Early Cheshire Churches*, Batsford, 1947), there was a very powerful guild in Nantwich, dominated by the leading families: 'The gild known as Holy Cross was all powerful, a brotherhood established for the better regulation of the town. Persons not incorporated in any of its respective confraternities were not allowed at their decease to have any ornaments of the church, or to have more than a third bell rung for them. From its contributions six chaplains were provided to say mass for the brethren and sisters composing it, as appears by a deed dated 1461. In no case had Combermere anything to do with the building of the church, their part being extraction of money from the chapel for themselves.'

According to Richards, it is to the guild and not to Combermere Abbey that one should look for responsibility for the magnificent growth of Nantwich church with its great octagonal tower before the Reformation: 'The quire is a fine example of the later free design of the fourteenth century, the production of no mean intelligence, a Master-Mason whose work will stand comparison with anything of its style to be found elsewhere.' (Richards, p.7)

We can get a small glimpse of the rivalry between the families from looking at what happened to the lands owned by the abbey of Combermere after the dissolution of the monasteries in the 1530s. (The following decade also saw the guild and confraternity system attacked by plunder and suppression.

Nantwich church was left penniless.)

Inter-family rivalries were best resolved through marriage, when such was possible. Ashmole's own life at the time shows that he had received this message loud and clear. He went courting Minshulls, Mainwarings and Fittons (the Fittons of Gawsworth were also closely related to the Minshulls and Mainwarings).

In 1541, the rector of St Bartholomew's, Church Minshull, was one John Minshull. However, the church and lands formerly belonging to Combermere were now in the hands of different families – and the old families were keen to re-establish the cosy arrangements that they had once enjoyed through association with the monks of Combermere. But they could not; the old order had changed.

After the dissolution, Henry VIII granted the advowson of Acton to the Wilbrahams. That made the Wilbrahams even more powerful. In the case of Church Minshull, however, the Minshulls did not fare as well. Whereas before the dissolution, Church Minshull had been leased to Edward Minshull of Minshull, Esq., following the seizure of Combermere, one John Daniel of Daresbury acquired the property.

Church Minshull had gone to the Daniels! This must have been a blow for the Minshulls. They had had many years' experience of dealing with the Cistercians. The new order brought disturbing pressures. In the event, Edward Minshull bought the land from Daniel, and Church Minshull remained Minshull territory. John Minshull stayed rector until 1568, an appointment that must have been a comfort for the family.

Change appears to have been no less discomfiting to the Mainwarings of Nantwich as it was to the Minshulls after the monastic dissolution and subsequent wasting of many the old guilds and confraternities. To this day one can still see the magnificent tomb at Acton (St Mary) of William Mainwaring of Baddiley and Peover who died in 1399. Recumbent in armour, carved with amazing skill by a freemason in alabaster and sandstone, the monument dominates the Mainwaring chapel in the church. It is very similar to monuments in the church of St Lawrence at Upper Peover, including the collar chain, inscribed '*Jesu Nazarenus Rex*' – perhaps a chivalric order.

In 1660, another monument appeared in the church at Acton, of surpassing magnificence. This was the tomb monument of Sir Thomas Wilbraham (1601-1660) and his lady.

Katharine Esdaile, in her book *English Church Monuments 1510-1840*, considered the monument to be the work of leading London freemason, Edward Marshall – and his masterpiece. I am not altogether convinced. The work is extremely similar in style and workmanship to Ellen (*née*) Minshull's monument to herself and her husband fashioned in alabaster by John Stone at Over Peover.

Whoever of the two was responsible, Edward Marshall was himself in any case very well known to the Stone family. Marshall was appointed King's Master Mason at the Tower of London in 1661, and was a chief competitor for royal work with the Stones. In fact, John Stone was reported to have referred to Edward Marshall as a pretender to the place of honour once held by his father. (Could the rivalry between master masons have been reflected in the choices of Mainwarings and Wilbrahams to be their respective tomb-makers?)

Anyhow, there is no doubting that the Stones and the Marshalls were among the handful of 'best men' in the business, brought up from highly lucrative work in the capital to adorn the lives of ancient Cheshire families. It is surely significant that we find them working in a part of Cheshire wherein we know a form of Free Masonry existed, dominated by gentlemen.

According to visitation records, Edward Minshull of Nantwich (Stoke Hall was the country residence just outside the smelly town) died in 1627. His widow was Margaret (*née*) Mainwaring, and it was their surviving daughter Ellen who built the neat mortuary chapel of stone on the north side of the chancel of St Lawrence, Upper Peover.

After her husband's death, Lady Ellen left Peover and went back to live at Nantwich (presumably at Stoke Hall). On 14 October 1656, her son Thomas Mainwaring recorded in his diary that, 'This day my deare mother was interred at Peover'.

It may be imagined that before she died, she may have had cause to look on a pair of chairs apparently commissioned by her father, Edward Minshull. On that chair dated 1597, appeared a bold cross. May this have been in reference to the Holy Cross guild that had dominated the civic life of the township of Nantwich? And might not this connection in part explain why gentleman Edward Minshull might have come to sit as master or warden over a symbolic lodge or fraternity of Free Masons?

A codicil. In Ashmole's notes on botany, recorded in his diary (Josten, *Ashmole*, vol. iii, p.1286, note 5), there is found reference to a 'white greene' near Nantwich. On it grew a thorn tree, which, like the famous thorn of Glastonbury, flowered at Christmas and at Easter. Could the name 'white green' have come from the 'white monks' (the Cistercians) who once owned the land? And could, I wonder, the cross on the second chair have been made from the wood of this thorn, thus making it truly a holy cross?

One could well imagine such an act being accomplished by a man who had been party to recovering lands once leased in apparent perpetuity from the old Cistercians of Combermere. Was symbolic Free Masonry, with its hypothetical symbolic 'lodge' of transformation, a knowing throwback to a perceived 'golden age' before the terrible events of the so-called Reformation systematically wrecked the ancient polity of England?

Edward Minshull may well be the first non-craftsman of whom we may say, with a reasonable degree of probability, that he was a Free Mason in 1595. This strongly suggests that Lord Northampton's chair is the oldest symbolic Masonry artifact in the world – and Edward Minshull the first known symbolic Free Mason.

Towards the Modern Lodge

It now appears that by the end of the 17th century we have several features familiar to those enjoying or enduring the experience of the modern lodge system. We have the chequered pavement, almost certainly the blazing star, as well as the presence of pillars and arches. We may also have the theme of angels descending, which may later (perhaps) suggest the ladder to heaven. We may also have the phenomenon of the master's chair. We may now ask, 'Did the Acception lodge go *on tour?*'

The plethora of 17th and 18th century images and symbols familiar to masonic museum keepers all over the country must have come from somewhere. Is it possible that the cloths or painted boards began, in part, as a way of taking the chief features of a fixed location to temporary locations where freemasons were assembled? This might explain the ubiquity of certain images and features.

However, it is also possible that the modern lodge simply evolved, becoming more sophisticated rather than less so. In this view, the idea of a fixed 'Acception lodge' or basic model is simply a casting back to an unknown past something from a known future. This tendency is, after all, quite common – to project the known into the unknown.

For example, it is quite common for masonic historians to deny the possibility of symbolic Masonry existing in the middle ages because they cannot recognise in that era the form of it that they know already. Sceptics of such a possibility can say that the surviving data of the 'middle ages' offers no evidence for lodge rooms, esoteric symbolism (whatever that might have meant in the middle ages) or the rituals 'as we know them'. However, as we have understood Freemasonry, these outward signs are not necessary in themselves.

The way Freemasonry has manifested has changed, clearly. Indeed, were it not for the iron grip that has been exercised by the grand lodge system, it is fairly certain a great deal more evolution would have taken place as the philosophy and practice of Freemasonry met new challenges and received fresh imaginative impulse and general creative input.

After all, the practice of architecture, in its substance, self-understanding, and in its organisation has changed beyond recognition in the last 300 years. One wonders what

Sir Christopher Wren would have thought of RIBA, for example.

What would the fresh breeze of early 20th century modernism have done for Freemasonry, had it been permitted to blow through the old halls, nooks and crannies of what came to be called 'the traditional system'?

King Solomon

One aspect of lodge manifestation has certainly changed over time. That is the significance given to King Solomon and his temple. It is difficult to know whether Solomon's reputation, masonically speaking, has more to do with his being an epitome of wisdom, than his commissioning a temple for the Jewish priesthood.

Most Freemasons today, for example, would probably think, if asked about the square pavement, that it derived in some way from Solomon's 'Porch', or part of the interior of the temple. This is chiefly because the familiar second degree tracing board, designed by John Harris around 1845, gives Solomon's temple (as conceived symbolically for masonic usage) a nice chequered floor.

Freemasons have become accustomed to thinking of the lodge as being in some sense a version of Solomon's temple. It is widely believed (though with how much conviction it is impossible to know) that 'speculative Freemasonry' began with Solomon's temple. Even the master's chair in a lodge room, or masonic temple, is sometimes called the chair of King Solomon – though how many masters have ordered babies to be cut in two to satisfy competing mothers from this vantage point must remain a matter for the lowest kind of speculative sensationalism.

It might come as a surprise to many to learn that the significance of Solomon, his famous temple and his celebrated worker of brass, Hiram 'Abif', apparently used to play a relatively small part in freemasons' self-understanding. This is the logical inference to be gained from reading the oldest documents of the freemasons, the so-called 'Old Charges' and early catechisms.

At Ashmole's initiation, for example, Ashmole will only have heard that there was a 'King called Hyram who loved Solomon well' and gave him timber for his work – there is nothing about an architect (which is, in fact, not Hiram's role in the temple according to the Bible).

Those who experienced the early English catechism as contained in *Sloane* MS. 3329, for example, will have learned that 'the first word' was given at the 'Tower of Babylon' where the masons convened their lodge 'at the holy Chapel of St John'. Lodges stand eastwest, the catechism maintains, as the 'said Chapel and all other holy Temples stand'. Nobody has yet come up with a thoroughly convincing idea of why St John has become so significant a figure in Freemasonry, though there are a number of quite rational suggestions.

The growing importance of King Solomon's temple may have come about for several reasons.

First, the new order of the 'Grand Lodge', some time after 1716, was looking for a fresh model, once the break with the trade was foreseen.

Second, Freemasonry began its long loosening of exclusive relations with Christianity.

Jews had been permitted to reside in England since the 1650s and the new grand lodge did not wish to exclude them. The figure of 'Hiram Abif' would replace (or symbolically encompass) Jesus Christ as a focus for masonic idealism. To be sure, there was some quasi-scriptural warrant for this interpolation, if we may call it so.

As we saw in chapter two, there is a note to the 1607 'Geneva' or 'Breeches' Bible, issued by authority of King James I, declaring, when dealing with King Hiram of Tyre: that 'in him' (Hiram) is 'prefigurate' the destiny of the Gentiles, who should build 'the spiritual temple'. This was (and is) mighty testimony, but alas, we have no evidence for the reasonable supposition that this was the kind of warrant for change the new order sought.

Third, Isaac Newton, the hero of Grand Lodge's third grand master, Desaguliers (1719), believed the proportions of the temple of Jerusalem contained a code of cosmic proportions.

Newton believed the temple had been constructed to encode not only the mathematical wisdom of the creator – the primal and universal knowledge of mankind (that had fallen with man into sin) – but also a universal symbolism.

Newton's code makes *da Vinci's* look a trifle tame. The temple's dimensions, according to the 'father of modern science', not only related to fundamental cosmic patterns, but also contained prophecies for the future destiny of mankind.

Righteous man needed raising back to the ancient antediluvian and paradisal science (simultaneously practical and spiritual) that Newton believed had been vouchsafed to the 'mighty men of renown' known as the Patriarchs (see the book of *Genesis*). This was a powerful theme easily reinforced by nascent claims for the craft's antediluvian credentials to be found in the *Old Charges*, as we shall see.

Linking Freemasonry closely to this matrix of advanced possibilities and advanced science and theology would have been attractive to Desaguliers, who had a hand in (and over) the first printed *Constitutions*. Grand Lodge was inculcating a new order. The new order was in a position to take elements of traditional freemasonry and, as it saw it, build on them. In the process, fundamental emphases changed. To take one example, the golden age of freemasons in England (the building of her abbeys, castles and cathedrals) was reduced by the author of much of the first *Book of Constitutions* (James Anderson, in 1723) to the phrase 'Gothick rubbish'. A new gang was, literally, on the block. And they were cutting it their way.

Thus it was that when the practice of meeting in public houses (upper rooms) and other temporary accommodation slowly gave way to permanent places of convening, the buildings tended to be considered in terms of the dimensions of Solomon's temple. How many noticed the extraordinary and peculiar reversal of meaning that took place thereby?

The 'lodge' by its very definition was a temporary place; one's passage through it a sojourn. Its foundations were but symbolic. It left no mark, no record – like the wind.

The 'holy Chapel of St John' was, of course, the wilderness. John's encounter with God was – like Golgotha – outside the city walls. His lodge was any place where the fire of holy spirit was manifest.

He was *in the Presence*, in the lowest valleys and the highest mountain.

'John' was one of *them*, a spiritual Free Mason, building a new Israel by burying sin in water. John's head had become a centre of divine life, full of fire and love and energy; little wonder the slut Salome wanted it on a platter!

Nevertheless, before we part from *terra firma*, we must admit that the symbolic character and possibility of the Solomonic temple was not a totally new idea to freemasons.

The chair discussed earlier, dated 1595, appears to depict something akin to Solomon's first temple to one God. There appears to be a 'Holy of Holies', a tabernacle or sepulchre, within its depth, and even a veil covering it, identified mystically with death (by the great skill of the carpenter). That veil may be supposed to be equivalent to the veil of the temple that John's gospel declares was rent from top to bottom as Christ accepted death and surrendered spirit to His Heavenly Father's care.

But again, this idea is more resonant in the creative imagination, than laid out in wood and stone.

It is worth reflecting that the modern lodge may have asphyxiated the old masonry. Certainly it is hard to find the freedom and wildness of the holy desert in a suburban lodge on a wet night! But good men have overcome even these restraints, and some of the most powerful masonic experiences on record came to men who had to carve working tools out of scraps and who convened lodges behind the Japanese army's barbed wire. But then, that rather proves the point, doesn't it?

Still, the modern lodge had to come – and it had to have a shape and a mailing address. To find the mailing address, you may consult a telephone book. To understand the shape, we need to look more closely at the symbols to be found in the modern lodge.

Chapter Four

Lodge Symbols

In chapter three we attempted to trace the process by which permanent lodge rooms came to be identified with Solomon's temple. The identification with proportions borrowed from Solomon's temple is particularly noticeable in the fact that the length of many lodge rooms is an oblong square or double cube, following the first Book of *Kings*, chapter six, verse two. (There are also some rare cubic lodges, particularly in the United States.)

However, the adoption of the Solomon's temple model has caused some confusion, particularly with regard to the status of certain pillars that are such a noticeable feature of masonic lodges. Alongside the question of 'Whose pillars are whose?', there is also the question of orientation, related to the positioning of the famous pillars in Solomon's Porch.

The Pillars

The entrance to Solomon's temple, according to the Bible, was in the east, but entrances to lodges are, symbolically speaking, in the west. This is almost certainly a result of the tradition of the master being seated at the point of the rising sun, to the far end of the lodge. Accompanying this tradition goes the charming idea of the master rising first to set his masons to work. One must also take into account the long established Christian church tradition of entrance at the west with the altar in the east. We are accustomed to look to the east for the star of salvation, the rising sun.

Unfortunately, it is an inherent problem of allegories that once you begin the allegorical process, every detail may be supposed to represent something else. Allegorical representations and genuine symbols easily become confused – especially where numbers are involved. The fancy is free to roam – within the general confines of the chosen allegory anyhow.

The fact seems to be that the lodge was from its start never intended to represent Solomon's temple. Though it might allude to it, the temple is just an element of the accreted tradition. Besides, the finished temple should hardly have been an object of especial focus since it is the *process of building it* that is more properly the masonic concern. Nevertheless, the temple stands as a masonic ideal and is now inseparable from Masonry's self-understanding.

During the first half of the 18th century it was customary for the wardens of the lodge (junior and senior) to each carry a pillar. This practice (how old we know not) bore some reference, presumably, to the Solomonic pillars – or had the portable pillars once represented perpend ashlars?

An added inference was that the wardens were themselves to be perceived as the upright pillars of the lodge – allegorically of course – being stationed at the lodge entrance, though this positioning is disputed.

Further confusion was added to the mix when the notion arose that the principles by which the lodge stood – and by which the masonic life was vitalised – were those of 'Wisdom, Strength and Beauty'. These principles were contrived to apply to each pillar, indeed to account for the very form and meaning of the pillar. That is to say, the pillar's base represented wisdom; the shaft, strength; the chapiters, beauty.

Architecture then was neatly explained as being no more than the direct application of the abstract eternal principles kept safe through time by Freemasonry. Freemasonry, operating in the sphere of divine ideas, had hovered above the old freemasons and looked down on them; Freemasonry had been there through all time.

It was 'perfectly obvious' that Moses was a Freemason – and such genius as Greece enjoyed was, at its most exalted, masonic also. In the 18th century, Freemasonry became – or tried to become – a *classical* idea, newly proud of its sublime geometrical status, as one of the seven arts of the classical, liberal education. Liberal education was the education of free men. Were not the new Accepted Masons *Free*?

By the end of the 18th century, the allegory of moral and aesthetic principles had been taken to the point where wisdom, strength and beauty were to be perceived as the 'pillars' of the lodge, its essential principles. So now there were three pillars, or, should we say, three more pillars. They can often be seen on masonic tracing boards, labelled at the base: W, S and B, three letters, pregnant with meaning and understood by those 'in the know'.

Abstract principles had become the proper names of a group of pillars.

Grand Lodge Freemasonry wished its work to be associated with fashionable ideas of architecture, its exalted principles, rather than its business. Thus, the quasi-Platonic principles of wisdom, strength and beauty, were applied to three of the five 'noble schools' of classical architecture: Doric, Ionian and Corinthian. Lectures were contrived as to their virtues, based in part on polite architectural manuals for the embellishment of monuments to the new age of dawning reason.

Architecture had become part of a gentleman's education. The new Paladian country house would echo visions of classical Arcadia, with the number of actual shepherds kept to an aesthetic minimum, wherever the capability of Brown or the genius of William Kent could so contrive it. This was the golden age of the 'Whig' landowner: a plutocracy of progress, at the dawn of the industrial revolution.

Architecture had now to be brought to Freemasons' attention as an 'add-on' discipline. This was cleverly achieved by keeping to the allegorical interpretations of architecture, with the conceit that these high principles came before, and indeed transcended, the grubby business of building. Freemasons kept their spotless aprons clean.

Truth levels the foundation; Justice plumbs the upright, and Charity squares the covering. The cement is Love and Friendship; Unity gives the bond. The ornaments of the pure lodge represented Virtue, Concord. Everything within the lodge is striving for perfection.

The four cable ropes have become the four cardinal virtues, likewise capitalled and personified: Justice, Prudence, Temperance and Fortitude. Silence locks the Door, depositing the Key in every true, just and honest Mason's Heart. Every Mason stands upright on the Square. And so on.

Some must surely have felt smothered in the torrent of blameless pieties. But piety was a vital component of 18th century religious revival: the only known cure – other than the gallows – for the horrors of Gin Lane and the terrors of syphilis.

The new Freemasonry met a social need.

But which pillar was Ionian, Doric or Corinthian? Surely, all three bore elements of wisdom, strength and beauty. There were differences of interpretation that would have to be sorted out. Masonic orthodoxy had to be established, or people might think they were not sure of what they were talking about.

Furthermore, what had happened to the pillars of Solomon's temple – Jachin and Boaz? How convenient it would have been if there had been three! This was tried too. Were the wardens about to lose their allegorical status as holders of the pillars and upholders of the temple of Solomon? Yes, and no. The wardens would still represent the pillars of the lodge. The lecture symbolism of the first degree would concern itself with the wardens – and the master. The master now represents Wisdom – and hence sits in the chair of Solomon. His wardens are Strength and Beauty.

Today, the senior warden is close to the lodge door (in the west) – to mark the setting sun. The junior warden sits in the 'south' of the lodge, to mark the sun at its meridian. Allegory is applied to these positions too, of course.

The junior warden, representing the pillar of Beauty is placed at the meridian, for it is when the sun is at its height in the south that the greatest light – and therefore beauty – is shed upon the earth.

Furthermore, even greater dignity could now be applied to this allegorical trio. Did the master and his wardens not also represent the three original grand masters?

Three original grand masters? Yes, there were three original grand masters of the craft: Hiram Abif, his suzerain King Hiram of Phoenicia, and, of course, the voice of Wisdom herself, King Solomon. All three were necessary to the application of the principles of wisdom, strength and beauty in the construction of Solomon's temple.

Having satisfied the dignity of the wardens' position, it would be necessary to decide which of the three noble orders of architecture (of the possible five) should be applied to which transcending principle.

Before 1813, William Preston's highly influential lectures referred to the Ionic as representing Beauty and the Corinthian, Wisdom. But after the union of the competing 'Antients' Grand Lodge (established in 1751) and the so-called 'Moderns' Grand Lodge (established 1716–1717), the assignations were changed.

Wisdom was permanently identified with the Ionic, Strength with the Doric, and Beauty with the Corinthian – and these three columns were formally identified with the master and his two wardens. This may have reflected the practice of the 'Antients', some of whose variant customs were adopted by compromise at the creation of the United Grand Lodge of England in 1813.

The union of 'Antient' and 'Modern' took place a year after Napoleon's Retreat from Moscow: the death knell for European republican and revolutionary fervour (until its recrudescence in 1848) – and, arguably, the effective end of masonic experimentation in Britain.

This still leaves us with the twin pillars of Solomon's temple, as described in I *Kings* VII.15–22 and II *Chronicles* III.15–17. Visually speaking, many lodges leave their representation to the second degree working (fellow craft ritual), where the pillars appear on the tracing board designed for that degree. The three columns mentioned earlier are very prominently displayed on the first degree tracing board (entered apprentice).

It seems likely that it was in the 18th century that the names of the two pillars became significant in masonic rituals, providing candidates for the entered apprentice and fellow craft rituals with pass words. 'Jachin' or better *Yakhin*, which means 'May the Lord establish'. 'Boaz' or better (in Hebrew) *be'oz*, means strength or energy. Freemasonry has given these words an architectural allegorical twist – building with the Lord in strength – whereas most Jewish historians would apply the words to references to the establishment of the Davidic kingdom. Both interpretations share the idea that the *Lord* is the securest foundation.

Again, there is some confusion over the orientation of the pillars. The right pillar (called Jachin by Freemasons) and the left pillar (known as Boaz) are only 'right' or 'left' depending on which direction a person would be standing in the temple porch. However, the first century Jewish historian Josephus informed his readers that his people faced the east (the rising sun), where north was to the left hand, and south to the right hand. So we may take it that 'Jachin' was, as it were, to the north (being left), and 'Boaz' was to the right (being 'south').

That being said, where modern lodges do contain representations of the two pillars, they tend to be placed in the east of the lodge. Their 'leftwards' or 'rightwards' position depends usually on the visibility of the letters 'B' or 'J', sometimes affixed to them, seen from the west looking east. It is not at all unusual for Freemasons to get very confused about this sort of thing. Perhaps this is why pillars of Solomon are less common – especially as they cannot be identified with lodge officers.

Where there are no pillars of Solomon, sometimes there may still be seen a pair of globes, one showing terrestrial geography, the other showing the stellar constellations. The appearance of these globes seems to have come about as a result of further confusion over the nature and meaning of lodge pillars. It was customary on some early tracing boards to depict the Solomonic pillars as being each capped by a large spherical ball. These balls or 'globes' soon appealed to the imagination of

Freemasons as being a reference to two levels of existence, the earthly and the heavenly – the divine creation in fact.

In William Preston's *Illustrations of Masonry* (1772), the significance of the globes is given emphasis. The globes are, Preston informs us, 'the noblest instruments for giving us the most distinct idea of any problems or proposition, as well as for enabling us to solve it'. Clearly, there was some kind of scientific discussion going on in lodges. However edifying this may have been, reference in I *Kings* VII, and II *Chronicles* IV to the pillars' crowning features restricts itself to calling them, not balls – or globes – but *bowls*.

Ironically, where the pillars have gone, the globes remain.

We now come to the remaining dominant features of lodge ornament and furniture. Again, we cannot be very sure of the original meaning ascribed to these images and objects. Elements of the original kit were acquired, over time, but the instruction manual appears to have been denied, mislaid, or suppressed.

The Letter G and the Blazing Star

In many lodges, a letter G the size of a hand is suspended over the centre of the lodge floor or over the master's pedestal. It is nowadays properly displayed during second degree ceremonies.

The letter G may also appear set within 'the Blazing Star or glory in the centre' that may be woven into the centre of the chequered 'pavement' carpet. The 'Blazing Star' is sometimes depicted geometrically as a pentagram, a frequently encountered figure in Freemasonry, and one with an even longer – and considerably more illustrious – pedigree than the use of the letter G.

The Pentagram

Briefly, the regular pentagon (in which the star-like pentagram is formed) contains a number of curious geometrical symmetries. It also contains some numerologically significant properties that mark it out from other geometrical figures. Its geometry is central to the fifth Platonic solid, the dodecahedron (constructed from 12 pentagons), representing the ultimate 'fifth element' by which the 'Great Geometrician' completes the universal creation (the other four solids representing the classical elements of earth, air, fire and water).

The pentagram is generated from the 'Golden Mean' (described in Euclid's *Elements*, Book VI, Proposition No 30) and involves a fascinating exposition of mean and extreme ratios – the golden mean being the most perfect of the incommensurable ratios. Such were its properties that the Greeks gave each of the pentagram's five points a letter, spelling the word *HYGITHA* from the verb '*hygiazo*', meaning to cure, to make whole or make sound. The figure enjoyed magical and positive medical qualities and was found suitable as a talisman. It is also a fairly common 'mason's mark' to be found on stonemasons' work over many centuries. It is not a wicked symbol.

There is a notable illustration in Henry Cornelius Agrippa's *Three Books of Occult Philosophy* (English version, 1651) where we see the figure of a man within a circle. His arms are stretched forth like dividers. Each hand thrusts forward a pentagram. There is a plumbline at his solar plexus and the upright builder's square at his feet. His feet are placed with his left heel in the ball of his right ankle at a 90-degree angle, a posture familiar to Freemasons today. He stands upon an ashlar with a perfect circle upon his head.

The design would serve as a perfect illustration of the masonic axiom that 'at the centre of the circle the Master Mason cannot err'.

The figure depicted is a being of power. A line bisects the circle at the solar plexus. The figure is balanced betwixt two worlds that together make a unity, at the centre of which is Man – poised between the temporal and the eternal: a microcosm of the universe. This figure is a classic condensation of Renaissance Hermetism and its positive estimation of human potential.

Hermetism represents the collection of philosophical insights attributed to the gnostic patriarchal figure, Hermes Trismegistus.

This legendary personage is named as 'the father of wise men' in a 17th century copy of masonic charges (containing a traditional history of the craft). It is easier in a sense to trace the background to the use of the five-pointed star than it is to understand why the letter G has come into lodge usage.

Does the 'G' stand for 'God', or as Freemasons sometimes call the supreme being, 'the Great Architect'? Does it stand for the creator as *Grand Geometrician*? Or does it simply stand for 'geometry' – which the Pythagorean schools understood as having a practical and a mystical side? (Pythagoras is also named in the *Cooke* MS. of 'Old Charges' as an ancient patron of the craft. This version of masonic charges was written down in about 1420.)

Geometry has been understood as providing proof of God's design in Nature, containing properties of harmony, truth, regularity, music and so on. (It is noteworthy that geometricians are more likely, in my experience, to accept the idea of an intelligent creator, than are some famous biologists, for whom 'natural selection' suggests an auto-efficiency precluding deity.)

Obviously, geometry offers many basic concepts to the one who wishes to allegorise the process of self-development. There is the regular progression from a point (or centre) to a line, to a superfice or plane, to the next dimension: a solid. The most 'perfect' example or ideal of this progress is a cube, and the masonic 'ashlar' or perfected stone is usually cubic. Was Picasso a Freemason?

Geometry means 'earth measurement' but of course it has also linked man to the stars above, by degrees. Measurement makes architecture possible, obviously – and humankind may likewise be measured in accordance with cosmic law. He had better advance in a regular movement of ascending degrees if he is to attain the proportions his maker had in mind.

How high is your lodge? It reaches to the heavens.

As the prophet has divided the sheep from the goats, man is faced with the choice – if he would know himself – between being a 'superficial flat' or becoming a lively perpendicular! Judging from some dominant elements in popular culture in east and west, the former option is, predictably, still an attractive one. But it can get pretty boring down there, with only crime to pass the time and self-destruction to fill the empty spaces.

After that little peroration, it seems a bit of a comedown to add the post-script that G is the third letter of the Greek alphabet. The Greek letter 'gamma' (capital) is in the form of a builder's square – one stroke up and then to the right: Γ. It is indeed a Capital Letter.

Freemasons are not compelled to favour one interpretation of the letter G over another; they all drink from the same cup.

In the first part of the first book of masonic *Constitutions* (Rev James Anderson, 1723), the author begins his history of the craft with the observation that God must have inscribed geometry on Adam's heart at his creation. This is akin to saying, today, that geometry is built into the human subconscious. Releasing its secret power releases Man.

Rockets to the Moon? Geometry gives us a rocket to the soul.

The Jewels

It has come to be accepted as a tradition (in English Masonry) that there are six jewels present in the lodge, three movable and three immovable. The former are today understood as being the square, the level and the plumb-rule – the 'working tools' of the second degree (fellow craft).

The immovable jewels are taken to be the tracing board and the rough and perfect 'ashlars'. In fact, an ashlar is a squared stone, so the unperfected or unpolished precursor of it, which represents the man before perfection, should perhaps better be called the rough stone.

Why immovable? Perhaps because of their 'fixed place' in the lodge. Perhaps because of the archetypal nature of the cubic stone – the first Platonic solid in the Grand Geometrician's mind, so to speak, before projecting the cosmos. It is certainly not a reference to the weight of the stones! The symbolic stones are generally little bigger than paperweights. Cubic stones have apparently replaced the older perpend ashlars which may have been 'double cubed' or oblong in shape. (The double cube may also be expressed by placing one cube on another at 45 degrees, producing the octagonal form, and, from above, the eight pointed star – a basic design for many ancient towers and ubiquitous to masonic ornament).

The first and second degree tracing boards now generally follow the designs of John Harris who completed these still resonant works for the United Grand Lodge's Emulation Lodge of Improvement (dedicated to ritual excellence) in 1845.

The third degree tracing board design was to be found on earlier boards and cloths. It involves a coffin, the skull and crossed bones and other grim motifs associated with the reality of death. After 1813 and the union of the 'Moderns' and the 'Antients', the three degrees of craft Masonry were fully separated. Before that, entered apprentice and fellow craft degrees could be conferred in a single ceremony. Each degree now had a separate tracing board.

Most of the elements combined to produce the standard first and second degree tracing boards can be seen in the frontispiece to Stephen Jones's *Masonic Miscellany* (1797). These include the following emblems and symbols: the two Solomonic pillars (surmounted by globes); a squared pavement (not chequered); a tessellated pavement (indented or 'zig-zagged' in contrasting black and white); a warden (holding a staff) standing by a seven-stepped staircase ascending to a domed structure. Within the domed structure and beneath an arch appears a seated figure also carrying a staff (master or senior warden).

There are three pillars in descending height, a key (to the lodge), an ashlar with the square and compasses inscribed upon it, a rough lump of stony *prima materia*, a geometrical figure resembling a ground plan in oblong square form. There is a circle with a point at its centre, bounded to its left and right by descending 'staves'. Between the lower parts of the staves is a blazing eight-pointed star with a G in its centre. Above the circle with the centre point is the Bible (VOSL) with the square and compasses placed over it.

From the Bible a three-rung ladder ascends heavenwards. The top rung is indicated with a 'C' (Charity), the middle, 'H' (Hope'), then the first step: 'F' – Faith (this is another way of expressing three progressive degrees – from faith to love through hope (the knowledge of things not seen).

Interestingly, it was the second century Father of the Church, Clement of Alexandria, who expressed the divine pattern of life as a progressive ascent from faith to *gnosis* (knowledge), culminating in divine love.

To the left of the ladder is a plumb-rule, square and gauge, to the right: the square and compasses. Above are seven stellar angels, then a cloudy firmament, within which are the familiar emblems of the sun and the moon (with seven stars). Moisture falls from the cloudy firmament upon a shaft of corn that grows next to a serpentine figure (weed? serpent?) that, crossing it beneath its leaves, seems to be making the corn bend. At the top of the frontispiece is the letter 'E' for East; West is below. If this is a kind of diagram of the 'lodge' as symbol, it follows the old tradition and 'reaches to the heavens'.

Contemporary lodge cloths belonging to the 'Antients' Grand Lodge show some figures which have fallen into disuse: Aaron's rod (that could explain the 'serpent'), a pot of manna, the tablets of the Law (Ten Commandments), and the trowel.

The Ladder

Anyone who has seen Powell and Pressburger's magnificent film *A Matter of Life and Death* (1946) will have been struck by a powerfully graphic interpretation of the moving staircase that leads to heaven. As in Jacob's dream, on which the image is based (an escalator has replaced the ladder) beings can go up and down on its steps. Jacob did not try to follow the angels in either their ascent or descent, but Freemasons are encouraged to rise.

Jacob was so struck by his dream of a ladder to heaven that he said of the place where he envisioned the scene: 'This is the house of God, and the gate of heaven.' Not surprisingly, masonic designs have not neglected the inference by putting a winding staircase into their representations of the temple of Solomon: an ideal masonic structure.

It may have been the influence of 18th century Pietism – a movement stemming from Germany and France – that gave the masonic ladder the three rungs of faith, hope and love, St Paul's spiritual trinity of ethical imperatives.

Faith, hope and love play a significant part in the 18th degree of the Ancient & Accepted Rite, where life is seen as a journey in search of these divine and vital principles. We rise by virtue, but above all, by the attraction of better things, the call of the spirit.

Climbing the ladder also means letting things go, leaving things behind. If we are to be reborn in the spirit, we must die to the flesh. This is hard, but the prospect and certainty of death is hard also, and cannot be avoided. The ladder is there.

The Point within the Circle

The image of the point within the circle, bounded by two perpendicular staves is one of the most intriguing symbols (if that is what it is) in masonic tradition. No one today can be certain of what was originally intended. It was obviously important for some people, for, obscure as it first appears, there has been no willingness to let it go the way of Aaron's rod! It is now mostly seen (if it is noticed) inscribed on the table or lectern on which the VOSL is opened, on the first degree tracing board. Thus it seems to support the three 'Great Lights of Masonry', though this may be incidental.

What can it mean? First, it encodes the method whereby a circle may be squared.

Suspend a plumbline the length of the radius of the circle from the extreme right and left of that circle. Join the ends of the two lines by a straight line. You have thus created two perfect squares. Thus, one can demonstrate that the square (which traditionally represents earth-bound measurement) is derived from the circle (which describes – like the compass – celestial movement: the stars, sun and moon).

In squaring the circle, you have unified both material and heavenly (spiritual) dimensions and shown the former's dependence on the latter. This demonstration shows practical and symbolic Freemasonry as one process.

I should add that there are other interpretations, some symbolic and mystical. For example, as the circle is the 'perfect figure', having neither beginning nor end, wherein all its degrees are equidistant from its centre, so it represents *eternity expressed* (or the pure creative act – *Fiat Lux!* – 'Let there be Light!'). Circular motion was held in classical times to be perfect motion – though this cannot be said to be true as regards all our buses.

The material dimension, represented by the two staves or lines on either side of the circle, is the constraint of that perfection in a dualistic system, that is, the cosmos. The almighty has constrained itself in order to create the 'square' world, the world of the four elements. This idea has resonances in Lurianic Cabala.

Cabala (or Kabbalah) is a form of Jewish mysticism or *gnosis* tradition that hopes to show the divine character in man and in the universe – a 'secret' insight. Lurianic Cabala tries to explain the limitations of the universe as being a result of a contraction in the being of God, whereby the supreme principle of being makes a space within his being, from which he, in a sense, 'withdraws'.

This interpretation is only one of any number of interesting speculations, but it does not seem, to this author anyway, to be what was originally intended. Indeed, the simplest explanation for the 'symbol' is that it simply shows the principle of drawing the foundation line for a circular structure. To do this, the builder can employ a point in a centre in which one staff is placed, while another staff is extended on a line to its limit. Thus the mason describes the outlying circle in the dust – the two men performing the task of two points of a compass, the two operations becoming, as it were, one.

The staves could then have come to be associated with the two wardens, or the master and his warden, each holding a staff.

(Nowadays the wardens may carry 'wands'.)

The point in the centre was probably used to illustrate the third degree teaching wherein the master mason cannot err when he is 'at the centre of the circle'. This has, again, a purely practical and a spiritual meaning. At the centre or point, is both God – the point from which time and space derives – and the heart of the mason, wherein his conscience is pricked, and where the spirit of God and his eternal love is to be found.

There are alchemical implications too. In alchemy, the symbol of the sun is the circle with a point at its centre. In Freemasonry, the master is associated with the sun, and the sun, of course, is the source of light. The sun is also, mystically and philosophically, the source of enlightenment. 'The jewel [the sun] resteth on him [the Master] first.'

Esoteric speculation regarding the point in the circle can be found in a book by John Dee, the famous Elizabethan astrologer and mathematician. It is called the *Monas Hieroglyphica* (1564): a book on the unity of the cosmos. Dee hoped it would be read and eventually applied by practical men. The book is very hard to understand, blending, as it does, Cabala, alchemy, mathematics and philosophy.

In fact, it was a visionary work and Dee probably tried to veil what he was really getting at, as he seemed to think he was on to something so important he could only hint at its real meaning. Unfortunately, he is no longer available for interrogation. We must get by with hints, inferences and allusions – and such light as we may attract to our endeavours.

It is worth mentioning that the book was much appreciated by persons attracted to the early 17th century Rosicrucian vision of global reform, with which Freemasonry has been often linked. One thing at least is clear. Dee saw a profound connection between alchemy, architecture and, indeed, all the arts and sciences. His 'one hieroglyph' was a magical attempt to symbolise and encompass this unity.

Dee's intriguing figure is based on the circle with the point at its centre, joined to the alchemical symbol for mercury, together with two semi-circles. In fact, the symbol could be geometrically constructed from the circle with the point at its centre, together with the two staves we see on the tracing board. This implies that whether the Freemasons knew it or knew it not, they had the universe at their fingertips! It seems possible that some such insight had somehow 'got into' 18th century Freemasonry, but no one can be sure how, or what it might mean.

Certainly there have been some not-very-convincing attempts to explain what it might mean. A long popular masonic teaching was that the two staves or lines represented John the Baptist and John the Evangelist respectively. Their 'days' are close to the solstices and were occasions for masonic feasts: 24 June for the Baptist and 27 December for the Evangelist. The role of the two Johns – which many identified as one – is one of the fascinating unexplained mysteries of masonic tradition. That does not mean of course that no one has tried to explain the mystery.

Some time after the union of 1813, Masonry was encouraged to become non-denominational and its most obviously Christian elements were removed. The Johns were changed to Moses and King Solomon: Law and Wisdom.

In keeping with the Solomonic interpretation, one compelling insight into the figure of the circle with a point bounded by two staves comes from the Bible. In I *Kings* VIII.8, we read of how, when the Ark was placed in the newly built Holy of Holies, 'they drew out the staves [by which the Ark was made portable], that the ends of the staves were seen out in the holy place before the oracle, and they were not seen without: and there they are unto this day.'

If the two staves before the 'oracle' are compared to those in the masonic symbol that would make the circle with the point in the centre nothing less than the Ark of the Covenant.

The Ark contained 'nothing...save the two tables of stone put there at Horeb'. (v.9) These 'volumes' of sacred law would then have been bounded by the staves, so the circle with the point at its centre could signify both the universal law – and more, the divine presence itself. For we hear in the book of *Kings*, that immediately after the removal of the staves from their former position, 'the cloud filled the house of the Lord'.

We are told that 'the glory of the LORD had filled the house of the LORD'. I think there is more to the phrase, 'There was nothing in the ark save the two tables of stone' than meets the eye. The phrase is linked to the manifestation of the glory of the Lord that followed. This 'nothing' in the ark is, I would suggest, that perfect medium by which the 'glory' is manifested.

This interpretation is consistent with the kabbalistic conception that the essential nature of God, prior to manifestation, may be expressed as a *zero*. Furthermore, this 'glory of the LORD' is not itself 'light' – though it is the source of spiritual light (awakening) – but quite plainly, in the text, it is darkness. The 'cloud' that fills the holy place is so dense that 'the priests could not stand to minister'.

Solomon himself then speaks (v.12): 'The LORD said he would dwell in the thick darkness. I have surely built thee an house to dwell in, a settled place for thee to abide in for ever and ever.' This interpretation, so rich in mysterious paradox, explains two notable masonic axioms at a stroke.

First, that 'at the centre of the circle, the Master Mason cannot err'. This would be because he is at the zero point; he is in the presence of God, where there is nothing – no force to compel movement from the point, no distraction and no thing – not even 'himself'. This dynamic of negative presence (or the Point) may be compared to Newton's axiom that perfect rest is only possible when no force on that point is impressed. The Holy of Holies is the still centre; men cannot see it. To them, it is darkness.

Second, as we shall come to see in respect of the third degree, we learn that 'the light of the Mason is darkness visible'. This only becomes 'clear' in the Holy of Holies: the third part of the temple, when its 'veil' has, as it were, been rent from top to bottom.

To understand this 'darkness' better I should recommend determined readers consult Pico della Mirandola's *Oration on the Dignity of Man* (1486) where the great Florentine genius speaks of inspiration being gained 'in the solitary darkness of God', to be gained only when men have flown heavenwards 'like earthly Mercuries'.

Keen observers of the New Testament may note that Christ's disappearance from the vision of the disciples occurred when a 'cloud' removed him from their sight. It is, as they say, all in the Mind. Literalists simply don't get the Point. The point is brought to the candidate's heart even before he has crossed the threshold of the lodge for the first time.

The Heart

One other meaning of the circle and the point: the German theosopher, Jacob Böhme, who died in 1624 and who was very influential on third grand master Desaguliers' hero Isaac Newton, sometimes portrayed the heart as the point in a circle.

Böhme thought of the heart as the 'organ' of man (the seat of feeling and the hall of conscience), that could most properly respond to the call of salvation, and the return of man to his pre-Adamic (innocent) state.

The ladder was another way of showing the path man must ascend by degrees to undo the work of the Adamic fall (out of Eden) into ignorance and darkness. Thus, the perfected ashlar could be seen in Jacob Böhme's terms as the 'New Man'. Many who have studied the works of Böhme have noticed a curious relationship between them (especially the famous engravings that first accompanied them) and the images associated with 18th century Freemasonry. There is much more in this treasure box still to be explored, I think.

The Tools of the Craft

How is the creation of such a *New Man* to be effected? In Freemasonry, there are tools to help in the quest for self-knowledge and self-development, with all its side-benefits for charity and for society. It appears to have been the premier Grand Lodge of England's rivals, the *Antients*, who made most of the running during the 18th century in providing the moral explanations of the working tools of the first and second degree.

The first degree tools acquiring moral explication were the 24-inch gauge, the square and the common gavel or setting maul. Anderson's *Constitutions* of 1738, on the other hand, mentioned the hammer (to separate) and the trowel (to join). Anderson made no references to ritual practice so we cannot be sure what was being taught on the subject among the 'Moderns' at this stage. There did exist standard references to the square, level and plumb-rule as jewels of the lodge, while the square and compasses were related to the Bible whose sacred rule encompasses the universe and the bounds of man's conduct. The concept of restraint is very strong in masonic moralising discourse based on the working tools.

In 1775, William Preston's famous *Illustrations of Masonry* gave moral explanations of the rule, trowel, plumb-line, square, compasses, chisel and mallet – and it all adds up to knocking chips off the disordered man on his path to (hopefully) perfection. The tools show the paths of virtue, restraining the disharmonious tendencies. There is something of the 'nanny state' in all of this. Eternity must always be kept in view – that limits ambition. What has the world to offer, but death at its end, the loss of worldly advantage? But in the light of eternity, the earth itself becomes a tool for the highest labour.

The chisel demonstrates the advantages of discipline and education. Even jewels need cutting and polishing to reveal their true beauty. This line is not followed quite as positively as we should expect today. There is not much stress on the beauty within – but then, the 18th century was not altogether convinced that we were 'worth it', to paraphrase a contemporary cosmetics advertisement. They were rough and ready times. Human beings are wayward creatures, and as the *Proverbs* tell us, a good man will welcome an honest rebuke. Never, says the proverb, scorn a dishonest man; he will hate you for it. Save your guidance for those who would be good. Freemasons welcome the message of restraint.

The 18th century 'Enlightenment' (with which continental Freemasonry especially is often linked) is widely believed to have based much of its rational optimism on the idea of 'the perfectibility' of man. However, there was in the masonic discourse much more moral stress on the imperfection of man than current conceptions of 'progressive Enlightenment' philosophy might suppose. There was no Rousseauesque 'noble savage' in English Freemasonry! The imperfections in man are to be treated from without, by discipline and more discipline. Self-discipline is welcomed by the wise. The message would be something like: 'Boy, it's tough! But you can make it!' Not altogether bad advice in any era.

The change of heart that comes from a moral challenge is generally supposed to come from an act of will rather than a 'spiritual experience'. The universe is rational and its laws are expressions of divine will. By will were they made, and by will they will be obeyed. A better society could only come from better men; social conditions were the product of the wickedness or otherwise of men, not impersonal economic determinants. Of course, all measurement is something of a restraint in property and in law.

The Freemasons were simply describing the facts of life and the pearls of wisdom. You don't get anything for nothing. According to the Prestonian vision, the tools of Masonry were, basically, to make a perfect temple and world order: a universal house of wisdom for all who would choose to enter therein.

On the Square

The square is the jewel of the master – the one who would master himself. He who has not achieved this is in no position to guide others. The square has become a by-word for honest dealing, sincerity of purpose and good practice. The master is thus erect, upright, with no weakness in his foundation; his eyes are fixed on higher things. His hands are open in charity; his heart is warmed in fellowship. The square shows us the summit of the degrees of elevation.

When the square is applied, it reveals weaknesses and strengths straight away. Without equivocation or need of argument the square conquers untruth and pretension. Nothing that will stand can be built without it. In its absence, man is stunted, incapable; he is not full-grown. He is immature and weak. He bends with the wind and his sight is therefore warped. He gazes away from life's challenges; he looks at the ground and stumbles. He falls.

The square is within. The square and compasses are the sun and the moon.

The one is the light, the other the light reflected. In the lodge, it was hoped that the light would be seen in all its phases – from its rise to its setting and round the infinite sphere to its rebirth.

The just and perfect lodge is the *House of Wisdom*, nothing more and nothing less.

Chapter Five
Genesis of Freemasonry

Readers will by now be familiar with the terms 'mason', 'Freemason', 'Free Mason', 'freemason', 'Masonry', 'Freemasonry', 'Free and Accepted Masonry'. Forgive me for throwing in some more: Free-mason, freestone, freestone mason, master mason of freestone, speculative Freemason, operative freemason.

Is it any wonder there is so much confusion about the origin of the craft?

When Adam named the animals in Eden, each knew his name and heeded his call. To know the true name of a thing, the old magi believed, was to call into its inner nature. How can one get to the reality of Freemasonry if one does not know how to call it? When terms get confused, it is generally because someone has a vested interest in twisting a conventional usage into something else. Terms may simply be misunderstood, and, in an attempt to clarify them or make them fit the user's notion, they become distorted. This happens all the time; it has certainly happened where Freemasonry is concerned.

London AD 1212: the first known use of the Latin expression, *sculptores lapidum liberorum*. The phrase refers to sculptors of freestone.

Freestone is a kind of stone suitable for fine carving. Freestone does not develop faults when carved with or against the grain and is soft and refined enough for detailed work. Sandstone and limestone are more suitable for the purpose than granite.

In London, in 1351, an Anglo-French expression appears: *maître maçon de franche peer*. Forty years later, in Oxford, we find the expression, *magister lathomus liberarum petrarum*: a

Latin equivalent for the Anglo-French. The expression means a 'master mason of free stone'. The occupation of 'freestone mason' gradually got shortened to 'freemason', a term that was in general use in England for a sculptor and mason until at least the 18th century. When Lichfield cathedral was repaired after the civil war, the Dean and Chapter employed a local freemason to rebuild and carve.

The term 'master mason of freestone' would now be expressed simply as 'architect'. Had that term been in general use in the 16th and 17th centuries, Freemasons today might have been called 'the architects' – and one may wonder what the relatively *arriviste* Royal Institute of British Architects would have thought of that!

The term 'freemason' was a specifically English term before 1600; the Scottish term for the same job was simply 'mason'. When 'Freemason' entered Scottish usage, Freemasonry had already become an order of symbolic rituals, in England, and was applied to lodges with loosening ties to the trade.

Before 1654, the *London Company of ffreemasons*, dominated the practice of the art, science and trade in London. After that time, the company called itself the *London Company of Masons*.

In general usage, mason and freemason meant the same thing: a craftsman in stone. It might be significant that when Elias Ashmole (1617–1692) twice refers to the organisation of which he was a member (in 1646 and in 1682), he refers to himself as a *Free Mason*. This usage might be to distinguish his status from a person who earned his living solely from stonework and construction (a freemason), but I don't think we should build too much on this. Usage of capitals and variant expressions was customary in the English of the period.

Furthermore, I think it likely that Ashmole genuinely considered himself as having a bond with the whole world of practical freemasons. He was a mathematician and in due course would be involved in construction (the *Musaeum Ashmoleanum* in Oxford). The theoretical side of the 'trade' was geometry, one of the seven liberal arts – and an art familiar to Ashmole, as was drawing. He would probably have agreed with Rudyard Kipling's statement that 'all art is one'; one should.

'*Ex Uno Omnia*' was Ashmole's pansophic motto.

In 1686, Dr Robert Plot's *Natural History of Staffordshire*, refers to lodges of '*Free-masons*' in that county – referring to lodges clearly dominated by trade work, but nonetheless attracting 'persons of quality' who had never served the five or seven year apprenticeships common to working freemasons.

Nevertheless, it might also be significant that when Ashmole adds an adjective – in 1682 he breaks up the usual expression (Free Mason) to 'New-accepted Masons' – the word 'Mason' can stand alone.

By 1723, Anderson refers to the grand lodge as one of Free Masons, or Free and Accepted Masons, who practise Masonry. So it is most likely that the period 1654–1723 is the one when most confusion seems to have entered the terminology – a confusion that masonic writers have often tried to clarify, but frequently muddied even further. It is obvious that the fundamental reason for the confusion is the development of a body or bodies who were not reliant on stonemasonry for their income.

Thus we find in modern Freemasonry that members are encouraged to think of themselves as 'Free and Accepted' or 'speculative' masons, distinct from the 'operatives'. There is much play on the word 'free' – its link with freestone being apparently long forgotten or dispensed with as being past and of no consequence.

Modern (post-1813) ritual links the word 'free' to being 'free born' – that is, not in service or slavery – that is, financially independent. Severed from its practical and earthy context, the word 'Free' in 'Free Mason' has also been supposed to refer to notions of the medieval guild system (its leaders not being 'bonded' but freed by redemption from apprenticeships). The word has also been linked to civic distinctions such as being 'given the freedom of the city'.

The word 'free' is also linked to the 'liberal arts' – liberal meaning 'free'. The seven liberal arts were those learned by citizens of Rome able to participate in the voting and representative procedures of civic life. By contrast, the old masons were frequently itinerants, 'free to roam' (to their next job) and sometimes outside of burgher control (dwelling in the 'holy chapel of St John' perhaps).

The mason 'companies' were the means by which the cities gained a measure of control over masons' practices, particularly as regards wages. Of course, there were perks for those that 'played the game'. The fact is that masons needed the work – and those with money needed the masons.

The problem with all this play on the word 'free' is that it has generally served a single and to a large extent misleading purpose. That is to say, it has served to sever the links between symbolic Freemasonry and the practical (and theoretical) business that originally fostered it.

Nowadays, it is (outside of scholarly circles) normal throughout the world to speak of 'speculative Freemasonry' and 'operative Freemasonry' as distinct entities. Proponents of various theories in masonic history thus tend to fall broadly into two camps. There are those that believe speculative Freemasonry was basically a new thing that used some of the old practices of stonemasons, but whose theoretical superstructure (moralising on the tools with – possibly later – esoteric developments), was original.

According to the argument, this originality crystallised with the 'foundation' of the Grand Lodge of England, supposed to have taken place in 1716-1717, but whose development before that might or might nor go back to the 16th century at the earliest.

In the other camp, broadly, are those who tend to see the story of Freemasonry as something of an unbroken chain, supposing that the distinct practices of symbolic Freemasonry evolved out of the old guild and company systems as more 'gentlemen' chose to join. Each camp has generated sufficient historical problems to keep them writing research papers for many years to come. *Solving* this problem may not be the highest priority. Many regard the problem as insoluble, unless startling new evidence comes to light.

My guess is that we have all the evidence we require, so long as we truly see – blinkers off – what we have. It is fairly accurate to say that we lack the key evidence to support any single theory of masonic origins – that is to say, a single theory that would convince everybody (especially those who do not wish to be so convinced). Such evidence as we are presented with involves, necessarily, questions of interpretation. One man's interpretation is compelling evidence; for another it is 'subjective opinion'.

I do not think evidence should be used simply to support any particular theory; we are not trying to prove by experiment a formula for the phenomenon of electromagnetism. Nor are we trying to convict – or release – a theory in a court of law. Theories do not have to be 'wrong' or 'right'. They only have to be useful. The word 'theory' means to 'open up' something, not to 'wrap it up'. A theory is a means of getting at the truth, not the name given to a conclusion. If we come to the conclusion of a search for truth, what we have is truth, not theory.

We are trying to understand something that has happened in history and that is still happening, albeit in a different form. *Understand* – not know for sure; we can never achieve that, since the witnesses are incapable of being cross-questioned – and people do not behave with the formulaic neatness of mathematical digits. Most ancient histories were composed of hearsay, but without them, what would we have? We should have archaeological 'evidence', but no *story* to hold the fragments together.

Evidence should be looked at in its own terms. That is to say, that which we call 'evidence' (something to be used to make a case) is not what the so-called 'evidence' was itself created for in the first place. A body may prove that a murder has occurred, but that is not what the body was made for. Historical evidence is just a bit of the past that has survived. What we make of it simply depends on what it means to us. Some 'evidence' stares people in the face for years and years until one person suddenly 'sees' it; this perceptiveness is an art, not a science as we generally understand the word.

Perception is not democratic. Now, it is also clear in the issue of finding out where 'Freemasonry' came from, that meaning is influenced by motivation: what somebody wants. Personally, I want to know what happened, because I am curious and like to get to the truth of things, if it's possible. Some people have vested interests in disinclining people to look in certain directions.

For example, can we trust the Roman Catholic Church to provide a completely unbiased and totally objective account of the origins of Christianity? Of course not. Any evidence that might come forward has already been interpreted over a thousand years ago. If someone finds bones beneath the Vatican, it is always St Peter or St Paul!

The creeds cannot be wrong because they are, *a priori*, true. To think otherwise is to trust your own reason over the authority of the ministers of right belief. The Church is interested in what people believe more than in what they know, since the Church has little faith in man's potential to know anything worth knowing without the Church. The Church is in the salvation, not the science business.

The Church has a nice distinction for really annoying problems: there are statements of faith, and there are statements of science. Faith is everlasting; science is transitory – new theories come into play every year. Guess which statements should hold the attention of catholics? Whoever's playing the game, the Church must win.

I hope this is not too big a sledgehammer for our little historical nut. But there is a useful analogy here. The search for masonic origins has very largely been the work of members of masonic organisations. The findings of research tend to support the organisations that have fostered them. This is not particularly sinister; it is natural. You would not expect the state educational system in England to suggest to people that democracy was emphatically a Greek drollery that wiser minds had dispensed with – or, in present circumstances, that 'justice' in socialist states was a means of state theft with no appeal. Every order has its so-called 'heretics', Freemasonry included.

The United Grand Lodge of England is a masonic authority; it is often regarded as *the* authority in masonic matters. And why not? It was the first 'Grand Lodge' in the world. The original is often the best. However, its justification requires an historical distinction between *its* kind of fraternal association plus symbolic or allegorical rituals, and that preceding it. Had it chosen to call itself something other than 'Freemasonry' the problem might have been avoided, but that just wasn't an option. Why? *Because what it was offering already existed.*

Therefore, it is in that institution's interest to perceive a clear distinction between so-called 'operative' and so-called 'speculative' Freemasonry. Why? Because 'speculative Freemasonry' is the 'USP' or 'product' of the grand lodge; this is what the grand lodge fostered that the 'older guys' did not, or could not, offer. They were only 'operatives'.

However, there was a problem if one took this view as being the whole matter. Namely, the grand lodge needed to acquire not only the 'title deeds', as it were, to use the name, but, more importantly, it had to acquire the history as well. How else could it be the ancient and honourable order it claimed to be? It was, theoretically speaking, stuck in something of a conundrum.

How could it be both distinct from what had preceded it, and yet also, the very same as what had preceded it? This problem, one might think, would tax the finest spin-doctors in history, but the age of reason provided a solution, one of exceeding cleverness. The Whig mentality is masterful in the art of dissembling.

In the first *Book of* (Grand Lodge) *Constitutions* (1723), the claim to be 'above' the mere practice of stonework is antedated to cover the whole history of civilisation. Thus, what the *Constitutions'* chief author James Anderson calls 'Masonry' in his peculiar history of the craft was always the profound ethical system brought into the world by God and exercised in time by God's chosen masters. Who could argue with this? The moral system – called Masonry – was effectively – to borrow a distinction from the world of alchemy – the *ergon*, (the 'work') of which the building part was the *parergon* (or by-product). Free and Accepted Masons needed to offer no apology for not serving time on the building site.

A brilliant stroke!

Now, Anderson's distinction between Masonry as ethics and

Masonry as architecture may or may not be the case. It is true that some writers have talked about distinguishing 'art mysteries' from 'craft mysteries' in the ancient world – but the point is that Anderson makes this distinction the basis for the authority of a grand lodge, independent of trade control.

One can only speculate as to whether in the early days of London's new grand lodge there might have been some dim dream of eventually 'taking over' the trade bodies! That is far-fetched, but of course, Grand Lodge did not need to do any such thing. If all the best architects joined the grand lodge (as did architect Sir John Soane for example) then the ancient vows of marriage between moral theory and practical outcome could be renewed in every generation.

Had the grand lodge taken a thoroughly élitist path, keeping membership strictly to the most brilliant members of creative society, then such might have been the case. It is perhaps to its lasting credit that such was not the direction that it took.

Grand Lodge was not established to foster architecture and keep a succession of dilettante princes of Wales engaged in public building works! Such an itinerary would have been quite reasonable for the old master masons, but Grand Lodge embraced a broader social dimension – another dimension that would in time also powerfully distinguish it from what had preceded it.

Nevertheless, however fecund a development the grand lodge idea has been in so many areas of culture around the world (not least in the culture of giving and sharing), the supposition of a clear distinction between 'operative' and 'speculative' is not necessarily its best argument.

To be fair, this particular verbal distinction was not even part of its original self-designation. Rather, the operative/speculative duality may have come about by a series of 'happy accidents'.

Apparently, the very first use of the term 'speculative' in this distinct way comes as late as 12 July 1757. According to the distinguished late masonic historians Knoop and Jones, a letter from Dr Manningham, deputy grand master of the 'Moderns', to a 'Brother Sauer' at Den Haag in Holland, attempted to assure the recipient that there were only three genuine degrees in Masonry.

Manningham insisted that, 'Lodges heretofore consisted of Operative not Speculative Masons'. In other words, if there were any degrees going about that people were saying were older than the grand lodge system, then they couldn't – if indeed they were older – be suitable for adherents to speculative Masonry.

As far as we can tell, Manningham's use of the word 'speculative' was a novel twist being wrought on a word of very old usage. The context of the word 'speculative' before that time – in building circles – simply referred to geometry, as we have observed in chapter one. The 'speculative' part of Freemasonry was the drawing, designing, mathematical and geometrical side of the art, contrasted (unfairly) with much of the building site work.

Obviously, what Manningham was getting at was that 'speculative Freemasonry' dealt (he believed) with the ideas behind architecture, architecture's conceptual superstructure; they were not going to train apprentices in using tools and so on. However, in making the distinction, it was soon to be forgotten – as the term 'Speculative Freemasonry' entered into masonic currency – that the so-called operative masons (and later 'Freemasons') had been speculating for thousands of years! Speculative activities – including moralising on the tools – had always been part of the craft. Furthermore, the craft had never existed in a vacuum; no one who has walked around York Minster can be in any doubt that the freemasons' work represented a synthesis of all learned culture; many of the 12th century builders came from the cloisters.

The problem for the grand lodge was that explicit links with the art and craft had been severed. They had struck out to sea, as it were, on their own, forgetting perhaps that half of their justification was still sitting on the quayside. It would be a problem for Freemasons ever afterwards, and to a significant extent, it still is. The continued success of 'Mark Masonry' (whose symbolism has a more pronounced 'trade' flavour to it) – while still being 'speculative' – proves the abiding need of some Freemasons to connect more strongly with the older conceptions of what a mason really was and ought to be.

However, we need not feel constrained to support any particular theory or to please any particular body. We are here to examine the origins of the modern movement – and while we cannot point to continual, unbroken lines of evidence – we can be certain that Freemasonry as it is now known simply could not have existed without the developments which preceded it.

Contrary to the assertions of some historians of the middle ages, links between the old architects, or (as they were called) master masons, and modern Freemasons are quite genuine.

Grand Lodge Freemasonry may certainly be regarded as an incident in the total history of architecture, even though the first grand lodge apologists would prefer to see architecture as incidental to the history of Freemasonry!

Even if, in retrospect, the early 18th century developments in London look like a definitive split, pressured into existence from the outside, Freemasonry may properly be regarded as a mighty – and extraordinarily curious – achievement within the total history of architecture. How many arts and crafts have been, if only in part, responsible for the birth of what has become for many a philosophy of life, binding men and women to common ideals throughout the world?

However, we should be foolish if we took the view that we can delve back into distant history and find, even in embryo, what we have now. It was, remember, the masons themselves who offered the means by which it could be said – and truthfully – you do not need to be a freemason to be a Free Mason. It was undoubtedly the 'trade' lodges that permitted the 'gentlemen' to join them as brothers.

It is also possible that the first progenitors of a trade-free grand lodge had been ejected from lodges, or a lodge, of working freemasons. However, the account written by the main author of the Freemasons' *Constitutions* for the second edition of that work (1738) was in no doubt that the idea for a 'grand lodge' had been dreamt up as a way of organising a midsummer shindig some time in the year 1716.

Since it was the rule at the time that lodges should contain at least one working freemason, then it is most likely that the persons who initiated the development were intimate with customs of practical freemasonry.

When the grand lodge was attacked by interested parties (old masons) in the 1720s, it was not because the new organisation had no business using old customs, but that they had changed some of them. Even today, grassroots masons are watchful over the 'landmarks of the craft' and jealous over their distinct practices. Rebellions happen from time to time; compromise usually resolves them. Harmony is all.

So, having traversed the pockmarked terrain of this scholars' battlefield, and succeeded in getting to the other side without falling into a crater, we may now look for the genesis of Freemasonry quite legitimately within the world of the medieval craftsmen, if not before.

The Charges

Sometimes called the 'Old Charges', the charges given to fellows of the craft of freemasonry, show us how the old masons liked to see themselves. We especially see this in the traditional histories of the craft, attached to the charges. While observers of the histories have often scoffed at the very loose approach to chronology and legend in these medieval craft histories – and those that came after them – they nonetheless demonstrate a long reach into ancient history and a determined sense of status. They are rather like cartoons, so colourful in manner and so quick to change from one dramatic scene to the next. They are verbal tapestries, written for people used to going from one emblematic fixed point to another.

Masons told stories in stone and, in doing so, animated their material.

Anderson's argument for a moral 'Masonry' going back to Adam owes its whole edifice to the vision of the past vouchsafed to the old masons and noted in their history. God had a special care for masons; they found plenty of 'evidence' for this in the Bible and liked to think they were also 'men of the world' and able to embrace the achievements of non-Jewish and non-Christian cultures.

Masons were aware that the craft was practised by Muslims, pagans and persons even farther afield. Some of the masons may even have come from Muslim dominated parts of the east. The masonic histories, useless in terms of history as we know it, nevertheless had the principle of universality built into them. Great things encourage legends.

How was this principle of universality made possible? Because the old masons took their cause back to the very first heroes of the human species, before there was any other religion but that which God had planted in the breast of the first human being. You do not need prophets when God speaks to you directly, as was the case with Adam in the Paradise.

Furthermore, the masons had their own 'take' on the biblical narratives. If the book of *Genesis* told you that the Tower of Babel was destroyed as a potential affront to God, the masons would tell you: 'But Ah! What a structure! Its architect may have been all the things the Bible says about him, but – what an architect! Great Nimrod – a prince among men!'

The masonic histories showed a keen selectivity in their choice of heroes. As we have seen, the older masonic interest was not so much in the figure called 'Hiram Abif' but in King Hiram of Tyre. The Charge histories were interested in the quality of the patrons – surely there was some canny self-serving going on here.

Anyone who commissioned great work joined the ranks of the celebrated patrons of all time. In matters of architecture, rich princelings or dukes could behave like mighty emperors. Buckingham Palace was built for a duke, not a queen. King Hiram had the means. So, he was not a card-carrying member of the Jahveh movement (the faith of the Hebrew prophets). For all King Hiram knew, Solomon was building a temple to '*Adon*', the 'Lord', who had a wife, the goddess of love. *What's in a name?*

This proto-universality is there in the *Old Charges*. As we shall see, Anderson picked up on it and ran as far as he could with it, producing, in the process, what has been described as a 'manifesto' for the Enlightenment – Masonry holds to that religion 'on which all men can agree'.

It is no mean claim to suggest that vital principles of the Enlightenment were there in seed-form in the middle ages, carried through from place to place by the freemasons! 'All men are created equal' was probably not on the lips of the freemasons who built Westminster Abbey, but in presenting a picture of the world and its wonders that emphasised what the great civilisations had in common, the freemasons appear surprisingly modern.

It is time to hear from some of these traditional histories themselves. The most famous document to deal with the history of Masonry is the *Regius* MS. or *Regius Poem* (British Library). The poem is thought to have been written in about 1390, possibly at Lanthony Priory in the Marches west of Gloucester, because the last abbot consigned manuscripts to the ancestress of John Theyer (1597–1673) whose library, after his death, was purchased by Charles II. King George III donated the manuscript to the British Museum in 1757.

It is not wholly a 'masonic' work. The *Regius* MS. not only contains a history of the craft, her 'Articles' and 'Points', an account of the Tower of Babel, the seven liberal arts and the Four Crowned Martyrs, but also includes parts of John Mirk's *Instructions for Parish Priests*, as well as the whole of *Urbanitatis*. The latter work was a metrical treatise on good manners – always useful in any trade. For this reason, some sceptics have considered that the master masons did not necessarily know their onions, making the jibe that their friends in the monastic orders wrote up their stuff for them on account of the masters being illiterate. This presupposes that the masons were jacks presented with a kit and set of instructions by super-intelligent monks. Most monks were pretty thick too, by all accounts.

The work of the medieval masters was made possible through collaboration with the most intelligent men in the religious orders. This whole debate is built around misconceptions about the real *sitz im leben* of medieval masters and their patrons that owes much to much later middle class ideas about divisions between trades and intellectuals, imitated from their social 'betters', many of whom should have known better.

A great deal of masonic history has been warped by this dreadful class-consciousness, applied to times when the system and psychology were quite distinct. That monks habitually worked as scribes for guild masters and wardens for example, does not mean that they invented what they wrote. That masters could employ monastic scribes merely points to the masters' high status. A master could extract money from a noble patron; this was rare indeed!

The *Regius Poem* itself is in no doubt of the educational background of the masters. The opening verses quite plainly tell that clever clerks got together to turn the science of geometry into the art of Masonry as a way of finding useful occupation for the sons of nobility whom it was their business to educate!

And one noble son in particular was chosen as fit for knowledge and his name was Euclid.

Euclid (c.330–260BC)

Here begin the constitutions of the art of Geometry according to Euclid.

> Whoever will both well read and look
> He may find written in old book
> Of great lords and also ladies,
> That had many children together, y-wisse; (certainly)
> And had no income to keep them with,
> Neither in town nor field nor frith; (enclosed wood)
> A council together they could them take,
> To ordain for these children's sake,
> How they might best lead their life
> Without great dis-ease, care, and strife;
> And most for the multitude that was coming
> Of their children after their ending
> They send them after great clerks,
> To teach them then good works;
> And pray we them, for our Lord's sake.
> To our children some work to make,

That they might get their living thereby,
Both well and honestly full securely.
In that time, through good geometry,
This honest craft of good masonry
Was ordained and made in this manner,
Counterfeited of these clerks together;
At these lord's prayers they counterfeited
geometry,
And gave it the name of masonry,
For the most honest craft of all.
These lords' children thereto did fall,
To learn of him the craft of geometry,
The which he made full curiously;
Through fathers' prayers and mothers' also,
This honest craft he put them to.
He learned best, and was of honesty,
And passed his fellows in curiosity,
If in that craft he did him pass,
He should have more worship than the lasse, (less)
This great clerk's name was Euclid,
His name it spread full wonder wide.
Yet this great clerk ordained he
To him that was higher in this degree,
That he should teach the simplest of wit
In that honest craft to be parfytte; (perfect)
And so each one shall teach the other,
And love together as sister and brother.
Furthermore yet that ordained he,
Master called so should he be;
So that he were most worshipped,
Then should he be so called;
But masons should never one another call,
Within the craft amongst them all,
Neither subject nor servant, my dear brother,
Though he be not so perfect as is another;
Each shall call other fellows by cuthe, (friendship)
Because they come of ladies' birth.

> On this manner, through good wit of geometry,
> Began first the craft of masonry;
> The clerk Euclid on this wise it found,
> This craft of geometry in Egypt land.
> In Egypt he taught it full wide,
> In divers lands on every side;

The author may not have been the world's greatest historian but he got one thing right. Euclid did come from Egypt. In particular, Alexandria, and masons ever afterwards – if not ever before – would have reason to think of themselves as having roots of some kind in ancient Egypt, as well as other places in the east. Indeed, the University of Pennsylvania's Museum of Archaeology and Anthropology has a papyrus fragment from Euclid's *Elements* (II.5), dug up at the end of the 19th century at Oxyrhunchus, in Egypt. Strangely enough, a manuscript dug up in the late 1970s also has links to that place. It is a mathematical manuscript and was discovered along with the world's only known copy of *The Gospel of Judas*.

Judas, of course, got all the headlines, but I wonder how long it will be before the importance of the mathematical manuscript is recognised. Scholars have not yet released information as to whether it too has any links to Egypt's great geometer.

There has long been a link between Euclid and the freemasons. Some old prefaces to Euclid's work have stylistic similarities to the accounts of Euclid in the *Old Charges*. John Dee's *Mathematical Praeface* of 1570, for example, which includes an English translation of Euclid's *The Elements*, refers to 'our heavenly Archemaster' and sees in geometry a path to the knowledge of God:

> Many other artes also there are which beautifie the minde of man: but of all other none do more garnishe and beautifie it, then those artes which are called Mathematicall. Unto the knowledge of which no man can attaine, without the perfecte knowledge and instruction of the principles, groundes, and Elementes of geometrie.

> ...from henceforth in this my [John Dee's] Praeface,
> will I frame my talke, to Plato his fugitiue Scholers: or
> rather to such who well can, (and also will), use their
> utward senses, to the glory of God, the benefit of their
> Countrey, and their owne secret contentation, or
> honest preferment, on this earthly Scaffold.

Dee was of course the greatest mathematician of the Elizabethan
era and a great hero of Accepted Free Mason, Elias Ashmole,
who did so much to preserve his memory and his manuscripts
from the depredations of the vulgar. But how did Euclid become
part of medieval (and Renaissance) masonic lore?

The Sabian Legacy

In the ninth century, Baghdad was home to a community of
'Sabian' polymaths who had originally flourished in Harran in
northwestern Mesopotamia. These so-called 'Sabians' took as their
prophet Hermes Trismegistus (renamed Enoch or Idris to bring
them in line with approved Koranic sources and so avoid
persecution) whose writings were regarded by them as sacred law.
Hermes was central to medieval masonic lore – a fact we shall
explore in more detail in due course.

The most important of the Baghdad polymaths was Thabit ibn
Qurra (835–901), described in Wolfram von Eschenbach's *Parzifal*
(*c.*1200, chapter 13) as a philosopher 'who fathomed abstruse arts'
and an apologist for the scientific knowledge of the old pagan world.

Among the many late pagan (and frequently Neoplatonist)
works translated into Arabic by Thabit was an improved
translation of Ishak bin Hunain's version of Euclid's *The Elements*.
It was the contents of Thabit's translation which encouraged
Gérard of Cremona (1114–1187) to travel to Toledo in search of
the magico-scientific work, the *Almagest*, over 200 years later.
Indeed, many of the Sabian works finally reached the minor
renaissance of the west in the 12th and 13th centuries in Latin
translations, made at the Toledo school founded by Archbishop
Raymond under Archdeacon Dominico Gundisalvi.

According to the late Professor Max Meyerhoff, 'Belonging to the pagan sect of the Sabians and at heart deeply attached to paganism, Thabit is one of the most eminent representatives in the Middle Ages of the tradition of classical culture.' It is even possible that Thabit's work reached England long before that.

All of the *Old Charges* speak of an assembly of masons held at York under the reign of King Athelstan. Often treated as purely legendary – while naturally a source of pride to the independent spirit of Yorkshire Freemasons – there is no reason to think that Euclid's work, translated from Thabit's Arabic into Latin, could not have reached England in the reign of Athelstan.

The *Regius Poem* goes straight from Euclid to King Athelstan, which would make sense if the great traverse of time between Euclid and Anglo-Saxon times had been made by means of a book:

> Ere that the craft came into this land.
> This craft came into England, as I you say,
> In time of good King Athelstane's day;
> He made then both hall and even bower,
> And high temples of great honour,
> To disport him in both day and night,
> And to worship his God with all his might.
> This good lord loved this craft full well,
> And purposed to strengthen it every del, (part)
> For divers faults that in the craft he found;
> He sent about into the land
> After all the masons of the craft,
> To come to him full even straghfte, (straight)
> For to amend these defaults all
> By good counsel, if it might fall.
> An assembly then he could let make
> Of divers lords in their state,
> Dukes, earls, and barons also,
> Knights, squires and many mo, (more)
> And the great burgesses of that city,
> They were there all in their degree;
> There were there each one algate, (always)
> To ordain for these masons' estate,

> There they sought by their wit,
> How they might govern it;
> Fifteen articles they there sought,
> And fifteen points there they wrought,

Alfred the Great's son Edward (who ruled from 899–925) was Athelstan's father. Athelstan and his son Edgar annexed Northumbria, which had been heavily settled by Norwegians, and revived the ravaged monasteries. The revival of monastic life would have required some construction expertise. And that is all that history can tell us.

The late, great medievalist Jean Gimpel gave to the Arabs – especially with reference to their geometrical knowledge – the greatest possible credit in making the medieval architectural explosion possible. And it was Thabit who gave the geometrical benefits of the classical world to the Arabs and – who knows? – to the masons of old Saxon England as well.

It should come as no surprise therefore to find the name of Euclid high up in the pantheon of masonic heroes, and little wonder that both medieval masons and Renaissance-influenced 17th century scholars and gentlemen interested in joining the Free Masonry should have regarded Euclid as one of their own.

On the frontispiece to Anderson's *Constitutions* of 1723, below the image of the Duke of Montagu passing on the masons' constitutions to Philip, Duke of Wharton, can be seen the famous diagram illustrating Euclid's 47th Proposition. This proposition, also known as Pythagoras's Theorem, was long considered a 'trade secret' of freemasonry and even today may be found in the form of the past master's jewel.

The Secret of Euclid's 47th Proposition

It may be the innocent works of Euclid that gave to Masonry in the middle ages the first idea of a specifically masonic secret – a special form of knowledge, not merely useful as a mode of recognition among fellow masons, but a genuinely wonder-working secret.

The 47th Proposition of Euclid demonstrated a principle that could undoubtedly work its magic on cold stone. A manuscript called the *Regensburg Document* of 1459 describes the unification of the majority of German lodges, including those of Switzerland and Alsace (confirmed by the Emperor Maximilian I in 1498). The document contains the instruction that 'no workman, nor master, nor parlier, nor journeyman shall teach anyone, whatever he may be called, not being one of our handicraft and never having done Mason work, how to take the elevation from the ground plan'.

While evidently a trade secret, it could still be communicated in specialist writings. Matthaus Roriczer was given permission by the Bishop of Regensburg to publish the secret in a small book of 1492. Roriczer's book shows how the construction of a right-angled triangle enables one to project the right angle: a construction necessary to bring the height of an architectural element from the drawing of its base. This construction is described in Anderson's *Constitutions* as 'that amazing Proposition which is the foundation of all Masonry'.

While the uses and meanings doubtless change over time, the history of this secret links the Babylonians, Thales, Pythagoras and his school, medieval masons and Freemasons. Euclid had understood something of the 'hidden' order of the universe, the experience of which initiates the understanding observer into the sphere of reasoning. The secret is the knowledge of how to use something that is visible to all. It is something simple, but which can be employed in the most complicated tasks. This curious kinship between considered idea and practical usefulness, or operation and speculation, was at the heart of the work of medieval masonry.

You could argue that 'Freemasonry begins here' – but if you did, you would not find yourself in agreement with the earliest known masonic documents.

Euclid was a master, for sure, but he was neither the only one, nor the first. The masons' own lore linked them a good deal further back than the Graeco-Egyptian culture of Alexandria.

The secret knowledge, according to the Pythagorean

tradition, is that which is transmitted through the cultivation of the spirit, depending ultimately on the trust flowing between the apprentice and his master. Pythagoras did not claim to have invented his system; he had inherited it from the east.

Freemasonry was, above all, an *oral* tradition, and while scholars tend to disparage traditions that do not generate copious quantities of written records (indicating, allegedly, culture and intellectual sophistication), an oral tradition is what Freemasonry was. Its written elements are its detritus. *Look* on their *works* ye scholars, and despair!

Now let us look at the works of one of the great medieval master masons, so that we can put all this theoretical knowledge into some kind of practical context.

Henry Yevele (b.1320-30 d.1400)

Yeaveley is now a tiny village between Sudbury and Ashbourne in southwest Derbyshire, close to the River Dove's border with Staffordshire. We first hear of freestone mason Henry living at Uttoxeter in the latter county, some ten miles southwest of Yeaveley. He was the son of Roger de Yevele (who may have been one of the family of John le Mazon de Iueleg [Yeaveley], recorded as being a freestone mason in about 1278).

Young Henry de Yevele was apprenticed to King's Master Mason, William Ramsay. He followed his master well and distinguished himself by his labours on Uttoxeter church and, between 1334 and 1336, by his alterations to the abbot's lodging at Croxden abbey (founded by the knight Bertram de Verdon in the Staffordshire moorlands in 1176). The startling ruins of Croxden abbey may still be seen, a few miles south of the now more famous Alton Towers.

From 1337 Henry was involved in work on the presbytery of Lichfield cathedral, also in Staffordshire. He also worked on the spire of Ashbourne church and Tutbury abbey church (1340–60) across the county border.

The Black Death struck England between 1348 and 1349, but did not decimate the Midlands as it did the south. Masons with northern names came to London after the pestilence;

Yevele was among them. In 1353 he was given the freedom of the city of London and became the leading mason in the capital. In 1356 he was chosen by the good people of the craft to be one of the six freestone masons given the task of ordering and caring, 'viewing' the craft of masonry. He became the leading master mason in the country.

Henry Yevele designed Canterbury cathedral's nave; Durham cathedral's nave screen was also his work, as was St Alban's abbey's rood screen. Back at St Paul's, Henry made the tomb of John of Gaunt.

John of Gaunt – who ruled England in the minority of Richard II – was patron of Yevele's friend Geoffrey Chaucer, the author of *The Canterbury Tales* and, less famously, Clerk of the Works over the King's Masons (1389-1391). Chaucer also ran secret missions on the continent for the government.

This gives us some idea of the kind of cultural background familiar to this master mason of freestone.

In 1361 Henry Yevele lent his expertise to London's Bloody Tower. A year later he worked on the abbot's house at Westminster abbey. 1370 saw Yevele directing and executing work on Cobham church and college. In 1371 he was busy at London's Charterhouse.

In 1377 Henry worked on the nave of Westminster abbey, as well as on the Black Prince's tomb at Canterbury. Rochester bridge occupied his well-rewarded time in 1383, while in 1384 the south front of St Paul's cathedral received his attention. In 1394, now an old man, Henry Yevele was responsible for the tomb of King Richard II. He was a busy man, with only a lifetime to make his mark. He made it, sure enough. That lifetime saw some interesting changes in the lives of the freemasons of the period, changes with which he was on some occasions a direct witness.

Attempts to control masons

In 1356 a dispute arose between the 'Layer Masons' or Setters, and the 'Mason squarers'. Each group sent six members before the

Mayor, Sheriff, and Aldermen of the city of London. Among the representatives of the 'Mason squarers' was Henry Yevele.

It fell to the civic authorities to adjust their organisation. Was the civic power involved as a result of an ordinance of 1350 that forbade 'all alliances, covines, congregations, chapters, ordinances and oaths' amongst masons, carpenters and artisans?

After consultation, the mayor drew up a ten-rule code that allowed the two bodies virtually identical privileges and regulations. A seven years apprenticeship was ordered. In either case, a master, taking any work in gross, was to bring four or six sworn men of the 'Ancients' of his trade to prove his ability and to act as guarantors. They were to be ruled by sworn overseers. Twelve masters were sworn, effectively uniting both bodies.

Thus was born the 'Craft and Fellowship of Masons', a body that would in the following century become the London Company of Masons.

> At a Congregation of Mayor and Aldermen holden on the Monday next before the purification of the Blessed Virgin Mary (2 Feby.) in the thirtieth year of the reign of King Edward III, etc., there being present Simon Fraunceys the Mayor, John Lovekyn, and other Aldermen, the Sheriffs, and John Little, Symon de Benyngtone, and William de Holbeche, commoners, certain Articles were ordained touching the trade of Masons, in these words:
>
> 1. Whereas Simon Fraunceys, Mayor of the City of London, has been given to understand that divers dissensions and disputes have been moved in the said City, between the Masons who are 'hewers' on the one hand, and the layer-Masons and 'setters' [Norman French: les masouns legers & setters] on the other; because that their trade has not been regulated in due manner by the government of Folks of their trade in such form as other trades are. Therefore

the said Mayor, for maintaining the peace of our Lord the King, and for allaying such manner of dissensions and disputes, and for nurturing love among all manner of folks, in honour of the said City, and for the profit of the common people, by assent and counsel of the Aldermen and Sheriffs, caused all the good folks of the said trade to be summoned before him, to have from them good and due information how their trade might be best ordered and ruled, for the profit of the common people.

2. Whereupon the good folks of the said trade chose from among themselves twelve of the most skilful men of their trade, to inform the Mayor, Aldermen, and Sheriffs, as to the acts and articles touching their said trade; that is to say Walter de Sallynge, Richard de Sallynge, Thomas de Bredone, John de Tyringtone, Thomas de Gloucestre, and Henry de Yevelee [Henry Yevele], on behalf of the 'Mason Hewers'; Richard Joye, Simon de Bartone, John de Estoune, John Wylot, Thomas Hardegray, and Richard de Cornewaylle on behalf of the 'layer-Masons and Setters'; which folks were sworn before the aforesaid Mayor, Aldermen, and Sheriffs, in manner as follows:

3. In the first place that every man of the trade may work at any work touching the trade, if he be perfectly skilled and knowing in the same.

4. Also, that good folks of the said trade shall be chosen and sworn every time that need shall be, to Oversee that no one of the trade takes work to complete, if he does not well and perfectly know how to perform such work, on pain of losing, to the use of the commonality, the first time that he shall by the persons so sworn be

convicted thereof, one mark; and the second time two marks; and the third time he shall forswear his trade for ever.

5. Also, that no one shall take work in gross, if he be not in ability in a proper manner to complete such work; and he who wishes to undertake such work in gross, shall come to the good men, of whom he has taken such work to do and complete, and shall bring with him 'Six' or 'Four' Ancient men of his trade, sworn thereunto, if they are prepared to testify unto the good men of whom he has taken such work to do, that he is skilful and of ability to do such work, and that if he shall fail to complete such work in due manner, or not to be of ability to do the same, they themselves who so testify that he is skilful and of ability to finish the work are bound to complete the same work, well and properly, at their own charges, in such manner as he undertook; in case the employer who owns the work shall have fully paid the workman. And if the employer shall then owe him anything let him pay it to the persons who have so undertaken for him to complete such work.

6. Also, that no one shall set an apprentice or journeyman to work, except in the presence of his Master, before he has been perfectly instructed in his calling; and he who shall do the contrary, and by the person so sworn be convicted thereof, let him pay the first time to the commonality half a mark, and the second time one mark, and the third time 20 shillings; and so let him pay 20 shillings every time that he shall be convicted thereof.

7. Also, that no man of the said trade shall take an Apprentice for a less time than seven years,

> according to the usage of the City; and he who shall do the contrary thereof, shall be punished in the same manner.
>
> 8. Also; that the said Masters so chosen, shall see that all those who work by the day shall take for their hire according as they are skilled and may deserve for their work, and not outrageously.
>
> 9. Also, that if any one of the said trade will not be ruled or directed in due manner by the persons of his trade sworn thereto, such sworn persons are to make known his name unto the Mayor, and the Mayor by assent of the aldermen and sheriffs shall cause him to be chastised by imprisonment, and other punishment, so that rebels may take example by him, to be ruled by the good folks of their trade.
>
> 10. Also, that no one of the said trade shall take the Apprentice of another to the prejudice or damage of his Master, until his term shall have fully expired, on pain of paying, to the use of the commonality, half a mark each time that he shall be convicted thereof.
>
> (Source: Gould's *History of Freemasonry*, I, 341; corrected by Knoop & Jones, *Handlist of Masonic Documents*, 1942, p.6)

In 1377 – the year of the eleven-year-old King Richard II's accession to the throne – the guilds of London were reconstituted as livery companies, the name on account of their livery or dress. The general term for the companies was 'Crafts and Mysteries'. Masters or wardens replaced the old Saxon term 'Aldermen'.

The masons had sent four members and the 'Free Masons' two members to the municipal council, but, according to John Yarker's *Arcane Schools* (Belfast, 1909, p.336), an old list (source not given) shows that an erasure was made to credit all the delegates as 'Masons'.

The 'Wardens' Oath' required them to oversee the craft of Masonry, to observe its rules, and to bring all defaulters before the city's chamberlain. No favours were to be shown to any man (an attack on fraternal obligations?) and nothing was to be done that might disturb the king's peace 'So help you God and all Syntes [Saints]'.

It would appear that the charters of city companies of masons (later to be causes of pride) were, as Yarker puts it, 'clearly a legalised usurpation of the Saxon right of Assembly, and modelled upon the older 'Fraternities' of France'. Well, the Saxons had not enjoyed rights as such for 300 years, so that aspect of Yarker's treatment – like so much in his *Arcane Schools* – is somewhat romantic in outlook.

However, there may be something in his observation that 'where such City Companies were chartered the result might be the withdrawal of the Masters into the Livery, leading to the continuation of the Assembly by journeymen and amateurs'.

> To put the question in other words, some Assemblies may have become Livery Companies, whilst York, and other northern towns, continued the ancient right of Masonic Assembly; and in regard to this the views of Brother Speth [a member of the premier Lodge of Masonic Research No 2076 who wrote a notable commentary on the Cooke MS published in 1890] that the Masonic Assembly, and the Charges belonging thereto, is a claim that they were free from the Guilds is worthy of close consideration. Brother Gould has mentioned several instances where Journeymen attempted to establish Guilds for their own enjoyment and protection, but were speedily suppressed by the Masters; in 1387 three Cordwainers [shoemakers] had been promised a Papal brief for this purpose, but only obtained the privilege of the London prison of Newgate; a similar attempt of the Journeymen Saddlers was suppressed in 1396; the same befell the Journeymen Tailors in

> 1415; also the Journeymen Guild of St. George at
> Coventry in 1427. Unfortunately all the documents
> of the London Company of Masons prior to 1620
> have been lost, or we should have had valuable
> information as to the working of that Guild.
>
> (Yarker, *Arcane Schools*, p.336)

It has long been rumoured that freemasons had something to do
with organising (if that word is appropriate) the peasants' revolt
against the government's poll tax in 1381. We know that
apprentice boys from London joined Wat Tyler's march from
Kent to Blackheath to declare their grievances to King Richard II.
Perhaps some of them were disgruntled young apprentice
masons, fostering resentments against loss of assembly rights.

Such would be perfectly understandable, and might explain
the continual refrain of masons' charges after the 14th century
that masons do nothing to upset the king's peace and even
'welch' on anyone – however close – should they be suspected
of planning any act of rebellion. This was the indirect origin –
and 'charge justification – for the Anderson ban on discussion
of politics in 1723.

It is hardly necessary to say that this period gave England
some of the finest architecture that she is ever likely to see,
architecture that has shaped the imaginations of Englishmen
and women – as well as the men and women of many other
countries – for many centuries. However, we are talking about
the middle ages and important as they were, artists – even
successful artists – were not given the kind of veneration that is
now accorded them. Indeed, it does seem that there is some
kind of inversion ratio between quality and appreciation.

The fact is that masons were attacked in the middle ages –
and it would appear that it is only as a result of these attacks
that we have any written documentation about what they
thought about themselves at all. This is what we should expect
of an oral tradition challenged – incomprehensibly to its
members – by jealous or hostile outsiders. An attempt will be
made by the craft's authorities to address the concerns.

What were the concerns?

Masons under Attack

At Westminster on 1 November 1388 (according to the Calendar of Close Rolls) a writ was issued by King Richard II and sent to all the sheriffs throughout the land.

> To the sheriff of Lincoln. Order, for particular causes declared in the parliament last holden at Cantebrigge [Canterbury], on sight &c. to cause proclamation to be made, that all masters and wardens of guilds and fraternities shall before the Purification next certify in chancery the manner, form and authority for the foundation of such gilds, the continuance and ruling thereof, the oaths of the brethren and sisters, their meetings, the liberties, privileges, statutes, customs &c. thereof, their lands, rents &c. mortified and not mortified, their goods and chattels, the value of their lands and price of their goods, and all circumstances relating to the same, under pain of forfeiture of their lands, goods &c., bringing before the king and council any charters [Note] and letters patent of the king or any of his forefathers concerning the same under pain of revocation thereof, and annulment of the liberties, privileges and grants therein contained; and order to certify before the octaves of St Hilary next the days and places where proclamation was made, and the names of those who made it. The like to singular the sheriffs throughout England. To the sheriff of Lincoln. Order to make proclamation ordering all masters, wardens and overseers of misteries and crafts likewise to bring charters &c. concerning the same. The like to singular the sheriffs throughout England.

The king, it appears, needed money, hard pressed as ever to

fund his military activities. We may note that not only were the guilds included – but the 'misteries and crafts' as well; that would include the London livery companies. Interestingly, the date of the order is very close indeed to the approximate dating of the *Regius Poem* (*c*.1390) which seems to be based in part on a prior document indicating the 'privileges, statutes and customs' of the craft.

The perhaps high-handed nature of masons' privileges outlined in the *Old Charges* – that Masonry's special status had been anciently ratified by saints, sages and ancient kings – might suggest an irritation with royal demands for specifying their exact legal status. The *Regius* MS. may represent a metrical version of a serious response to Richard II's order.

One may wonder how Henry Yevele felt when working on King Richard II's tomb (the king suffered death in 1399); did he wonder whether masonry always had the last word? Less than forty years after King Richard's writ, masons were in more serious trouble. We know this from an act headed *Statutes made at Westminster, Anno 3 Henrici VI. And Anno Dom.1424.*

Masons shall not confederate themselves in Chapters and Assemblies.

FIRST, whereas by the yearly congregations and confederacies made by the masons in their general chapters and assemblies, the good course and effect of the statutes of labourers be openly violated and broken, in subversion of the law, and to the great damage of all the commons; (2) our said Lord the King willing in this case to provide remedy by the advice and assent [of parliament] aforesaid, and at the special request of the said commons, hath ordained and established, That such chapters and congregations shall not be hereafter holden. (3) And if any such be made, they that cause such chapters and congregations to be assembled and holden, if they thereof be convict, shall be judged for felons. (4) And that all the other masons that come to such chapiters and congregations, be punished by imprisonment of their bodies, and make fine and ransom at the King's will.

A document such as the *Cooke Manuscript* (*c*.1420) of masonic charges (which we shall discuss in the next chapter) may have been not only a response to attack but also a confidence-building exercise for masons. The statute may explain a certain reticence thenceforth to reveal meetings of masons to the public. Clearly, if they were to meet with the knowledge of the commons, there might be problems.

The act is mentioned in William Preston's *Illustrations of Freemasonry* (1772). Preston says that it was never put into execution, but does not tell us why. Preston also says that, later, the king was initiated with ministers and nobles following his example. There is no evidence for this. In fact, Henry VI (b. 6 December 1421) was only three when the act was passed. Henry V's brother, Gloucester, was regent of England and the act appears to have been a commons initiative.

This act of Henry VI was well known to Elias Ashmole's colleague Dr Robert Plot. Plot makes special reference to it in chapter eight of his *Natural History of Staffordshire* (1686).

In that work, Plot describes lodges of 'Free-masons' operating in the Staffordshire moorlands (and over the rest of the country) who accept gentlemen as part of their fraternity, give advice on building materials, have secret passwords and who mutually support one another in times of need. Plot is in no doubt that he is talking of the same society, which came under pressure for setting independent wage schemes in the 15th century. Plot further states that Henry VI's act against masons was repealed in 1563 by order of Elizabeth I – and one would like to know more about the background to this intriguing detail.

Plot, furthermore, refers to what he regards as the Free-masons' spurious (we might say legendary) history of Freemasonry whose elements tally well with what we know of the late medieval *Old Charges*.

Plot is even keen to add that the practices of 'the Society of Free-masons', with regard to their independent wage setting, warrant scrutiny in his own time. Of course, Plot could have been wrong about all this, but there is no persuasive reason to think so. One certainly wonders if he showed this part of his manuscript to his ageing employer, Ashmole, before publication! Ashmole would not have been amused at the calumny aimed at a body of men whose genuine history was of great interest to him (he himself projected a history of the craft, but his notes have gone missing).

There are parallels with our times. First, external opposition necessitates writing down, perhaps unwillingly or defensively, something of the mysterious nature and origin of the craft. (The danger of ossification, once this has been done, is obvious).

Second, Masonry is attacked because it is 'different', somehow apart from mainstream society. It is neither a religion nor an ordinary social grouping. It has an exalted sense of its individuality and purpose. Some eras are friendly to it – seeing the many benefits of its work – others are blind to them.

It seems quite possible that the old tradition of Freemasons meeting in secret goes back to the time when free assembly was officially forbidden by statute. Security-conscious government is always wary of free assembly. Those who automatically condemn all private assemblies ought to remember that the dissident resistance to communist oppression in the 'Eastern Bloc', not so long ago, was perforce enacted in secrecy. These groups were praised by 'freedom-loving' western states.

One should not take this analogy too far. It is a certainty that Freemasons in Britain and America have never threatened the legitimate government of the day. Freemasons do not have a unified political or religious outlook. That is one of the pristine beauties of the modern, and ancient, fraternity.

Chapter Six

The Old Charges and Gnostic Lore

In 1861, Matthew Cooke reproduced an early 15th century version of the *Old Charges* in facsimile as *The History and Articles of Masonry*. British Library *Additional MS. 23198* has been called the *Cooke* MS. ever since.

We know nothing of its past before 24 June 1721. On that day, George Payne, Grand Master of the Grand Lodge of England, presented it before the annual assembly of Grand Lodge. Payne is known to have requested brethren to hand in to Grand Lodge as many old documents concerning the craft as could be found. This order undoubtedly caused suspicion among old members for whom the phrase 'Grand Lodge' was a novelty. Nevertheless, the arrival of the manuscript may be attributed to Payne's interest in forming new constitutions (his 'General Regulations' of 1720), a work completed three years later by the presbyterian minister, James Anderson.

The Cooke Manuscript

The manuscript is almost certainly a document coming from within the authority structure of the late medieval craft. Apparently written by a mason in a southwest Midlands' dialect (though this detail is uncertain), the manuscript appears to be a transcript of an older document. However, it may also be the work of a monk or other educated person, employed perhaps to show the scholarly *bona fides* of the masons' history. There are plentiful references to scholarly sources familiar to the better-educated clergy, and these sources are repeated as the authority (if not necessarily the ground) for the history.

The use of scholarly sources is reminiscent of the famous comic scene in Shakespeare's *Henry V* when the King brings in senior clergy to show from past records that he has a right to invade France (the 'law Salic')!

By the end of the scene, the court is strewn with scattered documents, a vellum *massa confusa* summed up by the archbishop with the straight-faced and outrageous claim that now 'everything is as clear as day'!

The aim of the references was to impress and to add authority. Unfortunately, we cannot be sure of how much of the history of the craft was known to masons or their masters independently of the established scholarly sources. This creates virtually insuperable problems in trying to ascertain for how long these English freemasons had identified themselves with the classical and biblical characters referred to in the traditional histories. All we can say is that the masters wished to be identified with these characters while the rank and file had no qualms about seeing themselves in all the worthy building projects of the past. *God loves 'is masons, and all them as loves 'is masons does God's will*, so to speak.

According to masonic researcher George William Speth's 19th century study, the manuscript is 'far and away the earliest, best and purest version of the 'Old Charges', which we possess'. Our only problem is that it is not as old as we should like. Nevertheless, we should learn from it what we can.

Mentioning nine legally enforced 'articles' and nine morally binding 'points', the manuscript indicates that masons under its jurisdiction met in 'Congregations' which might be simply a general and deliberately non-specific name for a gathering.

According to Speth, 'Many of our [Freemasonry's] present usages may be traced in their original form to this manuscript.' This must stand as being particularly true as regards the emphasis shown to the seven liberal arts.

The arts are listed and explained first of all in the manuscript. The place of geometry is held to be paramount, being the means of creation discernible in the creation itself, and without which, the movements of the heavens would be matters of superstition. The loving fellowship expected of masons amongst themselves is also emphasised.

It is important to realise that the *Cooke* MS. is not a work of symbolism and tells us next to nothing about masons' rituals of communication or favourite themes, in-jokes, myths, ulterior interests, visual aids or even dress. It cannot be used to dismiss any speculations about such matters derived from other sources. The *Cooke* MS. is important, above all, because it gives us a basic form or even template for the craft's vision of its own historical legend. There were other old versions of the charges and history, but this is the oldest prose version now left to us. Its basic format was to be remembered and repeated, with numerous additions and subtractions (especially and notably as regards historical sources), for the next 300 years. In its pages we can discern some possible roads as to whence the craft's self-understanding may have come, but not so many as we might wish for.

> Ye shall understand that among all the crafts of the world, of man's craft, Masonry hath the most notability and most part of this science, geometry, as it is noted and said in history, as in the Bible, and in the master of history. And in [the] Policronicon a chronicle printed, and in the histories that is named Bede. De Imagine Mundi; et Isodorus Ethomolegiarum. Methodius, Episcopus et Martiris, and others, many more, said that masonry is principal of geometry, as me thinketh it may well be said, for it was the first that was founded, as it is noted in the Bible, in the first book of Genesis in the 4th chapter; and also all the doctors aforesaid accordeth thereto, and some of them saith it more openly, and plainly, right as it saith in the Bible, Genesis.

The *Polychronicon* was a history of the world by Benedictine monk Ranulf Higden (*c.* 1299-*c.*1363), from the monastery of St Werburg, in Chester, a great centre of guilds, fraternities and confraternities. Composed in Latin, John of Trevisa's translation was completed on 18 April 1387; Caxton printed it in 1482. At the time of the *Cooke* MS., the *Polychronicon* was a modern history.

Bede's *De Imagine mundi* was a commentary on the book of *Genesis*, written by the saintly chronicler, Bede (d.735). Bede flourished in Northumbria before the Norwegian and Viking invasions mentioned earlier. The *Cooke* MS. continues (those who find Old English a bit irksome might wish to skip the quotation in its entirety):

> Adam's line lineal son, descending down the 7th age of Adam before Noah's flood, there was a man that was named Lamech the which had 2 wives, the one hight Adah, and another Zillah; by the first wife, that hight Adah, he begat 2 sons that one hight Jabal, and the other hight Jubal. The elder son, Jabal, he was the first man that ever found geometry and Masonry, and he made houses, and [is] named in the Bible Pater habitancium in tentoris atque pastorum, that is to say, father of men dwelling in tents, that is, dwelling houses. And he was Cain's master mason, and governor of all his works, when he made the city of Enock, that was the first city; That was the first city that ever was made, and that made Cain, Adam's son, and gave to his own son Enock, and gave the city the name of his son, and called it Enock. And now it is called Ephraim, and there was [the] science of Geometry, and masonry, first occupied, and contrenid, for a science and for a craft, and so we may say that it was [the] cause and foundation of all crafts, and sciences, and also this man, Jaball, was called pater pastorum.
>
> The master of stories saith, and Bede, De Imagine Mundi, [the] Policronicon, and other more say that he was the first that made depercession of land, that every man might know his own ground, and labour thereon, as for his own. And also he departed flocks of

sheep, that every man might know his own sheep, and so we may say that he was the first founder of that science. And his brother Jubal, or Tubal, was [the] founder of music and song, as Pythagoras saith in [the] Policronicon and the same saith Isodore in his Ethemologies, in the 6th book, there he saith that he was the first founder of music, and song, and of organ and trumpet, and he found that science by the sound of ponderation of his brother's hammers, that was Tubal Cain.

Soothly as the Bible saith in the chapter, that is to say, the 4th of Genesis, that he saith Lamech begot upon his other wife, that hight Zillah, a son and a daughter, the names of them were called Tubal Cain, that was the son, and his daughter [was] called Naamah, and as the Policronicon saith, that some men say that she was Noah's wife: whether it be so, or no, we affirm it not.

Ye shall understand that this son Tubal Cain was [the] founder of smiths' craft, and of other crafts of metal, that is to say, of iron, of brass, of gold, and of silver, as some doctors say, and his sister Naamah was finder of weavers-craft, for before that time was no cloth woven, but they did spin yarn and knit it, and made them such clothing as they could, but as the woman Naamah found the craft of weaving, and therefore it was called women's craft, and these 3 brethren, aforesaid, had knowledge that God would take vengeance for sin, either by fire, or water, and they had greater care how they might do to save the sciences that they [had] found, and they took their counsel together and, by all their witts, they said that [there] were 2 manner of stone[s] of such virtue that the one would never burn, and that stone is called marble, and that the other stone that will not sink in water and that stone is named latres, and so they devised to write all the sciences that they had found in these 2 stones, [so that] if that God would take vengeance, by fire, that the marble should not burn. And if God sent vengeance, by water, that the other should not drown, and so they prayed their elder brother Jabal that [he] would make 2 pillars of these 2 stones, that is to say of marble and of latres, and that he would write in the 2 pillars all the science[s], and crafts, that all they had found, and so he did and, therefore, we may say that he was most cunning in science, for he first began and performed the before Noah's flood.

Kindly knowing of that vengeance, that God would send, whether it should be by fire, or by water, the brethren had it not by a manner of a prophecy, they wist that God would send one thereof, and therefore they wrote their science[s] in the 2 pillars of stone, and some men say that they wrote in the stones all the 7 science[s], but as they [had] in their mind[s] that a vengeance should come. And so it was that God sent vengeance so that there came such a flood that all the world was drowned, and all men were dead therein, save eight persons. And that was Noah, and his wife, and his three sons, and their wives, of which three sons all the world came of, and their names were named in this manner, Shem, Ham, and Japhet. And this flood was called Noah's flood, for he, and his children, were saved therein. And after this flood many years, as the chronicle telleth, these 2 pillars were found, and as the Policronicon saith, that a great clerk that [was] called Pythagoras found that one, and Hermes, the philosopher, found that other, and they taught forth the sciences that they found therein written.

Every chronicle, and history, and many other clerks, and the Bible in principal, witnesses of the making of the tower of Babel, and it is written in the Bible, Genesis Chapter x., how that Ham, Noah's son begot Nimrod, and he waxed a mighty man upon the earth, and he waxed a strong man, like a giant, and he was a great king. And the beginning of his kingdom was [that of the] true kingdom of Babylon, and Arach, and Archad, and Calan, and the land of Sennare. And this same Nimrod began the tower of Babylon... and he taught to his workmen the craft of measures, and he had with him many masons, more than 40 thousand. And he loved and cherished them well. And it is written in [the] Policronicon, and in the master of stories, and in other stories more, and this in part witnesseth [the] Bible, in the same x. chapter [of Genesis] where he saith that Asur, that was nigh [of] kin to Nimrod, [and] went out of the land of Senare [Shinar] and he built the city [of] Nineveh, and Plateas, and other more, this he saith *de tra illa et de Sennare egressus est Asur, et edificavit Nineven et Plateas civitatum et Cale et Jesu quoque, inter Nineven et hoec est Civitas magna.*

Reason would that we should tell openly how, and in what manner, that the charges of mason-craft was first founded and who gave first the name of it of masonry. And ye shall know well that it [is] told and written in [the] Policronicon and in Methodius episcopus and Martyrus that Asure, that was a worthy lord of Sennare, sent to Nimrod the king, to send him masons and workmen of craft that might help him to make his city that he was in will to make. And Nimrod sent him thirty hundred of masons. And when they should go and [he should] send them forth he called them before him and said to them— 'Ye must go to my cousin Asur, to help him to build a city; but look [to it] that ye be well governed, and I shall give you a charge profitable for you and me.

'When ye come to that lord look that ye be true to him like as ye would be to me, and truly do your labour and craft, and take reasonable your meed therefore as ye may deserve, and also that ye love together as ye were brethren, and hold together truly; and he that hath most cunning teach it to his fellow; and look ye govern you against your lord and among yourselves, that I may have worship and thanks for my sending, and teaching, you the craft.' And they received the charge of him that was their master and their lord, and went forth to Asur, and built the city of Ninevah, in the country of Plateas, and other cities more that men call Cale and Jesen, that is a great city between Cale and Nineveh. And in this manner the craft of masonry was first preferred and charged it for a science.

Elders that were before us, of masons, had these charges written to them as we have now in our charges of the story of Euclid, as we have seen them written in Latin and in French both; but how that Euclid came to [the knowledge of] geometry reason would we should tell you as it is noted in the Bible and in other stories. In the twelfth chapter of Genesis he telleth how that Abraham came to the Land of Canaan, and our Lord appeared to him and said, I shall give this land to thy seed; but there fell a great hunger in that land, and Abraham took Sarah, his wife, with him and went into Egypt in pilgrimage, [and] while the hunger [en]dured he would bide there. And Abraham, as the chronicle saith, he was a wise man and a great clerk, and couthe all the seven science[s] and taught the Egyptians the science of geometry. And this worthy clerk, Euclid, was his clerk and learned of him. And he gave the first name of geometry, all be that it was occupied before it had no name of geometry. But it is said of Isodour, Ethemologiarum, in the 5th booke Ethemolegiarum, capitolo primo, saith that Euclid was one of the first founders of geometry, and he gave it [that] name, for in his time that was a water in that land of Egypt that is called [the] Nile, and it flowed so far into the land that men might not dwell therein.

Then this worthy clerk, Euclid, taught them to make great walls and ditches to holde out the water; and he, by geometry, measured the land, and departed it in divers parts, and made every man close his own part with walls and ditches, and then it became a plenteous country of all manner of fruit and of young people, of men and women, that there was so much people of young fruit that they could not well live. And the lords of the country drew them [selves] together and made a council how they might help their children that had no livelihood, competent and able, for to find themselves and their children for thy had so many. And among them all in council was this worthy clerk Euclid, and when he saw that all they could not bring about this matter he said to them – 'Will ye take your sons in governance, and I shall teach them such science that they shall live thereby gentlemanly, under condition that ye will be sworn to me to perform the governance that I shall set you to and them both.' And the king of the land and all the lords, by one assent, granted thereto.

Reason would that every man would grant to that thing that were profitable to himself, and they took their sons to Euclid to govern them at his own will, and he taught to them the craft, Masonry, and gave it the name of geometry, because of the parting of the ground that he had taught to the people, in the time of the making of the walls and ditches aforesaid, to close out the water, and Isodore saith, in his Ethemologies, that Euclid calleth the craft geometry; and there was this worthy clerk gave it name, and taught it the lords' sons of the land that he had in his teaching. And he gave them a charge that they should call here each other fellow, and no otherwise, because that they were all of one craft, and of one gentle birth born, and lords' sons. And also he that were most of cunning should be governor of the work, and should be called master, and other charges more that are written in the book of charges. And so they wrought with lords of the land, and made cities and towns, castles and temples, and lords' palaces.

What time that the children of Israel dwelt in Egypt they learned the craft of masonry. And afterward, [when] they were driven out of Egypt, they came into the land of behest, and is now called Jerusalem, and it was occupied and charges there held. And the making of Solomon's temple that king David began. (King David loved well masons, and he gave them right nigh as they be now.) And at the making of the temple in Solomon's time as it is said in the Bible, in the third book of Regum in tercio Regum capitolo quinto, that Solomon had four score thousand masons at his work. And the king's son, of Tyre, was his master Mason. And [in] other chronicles it is said, and in old books of masonry, that Solomon confirmed the charges that David, his father, had given to masons. And Solomon himself taught them there manners [with] but little difference from the manners that now are used. And from thence this worthy science was brought into France and into many other regions.

Sometime there was a worthy king in France that was called Carolus secundus, that is to say, Charles the Second, and this Charles was elected king of France, by the grace of God and by lineage also. And some men say that he was elected by fortune, the which is false, as by [the] chronicle he was of the king's blood royal. And this same King, Charles, was a Mason before that he was king, and after that he was king he loved Masons and cherished them, and gave them charges and manners at his device, [of] the which some are yet used in France; and he ordained that they should have [an] assembly once in the year, and come and speak together, and for to be ruled by masters and fellows of all things amiss. And soon after that came Saint Adhabell into England, and converted Saint Alban to Christianity. And Saint Alban loved well masons, and he gave them first their charges and manners first in England. And he ordained convenient [times] to pay for the travail. And after that was a worthy king in England that was called Athelstan, and his youngest son loved well the science of geometry, and he wist well that hand-craft had the practice of the science of geometry so well as masons, wherefore he drew him to council and learned [the] practice of that science to his speculative, for of speculative he was a master, and he loved well masonry and masons. And he became a Mason himself, and he gave them charges and names as it is now used in England, and in other countries. And he ordained that they should have reasonable pay and purchased a free patent of the king that they should make [an] assembly when they saw a reasonable time and come together to their councillors of which charges, manners, and assembly, as it is written and taught in the book of our charges, wherefore I leave it at this time.

One thing we can note straightaway is that the emphasis given to the pillars of antediluvian knowledge discovered by Hermes and Pythagoras, far outweighs any great interest in the temple of Solomon (antediluvian means before the Great Flood). These cataclysm-surviving pillars were of great symbolic interest, being the means by which the craft actually survived through time.

We may suppose, especially as the same story held equal weight right up to the end of the 17th century, that these – not those of the Solomonic temple – were the pillars venerated by masons. It may be that the pillars of 'Jachin and Boaz' simply superseded them, as the Solomonic temple model for a 'lodge' grew in dominance in the 18th century.

Furthermore, masonic writers such as the Rev Neville Barker Cryer have taken the view that it could well have been an 'antediluvian' Masonry that was the pure and original masonic *mythos*, and that this was superseded by 18th century innovation.

Barker Cryer is inclined to think that the *Royal Ark Mariner Degree* symbolism, for example, with all its colourful interest in the symbolism of the Ark, rainbow and Flood – and the patriarchs who inhabit the 'before' and 'after' of the Flood story – goes back to older rituals of the 'Mark' kind.

Mark rituals refer to the supposed means by which masons acquired their personal 'mason's mark', many of which are still to be seen on buildings throughout the country.

Barker Cryer believes the roots of the rituals go back to the old guild mysteries, or plays. Such rituals, if they ever existed, are now lost, although, if we think of them as an oral tradition, it is to an extent plausible to suggest that currently acceptable Mark rituals may represent something of a recovery.

Barker Cryer is mindful of the claims of York (members of whose 'Provincial Grand Lodge' have on occasion struck out for independence following ancient precedents) in this respect.

York's essential claims go back to the statement in the *Cooke MS.* – and subsequent versions of the *Old Charges* – that King Athelstan gave masons assembled at York right of free assembly.

There is evidence for some degree of apparent autonomy in old Yorkshire masonic practices. Barker Cryer relates 'antediluvian' and Noachite masonic symbolism (to do with Noah and the Ark) to the York guild plays that were such a feature of late medieval life.

Our word 'nave' comes from the Latin for ship. Noah's Ark then becomes the hub of the idea of the abbey church. So if Noah was a master mason, then masons didn't simply build churches, they invented them.

I think there is something in Barker Cryer's analysis to suppose some kind of growing neglect of older masonic forms as the 'Moderns' took over the craft. Barker Cryer refers to 'Past Librarian' of Grand Lodge, Henry Sadler, a keen masonic historian who:

> In his Inaugural address to the Quatuor Coronati Lodge [of Research], drew attention to an advertisement of 1726 which was headed Antediluvian Masonry and which was mentioned briefly in our examination of the emerging Mark Degree. It announced a lodge to be held at the Ship Tavern in Bishopsgate Street, on the Feast of St John the Baptist. There were to be 'several lectures on Ancient Masonry, particularly on the signification of the Letter G, and how and after what Manner the Antediluvian Masons form'd their Lodges, showing what Innovations have lately been introduced by the Doctor (Desaguliers; Grand Master 1719) and some other of the Moderns... ... There will likewise be a Lecture... shewing that the two Pillars of the Porch were not cast in the Vale of Jehosophat but elsewhere; and that neither the Honorary, Appolonian, or Free and Accepted Masons know anything of the matter; with the whole History of the Widow's son [Hiram Abif] killed by the Blow of a Beetle...
>
> (*The Arch and the Rainbow*, Neville Barker-Cryer, Ian Allan Publishing, 1996, pp.348–349)

While this interest in the legends of 'antediluvian masonry' tells us something about the cherished beliefs of masons at least in the late middle ages, there are some other important inferences to be gained from the legend. That is to say, there exist some striking co-incidences of interest shared by the old histories with some remarkable independent spiritual movements. Such movements may or may not have informed the development of Masonry.

Gnostic Traditions

While anyone who studies Freemasonry is aware that, at least in the 18th century, Freemasonry on the continent became attractive to movements of 'neo-gnosticism' – spiritual, magical and alchemical movements – it is generally held that these interests were entirely imported from the outside.

French masonic scholar, Roger Dachez, for example, believes that Freemasonry was not a gnostic tradition. According to Dachez's analysis (*Dictionary of Gnosis & Western Esotericism*, E. J. Brill, Leiden, 2005) Freemasonry was to an extent mistaken for one by esotericists in the 17th century (the 'Mason Word'). It was then transformed into one by esotericists in the 18th and 19th – at least within the spheres of so-called 'fringe Masonry'.

A concomitant of this conclusion is that there was nothing 'esoteric' about Freemasonry in the middle ages. Unfortunately, the understanding of the word 'esoteric' is linked to the notion of 'secrets' or even 'the great Secret' (the grail, holy *gnosis* and so on). But the middle ages were rich in powerful spiritual symbolism and it would be remarkable if masons had not been touched by such symbolism – the very imagination of the period was highly sensitive to symbolic and 'supernatural' visualisations. The holy grail stories were, after all, distinctly medieval 'products': a confluence of popular mythology and eucharistic idealism (the holy cup).

However, short of Thomas Norton the alchemist's observation that freemasons were interested in alchemy (which had both a technical and a gnostic side) in his *Ordinall of Alchemy* (1477), explicit evidence for the transmission of esoteric ideas through masonic circles is – perhaps by its very nature – a question of interpretation.

Esoteric ideas have tended to be associated with heresy because they suggest people can look at religious statements from different points of view; that people can think for themselves and gain religious experience without teacher being always looking over one's shoulder. In the middle ages, accused heretics were burnt at the stake. We have no evidence, however, of masons being accused of heresy. Their greatest 'crime' seems to have been an independence that irked civic powers. The Church was glad enough of their services, as were the nobles who wanted new castles and houses.

Furthermore, to read the gnostic words of Hermes was quite acceptable to scholars, since the Christian Father Lactantius had declared Hermes a prophet of Christianity. His works posed no obvious threat to the *status quo*.

As St Paul wrote, 'spiritual things are spiritually discerned'. Some have seen Chartres cathedral, for example, as a cornucopia of spiritual and esoteric symbolism. Those who are hostile to spirituality within themselves or in others are unlikely to see spiritual things in the world around them.

One of the most striking areas of legend and mythology shared by freemasons and gnostic sources is a profound interest in the patriarchal narratives related in *Genesis* and elsewhere. The key figures, following Adam, are Seth, Jabal, Tubal-cain, Enoch, Hermes, Noah, Nimrod and Abraham – of whom the most significant for our purposes are Seth and Hermes.

Genesis knows not of Hermes as being a patriarch, but the freemasons were taught otherwise (in variant traditions) that Hermes was son to the biblical Cush. A copy of the *Old Charges*, *Sloane* MS. 3848, dated October 1646, re-tells the story of the famous pillars erected by the children of Lameth:

> . . . and these children did knowe that god would take
> vengeance for sinne eather by fire or water;

> Wherefore ye writ ye Sciences wch weare found in 2
> pillars of stone; yt ye might be found after the flood;
> The one stone was called Marble that cannot burne
> with fire; The other was called Letera that cannot
> drowne with water; ... Hermenes that was sonne to
> Cus, & Cus was sonne to Shem wch was ye son of
> Noath: The same Hermenes was afterwards Hermes;
> the ffather of wise men, and hee found out ye 2
> pillars of stone where ye Sciences weare written, &
> taught him forth.

This is substantially the same account as that found in the *Cooke*
MS. The *Cooke* MS. adds the name of Pythagoras to that of 'the
philosopher Hermes' as the discoverer of the pillars. The masonic
tradition is clear that the earliest knowledge of science – including
geometry – was to be found on these pillars. That science was
inseparable from the supposed pristine theology, or *gnosis*.

When Ficino's translations of the *Corpus Hermeticum* burst
onto the Italian humanist scene after 1463, the revived claim
for the sublime status of Hermes' revelation was posited on the
supposition that Hermes stood with the fathers of revealed
religion. He was near the head of a chain of *prisci theologi*
(pristine witnesses of God's nature) that went back to the
spacious days before the Flood.

Before the Flood, there was supposed to have existed a race of
sons of God. The sons of God were the children of Seth. Seth
was the new hope for mankind, born to Adam after Cain
brought murder into the world. Seth – called 'another seed' in
Genesis – had the original *gnosis*, the primal understanding, a
word translated by Ficino as *contemplatio Dei* – divine
contemplation. It was believed to have flourished among Seth's
inspired descendants – and survived the Flood, through the
miracle of science.

Seth was the kind of son Adam – and God – wanted: a kind
of second Adam, made in the image of he who was made in the
imago dei: a little universe and universal man, a son of God. To
Seth we must return. As regards Hermes, dignified with the title

Thrice Greatest since Graeco-Egyptian times, he is both patron of science and of pristine spiritual philosophy. Science and God-consciousness were fused together in the supposed original pristine revelation.

According to Professor Frans Janssen: 'The Hermetic philosophy departs from the conception that there was once a unity between man and God – and this unity has been lost.'

Masons today might look to the tragic drama that is enacted in the third degree and contemplate the meaning of the 'lost secrets' or 'Lost Word'. A tragedy has occurred. The original unity has been lost. Therefore, the aim of the most essential Hermetic philosophy is to re-awaken the *gnosis* that resides in man as his immortal component, the knowledge of the original divine nature. This realisation enables him to see his destitute condition, his state of darkness, as one who has fallen from a life of divine plenitude, having fallen in love – like Narcissus – with his ego or image, reflected in the waters, far below the heavenly realms. Fascinated by his image, a mere reflection, he loses touch with his true nature.

Sinking into a heavy state, progressively wrapped in sins like barnacles about an old wreck, primal Man (*Anthropos*) becomes imprisoned by the consequences of an all-enveloping self-love that has separated him from the supreme God. Instead of flying freely in heaven, he is seized by the jealous powers of lower nature and bound to an earthly existence: a pathetic fellow in a state of darkness.

Nevertheless, some dim gleam yet penetrates the gloom of one fallen into this worldly grave. According to Hermes, the world, having ultimately derived elements of its being from imitation of the spiritual realm, yet contains keys and doors hidden within the gross natural fabric of the universe. To uncover those keys, Man will need precious enlightenment and much toil. According to the philosophy of Hermes, his reward will be to enact a re-ascension in this life.

There are even a few divine 'leftovers' in his heart from a higher realm: one such, as Anderson points out in his *Constitutions*, is geometry.

When Man truly knows his spiritual, divine nature and source, the task of securing his rise from the cold bosom of earth is eased considerably. He begins to work, as it were, under the sun – and in the sun. He may yet uncover the proper *Dignity of Man* and find that man is not the 'worm of 60 winters', but rather, a great miracle.

Magnum miraculum homo est – as the Hermetic tract *Asclepius* declares: the manifesto text of the Renaissance, according to Ernesto Garin.

Surely, this Hermetic philosophy makes perfect sense of the three degrees, as we currently know them. We begin with *purification* – the candidate enters the cosmos in a poor benighted, blind state. A door is opened to him; he learns the call of his neighbours upon his heart and the presence of a larger universe than his unenlightened, or unopened, self.

As a fellow, he approaches *illumination* – he learns the seven liberal arts (geometry, grammar, logic, music, mathematics, rhetoric, astronomy), these pillar'd arts and sciences vouchsafed by Hermes' legendary discovery of antediluvian wisdom.

Thirdly: *benediction of the spirit* – transformation. He learns how to die, and that to know how to die is to know how to live. Through the veil, beneath the Arch, beyond the pillars is eternal life.

As the pre-Socratic philosopher Heraklitos put it: the soul's death is our life and our death is its life. Or, as an unknown Gnostic wrote some time in the third or fourth century AD: *The dead are not alive – and the living will not die.*

All very well, no doubt, from our perspective. But we know nothing of any formal degree system in the Masonry of the middle ages. We certainly know nothing of any esoteric teaching or special symbolism being given to masons, save, arguably, the craft of geometry.

It is unlikely that men in pre-Reformation Europe needed to be brought to a state of spiritual awareness; it is arguable that some kind of spiritual awareness constituted the daily consciousness of the period, however 'unenlightened' people may have been from our perspective. Philosophers there were in those days, but they were invariably clergymen. Master masons may have been relatively learned men but freemasonry did not, as far as we can tell, own a philosophy peculiar to itself.

Nevertheless, modern Freemasonry inherited some unusual fragments of old lore. For example, if we return to the figure of Seth, the progenitor of the new race, James Anderson makes mention of him in the 1738 edition of the *Constitutions* of Free and Accepted Masons.

Seth is there described as 'the Patriarch of the other half of Mankind, who transmitted Geometry and Masonry to his late Posterity...' Regarding the pillars discovered by Hermes, Anderson notes that 'some call them SETH's Pillars, but the old Masons always call'd them ENOCH's Pillars, and firmly believ'd this tradition'.

Enoch is of course another significant figure in gnostic traditions. The Harranian Sabians had identified Enoch with Hermes in works available to the west after the 12th century. Enoch, according to *Genesis*, was great, great, great grandson of Seth, and was the grandfather of Noah: 'And Enoch walked with God: and he was not; for God took him.' (*Genesis* V, 24 has Enoch raised alive to God's bosom).

However, those who called them 'Seth's Pillars' might have been intrigued to read a work discovered near Nag Hammadi, Upper Egypt, in 1945. The work is called *The Three Steles of Seth*. The author, for esoteric reasons, has added a third stele to the two reported as the work of Seth's descendants by the Jewish historian Josephus (Josephus was read by scholars in the middle ages – as incidentally, was the *Asclepius* of Hermes).

The Three Steles of Seth is a justification and promise to those who followed 'Seth, the Father of the living and unshakeable race', as those of the Sethian generations describe themselves – a holy company, according to the newly discovered *Gospel of Judas*.

In the Gnostic *Second Treatise of the Great Seth*, the 'Great Seth' manifests as Jesus Christ, the symbolically (but not actually) slain Master.

Sethian *gnosis* (Greek for spiritual knowledge) is now

159

understood as a central inspiration at the core of the Gnostic explosion of the second and third centuries AD. The *Gospel of Judas*, for example, speaks of the 'incorruptible' generation of Seth. Seth is 'of another seed'. This sense of being of a race apart – a holy, purified race – was central to Gnostic self-definition, with the added meaning of the Greek word *allogenes*, that is, aliens, or strangers – wanderers in the world, not bondsmen. The Sethians were strangers in the world that they knew too well.

But Sethians were not freemasons. Or were they?

A passage in the *First Stele of Seth* reminds us that Gnostic literature is not simply a vast 'Farewell letter' but also encompasses a technical vision of the world: 'Thou [the Great Mother Barbelo – gnostic goddess of wisdom] hast empowered this (one) in knowing; thou hast empowered another one in creating.'

Knowledge of God inspires on many levels of being. Creative power – imagination – is central to *gnosis*. How else could one perceive? The final words of the *The Three Steles of Seth* are striking: 'Know therefore, as those who live, that you have attained. And you taught yourselves the infinite things. Marvel at the truth that is within them, and (at) the revelation.'

The Sethian line was most notable in the sciences, as one might expect – the genealogy of Jesus in Luke's gospel gives us a straight son-to-father run from Noah through to Seth, 'the son of Adam, the son of God'.

In the 1738 edition of the *Constitutions*, Anderson seems aware that the perpetuity of an alleged universal and antediluvian principle in Masonry is vouchsafed by geometry having been written in Adam's heart, together with the preservation of 'the Knowledge of the Arts and Sciences' by Noah and his three sons. Anderson even drops a footnote in to the effect that the so-called *Noachidae* was 'The first Name of Masons, according to some old Traditions'. Professor David Stevenson reckons this group – the *Noachidae* – is an invention; I do not see why it should have been.

Now, 'Father Noah' as Anderson calls him, was a holder of the pristine theology before the Flood and the Babel catastrophes divided the (already divided) human race. Was this knowledge 'salvific'? Was it salvation? Well, it saved the Sethian seed from destruction in the universal Flood!

The survival of Noah's Ark was certainly a pivotal event in the 'salvation history' of monotheism. But was this ancient knowledge *esoteric*? It certainly was for those who did not have it: those 'experts' who stood by and abused Noah and his kin when he built the Ark with no rain in sight. Noah was shown the signs. We should also recognise that for most people living before reading and writing became a widespread accomplishment, a mathematical diagram was frequently viewed as a magical secret – even a demonic exercise.

'Esoteric' is an adjective referring to the inside of things – knowledge that goes 'beneath the surface' – as opposed to externals: the deeper and essential *meaning*. In Masonry, the movement is from the point, to the superficial to the cube. The cube is capable of containment – and infinite expansion – all from a Point. *Ex Uno Omnia*! Hence the cubic lodge.

Was technical knowledge spiritual? See the Book of *Job* XXXVIII.1–7 following:

> Then the LORD answered Job out of the whirlwind, and said, Who is this that darkeneth counsel by words without knowledge? Gird up now thy loins like a man; for I will demand of thee, and answer thou me. Where wast thou when I laid the foundations of the earth? Declare, if thou hast understanding. Who hath laid the measures thereof, if thou knowest? Or who hath stretched the line upon it? Whereupon are the foundations thereof fastened? Or who laid the corner stone thereof; when the morning stars sang together, and all the sons of God shouted for joy?

Speculation on the tools of the craft did not begin after the Reformation. Symbolic values for the ordinary terms of architecture were repeated throughout the Bible. Even Jesus, looking hard at Peter, said: 'You are a stone.' This is what gave masons their special dignity. There they were – in the heart of God's eternal word, time and time again.

And who were the 'sons of God' who shouted for joy in the quote above from the book of *Job*? Could they have been the 'sons of God' of Seth's special lineage, in whose time, *Genesis* tells us, men first called upon the name of God? Are they the same 'sons of God' mysteriously referred to in Paul's letter to the *Romans* (VIII.19–22): 'For the earnest expectation of the creature waiteth for the manifestation of the sons of God ... Because the creature itself also shall be delivered from the bondage of corruption into the glorious liberty of the children of God. For we know that the whole creation groaneth and travaileth in pain together until now.'

Where did Paul obtain this tradition of the 'sons of God' re-appearing at the end of time? And why does he call himself an architect in I *Corinthians* III.10ff.? 'According to the grace of God which is given unto me, as a wise architect, I have laid the foundation, and another buildeth thereon. But let every man take heed how he buildeth thereupon. For other foundation can no man lay which is laid, which is Jesus Christ ... Know ye not that ye are the temple of God, and that the Spirit of God dwelleth in you? If any man defile the temple of God, him shall God destroy: for the temple of God is holy, which temple ye are.'

Is it possible that Paul was aware of esoteric traditions concerning building?

In *Acts* XVIII we are told how Paul met the Jew, Aquila of Pontus, 'And because he was of the same craft, he abode with them, and wrought: for by their occupation they were tentmakers.' Aquila, we are told, even perfected the teachings of the already eloquent Apollos of Alexandria, a follower of John the Baptist, by showing him 'the way of God more perfectly'. Check your Bibles; it's all there.

Much of Paul's mystical teaching of the 'Second Adam' raised as Christ would have been perfectly comprehensible to a Sethian Gnostic who saw in Adam's new son, his 'other seed', Seth, the archetype of Jesus. Sethians could use the names 'Seth' or 'Jesus' interchangeably.

And Paul was a tentmaker. The father of tentmakers, according to *Genesis*, was Jabal. Anderson's *Constitutions* is at pains to point out that tentmaking was a geometrical art: the very basis of architecture.

Sloane MS. 3848 of the *Old Charges* (1646) explicitly states that Jabal 'found ye Craft of Geometry' and with his kin erected the pillars of knowledge later discovered by Hermes. Every craft has its secrets. Paul never revealed his whole hand. He had milk for the children – and meat for his 'co-masons'. Sethians recognised him as one of their own.

As Elaine Pagels has shown, Paul's writings are wide open to gnostic exegesis, and it is never more gnostic in outlook as it is in those moments when his imagery has been seized upon by masonic traditions. II *Corinthians* V.1ff., for example, furnishes a key quotation in the spiritual understanding of Freemasons to this day: 'For we know that if our earthly house of this tabernacle were dissolved, we have a building of God, an house not made with hands, eternal in the heavens.'

In the Sethian *Gospel of Judas*, this house is shown to be the beautiful house of the incorruptible generation of Seth. In the 17th century writings of Rosicrucian-enthusiast Robert Fludd, as applied by Freemason Robert Samber in the 1720s, Paul's spiritual house represents nothing less than the spiritual work of the spiritualised Freemason – the temple not made with hands: God with us.

Paul's language in II *Corinthians* is very similar to that in his epistle to the *Romans* where he envisions the creation groaning like a mother giving birth, yearning for the manifestation of the sons of God. To the Corinthians Paul writes: 'For in this we groan, earnestly desiring to be clothed upon with our house which is from heaven.' He says plainly that 'whilst we are at home in the body, we are absent from the Lord' (v.6) – a classic Gnostic perspective.

The Judas of the *Gospel of Judas* also begs the Lord to be reunited with the spiritual house, to be clothed not with the vestments of decay but with the eternal body. (Masons today, it is worth noting, think of the best death as being one in which the mason's soul is translated to the great, archetypal Lodge in the heavens.)

In II *Corinthians* IV, Paul explains the reason why perception of his message is hidden, esoteric, to those outside it. This is not intentional, he insists, but it is inevitable. For those who will not believe, there is blindness: 'if our gospel be hid, it is hid to them that are lost: In whom the god of this world hath blinded the minds of them which believe not, lest the light of the glorious gospel of Christ, who is the image of God, should shine unto them.'

We even have here in this text the 'god of this world' whom Sethian Gnostics called *Saklas*, or fool. If we recall the modern charge of the master mason, the master needs that light which is from above so that he can 'trample the King of Terrors' – the fear of death – and so penetrate the veil of understanding and enter the house of wisdom.

In the third degree, the light of this world is insufficient; he stands in need of the 'Light which is from above'. One simply cannot know whether speculation on the total existence of the master mason and his craft had reached such heights during the middle ages, but the raw material was available to those 'in the know'.

It has not been recognised that the craft of Masonry perhaps engendered the first experience of 'comparative religion'. The masons' brethren in time had erected temples for Nisroch of the Assyrians, Seth of the Egyptians, Zeus of the Greeks, Jupiter of the Romans, YHWH of the Jews – and so on. In a sense, Masonry transcends all religions as historical events. As Albert Pike wrote in *Morals and Dogma* (1871): 'Masonry, of no one age, belongs to all time; of no one religion, it finds great truths in them all.'

The first chapters of *Genesis* give us a time when there was only one religion: the knowledge of God and no nations. As we have seen, the Hermetic philosophy aimed to restore a lost unity between man and God. Masons were employed to build temples whose purpose, ideally, was to restore man to union with divinity, even to house that divinity. The geometrical principles on which they were built must on occasion have appeared as divine secrets or revelations.

Pythagoras explicitly linked the technical and the symbolic, the material and the spiritual. Already there was a symbiosis between Hermetic revelation and the phenomenon of the religious builder, working his way back to the heavens. Even Nimrod, son of Cush, identified as the impertinent ruler behind the Tower of Babel, was a masonic, patriarchal hero.

Babel might have been blasphemous cheek – but it was magnificent. Masons saw things in their own way, from their unique perspective. Would not the Holy of Holies look different to the man who had squared the cornerstone, than to the priest who entered it complete for the first time? But the masons were vulnerable; they had to conform to the wills of their employers. Periodically, we know that they came under suspicion. Were they too independent – or too expensive? Like the Jew of legend, they wandered. They desired to assemble according to their own patterns. They longed for wise patrons. And who could blame them? Their standards were high.

Sloane MS. 3329, the earliest known English masonic catechism, asks: 'Who is it on earth that is greater than a freemason?' The answer: 'He it was carried to ye highest pinnacle in the Temple of Jerusalem.' Only Jesus was greater than a freemason! *If you don't like us*, they seem to say, *argue with Him!*

If this represented a genuine attitude as to the true dignity of the craft, then we can understand better why at the head of the *Old Charges*, there was an instruction for brethren to abjure heresy and keep their mouths shut. You would not I think put such a charge in, unless it had become necessary, either by fact or by suspicion. What circumstances lay behind the charge we shall probably never know.

The masons' was an oral tradition of men bound by honour, suspicious of outsiders; we can be sure that not all secrets were divulged in the 18th century. The modern third degree refers rather self-consciously to substituted secrets; the real ones await the finding. In an oral tradition, some would know, and some would not. Unfortunately, as regards the key question of a *gnosis* among medieval master masons, we appear to be firmly in the latter category. We do not know.

The Holy Chapel of St John

The earliest detailed account of the 'Society of Free-masons' in the post-medieval era is to be found in Dr Robert Plot's *Natural History of Staffordshire* of 1686. In chapter eight, Plot states that while the society was to be found throughout England it was 'of greater request in the moorlands' of Staffordshire 'than anywhere else'. Plot also gave accounts of the great Staffordshire quarries at Cheddleton, Cheadle, Biddulph and Wetley Rocks.

Forty years earlier, Dr Plot's employer, Elias Ashmole (1617–1692) of Lichfield, Staffordshire, was initiated into the first known lodge of an apparently 'non-operative' nature in the company of Colonel Henry Mainwaring, a gentleman of Karincham, Cheshire, within sight of the moorlands.

Within the Staffordshire moorlands, near to a rocky outcrop called the 'Roaches' on the Leek-Buxton road, a chasm opens up near to a wood. It is nowadays called Lud's Church (Lud being a Celtic god of light), but it may also be the origin of the colourful place described in the medieval story *Gawain and the Green Knight*, thought to have been written by a Midlands monk. Gawain must meet the Green Knight (a variant on the Green Man so often depicted by freemasons in medieval churches) at a place called the Green Chapel.

'Green' means Nature. That's why 'Robin' of Loxley (in Staffordshire's Needwood forest) and his 'merry men' wear green. They represent the spirit of Nature and the old ways before the Normans came. I thought of this when I was first confronted with an old masonic catechism preserved in the *Sloane* MS. (3329). We have already had cause to mention that according to this rare catechism (late 17th century), the first lodge is called at 'the holy chapel of St John'; the 'first word' being given (not in Jerusalem) but at the Tower of Babylon.

I have suggested that the 'holy chapel of St John' was a medieval 'in-joke' for the wilderness – the deepest valleys and the highest mountains – where God was most present. This is where St John (the Baptist) communed with God, living on locusts and wild honey and wearing skins (lambskins?). Was Jesus John's 'apprentice'?

John was also famous for having his head removed (at the request of the alluring Salome) – as the green knight must also be beheaded. The 'key' to the lodge, says a late 17th century Scottish catechism, lies in the 'bone box', the skull. Veneration of heads has been an ancient custom found throughout the world. The 'word' comes from the head. This is where transcendent lodge is imagined.

I can think of two kinds of wilderness experienced by masons in the middle ages. First: the Staffordshire moorlands. The Cistercians, who settled the moorlands to the north of the massive old diocese of Lichfield (which covered Staffordshire, Cheshire and much else), were particularly encouraged to establish their monasteries and agricultural control in wildernesses.

The white-mantled monks were famous for this. Anyone who visits the moorlands of the county today can see that they had their work cut out for them. But that is what they wanted. Their founder, St Bernard of Clairvaux, wanted the order to be more austere in outlook than the Benedictines. They were to take on the 'big jobs'. Little surprise that it was St Bernard who would write the rule for the kindred order known as the 'Knights Templar' in 1119 – many of whose knights retired into Cistercian abbeys after armed service. There were three Cistercian abbeys in the Staffordshire moorlands, all founded under the patronage of Norman barons. Croxden was founded in 1176 by Bertram de Verdon, a crusader knight. Dieulacres, near Leek, was founded by Ranulf de Blondeville, Earl of the Palatine of Chester, in about 1214, while the knight Henry de

Audley founded Abbey Hulton in 1223 near Stoke, close to the Knights Templar preceptory at Keele.

Does the presence of these three monastic establishments in the moorlands explain, at least in part, why Plot found so many 'Free-masons' there than anywhere else in the country?

What of the other 'wilderness' experienced by masons in the middle ages? I am referring of course to the deserts of Syria, Palestine, northern Mesopotamia and Egypt. Here was to be found not only 'the holy chapel of St John', but actual groups of people who believed that John, not Jesus, was the true divine messenger, the gnostic Mandaeans, or – as they were called by Muslims – Sabians. Crusaders and travellers undoubtedly came into contact with such people among a host of other persons with what must have been to westerners, startling beliefs and extraordinary skills. There were Nosairis in Lebanon and Sufi (mystic) orders of many kinds.

The followers of Sheykh Adi, a Sufi, from the Bekaa Valley who in the early 1200s travelled to what is now the Kurdish Autonomous Region of Iraq, led a gnostic kind of mystical faith that is still practised and persecuted today. The Yezidis' surviving hymns resonate strongly with masons' symbols and an account of the creation emphasising the principles of 'cornerstones' and 'points'.

Could ancient practices and ideas have come into English Masonry, not just from readings of the Bible and book knowledge, but also from actual encounters with oriental masons?

It would be absurd if such had not been the case. Western travellers had been visiting the near and middle east since Saxon times. The first crusade of 1099 made it much safer in some respects to do so. Jerusalem was then governed by Norman and Frankish barons until the disastrous Battle of Hattin in 1187 put the crusaders on the defensive.

In the meantime, a series of extraordinary crusader castles had been constructed and were still under construction. The knowledge gained in the process was certainly brought back to Europe. Saracen masons were employed and intelligent

Saracens could rise in the ranks of Norman government. The amazing castle at Beeston in Cheshire, for example, has been compared closely to the crusader castle of Sayoun in Syria. A knight called 'John the Syrian' was buried at the church of St John the Baptist in Chester, and Chester had a Saracen mayor in the 1200s.

John Sleigh's *History of the Ancient Parish of Leek* (London, 1862) includes an account of a knight crusader of Biddulph (Staffordshire moorlands) returning from the crusades with 'Paynim' (Saracens) – one of whom was a mason – and who established themselves on Biddulph Moor where their descendants dwell to this day.

The influence of Syrian or Phoenician styles is extraordinarily evident in the church of St Chad in Stafford. Some of the sculptures would not be out of place on an Egyptian temple. There are not only florid and mysterious representations of the green man, but on one chapiter, there is a carving depicting a goddess with a crescent for a crown joined bodily to a bearded man who is rising from beneath the corn. She/he is perhaps the origin of the she-male (or 'Maid Marion') who is such a striking feature of the ancient dance enacted annually at Abbots Bromley, Staffordshire.

The feminine aspect of the figure at St Chad's holds two stalks of corn apart like gateways. This carving seems to depict the myth of Ishtar (or Venus, the Morning Star) who descends into the underworld to recover her loved one, Tammuz, the god of vegetation (green man). In English folklore she survives as the 'corn dolly' and he is, in a sense, 'John Barleycorn' or the 'green knight' who must be beheaded at harvest time to ensure rebirth in the Spring. This myth was not just a fairytale in the middle ages; this was a living subculture, especially in Syria and Mesopotamia. Dramas of rebirth and raising had been celebrated since biblical times, along with the ancient custom of walking east and kissing the earth to greet the rising sun (in masonic terms, the master).

To cap it all, above the chapiter at St Chad's is the Latin inscription *ORM VOCATUR QUI ME CONDITIT*, 'The one who established me is called Orm'.

Ormus le Guidon was an early 12th century knight of Biddulph, son of the Earl of Chester's Forester, Ricardus Forestarius. They happened to be distant ancestors of Elias Ashmole, and of a number of other leading Cheshire and Staffordshire families, such as the Mainwarings and the Minshulls.

Why is all this important for understanding the genesis of Freemasonry?

Because for as long as can be remembered the Freemasons have been linked in popular folklore with ancient practices and curious interests, often derided by the ignorant as 'pagan' (which simply means the practices of country-dwellers). Some continue to believe that 'behind' the rituals of Freemasonry may be intuited older strands of spiritual understanding. Masons today are disposed to say that since there is no masonic orthodoxy as regards beliefs or the depth of symbols, people are free to interpret these things for themselves. Quite so.

However, by making so much of interpretation a matter of subjectivity, there is the possibility that any meaning beyond the superficial may be dismissed as objectively meaningless. If Freemasonry were ultimately meaningless, would so many people, often perceptive and intelligent people, have been attracted to it? Could it have achieved so much?

The information I am passing on simply suggests that there may be more than 'rumour' to some of the old rumours that surround the origins of the craft. Furthermore, there are some quite notable and well-attested influences from the east in the architecture of the time.

At the end of the 19th century, Professor T. Hayter Lewis FSA, a member of RIBA and chairman of the Palestine Exploration Fund, demonstrated that the builders of the early 'Pointed Gothic' of the 13th century were of a different school to those who preceded them in the 12th century. (*Ars. Quat. Cor.* iii; v, p.296)

Hayter Lewis showed that not only the style but also the masons' marks, and the methods of tooling the stones, was distinct from older work. He saw significance in his observation that the older was wrought with diagonal tooling while the later was upright, employing a claw adze. Hayter Lewis traced the changes in methods and marks through Palestine to Phoenicia. He concluded that it was brought into this country by masons who had learned it amongst the Saracens. While masons' marks were in use in this country long before, they became more sophisticated after eastern experience.

The transactions of the 'premier Lodge of Masonic Research' (*AQC*, viii, 1895) also records evidence of the presence of oriental masons in this country. Engravings made from drawings of two wooden effigies, said to be of the time of the crusades, formerly in the manor house of Woburn in Buckinghamshire, were shown to the Society of Antiquaries in 1814.

The effigies were life size, one representing an old man with quadrant and staff, the other a young man with square and compasses. Their 'attire, head-dress, and even features, indicate Asiatic originals'. Interestingly, Professor Hayter Lewis's views were supported in an anterior fashion in the 17th century by Sir William Dugdale (Ashmole's father-in-law). Dugdale considered the reign of King Henry III to be the time when the 'Society of Freemasons' was introduced into England by travelling masons, protected by Papal Bulls. It is still generally held today that 'pointed Gothic' (late perpendicular) was of Saracenic origin.

Ashmole, however, was convinced that Masonry was not so recent an arrival in England. He followed the *Old Charges'* traditional history that the society had been in England since Roman times (the time of St Alban).

Gould's *History of Freemasonry* takes the view that the story of the society coming in the time of Henry III (early to late 13th century) derives from papal bulls given to the Benedictines and other monastic fraternities who were builders. That is, that the bulls applied to masons as lay brothers of the monasteries and other orders, such as the Templars, who also employed masons. And since we have had cause to mention the famous Templars of legend and popular fascination, we had better address the time-honoured question of whether Freemasons may trace their origins to the Templars.

The Knights Templar and the Freemasons

Of all the theories of masonic origin, the one that seems to ignite the imaginations of people today is that by which the masonic movement is supposed to have emerged from the still-warm ashes of the suppressed Templar order. It must be said that this idea did arrive rather late in the day. The mother of all conspiracy theories was not the product of a New Age novelist's imagination, but the work of an ex-patriot Jesuit priest, living in England, working on some colourful statements made by a Scottish masonic 'evangelist' in the 1730s.

The Abbé Barruel had taken refuge in England from the ravages of the French Revolution. He seems to have been the first to propose that the revolution was the result of a secret conspiracy on the part of some sinister, occult groups. His huge, four-volume work, *Memoirs Illustrating the History of Jacobinism*, was published in English translation in 1797. He begins thus:

> At an early period of the French Revolution there appeared a sect calling itself Jacobin, and teaching that all men were equal and free! In the name of their equality and disorganising liberty, they trampled under foot the altar and the throne; they stimulated all nations to rebellion, and aimed at plunging them ultimately into the horrors of anarchy...

> Whence originated these men, who seem to arise from the bowels of the earth, who start into existence with their plans and their projects, their tenets and their thunders, their means and ferocious resolves; whence, I say, this devouring sect? Whence this swarm of adepts, these systems, this frantic rage

against the altar and the throne, against every
institution, whether civil or religious, so much
respected by our ancestors?

In a long, painstaking argument Barruel depicts a conspiracy
that, he claimed, began with the anti-Christian propaganda of
Voltaire and the rationalist 'Encyclopaedists' and ended with
regicide and the wasting of the Church. Freemasonry plays a
significant role in his story.

He describes a hilarious attempt to initiate him, which he
took rather too seriously, by French masons. In spite of his
assertion that Freemasonry aimed at subverting established
society, he had enough grace to note that, 'In justice I am bound
to declare, that, in excepting the Venerable [Worshipful
Master], who turned out a violent Jacobin, they all showed
themselves loyal subjects at the Revolution.'

Barruel also makes pains to point out that English
Freemasonry cannot be tainted with any anti-establishment
accusations; it is an honourable institution. Of course, liberty,
equality and fraternity were correctly seen as inimical to a
paternalistic society run by the aristocracy and the Church.

Barruel's argument was that the unholy trinity of liberty,
equality and fraternity might sound like a good idea, but in
practice they created the precise opposite. You can't have liberty
if there's a war on; you can't have equality when you're
commanded to serve in that war, and you can't have fraternity
when you've got to fight your neighbour.

Your best bet is to stick with the old order and try to make it
better from within by practising Christian virtues. This is an
aristocratic, catholic idea in which Church and aristocracy
found common cause: they were both threatened. This is also
the essential gospel of conservatism, and the arguments have
hardly changed in essence in two and a half centuries.

Barruel's work began a line of conspiracy books that have
excited readers ever since. In 1818, Joseph von Hammer-
Purgstall's *The Mystery of Baphomet Revealed*, took the basic
theory even further and linked the Freemasons to the

medieval Knights Templar. According to the theory, the Templars belonged to a subversive group who had been influenced by the Gnostics! The works of Barruel and von Hammer-Purgstall created the line that there was an unbroken tradition of anti-clerical teachings stretching from the third century *gnosis*-influenced Persian teacher Mani, through to the Cathars, the Templars and the founders of the French Revolution. And they all carried disturbance and misery in their wake! And watch out! They're still with us: illuminists and Freemasons are all part of the subversion, allegedly. Knowledge is always subversive of ignorance.

This is the murky stream from which all the current tributaries of Templar-masonic conspiracy flow. Suffice to say that there is not a shred of evidence to be found between the demise of the historical Knights Templar in 1314 and the appearance of masonic-style continental neo-Templars in the 1760s to support the conclusion that an (allegedly) surviving leadership of the Templars transformed themselves into 'Freemasons' or their order into 'Freemasonry'. That the descendants of families who had favoured the Templars in the 14th century later (*centuries* later) included members of masonic or masonic-Templar orders is simply irrelevant to the discussion; there was no institutional transformation.

Common sense ought to indicate that in the 14th century, the very notion would simply have been absurd – the employers of masons becoming their own employees! It is hard to imagine a knight swapping his broad sword permanently for a trowel. Imagine it: 'Last year I was fighting Saracens. This year I'm building Westminster abbey. It's a great life!'

It's a great joke too.

No, the connection between the two was, and is, a romantic one. The link-word is of course *temple*. But as we have shown, what little we know of medieval freemasons shows relatively little specific, iconic interest in the temple of Jerusalem (close to the ruins of which the Knights Templar had once enjoyed a base).

It is also noteworthy that Anderson in his *Constitutions*

(1723) reckoned that chivalric crusading orders derived their basic order and ethics from Masonry! All you have to do to create the 'modern' conspiracy story is to reverse the statement. The symbolic value of the temple of Jerusalem was developed masonically in the 17th and 18th centuries, rather at the cost of the older *loci* of masonic interest – namely, the pillars of Seth, the Tower of Babylon and the Ark.

However, since absolute proof that a hypothetical scenario did not occur is hard to achieve, rational argument cannot hope to convince those who do not appreciate that it is *their* job to furnish proof for strange ideas. When the very subject is secret sodalities, the expectation of any kind of proof must be very low indeed. That very mystery becomes for some people a kind of proof of its own. There is no doubt that those who crave the connection will find plenty in the cross-mythologies and shared symbols of the middle ages to suggest some kind of 'spiritual link'. This kind of thing gives spirituality a bad name. Reason is a gift of the spirit and Occam's razor could save your life.

Frankly, the whole thing becomes a bit of a jamboree bag of disparate and desperate speculation once you take away the main theoretical pillar. That pillar is the idea of an institutional takeover in Scotland.

What is all this about a takeover?

It goes like this: old Scottish families (Sinclairs, Setons and others) foster happy memories of glorious Templar days, hug their old swords, establish new Templar rites, seek ultimate revenge on the 'corrupt' papacy, cherish old links with 'Templar lands' and use the lodges to recruit their tools for the trade.

The buzz words of neo-Templarism begin to fill the (not very) illuminated manuscripts of late 18th and 19th century masonic orders: Kilwinning, Heredom, Rosslyn, *Rose Croix*, Knights of Kadosh… All dreamt up in the Age of Reason: a last dugout in the long war against materialism.

It was the Chevalier Ramsay's famous *Oration* of 1736 that first excited Freemasons in Paris to the potential for going a step beyond English Freemasonry, if one could argue a link between, first, medieval masonic sources, and second,

Scottish 'traditions'. The political context for this attraction was of course the romantic (and bloody) cause of the Jacobites or Stuart exiles, nourished in France by those opposed to the unromantic Hanoverian regime in England. No 'Farmer George' could ever compete with Bonnie Prince Charlie in the great pin-up test of romantic politics.

Furthermore, French history was fully familiar with the double curse of the last Templar *Grand Master* (another key word-link), Jacques de Molay, who was alleged to have condemned both the French crown and pope while slow-roasting in Paris on the banks of the Seine before the eyes of his enemies. Were not the Templars the vanguard of enlightenment in their time: internationalist, tolerant of Islam and respectful of oriental knowledge? Were they not harbingers of international republicanism before their time (like the Freemasons), building a temple of humanity wherein (as Ramsay's mentor, Fénelon, put it) the world was a republic, and every nation a family?

Well, not really. The Templars were not like that at all. But let us not allow facts to get in the way. Masonic-Templarism was building up for a roll, but where was it rolling?

Surely, it was surmised, there had been in Europe some slow progress towards a more enlightened time. The virtuous perpendiculars of classicism were everywhere to be seen. Progress was plain to the eye; perhaps it was inevitable; perhaps it was being directed. *Who was behind it?*

Had that progress not been delicately directed by wise and invisible *masters*, like the invisible *Rosicrucian Brotherhood* who, their task set in motion, had disappeared again? Had not the Templars and the Freemasons got all this idealism in common? Secrecy? Equality? Fraternity? Enlightenment?

And was it not therefore a strange coincidence that not only had the pope been brought to dissolve the Templars in 1312, but, in 1738, his successor would condemn Freemasonry as well? What's a mere 400 years between conspiracies? To European revolutionaries, moderate and not so moderate, such contradictory ideas lit the requisite dark and light energies of the soul and . . . well, they just grew!

What can mere history do when confronted by such a vast ideological battering ram? It can get out of the way or get trodden on; it got trodden on.

Just a note about Ramsay's *Oration*: Ramsay never mentioned the Templars by name. He referred to knightly orders being linked with the masons of old – building new worlds. His interest seems to have been to suggest a new ideologically driven, moral – not military – chivalry: men dedicated to the formation of a better world for all. He was not suggesting an armed crusade of mason-knights dedicated to rebuilding the power of the Templars in Jerusalem or even a physical temple.

Ramsay's main interest seems to have been to inspire Freemasons who might have been finding the sober English format of Masonry a bit lacking in mystery, fervour and romance.

Templar Masonry in its continental form was very colourful indeed. The political subtext was perhaps that England needed to be redeemed from Hanoverian dullness. Grand Lodge's view was that England needed to be saved from Jacobite bullshit.

Thus we come back to our old letter of 1757 from Dr Manningham to Brother Sauer in Den Haag. Manningham distinguished between the three degrees of the 'speculative' Freemasonry and the old and distinct 'operative' masons. I think the ideological subtext is this: '*Don't go back to the middle ages. That's where the Jacobites come from!*'

History is full of strange twists. Here's a last one.

At the Canonbury Masonic Research Centre's 2006 international conference on Freemasonry, Professor Thierry Zarcone of the *Centre National de la Recherche Scientifique*, Paris – an expert on Islam in the Turco-Persian area – delivered a paper entitled *Gnostic and Sufi symbols and ideas in Turkish and Persian Freemasonry*.

The paper revealed how Freemasonry and Islamic Sufi orders had interacted in the late 19th and early 20th centuries. Zarcone told of how, when in Istanbul, European Freemasons were visited by representatives of Sufi *turuq* (spiritual paths). Mutual astonishment cleared into enlightenment as both groups saw powerful elements of themselves in the other.

From the Sufi point-of-view, the arrival of Freemasonry appeared as the curious return of a lost relative. This was particularly the case with respect to the Bektashi Sufi order. Initiates into Bektashism, for example, had a belt around their neck and were led around their meeting room by a guide in candlelight, practices reminiscent of western masonic customs.

The Sufi 'Unity of Being' movement emphasised the symbol of several worlds coming down from the absolute, depicted as the centre of a fourteen-ringed circle in some images. The masonic concept of belief in supreme being or a supreme being was accepted as a basic spiritual insight and necessity.

Sensitive to the multi-dimensional nature of reality, Bektashi Sufis, such as Ahmed Rifki, resisted religious fanaticism. Freemasonry came into the Ottoman Empire as the equivalent of a Sufi society. The phrase 'Masonic rite' was translated as 'Sufi path'. The 'Ancient & Accepted Rite', for example, became the 'Ancient & Accepted Sufi Path': a path that in Sufism had seven stages. The symbolism crossed cultures perfectly. The word for 'lodge' in Turkey became a 'tarikat' from '*tariqa*', a path.

Professor Zarcone revealed the existence of a truly esoteric 'Freemasonry' that appears to have existed in Turkey and Iran since the middle ages, at least. According to Zarcone, this Freemasonry 'was concerned with Gnosticism, mysticism and Hermetism'.

In *Sloane* MS. 3329 (*c*1700), the secret word imparted to the masonic initiate – while observing a prototype embrace of the 'five points of fellowship' – is '*mahabyn*'. This word sounds uncannily like the Sufi's fraternal greeting: *Muhabba*. And what is the secret?

Muhabba means *love*.

Interlude One
Calcutta, 1824

Picture yourself in Calcutta, India, in the year 1824. Reginald Heber DD (doctor of divinity), has come to take up his post as Bishop of Calcutta (anglican communion). He is keen to meet local worthies, to learn from them and to impart knowledge of the Church of England's doctrines to those who are curious. One day, Bishop Heber receives a visit from Rhadacant Deb.

Deb is the son of a man of fortune, rank and consequence in Calcutta. He is also secretary to the Calcutta School Association, an organisation in which an English bishop in this wealthy outpost of the British Empire may properly claim an interest.

Heber and Deb speak about the Christian religion. The conversation is polite. The Indian listens with sober interest, but the Bishop soon becomes aware that another subject has caught Rhadacant Deb's fascination. As Heber will write, in his three volume work, *Narrative of a Journey through the Upper Provinces of India, from Calcutta to Bombay* (1828):

> His [Deb's] greatest curiosity, however, was about the Free-masons, who had lately been going in solemn procession to lay the first stone of the new Hindoo College.

> 'Were they Christians?' 'Were they of my [Heber's] Church?'
> He could not understand that this bond of union was

179

purely civil, convivial, or benevolent, seeing they made so much use of prayer; and was greatly surprised when I said that in Europe both Christians and Mussulmans [Muslims] belonged to the Society, and that of the gentlemen whom he had seen the other day, some went to the Cathedral, and some to Dr Boyce's [nonconformist] church.

He asked at length, 'If I was a Mason?' 'If I knew their secret?' 'If I could guess it?' 'If I thought it was anything wicked or Jacobinical [revolutionary]?'

I answered, that I was no Mason; and took care to express my conviction that the secret, if there was any, was perfectly harmless; and we parted very good friends, with mutual expressions of anxiety to meet again.

This tantalising anecdote, old as it is, tells us a good deal about how Freemasonry has been, and still is, perceived by outsiders. It also tells us something true about its nature and source of attraction. Deb's questions reveal that Freemasonry is perceived to have a peculiar relationship to religion, making much use of prayer, but being of no denomination, or even specific religion. Freemasonry brings together into civil fraternity men of differing and even, at sundry times, warring faiths. We learn that a man knowing little of the craft had yet heard that it contained a 'secret', that the secret might be of a dark or even revolutionary nature.

We learn that Freemasonry was perceived as having a peculiar relationship both to public morality and established societies. We also learn that an educated man, for such Reginald Heber undoubtedly was, had reasonable grounds for considering anxiety about Freemasonry baseless, its alleged 'secret' harmless.

How could Heber be so sure, when he did not know what their 'secret' was – or even whether such a thing might exist? If, as seems likely, Heber had observed Freemasons in his own experience, then we can say he took it that Freemasonry is best judged by a mason's life and practice. We may judge a tree by its fruit. Freemasons are expected to set as good an example as their merits permit.

We learn two further things, perhaps of greater importance than the very old debate around Freemasonry's alleged dark side.

First, that Freemasonry is simply *intriguing*. In this anecdote, Freemasonry is presented as being intriguing in a way that even the extraordinary doctrines of Christianity would not be to an educated Hindu – who, it might be argued, could lay claim to sufficient extraordinary doctrines of his own. Second, that Freemasonry's intrigue and even intense curiosity value crosses both racial and faith boundaries. That is to say, Freemasonry holds within itself a quality of universality, giving it an appeal to people of whatever background or spiritual conviction, although education certainly has a bearing on the nature of that appeal.

For example, an Indian Freemason wrote some years ago to inform me that uneducated people in his district still referred to masonic lodges as 'magic houses' (*Jadu Ghar*) – magic being associated among the poor with higher (out of reach) or esoteric knowledge.

This fabled universality can bring people together who might otherwise never have met and come to a common table. The ability to take people beyond the mental confines of race, faith and nation, while denying nothing to these relative claims (as, say, communism does), is extraordinary.

Freemasonry then seems to have something to say about life itself. For whatever might separate us, all human beings share life on earth.

Chapter Seven
Accepted Freemasonry

Freemasons today will often describe themselves as 'Free and Accepted Masons'. How did this curious distinction come about? Accepted by whom? Or, conversely, what did masons have to accept?

The fact is that Freemasons today have very little idea of what the term 'Accepted Freemason' signifies and what idea they do have is very uncertain. You might think there would be a generally understood explanation, since the word is used specifically to separate symbolic (so-called speculative) Freemasonry from that whereby one might earn a living.

In the modern 'Emulation' rituals, the initiate learns that the working tools are to be understood morally and allegorically, because he has just joined a lodge of masons who are 'free and accepted'.

This distinction might suggest that the 'operative' mason is neither free nor accepted! In point of fact, the initiate can think more or less what he likes because he is not going to receive any more explanation on the matter. He is free and accepted and he had better just accept it.

In old masons' practices, a man was made 'free' when he had paid his redemption fee at the termination of his apprenticeship. At this point he would join – if he was in London for example – the Masons' Company as a yeoman and begin paying his dues, attached either to a masons' yard, or otherwise earn his income as a journeyman freemason.

The word 'free' in this context (redemption at the end of apprenticeship) had nothing to do with the word 'freemason' which was, as we have seen, the general term for the trade. But you might not expect a person with scant knowledge of the trade to understand that.

As we have seen, the determinedly non-operative Grand Lodge Masonry tried to 'get round' this by suggesting that the *Accepted Mason* was 'free' on account of being of full age (21). This was not enough. He was also 'free' because he had an independent income – and was thereby able to make free decisions – and a predisposition thereby to take an interest in the 'liberal' (free) arts.

The qualification 'accepted' was not in use in Scotland (any more than the word 'freemason') when Grand Lodge got off the ground after 1717. However, the distinction is still made today that whereas a gentleman joining Masonry in Scotland was called an 'admitted' mason; in England the word for this status was 'accepted' mason as if this was the accepted meaning of the word 'accepted'! Well, it may surreptitiously have become the meaning of the word, but it was certainly not its original meaning as far as we can tell.

Readers may also be aware of the phrase 'Ancient and Accepted Rite' describing a thirty-three degree system particularly significant in the United States. Here the word 'Accepted' has been linked to the word 'Ancient'. The implication is, at first sight, that it is the particular rite that has been *Accepted*, perhaps because it was so *Ancient*! Again, any such idea is a misunderstanding.

When the new Grand Lodge organisation published its *Constitutions* in 1723, it dignified the craft with the term: the Ancient Fraternity of FREE MASONS. So that's where the 'Ancient' bit came from. This was not a new order; it was as ancient as mankind.

It is also clear from the curious stance of James Anderson's 'History' of the craft that 'Masonry' somehow transcends building, being the divinely created wisdom – or 'art' that is manifested in the craft. It is the 'art' that 'Accepted' Free Masons are primarily concerned with. Fine perhaps, but do they have it?

It must be plainly stated at the outset of this chapter that this distinction between Accepted and trade masonry is at best a twisting of an established term and at worst an error, which may or may not have been intentional.

In order to understand how such confusion may have arisen, we need to travel back in time to that critical era in masonic development, the 17th century.

The London Freemasons' Company

The century began well for freemasons in London. The accession to the throne of England of the Stuart James VI of Scotland in 1603 augured well for the craft. The new king was already well known as a 'new Solomon', dispensing wisdom, with a particular penchant for poetry with a serious religious or moral theme. In Scotland King James had patronised masons, and masonic tradition holds that the king was an 'Admitted Mason' to Scottish Masonry. Coming to England, poets in search of patronage made as much as they could of this Solomonic image.

Joshua Sylvester translated the Calvinist French poet Guillaume de Salluste du Bartas's *Devine Weekes and Workes* into English (1608), knowing that it was one of the king's favourite poetic works. The king had already translated sections of it himself. *His Majesties Poetical Exercises at Vacant Houres* was published in Edinburgh in 1591.

Du Bartas's poetic rendering of the creation narrative from *Genesis* contained a section called 'The Columnes'. This section concerned Seth and his descendant Heber and Heber's sons, Joktan and Phalec. Of Phalec, *Genesis* tells that 'in his days the earth was divided' after the catastrophe of Babel. Fortunately, after the scattering of mankind and in the wake of the loss of the ancient unity, Seth's pillars of brick and marble had yet withstood the test of time. Surviving on the pillars, Heber is able to point out to his sons the wonders of mathematics, astronomy and geometry: the latter of a Platonic kind. Du Bartas writes:

> See heere the Solides: Cubes, Cylinders, Cones,
> Pyramides, Prismes, Dodecahedrons:
> And there the Spheare, which (Worldes Type) comprehends
> In 'tselfe it-selfe; having no midst nor ends:

The book is full of Cabalistic and Hermetic knowledge. Du Bartas was himself so struck by the reputation of King James that he travelled to Scotland. What he found – 'a gray-beards Wisdom in an amber-bush' – enthused the French poet from the court of Navarre to commemorate the visit in the final section of 'The Magnificence'. It deals with Solomon's temple.

And so the Jacobean era was truly launched: an adjective we now chiefly associate with a period of architectural style. And what style! King James's reputation spread throughout Europe and great hopes were placed on the shoulders of this (for the time) enlightened protestant monarch, son of the tragic Mary Queen of Scots, with a firm grasp of political reality and a wish to see an amelioration of religious intolerance, wherever politically possible. His eldest son Henry was a paragon of chivalric virtue; his daughter Elizabeth the image of beauty and advanced learning.

Over a century later (in Anderson's masonic history), the shorthand for all this enthusiasm for building, largely funded by wealthy nobles and gentlemen, was that King James had 'revived the lodges'. Indeed, the fresh air of patronage could be felt blowing about the nation's mason yards.

Foreign trade was bringing in money, and merchants and nobles desired to spend, to rise to the magnificence of the new Solomon. And if the gentlemen cared for the classics and were touched by the imagery of the Renaissance, then it was the leading masons' task to travel abroad and bring back the treasures of knowledge and understanding. The masons had to learn some new tricks.

While most building was done in brick (not governed by the Freemasons' Company), the best structures were raised in stone. There was much work for sculptors in marble and alabaster; churches were filled with monuments; even brick buildings required carving of arms, ornaments, quoins and porticos. Tombs, chimneypieces and statues were made by members of the company, some of whom – before 1585 – would have been members of the Marblers' Company. The Marblers of London merged with the freemasons in 1585.

The Company of Freemasons tried to govern the quality of materials and workmanship in London. By a municipal ordinance of 1481, the government of the 'mistery' (or knowledge) was vested in two wardens elected by freemen of the craft. In 1607, a new municipal ordinance determined the company would be led by a master and two wardens elected annually by the Livery. However, it is clear that there was also an inner circle of Livery members.

The first entries made in the *Quarterage Book* set out the membership in 1663 as being: Mr Thomas Shorthose, master; Mr Stephen Switzer, Thomas Shadbolt (wardens); then Edward Marshall (whom we last encountered in Cheshire) and fourteen more names of the Livery. Twenty-five more names follow, designated as 'the rest of the Livery'.

In 1677, a royal charter incorporated the London Masons' Company. Control was then vested in a master, two wardens and a 'Court of Assistants' of 24 or more. The first meeting of the court was held on 27 March 1677.

Beneath the members of the court were the liverymen, and beneath them were the yeomanry. Any of these people might own masons' yards or shops, but if the owners were yeomen, they were also called 'Shopkeepers' and were required to pay more dues than yeomen without shops. The wealthiest members of the company were the 'Court Assistants' (along with the master and wardens) and the liverymen. These would have been the people with the greatest cultural contacts.

Other towns and cities had different arrangements for the control of the trade but all being built on patterns established in the middle ages, the systems had much in common, especially as regards the training and freeing of apprentices and a concern with maintaining monopolies and wage control.

The latter interests drew frequent negative attention from other guilds, companies and civic authorities. Privilege meant money and both were guarded jealously.

In London, following visitations by senior members, those who employed 'foreign' labour were, if necessary, punished. 'Foreigners' were persons who had not become 'free' within the company system or who had come into London from outside and had not paid their dues to the company and established themselves within it. Fines were levied and persistent offenders were taken to court. Before the dominance of the great mason-contractors in the later 17th century, there were still the great master masons and masters of works, the latter-day 'descendants', as it were, of Henry Yevele and Walter of Hereford. One of the most distinguished of these men, who both designed and built their works in the Jacobean period, was Nicholas Stone.

Nicholas Stone (1586–1647)

Nicholas Stone was born in 1586, the same year as the creator of the Rosicrucian legend, the German Johann Valentin Andreae, of whom more anon. Nicholas Stone appears to have been the son of John Stone, Freemason of Sidbury near Exeter, who died in 1617. An epitaph to John Stone's memory survives in the church of St Giles, Sidbury. The commemorative plaque exhibits a stimulating and charming blend of craft and symbolic inferences:

> An epitaph upon ye Life and Death of JOHN STONE, FREEMASON, who Departed Y's Life ye first of January, 1617, & Lyeth heer under buried. On our great Corner Stone [Christ] this Stone relied, For blessing to his building loving most, to build God's temples, in which workes he dyed, and lived the Temple, of the Holy Ghost, in whose lov'd life is proved and Honest Fame, God can of Stones raise seede to Abraham.

Nicholas Stone served two years of his apprenticeship and one year as a journeyman under London monumental mason, Isaac James, having been, and presumably 'turned over' by another mason to whom he would originally have been indentured.

In 1613, Nicholas married the daughter of Amsterdam

sculptor and architect Hendrik de Keyser, with whom Stone had worked since 1607. Unable to travel to Amsterdam, Stone's father gave his consent *via* the vicar of Sidbury. The couple thence journeyed to London.

Stone acquired premises in Long Acre, took up his freedom from the Freemasons' Company and took on two apprentices from Sidbury. By 1615 he was known as a 'citizen and ffreemason of London'.

From 1619–1622, Stone was employed as King's Master Mason on the new Banqueting Hall, Whitehall, to be constructed in a stunning, new classical style. In overall charge was the king's Surveyor of Works, Inigo Jones, but things went awry as masons absconded to work on more profitable projects, while Stone himself, frustrated by poor delivery of Portland stone and the inconstant labour supply, was also compelled to work elsewhere to earn his living. In order to keep him to the site, Stone was appointed master of the work.

The Banqueting House stands as a monument to the brilliance of both Stone and Inigo Jones. Jones went on to make designs for the entirety of Whitehall Palace, having already exhibited his brilliance at combining symbolism, mechanism and design in a series of extravagant court masques. His colleague Nicholas Stone went on to hold high office in the London Company of Freemasons in the reign of King Charles I.

Warden in 1627 and 1630, Stone also served as master in 1633 and 1644. During his first year as master he worked under Inigo Jones again in the construction of a portico at the westend of old St Paul's Cathedral. During the same period Stone worked on three gateways to the Oxford Physic Garden on Cornbury House (in the same county), and, in 1634, on the rebuilding of Goldsmiths' Hall, London.

A year after King Charles I's accession, he was appointed King's Master Mason and architect for Windsor Castle (Inigo Jones had pushed for the recognition of design as a 'liberal art'). In 1632, Stone was appointed master mason to the Tower, and supplied stone to Windsor Castle, as well as building work on other royal residences, Somerset House, Oatlands and Greenwich. By sub-contracting supervision work, he was able to work on several projects at once, thus ensuring a reasonably regular supply of income. Securing payment was a notoriously fraught matter in this period.

Nicholas Stone was also responsible for one of the classic examples of English Jacobean sculpture, the powerful effigy of poet and Dean of St Paul's, John Donne (1571–1631) – author of the famous poem: 'No man is an island', a phrase with a definite masonic ring to it.

Stone's profound work of marble, like Seth's pillar, survived the Great Fire of London that destroyed the old cathedral. The sculpture of Donne in his burial shroud may still be seen at Wren's 'new' St Paul's Cathedral, for which Caius Gabriel Cibber (1630–1700) provided the sculpture of the phoenix above the rubric, *RESURGAM* (I will rise again).

Cibber (father of theatrical impresario Colley Cibber) worked as a journeyman mason and then foreman to Nicholas Stone's son, John (d.1667) who had been educated for the Church of England.

In 1638, Stone sent his eldest son Nicholas to Rome to under-study the work of Italian masters, among whom was Gianlorenzo Bernini. Nicholas Stone *jr.* also dispatched, via the English 'factory' at Leghorn, plaster casts of classical figures, marbles and rare books on such subjects as the architecture of Vitruvius and perspective as seen by Vignola.

Nicholas, like his father, was an artist.

The Accepcon

In the same year, while young Nicholas was doubtless dreaming of things Italian, his father attended, according to the Renter Warden's accounts for the London Company of *ffreemasons* (Guildhall Library), some kind of special event:

> Pd [paid] wch [which] the accompt [accountant]
> layd out wch was more than he received of them wch

were taken into the Accepcon whereof xs [10 shillings] is to be paid by Mr Nicholas Stone, Mr Edward Kinsman, Mr John Smith, Mr William Millis, Mr John Colles

And this is our first positive record of the word '*Accepcon*' (Acception) within the context of Freemasonry. We cannot say that Nicholas Stone was one of the first 'Accepted Freemasons' because the relevant records of the company before this time have, most regrettably, been lost, or destroyed, or stolen; he may have been one in a long line. Alternatively, the 'Accepcon' may have been a fairly recent innovation. We know not. We have no 'substituted secrets' to put in their place; we must use our brains instead.

Here was Nicholas Stone, a *bona fide* 'ffreemason' and about as 'operative' as you could ever expect to see, paying (or owing) ten shillings to become an 'Accepted ffreemason'. At a stroke, we see that you cannot properly use the word 'accepted' to differentiate between a member of the or any other 'grand lodge' and a person who earns their living from practising the 'craft and mystery' of Masonry.

Furthermore, according to the understanding of the master and wardens of the London Company of Freemasons in Stone's time, it would appear to be absolutely illegitimate to tear this dignity – whatever it may have been – from the privileges of the trade.

The question then must arise. Did the early grand lodge know what the word 'Accepted' actually meant? We must ask this question because it is now highly probable that it did not mean what subsequent generations of so-called speculative masons have been told it meant.

How can we be sure of this? For the simple reason that all of the men mentioned in the above entry were craftsmen and members of the London Company of Freemasons. Stone himself had been master of the company four years earlier (and still not 'accepted'!). He had also worked with Edward Kinsman who had been employed on Syon House as a 'freemason' in 1604-05. Kinsman had succeeded Stone as master in 1635.

Frankly, these were among the top men in the profession, and yet with all their advancements, long since apprenticed, they had to wait until their mature years to be 'taken into the Accepcon'. This is extraordinary and should give us pause. Do we see here something like the first tangible signs of the genesis of a form of Freemasonry that is not accessible to those who are learning their craft – but only to those who have had a long time to consider the meaning of it? That is to say, is there not something here of the marriage of the art and craft with the philosophy, or spiritual underpinning of the trade?

It is reasonable to think on these lines, but only because we have so long accepted the notion that an 'Accepted Mason' was one who moralised on the allegorical interpretation of architecture in terms of some kind of self-knowledge. It is possible that this interpretation (misleadingly called 'Speculative Masonry') if not actually in error – that is to say, wrong – may simply be too limited a conception. That is to say, divining the true nature of Accepted Masonry may have been guesswork, once we suppose that those who had been 'taken in' to the Acception were absolutely compelled never to speak or write about it.

Is this what the 'substitute secrets' were substituted for? Is there something of an Oedipus Complex lurking behind the modern tale of the third degree? That is, was the old Accepted Freemasonry the 'Hiram Abif' who refused to give up 'his secrets' so was 'slain' by the new order? They 'tried to raise him' (revivify the secret) but could only manage the 'five points of fellowship'? Far-fetched? We shall see.

Back to Nicholas Stone and his brethren in 1638...

Who 'took them in' to the Acception? What might it mean to be 'taken in' to such a thing? It seems reasonable to suppose that the accountant at the company had at least some idea of what he was referring to. He appears to have still been unpaid for some of the required dues and ten shillings was a lot of money in those days.

The *Accepcon* appears to have been, in a sense, part of company business but for how long? We cannot tell. One thing appears to be clear at least – and will become clearer when we investigate further into the fragments of records concerning 'Acception' in the 17th century – this was not for every freemason. Did every freemason know about it? We do not know. Certainly, this *Accepcon* appears to have been a high privilege.

The great question still remains – who was in a position to grant this privilege (if that is what it was)? Stone had already been master of the company – he had not been 'taken in' then. Kinsman had been master; he had not been 'taken in'.

Was there a religious angle? That is to say, was there some kind of company chaplain, spiritual overseer or overseers of the company? As things stand, we cannot say. (The old guilds and confraternities used to employ priests for both liturgical and scribal duties.)

Masonic historian Matthew Scanlan has drawn attention to an entry in James Anderson's revised *Constitutions* of 1738 (p.111). The entry refers to something that happened in the year 1720 (before the first *Constitutions* were published). The entry may have been connected with an alleged call made by Grand Master George Payne on 24 June 1718.

Payne 'desired any Brethren to bring to the Grand Lodge any old writings and records concerning Masons and Masonry in order to shew the Usages of antient Times: And this Year several old Copies of the Gothic Constitutions [Old Charges] were produced and collated.'

It is noteworthy that Grand Master Payne and his colleagues seem to have required educating in these matters. The telling entry (according to Scanlan) refers to the second term under the grand mastership of George Payne (John Theophilus Desaguliers held the grand mastership during the intervening year). According to Anderson's account:

> This Year, at some private Lodges, several very valuable Manuscripts (for they had nothing yet in Print) concerning the Fraternity, their Lodges, Regulations, Charges, Secrets, and Usages (particularly one writ by Mr. Nicholas Stone the

> Warden of Inigo Jones) were too hastily burnt by
> some scrupulous Brothers, that those Papers might
> not fall into strange Hands.

In a serious article written for *Freemasonry Today* magazine (Summer 2000), Scanlan strongly implied that the 'strange Hands' that the 'scrupulous Brothers' wished to avoid were none other than those of Grand Master Payne and his colleagues.

This would seem to be a quite logical inference from Payne's earlier call for manuscripts showing ancient usages. Payne was in the process of drawing up fresh regulations, presumably on no authority other than that of himself and his colleagues (such as Desaguliers) in the grand lodge venture. The reference to the manuscript by Nicholas Stone stands out. Why was this one drawn out as being a particular loss? The possibility stands that information was being sought on the true nature of the 'Acception' and older members (from private lodges, note) were loath to let anyone tamper with the 'Regulations, Charges, Secrets, and Usages' in their possession.

Indeed, such was their suspicion of the lengths some person or persons might go to get hold of their material, that they were prepared to burn it so as to maintain secrecy. The scrupulous brothers may indeed have destroyed the only clue we might have to determining the nature of the privileged Masonry to which Stone and senior members of the company were attached.

In the absence of such a manuscript, the only clue I can suggest is that one should look again at Vaughan's engraving from Ashmole's *Theatrum Chemicum Britannicum* (1652) of the seated master enjoining his alchemical son and heir to 'Accept' his secrets (see chapter three). And since we have mentioned Ashmole, we had better look at his unique record of having been 'made a Free Mason' on October 16, 1646. Does his record help us in any way to understand what this 'Acception' phenomenon was all about?

Did Elias Ashmole become an 'Accepted Free Mason' eight years after Nicholas Stone?

Elias Ashmole and Robert Moray – A Curious Anomaly – or two

Five years before Ashmole's initiation, Robert Moray (*c.*1607-1673) was made an admitted mason at a Scottish lodge assembled at Newcastle in 1641.

Moray was the son of a Perthshire laird, Sir Mungo Moray. He had a lifetime interest in every aspect of science, in himself (he tried to calm his passions by a conscious application of Stoicism and Christian ethics) and in secret adventures. He would serve a number of masters, some of them apparently contradictory. The Scots Covenanters army, for example was raised to oppose the religious policy of King Charles I. Not very long afterwards, he would find cause to serve the King (who knighted him in 1643) and later, his son, Charles II, on secret missions in France, the Netherlands and in Scotland. Charles II quipped in later years that such was his modesty and tolerance of other people's religious standpoint, that Moray had a religion of his own, of which he was the head. Sir Robert was incorruptible and had a sacred conception of the value of friendship.

A key principle of his life (which tied in with his masonic interest) was that one must not judge people by appearances. A person was like a star, he wrote to a friend. Ignorance of its true position in relation to others might deceive one into underestimating its size and significance.

Furthermore, the most important dimension of a stellar ray was invisible to the eye. There was a certain conceit here; it was good not to appear as one was. How one appeared to others was not truly important; one must be absolutely true to oneself. Moray was suspicious of the poor judgements people made of one another. And yet, it was widely observed that Moray was himself a man without affectations of any kind. He was 'himself' and was sensitive to any idea that his ego had got the better of him.

All this, not to mention his serious alchemical, Hermetic and Rosicrucian interests, might lead one to suppose that he may have derived something of his orientation from Masonry. The evidence does not hold this out, however. Rather, it was the way his mind worked that gave him a respect for Masonry, among his other interests.

For example, Moray was extremely fond of the symbol of the pentagram and, following classical precedent, associated it with health, as well as friendship. Around the points of the star, he put the Greek letters AGAPA (based on the Greek verb *agapein*, to love). The word was compounded in its turn from some awkward forms of Greek verbs: *AGAPA*; *GNOTHI*; *ANECHO*; *PISTEUEI*; *APECHO*.

The acrostic may be read as indicating the following moral instruction: 'love God and your fellow men; know thyself; be constant; have faith; be temperate or 'exercise restraint'. The 'five points of fellowship' might have been implied, thus conforming to Moray's idea that things are not always as they seem. How much of this was masonically inspired is unclear since Moray had already begun to identify himself with the pentagram before his initiation. Nevertheless, Moray was apt to describe his seal as his 'Mason's mark'. In fact, the pentagram was indeed used as a mason's mark in the period. An example may be seen on the church tower at Lapley, Staffordshire, dated 1637, next to the name of William Tonck, perhaps the freemason who restored the tower. Such a happy coincidence between his own intuition and Masonry would undoubtedly have lit Moray's magical fire.

> At Neucastell the 20 day of May 1641
> The quilk day are serten nomber off Mester and othere bing lafule Conuined doeth admit Mr thie Right honerabell Mr Robert Moray Generall quarter Mr to the Armie off Scotlan and the sam bing apreuen be the hell Mester off the mesone off the Log off edinbroth quherto they heave set to ther handes or Markes.
>
> (*The Lodge of Edinburgh Mary's Chapel No. 1, Quatercentenary of Minutes 1599-1999*, Ed. J.E. McArthur, Edinburgh, 1999)

This is the record of Moray's initiation into the brotherhood of Masonry that took place, uniquely, on English soil, at a ceremony in which his comrade in arms, Alexander Hamilton, general of artillery, was also initiated, in the presence of James Hamilton, Deacon, and John Mengenes, Warden.

According to Professor David Stevenson (*The Origins of Freemasonry, Scotland's Century 1590–1710*, Cambridge, 1988), the admission of these men into Masonry was not simply to satisfy antiquarian interests any one or both of them might have had. Rather, it was done in view of the mathematical, geometrical and technical expertise that went along with the men's role in the Covenanting Army.

This is quite possible, but not certain. Nor is it clear why the Lodge of Edinburgh should have travelled to Newcastle for the purpose.

Was there any other way that becoming admitted masons might help them in the armed struggle with Charles Stuart and his 'High Church' policies? We do not know. One thing is certain. Moray did not become an 'Accepted Free Mason'. There is no record of the 'Acception' in Scotland. The lodge that Moray was sworn to was part of the business of Masonry in Edinburgh, as we have seen in chapter three. Moray is usually called an 'Admitted Mason', not having served an apprenticeship in the craft. This term is usually held to be the Scots equivalent of 'accepted', but such was not originally the case.

Nevertheless, the fact that Moray and Elias Ashmole (initiated five years later) knew each other, shared many profound interests, and were both founder members of the Royal Society (Moray was its first president) has led to a general sense of equivalence in their position as regards Freemasonry.

Stevenson has even gone so far as to suppose that the lodge into which Ashmole was initiated may have owed its origin to Scottish incursions during the Civil War period. This contention shows, I think, the effect of a most doubtful preoccupation in Stevenson's work, namely, to show that concerning the origins of 'speculative Freemasonry', the 17th century was 'Scotland's century' (*ibid*.p.219ff.).

Elias Ashmole – Free Mason

1646

Oct: 16. 4.30. p.m. I was made a Free Mason at Warrington in Lancashire with Coll: Henry Mainwaring of Karincham in Cheshire.

The names of those that were then of the Lodge, Mr: Rich Penket Warden, Mr: James Collier, Mr: Rich. Sankey, Henry Littler, John Ellam, Rich: Ellam & Hugh Brewer.

(See my book *The Magus of Freemasonry – The Mysterious Life of Elias Ashmole*, Inner Traditions, Vermont, 2006, p.92ff.)

Of all Ashmole's extensive esoteric interests, his decision to become a 'Free Mason' has perhaps aroused the greatest controversy. Ashmole's brief memorial note has long been considered to be the first record of initiation into 'speculative Freemasonry', its date of 1646 strangely in advance of the generally accepted date for the establishment of 'speculative Freemasonry' as an organisation.

The occasion followed on from Ashmole's defeat at the battle of Worcester in July 1646 – and a summer spent wooing 'Ellinore' (as he styled her name) Minshull. Interestingly, Ashmole (like Hamilton) had been in charge of artillery defences. (Stone's son, Nicholas Stone the younger – a royalist was the author of the *Enchiridion of Fortification*, published in 1645).

Having lost his mother in a plague after parliamentarian forces besieged royalist Lichfield, Ashmole had been kicking his heels around his in-laws' (the Mainwarings) territory in Cheshire.

What had Elias Ashmole joined in his darkest hour? We cannot be certain. Late 17th century English evidence suggests initiation involved an entered apprentice, followed by a fellow craft ritual. A secret word and grip may have been given.

All we can be reasonably certain of is that at Ashmole's initiation, he was read a traditional history of the craft, enjoined to swear his allegiance to the craft charges, and became a fellow of the society. That does not mean that that is all that happened, but it is all we can be fairly sure happened.

After Ashmole established his pioneering museum in Oxford in 1683, he approved the appointment of Dr Robert Plot as its first curator. Plot was to be the author of *The Natural History of Staffordshire*, published in 1686. In chapter eight, Plot gave the following account of 'Free-masons' in the moorlands of Staffordshire:

> To these add the Customs relating to the County, whereof they have one, of admitting Men into the Society of Free-masons, that in the moorelands of this County seems to be of greater request, than anywhere else, though I find the Custom spread more or less all over the Nation; for here I find persons of the most eminent quality, that did not disdain to be of this Fellowship. Nor indeed need they, were it of that Antiquity and honor, that is pretended in a large parchment volum they have amongst them, containing the History and Rules of the craft of masonry. Which is there deduced not only from sacred Writ, but profane story, particularly that it was brought into England by Saint Amphibal, and first communicated to S.Alban, who set down the Charges of masonry, and was made paymaster and governor of the Kings works, and gave them charges and manners as St. Amphibal had taught him. Which were after confirmed by King Athelstan, whose youngest son Edwyn loved well masonry, took upon him the charges and learned the manners, and obtained for them of his father a free-charter. Whereupon he caused them to assemble at York, and to bring all the old books of their craft, and out of them ordained such charges and manners, as they then thought fit: which charges in the said Schrole or parchment volum, are in part declared: and thus was the craft of masonry grounded and confirmed in

England. It is also there declared that these charges and manners were after perused and approved by King Hen.6. and his council, both as to Masters and Fellows of this right Worshipfull craft.

Into which Society when they are admitted, they call a meeting (or Lodg as they term it in some places) which must consist at lest of 5 or 6 of the ancients of the Order, whom the candidates present with gloves, and so likewise to their wives, and entertain with a Collation according to the custom of the place: This ended, they proceed to the admission of them, which chiefly consists in the communication of certain secret signes, whereby they are known to one another all over the Nation, by which means they have maintenance whither ever they travel : for if any man appear though altogether unknown that can shewe any of these signes to a Fellow of that Society, whom they otherwise call an accepted mason, he is obliged presently to come to him, from what company or place soever he be in, nay tho' from the top of a steeple, (what hazard or inconvenience soever he run) to know his pleasure, and assist him; viz. if he want work he is bound to find him some; or if he cannot do that, to give him mony, or otherwise support him till work can be had; which is one of their articles; and it is another, that they advise the Masters they work for, according to the best of their skill, acquainting them with the goodness or badness of their materials; and if they be in any way out in the contrivance of their buildings modestly to rectify them in it; that masonry be not dishonoured: and many such like that are commonly known: but some others they have (to which they are sworn after their fashion) that none know but themselves, which I have reason to suspect are much worse than these, perhaps as bad as the History of the craft it self; than which there is nothing I ever met with, more false or incoherent.

(*The Natural History of Staffordshire by Robert Plot. LLD. Keeper of the ASHMOLEAN MUSAEUM And PROFESSOR of CHYMISTRY in the UNIVERSITY of OXFORD*, 1686. Ch.8.)

The historical information which Plot dismisses (some references are plainly legendary) coincides with a document that has come down to us from the Sloane Collection. It is of the same 'family' of 'Old Charges' as the *Cooke* MS. discussed in chapter six. By a curious coincidence, the manuscript copy dubbed the 'Constitutions of Masonry' formerly in the possession of Sir Hans Sloane (*Sloane* MS. 3848 British Library), ends with the following autograph: '*ffinis p.me Eduardu : Sankey decimo sexto die Octobris, Anno domini 1646*' – the very day on which Ashmole and his late wife's cousin Colonel Henry Mainwaring were made Free Masons.

Warrington church registers record the baptism of 'Edward son to Richard Sankeay [sic], gent., 3 ffebruarie, 1621/2'. It seems highly likely that this was the son of the Richard Sankey recorded by Elias Ashmole as having been present at his initiation. We may be permitted to imagine Edward Sankey writing out the Charges – perhaps from memory – as part of his father's preparation for the ceremony. Edward Sankey wrote as follows:

> Good brethren & ffellows, our purpose is to tell you, how and in what manner; this Craft of Masonrie was begun; and afterwards founded by worthy Kings and Princes; & many other worshipful men; and also to ym that are heare; wee will declare to ym the Charge yt doth belonge to every true Mason to keep ffor good sooth if you take heede thereunto it is well worthie to bee kept; or a worthie Craft and curious science, ffor there bee seaven liberall sciences;

before Noes flood was a man called Lameth as it is written in ye 4 chapt of Gene, and this Lameth had 2 wives; ye one was called Adar; ye other Sella: and by Adar hee begott 2 sonnes. The one was called Jabell ye other Juball; And by ye other wife hee had a sonne & a Daughter; and these foure children found ye beginninge of all Crafts in ye world; This Jabell was ye elder sonne; and found ye Craft of Geometry;

and these children did knowe that god would take vengeance for sinne eather by fire or water; Wherefore ye writ ye Sciences wch weare found in 2 pillars of stone; yt ye might be found after the flood; The one stone was called Marble that cannot burne wth fire; The other was called Letera that cannot drowne with water; Our intent is to tell you truly how & in what manner these stones weare found; where these Crafts were written in Greek; Hermenes that was sonne to Cus, & Cus was sonne to Shem wch was ye sonne of Noath: The same Hermenes was afterwards Hermes; the ffather of wise men, and hee found out ye 2 pillars of stone where ye Sciences weare written, & taught him forth.

when Abraham and Sara his wife went into Egypt; there weare taught the seaven sciences unto ye Egyptians; And hee had a worthy Schollar called Euchlid and hee Learned right well and was Maister of all ye 7 Sciences;

And there was a King of an other Region yt men called Hyram and hee loved well Kinge Solomon; and gave him timber for his worke; And hee had a sonne that was named Aynon & he was Mr of Geometry; and hee was chiefe Mr of all his Masons; and Mr of all his graved works; and of all other Masons that belonged to ye Temple; & this Witnesseth the Bible in libro 2 Solo capite 5.

And soe it befell that a curious workman; who was named Nimus Graecus & had beene at ye makeinge of Solomons Temple; and came into ffrance; and there taught ye Craft of Masonrie; to ye man of ffrance that was named Charles Martill;

And all this while England was voyde both of any charge or Masonrie; until ye time of St.Albans; And in his time ye King of England that was a Pagan; and hee walled ye Towne wch is now called St. Albans;

until ye time of King Athelstone; yt was a worthy King of England; and hee brought ye Land into rest and peace againe; and hee builded many great workes & Castles & Abbies; and many other Buildings; and hee loved Masons well; and hee had a sonne yt was named Hadrian:

And hee held himself assembly at Yorke and there hee made Masons, and gave ym Charges and taught them Mannrs of Masons; and commanded that rule to bee holden ever after: And to them took ye Charter & Commission to keepe;

And from time to time Masonrie until this day hath beene kept in yt forme & order, as well as might gov'ne ye same; And furthermore at dyvrs assemblies hath beene put to and aded certaine Charges; more by ye best advices; of Mastrs and fellowes; Heare followeth the worthie and godly oath of Masons; Every man that is a Masonn take Heede right well; to this charge; if you finde yo'self guilty of any of these; yt you amend you; againe especially you yt are to bee charged take good heed that you may keepe this Charge; for it is a great perill for a man to foresweare himselfe on a book;

These are almost certainly the exact words that Elias Ashmole and Col. Henry Mainwaring heard at their initiation into the craft. But was this an initiation into 'Accepted' Freemasonry? Did Warrington contain an 'acception' ceremony?

Plot, writing forty years later, refers to Freemasons being called 'a Fellow of that Society, whom they otherwise call an accepted mason'. He does not tell us what precisely he means by an 'accepted' mason. Plot notes that particular practices – especially as regards a 'Collation' – depended on 'the custom of the place'.

There seems nothing fanciful or outside of known evidence in what he next has to say: 'This ended, they proceed to the admission of them, which chiefly consists in the communication of certain secret signes, whereby they are known to one another all over the Nation, by which means they have maintenance whither ever they travel: for if any man appear though altogether unknown that can shewe any of these signes to a Fellow of that Society, whom they otherwise call an accepted mason...'

As far as Plot is aware (he is not a member) the words 'Fellow' and 'Accepted Mason' may be used interchangeably. And yet, Plot is clearly referring to a so-called 'operative' context; the lodges he describes are run by the 'ancients of the order', even though they admit gentlemen. How does the lodge of Ashmole conform to this picture?

The Warrington Lodge

The lodge at or near Warrington on the Lancashire-Cheshire border was not a coven of esotericists, at least as far as we can tell! Nor was it a discussion group for the latest philosophical 'discoveries'. The Warrington lodge was largely made up of landed gentlemen from Cheshire and from that county's border with south Lancashire: royalists and parliamentarians both with a significant number from families with traditions of faithfulness to the 'old religion', that is, Catholicism. It is not unreasonable to conclude that for Ashmole the contact came through the Mainwaring family and that family's connections with the gentility, craftsmen, and religion of the old County Palatine of Chester.

Intriguingly, the name Stone was not unknown to the Mainwaring family. As we have seen in chapter three, two years after the initiation of Col. Henry Mainwaring and Elias Ashmole, Ellen (*née*) Minshull, the widow of Sir Philip Mainwaring, erected a mortuary chapel at the church at Upper Peover. The lifesize marble effigies of herself and her husband were the work of John Stone (d.1667), son of Nicholas Stone and a man originally trained for the Church, but who inherited his father's yard (along with his brother Henry, d.1653) when their father died in 1647. It should also be recalled that the possibly masonic chair owned by Lord Northampton was almost certainly in the possession of Edward Minshull in 1595. Ellen Mainwaring's father was Edward Minshull, from Stoke Hall, near Nantwich.

But why Warrington?

If, as seems most likely, Ashmole's reference to 'Mr: Rich Penket Warden' means that Richard Penket was warden of the lodge (he is mentioned first), then the Penket family name may give us a clue.

Friar Thomas Penketh (d.1487: one of the Penkeths who held lands from the lords of Warrington, the Boteler [Butler] family) was Head Hermit at the Priory of St Augustine, Warrington. The Penketh coat of arms used to adorn a window in the Warrington Friary; there was also a window bearing their coat of arms in Warrington parish church. The Penkeths also patronised the church at Farnworth, to the west of Warrington.

We see here a repeated connection between gentlemen landowners and the monastic and confraternal system. This was also the case with respect to the Mainwarings in Cheshire and Staffordshire. Who but the pious gentility would have the greatest concern with old family chapels and their ornamentation, never mind the pre-Reformation monastic world to which 15th century members of the Mainwaring family were bound by deeds of confraternity?

The Penkeths lived at Penketh Hall, Penketh (a hamlet of Great Sankey) in the time of James I, as they had done since at least the early 1200s, but after 400 years, Richard Penketh sold Penketh Hall to Thomas Ashton in 1624. The sale appears to have marked the demise of the family's fortunes. It is perfectly possible that this Richard Penketh (or possibly his son) was the same Richard Penketh who was warden of the lodge Ashmole describes as having gathered at Warrington.

Ashmole refers to a Henry Littler as having been present at his being made a 'Free Mason'. The Littlers were a family of Cheshire gentry.

The Sankeys held manors under the lords of Bewsey at Great and Little Sankey and were of sufficient consequence to have had their arms emblazoned in the windows of Warrington church. The old family seat was the Hall at Sankey Parva or Little Sankey. Once a hamlet of Warrington, it may be that the lodge joined by Ashmole and Col. Henry Mainwaring on that late October afternoon came alive at that place.

We have mentioned the Edward Sankey who wrote out the masons' charges and traditional history in October 1646. He was possibly the son of Richard Sankey born in early 1621. It is also possible that this was the Edward Sankey described by William Beaumont in his *The Chapelry of Sankey* (Warrington, 1882). Beaumont called Sankey: 'the last of his ancient house of whom we hear, a man well born and well educated, and who had lately been abroad and seen something of military affairs'.

Having joined Sir William Brereton's regiment of horse in 1642, this Edward Sankey received a commission to command a company. He was one of the party who, on New Year's Day, 1643, searched the house of Mr Davenport of Bramhall. He also joined in the attack upon Withenshaw, the house of Mr Tatton. Edward Sankey even appears in a contemporary lampoon verse – a verse that, intriguingly, includes a Mainwaring at arms. This could equally have been Edward Mainwaring of Whitmore, Sir Philip Mainwaring of Peover, or Colonel Henry Mainwaring of Karincham:

> Lancaster's mad,
> And Eaton's as bad,
> Mainwaring looks like an ape;
> Oxley is naught,
> And Sankey was caught
> When he was in a captain's shape.

One can only speculate as to what might have kept Edward Sankey from joining his supposed father at a lodge that might well have been convened at the family home. Since Edward Sankey almost certainly wrote out the copy of the *Old Charges* used at Ashmole's initiation, it is practically certain that the scribe was an Accepted Free Mason. On the other hand, Edward Sankey may indeed have been present and Ashmole simply omitted his name for some reason unknown.

Ashmole recorded that one Hugh Brewer attended the initiation. Hugh Brewer may have been the man of Lancashire yeoman stock who distinguished himself as a sergeant major in Lord Derby's royalist regiment of horse (the burial of a Hugh Brewer is recorded in Warrington parish records on 29 May 1658).

Mr James Collier may have been the James Collier of Newton, gentleman, reported in a certificate taken by Randle Holme II of Chester (*Deputye to the Office of Armes*). This Collier, on 3 June 1640, at the age of 32, married Elizabeth, daughter of Sir Edward Stanley of Bickerstaffe, Lancashire. Elizabeth's grandfather was Sir Randle Mainwaring of Peover, a relative of Colonel Henry Mainwaring, and distantly thereby of Elias Ashmole himself. Whether or not this was the man, it seems likely that the James Collier of the Warrington lodge did come from Newton and was a royalist.

The case of John Ellam's brother, Richard, is particularly interesting. It shows how the Warrington lodge did not operate independently of the operative world of freemasons but was controlled by its customs and regulations.

17th century Cheshire wills records reveal a Richard Ellom of Lymm, with a brother called John. Richard Ellom's will (7 September 1667) describes him plainly as a 'freemason', and shows that he had property to dispose of in a gentlemanly fashion. Freemasonry could be reasonably lucrative, as one might expect of such a vital craft.

If this was the same Richard Ellam referred to by Ashmole, it seems likely that his singular presence at a lodge of accepted gentlemen fulfilled a stipulation of contemporary trade practice. When a number of London Freemasons attempted to establish a system of lodges beyond the control of craftsmen freemasons between 1720 and 1730, a chief instrument in their purposes was the publication of Rev James Anderson's *Constitutions of Free and Accepted Masons* (1723). As if to preempt Anderson's work, Freemason J. Roberts, about whom nothing else is known, published another set of *Constitutions* in 1722. Significantly, he repeated the charge of *Grand Lodge MS. No 2* that a properly constituted lodge must contain at least five brethren and a minimum of one brother who was an active master of the trade.

Grand Lodge MS. No 2 is a copy of the *Old Charges*, held by the United Grand Lodge of England. It dates from the 1660s and is possibly a product of an assembly of masons believed by both Roberts and Anderson to have been held in 1663. Ashmole's 'mother lodge' at Warrington in 1646 conforms to the rule regarding a properly constituted lodge. It also shows that the leaders of the trade craft of Freemasons encouraged the existence of lodges constituted primarily of gentlemen for purposes other than training apprentices; a symbolic and learned Freemasonry running side by side with the trade seems to have been intended. John Ellam was almost certainly the statutory working freemason.

Ashmole's introduction to this system must surely have come from his kinship with the Mainwaring family. Colonel Henry Mainwaring lived near to the road that joins Smallwood (where Ashmole was staying at the home of his father-in-law, Peter Mainwaring: the colonel's uncle) to Warrington.

Col. Henry Mainwaring was the squire of Karincham (now called Kermincham and pronounced by locals as 'Kermidgum'). Kermincham is close to Swettenham, where Mainwarings were interred for many years. Records from the Consistory Court in Chester reveal that Henry Mainwaring of Karincham, husband of Eleanor (*née*) Minshull, the colonel's grandfather (and Ashmole's father-in-law's father) was involved in a dispute over burial places and seats at the church of St Luke, Goostrey, two miles away. Henry Mainwaring was permitted to build an out aisle or aisles on the north side of the chancel. One wonders who undertook the masonry.

The advowson of Goostrey, incidentally, had been held by Dieulacres, a great abbey of the Staffordshire Moorlands founded by Ranulphus, earl of Chester in 1214. Roger de Mein-warin (Mainwaring) along with William de Venables, witnessed the earl's instruction to his barons regarding its founding. As we have seen, Ashmole was a distant relative of the Venables family, as was his first wife, Eleanor Mainwaring.

Eleanor's forebear, Margery Mainwaring, was the daughter of Hugh Venables, baron of Kinderton, and it was Margery who erected the unusual chapel at the church of S.Lawrence, Upper Peover, over the tomb of her husband Randle Mainwaring, who died in 1456.

There are – as we have seen – numerous other monuments in St Lawrence's that testify to a longstanding relationship with fine sculptors and architects – freemasons – from the 14th century right into Ashmole's time.

Six miles north of Upper Peover (on land given by the Conqueror to the Venables family) is that church's mother church of Rostherne, some six miles southeast of Warrington. In 1578 an arbitration award was made to Thomas Legh against Sir Randle Mainwaring who had claimed possession of the Legh chapel in Rostherne church.

According to Raymond Richards (*Old Cheshire Churches*, Batsford, 1947, p.874): 'The Legh Chapel at Rostherne stood ruinous in the sixteenth century for want of glass, [and] Sir Randle Mainwaring repaired it at his own expense,' assuming possession for himself and his family 'only to be turned out by Thomas Legh'.

The passion for building continued. In 1585 the stately home of Peover was completed and still stands, unspoilt, in the midst of Peover Park, overlooking the church of St Lawrence.

One further fact regarding Ashmole's initiation may be noted. Colonel Mainwaring had in 1643 taken a leading role in the defence of Nantwich, against the royalists, with 2000 men and a furiously constructed, but well designed trench and earthwork system. Mainwaring's later commitment to the parliamentarian cause seems to have wavered considerably (*The Civil Wars in Cheshire*, R.N. Dore, Chester, 1966, p.72), as the plot thickened, but he was, like all the fighting-age Mainwarings of whom we have knowledge, associated with parliament.

Attempting to keep civil war destruction and bloodshed out of Cheshire, Colonel Henry Mainwaring was responsible for organising the Peace of Bunbury, whereby men on opposing sides agreed to exercise restraint in arms. This peace was overturned by parliamentarian commander, Sir William Brereton, who soon advanced north in an orgy of destruction that extended across from Staffordshire to Cheshire.

There is no record of Ashmole's regarding the Mainwarings's disloyalty to the person of Charles I with censure. Perhaps there was something in him that he felt to be above such partisan concerns. Perhaps he simply understood too well the profound complexities of the war. In the lodge to which he would be fraternally bound he encountered a catholic, an anglican, a parliamentarian and himself: a royalist. All of this strongly militates against David Stevenson's notion that Freemasonry derived from Scottish sources. But the question remains, was this 'Accepted' Freemasonry?

We have very little to go on and certainty is out of the question.

In a diary entry concerning an event at Masons' Hall in London in March 1682, Ashmole describes those attending as 'Fellows', and himself as 'Senior Fellow' on account of the early date of his initiation (and age). Ashmole writes of those admitted to their fellowship as being 'New: accepted Masons' after the meeting.

It is reasonable to assume that the meeting was called for the purposes of an 'Acception'. If Ashmole was invited, then we must presume that he was himself already 'accepted'. Ashmole dates his admission into the 'Fellowship' as having taken place 35 years before. This could give us a date of 1647, or 1646, depending how precisely Ashmole was computing his 35 years. (Ashmole was a keen mathematician and professional accountant for His Majesty's Excise).

It is possible that Ashmole experienced a ceremony subsequent to that held in Warrington, for after the Warrington episode, Ashmole left Cheshire for London where he stayed for a considerable time. The distinguished editor of Ashmole's published manuscripts, C.H. Josten, noted that Ashmole's arrival in the capital brought him a sudden rush of meetings with, and invitations from, mathematicians and astrologers. Josten wondered if this might have been on account of Ashmole's newly forged masonic connection. Ashmole could have been 'accepted' at this time, rather than at Warrington. There is something, however, which makes one consider that the Warrington event was itself an 'acception'. That 'something' is the social status of the men involved with the lodge.

We have seen from the London Freemasons Company records that those taken in to the 'accepcon' (earliest spelling) were distinguished members of the craft, high earners, not yeomen or journeymen. They could live as gentlemen. Now it may be that in different parts of the country, customs differing, terms became confused. It may be that ordinary masons wished not to be left out of the term 'Accepted Mason' and did their own version of what they supposed the term to mean.

Bearing this possibility in mind, we are at liberty to imagine that there were possibly three classes of lodge meeting occurring in England during the 17th century. These would be, first, lodges where freemasons met for trade purposes (as in Scotland). Such lodges would offer exclusive brotherhood and discipline to masons.

Second, lodges – or additional ceremonies – convened by

tradesmen for the purpose of inviting gentlemen into their midst.

Third, lodges primarily for gentlemen, and run by gentlemen, offering a symbolic emphasis and fraternal enjoyments, but nonetheless linked to, and approved by, senior members of the trade. Such a lodge as latterly described would represent a kind of 'platinum' masonic membership, coveted by and accessible only to the most distinguished company.

This model of lodge variants could explain how there came to be an 'Acception' at the London Masons' Company that could bring in the top men of the business, and yet still be run by persons not primarily concerned with trade business, but with longstanding business involvement nonetheless. This would also explain how someone like, say, Edward Minshull, could come to sit in what may be a 'master's chair' – and would further allow a space for the indulgence and development of Renaissance, biblical and alchemical symbolism, of the kind that strongly attracted men like Ashmole and Moray.

Readers familiar with the cross-over between masonic and Rosicrucian interest in the 17th century (see my book *The Golden Builders, Alchemists, Rosicrucians and the First Free Masons*) will also see how such a model accommodates so many of the anomalies and contradictions that abound in treatments of 17th century 'Freemasonry'.

To give just one example of how this model explains an anomaly in the records of Masonry, let us examine the famous lodge of Randle Holme III that existed in the ravaged city of Chester after the end of the civil war. If the model I have suggested is correct, this lodge should fit comfortably into the second kind of lodge and explains why nowhere in the Randle Holme's surviving notes is it described as being a lodge of 'accepted' Freemasons.

Randle Holme and Chester's Society of Freemasons

Randle Holme III, born in 1627, was the son of Alderman Randle Holme JP, painter, Herald, and Mayor of Chester

(1643). At the age of 21, the ex-mayor's son was admitted into the Painters, Stationers and Glaziers Company. Holme was one of the stewards of the company and entered up its accounts, one surviving example of which shows the costs for rebuilding the Phoenix Tower on the city walls, ruined in the 'late [Civil] Wars'.

The Phoenix Tower (later known as King Charles' Tower) was for over 164 years after 1609 the meeting place for many of Chester's trade guilds. Randle Holme's society of 'Free-Masons' met at the Phoenix Tower.

In 1659, Randle Holme was elected Alderman of the Painters, Stationers and Glaziers Company, entertaining the members at his house with 'Beare and Tobacco' for the grand sum of five shillings and sixpence. In 1664, some court influence gained him the sinecure of Sewer of the Chamber in Extraordinary to His Majesty King Charles II: a valuable post with excellent privileges such as being secure from arrest unless under direct order of the king.

Given Holme's comfortable setting in the latter company, it seems surprising that he should have joined another trade fraternity. We know that he did so from an entry in his four volume work, *The Academie of Armory* (Chester, 1683) and from 'Notes and Charters, with generall things which concerne the Companyes and occupations with in the Citty of Chester' (*Harleian* MS. 2054 British Library).

These notes deal with practically every aspect of the city of Chester's trade guilds and companies, as well as containing three items specific to 'Free-Masons'.

First, the *Constitutions of Masonry* (in Holme's handwriting, from the middle of the 17th century); second, a scrap of paper referring to the 'Words and Signes of a free-mason'; third, a list containing twenty-six names, together with certain fees due (or received) from each.

The scrap of paper regarding the 'Words and Signes' contains the injunction that they are to be kept secret. Failure to do so will be answerable on God's day of judgement. They should be revealed only 'to the Master and fellows of the said Society of free masons so help me God…'

It should be noted that very similarly worded oaths to

maintain secrecy were used by other Chester companies. In volume three (p.393) of his *Academie*, Randle Holme writes: 'I cannot but Honor the Fellowship of the Masons because of its antiquity: and the more, as being a member of that society called Free-Masons: In being conversant amongst them I have observed the use of these several Tools following some whereof I have seen born in coats armor.'

This passage opens a section on masons' tools, and tools – not morals – is what we get: shovel, masons' hammer and maul. (On p.111 Holme had already given 'Terms of art used by Freemasons stone cutters'). As S.L. Coulthurst notes (*The Lodge of Randle Holme at Chester*, AQC, p.63), the use of the term 'Free mason' is used in its 'operative sense'. When Holme lists twenty-six members of his lodge, he uses the term 'Free mason'. Nevertheless, there does seem to be a possible and subtle distinction made by Holme when he refers to his membership of 'that society called Free-Masons'. Was this distinct in some way from the 'Fellowship of the Masons'?

The old error ('operative' vs. 'speculative'), interestingly, appears at this point in Coulthurst's account. Freemason Coulthurst takes it that while the lodge contains working masons, some of the 'Free-Masons' are not masons and therefore 'must be speculative'.

Not a bit of it! What seems to me to be most likely here is that the 'Society of Free-Masons' was a means by which 'real' freemasons established bodies of value to the trade. They could invite in to the ancient brotherhood men who, it was hoped, might further their trade interests in the manner of the medieval confraternities by which lay persons attached themselves to religious orders. They were prepared to share some of their secrets, provided they go no further. That explains the extreme penalties to the soul of revealing what has been learned to outsiders; the trade must be protected.

Once the gentlemen, or other tradesmen, had learned some basic words, signs and the history and charges, they could then (if they wished) set up their own occasional lodges for purposes of pleasure, fraternity and possibly profit, so long as they had at least one working mason present as 'guide'.

It was understood that the fount of the body was the authentic tradition of freemasonry, or so much of it as the mason or masons present were acquainted with. There is no great reason to think such bodies necessarily pursued profound symbolism, unless the members enjoyed that aspect of the whole art and science of freemasonry. This picture fits all of the evidence and I am confident therefore to describe Randle Holme's lodge as one fitting my second class (no sourness intended) of lodges. This picture is borne out fully by examining the membership of Randle Holme's lodge at Chester. The information appears to come from a date of about 1673 or 1674.

Robert Morris, glazier. He was 'free' in 1659/60 as a glazier. (Note the modern masonic requirement that a brother be 'free and of good report'; it almost certainly refers to craftsmen having been freed after apprenticeships (usually at 21). Morris appears to have been elected 'Alderman or Master of the Lodge or Company' at the election for which the list, according to Coulthurst, was devised.

Alderman (of the City) *William Street*, JP (Justice of the Peace). Street, who made his money as a 'Beerbrewer' was Sheriff of Chester in 1657 and Mayor in 1666, 1683 and 1688.
John Hughes, slater.
Samuel Pike, tailor.
William Wade, bricklayer.
William Harvey, bricklayer and linen draper. Harvey was sheriff in 1667, and mayor in 1678–9.
Michael Holden, status unknown.
Peter Downham, freed in 1668 as a mason.
Thomas Foulkes, carpenter.
William Hughes, bricklayer.
John Fletcher, carpenter. Fletcher renewed the roof of St Mary's, Chester in 1657, when Holme was churchwarden.
Seth Hulton. He was free as an apprentice to Ralph Downham, mason on 12 February 1671/2.
Randle Holme, painter.
Richard Taylor, free as a *glazier* on 9 October 1672.

Richard Ratcliffe, Gentleman. Ratcliffe was the son of John Ratcliffe, MP for Chester 1646–53, 1666–72; Recorder for Chester 1646–51, 1656–72, and was assessed (for taxation purposes) on ten hearths (a large number) in Chester's Northgate Ward in 1664. Richard Ratcliffe matriculated at Brasenose College, Oxford, on 20 November 1663, aged 20. He was removed on 17 September 1664 and entered as a student of law at the Middle Temple. He boarded in Chester with Alderman Street, and died unmarried.

William Woods, mason. Many Woods were masons, then and after.

John Parry, carpenter (died 1682).

Thomas Morris, bricklayer and linen draper. Morris was the son of a butcher killed at Boughton, Chester, during the first attack of the siege of Chester, and buried on 19 July 1643.

Thomas May, mason.

William Robinson, slater and plasterer.

James Mort, mason.

John Lloyd, mason.

George Harvey, bricklayer and linen draper.

William Jackson, plasterer.

Robert Harvey, bricklayer.

John Maddock, tanner.

So, among the twenty-six brethren, six were masons, six bricklayers and three were carpenters. There were also glaziers, tylers and plasterers. Clearly, all of these trades worked closely together, given the nature of the fine houses built during this period. They had common economic interests. If a house was not built, they were all out of pocket. They would undoubtedly have met on site. Furthermore, these were the leading trade employers in the city. The hearth tax returns show they were mostly quite well off; half of them had three or more hearths. Two hearths might be expected of a yeoman, three or more for a gentleman. Eight of the members were armigerous; the Harveys were an old Cheshire family.

Coulthurst advanced the hypothesis that what had brought

them all together was the devastating long-term effect of Sir William Brereton's savage attack on the city during the civil war. Could this have compelled the trade units to join hands as a 'Society of free Masons'? Or was this an initiative of the masons, to prevent infra-trade rows and secure a more harmonious future for the trade?

In London during this period, for example, there were frequent serious disagreements between masons and plasterers. Plasterers were accused by the Masons' Company of plastering over faulty stonework in churches, thereby preventing masons from seeing or amending damage. The issue went to court.

It is noteworthy that nowhere does Holme describe being a member of a 'lodge', always a 'Society'; this may or may not be significant. Attempts to classify the 'Society' definitively would be helped immeasurably if we knew whether the society had been established by the large number of masons in the first place, or whether, the masons had been invited in by others (which seems unlikely).

On the other hand, was the society simply a common enterprise, modelled on something they had heard about existing in London? A kind of 'accepted' mason enterprise, without the specific knowledge of the London 'Acception' itself? London, after all, had no authority over freemasons operating beyond its boundaries. Chester masons could do what the law and custom permitted, even introduce new customs if the freed mason contractors agreed.

It is well observed by Coulthurst that Randle Holme had been alderman of the Painters and Glaziers Company (like his father and grandfather before him) between 1659 and 1673, but in 1673 he was not re-elected. Was it because he had pinned his colours to the mast of a novel 'Society of free-Masons'?

In 1679, Holme was re-elected alderman of his old company, an office he held until 1699. Was this because the new body had failed to retain its members, or because Holme had otherwise ironed out any supposed discord with the Painters, Stationers and Glaziers Company? Did the other glaziers leave also? Did the society disband?

We have no other contemporary record of the existence of this 'Society of free-Masons' in Chester. As far as the evidence permits us to tell, Randle Holme does not seem to have been aware of, or felt able to use, the qualifying word 'accepted' within his sodality. Looking at the Randle Holme evidence has, nevertheless, enabled us to get a clearer understanding of the kinds of masons' assemblies that existed in the 17th century. There appear to be three:

1. freemasons' lodges concerned with working masons' welfare.
2. Lodges or societies organised with co-operation of masons to promote, broadly, trade interests, but whose content of activity would also suit non-masons.
3. Acception Freemasonry. This appears to have been primarily a London-based phenomenon and was accessible open to the upper echelons of mason trade structure and to persons distinguished as being of interest to Accepted Free Masons.

These three categories were not isolated but shared a common basis (the charges, history and some secret signs and words) and there was necessarily some social inter-action between them at the level appropriate to the persons concerned. We may say that a 'lodge' was actuated when masons met for the purpose. There need have been no fixed address or great regularity of attendance: twice a year may have been a traditional minimum. Members of category one or two may never have known of category three, though by the late 17th century, the word 'accepted' appears to have 'got out', as these things will. Its first appearance, a little after Randle Holme's society met, is rather striking.

Poor Robin's Intelligence

These are to give notice, that the Modern Green-

ribbon'd Caball, together with the Ancient Brotherhood of the Rosy-Cross; the Hermetick Adepti and
the Company of Accepted Masons, intend all to dine
together on the 31st November next, at the Flying-
Bull in Windmill-Crown-Street . . .

(Knoop, Jones and Hamer, *Early Masonic
Pamphlets*,
Manchester, 1945, p.30)

'All idle people' who could spare time from frequenting the
coffee house were encouraged by the comic advertisement to
attend. However, they would need 'to provide themselves
Spectacles of Malleable Glass; for otherwise 'tis thought the
said Societies will (as hitherto) make their Appearance
Invisible'. This burlesque (note the date: 31st November!)
appeared in 1676 in a sheet dedicated to satirical imitations of
current advertisements and notices – a kind of *Monty Python* of
its day. There is nothing new under the sun.

The aim may have been to lampoon a discreet association of
Whigs who opposed the increasing power of the monarch and
his closest advisors. The 'Cabal' was the nickname given to five
of King Charles II's closest advisors: Lord Clifford of
Chudleigh, Anthony Ashley, first Earl of Shaftesbury, George
Villiers, second Duke of Buckingham, Henry Bennet, Earl of
Arlington, and John Maitland, first Duke of Lauderdale.

The word *CABAL* suggested secrecy and mystification (the
mystical Cabala) as well as wickedness (a cabal is another word
for coven). A number of those who opposed the king's policies
of alliance with France (and tolerance of Roman Catholicism),
along with neglect of parliamentary will, wore a green ribbon
and were in favour of the 'Whig' faction in parliament.

The lampoon therefore seems to be identifying the invisibility
of the government's opposition (a green-ribbon'd Cabal) with
the mysterious 'cabals' associated with 'Rosicrucian' enthusiasts,
Hermetic philosophers, and, remarkably, 'the Company of
Accepted Masons'.

Perhaps the advertisement was saying that the opposition was so invisible (and unrealistic) as to be of no use; all satirists expect others to suffer in their place.

We will never be sure of exactly where the joke lay for the writers of the advertisement, but it is plain that the *Company of Accepted Masons* was not the same in the writer's mind as the London Company of Masons.

Frances Yates in her book *The Rosicrucian Enlightenment* (Routledge, 1972) remarked on the precision of the association. Whoever wrote the advertisement, ludibrious as it was, seems to have known a lot about esoteric circles in London, she observed. How well known was it in London that during the 'Rosicrucian Scare' in Paris in 1622, placards had appeared declaring an imminent visit from the 'Invisibles' of the Rosicrucian Fraternity? This old joke (invisibility) was based on the injunction in the first Rosicrucian manifestos (the *Fama*, first published in 1614; and the *Confessio*, published in 1615) that a brother of the order should not be recognised as such when travelling. By the time the enemies of the movement had finished with this innocent directive, the Rosicrucians had become witches, supernaturally attending Satan's Sabbaths and perverting the innocent everywhere.

A similar idea – in its first innocence, that is – was expressed in Sir Francis Bacon's *New Atlantis*, published in 1627, where the 'merchants of light' from 'Saloman's [Solomon's] House' travel *incognito* through the world gathering and dispensing knowledge.

There had been a veritable blitz of Rosicrucian, occult, Hermetic (alchemical) and astrological works in London during the 1650s. Elias Ashmole himself and a number of his friends and associates had been associated with some of the more distinguished publications. We have had cause to mention his *Theatrum Chemicum Britannicum* (1652). Other writers, such as John Heydon, were not so scrupulous. His *Holy Guide*, *Rosie Crucian Physick*, *Idea of the Law* and *Voyage to the Land of the Rosicrucians*, published in the 1650s and 1660s attacked Ashmole (for plagiarism!) and freely linked ideas from Bacon's utopian allegory with concepts and images taken from fringe Rosicrucian texts and his own imagination.

After the Restoration of King Charles II in 1660, poet and satirist Samuel Butler had attacked 'Rosicrucians' and others as having brought about national ruin under Oliver Cromwell with crackpot idealist and utopian schemes (*Hudibras*, 1662).

Butler may have been thinking about Philip Herbert, Earl of Pembroke, who maintained interests in alchemy and kindred traditions. The Earl of Pembroke was President of the Council when he bought from Ashmole the first (sold) copy of the *Theatrum Chemicum Britannicum* (1652). The word 'Rosicrucian' had for some acquired a negative tinge that it did not have when the first news of the fictitious Rosicrucian (or Rose Cross) Fraternity arrived in England in the second decade of the 17th century. Then, it was the preserve of a small number of men, men like Paracelsian Doctor Robert Fludd, whose *Tractatus Apologeticus Integritatem Societatis de Rosea Cruce* (Leiden, 1617) linked the brotherhood to those who would build a spiritual house 'not made with hands' (*Mark* XIV.55–58; II *Corinthians* V.1ff.).

We know that two leading Freemasons were deeply interested in the Rosicrucian movement (Moray and Ashmole). This and other associations led Frances Yates – and other writers since – to suppose some profound unity of purpose between a Fraternity of the Rosy Cross and a fraternity of Accepted Free Masons. Is there anything in this association?

Let us see.

Chapter Eight

Rosicrucians and Accepted Freemasonry

There is a great deal of symbolic resonance between symbolic Freemasonry and the first so-called Rosicrucian manifesto, the *Fama Fraternitatis* (or 'Fame of the Fraternity').

First composed in about 1610 for private distribution as a manuscript in Germany, the *Fama* was published in Cassel in 1614 (without the author's consent) and immediately generated a furore in Germany that lasted beyond the outbreak of the Thirty Years War (1618–20). I recommend that readers consult it (a translation is reprinted in Yates's *The Rosicrucian Enlightenment*).

For those unfamiliar with the Rosicrucian story, there follows a brief summary of the main ideas.

The *Fama* – almost certainly the work of brilliant Lutheran theologian Johann Valentin Andreae (1586–1654) – tells an allegorical story of a figure called C.R. or Father C.R.C. It is supposed that these letters stand for 'Christian Rosenkreuz' because another writing by Andreae was called 'The Chemical Wedding of Christian Rosenkreuz' (*Chymische Hochzeit*, Strasbourg, 1616).

Brother C.R. leaves his dull German monastery in the late 14th century and goes to the east in search of wisdom. Enlightenment is sought and obtained from the wise men of 'Damcar' in Arabia (probably meant to be the Islamic School of Damar in the Arabian peninsula) who have long expected the young Christian. They teach him all they think he needs to know.

Christian then goes to Fez, encountering the spirits of the

elements, while perfecting his knowledge of science, mathematics, medicine and *magia*. He is surprised to see how the savants of the east meet regularly to share their knowledge and to improve it. The *Fama* lambasts the 'covetousness and envy' of European scholars who would rather lose knowledge than share it. The author wants openness, communication, intellectual honesty and spiritual idealism: rare things in the universities of his day.

Ever optimistic, Christian Rosenkreuz (Rose, or Rosy, Cross) returns to Germany in the hope of reforming the entire knowledge base of Europe. Like Marco Polo before him, however, he is laughed at, and so retires, taking a number of 'Brothers' into his confidence. They form a fraternity on a monastic model but dedicated entirely to pious science. They meet in his house, called 'Holy Spirit' and plan the gradual dissemination of wisdom that will lead to a general reformation.

Knowledge earthly and heavenly is linked to the 'last light' – a final outpouring of revealed knowledge from God, showing how God's presence and *Word* is diffused in nature. The *Fama* is going to 'turn the world on', like a bright light pulsing in every vein of its being. That presently occluded from view ('occult' – or scientific – knowledge) will become visible to the true men of heart and head who unite in a fraternal quest for liberating and ennobling knowledge.

The final revelation before the end will consist of the 'mysteries of science and Nature' that a second degree Freemason is supposed to make his business to investigate.

Father C.R.C dies at a great age and it is implied that the stunning scientific, technical, medicinal, theological, explorative and artistic advances begun in that period which we call the Renaissance were somehow connected with the discreet work of the brotherhood. They were behind it all – invisible men, unseen by the blind eyes of the world.

But greater things are to come. However, there must first be a 'cleaning out' of the conceits and hostilities that prevent men of science and goodwill from working together and bringing the worthy to the *Light*.

The story goes on to tell of how an architect brother (of the order), when repairing his own 'house' comes upon the hidden vault that contains the perfectly intact body of Father C.R.C. The seven-sided vault is designed geometrically as a compendium of the universe. The next day the Rose Cross brothers arrive at dawn to see this strange vault, lit by 'another sun'.

The date is 1604.

The disclosure of the vault's contents marks the beginning of the new age. On the Hermetic principle of 'as above, so below', new stars have appeared in the constellations of Serpentarius and Cygnus, forming a *trigonus igneus* or 'fiery trigon': a certain sign of great and innovative change.

Worthy persons who read and recognise the value of the story are invited to declare themselves to the Brotherhood. The Brothers will sort out the wheat from the chaff and initiate the chosen into the knowledge they need to enable them to play their part in the universal reformation.

One of the men who wrote a pious – and doubtless symbolic – prayer to the 'illuminated fraternity', humbly soliciting its attention, was Elias Ashmole, Free Mason.

In an issue of the *London Magazine* (1824), Thomas de Quincey (the 'Opium Eater') concluded from his studies of the German historian J. G. Buhle, that Rosicrucianism gave life to 'Speculative' Freemasonry. Dr Robert Fludd – with his copious continental contacts – was named as the progenitor of a transformation accomplished between 1630 and 1640. It is not difficult to see why de Quincey could arrive at this conclusion.

How was one to account for the apparent discrepancy of priorities shown in the world of Freemasonry once you had divided so-called 'operative' from so-called 'speculative' Masonry?

By the time De Quincy was writing, the 18th century had already seen Freemasonry drenched in a bewildering, and frequently bizarre array of mystical ideas that would have seemed quite remote even from those who established a grand lodge in London at the beginning of the century. Something had to account for this strange *mélange* of ideas and confusion of mystical and moral categories. Did the arrival of Rosicrucianism give the spur for the secret Masonry to wake from its slumbers and, finally, announce itself?

The fact is that there is simply insufficient evidence to support or refute such a theory definitively. That does not mean, however, that we have to give up our search.

The question we are trying to answer is what Acception Masonry consisted of, if I may use such a loaded phrase. The expression 'Free and Accepted Masonry' was obviously used after 1723 to distinguish what had gone before from what had come after it. It is also clear that the idea that 'accepted' simply meant something to call a gentleman who had been admitted (or accepted) into the brotherhood of Freemasons is both misleading and erroneous. Even modern Freemasonry regards the word 'accepted' as delineating something of the content of the Freemasonry. For example, whereas the tools for operatives are for chiselling, squaring, knocking and so on, for 'accepted' or 'speculative' masons the tools are full of moral implications – signals for another lecture.

Did those in the 18th century who tried to understand the content of what 'Accepted' Masonry was, look to the Rosicrucian tradition for ideas of a symbolic path to moral and spiritual perfection? We can answer a qualified 'yes' to this.

We know that the Rosicrucian tradition inspired, to varying extents, Freemasons in England and, more notably, on the continent. Neo-Rosicrucian societies blended with masonic societies until it was hard to tell them apart. But inspire is one thing; create is another.

People who shared this inspiration seem to have intuited that the essential spiritual component of Freemasonry was somehow linked to a mystery enshrouded in Rosicrucianism. Why did they believe this to be so? Was it just that there was so much in common, symbolically speaking, between the two traditions? Or was it primarily because they believed, like Buhle and De Quincey, that it was simply a question of Rosicrucianism being the parent of 'speculative' Freemasonry?

I wonder if they ever considered the other possibility. Could there have been something in English Freemasonry that inspired the Rosicrucian movement?

Could the *Acception* have had anything to do with a conception of spiritual perfection and social improvement that inspired the creators of the Rosicrucian mythology?

Well, as far as Germany is concerned, the answer is almost certainly, probably not. Andreae did admire the burgeoning English theatre of his time; he found the dramatisation of ideas inspirational.

Some of his colleagues and associates may have been familiar with the mission of Euclidean geometer and angel scryer John Dee to wake the Holy Roman Empire up to a coming judgement during the 1580s.

These influences testify to the communications flowing between England and Germany during the 'Rosicrucian' period (James I's daughter Elizabeth married the Elector, Frederick, of the Palatinate in 1613). But none of this detracts from the fact that the largest inspiration for the *Fama Fraternitatis* was the figure of the Swiss physician Paracelsus (1493–1541).

The Rose Cross doctrine (according to the *Confessio Fraternitatis*) – *much medicine, some theology (little law)* – is Paracelsian. That Paracelsus shared traditions with the esoteric minded people of the Elizabethan era is again indicative of how it came to be that Freemasons' and Rosicrucian works would meet in private libraries. They had all been baptised in the spirit of the Renaissance – that spirit announced in 1486 in the *Oration on the Dignity of Man*, by Giovanni Pico della Mirandola: *Man is a Great Miracle* – and he can reach the Top if he wants to.

British Rosicrucianism, however, was rather different to its German cousin.

British Rosicrucianism

Once we remove the idea that there ever was a real Rose Cross Fraternity, we can save ourselves the trouble of trying to find its agents anywhere – even in the upper echelons of British Masonry. That does not mean, however, that the ideology associated with it did not represent a living force in the minds of people at the time. On the contrary, the strength of the influence was more potent perhaps for being so subtle. Such, surely, was the original intent of Andreae, the creator of the mythology: to fashion an invisible presence. We have already seen how Sir Robert Moray, for one, liked the idea of 'invisible presence': being felt but not seen, like the wind. And wind, of course, was the ancient metaphor for the spirit.

The phenomenon of British Rosicrucianism in the 17th century bears markedly different characteristics to its European, especially German, counterpart. This is principally a result of the missing religious context that enlivened and inspired the original manifestos. That context was principally connected to the special position of Paracelsus and radical spiritual reformers in continental religion.

The English and Scottish religious settings were quite different. The English Reformation had produced a new national spiritual establishment, if not a theological consensus. Roman Catholicism was severely under the government heel; the leading figures of the continental *radical* Reformation remained relatively unknown.

The radical reformers of greatest significance were Caspar Schwenckfeld, Valentin Weigel, Sebastian Franck and, surprisingly perhaps, Paracelsus who wrote a great deal on religion that was to be kept secret until after his death. Only elements and tinctures of the radical reformers' striking (and not infrequently 'gnostic') spiritual doctrines entered the English religious scene.

Protestantism meant two things in England: the reformed catholic ('universal') Church under the monarch (with some 'abuses' removed and the monastic system abolished), or non-conforming – or reluctantly conforming – followers of Calvinist, Lutheran, Zwinglian or other preachers.

The famous division of puritans and cavaliers is a broadly accurate picture, though puritans could be presbyterians, conventiclists or 'independents' and cavaliers might be reformed catholic or Elizabethan chivalrous (and tolerant) puritans of an intellectual and mystical stamp. It wasn't a question of hairstyle.

The consequent loss of original religious context deprived the Rosicrucian manifestos of their explosive character when transported to England. There was no furore; the establishment was not offended or challenged. From the first discreet appearance of the Rose Cross writings, they tended to be seen and appreciated by antiquarians, natural philosophers (mathematicians, astrologers, alchemists, mechanicians), students of occult philosophy and doctors practising Paracelsian medicine, such as Dr Robert Fludd (1574–1637). They were foreign works; their ironies and ludibrious qualities could be, and were, lost in translation.

It is characteristic of this period that the most significant men in British Rosicrucianism embraced all or most of the above disciplines. Fludd, the Paracelsian doctor and first British defender of the Rose Cross (*Apologia Compendiaria*, 1616), was also the author of a series of elaborately illustrated 'pansophic' books attempting to integrate all knowledge within a micro/macrocosmic system of divine correspondences.

Fludd's pansophic accounts of man and the universe frequently involved a magical theory based on a universal sympathy operating between all – apparently separate – things. Man was, in himself. a mini universe, and could therefore be linked in mind to all phenomena. Eventually, through absolute purification and the gift of divine insight, he would learn to control the hidden powers of Nature.

The feature in common with all those who warmed to the Rosicrucian cause in Britain was a common devotion to the Hermetic spiritual stream. Study was a protracted ritual of self-initiation or, as Newton believed, the universe was a divine cryptogram that only the pure could decode. Since the *fratres R.C.* claimed to have achieved just that, they were of interest to British Hermetic scholars and cosmic theorists.

British enthusiasts of the Rose Cross mythology tended to believe that the fraternity did actually exist somewhere in Germany, paranormally 'listening in' to their higher thoughts (an intuition perhaps of Jung's conception of the 'collective unconscious'). Hermes and the Rose Cross Fraternity were the kings of the 'collective unconscious' for those who sought higher and deeper knowledge of human and divine existence. The universe was a secret symbol open to the pure: the keys, knowledge of secret symbols, of which symbolic world, mathematics was a cabalistic part.

Central to British Rosicrucianism was the figure of John Dee (1527-1608), arguably the greatest mathematician of his day (his *Mathematicall Praeface* to Euclid's *Elements*, 1570, was highly influential), and one whose name has been linked to the genesis of Rosicrucianism itself.

Dee's *Monas Hieroglyphica* (1564) was even more influential on continental magi. It was possibly Dee's famous tours of central Europe accomplished in the 1580s that alerted continental enthusiasts to the value of English alchemy. Perhaps such interest explains in part the visit of Count Michael Maier to England in 1611. This visit has high candidate status for being seen as the birth date of British Rosicrucianism. It was recalled 40 years later in Elias Ashmole's *Theatrum Chemicum Britannicum* (*Prologomena*, sigs A 2 *recto* and *verso*):

> Our English Philosophers generally, (like Prophets) have received little honour... in their owne Country: nor have they done any mighty workes amongst us, except in covertly administering their Medicine to a few sick, and healing them... Thus did I.O. (one of the first foure Fellowes of the Fratres R.C.) in curing the young Earle of Norfolke of the Leprosie [a tale lifted straight out of the *Fama*]... But in parts abroad they have found more noble Reception, and the world greedy of obteyning their workes; nay, (rather than want the sight thereof) contented to view them through a Translation, though never so imperfect. Witnesse what Maierus [Michael Maier]... and many others have done; the first of which came out of Germanie, to live in England; purposely that he might so understand our English

Tongue, as to translate Norton's Ordinall into Latin
verse, which most judiciously and l; earedly he did:
Yet (to our shame be it spoken) his Entertainment
was too coarse for so deserving a scholar.

While Ashmole seems to think that *frater* I.O. was English, if
ever there was a moment to state that the fraternity had its
origins in Britain, here was that opportunity. Rather Ashmole
speaks of Britain having the substantial insights, but lacking in
willingness properly to understand and exploit them. Ashmole
wishes to amend this one-sided situation and perhaps 'catch
up' with his continental counterparts, while showing them
(and England herself) that Britain ought to be proud of her
alchemical tradition.

It was hoped by men of a Rosicrucian-touched outlook that
the establishment of the Royal Society in 1661 might make up
for so much lost time in demonstrating the inter-relation of
spirit and matter as matters of science.

Disappointment would take a while to sink in.

As a good antiquarian, Ashmole resisted the temptation to
make the Rosicrucian apologist Maier a Rosicrucian Brother.
This temptation was not resisted in France where Maier's
proximity to the R.C. cause had a French writer condemn him
as the incarnate secretary to the infernal brethren (François
Garasse, *La doctrine curieuse des beaux esprits de ce temps*, Paris,
1623). Garasse was a Jesuit.

We know that Maier met Sir William Paddy, James I's
physician on this visit to England. Since Paddy was a lifelong
friend of Dr Robert Fludd, most writers on the subject take it
as likely that Maier met Fludd as well. They were, after all, both
Paracelsian physicians. One may further speculate as to whether
Maier made a manuscript of the *Fama* available to Fludd, so
launching the latter's interest in the Rosicrucians. We do not
know. Nor do we know for sure the essential purpose of Maier's
visit. It seems a long journey to undertake simply to translate
Norton's *Ordinall of Alchemy* (which speaks of the freemasons'
appreciation of alchemy).

Perhaps Maier sought a patron. Having been made a count by the Emperor Rudolf, Maier could not work for a living in a conventional way. Why did Maier send a famous Christmas card – from those who cared for the 'Rose' – to James I? Was he on an eirenic mission for the Protestant cause? We do not know.

Fludd and Maier would later come to share temporarily a printer in Oppenheim in the Palatinate: the De Bry firm. The De Bry firm was top notch and well funded. Furthermore, there was a kudos factor. It seems likely that after the marriage of James I's daughter Elizabeth and Frederick of the Palatinate, its capital Heidelberg became a 'Venice of the North' to pansophic optimists before Frederick's crushing defeat at Prague in 1620. Perhaps it enjoyed a 'buzz' like San Francisco did for a year or so in the 1960s when a few visionaries or would-be visionaries there sought an objective correlative for the utopian idealism that besets happy/sad, blinkered youth.

Fludd wanted to be part of the new world. That world was a pansophic world, inspired by Paracelsus, later called 'Rosicrucian': a new world false dawning. By 1623, Heidelberg and the dream it represented lay in hopeless ruins; the Rosicrucians were witches, evil, mad scientists hell-bent on the destruction of the true faith and her papa in Rome.

It is difficult to think of Robert Fludd's Rosicrucianism as being 'British'. His famous debates were with continental philosophers Andreas Libavius and Marin Mersenne; his pro-Rosicrucian publications were printed in Oppenheim, Amsterdam or Leiden; his ideal world seems to be northern Europe, intellectually kissed by a Florentine sun.

In England, Fludd's researches suggested one thing above all: magic. James I did not really approve, and neither did the king approve of grandiose, expensive schemes to make northern Europe the epicentre of apocalyptic Protestant enlightenment. This is probably why Ashmole informed his readers in 1652, that England had dishonoured her own prophets, and even failed to recognise those from abroad. It was tough being an English Hermetist.

It is a fascinating fact that the majority of British Rosicrucian texts were published in the early 1650s when the established order of learning had to some extent broken down or appeared to be in the process of being transformed.

Between 1617 (Fludd's *Tractatus Apologeticus Integritatem Societatis de Rosea Cruce defendens.*, Godfrey Basson, Leiden) and 1629 (Fludd's *Summum Bonum, Quod est Verum Magiae, Cabalae, Alchymiae, Fratrum Roseae Crucis verorum Verae Subiectum, o.O., o.D.*, 1629), there is very little indeed of a Rosicrucian character published in England. Likewise between 1629 and 1651, at which latter date Robert Moray's protégé Thomas Vaughan's *Lumen de Lumine: Or a New Magicall Light Discovered* appeared, containing *A Letter from the Brothers of R.C. Concerning the Invisible, Magical Mountain, And the Treasure therein Contained* (H. Blunden, London 1651).

This work, along with those of Fludd, would inspire another early 18th century Freemason, Robert Samber, as we shall see. This Freemason was in fact so inspired that he believed its vision of spiritual transformation held Grand Lodge up to ridicule by sheer contrast. This man believed that Accepted Free Masonry was losing contact with its roots. He obviously believed that Accepted Free Masonry was founded upon a profound spiritual ideal.

Was he right?

How could such an ideal have penetrated the upper echelons of the London Masons' Company and taken the ancient spiritual, symbolic and geometrical content of the craft into a far more idealist, even utopian, direction?

As we have seen, de Quincey, following Buhle, reckoned a re-focusing of craft symbolism coincided with the genesis of the British Rosicrucian experience. He dated the change as having taken place sometime between 1630 and 1640. Provocatively, these dates would include our tantalising record of Nicholas Stone's being 'taken in' to the 'Accepcon' in 1638.

A Merchant of Light

In 1628, a Prussian scientist and reformer left the ravages of the Thirty Years War and came to England, thinking it a good place to launch his enterprise. Samuel Hartlib (*c.*1600–1662), having studied at Königsberg University, briefly attended the university of Cambridge. Living in London, a neighbour of Samuel Pepys in Axe Yard, he soon established himself as one of the most inspiring and brilliant men in London. Hartlib enjoyed excellent connections to the leading intellectual figures of the time, while receiving encouragement from Elizabeth of Bohemia's court-in-exile in Den Haag.

Hartlib's glory days were those before the civil war when, inspired by the works of Sir Francis Bacon and the *Fama Fraternitatis*, he lectured politicians on their duties to reform the world and succeeded in getting the great Czech genius of educational reform, Comenius, to come to England.

Hartlib produced mechanical patents, encouraged agricultural development, practised alchemy for medicinal purposes and did all he could to live out the ideals he found in the works of Bacon, the *Fama* and Comenius. As a designer of calculators, double-writing instruments, seed-machines and siege engines one might have expected him to be a suitable candidate for a masonic lodge. There is no record of his having so joined, but records at this time are the exception, not the rule.

Hartlib took an interest in the work of Free Mason Ashmole; the two first corresponded in 1656. Hartlib's circles of contacts would embrace many of those who came together to form the Royal Society in 1661, an institution made especially possible due to Robert Moray's excellent relations with King Charles II and Hartlib's and others' tireless work. Unfortunately, that role was to be somewhat muted, since Hartlib was so closely associated with Cromwell and the Commonwealth, from which he hoped too much. Sidelined after the Restoration, Hartlib died a poor man in 1662. Hartlib's goal was 'To record all human knowledge and to make it universally available for the education of all mankind'.

A Fraternity of Knowledge

Comenius first met Hartlib when he went to Poland in 1628 to form a community of exiled Bohemian Brethren. There, Hartlib had also met the Scot John Dury at Elbing. Dury shared the view that England was the best place to get the new reforms under way, encouraged by the writings of Dr Robert Fludd and Sir Francis Bacon. Among Dury and Hartlib's excellent contacts was Sir William Boswell, Queen Elizabeth's diplomatic supporter in England. Boswell was not only Britain's ambassador to The Hague but was also Sir Francis Bacon's executor (Bacon had died in 1626).

Was it coincidence that Hartlib set out for England within a year of the publication of Bacon's fable of a perfected spiritual and scientific society, the *New Atlantis* (1627)?

The story told in Bacon's *New Atlantis* is strongly reminiscent both of Andreae's *Christianopolis* (1619) and the *Fama*. For example, Bacon included a journey by sea to reach his mythical utopia, where its representatives bear a red cross on their turbans. A cross and cherubim's wings also appear on their official scroll (the Fraternity of the Rose-Cross was 'under Jehovah's wings'). The *New Atlantis* also presents us with the image of a new temple of science:

> Ye shall understand, my dear friends, that amongst
> the excellent acts of that king [of the island], one
> above all hath the pre-eminence. It was the erection
> and institution of an order, or society, which we call
> Saloman's House; the noblest foundation, as we
> think, that ever was upon the earth, and the lantern
> of this kingdom. It is dedicated to the study of the
> works and creatures of God.

'Saloman' is explained as a corruption of 'Solomon'. The House (so similar in concept to the vault of Christian Rosenkreuz: 'a compendium of the universe') is a kind of distant temple, housing not so much God Himself as the knowledge of His creation in all its aspects, physical and spiritual.

New Atlantis sends out agents – 'Merchants of Light' – (again like the fraternity of Christian Rosenkreuz) to gather new discoveries.

In 1640, Hartlib addressed his *Description of the Famous*

Kingdome of Macaria to the newly instated 'Long' parliament. Hartlib compared his ideal tolerant state to the Macaria of Pico della Mirandola-enthusiast St Thomas More's *Utopia*, and to Bacon's *New Atlantis*. Hartlib, in telling words, hoped that parliament would 'lay the corner Stone of the world's happinesse before the final recesse thereof...'

Was the 'corner Stone' a clue to those who would understand?

A mason's grave from the west of England, dated 4 May 1639, bears these words:

> Christ was thy Corner-stone, Christians the rest,
> Hammer the word, Good life thy line all blest,
> And yet art gone, 'twas honour not thy crime,
> With stone hearts to worke much in little time,
> Thy Master saws't and tooke thee off from them,
> To the bright stone of New Jerusalem,
> Thy worke and labour men may esteem a base one,
> Heaven counts it blest, here lies a blest free-Mason.
> (W. J. Williams, *AQC*.48, 1935, p.256)

Cornerstones at the Royal Society?

According to Royal Society member John Wallis, writing in 1678 and 1697, the Royal Society grew out of meetings held in London in 1645 in private homes and at Gresham College. The meetings included founder members Dr John Wilkins (later bishop of Chester), but then chaplain to the Prince Elector Palatine in London, and Theodore Haak, a German from the Palatinate. These men were, like Comenius and Hartlib, patronised by Elizabeth of Bohemia.

According to Wallis, it was Haak 'who, I think, gave the first occasion, and first suggested these meetings and many others'. Further suggestive evidence comes from the letters (1646-1647) of alchemist, Christian evangelist, and experimental scientist Robert Boyle.

Boyle, a correspondent of Hartlib, mentions an 'Invisible College', a phrase with which we should be familiar. The philosopher Descartes was held in suspicion in Paris in the 1620s for being a member of the 'Invisibles', that is, the

Fraternity of the Rose-Cross.

In one letter, Boyle asks his former tutor to send him some books, a favour 'which will make you extremely welcome to our Invisible College'. In a letter to a friend of February 1647, Boyle writes excitedly about his having made the acquaintance of a quite remarkable group of people:

> The best on't is that the cornerstones [my emphasis] of the Invisible or (as they term themselves) the Philosophical College, do now and then honour me with their company... men of so capaceous and searching spirits, that school-philosophy is but the lowest region of their knowledge... as they disdain not to be directed to the meanest, so he can but plead reason for his opinion; persons that endeavour to put narrow-mindedness out of countenance, by the practice of so extensive a charity that it reaches unto everything called man, and nothing less than an universal good-will can content it. And indeed they are so apprehensive of the want of good employment, that they take the whole body of mankind to their care.
>
> (Robert Boyle, *Works*, ed. Thomas Birch, 1744, I, p.20; Yates, *Rosicrucian Enlightenment*, Ark, 1972, p.182)

To be fair this does not sound quite like the Royal Society, but it does sound like the kind of atmosphere in which such an undertaking could develop. Who were these 'cornerstones'?

According to Thomas Sprat's official history, the Royal Society grew out of meetings held in John Wilkins' rooms at Wadham College, Oxford, between 1648 and 1659. Regular visitors included the polymath Christopher Wren, William Petty and the famous diarist and botanist John Evelyn. Evelyn described the rooms as having been filled with 'many artificial, mathematical and magical curiosities'. (Evelyn enjoyed an interesting correspondence with Boyle and Sir Robert Moray concerning a 'metaphysical alchemy of friendship' after 1660, outlined in David Stevenson's, *The Origins of Freemasonry*, Cambridge, 1988, p.183).

Wilkins, chaplain to Elizabeth's son Charles Louis, was also the author of a book called *Mathematical Magick* (1648) based on the work of both John Dee (*Mathematical Preface*, 1570) and on a section on mechanics from Robert Fludd's *Utriusque Cosmi Historia* (Oppenheim, 1619). Wilkins cites the magician-scholar and Hermetic enthusiast Henry Cornelius Agrippa (1486–1535) as his authority for employing the term 'mathematical magick' for that branch of science dealing with mechanical invention. This was a fairly bold statement to appear in an era of regular witch trials for both Agrippa and Dee had been accused of diabolical pacts.

The fact that Boyle says that the 'cornerstones' take the whole world for their care suggests the universal reformation ideal familiar to *aficionados* of the *Fama Fraternitatis*, as is the emphasis on a path of love and knowledge. Moray's discreet cult of friendship referred to by Stevenson (symbolised in his pentagram seal or 'Mason's mark') is also suggestive of the hope that Europe's wars of religion might yet be transcended by a path of friendship and the cultivation of spiritual love. Boyle's charity that 'reaches unto everything called man' suggests the pansophic vision endowed in the human microcosm that we find in Fludd, and in the Renaissance works of Pico and others. In the words of the *Fama*, God has:

> *raised men* [my italics] imbued with great wisdom who might partly renew and reduce all arts (in this our age spotted and imperfect) to perfection; so that finally man might thereby understand his own nobility and worth, and why he is called *Micro-cosmus*, and how far his knowledge extendeth into Nature.

Such a speech would not be out of place methinks in an inspired gathering of Accepted Masons.

If such a summit of spiritual and material concerns

characterised something of an 'Accepted Masonry' by the 1640s, it appears to have been in short supply by the time that the Rev James Anderson was reconstituting the *Constitutions* of Free and Accepted Masons in 1722.

The Mountain of Light

According to a report published in 1723, Robert Samber, a prolific translator, attended the raucous celebration dinner for the newly elected Grand Master of Free and Accepted Masons, Philip, Duke of Wharton, held at a London inn.

Samber is 'the man' we heard of earlier, a man who felt he could judge the activities of the new 'Grand Lodge'. Samber was not very impressed by what he witnessed at the celebration dinner. How, he asked, 'demolishing huge Walls of Venison Pastry...after a very disedifying Manner' contributed to 'building up a Spiritual House', he did not know.

The reference to the *Spiritual House* seals his acknowledged identity with the *Eugenius Philalethes Junior* who translated a French book on longevity known as *Long Livers: A Curious History of Such Persons of Both Sexes Who Have Liv'd Several Ages, and Grown Young Again* (1722).

Eugenius Philalethes (Philalethes means truth lover) was the name taken by Rosicrucian *aficionado* Thomas Vaughan. In Vaughan's *Lumen de Lumine* published 70 years before, he echoed Robert Fludd's view that he who stood on the corner-stone of Christ should be a builder of the spiritual house, an ideal celebrated in the aforementioned Freemason's grave inscription.

Eugenius Philalethes FRS's translation of De Longeville Harcouet's book, gave Samber the opportunity to pen a 'Dedicatory Letter' from a 'Brother' mason to 'the Grand Master, Masters, Wardens and Brethren' of the Freemasons of Great Britain and Ireland, who 'are a chosen Generation, a royal Priesthood'.

Samber claims Freemasonry represents 'an uninterrupted Tradition'.

'Ye are living stones, built up a spiritual House, who believe and rely on the chief *Lapis Angularis* [cornerstone], which the refractory and disobedient Builders disallowed...'

Freemasons are 'a chosen Generation, a royal Priesthood', as well as 'imprisoned...exiled Children...' and 'Sons of Science...who are illuminated with the sublimest Mysteries and profoundest secrets'.

God is described as 'the Centre of all Things, yet knows no Circumference'.

Samber refers to several levels of masonic understanding. He alludes to 'those of you who are not far illuminated...and are not worthy to look behind the Veil', contrasting them with 'those who are so happy as to have greater Light' who 'will discover under these Shadows somewhat truly great and noble, and worthy the serious Attention of a Genius the most elevated and sublime'.

Samber not only refers to the 'Arcane disciplines' of the early Christians (the *cubic stone* of the book of *Revelation*) but also to alchemy, to the Paracelsian tripartite distinction of principles of salt (body), sulphur (soul), and mercury (spirit). Clearly, for Samber, the mercurial, or third, level (Ashmole called himself the *Mercuriophilus Anglicus*) was for those who had seen beyond 'the Veil'. He says he is addressing 'a higher class who are but few'.

We have seen this 'veil' somewhere else, have we not?

Samber is well acquainted with the Renaissance idea familiar to Pico that there had always been a doctrine of *Unity*, vouchsafed by a continual brotherhood from Moses through the schools of the prophets, and the rabbis.

Samber regards Christ as the reorganiser of a masonic brotherhood, along with 'holy brother St Paul.' This is a theme that would be taken up later in the century with the development of Christian Masonry in the so-called 'Ancient & Accepted Rite'.

In a recent paper, *William Stukeley: Science, Religion and Archaeology in Eighteenth-Century England* (2001), David Boyd Haycock has drawn attention to an 1892 reprint of the preface to *Long Livers*. According to Haycock, masonic historian R. F. Gould 'noted previous speculations on the book's bearing to the history of Freemasonry, referring to its possible relationship with the obscure 17th century Protestant order of Rosicrucianism'.

Haycock continues: 'A letter published in the *Freemason* [magazine] on 16 April 1887 reflected that 'during the decade from 1720 to 1730, a kind of Rosicrucian or Hermetic influence must have taken place in the Lodges of London, and there are indeed some things in the ritual and terminology of Masonry after 1730 that cannot be derived at all from Operative Lodges, but are taken from the works of Rosicrucians and Cabbalists'.

Gould suggested that it was possible that some high-ranking masons were members of another Hermetic Society, and it was to these that *Philalethes*' work applied.

It seems more likely to this author that Samber's insight represented a survival of an older representation of the spiritual essence of the craft, as Samber himself suggests. If any 'high ranking Masons were members of another Hermetic Society', then that 'Society' was that associated with the meaning of 'Accepted' Freemasonry. The raw material for such an exalted insight had been in existence for 1700 years. Samber would not have to look very far in the Bible for references with a distinctly masonic, even alchemical, ring to them.

The Holy Stone

Jesus of Nazareth based much of his radical doctrine on a precise re-interpretation of the nature of the temple.

> And he beheld them [in the Temple], and said, What is this then that is written, The stone which the builders rejected, the same is become the head of the corner? Whosoever shall fall upon that stone shall be broken; but on whomsoever it shall fall, he shall be winnowed. *(Luke* XX.17ff.)

The stone that falls from heaven has left a traceable pedigree within Jewish apocalyptic and prophetic literature. It appears in the prophecies ascribed to Daniel (*Daniel* II.34–35. *c*.160 BC) as a fatal projectile sent by God against the great image symbolising the empire of Nebuchadnezzar. The false image with 'feet of clay' is smashed on impact. Transformed into a mountain, which covers the whole earth, the mountain reminds us that it is God who 'rules the heavens'. The polyvalent stone is supernatural.

In the quotation from *Luke* above, the falling stone of heavenly origin 'winnows' the one on whom it falls; it divides the grain from the chaff. (Grain has a long-standing alchemical association with gold; Christian Rosenkreuz is described in the *Fama* as a grain hid in Christ, for example). This process of winnowing occurs when the wheat is tossed into the air for the wind to do the work of division. The Hebrew word for 'wind' or breath is *ruach,* the word for spirit. The winnowing by the stone may be seen as a spiritual process, equivalent to the action of the philosopher's stone in alchemy.

The coming of the stone is a salvific operation; it would be consistent for the believer to say that the best thing is to be hit by the stone and remade into a new being. This is spiritual alchemy. In the alchemical context, the stone releases the divine spirit. Jesus identifies himself with the cornerstone of the temple, the 'precious' corner stone referred to by Isaiah (XXVIII.16).

> And the chief priests and all the council sought for witness against Jesus to put him to death; and found none. For many bare false witness against him, saying, We heard him say, I will destroy this temple that is made with hands, and within three days I will build another made without hands. (*Mark* XIV. 55–58).

The reference here to Christ raising a new temple 'without hands' is directly parallel to the account of the stone in *Daniel* II.34–35:

> Thou sawest till that a stone was cut 'without hands'
> [my emphasis], which smote the image upon his feet
> that were of iron and clay, and broke them to
> pieces . . . and the stone that smote the image became
> a great mountain, and filled the whole earth.

This stone can transform itself and anything with which it comes into contact.

The *Gospel of John* is more explicit. Following Jesus's rout of the temple commerce, his enemies ask Jesus for an explanation:

> Jesus answered and said unto them, Destroy this
> temple, and in three days I will raise it up. Then said
> the Jews, Forty and six years was this temple in
> building, and wilt thou rear it up in three days? But
> he spake of the temple of his body.
>
> (*John* II.19ff.)

The 'temple of his body' is raised in three days; do we see here the tripartite division of body, soul and spirit? Do we have an origin for a three stage masonic system?

Should we follow the *Gospel of John*'s symbolism literally, Jesus is responsible for his own raising: 'I will raise it up'. Jesus appears to have the art of building at its highest degree. He can raise stones; He can raise himself. He can raise himself in another; he is an initiator:

> And he [Andrew] brought him [Simon] to Jesus. And
> when Jesus beheld him, he said, Thou art Simon the
> son of Jona: thou shalt be called Cephas, which is by
> interpretation, a stone.
>
> (*John* I.42).

The new temple envisioned by Jesus is made up of living stones, rejected by prevailing powers, but yet set in place by the appearance of the keystone within themselves, those who have been, as it were, 'hit' by the Stone, and become divine.

Was one such Stone raised thus called Nicholas?

And what of that temple and stone cut 'without hands'? Does this image explain why masons wear gloves in the infinite lodge?

11 March 1682

Perhaps it is time to come back down to earth. The most striking account of fellowship in Accepted Freemasonry comes again from the diary of Elias Ashmole, a man by now distinguished as the country's leading antiquarian, and as the founder of the first purpose-built public museum *cum* chemical laboratory in the world. Ashmole was almost sixty-five years old when on 10 March 1682:

> About 5pm I received a summons, to appear at a Lodge to be held the next day at Masons Hall London.
>
> Accordingly I went, and about Noone were admitted into the Fellowship of Free Masons,
>
> Sir William Wilson Knight, Capt. Rich: Borthwick, Mr Will: Woodman, Mr Wm Grey, Mr Samuell Taylour & Mr William Wise.
>
> I was the Senior Fellow among them (it being 35 years since I was admitted). There were present beside my selfe the Fellowes after named. Mr Tho: Wise Mr [Master]: of the Masons Company this present year. Mr: Thomas Shorthose, Mr: Thomas Shadbolt, Waindsford Esqr Mr: Nich: Young. Mr: John Shorthose, Mr: William Hamon, Mr: John Thompson, & Mr: Will: Stanton.
>
> We all dyned at the halfe Moone Taverne in Cheapside, at a Noble Dinner prepared at the charge of the New: accepted Masons.

The occasion? In March 1682 William Wilson (1641–1710) was knighted for his services to architecture. As well as having worked on the restoration of Lichfield Cathedral, he had also worked on the rebuilding of Nottingham Castle (where King Charles I had first raised the Royal Standard of resistance to parliament).

It seems that the Accepted Fellows wished to add their own distinction to that bestowed by His Majesty, and – at the same time – admit some new members to the fellowship.

An example of Wilson's work (now weathered of course) is a larger than life statue of the king that stood above the west door of Lichfield Cathedral until the last century; it now stands by the south door. It is stated on the inscription attached to the plinth that Charles II provided timber for the work of restoration – like King Hiram of Tyre. It was Ashmole who referred to the cathedral as a 'temple'.

Sir William Dugdale's *Antiquities of Warwickshire* (vol.ii, 1730 edition, p.916) informs us that in the church of Holy Trinity, Sutton Coldfield, was once the following inscription:

> Near this Place lieth the Body of Sr WILLIAM WILSON Knight, interred here by his own desire. He was born at Leicester; but after his Marriage with his well beloved Lady JANE, Relict of HENRY PUDSY Esq; he lived many years in this Parish, where he also died the 3d Day of June 1710 in the 70th year of his age, and generally beloved, and very much & no less deservedly lamented: being a Person of great Ingenuity, singular Integrity, unaffected Piety, and very fruitful in good Works, the only issue he left behind him.

Sir William Wilson is not the only man of whom we have knowledge from this gathering on an early spring afternoon in 1682. Looking at the names of those gathered we can come to only one conclusion, namely, that this fellowship of Accepted brethren was dominated by leading members of the London

Company of Masons. As to who was 'in charge' of it, we simply cannot tell. It was perhaps organised in a rotating manner. Certainly it was unusual to have a regular occurrence to get the cream of mason-contractors all together at the same time and at such short notice.

The site for the ceremony was significant. Masons' Hall used to stand in Masons Avenue, Basinghall Street, in the City of London. The hall had been the headquarters of the London Company of Masons since 1463. (The company was awarded its arms in 1472, its main feature being the outstretched compasses so familiar to students of the craft.)

It is noteworthy that Ashmole received his summons to attend Masons' Hall only nineteen hours before the event; he came as instructed. There were very few fellows of this sodality within London, it would seem – a highly exclusive gathering.

Let us see just how exclusive a gathering this was.

William Wilson was originally a freemason from Sutton Coldfield; he was not a member of the Masons' Company of the City of London, though there was a William Wilson who was master of the company in 1625–1626. The two men may have been relatives. William Woodman, on the other hand, took the freedom of the London Masons' Company on 21 July 1678.

In a 'General Search' undertaken by the company in 1694, 'Mr Woodmans' shop in Queen Street employed one apprentice, two masons, and two 'foreigners'. Woodman was to be master of the Masons' Company in 1708. He is, interestingly, mentioned in Grand Lodge lists in 1723 and 1725.

William Grey was probably the youngest candidate. He was a member of the Masons' Company who became its master in 1703.

Of those who were already accepted fellows, Thomas Wise was elected Master of the Masons' Company on 1 January 1682. Wise, possibly from the Isle of Portland (where the stone came from), had been admitted to the freedom of the Masons' Company by redemption on 7 February 1671–1672. He joined the Livery on 29 October 1672, and was made a court assistant in 1675. His rise through the ranks had been swift.

Thomas Wise did paving work at Whitehall between 1669 and 1670, holding masons' contracts for the rebuilding of St Michael's, Wood Street (£1,019); St Benet's, Gracechurch (£2,658) and St Nicholas, Cole Abbey (£3,141). Wise was one of the early contractors at St Paul's.

By the end of 1678, he had laid foundations for two southwest legs of the dome, and for the great staircase. Wise continued working at St Paul's until his early death in 1685. He left three sons: Thomas, William and John.

William was apprenticed to his father on 12 August 1673, admitted to the freedom of the company on 5 October 1680 and appointed warden for 1695-1696. John Shorthose was admitted to the Livery in 1662–1663. Warden in 1676 and 1681, Shorthose became Master of the Company in 1686, and was named as a court assistant as late as 1700. Records show he was paid £145 jointly with Thomas Shadbolt for masons' work at Masons' Hall, in 1668–1689, earned sums up to £360 for work at the Guildhall, and received £1,060 for work on Fleet Bridge from 1668 to 1672.

He worked on the church of St Michael, Cornhill, in 1670–1677; was mason-contractor for St Olave's Jewry in 1670–79 (£3,366), and was a contractor for Christchurch in 1677–1691 (receiving £6,648 jointly with John Crooke). Work on St Clement Danes in 1680–1682 netted £3,200, held jointly with fellow contractor Edward Pearce. These were very significant sums. John Shorthose could walk tall in London society.

John Shorthose was possibly the son of Thomas Shorthose. Thomas Shorthose was renter warden of the company in 1656 and 1662, and Company Master in 1663-1665. An old man, it seems he accompanied his son to the March 1682 Acception.

Thomas Shadbolt (or Shotboult) was apprenticed in 1639, admitted to the Livery in 1654, elected warden in 1664, and again in 1666, and became Master of the Company in 1668. Mr Shadbolt was still a court assistant in 1676. We know he did masonry work at the Sessions House just after the Great Fire of 1666 and also worked on Billingsgate Dock.

Regarding '[blank] Waindsford Esq', the man was probably Rowland Rainsford, described in the records of the Masons Company as 'late apprentice to Robert Beadles' and was 'admitted a freeman' of the company on 15 January 1668.

Nicholas Young was Master of the Masons' Company in 1682 and 1683. William Stanton was born 6 April 1639, the son of Edward Stanton. He was apprenticed to his uncle Thomas Stanton and made free of the company on 30 June 1663. Stanton was admitted to the Livery on 22 June 1668. He joined the Court of Assistants in 1674. Made warden in 1681, Stanton was Master of the Company in 1688 and 1689.

Working as a mason contractor during the 1680s at Belton House near Gainsborough, William Stanton received £4,921, six shillings and sixpence. Mr Stanton was also responsible for fine monuments and mural tablets. He died on 30 May 1705.

William 'Hamon', as Ashmole wrote his name, was probably the William Hammond who was a member of the Yeomanry when the company's *Quarterage Book* commenced in 1663. A 'William Hamon' was working on London Bridge in October 1652, at nine shillings per week.

Hammond joined the Livery in 1669, and the Court of Assistants in 1672. He was warden in 1680 and 1683. He held masons' contracts at St Anne's and St Agnes (1676–1687) for £130; at Allhallows the Great (1677–1687) for £337; and at St Michael's, Crooked Lane (1684–1694) for £2,533.

John Thompson was made free on 1 October 1667, being admitted to the Livery on 29 October 1669. He was a court assistant between 1674 and 1675 and warden between 1683 and 1686. Mr Thompson became Master of the Company in 1690 and again in 1695. He died in 1700 a wealthy man.

John Thompson had been masonry contractor for the parish churches of St Magnus (£6,313); the tower of St Mary le Bow (£6,172); Allhallows, Lombard Street (£4,399), and St Bartholomew Exchange (£3,223).

In 1683 Thompson held a contract at Winchester Palace. A petition by John Thompson and other 'workmen' engaged at Winchester survives. The complaint (a not uncommon one) was that after two years £500 was still owed to them. The matter was referred to Sir Christopher Wren in what appears to have been a common practice in disputes of this nature. (Wren is reported by both John Evelyn and John Aubrey as having been 'adopted' as a member of the Fellowship of Free Masons at a convention held at St Paul's Yard in May 1691.) Thompson, meanwhile, undertook repairs on Lincoln's Inn Chapel (£600), at Hampton Court Gardens in 1689 and 1696, and at Kensington Palace in 1690. Mr Thompson commenced work at St Paul's Cathedral (Wren's masterpiece) around 1688. A 'Company Search' of 1694 shows he was employing thirteen men there.

A Holy Mountain of Venison

Two things become immediately apparent from a survey of the membership of this Fellowship of accepted and 'new-accepted Masons'. First, contrary to what was held to be the case until very recently (and is still held in some quarters), this congregation was not gathering at Masons' Hall because some members of the fellowship 'happened to be associated' with the London Masons' Company. On the contrary, this was the absolute cream of the crop! This was as fair a slice of the governance of the company as you were likely to get at short notice.

As Knoop and Jones's *London Mason in the 17th Century* (Manchester University, 1935) most adequately demonstrates, these were the big names in London stone construction; they were very well off indeed and their money came from the industry.

Accepted Free Masonry was clearly an infra-trade phenomenon. It is not a transition out of 'operative freemasonry'; it is not a stage in the game; it is not a moment of evolution predestined to turn out as 'Grand Lodge'. It runs side by side with the industry. It is the manager's box at the Wembley of Masonry! This is where the Big Talent met.

Second, this was not a meeting of London's Rosicrucian mystics, or even the survivors of such a movement. Ashmole was one of very few people indeed who understood the dynamics of mind and spirit that joined masonry, science, art and mystical intelligence. The members would have been lucky to have Ashmole aboard; and he would have felt privileged to be at the coalface of the action that was making London a proud city of the world.

Free Masonry had a spiritual dimension, certainly. In 17th century Britain, *everything* had a spiritual dimension.

Free Masonry had an esoteric dimension, no doubt. The Freemasons had been saying this (in their own terms) for at least 300 years! Did whatever the 'new-accepted Masons' experience on 11 March 1682 involve a spiritual or esoteric or symbolic (or all three) dimension?

Was Robert Samber right to link the ideal craft with the ideal of man's highest spiritual potential?

I can only say this. Those men who entered Masons' Hall at noon, and who left for a noble dinner at another place on 11 March 1682, did not go into that building to learn about stonemasonry, in either practice or theory. They were the experts, and it may be rightly supposed that no grand lodge on earth could teach them their own business.

They must have been taken in for something else. And it still is taking them in; it has been taking them in for the last 300 years. And what is 'it'? It is called mystique – and you either have it, or you do not. Freemasonry has it.

Join it to sound, well-grounded life–principles and you have something called Accepted Freemasonry.

Chapter Nine
The Scottish Evidence

Generally speaking, lodges only become visible to the researcher when someone has tried to control them.

David Stevenson's excellent book on the origins of Scottish Freemasonry (misleadingly entitled *The Origins of Freemasonry – Scotland's Century 1590-1710*, Cambridge, 1988) analyses, amongst other relevant matters, the significance of William Schaw (*c.*1550-1602), Master of Works and 'General Warden of the Masons of Scotland'.

Schaw was a trusted servant of Scotland's King James VI (James I of England from 1603). He appears to have kept the monarch abreast of Roman Catholic interests in the country (being himself a catholic tolerant of the Reformation). In December 1583, the king made Schaw his Master of Works. One might have thought, given Schaw's importance to the king's court, that Schaw might have regarded the appointment as a sinecure.

However, Schaw seems to have taken the job very seriously, working hard for the interests of stonemasons and for the cause of fine architecture in general. Perhaps we should expect this of a catholic who had seen the ancient structures of that church suffer at the hands of protestant iconoclasts. The inscription on Schaw's tomb at Dunfermline Abbey, erected by Scottish nobleman Alexander Seton, gives us some idea of Schaw's reputation:

> To his most upright Friend,
> WILLIAM SCHAW,
> Live with the Gods, and live for ever, most excellent man;
> This life to thee was labour, death was deep repose.
> ALEXANDER SETON, Erected
> DEO OPTIMO MAXIMO [To God the Best and Greatest]

This humble structure of stones covers a man of excellent skill, notable probity, integrity of life, adorned with the greatest of virtues – William Schaw, Master of the King's Works, President of the Sacred Ceremonies and the Queen's Chamberlain. He died on 18 April 1602.

Among the living he dwelt fifty-two years; he had travelled in France and other kingdoms for the improvement of his mind; he wanted no liberal training; skilful in architecture; was early recommended to great persons for the singularity of his mind; and was not only unwearied and indefatigable in labours and business, but constantly active and vigorous, and was most dear to every good man who knew him. He was born to do good offices and thereby to gain the hearts of men; now he lives eternally with God. Queen Anne [of Denmark; the King's wife) ordered this monument to be erected to the memory of this most excellent and most upright man, lest his virtues, worthy of eternal commendation, should pass away with the death of his body.

(Reproduced in *The Rosslyn Hoax?*, Robert L. D. Cooper, Lewis Masonic, 2006, p.277)

In pursuit of a more organised workforce – and possibly a degree of independence for masons – Schaw issued two statutes 'to be observed by the Master Masons within this realm'.

The first was issued on 28 December 1598, the other precisely one-year later, both written the day after St John the Evangelist's day. St John the Evangelist was the Scottish craft's patron saint. As we saw in chapter three, the Lodge of St Mary's, Edinburgh, has minutes going back to July 1599, making those minutes the second oldest examples of masonic minutes in the world. Those of Aitchison's Haven, also in Scotland, go back a little earlier to 1598. The coincidence of dates between the statutes of Schaw and the survival of minutes from these lodges is doubtless due to the stipulation in Schaw's statutes that basic lodge records are kept. While a number of people over the centuries have shown a great willingness to write about Freemasonry, members of lodges in general do not like writing things down if they can avoid it; it savours of work and onerous responsibility. The masonic 'rank' system has partly grown up as a means of rewarding masons for doing things they might otherwise not be inclined to do.

In the old days (before the keeping of minutes became established custom) this unwillingness to keep records was a result of the craft being an oral tradition, coupled with the illiteracy of the vast majority of masons. Unfortunately, in my judgement, Stevenson makes too much of the fact that Scotland has the oldest evidence for lodges keeping minutes. Apart from a possible distortion of history, the claims built around this fact have added to the longstanding myth that there is a 'Scottish Masonry' of greater antiquity (and even authority) than that elsewhere. This myth has generated dire outcomes for those who prefer facts to romance where history is concerned (*The Da Vinci Code* could not have been written as it is without this myth-dressed-as-history).

Stevenson is in no wise responsible for this latter side effect of his idea of 'Scotland's century'. In the interests of scholarship, Stevenson just looked at the evidence at his disposal and made a perfectly understandable computation, expounded on p.7 of his *Origins of Freemasonry*:

> The claim that it is in Scotland in the late sixteenth and seven teenth centuries that the essentials of modern Freemasonry emerge is a large one, but the following list of 'firsts' that Scotland can claim on the basis of surviving sources is a crude indication of the evidence on which the claim rests:
>
> Earliest use of the word 'lodge' in the modern Masonic sense, and evidence that such permanent institutions exist

Earliest official minute books and other records of such lodges

Earliest attempts at organising lodges at a national level

Earliest examples of 'non operatives' (men who were not working Stonemasons) joining lodges

Earliest evidence connecting lodge Masonry with specific ethical ideas expounded by use of symbols

Earliest evidence connecting lodge Masonry as sinister or conspiratorial

Earliest references to the Mason Word

Earliest 'Masonic catechisms' expounding the Mason Word and describing initiation ceremonies

Earliest evidence of the use of two degrees or grades within Masonry

Earliest use of the terms 'entered apprentice' and 'fellow craft' for these grades

Earliest evidence (within the Lodge of Edinburgh) of the emergence of a third grade, created by a move towards regarding fellow craft and master not as alternative terms for the same grade but as referring to separate grades (or at least status)

To set alongside all these Scottish masonic 'firsts' England can claim:

Earliest copies of the Old Charges (no Scottish copies are known which pre-date the mid seventeenth century)

Widespread use of the word 'Freemason', and use of the term 'Accepted Mason'

Earliest lodge composed entirely of 'non operatives' (which can be interpreted as indicating how English Masonry was, much more than Scottish, an artificial creation, not something that grew out of the beliefs and institutions of working Stonemasons)

The earliest grand lodge

(*The Origins of Freemasonry*, David Stevenson, Cambridge, 1988, pp.7–8)

If this were a football match between England and Scotland, the score, according to this referee, would be Scotland 11, England 4: a resounding victory for the Scottish side! But what exactly is the game here? I for one was not aware that we were studying national claims to masonic primacy. The aim of the historian is to render the past as comprehensible and as intelligible as possible based on the available information. The information is interpreted (if necessary) in the light of the most likely scenarios, subject to revision in the light of additional evidence and better powers of interpretation. I should think we shall arrive at a better 'result' if we keep our terms to the study of 'Freemasonry', not 'Scottish Freemasonry', or 'English Freemasonry', for that matter. We can speak of 'stonemasonry in Scotland' and 'Freemasonry in England' or Freemasonry in other countries, towns, cities.

As for national language, I observe that the Schaw statutes are written in English, not Gaelic, and were issued before the two nations were joined at the crown (if not elsewhere). But is this a cultural issue? In fact, there are very few of Stevenson's categories of 'earliests' that are not subject to further analysis, rendering them impotent to secure the case that the 'essentials of modern Freemasonry' are to be sought in their origin in Scotland alone.

To give just one example, Stevenson claims that Scotland has 'the earliest use of the word 'lodge' in 'the modern Masonic sense'. Just what is this 'modern Masonic sense'? We have seen in chapters three and four that the word 'lodge' has always meant and still means different things to different people at different places and in different times. There has been an evolution of scattered concepts, a number shown to have been built on confusion and misunderstanding. There is no clear definition of a lodge in 'the modern Masonic sense'; the word's meaning depends on custom and usage.

The 'essentials of modern Freemasonry' are 'essential' to modern Freemasonry, not essential to its origins. One thing that is not essential to modern Freemasonry is stonemasonry. Likewise, the 'essentials of 17th century Free Masonry' (or freemasonry) are essential to the variety of practices discernible in the craft in this period; those 'essentials' may not be essential to 'modern Freemasonry'.

One thing that *is* essential to 17th century Free Masonry is stonemasonry.

Furthermore, the significant claim that Scottish records contain the earliest references to non-stonemasons joining lodges has recently been challenged by the Rev Neville Barker Cryer in his book, *York Mysteries Revealed* (2006). The *York MS*. No 1 (*c.*1600) contains a hand-written introduction containing:

> An Anagraime upon the name of Masonrie
> William Kay to his friend Robt Preston
> Upon his Artt of Masonrie as Followeth:

Barker Cryer sees good reason to consider these two names as being those of York Freemen, William Kay (freed as a spurrier in 1569), and Robert Preston, (freed as a fishmonger in 1571).

Barker Cryer regards these references as 'evidence that by about 1600 at least there was in York or thereabouts a lodge or lodges meeting to practise a different kind of Masonry'. (*York Mysteries Revealed*, p.157).

I am not sure that the latter conclusion is one that is definitively supported by the evidence, but the evidence does at least challenge Stevenson's assumption that Scottish records reveal the first entry of non-stonemasons into stonemasons' lodges.

One thing at least is clear to all serious scholars of the craft. 'Freemasonry' does not have a single point of origin – and certainly not a single national origin. Even the word 'Freemasonry' has no single origin, when we look at its several meanings throughout time. Even today, the word means a completely different thing to the editor of a Sunday newspaper than it does to me.

Stevenson has noted 'England's claim' that the earliest lodge composed entirely of 'non-operatives' was in England. He is referring to the Warrington lodge that 'made' Ashmole and his wife's cousin Free Masons in October 1646.

First, the statement is untrue. An operative freemason together with his brother was present at the Warrington lodge of October 1646. The presence of a working stonemason at a lodge appears to have been a stipulation of craft masters, as we have seen.

Second, Stevenson writes that the event itself 'can be interpreted' as indicating how English Masonry was, 'much more than Scottish, an artificial creation'. Indeed, it *can* be interpreted in this way. But the plea is simply absurd in the context of the study as a whole. The very point of interest in studying Freemasonry beyond its links to the trade of masonry, is that it does indeed appear to be an 'artificial creation' – because that is what modern Freemasonry clearly is!

When you sever the symbols and allegories from the business and make them the central subject of interest, you necessarily create a new thing – in so far as a child is 'new' compared to its parents. Freemasonry in the modern sense is a 'complex' of contrivance.

If you are looking for the origins of the 'essentials' of modern Freemasonry, then it would seem that this very artificiality is the precise thing that a scholar should be looking for. Whether or not you find it at Warrington in 1646 is still debated.

One place where you can be fairly sure to have found it is in the phenomenon of the 'Acception' as discussed in the last chapter. Stevenson himself admits that the term 'Accepted Mason' is, in the period he describes, not in use among the Scottish lodges he has studied; nor is the term 'Freemason' for that matter. This does seem rather significant to the case. To say that the practices of masons in Scotland *circa* 1600 were not 'artificial' is surely an argument to be used in support of the idea that the origins of the 'essentials' (however they may be defined) of modern Freemasonry are not to be sought among stonemasons' lodges! The background to this error of logic is the too well established distinction of 'operative' and 'speculative' Freemasonry, which Stevenson has inherited from a century and more of masonic history undertaken by Freemasons.

Thus, Stevenson takes the view that the 'speculative' is somehow less authentic than his alleged predecessor, the 'operative'. However, he wishes it to be known that the essentials of modern (or so-called 'speculative') Freemasonry: 'Masons's Word', catechisms, a lodge, minute books, the expressions 'entered apprentice' and 'fellow craft', and national organisation, are the creation of working stonemasons in Scotland. According to this logic, the creation of an artificial Freemasonry can be laid squarely (forgive the pun) at the door of authentic working stonemasons. This boils down to nothing more extraordinary than saying – along with the whole of masonic scholarship – that symbolic or 'accepted' Freemasonry has made use of practices familiar to fully trained stonemasons. Nobody would deny this.

The point is, what kind of use has been made of stonemasons' practices? As an analysis of the origins of Freemasonry in Scotland, Professor Stevenson's work is second to none, but what we get is knowledge not of the essentials of modern Freemasonry, but of stonemasons' lodge practices in 17th century Scotland.

Admittedly, this is a serious boon to scholarship; let us not be in any doubt of that. The one thing we do not get from the surviving 17th century evidence in England is first-hand knowledge of stonemasons' lodges. We have a great deal of evidence concerning the activities of the trade in London, but not of individual tradesmen's lodges. One thing we might conclude from this is that in the almost total absence of evidence for tradesmen's individual lodges in England, such lodges did not exist. This would lead us to conclude further that there were stonemasons' lodges in Scotland, but not in England. This does seem a trifle extraordinary. But then, Stevenson has made such a case for the importance of records concerning 'lodges' that such would be a reasonable inference from the surviving evidence. We might even begin to wonder whether there were any working freemasons in England at all – but surely, the stones testify. But perhaps they were put in place by artificial Freemasons! The trouble here is that we know from sources such as Dr Robert Plot (1686) and John Aubrey that assemblies of masons in some places in the country were called 'lodges'; but were not so called everywhere.

Why then do we know so little about them?

For the simple reason it is likely that such assemblies kept to the letter and spirit of the craft and did not keep records. Such evidence as might have been available (rare copies of masons' charges or traditional histories) was called in to the good offices of the new 'Grand Lodge' after 1720 where much of it seems to have disappeared in the course of time.

Besides, there is evidence in England for a mason's word, oath and catechisms, though it comes from late in the century; that the evidence is of late date may simply be because that is when it comes from.

No, the reason why the Scottish evidence appears in such relative abundance is quite simple. Masonic evidence tends to appear either when the craft is attacked, or when somebody tries to take control of it from the outside of a particular sodality. Interestingly, this phenomenon applies as much to working stonemasons as it does to symbolic 'Accepted' Freemasons today and in years gone by.

This explanation fits the Scottish evidence for stonemasons' lodges very well. William Schaw tried to organise the lodges on a national scale. Where the lodges were co-operative (recalling that he died very soon after issuing his statutes), there were minutes made on a more or less formal basis. It is to be supposed that those lodges that for a number of possible reasons (such as being satisfied with existing arrangements) did not wish to co-operate on a national level, kept such material as might have existed strictly to themselves. Thus, it may well be the case that the relative abundance of lodge evidence available to a scholar from the period in Scotland may have been greater had efforts *not* been made to organise the craft.

The Schaw Statutes

We have established already a variety of practices that obtained in different parts of England. Practices were bound to vary depending on their independence from outside control. This is a highly significant factor. During the 17th century there was no systematic attempt to dominate freemasons' customs in England. The same was not true in Scotland at the end of the 16th and beginning of the 17th centuries.

As we saw in chapter three, the lodge of St Mary's, Edinburgh, for example, was part of a civic 'Incorporation' that included the trade of wrights. Most towns preferred to control their masons when they could. We know that in Scotland during this period, lodges often officially met beyond the burgh boundaries. If similar conditions applied in England, this would explain why we hear so little of lodge activity, except perhaps in folklore.

In Scotland, even within the city boundaries, the masons still called their collective (that is, exclusive) meetings lodges, even though the meetings had little practical independence from civic bodies. Under these circumstances, it might be likely that those areas of practice beyond the control of the incorporations, secrets and symbols, might have dominated meetings constituted as 'lodges'.

The possible focusing of meetings on less practical matters than trying the work of apprentices, for example, is undoubtedly a feature that would lend itself to development towards the modern lodge system.

It appears to be the case that Schaw's attempt to establish rules governing a number of fixed-identity ('stated'?) 'lodges' (as opposed to occasional lodges on sites of work) under his 'General Wardenship' may have encouraged the development of independent masons' meetings. That is to say, his attempts at a common order may have encouraged the idea of a fixed lodge, and the lodge as the locus of masons' interests, civic and private.

Scholars always take institutions more seriously if there is a literate dimension to the phenomenon. Literacy signifies culture. In this case, this dimension is provided by minutes of meetings. Schaw stipulated that lodges list the names of those apprenticed or made 'fellows of craft', and the masters, deacons or wardens present.

Let us look in more detail at what Schaw attempted in 1598 and 1599.

This is a paraphrase of the statutes issued in Edinburgh in December 1598:

Masters should ensure that masons keep all the good ordinances set down by their predecessors of good memory concerning the privileges of the craft, especially that they be true to one another and live charitably together like brothers and companions of the craft. (The language used was very similar to the 'Old Charges' observed in England for many years.)

Masons should be obedient to their wardens, deacons and masters in all things concerning their craft. Masons must be honest, faithful and diligent in their calling, dealing uprightly with their masters or employers, adhering to all financial agreements. Masons should only take on work for which they are qualified to undertake, or else pay £40 or a quarter of the value of the work. Amends should be paid to the employer at the sight and discretion of the General Warden, or, in his absence, of the masters, deacons and wardens of the area where the work is undertaken.

No master should take another's work over his head once the first master has sealed his contract in writing or by word. The penalty is £40 for breach of this rule.

No master shall take on the work of another until the former master is satisfied with what he has done. Penalty for breach is again £40. Disputes over elections of lodge masters are to be settled by appeal to the Warden General.

No master shall take on more than three apprentices during his lifetime without the consent of wardens, deacons and masters of the shire where the additional apprentice lives. Apprentices must serve seven years as such and not be admitted as fellow in craft until he has served another seven years after the end of his apprenticeship, unless a special licence is granted by wardens, deacons and masters assembled for the purpose. Trials of skill, worthiness and qualification are to be set for those aspiring to be 'fellow of craft'. Transgression of this statute entails a £40 fine, in addition to penalties set down against the apprentice's person according to the order of the lodge of where he remains.

£40 will be charged to masters who sell their apprentice to another master before their seven years' apprenticeship is done. No master may receive an apprentice without leave of the warden of the lodge where he dwells. The date of indenture as apprentice should be orderly booked. No master or fellow of craft be either received or admitted without six masters (including the lodge warden) and two entered apprentices being present. The name and *mark* of the candidate must be entered in the book, with the names of those who have admitted him, along with the names of the 'intendaris' (guides) chosen to help the new fellow of craft. No one is ever to be admitted without an 'assay' or trial of his skill and worthiness in his vocation and craft. (Masons were 'professionals', having made a vocal 'profession', or sacred oath.)

No master should work under command of any other craftsman that takes upon himself masonry work. No master or fellow of craft may receive any *cowans* (unrecognised masons) to work in his society or company, nor send any of his servants to work with *cowans*, on pain of £20 fine.

A £30 fine is to be taken from anyone who lets an entered apprentice work beyond his qualification. Further enterprise will be forbidden without licence of the masters and wardens of where they dwell. If strife or variance on any question break out among the masters, servants or entered apprentices, then the parties to the quarrel must signify its causes to the wardens or deacons of their lodge within the space of 29 days, or pay £10 fine. The wardens, deacons and masters may remove the grievance, but if the parties are obstinate or wilful they will be deprived of the privileges of their lodge and will not be permitted to work until they have submitted to reason in the sight of their wardens, deacons and masters.

All masters and enterprisers ('Inte priseris') of works should be careful when erecting scaffolds and construction equipment to so set and place them that no one come to harm as a result of negligence. The penalty for failure is that the master spent the rest of his days serving under a principal master with no authority over his own work. Masters must not employ

Figure 1. The 'son' accepts the secrets from the master; engraving by Robert Vaughan in Ashmole's *Theatrum Chemicum Britannicum*, 1652.

Figure 2. Presumed 'Master's chair', probably owned by Edward Minshull, dated 1595, now in the possession of Lord Northampton, Pro Grand Master, United Grand Lodge of England (photograph used by permission).

Figure 3. Unique carving on chair of 1597, in possession of Lord Northampton, – possibly one of a pair formerly owned by Edward Minshull (photograph used by permission).

Figure 4. Entrance to Stoke Hall (private), near Nantwich, once home to Edward Minshull, father to Ellen Mainwaring.

Figure 5. Stoke Hall (private), near Nantwich, formerly home of Edward Minshull, as it is today.

Figure 6. Tomb of Sir Philip Mainwaring (d.1647) and Ellen (*née* Minshull, d.1656), by John Stone, King's Master Mason.

Figure 7. Combined arms of Mainwaring (left) and Minshull families; tomb Sir Philip and Lady F Mainwaring, churc Lawrence, Upper Cheshire, 165 Stone, King's Windsor

Figure 8. Acton church,
near Nantwich, Cheshire.

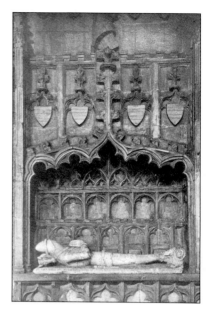

Figure 9. Tomb of Sir William
Mainwaring, of Baddiley and
Peover, (d.1399), Acton church,
near Nantwich, Cheshire.

. Tomb of Sir Thomas and Lady Wilbraham, Acton, Cheshire,
to be the work of Edward Marshall, King's Master Mason.

Figure 11. The octagonal tower of Nantwich church, Cheshire, once filled with monuments to the Mainwaring, Minshull and Wilbraham families.

Figure 12. 17th century brass plaque to Richard Minshull, Nantwich church, Cheshire.

Figure 13. The C·
Nantwich, whe
Dugdale hel
on 11 Se·

Figure 14. Elias Ashmole, Windsor Herald, after 1660, by Cornelis de Ne

e 15. Sir William
, by Wenceslas
m the
The

dale),

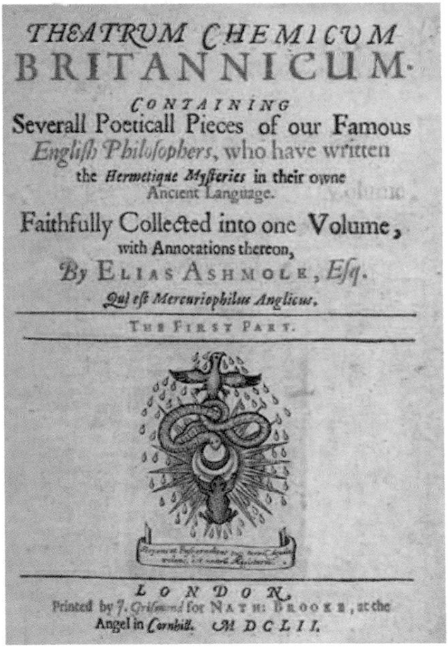

THEATRUM CHEMICUM
BRITANNICUM.
CONTAINING
Severall Poeticall Pieces of our Famous
English Philosophers, who have written
the Hermetique Mysteries in their owne
Ancient Language.

Faithfully Collected into one Volume,
with Annotations thereon,
By ELIAS ASHMOLE, Esq.
Qui est Mercuriophilus Anglicus.

THE FIRST PART.

LONDON,
Printed by J. Grismond for NATH: BROOKE, at the
Angel in Cornhill. CM DC LII.

Figure 16. Title page, *Theatrum Chemicum Britannicum*, 1652, Elias Ashmole (1617-1692).

Figure 17. Alchemical *Sol* and *Luna* combine as hermaphrodite, carrying square and compasses. Jamsthaler, *Viatorium spagyricum*, 1625.

Figure 18. One of the earliest boards known in Britain, *Faithful* lodge No 85, Harleston, Norfolk.

Figure 19. Second degree board from *Faithful* lodge No 85, Harleston, Norfolk.

Figure 20. Intriguing third degree board (dated 1800) from *Faithful* lodge, Harleston; note the five orders of architecture indicated below.

Figure 21. Cloth from *Unity* lodge No 321, Crewe, originally founded in 1806 with a different number; painted between 1832 and 1863.

Figure 22. Cloth from *Unity* lodge No 254, Coventry.

Figure 23. Cloth from *Paladian* lodge, Hereford (c.1820).

Figure 24. Cloth from the lodge of the *Marches* No 611, Ludlow, possibly originally from *Silurian* lodge, consecrated 1791; note the master's hand drawing a true tracing board.

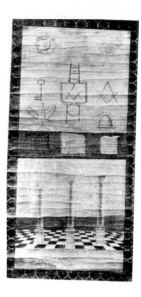

Figure 25. Cloth from the lodge of the 7th Light Dragoons.

Figure 26. Cloth from lodge of the 7th Light Dragoons; the three figures on the roof represent the three great masters.

Figure 27. Cloth from lodge of the 7th Light Dragoons; note the heavy 'beetle' – 80lbs of hard wood attached to a four foot handle – setting level and plotting pin.

Figure 28. Cloth from *Cestrian* lodg No 425, Chester, originally from *Feathers* lodge No 209 that met at t *Plume & Feathers*, Bridge street, Ches

Figure 29. Cloth from *Friendship* lodge No 100, Great Yarmouth (1809).

Figure 30. Cloth from *Friendship* lodge No 100, Great Yarmouth, originally meeting in Norwich (dated 1809).

Figure 31. Striking third degree cloth from *Friendship* lodge No 100, which used to meet in Norwich (dated 1809).

Figure 32. Tracing board found at Bristol (19th century).

Figure 33. Tracing board from Bristol (19th century).

Figure 33b. Unusual tracing board found at Bristol.

Figs.34-36. Unique circular boards (18 inch diameter) from lodge No 24, Newcastle on Tyne.

Figure 37. Board designed by Brother Jacobs of 3, Charles Street, Hatton Gardens, London.

Figure 38. Second degree board designed by Jacobs of Hatton Gardens; similar to a set in lodge *Freedom* No 77, Gravesend.

Figure 39. Fascinating design for a third degree tracing board by Brother Jacobs of Hatton Gardens, London (mid 19th century).

Figure 40. First degree tracing board from *Royal Naval* lodge No 59.

Figure 41. Second degree tracing board from *Royal Naval* lodge No 59.

Figure 42. Interesting oriental style third degree tracing board from *Royal Naval* lodge No 59 (19th century).

Figure 44. Second degree board from
All Souls lodge No 170, Weymouth.

Figure 43. Board from *All Souls* lodge
No 170, Weymouth.

Figure 45. Striking board showing Hiram lying in state in the temple;
All Souls lodge No 170, Weymouth.

Figure 46. Framed cloth
from the *Loyal
Cambrian* lodge No 110,
Merthyr Tydvil,
constituted 1810.

Figure 47. Framed cloth
from the *Loyal Cambrian*
lodge No 110, combining
Royal Arch and craft
Freemasonry.

Figure 48. Third
degree framed lodge
cloth from *Loyal
Cambrian* lodge No
110, Merthyr Tydvil.

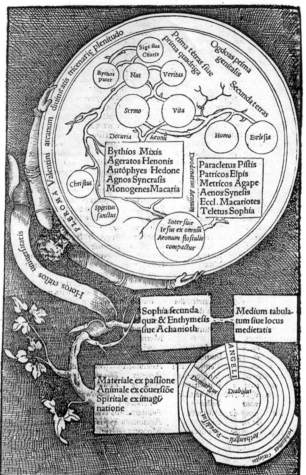

Figure 49. A very rare 16th century illustration of the Valentinian Gnostic creation myth; *Adversus Valentinus*, by 2nd century church Father, Tertullian.

Figure 50. A carving of the Green Man, Rosslyn Chapel, Scotland; photo by Matthew Scanlan.

Figure 51. John Yarker (1833–1913), author of *Arcane Schools* (1909) and many other masonic works.

Figure 52. John Dee's *Monas Hieroglyphica*, Antwerp. 1564.

Figure 53. Hermes Trismegistus, 'patron saint' of the old freemasons.

Allgemeine vnd General
REFORMATION,
Der gantzen weiten Welt.

Beneben der

FAMA FRA-
TERNITATIS,
Deß löblichen Ordens des Ro-
senkreutzes / an alle Gelehrte vnd
Häupter Europæ geschrieben :

Auch einer kurtzen RESPONSION,
von dem Herrn Haselmeyer gestellet / welcher
deßwegen von den Jesuitern ist gefänglich ein-
gezogen / vnd auff eine Galleen ge-
schmiedet :

Jetzo öffentlich in Druck verfertiget / vnd allen
trewen Hertzen communiciret worden.

Erstlich Gedruckt zu Cassel /

Jm Jahr / 1614.

Figure 54. *Fama Fraternitatis,* with Boccalini's satirical *Reformation of the whole wide world;* first printed by Wilhelm Wessel, Kassel, 1614.

Figure 55. An engraver's vision of the House of the Rose Cross fraternity; Theophilus Schweighart (Daniel Mögling), *Speculum Sophicum RhodoStauroticum,* 1618.

Figure 56. 'Damcar' (or is it Damar?) on a map of Arabia – where Christian Rosenkreuz sought wisdom. *Carta Marina*, M.Waldseemüller, Strassburg, 1516.

Figure 57. Johann Valentin Andreae (1586–1654), genius of the *Fama Fraternitatis*, aged 42.

Figure 58. Giovanni Pico della Mirandola, Conte di Concordia, author of the *Oration on the Dignity of Man* (1486) – manifesto of the Renaissance – and of Free Masonry.

Figure 59. Paracelsus (1493–1541) – medical pioneer and secret radical theologian.

Figure 60. Entering into the secrets of Nature, from *Amphitheatrum Sapientiae Aeternae*, Heinrich Khunrath, Hamburg, 1595.

Figure 61. Engraving of Elias Ashmole by William Fairthorne, 1656.

Figure 62. Letter from Samuel Hartlib to antiquarian John Aubrey, March 1655.

Figure 64. The Rose gives her honey to the Bees, from *Summum Bonum*, Joachim Frizius (Robert Fludd), 1629. Masons are meant to be busy bees.

Figure 63. Man the Microcosm, from Robert Fludd's *Utriusque Cosmi…Historia*, 2nd volume, Johann Theodore de Bry, Oppenheim, 1619.

Figure 65. Amazing presentation of man as universal co-creator and Free
Mason: 'At the centre of the circle, the Master Mason cannot err' – note the
square at his feet; *Three Books of Occult Philosophy*, Henry Cornelius Agrippa,
London, 1651.

Figure 66. Masons Avenue, off Basinghall street, city of London – former home of the London Company of Masons.

Figure 67. Site of Masons' Hall, Masons Avenue, Basinghall street, London.

Figure 68. Lifesize statue of Charles II, Lichfield cathedral, by Accepted Free Mason (1682), architect Sir William Wilson.

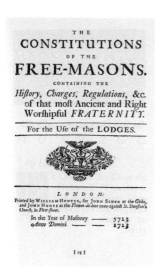

Figure 69. Title page, James Anderson's book of Free-Masons' *Constitutions*, 1723.

Figure 70. Frontispiece to Anderson's *Constitutions* (1723) showing the Duke of Montagu handing the constitutions to Philip, Duke of Wharton, watched (right) by Deputy Grand Master, JT Desaguliers.

Figure 71. Jacob Böhme, from Edward Taylor and Jacob Böhme's *Theosophick Philosophy Unfolded*, London, 1691.

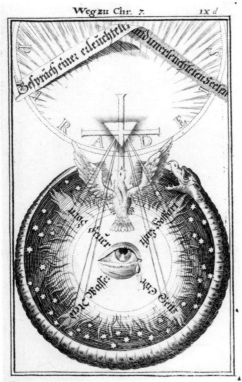

Figure 72. Illustration from Jacob Böhme's 'theosophick' *Way to Christ* – the geometry of the Heart.

Figure. 73. Alchemical emblem from Malachias Geiger's *Microcosmus hypochondriacus sive de melancolia hypochondriaca*, Munich 1651, engraved by Jan Sadeler (1568–1665), *Bibliotheca Philosophica Hermetica*, Amsterdam.

Please note the words closest to the name of God at the top: *Ab Uno Omnia* (From One, All); *In Uno Omnia* (In One, All); *Per Unum Omnia* (Through One, All). These principles encapsulate the micro-macrocosmic (pansophic) philosophy of the period. This philosophy has influenced Freemasonry profoundly. Freemasonry can accommodate differences because it looks to the principle of the One behind all diversity; it aims at the primary principle, contained *in potentia* in all things. Thus, bigotry is a sign of lack of consciousness – consciousness of the *whole*, in which the human being finds his or her proper place.

This image combines symbols familiar to symbolic Freemasons with alchemy and suggests the vital living cosmos that contains both geometrical form and living chemical and spiritual phases of transformation to higher principles. In fact, from the highest perspective, the alchemical and geometrical universes are one – extensions of the fundamental divine principle. Accepted Free Mason Elias Ashmole's motto – in the same period – was *Ex Uno Omnia: From the One: Everything*. This philosophy has universal applications.

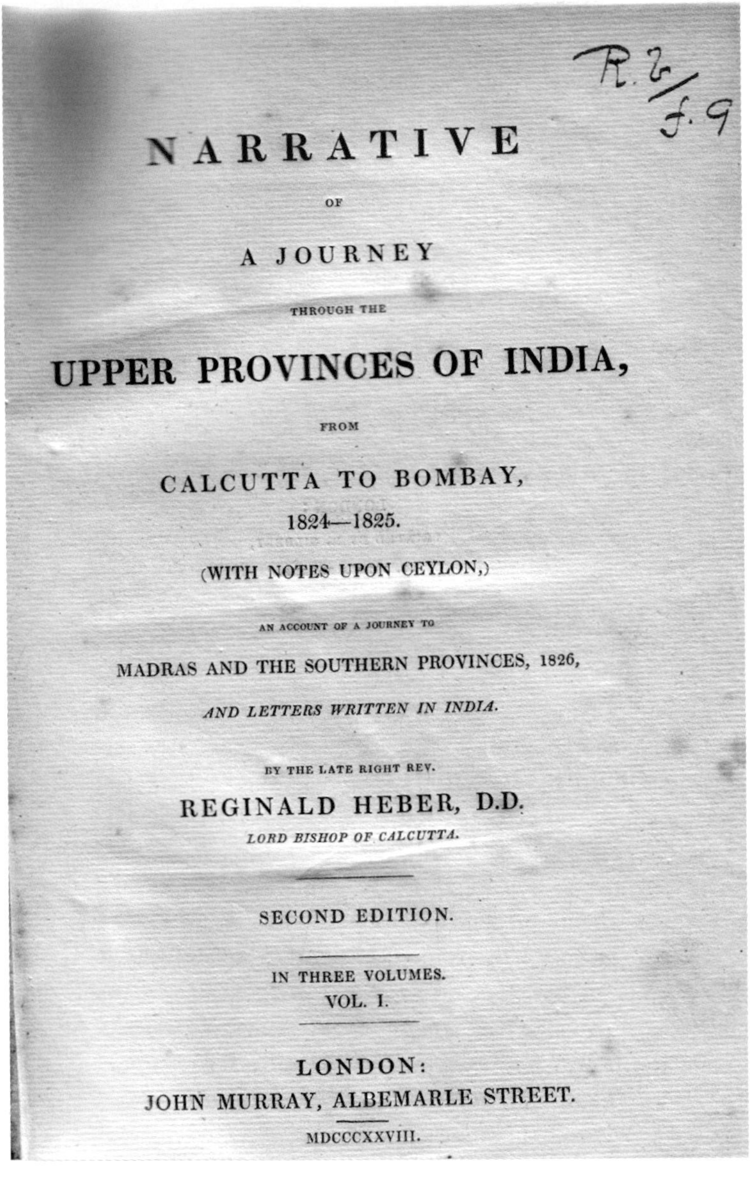

R. 2/
J. 9

NARRATIVE

OF

A JOURNEY

THROUGH THE

UPPER PROVINCES OF INDIA,

FROM

CALCUTTA TO BOMBAY,

1824—1825.

(WITH NOTES UPON CEYLON,)

AN ACCOUNT OF A JOURNEY TO

MADRAS AND THE SOUTHERN PROVINCES, 1826,

AND LETTERS WRITTEN IN INDIA.

BY THE LATE RIGHT REV.

REGINALD HEBER, D.D.

LORD BISHOP OF CALCUTTA.

SECOND EDITION.

IN THREE VOLUMES.
VOL. I.

LONDON:

JOHN MURRAY, ALBEMARLE STREET.

MDCCCXXVIII.

Figure 74. Title page: *Narrative of a Journey through the Upper Provinces of India*, by Reginald Heber DD, bishop of Calcutta, John Murray, 1828.

runaway apprentices from other masters, under pain of £40 fine. 11 persons of the masons' craft shall convene at a time and place as instructed, under pain of £10 fine. All summonsed masters to an assembly or meeting shall be sworn to a great oath that they shall neither hide nor conceal any faults or wrongs done one to another. Wardens, deacons and masters of the lodges where offenders dwell shall secure the penalty fines from those offenders and distribute the moneys to pious uses as good conscience advises.

William Schaw, Master of Work, signed the statutes personally and ordered authentic copies to be sent to 'every particular lodge within this realm'.

The Schaw Statutes of 1599

The statutes of 1599 were issued from Holyrood House, Edinburgh, after a meeting held the previous day. There had, judging from the contents, clearly been some dispute as to primacy of tradition, Kilwinning in particular asserting its ancient statutes and customs. The meeting ended with the hope that a further assembly would iron out outstanding problems.

Here is a paraphrase of the statutes:

It is ordained that the warden within the bounds of Kilwinning and other places subject to their lodge shall be chosen and elected annually by the majority of masters voting of the said lodge on 20 December, within the kirk (church) of Kilwinning, as the head and second lodge of Scotland, and that the General Warden be informed who is chosen warden of the lodge, immediately after his election.

It is thought needful and expedient by the Lord Warden General that every lodge in Scotland shall have in times coming the old and ancient liberties of use and wont of before, and especially that the lodge of Kilwinning, second lodge of Scotland, shall have their warden present at the election of wardens within the bounds of the Nether Waird [Ward] of Cliddsdail (Lanarkshire), Glasgow, Ayr, and bounds of Carrick (one of the three divisions of Ayrshire); with power to the said warden and deacon of Kilwinning to convene the remaining wardens and deacons within the aforesaid bounds whenever they have any need of importance so to do, and yea to be judged by the warden and deacon of Kilwinning when it shall please them to convene either in Kilwinning or within any other part of the west of Scotland and aforesaid bounds.

It is thought needful and expedient by the Lord Warden General that Edinburgh shall be in all time coming as of before the first and principal lodge of Scotland, and that Kilwinning be the second lodge as of before naturally manifest in our old ancient writings, and that Stirling shall be the third lodge, in conformity with the old privileges thereof. (All of this rather confirms my point that lodges become visible when attempts are made to control them.)

It is thought expedient that the wardens of every like lodge shall be answerable to the presbyteries (church district courts) within their shires for offences committed by masons in their lodges, and the third part of fines imposed for such offences shall be employed to the godly use of the lodge where the offence happened to be committed.

A trial to be taken yearly by the wardens and most ancient masters of every lodge extending to six persons, who shall take trial of the offence, the punishment may be executed in conformity to equity & justice & good conscience & the ancient order. It is ordained by the Lord Warden General that the warden of Kilwinning as the second in Scotland, elect and choose six of the most perfect and worthiest of memory within their bounds, to take trial of the qualifications of all the masons within the bounds aforesaid of their art, craft, science and 'antient memorie'.

The Art of Memory

This latter requirement to test the art, craft, science and 'antient memorie' of masons has been taken to suggest that masons may have had to study what the late Dame Frances Yates called 'The Art of Memory'.

Stevenson took the view that the cultivation of this art may have represented a genuine 'Renaissance' cultural input into the craft, in consideration of which, the Scottish craft may also have been open to other, more esoteric, branches of Renaissance philosophy, such as Rosicrucianism or related Hermetic strands.

Stevenson writes (*The Origins of Freemasonry*, p.49): 'The reference to the art of memory in the Second Schaw Statutes provides the only direct evidence, as opposed to strong circumstantial evidence, that in remodelling the Mason craft William Schaw was deliberately introducing Renaissance influences into the craft, and for that reason it is immensely important.'

It is a brave thought.

While I should not suppose the Scottish craft to have been immune to the cultural influences of the time – this was, after all, the late 'Elizabethan' period – I am not convinced that this test of 'Memorie' really adds up to an importation of a Renaissance 'Art of Memorie'.

The 'Art of Memorie', advocated as a form of metaphysical psychology by the Dominican friar, Giordano Bruno (1548–1600), was linked to his belief that the magus could stand foursquare upon earth with his higher mind illuminated by celestial and solar influences.

The Italian Bruno was the first person to promote the idea that the universe was infinite, containing many worlds and beings currently unknown to us. The magus could, *in potentia*, link his mind to this infinite space and total energy of the universe, present at a single point. I dare say Schaw had heard of 'the Nolan' as he liked to be called; Bruno was a famous visitor to England during the 1580s and Schaw had visited France where Bruno was also active, but this is conjecture.

Bruno took the old, medieval 'Lullian Art' of integrating knowledge in complex mind-pictures away from its basis as an aid to memory function, through visual links and associations placed in an imagined 'Theatre' construction, and on towards an illuminist parapsychology.

Bruno's meditation on archetypal, talismanic images could, in theory, lead the mind from this shadow-world of earth towards an ideal world experienced in cosmic states of consciousness. This is the 'Art of Memory' at its most florid, esoteric and exalted, bound in to pictures of God's creative nature, cabalistically expressed. However, this occult system was surely well beyond the capacities of most masters, wardens and prentices of stonemasons' lodges. Even had it been a private interest of the most daring and gifted masters, it was an unlikely candidate for a national masonic curriculum!

That some masons may have employed some kind of imaginative memory 'theatre' to help them remember 'their lines' or positions in a lodge is of course perfectly possible. It is also possible that the convening of one of these Scottish lodges required a kind of imaginative effort to render it into a more symbolically attuned environment (reaching to the heavens, for example).

However, on the basis of Occam's razor and the apparent logic of the original sentences – and even when one takes into account the later phrase 'the art of memorie and science thairof' – it would seem that the most likely meaning of the test was as a simple test of memory. This may have consisted of a recounting of old charges, for example, a traditional history, or of answers to catechetical questions. The latter we have evidence for; the vitality of a cultured, highly intellectual system of memory alive in the lodges, we do not have evidence for.

Furthermore, the world of the mason was an oral tradition. Words had to be memorised, geometrical concepts too, presumably. 'Antient memorie' does rather suggest statements inherited from past times that must be memorised to ensure the survival of the ancient craft.

That there was some mnemonic system used by some masons (including Schaw himself) cannot be discounted; they would have use for it. However, such systems had been available for many years and cannot be used to justify the idea of an importation of 'Renaissance', Hermetic or occult knowledge into the Scottish lodges by Schaw.

Taking into account the times, some forms of occult knowledge would have been current in the culture anyway. Shakespeare's plays are full of magic, of course, and Scotland had been touched by the French and Italian Renaissance experience for a century; it did not need Schaw to plug it in simply, as it were, to justify Frances Yates's view that Hermetism and Freemasonry were profoundly linked in some way. Of course they were linked! Architecture was a symbolic language: her ancient patrons; Hermes; Euclid; Pythagoras. Having said this, it is also worth raising the question as to why, if Schaw was concerned with 'educating the craft' into 'new' knowledge, the only writing permitted in the lodge by Schaw was that made by a lodge clerk. This we can see from the following paraphrased statutes of 1599:

> The warden and deacon of Kilwinning (as second lodge) are granted powers to expel all persons disobedient to acts and ancient statutes set down before 'of good memory', and all persons disobedient to kirk, craft, council and such statutes as follow made for the good order of the craft.
>
> It is ordained by the Lord Warden General that the warden and deacon elect choose and constitute a notary as ordinary clerk and scribe who shall write down indentures, discharges and other writings pertaining to the craft. Only the clerk shall write these down, and no other writing is to be admitted by the warden and deacon except writings made by the said clerk and subscribed with his hand.
>
> It is ordained by the Lord Warden General that the old, ancient acts and statutes made in former times by the predecessors of the masons of Kilwinning be faithfully observed and kept hereafter by the crafts in all times coming, and that no prentice nor craftsman, in any times hereafter be admitted nor entered but only within the kirk of Kilwinning as his parish and secured lodge, and that all candidates for entry of

prentice or fellow of crafts to be made within the said lodge of Kilwinning.

It is ordained that all fellows of craft at his entry pay towards the lodge banquet the sum of £10, with ten shillings'worth of gloves. And that he be not admitted without a sufficient essay and proof of memory and art of craft ('sufficient essay and pruife of memorie and art of craft') by the warden, deacon and quartermasters of the lodge, or else be answerable to the General Warden.

All prentices to be admitted are not to be admitted until they pay £6 towards the lodge banquet. It is ordained that the warden and deacons of the second lodge of Scotland present of Kilwinning, shall take the oath, fidelity and truth of all masters and fellows of craft within the bounds committed to your charge, yearly, that they undertake never to keep the company of cowans, nor work with them, nor any of your servants or prentices, on pain of paying the penalty contained in the former acts. It is ordained by the general warden that the warden of the lodge of Kilwinning, being the second lodge of Scotland, take trial of 'ye airt [art] of memorie and science yrof [thereof]', of every fellow of craft and every prentice; 'and in case hereat you have lost any point thereof died to them', to pay the penalty for your slothfulness: 20 shillings for fellow of craft, ten shillings for prentice, and that to be paid into the box for the common wealth yearly and hereat conform to the common use and practice of the common lodges of this realm.

'And for the fulfilling, observing and keeping of their statutes and all our acts and statutes made of before and to be made by the warden, deacons, and quarter masters of the lodges foresaid for good order keeping conform to equity justice and ancient order to the

> making and setting down whereof the General Warden
> [Schaw] has given his power and commission to the
> said wardens and yours abovewritten to set down and
> make acts conform as accords to the office law.'

The second statutes seem to have been made to placate Kilwinning, until such a time as a complete set of statutes could go before the king and be ratified and royal privileges granted, thus bringing the entire craft under a single order impossible to contradict without legal consequences. Kilwinning would not be placated, as we shall see.

Stevenson makes the interesting point that the second set of statutes does militate against the idea that Schaw himself somehow formed a new lodge system; for as soon as he tries to impose a unified system, voices arise from the footnotes of reality to make him think again.

Suddenly, the emphasis is all on the ancient rights and acts and customs.

These old 'writs' lack specificity; they were probably a varied collection of guild orders, local customs and constraints imposed by incorporations and burgh councils. Schaw probably was trying to do something new, but like all pioneers prepared to achieve something less than the ideal, King James's Master of Works seems to have been seeking a compromise – at least to begin with.

Schaw was probably trying to do the masons a favour, but some of them at least could do without it. 'What's in it for us?' would be the time-honoured cry. Besides, if an authority says 'follow the laws you have always followed – I insist!' where does the authority now lie for doing what you have always done? Once a liberty is given and practised, it can only be respected, not enforced. Privileges may be withdrawn, liberties not.

One wonders what would have occurred if Inigo Jones, for example, in England, had attempted to impose a nation-wide order on freemasons from Cornwall to Northumbria. Who knows? One thing seems likely, had he attempted such an imposition, we should probably know a great deal more about freemasons' lodges and assemblies in England. Perhaps the Schaw experience chastened any such ambition that might have lurked in the minds of English masters of works!

Rosslyn

The so-called 'Charters' granted by the masons of Scotland to William St Clair of Roslin and his heirs, dated 1601 and 1628, have been unwittingly responsible for the creation of a vast entangled orchard of myths concerning Scottish Freemasonry. That web of twisted branches and rotten fruits now extends about the world. The saddest thing about the whole matter is that, paradoxically, what began as a morale boosting exercise for freemasons has come full circle to render masons themselves victims of an international hoax of immense proportions. This, I suppose, is because it all began with a lie in the first place.

To the scholar, however, what is perhaps the most striking feature of the 1601 document, on first view, is that it is signed not only by representatives of the lodges of 'Edinburgh, Hadington, Aichison Haven and Dunfermline', but also by William Schaw.

Andrew Symson, John Robeson, P. Campbell, Jonathan Saw, J. Vallance, William Ayton, George Ayton, John Fawsetter, Thomas Petticrif, Robert Pest, Thomas Roberston, David Skowgall, Alexander Gilbert, David Spens, Andrew Alison, Archibald Angus, Robert Balze, Laurence Robeson and Henry Bannatyne all put their names to a document written 'with express consent and assent of William Schaw Master of Work to our Sovereign Lord' [James VI]. This does seem rather peculiar, if we accept the view that it had been Schaw's express intention to bring the lodges under his jurisdiction as 'Lord Warden General' of masons only three years before. For the letters dispatched to the laird of Roslin attempt to make the St Clairs (or Sinclairs) hereditary patrons and protectors of the craft in Scotland.

Something amiss here surely!

Stevenson wonders whether some kind of hereditary right or

custom had been asserted by William St Clair with respect to Scotland's masons, in a complaint against Schaw's plans akin to that asserted by the lodge of Kilwinning in 1599.

That is to say, Schaw, by signing the letter of 1601 was simply trying to accommodate current practice and make a working solution beneficial to the masons under his wardenship. 'Hereditary patron and protector' may have simply meant 'another useful patron of masons' enterprises': an honorary dignity with no institutional punch. Schaw then was doing the equivalent of a councillor meeting the representative of a foreign car firm who planned to bring a factory, and jobs, into a neglected area – not to invade the borough!

As we shall see, Robert Cooper, Librarian of the Grand Lodge of Scotland Museum and Library in Edinburgh, takes another tack; the so-called charters are just *begging letters* and carried very little institutional weight; the so-called hereditary rights of the St Clairs either never existed or were never asserted.

Either way, Schaw's participation in the 1601 letter is still puzzling. Schaw comes along for the ride, so to speak. There is no reference to his being 'Warden General'. Had he given up on his masonic plans? Was he hoping to hand over the reins?

Schaw would die in the following year. Did he know he was going to die – and had not found a fit successor? Was William St Clair a fit successor? All the evidence suggests not. Was Schaw too ill, or preoccupied, to understand fully what he was signing at the time? We do not know. In any case, Schaw could not have had any idea of how much mischief would arise out of this letter, and from the subsequent letter sent to the laird of Roslin in 1628, after Schaw's death. Like Topsy, it would just grow.

The Hoax Begins

You have not heard of the Great Rosslyn Hoax? I had better 'fill you in'. The legend had small beginnings, for sure, but a rolling stone gathers a lot of moss over 300 years. This one is so big, the little stone beneath has been forgotten. Do not take this metaphor for an allegory. You could call this legend a 'traditional history' of the Grand Lodge of Conspiracy and Social Dynamite.

The story, in its many variant forms, was made to please the members of this eternal lodge. And then one day, it gets out to the public. Then there's an appetite, and where there's an appetite, there's cash. So, it gets bigger and bigger until it finally gets completely out of control.

Legends and stories have been combined into what has become a myth. Myths get under the skin. Over 100,000 people visited Rosslyn Chapel last year. They came because *The Da Vinci Code* by Dan Brown suggested there was something of culture-shattering importance there. It was a novel, but today, fiction is truth untold.

It is as though someone had finally found the landscape of a million dreams, not hidden in the subconscious experience of an individual, but actually 'out there' – there, in Bonnie Scotland, land of romance, legend, rebels from Hollywood and Knights Templar.

Did I say Knights Templar? Oh yes, they come into it, too. Unlike the Spanish Inquisition, everyone now expects the Knights Templar. If we shared the Edwardians' delight in biscuit tins, the Templars would be on those too, along with Robbie Burns, Landseer's proud deer of the glen and Bonnie Prince Charlie heading over the sea to Skye.

In a nutshell, the hoax:

One of the lairds of Roslin's ancestors was a Knight Templar back in the 'glory days' of the 12th century. The Templars went to Jerusalem to dig up the site of Solomon's Temple. They found something. The Holy Grail? A Book? Christ's body? Depends which book you fancy. But the Knights Templar got too big for their boots. After all, they had a secret that could bribe popes and bring down the fabric of everything in the west. They were (like a famous lager) *probably* secret Gnostics, privy to the 'truth' of Christ's nature and even dedicated to preserving his 'bloodline': Jesus' and Mary Magdalene's (alleged) children. Remember them? This bloodline had been waiting a long time to get back what was rightfully theirs. They could wait a little longer. They had the Templars to protect them. And yea, even the Templars had a deeper secret. They were the outer group of a yet more secret body. So secret that we are told its name: *The Priory of Sion*. There they all were: floating helplessly in the pages of history, somewhere between myth, imagination and a royalty cheque. Just waiting for the right time to overturn the papacy and bring us back to some kind of hip rationally messianic utopia. Are you with me?

But, apparently, King Philippe le Bel of France hatched a wicked plan. This was in the early 14th century: knights, plague, peasants revolting, broadswords and goitres – all that medieval stuff you see in films. He was jealous, you see. *Who?* Philippe le Bel, King of France. He'd seen it. *Seen what?* All that boodle in the Templars' Paris preceptory where they kept a magic head and did odd rites with girdles, spitting on the cross and denying Jesus's divinity. These Templars were . . . *cool*. They were just spiritual existentialists, like some guys were back in the late Sixties. (These are the ones who didn't make it into the myth of Sixties 'radicalism': children of Nietzsche and astrology, the occult underground).

Philippe le Bel attacks the Templars in 1307 and succeeds in 'swinging' the Pope over to his cause too. Maybe he's got something on the pope: that 'myth of Christ' that had served the church so well. The old myth suited the French kings: keep the proles occupied with religion while we (the lords of the earth) do what we like. *Aux barricades, citoyens!*

Still with me? So the Templars are arrested. Thrown into dungeons. It starts getting sentimental. These warriors for *Apocalypse Then* are slow roasted by the beautiful, stinky Seine, and their smoke rises to heaven where it is recycled as revenge. If the last grand master, Jacques de Molay, wasn't exactly the new messiah (as one 'alternative history' book opined) then he was at least judge and jury on the French monarchy and the Pope.

The old legend: Jacques de Molay curses the French king – and the pope. They're both dead in a year. Must be magic. Rush the video forwards. It's the French Revolution and Louis XVI is guillotined. 'Jacques de Molay is avenged!' someone cries from the crowd of filthy *tricoteurs* who surround the bloody place: 'Jacques de Molay is avenged!' Another myth. Never mind, it all serves.

Meanwhile, back in 1307 – seven years before the last Templar grand master breathes his last. The Templars get wind of what the French king is planning. They've got to get the treasure out. *What treasure?* The Treasure. *You know*, loads of money, gold, silver, enough to buy your way out of anything. And then, that OTHER TREASURE. *Which one?* Oh, the one the Cathars escaped with from Montségur: the secret. *Who mentioned the Cathars?* They're all part of it. The truth about Magdalene and Jesus. They were a double act. And you ask *what treasure?* Gnostic books maybe. Gold. The secret treasure. Another book contract. It's an archetype, my dear. Deep in your unconscious. Read Jung? It's all about myths, you see. They're powerful. Touch the archetypes and the reader begins to tell his own story. This is getting personal. I can't put the book down; it's a page-turner, a mind burner.

So the Templars escape with the treasure. Where can they go? They're on the run like Paul McCartney and Wings. Didn't he go to Scotland? Oh Mull of Kintyre!

The powers that be are out to get them. Like they're out to get you, me and everyone else on this whole drunk, sleeping planet!

Templars are banned everywhere – *almost*. Robert the Bruce is having troubles with the Church. Who doesn't? In fact, he's been excommunicated. Bruce, that is. And he's a hero: the ideal candidate. After all, the Templars wouldn't have been too popular in the middle east. They'd rather soiled their own doorstep there. They'd lost Jerusalem.

So a group of Templars get a fleet and set sail for Argyll. Then they live there under the protection of the Bruce who does not persecute the persecuted Templars. Of course, the French Templars could perhaps have gone to Portugal where – having changed their name to the Knights of Christ – Templars carried on doing the very ordinary things that real Templars did for years. But there's not enough romance in that. No, these Templars (old as they must have been by the time of Bannockburn) fought for the Bruce and saved his skin by the skin of their teeth and the power of the red cross. Or was it, the *rosy cross*? No, that comes later.

But it wasn't Bannockburn that was the really important

thing. That was just a sideshow, guaranteeing the Templars permanent grazing rights in *Secret Scotland* where they lived invisibly for as long as you like. No, the Templars are important because of the French Revolution. The French Revolution was very bad for the Church in France. Margaret Thatcher didn't like it either. Anyone who's seen *The Scarlet Pimpernel* knows that. One of those who suffered was a priest called the Abbé Barruel. He fled from the murderous Jacobins to Merrie England where he wrote a book.

And this is what he wrote: The whole misery of the revolution was the work of secret continental Freemasons – not English ones (or Scots for that matter). It was the wicked, politicised Freemasons of France. They had inherited ancient doctrines of revenge against the Church, unbeknownst to most of the poor members. What the ordinary members couldn't see was that this Freemasonry thing was just an old heresy in new dress. Behind the dangerous prophecies of equality, fraternity and liberty (all self-contradictory), there was an upper bracket, secret conclaves. They were sorting things out from behind the scenes. That's what revolutionaries are like. Secret Societies.

Enter the German romancifier von Hammer-Purgstall. He takes the Jesuit Barruel's story and really dishes the beans. He got it down in a book: *The Mystery of Baphomet Revealed*. The Templars had survived! Secret Gnostics dedicated to the secret enslavement of humanity to a false and heretical religion. Watch where you walk; there might be a Templar in the shadows!

Meanwhile, over in Scotland, as we shall see, some Freemasons had heard something of a Templar-mason link. Maybe there was something in it. It had been told that the Templars back in the 14th century had come to Scotland, and then, by ingratiating themselves with leading families, with special orders and ceremonies had perpetuated a Templar identity through the medium of Freemasonry! There were...*higher* degrees. Scottish degrees. Freemasonry was Templarism cloaked. That would explain why there were new Templarist masonic orders at work in 18th century Germany and France. The Templars had never really gone away. They were *Secret Masters*, the hidden genius behind the tableau (now read *movie*) of the world. And Scotland was the place to be. The Templars were the good guys. They weren't spreading nasty heresies and trying to damage good religion; they were misunderstood, working for more enlightened times. Good guys. Like the Freemasons.

And what of Rosslyn Chapel? Well, thanks to the so-called *Charters* signed by William Schaw, everyone knew that the St Clairs had been hereditary 'Grand Masters' don't you know – yes, *Grand Masters*, of the Freemasons with all their symbolic orders. And that's why Rosslyn Chapel was filled with all kinds of clues. Admittedly, no one seems to have noticed these clues as being masonic until after World War II, so cunningly were they concealed for all to see. But Rosslyn is close to a Templar preceptory and, you see, that makes it Templar. And the carvings! They're sort of weird and must be masonic or Templar, or both.

Myths attract tourists.

Then there's the crypt. Full of dead knights ready to become dust at the touch, like in that Indiana Jones film about the holy grail. *What's going on down there?* Why can't we get into it? It's a conspiracy. They must have the proof, the final proof. The final proof like what is supposed to be hidden somewhere at Rennes le Château in Languedoc.

I didn't mention *Rennes le Château*? There was this French priest, you see, during the naughty 1890s when Paris went all sex and occultism. This priest, Saunière, he knew all about local Templars in the area and stumbled on to secret parchments, and they tell a secret about … well, probably about the bloodline sacred to the Merovingians and the Templars. And the Freemasons, if only they – and we – knew.

And the French priest went to St Sulpice in Paris, where he was transformed in the imagination of Dan Brown into the victim of a hideous albino murderer working zealously for a catholic organisation called *Opus Dei*. And it's all got to do with Rosslyn and the *Secret of the Templars* who also were the first to go to America and invented capitalism. Amazing!

And the whole thing, if you read the books, in the middle

east, explains why the Jews are in Palestine (Rosslyn Chapel is an imitation of the temple of Solomon) and how the west has been secretly manipulating Arabs for centuries, so that the revenge of the Templars on their old enemies from the crusades can be enacted. And the Jews and Freemasons want to rebuild the temple in Jerusalem and sacrifice something to 'the Masonic God', which is the devil or *Dajjal* of eastern lore, or something strange anyway. And the Fascists tried to stop this. They wanted the grail too and the *Spear of Longinus*, but they couldn't because of the power of Jews and American capitalists. And you see this Rosslyn Chapel and, well, there it is.

It's all because the St Clairs were given special rights over masons in Scotland. It explains everything, doesn't it? Except... It's a vast tissue of lies: incomplete and utter rubbish.

A Brief Account of the Making of a Myth

Stevenson suggested the possibility that William St Clair, laird of Roslin, might have been annoyed at the actions of William Schaw in trying to organise the craft without reference to himself. Robert Cooper (*The Rosslyn Hoax*, Lewis Masonic, 2006, pp.31ff.) makes it clear from his reading of the so-called 'charters' that nothing could have been further from the truth.

The 'St Clair Charters' were preserved by a poor catholic priest, Father Richard Hay (1661-*c*.1736). Hay went through the St Clair (or Sinclair) records (*Hay's Antiquities*; National Library of Scotland) in order to aggrandise the family. It was he who called them 'Charter[s] granted by the Masons to William Saintclair'. Other than taking note of the masons' interest in the family, Hay found nothing else worthy of mention in the matter.

Hay would doubtless love to have found that the Sinclairs were 'Grand Masters' of the masons of Scotland, or even that their ancestors were linked with the Knights Templar. He had nothing to say on such matters because there was nothing he found to make him think in such terms. The whole mythology of Sinclair-Freemasons-Templars was invented after his pauper's death in Edinburgh.

Cooper's analysis of the 'Charters' shows that they were letters begging for someone to help the lodges resolve their internal disputes because they could not afford a long legal process. They ask him to be again 'patron and protector' of their interests because the Sinclairs had enjoyed that honour in years past. They were presumably talking about the time that Sinclair's ancestor, William St Clair, Earl of Orkney (*c.*1404–*c.*1484), began building the family's collegiate chapel in 1446. This was a chapel for burying members of the family and for the use of priests to pray for the souls of the dead family members who might still be awaiting translation from Purgatory. Such collegiate chapels were not uncommon in Scotland in the period.

There was nothing unusual about the foundation other than the very ornate nature of the carvings employed, which was the wish of the laird. According to Hay, 'It came to his mind to build a house for God's service, of a most curious worke...'

The chapel was, unusually, dedicated to St Matthew. Perhaps the old laird was an eccentric. Outside of the building survives a carving of someone pulling another along with a rope round his neck, apparently blindfolded. This isn't a reference to masonic practices we have every reason to doubt existed in 1446; it is a graphic representation of Christ's parable (recorded in *Matthew*) of the blind leading the blind to their destruction. It's a pious warning. And very apt for this story.

The old laird was kind to masons and saw they were properly housed and paid; this was a family tradition relayed verbally to father Hay. Employing masons for such extensive carving work would have cost money indeed and this would, in the eyes of masons, have constituted sufficient 'patronage and protection' to render the service to the craft memorable and worthy of celebration.

Masons in their traditional history always felt free to call previous employers or people they admired (such as Euclid or Hermes) – 'patrons' or protectors of the craft. In fact, this attitude was amplified by James Anderson in the Age of Reason into the realm of the absurd. Anderson took the liberty of calling anyone who was famous and connected to architecture in the past either a warden or grand master. Even Moses gets the honour, but then, to Anderson, 'Masonry' meant more than housing masons. For him, 'Masonry' was the Platonic Idea (divine) of which building was the earthly shadow. For him, 'Masonry' was nothing less than the reflection on earth of God's creative nature.

Here lies the fundamental conceit of the masonic 'traditional history' – now translated into the public domain as 'alternative history'. The dynamic centres in the conceit that God's creation is a work of Masonry (or Geometry). Therefore, *Masonry* is a work of God's.

There's something weird in this: the potential for a cult built on a metaphor. The magnification of employer-into-patron-into-warden-into-master-into-grand master has caused no end of problems for historians, especially of Scottish Masonry. This is why one should be extremely careful in taking the word 'history' in the phrase 'traditional history' too seriously.

The crafts wrote their histories for themselves and their own purposes. If it was myth, then it was myth. If one was being very generous, one might call the traditional histories 'transcendent histories'. Masons under the eye of the Great Architect, so to speak: their works seen in the eye of heaven. They certainly transcend the realm of fact! Hollywood has never been ashamed of doing this; why should old Freemasons? After all, unlike Hollywood, they did not pen their legends for public acclaim, public broadcast or to achieve academic honours.

The masons needed the work. Furthermore, as Cooper shows, the masons tactically avoided the notion that the Sinclairs had desisted from such protection; the masons blame themselves for not having kept relations sweet. Now they hope they can entice the family back into some kind of working relationship with them. Not that they wanted William Sinclair to commission more carvings or even complete the design for the chapel. This might have been somewhere in their minds, (unlikely as such an event would have been after the Reformation) but no, the poor masons would just like him to bend his ear to judging some disputes. They humbly ask him to be their 'patron and judge'.

Again, it is difficult to understand why William Schaw would have put his name to such a request, unless he felt desperately unable to satisfy their needs himself.

Schaw's name is again respectfully given in the second letter of request of 1628. This one – over a quarter of a century later – addresses William Sinclair, the son of the previous laird, in much the same way as the previous letter. The masons must have had either long memories or extraordinary patience. It is perfectly evident that the previous laird had little or no inclination to accept the request of the stonemasons. There was no 'Charter'.

The second letter adds a new persuasive tool to the vanity of the hoped-for patron. It asserts that an unnamed Scottish monarch had previously granted 'letters of protection' of stonemasons to the Sinclairs. Unfortunately, the letters had been burned in a fire. Why was this not mentioned in the first letter? The whole thing looks rather strange, to say the least. As Cooper says, the letters do not provide the first link between the Sinclairs and Freemasonry, 'but with stonemasons of early 17th century Scotland'. It was the stonemasons who sought Sinclair out, not the other way about.

In 1628, the lodges seeking protection were Dundee, Edinburgh, Glasgow, Stirling, Dunfermline and St Andrews. Ayr is mentioned but not described as a lodge. William, the son of William Sinclair, was more inclined to see benefit in the lodges' offer than his father had been. He had had time to observe the masons' work while renovating his castle in the early 1620s. This William Sinclair took note of the stonemasons' unsubstantiated assertions that the Sinclairs had been given rights by a former king (unnamed and undated). He proceeded to send his letter to London, in the hope of getting recognition from King Charles I.

Charles wondered whether he should approve Sinclair's request of acceptance of the lodges' suit. Then he took advice as to its effect on present arrangements. A swift reaction from the King's Master of Works, Sir James Murray (d.1634) and Sir Anthony Alexander left the King in the awkward position of having to deny the double-request. Sinclair persisted but an internal court struggle between Sinclair's father-in-law (the king's chancellor) and Sir Anthony Alexander's father (the king's secretary) locked the matter up as the two countries' problems deepened.

Charles was angry at Sinclair's stirring up problems between chancellor and secretary. He accused Sinclair of 'pretending an heritable charge of the Masons of our said kingdom, though we have never given warrant for strengthening of any heritable right'. In short, the King did not accept any claim of hereditary rights vested in the Sinclair family.

Dying in 1650, Sinclair never received official sanction for the plea contained in the second so-called 'Charter'. It was, one might have thought, dead letter. Not so. The story is still told to this day that William Sinclair was granted the 'Charters' from 1630, recognising that the position of Grand Master Mason of Scotland had been hereditary in the St Clair family since being granted by James II (of Scotland) in 1441. We must, ultimately, thank James Anderson for the James II embellishment.

Anderson, 100 years after the second so-called 'Charter', was keen in his second *Book of Constitutions* (1738) to give Grand Lodge Masonry a good dose of pre-history among the ancient kings of Scotland long, long before the Union of 1707. 1441 was the Anderson date for the building of Rosslyn Chapel. All that later mythmakers had to do was put the date together with the reigning Scottish monarch and the 'Charters', and hey presto! The Myth is born. It's a short ride from there to bringing the Templars on home.

From such pips as these, the vast orchard of horror has grown.

One might think that the straight and categorical denial of the king would have been sufficient to scotch the story once and for all. But when has the truth ever been allowed to get in the way of a good story? Or scotch, for that matter? The founding of the Grand Lodge of Scotland needed a good story. They got one.

The Grand Lodge of Scotland

As Cooper writes in his scholarly account *The Rosslyn Hoax?* 'The documents [St Clair 'Charters'] were written by stonemasons for stonemasons.' They have got nothing, he says, to do with Scottish Freemasonry. They didn't then, but they have now.

I have to say something at this point that may seem peculiar. Is there not something counter-intuitive about this separation of masonry from Masonry (or Freemasonry)? It goes against the way our minds ordinarily work. We are used to the idea of words signifying something, yet here we have the discombobulating idea that you can have Masonry without masonry. This seems to have been the bizarre achievement of the Rev James Anderson, named author of the English *Constitutions* of Free and Accepted Masonry. But we're getting ahead of ourselves – or behind ourselves.

The grand lodge governing Free and Accepted Masons dates its inception from when four London lodges (according to Anderson in 1738) got together in 1716 to form a body to host a summer shindig in the June of 1717. They called the organisational umbrella a grand lodge, and elected someone to an office entirely new to Freemasonry: a grand master to oversee the midsummer fest. His name was Anthony Sayer for what it is worth because we know no more about this fellow. What followed, however, was momentous, but we're leaving that for the next chapter.

In 1736, twenty years after the four London lodges met to propose a grand lodge of some kind (according to James Anderson, a Scot, writing in 1738), four Edinburgh lodges imagined they could pull off a similar stroke – perhaps to prevent a feared encroachment from England. It was time for the world to recognise the existence of the 'Grand Lodge of Scotland', an institution not as new, its founders hoped, as might appear. And if you want to give the impression of antiquity, be sure to have some ancient manuscripts at the ready.

Robert Cooper explains the process crisply (*The Rosslyn Hoax?* p.96):

> Those who began the process, initially members of Lodge Canongate Kilwinning, which led to the creation of the Grand Lodge, followed the methods

employed at the formation of the Grand Lodge of England. Elements of Lodge Canongate Kilwinning formed a new Lodge, Lodge Leith Kilwinning, as part of the plans for the formation of the Grand Lodge of Scotland. Such a lodge was necessary because the English model dictated that only four Lodges could be 'founding' lodges. The lodges instrumental in the process were Lodge Canongate Kilwinning, The Lodge of Edinburgh and Kilwinning Scots Arms together with the newly created Leith Kilwinning. Surprisingly these Lodges did not meet officially until 15 October 1736 to decide on the procedure for the election of a Grand Master and the first regulations of the new Grand Lodge. William St Clair of Rosslyn (1700–1778), even at this late stage, was not seen as the automatic choice for Grand Master. This position was to be filled by election rather than appointment. It was not until 2 November 1736 that the members of Canongate Kilwinning recorded their desire to have St Clair as Grand Master.

As the founders of the Grand Lodge of England attempted to legitimise their operation by calling in any old documents connected with the craft, and, eventually, by Anderson's penning a 'history' to suit their purposes, the Grand Lodge of Scotland thought fit to do the same. The St Clair 'Charters' fitted the bill perfectly. Here was documentary 'proof' of an ancient unity that bound the lodges of Scotland together, now re-affirmed by the spruced-up Grand Lodge of Scotland (1736). What better idea than to pull off the smartest *coup* of all: persuade the current William St Clair to accept grand mastership! This would be seen as a legitimate, conservative act. Each side would get what they wanted. Accordingly, William St Clair was initiated into Freemasonry in Lodge Canongate Kilwinning on 18 May 1736.

On 20 October 1736, a circular issued by the four organising lodges informed other Scottish lodges of the intention to form a grand lodge; no mention was made of Sinclair's interest in the position of grand master.

On 25 November, St Mary's Lodge, Edinburgh, met to discuss the grand lodge idea. Their representatives were asked to vote for William, 8th Earl of Home (d.1761). Home had the support of Glasgow, Hamilton, Falkirk and Dunfermline, among other lodges. Nor was Home the only candidate in the ring. John, 20th Earl of Crawford, also gained support. He had experience. Crawford had been grand master of England's grand lodge only two years before. Then, the grand stroke was pulled. Just before the election, set for 30 November in Mary's Chapel, William St Clair of Rosslyn stood up to read nothing less than 'a renunciation and discharge' of his hereditary rights over the masons of Scotland.

Such magnanimity gained the swiftest reward. The electing body unanimously declared William St Clair of Roslin Grand Master Mason of the Grand Lodge of Scotland.

A letter first dispatched in 1601 had finally reached its destination!

The masons of Scotland finally had a Sinclair as protector and patron. But, of course, these masons were not masons; they were Freemasons – something quite different.

A change had been coming over the old stonemasons' lodges in Scotland over the previous century. Cooper records that 'the first admissions of non-stonemasons did not take place until 1634' (*The Rosslyn Hoax?* p.98). Since that time, gentlemen had taken an interest in the relics of what education was now declaring to be an ancient art with Hermetic and classical liberal-art status – with the hint of secrets, even magic of an indeterminate kind.

By the time the Grand Lodge of Scotland was constructed, the English usage of 'Freemason' had entered the field, or glen, though the word 'accepted' was understood as 'admitted', which to most must have appeared simply a semantic issue, as it does today.

With a marvellous sense of raw irony, Cooper has observed

that in 1628, Dundee, Edinburgh, Glasgow, Stirling, Dunfermline, St Andrews and Masons from Ayr had all signed the second so-called 'Charter'. How is it then that in 1736, these lodges had forgotten that they already had a 'hereditary Grand Master' and did not need to elect a new one?

In January 1737, Aitchison's Haven lodge (whose ancient members had signed the first St Clair 'Charter' (or begging letter) seems to have recognised this discrepancy. It might even have looked as though the Sinclairs had given up a traditional status for a 'mess of potage'. Aitchison's Haven lodge undertook 'not to trouble the Grand Lodge nor themselves farther, they choosing to stand on their own footing and rights as they have done these many years and ages past' (*The Grand Lodge of Scotland – Historical Sketch 1736–1986. The Grand Lodge of Scotland Year Book 1986*, p.73).

Many other lodges – nearly all of which were stonemasons' lodges – decided to avoid the new grand lodge. As Robert Cooper has written, 'This is hardly a ringing endorsement by lodges over which the Sinclairs were alleged hereditary Grand Masters!'

Kilwinning

Readers will recall how when William Schaw attended a meeting on St John's Day 1599 at the Royal Palace of Holyrood, issues regarding the status of the lodge of Kilwinning were clarified but not wholly resolved. Stung at not having been mentioned in Schaw's first statutes (1598), Kilwinning sent a commissioner to establish the lodge's superior time-honoured status.

The second set of statutes is heavily focused on Kilwinning's interests. This would not be the last time that the lodge at Kilwinning would be a thorn in the side of unitary authority. Indeed, the name of Kilwinning would come to appear time and time again in the documentation of a number of degrees associated (in the 18th century and beyond) with a supposed pre-Schavian golden age of antique Scottish (and Templarist) Freemasonry.

Some readers may be familiar with phrases such as 'the Rose Croix of Heredom of Kilwinning', or the 'HRDM of Kilwinning' or suchlike. Kilwinning has become a kind of Camelot within the myth of ancient Scottish Freemasonry, such that the very phrase 'Scottish Freemasonry' even today is used as an awe-struck guarantee of some great mystical secret tradition behind mere 'blue' (or craft) Freemasonry.

The 'Scottish Rite' has a particular history in France, Germany and the United States – and we shall look at aspects of it in due course (including its links with Jacobite, occult or magical masonic, or quasi-masonic systems). However, first we should be acquainted with some facts about Kilwinning: the real Kilwinning, not the mythic identity. The latter is not to be found on the banks of the River Garnock, some twenty-five miles southwest of Glasgow, but within the labyrinths of romantic imagination.

In December 1999, the 'Mother Lodge' of Kilwinning celebrated 400 years of known existence. For many of those years, Kilwinning had been more of a myth than a place. For example, after the foundation of London's grand lodge in 1717, writer and Freemason, Dean Jonathan Swift, published, anonymously, a letter in Dublin. The letter purported to come from the 'Grand Mistress of the Society of Female Free-Masons'. With Swift's characteristic humour, he linked the 'famous old Scottish lodge of Kilwinning' with 'the Branch of the lodge of Soloman's Temple', later known as the Knights of St John of Jerusalem and the brother order of the Templars. This story would run and run, without further endorsement from the *Grand Mistress* himself.

Less than a month after the declaration of Sinclair as the first 'Grand Master Mason of the Grand Lodge of Scotland', a banquet was held in a restaurant in the Rue du Paon, Paris.

On 26 December 1736, Scotsman Chevalier (Order of Lazarus) Andrew Michael Ramsay, whom we have encountered before, inspired his listeners with the vision of a Masonry that united all virtuous and enlightened men, men who possessed a love of the fine arts, science and religion. He prophesied that in time, 'the interests of the Fraternity shall become those of the whole human race'.

Ramsay saw parallels between Freemasonry and the mystery societies of classical and late antique times. He took the traditional view of Hermetic enthusiasts that the rites celebrated in the old mystery cults bore the remnants of the unpolluted religion of Noah and the Patriarchs. Progress would mean getting back to the original, pristine sources of power and understanding. Freemasonry had a role to play in restoring the primitive unity of humankind.

This was a big idea.

Ramsay stated that the order was revived during the crusades when 'many princes, lords and citizens associated themselves, and vowed to restore the Temple of the Christians in the Holy land, to employ themselves in bringing back their architecture to its first institution':

> The Kings, princes, and lords returned from Palestine to their own lands, and there established divers Lodges. At the time of the last Crusades many lodges were already erected in Germany, Italy, Spain, France, and from thence in Scotland, because of the close alliance between the French and the Scots. James, Lord Steward of Scotland, was Grand Master of a Lodge established at Kilwinning, in the West of Scotland in 1286, shortly after the death of Alexander III, King of Scotland, and one year before John Balliol mounted the throne. This lord received as Freemasons into his lodge the Earls of Gloucester and Ulster, the one English, the other Irish.
>
> (From the 'Grand Lodge' version of Ramsay's *Oration*, as reproduced in *Andrew Michael Ramsay and his Masonic Oration*, by Dr Lisa Kahler in *Heredom*, Vol.1, 1992, *Transactions of the Scottish Rite Research Society*, Washington DC).

As a result of this carefully worded propaganda, the myth

gathered new and exalted moss. It was easy to conclude from a superficial reading that Freemasonry had somehow descended from crusading orders; Ramsay associates it particularly with the Knights of St John of Jerusalem, which, for him, explained having St John as patron saint of the order.

Anderson seems to have been aware of the content of the speech when he put together his revised traditional history of Freemasonry, published in 1738. But there he was careful to insist that it was the virtues and order of Masonry that was recognised by the warrior knights as a model, not the other way around. That *Freemasonry was the parent model for the knightly order* was Anderson's emphasis. However, it did not take much twisting to come up with the opposite view; Freemasonry came from the knightly orders, especially if it was chivalric Masonry (so popular on the continent) that one was proposing.

This confusion has resulted in the very curious language to be found in chivalric masonic orders to this day. The mixture of masons' images, biblical themes and chivalric ones is decidedly odd, especially when admixed with alchemical language and Rosicrucian atmosphere (as it was). These were heavy-handed contrivances dressed in an exalted language that undercut what might otherwise have appeared ridiculous. One might have expected the orders to suffocate from surfeit of nomenclature; but many expect to pass the narrow gate loaded with honours. The only way found to make for some kind of clarity out of the confusion (universalist/Christian; masons/knights; alchemy/science; romance/philosophy) was to try and keep the orders apart. But who in the middle ages could ever have come up with a title like 'Prince Mason' or any of the variants on the 'Sublime Knight of the Royal Secret type' that permeate the degrees of the 'Scottish Rite.'

Contrary to Ramsay's stirring stuff, Kilwinning Lodge first appears not in the annals of post-crusading Scottish kingship, but in the Schaw Statutes, though it is perfectly clear from the contents that the lodge was older and that it clasped what it considered ancient rights to its bosom.

It is also clear that the kirk of Kilwinning was somehow

important to the lodge. This strongly suggests an old relationship with the now ruined abbey of Kilwinning, a kindred association that we have observed in looking at the craft in Cheshire and in the Staffordshire moorlands of England.

The lodge at Aitchison's Haven, for example, may have been connected with the Cistercian monks of Newbattle Abbey in Midlothian. The monks there received a charter from King James V in 1526. The charter gave them authority to build a harbour. The harbour was to assist the shipping of coal from the Barony of Prestongrange. First called Millhaven, the name changed to Aitchison's Haven. It is possible that the now defunct lodge may first have assembled for this purpose.

Likewise there is an oral tradition that the 'Mother Lodge' of Kilwinning owes its origin to the arrival of French monks in the 12th century. Previous records may not be adduced as evidence because perhaps there were no previous records. Kilwinning's chartulary (records) disappeared in the 1560s during the iconoclasm of the Reformation.

Kilwinning in myth still bears a magical dimension. There is the whiff of Celtic twilight about stories of a holy mountain that would have enticed the filmmaking skills of Powell and Pressburger. Whence might these associations derive? Apart from Vaughan's *Lumen de Lumine*, referred to in chapter eight, as the inspiration for Robert Samber's joke about 'mountains of venison' in 1722, there really is a Celtic angle to the Kilwinning story.

When in the early 12th century reformed Benedictine monks arrived in Scotland from France they encountered Culdees. These were Celtic monks who celebrated a Christianity of a distinctive kind with strong emphases on nature as a manifestation of God's will. Celtic Christianity explains the name of Kilwinning.

St Winnin was an Irish monk who arrived at the mouth of the Garnock in 715 AD. His arrival led to a community of monks. This community was called a 'kil' in Gaelic, from the Latin '*cella*' or cell. Kilwinning was the cell of Winnin. Irish manuscripts referred to these monks as *Cele De*, allies of God: in Latin, *Coli Dei*. The word was pronounced as 'Culdee'.

The monks began construction of their monastery in about 1140. Kilwinning grew into a rich foundation. In 1309, the Abbot, Bernard de Linton, became King Robert Bruce's Chancellor. It was he who, in 1314, recorded the Bruce's heroic words before the battle of Bannockburn secured Scottish independence. The same Abbot of Kilwinning was responsible for drafting the famous 'Declaration of Arbroath' in 1320.

The abbey was demolished by the 5th Earl of Glencairn, a follower of John Knox, zealous firebrand of Scottish protestantism. The catastrophe of the religious houses must have affected the incomes of masons in some areas. Perhaps this in part explains William Schaw, the catholic's interest in organising the lives of stonemasons in 1598.

Certainly, there existed no Knights Templar to come to the masons' aid. According to D. Murray Lyon's *History of the Lodge of Edinburgh*, (Tercentenary Edition, pp.9-11), by 1643, the lodge wished itself to be known as 'the antient ludge of Scotland'. It was apparently assembling in the upper room of an inn. For reasons that are not always easy to interpret, Kilwinning, like other lodges, began admitting people who were not earning their living from stonemasonry in the 17th century. Kilwinning's first entries for non-masons occur during the 1670s. The Earl of Cassillis became deacon of the lodge in 1672. Gentlemen Sir Alexander Cunningham and Joseph Cunningham of Carlurg were also admitted, to be joined in 1674 by the 8th Earl of Eglinton, Lord Cochrane.

Minutes made in 1686 state that initiations should take place only once a year. It may be presumed that some kind of ritual, or adapted ritual, was in place for the purpose of admitting non-masons who would not need to have their work tried or wait seven years to become a fellow of craft!

Kilwinning is mentioned in the earliest known ritual manuscripts of Scotland. At the formation of the Grand Lodge of Scotland in 1736, Kilwinning's presence and status again became an issue. As her pre-1642 minutes were unavailable, Edinburgh again gained primacy, with Kilwinning second. This situation mirrors somewhat the old disputes that flare up from time to time between Yorkshire Freemasons and the United Grand Lodge of England.

In 1743, Kilwinning, uncomfortable with secondary status, seceded from the Grand Lodge of Scotland. This independence, pursued throughout the remainder of the century, did nothing but assist a growing sense of Kilwinning's mythical status. It became a mountain far away, distant on a hill, shrouded in mist from the eyes of the vulgar, like Brigadoon. If you were in Paris, or Washington DC, Kilwinning was a long, long way away. Reality is obscured by distance.

For sixty-three years after secession, the lodge issued charters to distant lodges. The fun didn't quite end when, in 1806, the lodge finally succumbed to the Grand Lodge of Scotland's special inducement. In recognition of its ancient status, now hallowed in myth and legend and known throughout the world, Kilwinning was permitted the distinction of referring to itself as 'Lodge Number 0'. To this day, the lodge proudly carries this potent zero, coupled to the unequivocal title, 'Mother Lodge of Scotland'.

The Mason Word

Such knowledge as we have of Scottish lodge catechisms comes from the end of the 17th century. Three documents in particular have attracted the attention of scholars.

First, the *Edinburgh Register House* MS. dated 1696, was so called because it was found (in 1930) among the historical records of Edinburgh's General Register House. (There is a reproduction in *AQC*, xliii). The manuscript contains: 'Some Questiones Anent [about] the Mason word 1696', in two parts: 'Some Questiones that Masons use to put to those who have ye word before they will acknowledge them', and 'The forme of giving the Mason word'.

Its contents are very similar to the *Chetwode Crawley* MS. Like the previous manuscript, its early history is unknown. It turned up in a lot of second-hand works sold by a collector around 1900. In 1904 it was donated to the Grand Lodge of Ireland and named after the Irish masonic historian, W. J. Chetwode Crawley.

Entitled *The Grand Secret or The forme of giving the Mason-word*, a second part contains 'Some Questions that Masons use to put to those who profess to have the Mason word, befor they will acknowledge them'. Whether all of the contents of these documents were peculiar to Scotland is not certain. Nor is it certain whether their use was widespread or localised. Some of the terms, such as 'interprintices' for apprentices appear to be more Scottish than English. On the other hand, some of the catechetical questions and responses are similar to those found in *Sloane* MS. 3329 – an apparently English catechism from the end of the 17th century with elements in common with the Scottish catechisms.

Then there is the *Kevan* MS. This manuscript is again similar to the two already referred to, but was found in Berkshire and, as far as we can tell, was written in England. Before one rushes to the conclusion that Scottish (or Irish) practices formed the basis for (contemporary or later) English usage, it must be said that these manuscripts are isolated items. They have survived from a period where the collected evidence leads one to think that masonic material was shared among masons in England, Scotland and Ireland, with some colourful variants of terminology.

Considering the nature of contract work – especially large contracts – it would not have been much use having a secret mode of mutual recognition whose efficacy stopped at the borders of any of these countries in the old British Isles! When young James Anderson, for example, left Scotland for London soon after the Union of England and Scotland in 1707, his 'Scottish' masonic identity seems to have encountered no difficulty in being accepted by at least some English lodges. It would be interesting to know if there were any problems.

Such knowledge might help explain the mystery of Anderson's motivation, since he played such a significant part in the formation of the grand lodge system, over the head of previous practice. Professor Stevenson's conjecture that Scottish practice might have been used as a template to bring to London on account of visits made to Scotland by Desaguliers and Anderson gainsays the available evidence. These manuscripts give us insights but should be used circumspectly. We simply do not know what were the common internal practices of lodges in Scotland, Ireland or England as to words used, or how different customs were among lodges dominated by stonemasons and those dominated by gentlemen. We do not even know for what specific use the above manuscripts were prepared, or who prepared them.

Stevenson (*Origins*, p.136) takes the view that written catechisms were for the use of 'non-operatives' to learn, taken down from long memory, perhaps by the clerks of the lodge or by non-operatives themselves, presumably from stonemasons. This is logical conjecture. The only thing we can be sure of is that copies of the *Old Charges* begin to proliferate in England and Scotland as the 17th century advanced out of the worst of the civil wars, and as more gentlemen took an interest in the ancient craft.

We can be reasonably sure that the reading of the charges and traditional history of the craft constituted an element of initiation and, perhaps, of other meetings as well. The giving of a secret word also appears to be so common an idea associated with Masonry at the time that it may have formed the climax of a fellow craft ritual. Where there was no central authority, lodges could please themselves, within, presumably, an innately conservative tradition.

Professor Stevenson offers a kind of 'catholic' impression of a late 17th century catechism. He does this by combining the *Register House* MS. with some elements of the *Chetwode Crawley* MS., the *Sloane* MS., together with a manuscript from the early 18th century. The early 18th century manuscript is called the *Dumfries No. 4* MS., discovered in 1891 among the records of the 'Old Lodge of Dumfries'. The earliest known reference to the lodge of Dumfries (now the *Dumfries and Kilwinning* lodge No 53) is from 20 May 1687.

Stevenson's combination helps us to feel more a part of

proceedings that surely took place, perhaps at inns, private rooms or even ruined places around the time of persistent Jacobite rebellion after the failure of King James II to regain his throne following the 'Glorious Revolution' of 1688. Britain would suffer intermittent political turmoil, chiefly over questions to do with religious affiliation, for the next 50 years.

Are you a Mason?

Yes.

How shall I know it?

You shall know it in time and place convenient.

(Remark: The forsaid answer is only to be made
when there is company present who are not
Masons. But if there be no such company by, you
should answer by signs, tokens and other points of
my entrie).

What is the first point?

Tell me the first point, I'll tell you the second. The
first is to heill [cover] and conceall. Second, under
no less pain, which is then cutting of your throat.
For you most make that sign when you know that.

Where wes you entered?

At the honourable lodge.

What makes a true and perfect lodge?

Seven masters, five entered apprentices, a dayes
journey from a borroughs town without bark of dog
or crow of cock.

Does no less make a true and perfect lodge?

Yes, five Masons and three entered apprentices etc.

Does no less?

The more the merrier, the fewer the better chear.

What is the name of your lodge?

Kilwinning.

How stands your lodge?

East and west as the Temple of Jerusalem.

Where wes the first lodge?

In the porch of Solomon's Temple.

Are there any lights in your lodge?
Yes, three. The northeast, southwest, and eastern
passage. The one denotes the Master Mason, the
other the warden, the third the setter croft
[corruption of fellow craft].
Are there any jewells in your lodge?
Yes, three, perpend esler [ashlar], a square
pavement, and a broad oval.
Where shall I find the key of your lodge?
Three foot and a half from the lodge door under a
perpend esler and a green divot. But under the lap
of my liver where all the secrets of my heart lie.
Which is the key of your lodge?
A weel hung tongue.
Where lies the key?
In the bone box.

Stevenson makes the interesting observation (*Origins*, p.145)
that 'The key or secret contained in the grave is not openly
referred to in the very earliest catechisms, but the key that lay
below a green divot surely indicates a grave.' This comment
refers to the 'grave' idea behind the 'third degree', which
emerges in a 1726 copy of the *Old Charges* with reference to
Noah being 'raised' from the grave in search of a secret, which
is not found.

Stevenson continues: 'This becomes explicit in the
Dumfries No. 4 catechism. It includes a question about the
building of Solomon's Temple, and the answer emphasises
Hiram's part in the work. This is followed immediately by:

Where lies the master?
In a stone trough under the west window looking to
the east waiting for the son rising to sett his men to
work.

(Knoop, *Early Masonic Catechisms*, p.66)

If the setting of the grave referred to in the catechism were
indeed Solomon's temple (whose porch was in the east), the

grave under the west window, would put the 'master' within the Holy of Holies, where the secret is kept. If the Holy of Holies – wherein only the high priest could enter once a year – was the original setting for the master's rising, one might well intuit a certain gnostic influence within the conception.

In the modern 'Third', Hiram Abif is, notably, interred *outside* the Holy of Holies, lest the place of God's presence be defiled by a corpse. A master rising in the Holy of Holies then would not – or could not, theologically speaking – be dead. The secret key is alive in the holiest part of the inner temple.

The 'Word' is only the beginning; the quest for lost knowledge goes on. Such a secret, accessible by the 'Key', would be of far greater worth than the knowledge of a mere recognition word. But then, the key point about the 'Mason Word' is that it renders visible to the master what is invisible to outsiders. It seems to denote a way of *seeing*.

In this respect, the Scottish evidence concerning the mason word is notable for its linkage to the idea of 'second sight' or heightened powers of intuition, foreknowledge, perception and spiritual awareness.

The Muses Threnodie and Second Sight

In a famous poem called *The Muses Threnodie, or, Mirthfull Mournings on the Death of Master Gall* (1638), Henry Adamson, master of the Perth Song School, poses an imagined dialogue between two old friends. One of them, Mr Gall (a burgess of Perth who died in 1628) reassures a Mr Ruthven that the bridge across the Tay would yet recover from its destruction by natural causes in 1621:

> Thus Gall assured me it would be so,
> And my good Genius truly doth it know:
> For what we do presage is not in grosse,
> For we be brethren of the Rosie Crosse;
> We have the Mason Word and second sight,
> Things for to come we can foretell aright.

It makes a grand advertisement for joining the masons – or the brethren of the Rosy Cross – but it only serves to tell us that the author considered himself a man who listened to his deepest inner voice.

'My good Genius' refers to the Neoplatonic conception (widespread in Renaissance philosophy) of the extra-dimensional being, the *daemon*, or *genius* above the soul of the individual. What the poet, and those he associates his insight with, know, is not *in grosse*, that is things seen through the mortal eye.

Think of matter as a dense, dark substance that obstructs the higher light casting a shadow and you'll get the idea. The poet is seeing with the light of higher perception. He is perceiving through an enlightenment of the spirit, or inner eye. This leads him through the visible to the invisible. His conscious mind just receives the message.

The references to the 'Mason Word' and 'Rosy Cross' undoubtedly suggest the idea of seeing what is invisible to the ordinary 'vegetable' (material-seeing) eye, bound by time and space.

The mason word was believed to convey connections between masons unknown and invisible to those around them. The word need not, I think, be seen only as a spoken word, but also as a gesture and canny knack of knowing. Of course, as Stevenson has pointed out, in a social setting suffused with the seriousness of religion, the 'Word' already suggested the source of salvation and power.

In the 17th century, the implication of a 'canny knack of knowing' might suggest witchcraft, and the kirk would be quick to investigate. Thomas Aquinas in the 13th century had developed a doctrine of pacts between men and demons, affected through secret signs and words audible to demons and those who had congress with them. The making of such a sign or word presupposed an *ipso facto* pact.

Perhaps that is why Adamson adds the association of such powers with the brethren of the Rosy Cross. The brethren of the Rosy Cross were known to the wise as good Christians whose legendary invisibility only cloaked them from the gaze of the vulgar and the sinful. They were 'in the world but the world knew them not'. They were purified and reformed Christians bringing angelic knowledge to the true and unimpeachably worthy believer.

Even so, this was dangerous ground. The mason word could even suggest political conspiracy. John Stewart, Earl of Traquair was accused in 1637 of treachery by supporters of Charles I. They said 'he had the Masone word, among the nobilitie' (D. Laing, ed., *A relation of proceedings concerning the affairs of the kirk in Scotland, from August 1637 to July 1638*, Bannatyne Club, Edinburgh, 1830).

The implication is of some conspiratorial access to persons hostile to the king. The word then seems, by 1637, to have become a kind of slang word for 'a nod and a wink' with implications of membership of a secret cabal. Secrecy was power. There was discussion of the 'meason word' at the general assembly of the Church of Scotland in the summer of 1649. The extreme presbyterian 'kirk party' were on the look-out for anything that might have brought God's wrath upon the country. The church's district assemblies – the presbyteries – were asked for their opinion.

History has not left us record of their opinions on the matter.

In 1652, however, one James Ainslie's appointment to the ministry was frustrated by an enquiry by the elders of the kirk session of Minto in Roxburghshire. They had a poor opinion of the mason word. Resistance to appointing Ainslie was on the basis that he had the mason word. Requests for further information were sent out to neighbouring presbyteries. These resulted in reassurances that many in 'purer' times (presumably the 'golden age' of the Knoxian reformation) had had the word and been good Christians, respected, learned, pious and so on. This reassurance did not end the matter; the case was brought to the synod.

After much searching enquiry, Ainslie took up the ministry in Minto. He died, aged 94, in 1702.

Robert Kirk, minister of Aberfoyle in Perthshire, entrusted some of his knowledge of Scottish folklore to the pages of a treatise completed in 1691 entitled 'The secret commonwealth'.

An appendix headed *A Succinct Account of my Lord of Tarbott's relationes in a letter to the Honourable Robert Boyle* dealt with the subject of second sight, a phenomenon Kirk was sure was peculiar to the highlands of Scotland. Kirk did not believe second sight supernatural but rather an improvement of perception as one might find in animals' superior smell and hearing senses. In addition to second sight, Kirk added the mason word, brownies (faeries), charms and 'being Proof of Lead' (bullet proof) as five Scottish 'Curiosities' he had not observed elsewhere:

> The Mason-Word, which tho some make a Misterie of it, I will not conceal a little of what I know; it's like a Rabbinical tradition [he may mean Kabbalistic tradition] in a way of comment on Iachin and Boaz the two pillars erected in Solomon's Temple; with an addition of som secret signe delivered from hand to hand, by which they know, and become familiar one with another.
>
> (The secret common-wealth and A short treatise of charms and spells, ed. S. Sanderson, London, 1976, quoted in Stevenson, *The Origins of Freemasonry*, p.133)

This may, as Stevenson has observed, be the first British reference to a masonic handshake! But whether it was a peculiarly Scottish practice we cannot properly say. Kirk was a Scot. How much did he know of what occurred in lodges in England?

Kirk's work was written in the same year (1691) that John Aubrey reported the 'adoption' of Sir Christopher Wren by a convention of the 'Fraternity of Adopted Masons' at St Paul's Churchyard, London. One wonders whether Wren was given the mason word on this occasion.

1691...

Elias Ashmole's era was fast passing; the elder fellow of Accepted Free Masonry would be dead within a year.

It is time we returned to London to see what had been happening since we last visited Masons Hall, off Basinghall Street, London, in the company of Elias Ashmole, his fellows and their 'new accepted' brethren, on 11 March 1682.

The lives of the next generation of Accepted Masons in England were soon to be considerably affected by the appearance of a certain clergyman from Scotland.

Chapter Ten

The Great Masonic Hijack

> The United Grand Lodge of England is the governing body of Craft Freemasonry controlling subordinate lodges which work only the three degrees of Entered Apprentice, Fellowcraft and Master Mason.
>
> The Grand Lodge of England was formed on 24 June 1717 in London as the first Grand Lodge in the world.
>
> (John Hamill, Director of Communications, United Grand Lodge of England; *The Craft*, Crucible, 1986.)

It is highly likely that the spread of Free and Accepted Masonry around the world was a result of the establishment of the Grand Lodge of England. This event is customarily held to have taken place in London on John the Baptist's day, 24 June 1717. Nearly 300 years later, and with the benefit of hindsight, that is how it must appear to us. But the statement begs another question, one for which hindsight offers less than we might wish.

What was the establishment of the premier Grand Lodge of England the result of?

Accepted Free Masons before Grand Lodge

A note was found attached to a manuscript copy of the *Natural History of Wiltshire* (1685) in the hand of its author, antiquarian John Aubrey:

> This day (May 18th Being Munday 1691 after
> Rogation Sunday) is a great Convention at St Paul's
> Church of the Fraternity of the Adopted Masons
> where Sr. Christopher Wren is to be adopted as a
> Brother.

This is also reported in manuscripts of the contemporary
diarist, John Evelyn:

> Sir Christopher Wren (architect of S.Paules) was at a
> convention (at S.Paules 18 May 1691), of Free-
> masone adopted a Brother of that Society; shore have
> ben kings of this sodality.
> (John Evelyn, MS. 173, *f*9, British Library)

Wren, most famous as the architect of St Paul's Cathedral, had
been president of the Royal Society (1680–82). He was a
famous architect who himself found architecture considerably
less compelling than his other scientific interests, especially
microscopy and biology.

Wren was an artist. He liked a challenge, and most
architecture (once he had mastered the geometrical content)
bored him. If he was 'adopted' as an 'Accepted' Freemason, then
the very late date of that 'adoption' (whatever that may have
been) would be consistent with all that we know of 'Accepted'
Freemasonry fellowship practice.

'Accepted' Freemasonry, unlike the masonry of Scotland
that we have examined, was not, as far as we can tell, directly
connected to the process of educating stonemasons. On the
other hand, this 'adoption' granted to the great Wren may
have been more in the manner of the Scottish practice of
'admitting' gentlemen to a stonemasons' body, or lodge. Perhaps the assembled craftsmen experienced a fit of springtime
enthusiasm, offering a sign of thanks for the work Wren's
designs had provided for them.

This 'adoption' was certainly not an invitation to 'run the
business' of individual lodges. It was most likely a dignity

granted in gratitude for Wren's role in handling disputes between craftsmen and employers over matters of wages and contracts. We know that Wren was the place of last resort in such disputes during this period. Securing payment to a widow whose husband had died 'on the job', for example, was a matter of great importance to craftsmen working on long-term projects. That Wren's good offices were so used is attested in the rebuilding records of Lichfield Cathedral during the 1670s (Lichfield Record Office). It is even possible that Wren had formerly joined the 'Acception', but lower ranking stonemason lodge members were simply unaware of it.

Wren's connection with a distinct body of 'Free Masons' is attested elsewhere. At his death in 1723, several newspapers referred to the architect as that 'worthy Free Mason'. (viz: *Post Boy*, No 5245; see *New Light on Sir Christopher Wren*, Matthew Scanlan, *Freemasonry Today*, issue 18, p.22)

We know that Wren's son joined a lodge of 'Free and Accepted Masons'. Christopher Wren *junior* belonged to the Old St Paul's Lodge, which does not seem so surprising given the amount of time his father had to spend in the vicinity. The younger Wren served as the lodge's master in 1729, after his father's death. Since 1691 (the date in Aubrey's account of Wren's 'adoption' at St Paul's church), that lodge had met at the Goose and Gridiron tavern in St Paul's churchyard; the first 'Grand Lodge' was formed at the Goose and Gridiron.

Christopher Wren *junior* was present when mason-contractor Edward Strong, his son and other Accepted Free Masons placed the last stone on the lantern of St Paul's in 1708 (as reported by Stephen [grandson of Sir Christopher] Wren, in *Parentalia*). Edward Strong (1652–1723) was an Oxfordshire mason, the most important contractor to have worked on the cathedral. Strong was upper (or senior) warden of the Masons' Company in 1694.

Edward Strong *junior* belonged to a lodge of Free and Accepted Masons, which met at the Swan, East Street, Greenwich (1725 list), seven years after serving as Master of the Masons' Company.

In the same year as Wren's 'Adoption', John Thompson was the Master of the Masons' Company. Thompson's workshop supplied work for Wren. Thompson, an Accepted Free Mason was present at the 'Acception' of several brethren, which took place with Elias Ashmole as senior fellow at Masons' Hall, Basinghall Street in March 1682 (see chapter eight).

High on the south side of St Paul's Cathedral sits a huge carving of a phoenix, symbolising the rebirth of the cathedral after the Great Fire of 1666. The phoenix was an alchemical image. In Ashmole's transcription of alchemist Norton's *Ordinall of Alchemy*, 1477, (*Theatrum Chemicum Britannicum*, 1652), it is recorded that a number of professions, including the freemasons, 'love this profound philosophy'.

The phoenix carved on St Paul's was the work of Wren's expert carver, Caius Gabriel Cibber (pronounced 'Cibert' in the French manner). Cibber had been attached to the workshop of ffreemason and King's Master Mason Nicholas Stone ('accepted' at Masons' Hall in 1638).

Cibber's father inherited his workshop from the Stone family. Cibber's son was an Accepted Free Mason. The domination of mason-contractors within Accepted Free Masonry before the appearance of a grand lodge in London has only recently been recognised as significant for understanding anomalies in Grand Lodge's curious beginnings.

For example, Bernard E. Jones's *Freemasons' Guide and Compendium* (London, 1956) was not fully aware of the significance of this trade domination at the beginning of the 18th century. Jones perpetuated the old and comforting assumption that 'Accepted' Free Masonry was above all represented by 'gentlemen' even before the founding of the grand lodge. Regarding the highly aristocratic *Rummer and Grapes* lodge (later *The Horn*, or *Old Horn*) in Westminster, Jones concluded that it 'appears to have been a lodge of accepted and speculative masons who had no connection at that time with the mason trade'.

The *Horn* lodge, Westminster, apart from being one of the four participants in the formation of a grand lodge in 1716, was rich in government links. Some of its members appear to have played a lead part in the wresting of Accepted Free Masonry away from its trade context. As such, one might indeed think that this was a lodge of gentlemen pursuing 'speculative Freemasonry' entirely apart from the trade. However, an examination of the 1725 Grand Lodge list of its members reveals that William Woodman (c1654–c1731) was a member of the lodge. The presence of a senior working freemason in the lodge is telling, as we shall see.

Pre-1716 rules (repeated even by Anderson) state that it could not have been founded without the presence of at least one working freemason, along with at least five Accepted Free Masons.

Woodman's trade concerns went back a long way. He worked as a monumental sculptor on the monument to the 2nd Viscount Newhaven and executed other high quality masonry work for that family. He was a member of the Masons' Company in March 1682 when Elias Ashmole attended the Acceptions of a number of members of that company in Masons' Avenue, Basinghall Street.

It is now clear that a vivid world of Accepted Free Masonry existed at the top of the world of stone masonry craftsmanship before the establishment of a grand lodge. It is also clear that Anderson's second book of *Constitutions* (1738) involves a certain amount of special pleading to justify a doctored version of events. It is significant that the first 'victim' of the 'official story' was Sir Christopher Wren.

The Takeover

While in the 1723 *Constitutions* Wren is referred to respectfully as the architect of the extraordinary roof to Oxford's Sheldonian Theatre, references to Wren in the revised 1738 edition are less flattering. By 1738, Grand Lodge was well established.

Masonry, Anderson asserts in his second book of *Constitutions*, was apparently in need of 'reviving' in the early 18th century, especially after the 'neglect' of the lodges by supposed 'Grand Master' Christopher Wren. Wren had died in 1723 and was in no position to take this canard on. By 1738, the new regulatory body called 'Grand Lodge' was in full swing and in a position to re-write history – or rather to write it for the first time. The process was not accomplished in the spirit of an historical investigation but in a spirit informed by the fantasy-scape of the old traditional histories and the requirements of the new body. Anderson turned the history to suit the claims of the new grand lodge.

In fact, there is no evidence whatsoever that grand masters existed before 1717 (and even that date is arguable), no evidence that Wren was 'Grand Master', no evidence that Wren 'neglected' the lodges, and we only have Anderson's word concerning the first origins of a grand lodge. All the evidence points to a propaganda exercise. For example, everything we can glean about Accepted Free Masonry before 1717 suggests that it was not something that could be 'neglected' since bodies were intended to be highly selective and contained phenomena of specialised, exclusive interest. There was no interest in increasing membership for its own sake.

There was always a need in the craft for more patrons and funding for rebuilding London was winding down by the end of 1716, but that is hardly the point. The only persons who could have 'neglected' lodges were the members themselves!

In short, what Wren had 'neglected' to do was to transform the existing system into the (then) undreamed of 'Grand Lodge'. It's a bit like saying that medieval theologian Thomas Aquinas had 'neglected' to produce the Renaissance!

Anderson was a Whig, Wren a Tory. Politics was involved. Blame the old (pro-Stuart) order! The only administrative body for which we have any evidence in London is the London Masons' Company, and if Anderson thought they were doing a bad job, he should have said so. He shows no interest at all in the company, perhaps for legal reasons. We cannot be at all sure that 'Accepted' Free Masons even met outside Masons' Hall for anything other than congenial festive purposes.

The real setting of Masonry in London, the London Company of Masons, is airbrushed out of history without a murmur. Anderson does not seem to have understood Accepted Free Masonry as practised in London; he certainly has practically nothing to tell us about it. Anderson's 'Masonry' is a fantasy of Masonry based on his own experience and what he thinks people should know about it. This picture of 'Masonry' was not accomplished in innocence or even as a result of simple and admissible ignorance. There was Method in his fantasy, as we shall see.

It would have all been so much simpler if Anderson could have started his Masonry from the date he affixes to the grand lodge's first appearance. But, of course, he could not do this. He and his backers knew that the new grand lodge had to assert its *bona fides* as being a continuation, or 'revival' of something of 'time immemorial status' that had gone on before it. Therefore, every piece of evidence he brought to his bland account was subtly twisted. New practices were backdated; all information was re-digested and regurgitated to suit the new purpose.

It was, as Baldrick would say, 'a cunning plan'.

Thus, Anderson's *Constitutions of the Antient and Honourable Fraternity of Free and Accepted Masons* (2nd edition, 1738), tells new members that in 1693, eight lodges were working in London. There was, according to Anderson's information, an 'occasional' lodge headed by Sir Robert Clayton. There was a 'stated' lodge near St Thomas's Hospital, Southwark. There was the old lodge at St Paul's (presumably that held at the Goose and Gridiron). There was also one in Piccadilly over and against St James's church. There was a lodge near Westminster Abbey (possibly at the *Rummer and Grapes*, later called *The Horn* lodge).

According to Anderson, there was a lodge near Covent Garden, one at Holborn, and an eighth lodge at Tower Hill. There were also 'some more that assembled statedly'. We don't really know what Anderson was getting at when he distinguished 'occasional' lodges from 'stated' ones, apart, perhaps, from the idea that some lodges had a regular place of assembly, and some lodges met wherever the members freely and spontaneously decided. The Scottish practice – with which Anderson was familiar (his father, a glazier, had been admitted to a stonemasons' lodge in Aberdeen) – tended to interpret the word 'lodge' as being a specific place. We do not know if this was universal practice.

It may be that Anderson was trying to suggest that there had once been some kind of registry of lodges in days gone by. Registering approved assemblies was a key part of the strategy for establishing the rule of the new grand lodge. It would have been convenient to suggest that something of the practice already existed, or existed in embryo, ready for the 'new and better Method' Anderson first proposed to officials of the grand lodge in 1722. The distinction of 'occasional' and 'stated' may have been brought with Anderson from Scotland where, after 1736, there were lodges that met under the new grand lodge's authority, and those that decided to 'paddle their own canoe'. Whatever the meaning, there is no evidence that lodges in England had been distinguished by such terms before Anderson introduced them. Anderson was not a witness to the events he described regarding Freemasonry in London in the late 17th century, but he nonetheless felt free to appropriate its story for his purposes.

As we have seen, in the first edition of Anderson's work (*Constitutions*, 1723), Wren is mentioned only in a footnote as the architect of the Sheldonian Theatre's dome. Yet, in the second edition, it is Wren's alleged 'neglect' of the lodges that is said to have occasioned the need for a 'revival' that Anderson says took place in 1717 after a decision made, he says, in 1716 by four lodges.

This term 'revival' is used by Anderson specifically in terms of reviving quarterly assemblies – in particular, a midsummer assembly and feast. Anderson seems also to suggest that it was the lodge system itself that needed reviving; he does not say so, but that is the inference that has most been seized on in much masonic history. Thus, those who would wish to separate completely the institutional beginnings of symbolic or 'Accepted' Freemasonry from the business of working and contracting freemasons can suggest that 'speculative masonry' had an independent existence based on a 'revival' of old masons' customs, radically reinterpreted. The foregoing description of late 17th century Accepted Free Masonry should help us to see the fallacy of this position.

There are other reasons to doubt the gloss placed on the events of 1716 and 1717 as reported by Anderson. Wren *senior* died in 1723, the year in which the first edition of the *Constitutions* was published, and it may have been considered quite untimely to make criticism of the late masonic Brother's 'neglect' that had led, according to Anderson, to the 'decay' of the lodges.

Furthermore, at the time of his death, Wren was regarded by the British state's leading party as an old Tory, well out of favour with the new Hanoverian regime, acutely suspicious of Jacobites and their sympathisers. Prime Minister Walpole asserted that behind every Tory was a Jacobite in disguise. Anderson, a presbyterian, showed himself to have been a loyal supporter of the new regime.

Henry Jermyn, Earl of St Albans, would undoubtedly have been seen as a staunch supporter of the Stuarts. Becoming an Earl in 1659, Jermyn was a confidante of Charles II, close friend of Free Mason Sir Robert Moray, as well as being principal employer of masons in London. According to Anderson, Jermyn oversaw a great assembly of masons in London in 1663. But Jermyn was dropped from Anderson's history in 1746, the year after Bonnie Prince Charlie's Jacobite rebellion. (see *Henry Jermyn, Grand Master of the Freemasons?* Adolph, Anthony, *Freemasonry Today*, issue 6, p.46).

Wren's family did not, as far as we know, object to the references to Wren as grand master made in the 1738 edition of Anderson's *Constitutions*. The anomalies have not yet been fully explained. Anderson himself was far too close to his subject to have been objective.

In case anyone should think that evidence for freemasons' lodges was confined to the ten-mile jurisdiction area of the London Masons' Company, readers will recall Randle Holme (1627–1699) and the 'Society' of which he was a member in the 1670s. Twenty miles south east of Chester, Robert Plot's *Natural History of Staffordshire* (1686, Ch. VIII) reports how 'Free-masons', while spread about the country, were 'more numerous in the moorelands of Staffordshire than anywhere else'. Plot gave details of their ties of service to one another and of how men of understanding and of social position had been accepted among their number.

From 1694 comes the *York No 4* MS. of the *Old Charges*, which lists lodge members. The first official records of the lodge at York are dated 1705, in which year the Scarborough manuscript *Old Charges* lists members in that town. In 1710, George Grey was made a mason at Bedale. Three years later, the York Lodge made eighteen masons at Bradford.

Evidence is fairly sparse, but it is there. Anderson himself bemoans the lack of materials for his history. His explanation is characteristic. Some of the shortfall was a result of masons themselves protecting their privacy from outsiders, viz:

> ... many of the Fraternity's Records of this [Charles II's] reign and former reigns were lost in the next [James II's] and at the Rebellion [1688]; and many of 'em were too hastily burnt in our Time for fear of making Discovery so that we have not so ample an account as would be wished ...

Blame the old freemasons! The new, un-neglected, reviving order would *never* have permitted such a thing.

There was a particularly noticeable destruction recorded by Anderson only three years before publication of his *Constitutions*. That year of 1720 coincides with significant changes in the management of Grand Lodge. The destruction followed a request from the year 1718, when grand master George Payne required brethren to bring to Grand Lodge 'any old writings and Records concerning Masons, ...to shew the usages of Antient Time':

> This year [1720], at some private Lodges, several very valuable Manuscripts (for they had nothing yet in print) concerning the Fraternity, their Lodges, Regulations, Charges, Secret, and Usages, including one manuscript writ by Mr. Nicholas Stone the Warden of Inigo Jones were too hastily burnt by some scrupulous Brothers that those Papers might not fall into strange hands.
>
> (Anderson's *Constitutions*, 1738, p.111)

The account is positively loaded with possible inferences. Had these materials been lost in the manner described? Had they been destroyed at all? There are many reasons to suppose that there were Free Masons in London who wanted nothing to do with Anderson's history or the regulatory pretensions of the new grand lodge. Such objectors may well have asked, 'Where did this fellow Anderson come from?' We may ask the same.

Rev James Anderson DD (1679–1739)

James Anderson was the son of an Aberdeen glazier, an admitted mason to the lodge at Aberdeen. A surviving seal shows Anderson's respect for his father's masonic membership. Its crest depicts Anderson *senior*'s mason's mark at its head.

Anderson studied divinity at Marischal College, or at least he tried to. In the religious conflicts that marked the period of his education (the College's episcopalian lecturer in divinity had been replaced by a presbyterian), the presbyterians were running the Church of Scotland at the time. However, the presbyterians had not yet found a suitable candidate to fill this among many other (enforced) vacant posts. It was perhaps, this kind of experience that gave Anderson an insight into the folly of dividing men according to religious affiliation.

In any case, he so divided himself. He sought a presbyterian ministry.

Apparently unable to find a position in Scotland suitable for a young would-be minister, Anderson came south to London, after the union of England and Scotland in 1707. In London he married an English widow, providing him with sufficient funds to begin a small presbyterian ministry.

In 1710 he took over a former Huguenot chapel in Swallow Street, Westminster, and established himself as an occasionally controversial presbyterian minister, significantly beyond the control of the presbyterian Church of Scotland. The Swallow Street chapel had, interestingly, served the father of Huguenot *émigré* John Theophilus Desaguliers. Desaguliers would become the grand lodge's third grand master in 1719. Perhaps Desaguliers first met Anderson at the chapel while on a sentimental visit.

According to Professor David Stevenson's fascinating paper, *Anderson, Man and Mason*, the first of Anderson's printed sermons, delivered on 6 January 1712, well illustrates Rev James Anderson's attitudes. Anderson wrote of how the country was blessed by having a good protestant sovereign and a happy constitution, having been delivered from the jaws of 'Popery and Slavery' by the revolution (of 1688). But dangers threatened. The growth of popery was alarming, for by their principles catholics recognised a foreigner, the Jacobite pretender, as rightful king.

Danger also lurked within the 'Contagion of Scepticism and Deism'. There were 'too many, that either think God is an idle Spectator of the Affairs of the World, and will allow him no further Superintendency over it than a Clockmaker or an Architect'. This makes Anderson's Whig and Hanoverian sympathies clear. It also shows his notable antipathy to *deism*, a point-of-view sometimes associated with Anderson's famous *Charge Concerning God and Religion*, which he included in his *Constitutions*, and which, more than anything else perhaps, made the *Constitutions* something of a manifesto of the European 'Enlightenment'.

Anderson's own ministry was marked by a considerably less harmonious spirit than that he celebrated as emanating from a good protestant sovereign and a happy constitution. Anderson, poor Scots presbyterian in London, saw it his duty to comment on things that others felt were none of his business. Anderson drew fire for his practice of writing fair and balanced obituaries (as he saw them) of religious leaders of denominations other than his own. To those who disliked such presumption, Anderson appeared as a jumped-up, self-appointed religious commentator from a suspect source.

A man judged by anglicans as a priggish, 'superior' upstart, appeared to persons of his own denomination as a shameful latitudinarian, or even far worse, a snivelling 'Mass John': a provider of catholic masses. It was said after his death that presbyterians were wont to call the Scot, 'Bishop Anderson'. This jibe may have had more than one meaning. (One cannot help thinking of *Private Eye*'s satirical creation, the highly opinionated 'vicar of St Albion's' – ex-prime minister Tony Blair – who knows a catholic bishop's duty better than a catholic bishop, being himself intimate with the source of Christian truth).

To Anderson's outlook, it may well have appeared that a good presbyterian minister was equivalent (at least) to any bishop! This would not have gone down well among Tory Londoners. Nor would it have gone unnoticed by the *opponents* of Tory Londoners. Men such as Anderson can prove remarkably useful, so sure are they of their own position, so well insulated and so positively lagged by rational principle that they are blind to their vulnerability to manipulation; poverty only adds to that vulnerability.

Anderson was remarkably confident in his views. When we come to look at his novel ideas concerning Masonry and Religion, we may be astounded at his apparently guileless self-assurance. Anderson saw it his business to tell any religious person their business, if he thought it necessary. Not being subject to religious control, as he would have been in Scotland, the obscure Anderson felt at liberty to say what he thought, once he considered it principled and necessary. Once he felt something was right, it was right. Admittedly, he was not (in his own mind) a seeker after dissension or conflict on religious matters; was he not above all that? Anderson saw fit to educate those who read his usually pacific sermons that the martyrdom of King Charles I could not, as was often maintained, be laid at the door of Scottish presbyterians and presbyterians in general. This, from a man who would later forbid discussion of religion or politics in lodges, was a highly political statement, sure to enflame the opponents of one surely considered as another petty 'Dissenter'.

Anderson had a lot to prove.

In 1715, at the height of national agitation over the Jacobite rebellion against King George I (launched from Scotland), a sermon of Anderson's declared the innocence of presbyterians against the calumny of regicide. In the year of the rebellion, this assertion bore the implication that the Jacobites – being ready to war against the lawful king – were on a moral par with those who had seen fit to execute Charles Stuart in 1649.

The Jacobites had supporters in London and elsewhere. But Anderson did not only deliver the sermon to a committed presbyterian congregation, he chose to have it printed, so important was the subject to his heart. His critics were, predictably, infuriated. A pamphlet countered Anderson's measured and calm reasoning with words turned roughly on the lathe of rage. *No king-sellers: or, a brief detection of the vanity and villany in a sermon entitul'd, No king-killers. Preached by the Scotch-Presbyterian of Swallow-Street, Picadilly*, sent sparks flying in all directions.

Not only, the pamphlet spat, was 'Poor Jammy,' 'This Diminutive in Divinity, this little white-liver'd, red-headed Scot,' 'this Pimp of a Presbyter,' the author of 'the fraud of this Prig', he was also a master of fraud 'or a Crafts Master'. Anderson was nothing less than 'a fraudulent Brother'.

Fraudulent Brother... Admittedly, political pamphlets in this period seldom pulled their punches, but one would like to know what lay behind the abuse concerning Anderson's masonic identity. It is unclear from the language whether the writer or writers of the pamphlet were for or against the craft in general. Was Anderson, in their eyes, fraudulent because he was a 'Brother', or was he a masonic brother who was fraudulent, that is to say, a bad example or deceitful claimant to masonic privilege? Did the attack come from a Freemason?

We must, in fairness, conclude that these were insults showered on Anderson for cumulative effect, not biographical accuracy. However, it is interesting that something of Anderson's masonic identity was already known to his enemies at the period of the grand lodge's first gestation. What do we know of the origins of the body called a 'Grand Lodge'?

Momentous Events at the Apple Tree Tavern

This rubric should perhaps have served as the newspaper headline announcing an event that allegedly occurred some time, probably late in the year 1716. That neither it, nor anything like it, did make the 'late edition' should give us pause. That is to say, there is no corroborative evidence whatsoever for the report of the origins of the grand lodge.

Furthermore, that report only made its appearance twenty-two years after the event described. And in the space of those twenty-two years – a period punctuated with reports as to the Free Masons' affairs, both public and private – there is absolutely nothing to suggest that any such event ever happened. The general belief was that the 'Grand Lodge', or something very much like it, had always existed. Free Masonry is customarily described in newspaper reports as 'that honourable and ancient fraternity'. This itself shows just how effective the grand lodge 'spin' had been.

The pretence must stand as one of the greatest examples of 'sleight of hand' in history. And who wrote that account, when it did finally appear?

The one and only telling of the founding of a grand lodge came from the pen of the Rev James Anderson, while filling out his earlier (1723) history of Masonry. It does not purport to be the work of an eyewitness. There is no indication that the writer of the account was present. Nor is there any doubt in the writer's account that the reader is receiving truth in the form of established fact.

Here is the record as first printed in *The New Book of Constitutions of the Ancient and Honourable Fraternity of Free and Accepted Masons*, published by Caesar Ward and Richard Chandler, London, 1738, p.114:

> AD 1716, the few Lodges at London ... thought fit
> to cement under a Grand Master as the Centre of
> Union and Harmony, viz. The Lodges that met,

There follows a list of four lodges.

The *Goose and Gridiron*, St Paul's Churchyard. According to the official engraved list of lodges for 1729, the lodge was established in 1691. A lodge at the *Crown Ale House*, Lincolns Inn Fields. According to the above list, this lodge was established in 1712. A lodge at the *Rummer and Grapes*, Channel Row, Westminster, subsequently known as the Horn Lodge. The lodge at the *Apple Tree* tavern, Charles Street, Covent Garden, now the Lodge of Fortitude and Old Cumberland No 12. Its date of origin is unknown.

Anderson's account continues:

> They and some old Brethren met at the said Apple Tree, and having put into the Chair the oldest Master Mason (now the Master of a Lodge) they constituted themselves a GRAND LODGE pro Tempore in Due Form, and forthwith revived the Quarterly Communication of the Officers of Lodges (call'd the GRAND LODGE) resolv'd to hold the Annual ASSEMBLY and Feast, and then to chuse a GRAND MASTER from among themselves, till they should have the Honour of a Noble Brother at their Head. Accordingly
> On St John Baptist's Day, in the third year of King GEORGE I, AD 1717, the ASSEMBLY and Feast of the Free and accepted Masons was held at the foresaid Goose and Gridiron Ale-house.
> Before Dinner, the oldest Master Mason (now the Master of a Lodge) in the Chair, proposed a List of proper Candidates; and the Brethren by a Majority of Hands elected
> Mr ANTHONY SAYER, gentleman, Grand Master of Masons.
> { Capt. Joseph Elliot Grand
> { Mr Jacob Lamball, Carpenter Wardens

> who being forthwith invested with the Badge of
> Office and Power by the said oldest Master and
> install'd, was duly congratulated by the Assembly
> who pay'd him the Homage.
> SAYER Grand Master commended the Masters and
> Wardens of Lodges to meet the Grand Officers every
> Quarter in Communication at the Place that he
> should appoint in his Summons sent by the Tyler.

Astute readers will have observed that the constitution of this grand lodge took place in 1716, according to Anderson, and that a master mason was put in the chair. This man, whoever he was, appears to have been the first master of this grand lodge, if not given a title of 'Grand Master'.

All official masonic histories date the founding of the first grand lodge at 1717, the date of the 'Assembly and Feast'. It should be stressed that the assembly of officers called a grand lodge – a getting-together of four lodges (initially) for a single purpose, namely, to 'revive' the quarterly assemblies or 'communication' of officers – was not a regulatory or governing body. Its purpose seems solely to have been to reestablish four annual meetings in the tradition of the old guilds, which tended to assemble at the solstices and equinoxes. St John Baptist's Day brought together the masons' 'patron saint', St John (the Baptist) and the midsummer celebration. They appear to have been doing no more than planning a feast, a summer's day shindig.

John Hamill (*The Craft*, Crucible, 1986) and Bernard E. Jones (*The Freemasons' Guide and Compendium*, 2nd edition, London, Harrap, 1956) both assert that the claim of Anderson that the meeting of 1716 intended to 'revive' the 'Quarterly Communication' (an extant masonic tradition) is untenable: 'there being no evidence of either a Grand Lodge or any similar governing body having existed before 1717.' (Hamill, *op.cit.* p.42). This statement is flawed.

First, it does not address its pre-stated denial regarding the revival of the quarterly communication. It says that there has been no grand lodge or 'similar governing body' before 1717. But we have no evidence to suggest the grand lodge as constituted according to Anderson was a 'governing body' in any sense. That there emerged a governing body in the years following the meeting only begs further questions.

Second, there is evidence of assemblies of Free Masons being summoned. The *Roberts Constitutions* or 'Roberts Print' of 1722 (*Early Masonic Pamphlets*, Knoop, Hamer and Jones) refers to an assembly of masons called in London in the year 1663. Anderson's *Constitutions* of 1738 also refers to a general assembly of masons called in 1663 by 'Grand Master' Henry Jermyn to establish rules to reorganise masonry after disruptions ensuing from the civil war.

Incidentally, when Wren went to Paris in 1665 to meet the craftsmen of that city, it was Jermyn, then ambassador to Paris, who gained Wren the relevant introductions. (*Henry Jermyn, Grand Master of the Freemasons?* Anthony Adolph, *Freemasonry Today* No 6, p.46).

John Hamill states that the reason why a grand lodge 'came into existence in 1717 has never been answered satisfactorily.' (*The Craft*, p.42) This is reasonable, if not something of an understatement, but when one looks afresh at the perspective of a craft undergoing particular difficulties, reasonable suggestions may be advanced to account for the phenomenon. Again, it is vital to realise that Accepted Free Masonry was operating within the world of freestone masons, albeit as an élite grouping or coterie.

In 1670, Parliament passed an act for the rebuilding of London after the Great Fire, with specific taxes to be raised for the reconstruction of churches. Coal sent to London from the north, for example, was to be taxed for this purpose. This taxation measure required renewal.

On 29 September 1700 parliament passed the third and last measure. Sixteen years later, in September 1716, the measure expired. The money was drying up. St Paul's Cathedral was complete and the churches of London were mostly rebuilt. The world of London masonry was in trouble; masons were vulnerable. A reduction in the number of working masons in

London was clearly an issue for these, let us note, very small groups of interested parties. In this context, a 'revival' of quarterly assemblies does not appear altogether strange.

The feasts may have brought in new paying-gentlemen members who 'forked out' for some kind of association with the masons' fellowship, a place in a convivial society. This period saw a great growth in the number of clubs and occasional coffee house fraternities. (Note that the old religious context had all but evaporated.)

It is true that an aristocratic patron might assist the status and patronage of the craft in general. We may reasonably speculate that the four lodges met at the *Apple Tree* to plan a feast and assembly for midsummer, run by a novel (and perhaps temporary) organisational umbrella called a 'grand lodge'. A 'grand lodge' might host a 'grand party'. This conclusion is of course conjectural. It is also unclear as to what the specific status was of the lodges mentioned; we have no minutes from the lodges concerned at this time at all. Lodges in London probably did not keep minutes as a rule. Were they dominated by gentlemen, or by stonemasons?

Who was behind the gathering of four lodges? Did it ever really happen?

We are not compelled to believe it did.

It is worth noting that it had been the custom of English guilds to hold quarterly communications, usually held on Michaelmas Day (25 September), the Feast of St John the Evangelist (27 December) and Lady Day (25 March). According to Anderson, only annual assemblies were held in 1717, 1718 and 1719. The first quarterly communication of record was that on St John Evangelist Day in 1720. The reference to St John the Evangelist may or may not be significant, that saint being patron of Scottish Masonry.

We have no early records of the four lodges to aid scholarship, nor did the grand lodge allegedly formed in 1716 keep any minutes until 1723. We do not know who the 'oldest Master Mason' was who prepared the list of candidates for grand mastership.

Anthony Sayer, gentleman, called by Anderson the 'Grand Master' of this 'Grand Lodge', may have been a convenient choice simply because a family called Sayer ran a bookshop in St Paul's churchyard where the Goose and Gridiron lodge met (see *AQC* 88, 1975, and T. Beck's *Prestonian Lecture*, 1975).

The regulating body of 'Free and Accepted Masons' in England, following the union of 1813, has chosen to see the alleged events of 1716–1717 as significant. However, Free Masons in the 18th century did not, it should be understood, date their beginnings from this time – not in the least.

Anderson, and masonic verbal tradition itself, dated the craft as coming from an antediluvian past. Following Archbishop Ussher's famous dating of the creation to 4004BC, it became customary among 18th century masons to refer to a masonic dating system that added 4004 years to the Christian calendar, adding *Anno Lucis* (Year of Light) to the date, instead of using the established indices 'BC' and 'AD'.

During the 19th century, with all its enthusiasms for scientific progress, the antediluvian tradition had begun to look to scholars and investigators as romantic, unenlightened, fanciful and unscientific and so a great deal of attention has since been given to events of the early 18th century. Clean-cut distinctions of 'operative' and 'speculative' grew into the standard currency of masonic historical discourse.

A recent publication of the United Grand Lodge of England (*Your Questions Answered*, 2001, p.17) states boldly that 'Organised Freemasonry began with the founding of the Grand Lodge of England on 24 June 1717, the first Grand Lodge in the world. Ireland followed in 1725 and Scotland in 1736. All the regular Grand Lodges in the world trace themselves back to one or more of the Grand Lodges in the British Isles.'

We may note that the usual distinction of 'speculative' has apparently been omitted in favour of the relatively innocuous word 'organised'. But the quick-fix word-change doesn't really help do any more than shore up the leaking dam with temporary glue. It also sets up new, unnecessary problems, like all quick-fix deflections.

Apparently, Freemasonry before 1717 was *dis*-organised – not too difficult to prove once you have established subsequently that which would constitute 'organisation'! However you look at it, the attention given to the date 1717 has tended to encourage a comfortable (and misleading) split between so-called 'operatives' and 'speculatives'. The point at issue for the institution is, if there was a working Accepted Freemasonry before the appearance of a grand lodge regulating body, where was the need for a grand lodge at all? The Vatican is faced historically with a very similar question. If Christianity was practised (and organised) before centralised authority in Rome, what right has Rome to rule? The simple answer given to the devout is that it was the Founder's intention.

No such answer can be offered by Grand Lodge. Or can it? Anderson's lonely account implies that the existing organisation developed the idea as a way of promoting the existing organisation. Again, we are not compelled to accept this story at face value. We may ask, why bring lodges together for anything but temporary purposes? Simply to 'revive' the quarterly communication and feasts, as Anderson insists? To help gather patrons for the purposes of promoting construction, as the detail regarding import tax on coal might suggest? To launch an experiment in enlightenment philosophy and universal benevolence as certain other aspects of the *Constitutions* imply? Such possible motives are not as easily reconciled as might first appear.

Could it be that in the era of growing club membership, the social side of some lodges had altogether overtaken other reasons for assembly, and there was a wish to make the lodges more significant in the general run of convivial gatherings?

Perhaps, but were not lodges supposed to be entirely private affairs? Had some lodges been recruiting members without sufficient emphasis on absolute secrecy? Was the 'Grand Lodge' idea initially a means of 'reining in' lodges demonstrating embarrassing levels of independence?

It is a tempting thought, but it presupposes tendencies only found later, that is after a regulating body had been established. It is the kind of rationale Anderson would have found attractive.

Furthermore, the latter picture does not make sense in a period when, as far as we know, membership was still strictly secret.

The possibility then springs to mind, was there a wish in someone's mind to expose the existence of otherwise secret lodges by bringing them out into the open through a direct challenge, that is, a challenge to join an 'authorised' (by whom?) body? Creating state-neutral, non-political new 'orthodoxies' has been a method of government control since ancient times. Locate the perceived threat, then 'turn it' into an innocuous body by maintaining elements of its former attractiveness while taking the sting out of its potential to challenge elements of state policy and control.

The political situation in England during the period of the formation of Grand Lodge lends itself precisely to such a scenario.

The Whigs had, in 1714, secured the coronation of a deeply unpopular king and anti-Tory regime against which there was much active and passive resistance. Secret trade associations with conservative roots could certainly pose a threat to a new regime.

Put yourself in the shoes of an intelligence chief faced with possible civil war or at least serious civil disobedience. How would you view the existence in the capital of secret bodies, many of whose members were suffering from a shortfall of work? How would you go about neutralising the perceived threat?

Infiltrate, dominate, transform and recruit, recruit, recruit.

Soon, new members would outnumber the old. This picture has something to commend it, other than fitting much of the evidence as it stands. It is a realistic hypothesis, and would help answer the burning question regarding the appearance of 'Grand Lodge' – a question so hot that nobody seems to have asked it: *On what authority was a grand lodge declared and a grand master elected?*

Saying it was 'four London lodges' will not do, the idea being tautological; the rule for founding grand lodges based on a convention of four lodges (followed in Scotland in 1736) had not been written when the alleged gathering of four lodges took place in Covent Garden in 1716.

What had the London Masons' Company to say about all this?

In fact, there *was* no authority.

Authority – if that is what it was – was steadily *acquired* by a process of regulatory activities in line with state approval. However secret Free Masonry may have once been (before 1723) – and however many 'secrets' it might insist upon (after 1723), the fact is that after that date its known meeting places were available to the public, members appeared in public processions and newspapers reported proceedings.

The probable reason why nothing of the 'founding' of a grand lodge was reported in 1716 or 1717 was that at that time, Free Masons did not convey anything whatsoever of their private activities to outside scrutiny. The entire business could be established in absolute privacy. Again, the date cries out with significance: 1716. Only a year after the Jacobite revolt of the 'Old Pretender', with the threat of further insurrection in Ireland and interference from France, danger was very real.

Where was the support for these Jacobites? One man may have had an idea, having argued so strongly against their cause both in chapel and in print. If there was a government plan to infiltrate the world of secret societies during the period, we can hardly expect 'evidence' for such hypothetical covert activity to jump out and bite us! Effective covert action does not leave evidence – especially after nearly three centuries. As things stand, the suggestion may stand as one among several possibilities, all of which may, in truth, be mistaken.

Nevertheless, as we come to look at the origin of Anderson's first epoch-marking *Constitutions*, we shall surely find a considerably heavier degree of politics and politicking than we should ever expect to find in any regular lodge of Free and Accepted Masons.

The Political Background to Anderson's Constitutions

John Hamill's concise account of the history of the craft in England (*The Craft*, Crucible, 1986, pp.42ff.) gives excellent service in paring down the process of the formation of Grand Lodge as a regulatory body. Hamill notably observes that the reason why 'Grand Lodge came into existence in 1717 has never been answered satisfactorily'. This is, as we have seen, both honest and true. The appointment of the first succession of grand masters suggests a gradual 'upping of the stakes'.

First, one Anthony Sayer, about whom nothing is known: did he ever exist? Was he really a 'Grand Master'?

In 1718, the name George Payne appears as the 'revived' order's grand master. Payne certainly existed; he was a government official, working for the commission of taxes. This is the man who called for all documents connected with the craft and in the possession of lodges to be surrendered to Grand Lodge. This call went hand in hand with the establishment of new regulations to govern the craft and which would form the skeleton around which Anderson's *Constitutions* would be built. Payne would be grand master again in 1720.

According to Hamill, the year 1720 marked a watershed. 'In 1720 a change begins to be discernible. The catalysts for this change are believed to have been George Payne and the Reverend Dr John Theophilus Desaguliers.' (*The Craft*, p.42)

In 1719, Desaguliers succeeded Payne as grand master. He would serve as 'Deputy Grand Master' from 1722–3 and 1726. According to Hamill, Desaguliers 'is credited with introducing the aristocracy and men of intellect into the Craft.' The aristocrats brought in seem to have shown a remarkably unanimous political colouring; they were predominantly Whigs, courtiers such as the Duke of Montagu and the Duke of Richmond. Both men had the king's ear.

Interestingly, the figures most associated with the change all had connections with the *Rummer and Grapes* lodge, Westminster. Minutes of the lodge from 1723 show the Duke of Richmond as master, while other members were aristocrats and persons of 'social quality'. It is no surprise to find that Payne, Desaguliers and Anderson were all members of the lodge. This centring of transforming power in a single lodge can hardly be a coincidence. In 1721, John, 2nd Duke of Montagu, was appointed grand master. With an agreeable aristocrat at the helm, the little grand lodge began to grow. The government did not mind this at all; in fact, prime minister Robert Walpole would himself join at a time convenient.

John Desaguliers and the Recruitment Drive

The brilliance of Desaguliers (1683–1744) lay chiefly in science, or as it was still called, natural philosophy. Desaguliers was also extremely adept at public relations.

Born at La Rochelle, the infant Jean des Aguliers was brought to England at the age of two from an increasingly intolerant catholic France. The Edict of Nantes had once protected protestants. Louis XIV revoked it in 1685. Desaguliers (like Anderson) had both reason and experience to favour a doctrine of universal religious toleration.

Educated as John Desaguliers at Christ Church, Oxford, he lectured on experimental philosophy at Hart Hall in 1710 and graduated MA in 1712. Two years later he was made a fellow of the Royal Society where he occupied the post of curator, conducting experiments, often for the gaze of the interested public. He invented the planetarium and published works on physics, astronomy and mechanics. He speculated on the idea that corporeal nature would be changed if atoms ('original particles') were split (*A Course of Experimental Philosophy*, published in 1734).

Desaguliers was a great admirer of Newton. This admiration, verging on worship, is evinced in Desagulier's extraordinarily devoted poem, *The Newtonian System*, published in 1728. Devotion to Newton seems to some extent to have encompassed aspects of the vision of Newton's fervent, if heretical, spirituality and religious philosophy.

Newton did not believe in the holy trinity as understood in the Church of England's *Thirty Nine Articles of Belief* nor, contrary to what he has come to represent, did he believe in the 'deist' conception of an absent divine mechanician. Newton was exercised by the vision of a living universe in which the divine power was present at every level. His imaginative universe consisted of a great living, alchemical system whose lineaments could be revealed abstractly by mathematical physics.

Newton's questing mind was fascinated by the alchemically-informed, theosophic works of Jacob Böhme. Böhme described a universe that was an expression of divine spiritual dynamics in which the human being should look to his absolute centre, his heart. Images of the centre, often identified with the heart, emerge in masonic rituals after the time of Desaguliers. It may be conjectured that Desaguliers had at least a hand in the composition of the formerly (before 1725) unknown third degree ritual.

Mathematics, for Newton, was part of the divine code (a concept analogous to Masonry's apotheosis of geometry). Newton shared the alchemical view that the ancient keys to divine knowledge had become obscured with time as man lost intimacy with the inner life of Nature.

Newton regarded the conflicting faiths of the world and Christian sectarianism as signs of the falling away from and the search for an ancient pristine knowledge. He believed the structure of Solomon's temple contained fundamental insights into God's system of creation and gave keys to future knowledge. Newton's science, as Michael White's *Newton: The Last Sorcerer* (4th Estate, 1997) makes clear, was a spiritual quest for God's primal revelation.

After Newton, the world of science would come to embrace the mathematical structure but ignore the vision that inspired it. This was not the case as regards Freemasonry.

It does not take much imagination to see how such an almost 'evangelical' conviction of the need for a kind of revolutionary divine science could tie in with the traditions of the ancient craft. Such an idea may even, to the bright mind of Desaguliers, give Free and Accepted Masonry a purpose it either had not had before, or which could be said to have lain untapped within it. Furthermore, Desaguliers, a near-victim of religious persecution, understood as well as anybody the value of the masonic meeting-point: effectively an abstraction of high Christian principle.

Free Masonry was going to be different after Desaguliers.

As chaplain to the Prince of Wales, Desaguliers also had a

vested interest in the harmonious continuance of the protestant Hanoverian dynasty, considered by many a Whig as a defence of liberty – especially the liberty of Whigs.

The word 'harmony' meant a great deal to Desaguliers and it is prominent in Anderson's *Constitutions*. Desaguliers wrote the *Dedication*, and, some scholars believe, even more. Strangely, Desaguliers's correspondence, which must have been massive, has almost completely disappeared.

It is possible that Desaguliers came to the craft *via* the midsummer feast Anderson reports as having taken place at the Goose and Gridiron pub in 1717. With the expiry of a government measure to promote reconstruction in London in September 1716, the lodges may have been aware of financial constraints. If the alleged feast was an opportunity to attract new members, could Desaguliers have been one of them?

With all his social and political connections, Desaguliers was useful to the craft, or was it the other way around? The most widely known Free Mason of the time, Sir Christopher Wren, was an old Tory and the government did not care for old Tories. But Desaguliers was protestant, loyal and even grateful. His back was turned against the Stuart past of civil disorder and religious conflict: a man for whom the Reformation meant salvation from the dark ages.

In 1719, Desaguliers was elected grand master of the Free and Accepted Masons of London, seeing perhaps a peculiar potential within the craft. The potential had little to do with architecture. In his poem, *The Newtonian System of the World, the best Model of Government, an allegorical Poem*, published in 1728, Desaguliers is inspired by aspects of Newton's philosophy. Accepted Free Masonry's interest in geometry perhaps began to look more exciting, even prescient. Of course, it might need a touch of modernising: 'a new and improved Method' to rid the pristine essence of its discredited *Gothick* impurities; Anderson could see to that.

Anderson thought Gothic architecture was 'rubbish': a curious position for a promoter of 'Masonry'.

This seems to have been how Desaguliers saw it: Free Masonry had, throughout all the vicissitudes of history, preserved knowledge that could now – under a reasonable government – revolutionise the world. At the *fons* of religion was a divine science. That is to say, science and religion were originally one: both knowledge and consciousness of knowledge. The knowledge was God's, its language: geometry. The music of the spheres sang for everyone who had ears to hear, whether anglican, catholic, non-conformist, or heretic. The original religion was divine science: return to it and religious division might properly vanish.

> The Musick of his (Pythagoras) Spheres did represent
> That ancient Harmony of Government:
> When Kings were not ambitions yet to gain
> Other's Dominions, but their own maintain;
> When, to protect, they only bore the Sway,
> And Love, not Fear, taught Subjects to obey.

These were Desagulier's words. Geometry had no sects, no rival churches, no popes, no heretics. Geometry, the big 'G', was demonstrable to human reason everywhere. As Anderson would write in the 1738 edition of his *Constitutions*: 'Reason surveys the Lodge and makes us one.' God as Reason itself is the classic enlightenment *credo*, or assumption. To be guided into divine science, one needed a harmonious mind, enlightened by reason divine.

Newton, as we have seen, believed that the structure of Solomon's temple contained lost insights into God's system of creation, the keys to future knowledge. But, as Accepted Masons were told, the original secrets had been lost through an ancient tragedy. Newton and Desaguliers shared the view that the ancient keys to divine knowledge had become obscured with time, as man lost intimacy with the inner life of Nature. Newton regarded the conflicting faiths of the world and Christian sectarianism as signs of the falling away from an antediluvian, pristine knowledge. This concept had been an esoteric and Hermetic theme of continental renaissance since the late 15th century.

Knowledge was rediscovery. Antiquarians had a hand in science. Was it then Desaguliers who introduced the most famous antiquarian of the age to Free and Accepted Masonry?

William Stukeley – in Search of Ancient Mysteries

Rev Dr William Stukeley (1687–1765) was five years old when his great antiquarian predecessor, Elias Ashmole, died. Famous today for his pioneering work on Stonehenge, Druidism and the stones of Avebury, Stukeley was secretary and fellow (1717) of the Society of Antiquaries as well as being a fellow of the Royal Society, as was Desaguliers.

Like Desaguliers, Stukeley was well acquainted with Isaac Newton. They discussed science and Solomon's temple. He was, like Desaguliers, also friendly with John, 2nd Duke of Montagu, elected Grand Master of the Free and Accepted Masons on 24 June 1721. Montagu and Stukeley were made fellows of the Royal Society on the same day.

James Anderson shared Stukeley's view that 'Celtic' edifices like Stonehenge (built by Druids according to Stukeley) represented a branch of Masonry brought from the east. In an account of his life, published in 1753, Stukeley recorded that his curiosity led him to be 'initiated into the Mysterys of Masonry, suspecting it to be the remains of the mysterys of the antients'.

David Haycock, in the course of writing his recent excellent study *William Stukeley: Science, Religion and Archaeology in Eighteenth-Century England*, discovered a most interesting manuscript in the archives of the Wellcome Institute: *Palaeographia Sacra, or Discourses on Monuments of Antiquity that relate to Sacred History Number 11 A Dissertation on the Mysterys of the Antients in an explication of that famous piece of antiquity, the tables of Isis* (1735). The manuscript reveals in his own hand that Stukeley believed, like Ashmole, in the 'pristine religion' theory.

Stukeley held to the principle that there was an uncorrupted revelation before Moses and which Moses, and then Christ, tried to re-institute. According to Haycock, 'The function of this perception was to clear away constantly the debris of ignorance – brought about by mankind's perpetual tendency to corruption – by holding forth a vision of the original and true.' (*Stukeley on Masonic Origins*, David Haycock, *Freemasonry Today*, issue 6, p.22).

Stukeley accepted the image of the *Old Charges* of the primal knowledge inscribed on two columns built to survive deluges of flood and fire, writing in his *Palaeographia Sacra*:

> The origin of the mysterys (as we hinted before) is no other than the first corruption of true religion, when they [first] began to deviate from the patriarchal religion, into idolatry & superstition, & this was nigh as early as the renovation of mankind, after the noachian deluge...

The ancient patriarchal religion was linked in Newton's and Desaguliers's mind with the science of number and proportion, with geometry and mathematics. It does not take much imagination to see how such an almost 'evangelical' conviction of the need for a kind of revolutionary divine science could tie in with the traditions of Freemasonry.

Harmony is an idea central to Anderson's *Constitutions*. In addition to its Renaissance meaning as a fundamental characteristic of divine creation, 'Harmony' has political meaning also. Desaguliers, chaplain to the Prince of Wales, addressed the *Constitutions*' dedication not to the Tory Duke of Wharton (grand master, 1722) but to his predecessor, the Whig Duke of Montagu and his care for the Freemasons' 'Peace, Harmony and lasting Friendship'. Social Harmony was what the Whigs were offering. It was Walpole who was famous for 'letting sleeping dogs lie'. Desaguliers would doubtless have seen his calling as perfectly consistent, and complementary, with that of the dedicated antiquarian.

The task of the antiquarian was to bring back into the light the light that ignorance had shrouded in decay. 'This also was Stukeley's task and largely explains his and other enlightened men's enthusiasm for Freemasonry' (Haycock). 'The mysteries, therefore, had existed throughout the ancient world, and it was this secret religion – a fragment of the primeval patriarchal religion – which Stukeley believed the Druids had possessed, and which he had hoped to rediscover in the secrets of Freemasonry.' (Haycock, *FMT*, issue 5, p.25)

> It will be first inquired, what was the intent, the inducement of their initiation into these mysterys? The answer will be, they learnt thereby taciturnity, or the art of keeping a secret, a thing of great use in the political part of life: they learnt to cultivate an inviolable friendship: they learnt morality: and at length a sublimer notion of religion than the rest of the world enjoy'd... The friendship hereby sealed among the initiated, took a sacred and inviolable character: they were brothers ever after.
>
> *Palaeographia Sacra, or Discourses on Monuments of Antiquity that relate to Sacred History Number 11 A Dissertation on the Mysterys of the Antients in an explication of that famous piece of antiquity, the tables of Isis* (1735).

As Haycock summarises his findings: 'The antiquity of Masonry ... confirmed his [Stukeley's] picture of the past: the loss of knowledge and the corruption of an ancient pristine, patriarchal religion.'

From the point-of-view of government, of course, antiquarian study was a fit study for a pacific and pacified nation. As the 18th century wore on, many country gentlemen and educated clergy indulged an interest in the subject, keeping in touch with one another through organisations such as the *Society of Antiquaries* and the pages of *The Gentleman's Magazine*. A certain kind of Freemasonry blended very well with these self-educational priorities.

Stukeley's diary of 6 January 1721 records how he was himself 'made a Freemason at the Salutation Tavern, Tavistock Street

[Covent Garden], with Mr Collins and Captain Rowe, who made the famous diving engine. … I was the first person made a Freemason in London for many years. We had great difficulty to find members enough to perform the ceremony. Immediately upon that it took a run and ran itself out of breath thro' the folly of the members.'

Notwithstanding, Stukeley formed a lodge at Grantham, Lincolnshire, in 1726, independently, it would appear, of Grand Lodge. Stukeley was initiated in January 1721. In June, the Duke of Montagu became grand master. That would well account for the reference to what Stukeley regarded as an ill-fated recruitment drive. The serious question here would seem to be what was it, precisely, that constituted the 'folly' of the members referred to by Stukeley?

The period from June 1721 to June 1723 was one of the most tumultuous and difficult periods in Freemasonry's entire history. It was a period that later generations of Freemasons would hear little of, and those that knew what had happened – and whose purposes were threatened by it – would very much like to forget. Its stunning vividness has been buried in time, heaped over in saccharine myths, like the events related in Martin Scorsese's astonishing recreation of 1840s America, *Gangs of New York* (2003).

The period of tumult effectively ended, significantly, with the publication of Anderson's *Constitutions* in 1723. Once published, official minutes would begin to be kept, and the first secretary to Grand Lodge would be elected (perhaps after the Scottish model).

The first secretary to Grand Lodge was William Cowper. Cowper was 'Clerk of the Parliaments', a government official who ran his masonic business from his government office. Naturally, he batted for the Whig cause. Under the government of George I, if you were not a Whig, you were out of power.

As if to pre-empt the first *Constitutions* of Anderson, which came out in January 1722, Free Mason J. Roberts – about whom nothing else is known – published another set of constitutions (known as *The Roberts Print*). Significantly, Roberts repeated a charge from a copy of the *Old Charges*, dating from the 1660s, now held by the United Grand Lodge of England (*Grand Lodge MS. No 2*). It is quite possible that the manuscript represented the deliberations of an 'Assembly of Masons' believed to have been held – both by Roberts and Anderson – in 1663. The relevant charge stipulated that a properly constituted lodge must contain at least five Accepted brethren and a minimum of one brother who was an active master of the trade. (Incidentally, this is also consistent with the account given by Ashmole of his 'mother lodge' at Warrington in 1646 where John Ellam was almost certainly the statutory working freemason.)

Importantly, Anderson's *Constitutions* do not stipulate this requirement. What the 1723 Anderson *Constitutions* do stipulate is that a new lodge could be described as regular only if it had been created with the permission of the grand master. The lodge had to be personally constituted by him or his deputy or, in the case of provincial lodges, a suitably qualified local brother deputed by the grand master for that purpose. Only then would a certificate be issued and the lodge's name could appear on the books of Grand Lodge. Master masons of freestone had nothing to do with it.

According to John Hamill, 'Any lodge which had not gone through this process was considered to be irregular until it submitted to Grand Lodge, and its members were branded clandestine and not to be countenanced as visitors to regular lodges.' That did not seem to bother William Stukeley when he established his own lodge at Grantham, but Stukeley was a brother of distinctly independent mind, who entered the craft in the last breath of its old liberty.

However, before the final seal of domination of the old Free Masons could be affected, something of a rebellion seems to have occurred. The appearance of the *Roberts Constitutions* seems to have been connected to that rebellion. In order to understand the rebellion's significance, we need to travel back a little from 1723 to 1714, the last year of life granted to the Stuart Queen Anne and the fourth year of Anderson's preaching in his Swallow Street chapel.

A Change of Dynasty

On 1 August 1714, Queen Anne, daughter of the last Stuart king, James II, died. Whigs and Tories fought for the succession. While most Tories favoured the catholic James Francis Edward Stuart (the late queen's half brother), threat of civil war inclined parliament to unite behind a previous Tory undertaking: that the protestant George Lewis, Elector of Hanover, be considered heir presumptive.

Had James Stuart not been a catholic, he would certainly have come to the throne. And so a man who hardly spoke English and cared little for his surprising new acquisition became king of Great Britain, Ireland and a growing family of overseas possessions.

Nobody in England loved George, not even his supporters. But he was useful. He would maintain the 1688 settlement and keep the pope out.

George looked to the Whigs for support. He alienated Tory factions, including those who had supported his claim, by denying them preferment. His government was thus led by James, Earl Stanhope, secretary of state for the southern department. Charles, Viscount Townshend ran the northern department. Townshend's closest crony was Norfolk gentleman, Robert Walpole. Walpole was Townshend's brother-in-law. All three were Whigs, committed to the rights of the aristocracy and the landed interest to do as they pleased.

On 6 September 1715, misreading the Whig's determination to adhere to the new settlement, Jacobites (from the Latin '*Jacobus*', James) launched an ill-fated, ill-organised rebellion in Scotland. Without serious French help, the rebellion was, like its leaders, courageous, but doomed. James Francis Edward Stuart fled to France in February 1716.

Towards the end of that year, according to Anderson's *Constitutions* of 1738, four lodges of Free Masons met at the *Apple Tree* tavern, Covent Garden. At roughly the same time, Stanhope succeeded in getting his rival Townshend dismissed from his post as secretary of state for the northern department.

Walpole resigned in sympathy in early 1717. So it was Stanhope who governed England when (or if) the four lodges met again for their summer feast of St John the Baptist at the *Goose and Gridiron*, St Paul's, in June 1717.

The Arrival of the Duke of Wharton

Stanhope governed until his death in 1721. In that year, in hope of a Tory election victory, Irish peer Philip, Duke of Wharton, came to London. Looking for a political support base, he found the Accepted Free Masons of the city of great interest. Following initiation, the Tory Duke of Wharton proved popular among grassroots Accepted Free Masons. In the event, Wharton and his fellow Tories lost the 1722 election; Walpole and Townshend returned to power.

In May, the Duke of Orleans informed Walpole of a fresh Jacobite plot. This timely news conveniently helped Walpole to neutralise the Tory opposition and secure power. What better way to trash your opponents than by suggesting they were traitors? 'Scratch a Tory,' Walpole opined, 'and you will find a Jacobite.'

Meanwhile, on Monday 25 June 1722, Philip, Duke of Wharton, was elected grand master of the city's Accepted Free Masons. The Tory replaced leading Whig aristocrat John, 2nd Duke of Montagu FRS. This seems to have put a spanner in the works of plans dear to Desaguliers and Anderson.

According to the 1738 Anderson account, Montagu's supporters were not best pleased, on account, according to Anderson, of some procedural irregularities in the conduct of the assembly. This complaint may be taken with a pinch of salt. Rules regarding such 'procedural irregularities' were novelties, serving the new order.

By July and August, intelligence sources informed Walpole of Jacobite plans to capitalise on discontents within bodies of tradesmen in the city of London. Arrests were made. The Duke of Wharton's newfound masonic interests must surely have been of interest to the government. Walpole would have heard of everything that happened through the good offices of the Duke of Montagu and his supporters.

On 22 September, England's leading Jacobite advocate, Francis Atterbury, Bishop of Rochester, and a number of other English peers were arrested. Atterbury was placed in the Tower on a charge of high treason.

The Duke of Wharton, grand master of the Accepted Free Masons, gave an outstanding parliamentary speech in support of Atterbury in May 1723. Atterbury was exiled. Walpole was informed of how, assisting Atterbury to his ship, Wharton took Atterbury's chaplain under his protective wing and gave Atterbury his sword.

Walpole now broadcast the news that the peace of the nation was threatened by a new plot to assassinate King George while on a trip to his homeland in Hanover. Walpole worked the mob and played on the old propaganda: it was a *Popish Plot*. Try to imagine the scene in London. Thousands of armed troops marched into Hyde Park. The army was under the orders of a Whig government. Catholics were ordered out of the capital. Plans were laid to suspend *habeas corpus*. The requirements of state security aimed to curtail civil liberties, not for the last time, in the national interest, of course.

In the spring of 1723, Philip Duke of Wharton, grand master of London's Free and Accepted Masons, came under suspicion for collaborating with Jacobite conspirators. And while all of this was going on, the Rev James Anderson, a Whig, was finalising publication of his new *Constitutions* of Free and Accepted Masonry.

The *Constitutions'* frontispiece is telling. It shows the Whig past grand master, John, 2nd Duke of Montagu, handing over the *Constitutions* to his successor, Philip, Duke of Wharton, a Tory and a Jacobite. While Wharton accepts the *Constitutions* from the Whig peer, a certain past grand master – another Whig supporter – the Rev Dr John Theophilus Desaguliers, points to them with purpose.

Desaguliers was the brilliant back-room boy with the key to the front office. He was Anderson's chief supporter in a world otherwise hostile to jumped-up presbyterian preachers and would-be pundits.

David Stevenson suspects Desaguliers's openness to Anderson's interest in writing a history of Free and Accepted Masonry may have followed a dinner at *Canons*, the house of the Duke of Montagu in July 1721. (*James Anderson, Man and Mason*, in Freemasonry on both sides of the Atlantic: Essays concerning the Craft in the British Isles, Europe, the United States and Mexico, ed. R. William Weisberger, New York, Columbia University Press, 2002).

A number of Scots were present, including John Campbell, the 'Provost' (mayor) of Edinburgh. Desaguliers had been supervising the installation of a piped water system at Canons. A month later he was in Edinburgh, advising the burgh council on its water supply. He was present when Provost Campbell and a number of other Edinburgh worthies were admitted to the lodge of *St Mary's Chapel*.

Lionel Vibert (*Anderson's Constitutions of 1723*, L. Vibert, *AQC*, vol. 36 (1923), p.41) also attempted a reconstruction of how Anderson's *Constitutions* came to be produced. In his version of events, Anderson appears in Grand Lodge in 1721 and asks permission to write and publish a history of the order to be dedicated to the grand master, the 2nd Duke of Montagu, installed that year. Desaguliers perhaps associates himself with the proposition and Anderson is given permission.

Whichever version of events was most likely, matters undoubtedly moved at a pace. On 29 September 1721, according to Anderson, Grand Master Montagu and his masonic team, having found fault with all the copies of the 'old Gothic Constitutions' (collected by the previous grand master, George Payne), commissioned Anderson 'to digest the same in a new and better Method'. (*The New Book of Constitutions*, 1738, pp.113–114.)

What this digestion boiled down to was removing Freemasonry from its former trade context and putting its destiny entirely within the hands of a new controlling group. Why precisely Anderson was chosen we cannot be certain, but he seems to have fitted the bill rather well. One cannot avoid the suggestion that since Anderson had little significant reputation as a writer but did have a previously demonstrated desire to serve the British establishment, he would prove a malleable, sympathetic and useful jumping jack.

In what appears to be a collaboration of the two pro-Hanoverian protestants, it is clear that Desaguliers would be the ideological driving force. Nevertheless, the *Constitutions* would bear Anderson's name, and, to some, shame. According to his own account, Anderson presented his work at the next meeting of Grand Lodge, 27 December.

Fourteen 'learned Brothers' were appointed 'to examine Brother Anderson's Manuscript, and to make report'. According to Anderson's *Constitutions* of 1738, the committee reported back in March 1722, 'that they had perused Brother Anderson's Manuscript, viz. the History, Charges, Regulations and Masters Song, and after some Amendments had approv'd of it: Upon which the Lodge desir'd the Grand Master [Montagu] to order it to be printed.' The amendments included the addition of grand master George Payne's novel 'Regulations' of 1720:

> The General Regulations to the number of 39 Compiled first by Mr George Payne, Anno 1720, when he was Grand Master, and approved by the Grand Lodge on St John Baptist's Day, Anno 1721, at Stationer's Hall, London, when the most noble Prince John Duke of Montagu was unanimously chosen our Grand Master for the Year ensuing.

As Stevenson notes in his paper, the *Constitutions* 'had been commissioned, written, revised and approved for publication in a period of six months'. Some might observe an unusual haste. Assertion of a new regulatory power was in the air.

While the approval process took place, the Whigs Walpole and Townshend triumphed in the general election. In June, the Tory Duke of Wharton would be elected grand master at an installation later pilloried by Anderson as 'irregular'. 'Inconvenient' might have been a better word. Furthermore, the manifestation of 'Grand Lodge' and 'Grand Master' as a collective regulatory body (as this movement coalesces about the *Constitutions*) was a fundamental break – both 'heretical' (in terms of masonic practice) and 'revolutionary' (in terms of religion and philosophy) – with the established order of things in Accepted Free Masonry.

In order for those involved (and the finger of evidence points straight to the Whig-dominated Horn lodge of Westminster) to achieve this extraordinary vanishing and re-appearing trick, it was necessary to sever as far as possible the institutional links between the London Company of Masons and the novel body. This was accomplished by the *Constitutions'* maintenance that only regular or regulated lodges (that is, those approved by the grand lodge) could be granted certificates, and without a certificate a lodge was to be shunned by members. This measure was allied to a hasty recruitment drive (referred to by Stukeley) aimed specifically at the upper classes. Soon there would be more new lodges than old ones, with new attachments, loyalties and subtly adjusted perceptions of the past. As we have seen, the requirement of an alleged 1663 assembly of masons, for example, that a properly constituted lodge should have at least one member of the trade within it was ignored. Who, one might ask, could now teach the new members what it was all about?

The 1663 requirement had appeared in 1722, in the so-called *Roberts' Print*, a publication that seems to have been intended to pre-empt the innovations of Anderson, Desaguliers and the Duke of Montagu. By 1738 and the second edition of the *Constitutions*, it appears that the author was sufficiently confident and secure in the new order actually to reproduce this earlier charge and, by doing so, set it apart as merely an incident in the regulatory evolution of Grand Lodge. (*Constitutions*, 1738, chapter two, p.101).

Belated inclusion (while yet nullifying it) would also serve as a gesture of inclusiveness to those who might recall the earlier order. By this tactic, objection was appropriated and swiftly neutered. It appears that Desaguliers, ever busy to acquire authentic freemasons' manuscripts, was of the opinion that

Grand Lodge had sufficient material from the existing lodges to make Free and Accepted Masonry an independent order (that is, independent of the trade), while simultaneously absorbing the existing order.

The later flawed and misleading distinction between operatives and speculatives was forced upon the movement as a result of the severing of Accepted Free Masonry from its source and natural environment. (See *The Mystery of the Acception, 1630–1723: A Fatal Flaw*, M. Scanlan, in *Heredom* [The Transactions of the Scottish Rite Research Society], ed. by S. Brent Morris, Washington DC, vol. 11, 2003.)

Ironically, the *Constitutions* themselves show perfectly clearly that Accepted Free Masonry was no 18th century innovation – but, surely, that was cleverly to deny that there had ever been any fundamental innovation. The surface of the *Constitutions* is calm, but beneath the surface a revolution has occurred: an ideological and political *coup d'état*. The 'forces of conservatism' had to be… put in their place.

In a bold and extraordinary move, Anderson backdated the existence of grand masters to cover the entire history of the craft. *Didn't you know?* There had *always* been nobles and royals dominating the craft; it was how things ought to be.

It is as though accepted brethren awoke one morning to find they had a new government, a new government whose first act was to reassure the members that the government was the same as it always had been. Except, you understand, that it had had to be been cleaned up, polished, and brought into the glorious sunshine of the 18th century, shorn clean of 'hopelessly muddled' histories stemming from 'the dark illiterate Ages' (*Constitutions*, 1723, p.23), that is to say, Masonry's 'Gothick' past. After some past neglect, members had every cause to be grateful. Such happy and blessed times were these to live in! One might have felt inclined to declare: God bless King George! Masonry – *Free at last*!

But free it was not.

Stevenson has asked the question: 'Had they, in grand lodge, created an organisation that instead of serving [the brethren] was taking them over?... Moves towards promoting Freemasonry's public image jarred with the quiet, semi-private masonry of small groups of friends who had perhaps savoured obscurity as being related to their treasured secrecy.' (*James Anderson, Man and Mason*).

If the Duke of Wharton was attempting to exploit discontents within the trades of London, he would have found plenty to disconcert the city's small but growing number of Free Masons. All available evidence points to the realisation that Accepted Free Masonry had grown up within companies of freemasons, albeit as an élite inner body; masonry as a purely commercial practice could, in principle, exist without it. But until the first quarter of the 18th century, the reverse could not be said to be the case.

It is arguable then that Anderson, himself aware of discontents, swung the whole argument round to implicate the Tories. This might explain why in the first edition of Anderson's *Constitutions*, Sir Christopher Wren is mentioned only in a footnote as the architect of the Sheldonian Theatre. Yet, in the second edition, it is Wren's alleged 'neglect' of the lodges that is said to have occasioned the need for a 'revival' that Anderson says took place in 1717 after a decision made by four lodges.

Anderson is saying, if anyone objects to the changes, they were *a)* necessary for the lodges' survival, and *b)* brought about by the lodges themselves.

Again, did Masonry really need reviving?

In 1716, when the famous four lodges allegedly met in Covent Garden, the expiry of a tax on imported coal designated for London's reconstruction probably did leave lodges with straitened finances – but Anderson does not mention this. It was, after all, a trade issue. For Anderson, revival means effectively a re-institution of quarterly communications or assemblies, in particular, a midsummer assembly and feast, and the return of aristocrats to the helm of a grand lodge. The 'Grand Lodge' takes over from the Masons' Company as parent body. His history tries to show that 'Grand Lodge' – a kind of heavenly or Platonic *Idea* – had always existed above the vicissitudes, follies and will of man. *Grand Lodge* was, according to this spin on events, nothing less than a glorious restoration!

Anderson's Idea of Masonry

As Stevenson has noted, no 'Tory Brother' could be content with this situation, this theft of glory – and it was not just a matter of who was in charge. It is clear to the observant eye of the new *Constitutions* that what Anderson calls *Masonry* is not quite, well, *real*.

In Anderson's (or Desaguliers's) mind, 'Masonry' seems to be a kind of perpetual or even perennial moral philosophy: slightly otherworldly, up there in those blue Georgian skies with fluffy clouds above Palladian arches: universal, benevolent, transcendent, and, incidentally, linked by analogy to ...building.

What Anderson calls 'Masonry' (he persistently uses the Scottish term) is a rather Whiggish philosophy, favouring trade, rationalism, reasonable religion: edges smoothed, peaceful prosperity, the arts, sound government, the wise avoidance of war or interference in others' territories. It is all very reasonable, and decidedly as unspiritual as the style of presbyterian salvationism. In fact, Anderson's 'Masonry' serves as a kind of blueprint for a quintessence of a rational society.

The symbols are basically 'traditional'; it is the social utility that counts. One might want to call it *New Masonry*.

And this new Masonry, as Anderson or Desaguliers sees it, is not really committed to any particular religious polity. Tories favoured the reformed catholic Church of England, but Masonry favours 'that religion on which all men can agree', which as you know, has not been invented yet, since none could agree on what to call it.

A new attitude to Masonry is visible in two events. In 1721 the first public procession of Free Masons took place. This was to celebrate the first aristocratic grand master's 'Installation', a clear exercise in public relations. One can somehow imagine the old Free Masons turning in their graves. *Public processions*!

The second event took place the following year. According to the 1723 edition of the *Constitutions*, the laying of the foundation stone for the new church of St Martin's-in-the-Fields took place on 19 March 1722. Two months later a body of Accepted Free Masons laid their own stone with due ceremony, twelve feet above the original. Stevenson expresses the presumption, or awkward confidence, of this act: 'Laying a new stone, without permission, could be seen as an insult not only to the bishop [who laid the original stone] and his church but to the king himself. That the new stone lay exactly over the original one, but twelve feet above it, might seem to suggest symbolically that the first stone had been superseded. The masons had trumped the king.'

Well, I do not think that was quite the point. The Freemasons had trumped *the trade*! Masonry is superior to freemasons! You won't see an aristocrat getting his hands dirty, my dear.

The 1738 *Constitutions* manages to telescope the two stone layings into one. Stevenson suggests that embarrassment about the incident may explain a famous plea made to Viscount Townshend on behalf of the Free Masons' loyalty to the Hanoverian regime.

Soon after their St Martin's ceremony, 'a select Body of the Society of Free Masons' waited on Lord Townshend, notifying him of their forthcoming annual assembly. They 'hoped the Administration would take no Umbrage at that Convocation, as they were all zealously affected to his Majesty's Person and Government'. (See A. F. Robbins, *The Earliest Years of English Organised Freemasonry*, in *AQC* vol. 22 (1909), p.67. *Constitutions* (1723), pp.44–5 describes the laying of the first stone on 19 March).

Stevenson asks: 'Was it felt that presumption at St Martin's made a reassurance necessary?' This observation may be a trifle naïve in the context of the times. Frankly, I suspect that there was no chance of any umbrage being taken. This looks like plain toadying, with a nod and a wink. Of course, the government might have been interested to know what Philip, Duke of Wharton, was doing in their midst…

Was it, for example, true that that curious Irish peer, veteran of the disgraceful *Hell-Fire Club*, was tipped by some to be the next grand master? Townshend assured the delegation that brethren 'need not be apprehensive of any molestation'... 'so long as they went on doing nothing more dangerous than the ancient Secrets of the Society; which', he added, 'must be of a very harmless Nature, because, as much as Mankind love Mischief, no Body ever betray'd them.' (A. F. Robbins, *op.cit.*pp.70–71.)

Townshend was no fool. Look at that date again: the summer of 1722. In May and June of that year, intelligence concerning a Jacobite plot was trickling in. Very shortly after the toadying to Townshend, Philip, Duke of Wharton, was elected grand master by his supporters among the brethren.

It is quite possible that the delegation to the government was intended as a message to the rank and file: 'Don't rock the boat. The government is watching us. We have even had to reassure them of our loyal intentions'. It is reasonable to assume that Wharton would never have countenanced such a delegation, not being himself 'zealously affected' towards the foreign king and his Whig government. Was the delegation, therefore, pre-emptive?

Six months later, in January 1723, according to Anderson, Wharton signed off the *Constitutions* for printing. Aware of this date, Anderson has Wharton being regularly *re*-installed on 17 January, in full healed-up amity with his predecessor, the Whig magnate, Montagu, after earlier alleged irregularities. And about this time the new *Constitutions* received some late modifications. Discussion of religion and state policy was to be forbidden within lodge. Brethren should never be involved in plots against the civil power. The grand lodge still wished it to be known that brethren were zealously affected towards the king and his government. One can only wonder what passed through the Duke of Wharton's mind when he read these words, if, indeed, he did read them. It is ironic that politics and religion were forbidden topics in the lodges blessed by Anderson's *Constitutions*, since these influences shaped the *Constitutions* so profoundly.

Let us look again at the Wharton Affair, for set against it, the underlying arteries of the *Constitutions* are thrown into intelligible relief.

Jacobites in the craft

Philip, Duke of Wharton, (1698–1731) was godson to William III. He visited the 'Old Pretender' (James Stuart) in Avignon in 1716. Spied on by British government agents in Paris, they warned Wharton to steer clear of the Jacobite cause. In 1717, Wharton took his seat in the Irish House of Lords after promising good behaviour. The duke was president of the notorious 'Hell-Fire Club' (suppressed by royal proclamation in 1721).

In August 1721, Wharton was admitted into the Society of Free Masons. While he did not appeal to Messrs. Desaguliers and Anderson, he must have appealed to someone.

> Last week His Grace THE DUKE OF WHARTON was admitted into the Society of Free-Masons; the Ceremonies being performed at the King's Arms Tavern in St. Paul's Church-Yard, and His Grace came Home to his House in the Pall-Mall in a white Leathern Apron.'
>
> (*Applebee's Original Weekly Journal*, 5 August 1721)

Four days after the *London Journal* reported the masonic delegation to assert the masons' zealous affection for king and government, the following announcement appeared in the *Daily Journal* (20 June 1722):

> On Monday next, being the 25th Instant, will be kept at Stationers-Hall, the Grand Meeting of the most Noble and Ancient Fraternity of Free Masons, as usual.

In the same issue appeared another announcement, presumably issuing from the Duke of Wharton's supporters:

> All belonging to the Society of Free-Masons who
> design to be at Stationer's Hall the 25th Instant, are
> desired to take out tickets before next Friday; And all
> those Noblemen and Gentlemen that have took
> tickets and do not appear at the Hall, will be look'd
> upon as false Brothers.

This announcement was disowned in a notice in the *Post* next
day:

> Whereas there was an Advertisement inserted in this
> Paper Yesterday, design'd to be injurious, 'tis hoped
> no such sly Insinuation will have any Influence on
> the Fraternity.

On the same day, Grand Lodge requested the *Daily Journal* to
publish an announcement, asking members of the 'Society of
Free Masons' to obtain tickets for the Stationers' Hall meeting
of Monday 25 June from 'the most Ancient Branch of this
Society in Town'. This is a contemporary record. By 1738,
Anderson recalled things differently.

According to Anderson, Montagu's tenure was so popular
that 'the brethren' asked him to continue, and Montagu
accepted. However, Philip, Duke of Wharton, 'being ambitious
of the Chair', as Anderson pointedly puts it, persuaded a
number of brethren (presumably not those who craved another
year of the Duke of Montagu) to meet him at Stationers' Hall
on 24 June 1722 (Anderson's date is incorrect).

Anderson claimed that there were no 'Grand Officers'
present; that Wharton had not been master of a lodge or
properly nominated and proposed as grand master; that he had
not appointed a deputy and that 'the Noble Brothers and all
those who would not countenance such irregularities,
disowned Wharton's Authority.' By the time these irregularities
appeared in print (1738), Philip, Duke of Wharton, had
entered the Heavenly Lodge and was unable to defend himself.

On Monday 25 June 1722, (John the Baptist's Day had fallen on the Sabbath), Philip, Duke of Wharton, was duly proclaimed and installed as grand master. This is Anderson's account:

> And having no Grand Officers, they put in the Chair the oldest Master Mason (who was not the present Master of a Lodge, also irregular), and without the usual decent Ceremonials, the said old Mason proclaimed aloud PHILIP WHARTON, Duke of Wharton, Grand Master of Masons, and Mr. JOSHUA TIMSON, Blacksmith, Mr. WILLIAM HAWKINS, Mason Grand Wardens but his Grace appointed no Deputy, nor was the Lodge opened and closed in due Form. Therefore the noble Brothers and all those that would not countenance Irregularities, disown'd WHARTON'S authority, till worthy Brother MONTAGU heal'd the Breach of Harmony.'

In fact, the events in Stationers' Hall were reported in the *Weekly Journal* as well as in *The Daily Post* of 27 June 1722:

> On Monday last was kept at Stationer's Hall, the usual Annual Grand Meeting of the most Noble and Ancient Fraternity of Free-Masonry (where there was a noble Appearance of Persons of Distinction) at which meeting they were obliged by their Orders to elect a Grand and Deputy-Master; in pursuance whereof they have accordingly chosen His Grace THE DUKE OF WHARTON their Grand Master, in the room of His Grace THE DUKE OF MONTAGUE, and DR. DESAGULIERS, Deputy Master, in the Room of DR. BEAL, for the Year ensuing.

No irregularities were reported, but events after the meeting contained telling details. Writer Robert Samber – whom we have already met – had recently paid five shillings for initiation.

He reported in *Ebrietatis encomium*, published in 1723, that grand master Philip, Duke of Wharton, was hailed heartily at a grand drinking session at an inn after the installation. (R. Samber, *Ebrietatis encomium* (1723), quoted in Robbins's *Earliest years . . .*, in *AQC* vol. 22, pp.72–3).

Samber's account reveals Anderson's 1738 telling of Wharton's installation and subsequent humbling in January 1723 was very likely a politically inspired cover-up. Samber's account perhaps explains why. While praising the dinner's quality, Samber declared his inability to see how 'demolishing huge Walls of Venison Pastry', 'after a very disedifying Manner', could contribute to 'building up a Spiritual House'.

That Samber has been identified with the 'Eugenius Philalethes Junior' who wrote the 1722 pamphlet *The Long Livers* is significant. ('Eugenius Philalethes' [R. Samber], *The Long Livers*, London, 1922, 'Dedication', quoted in D. Knoop, G. P. Jones & D. Hamer: *Early Masonic Pamphlets,* Manchester University Press, 1945, p.50 and J. R. Clarke, *The Change from Christianity to Deism in Freemasonry*, in *AQC*, vol. 78, 1965, p.49). 'Eugenius Philalethes' was the name taken by Rosicrucian *aficionado* Thomas Vaughan. In his *Lumen de Lumine*, published seventy years before, Vaughan echoed Robert Fludd's view that he who stood on the cornerstone of Christ should be a builder of the spiritual house: an ancient ideal of the old freemasons.

Politics and religion were not discussed at the celebration. Samber suggests they were following the advice of 'that Author', doubtless a reference to Anderson, whose *Constitutions* had been published by the time Samber wrote.

However, at one point the band began to play *Let the King Enjoy his Own Again*, a popular Jacobite tune. As Stevenson remarks of the incident: 'Politics might be banned, but music could make a political point.' It is not at all clear that politics was banned from this meeting!

The feast was probably seen in the duke's mind as part of his election strategy. Events immediately subsequent to the playing of the radical song suggest as much. Fearful of charges of sedition – the king's army would soon fill Hyde Park – there arose a reprimand 'by a Person of great Gravity and Science,' as Samber describes a figure that can only be Wharton's compromising and compromised deputy, J. T. Desaguliers.

Decorum restored, the bottle went round and toasts were made to the king, the royal family, and the established 'Churches' (of England and Scotland). Prosperity received a toast, as did Old England 'under the present Administration'. A notable toast was made to 'Love, Liberty and Science'. Aleister Crowley would have liked that. The discomfited Desaguliers's agony would not last forever.

A year later, the first minute recorded in a grand lodge minute book, dated 24 June 1723, states that the *Constitutions* had been approved in manuscript by the grand lodge and so were printed and approved. There then follows an interesting minute:

> And the Question was moved That it is not in the Power of any person, or Body of men, to make any alteration, or innovation in the Body of Masonry without the Consent first obtained of the Annual Grand Lodge and the Question being put accordingly Resolved in the affirmative.

The minutes were actually written up in the November of that year in the hand of Desaguliers. The intention seems to have been to seal for all time the new constitutional identity of Free and Accepted Masonry, to put a line under the grand mastership of the Duke of Wharton and to establish the regulatory function of Grand Lodge, independent of any other body.

Of course, the whole statement could be viewed another way, as does Bernard E. Jones in his *Freemasons' Guide and Compendium*. It could be concluded from the minute 'that whatever was new in the Regulations was of no effect'. There was now a new grand master, Francis, Earl of Dalkeith, elected on 24 June 1723 at a fiery meeting at the Merchant Tailors' Hall. There was disagreement about novelties in the *Constitutions*. Furthermore, a motion was advanced asserting that the Duke of Wharton's grand mastership had been irregular.

The duke, enraged by the suggestion, refused to nominate the absent Dalkeith. Wharton then had a row with his deputy, Desaguliers, when he learned that Desaguliers was to be Dalkeith's deputy. Two Whigs were apparently too much for Wharton. He stormed out of the grand lodge, never to return. Wharton then went straight to a hustings meeting to support two Tory candidates standing for the position of sheriff of London. Five days later, Anderson wrote to the Duke of Montagu:

> The said Duke has been deeply engaged all this week among the liverymen of London in the election of Sheriff, though not entirely to his satisfaction, which I am sorry for, but none can help it except Mr Walpole, who, they say, thinks it not worthwhile to advise him.

The reference to Walpole, Britain's most senior minister, makes it reasonably clear that Anderson was spying on his former grand master and masonic superior, while Walpole himself bided his time.

Members of the *Horn* lodge had the ear of the highest government. It is not surprising that Anderson in 1738 should emphasise the handy canard of irregularity to disown the Duke of Wharton and look 'clean' in the government's eyes. For the time being, one can only guess at the measure or significance of Jacobite sympathy among the ten lodges listed as functioning in the 1723 *Constitutions*. Whatever that may have been, anti-government feeling would fall under the eye of clerk of the parliaments, William Cowper, first secretary of the grand lodge and government supporter.

The Wharton Affair can only have increased the tendency to 'control-freakery' around the grand lodge. New members would be needed: new members who would know only the new system.

Wharton himself may have been the author of a pamphlet published on 14 September 1724. *The Plain Dealer* refers to 'The late prostitution of that order'. 'Why,' the author asks, 'did they make so many proselytes in so cheap and prostituted a manner?'

In 1726 in Vienna, Wharton would declare for the cause of James III and continue to fulminate against those he regarded as the usurpers of Accepted Free Masonry. He died young in Catalonia in 1731, after having founded the first masonic lodge in Spain.

Philip, Duke of Wharton's tomb near Barcelona was desecrated by order of General Franco shortly before the dictator's death.

Chapter Eleven
The Anderson Revolution

The Rev James Anderson's 'new and improved Method' for suppressing the traditional charges of Freemasonry did not come out of an idealistic daydream. As we have seen, the *Constitutions* emerged out of a London reeling from years of political instability, religious turmoil and social discontent. So we should not be surprised to find two extreme positions available to those who have examined Anderson's *Constitutions*.

On the one hand, the charges (or rules) can be seen as positively revolutionary: innovative, enlightened and creative contributions to civilisation. On the other hand, they may be seen as heretical, not 'heretical' in terms of religious orthodoxy, but 'heretical' in so far as being a radical deviation from what we know of established beliefs and customs as laid out in the *Old Charges* familiar to freemasons.

Of course, these two positions may be combined. It may be that the *Constitutions* were both revolutionary and heretical: heretical because revolutionary, and revolutionary because they 'dared' to be heretical. The adjective 'heretical' is not employed entirely without religious implications.

There can be little doubt that besides institutionally severing 'Free and Accepted Masonry' from the business of freemasonry, the major issue that the new charges challenge us with, is the epoch-marking approach to religious allegiance and tolerance, issues that have, arguably, affected the polity of post-enlightenment democracies worldwide. It has already been implied that Desaguliers, the winner of the conflict with the Duke of Wharton and his supporters, may have had in mind a programme of social engineering by Freemasonry. May such a programme be discerned in the new *Constitutions*?

The Philosophy of the Constitutions

The opening of the first edition of the *Constitutions* informs us that Adam, created in the image of God, 'must have had' the liberal sciences, particularly geometry, written on his heart, for ever since the creation of man the principles of geometry have been 'in the Hearts of his Offspring'.

The word 'heart' here corresponds to what some psychologists would call the unconscious, wherein may reside the roots of our feelings, intuitions, thoughts and sensations: the 'archetypes' of thought. Anderson is saying that geometry is an *archetype* at the root of our mental experience, inseparable from man as a thinking agent.

The use of Adam as the original 'type' of Man and the root of masonic experience may reflect Desaguliers's interest in an Isaac Newton theologically motivated by the works of 'Teutonic Theosopher' Jacob Böhme (*c.*1575–1624).

In Böhme's thought, redemption comes through the 'New Man'. The *New Man* comes as a manifestation of the original type: the sinless Adam before the Fall. The *New Man* is also 'Christ' or the 'second Adam' (in whom there is no confusion of human and divine will). It is through 'Him' that man is brought back (redeemed) from 'original sin' to original bliss. At the last day, Man will rise as Adam was first created.

Böhme is famous for a conception called 'The Double Fall'. According to this idea, the first 'Fall' of Man was not that resulting from Adam's sin in Eden (as in the Bible); the first Fall had already occurred.

Before there was time or space, a spark of creative expression was emitted from the latent dynamism of God's original being. This spark, by degrees, generated the universe. Man's original, divine essence belonged with God, but that essence became involved with the creation – the relative world of change and time. Adam's second Fall – his loss of paradisal innocence – occurs when he mistakes his selfhood as a worldly being for his original essence. From that moment he becomes a slave of his ego, separated from himself. He has forgotten his source and original perfection.

The 'Double Fall' involves Man in a sleep, unconsciousness and amnesia. According to shoemaker-mystic Jacob Böhme, so long as man had 'stood in heaven his essences were in Paradise; his body was indestructible...the elements stood in awe of him'. Unfortunately, 'tired of unity, Adam slept and his imagination turned away from God... He brought will and desire from God into selfhood and vanity; and he broke himself off from God, from his divine harmony ... Sleep was succumbing to the world's powers, and Adam became a slave to just those powers which previously had served him. Now the elements ruled him.' (Dr Stoudt, *Sunrise to Eternity*, pp.264–66, on Böhme's *Mysterium Magnum*).

One can see from this outline – this process of de-perfection, if you like – how self-mastery and self-awakening can link the mystical with the allegorical and geometrical themes latent or explicit in Freemasonry. Geometry, says Anderson, must have been written on Man's heart from the beginning. The 'original type' (or archetype) of Man is latent in the unconscious: a being filled with primal divine knowledge. The essence of Man is asleep – or rather our conscious minds are asleep to what we really are.

Furthermore, when we speak of *Man* as an archetype, we find we are also talking in terms of the so-called 'Platonic solids', the geometrical principles and original *ideas* by which the universe has been (according to Platonism) constructed.

Think again of what we have said in chapter four about the pentagram as an image of human wholeness, its relation to the 'golden mean' and the dodecahedron (the Platonic solid made up of pentagons) by which the 'Great Architect' completes his creation.

By 'remembering' these ideas in his heart, Man may master his world, rather than be enslaved to it by ignorance. This is wisdom, the acquisition of which is the purpose of Freemasonry. Man may link the 'small architect' (the hidden mind of man) with the Great Architect (the *logos* or creative mind of God).

As St Paul said: 'We have the mind of Christ.' Indeed, but we do not use it. The candidate is made a mason in his heart. Geometry is within Adam's heart. His heart is the centre of the universe. That universe is projected as a lodge from the centre of the heart to the heavens.

For all that heady brew of mystical liberation, explicit mystical thought is absent from the *Constitutions*, though there are implicit clues for those of an explicitly spiritual cast of mind. However, if Desaguliers hoped for such conceptions to indwell Masonry, it seems Anderson preferred to depict men of all sorts turning to Freemasonry as 'a safe and pleasant Relaxation from Intense Study or the Hurry of Business, without Politicks or Party'. (*Constitutions*, 1738, p.115).

This is a Whig conception through and through, but may have been intended to allay potential fears of the ignorant as to what Masonry was really about. An idea intended to get above areas of religious conflict, the hostilities and fears of one man towards his neighbour, was unlikely to pitch its tent in the valley of religious doctrine.

The emphasis was on harmony: the 'original' harmony implicit in the geometry of the universe. Thus, Christ receives but passing recognition. 'God's Messiah' was born in the reign of Augustus (*Constitutions*, 1723, pp.24–15). Stevenson considers that the use of the term 'Messiah' was intentional, so as to permit entry to those that did not believe Christ was God incarnate or the second person of the Trinity. Newton could happily have subscribed to the idea of Christ as a teacher of the 'Way to the Centre'. Equally, trinitarians could hardly deny Jesus was the messiah. Deists and 'unitarians' could also be included. Like a government inclusiveness directive, distinctions were not stated directly. Was Anderson the first spin-doctor?

According to Stevenson,

> Though such Masonic attitudes were combined with full acceptance of denominational religion, nonetheless traditional views of religion were being directly challenged, for they claimed that their religious beliefs should be reflected in all aspects of

life, all the time. Freemasonry argued that there should be the possibility of a part-time opt-out from denominational religion, cooling-off periods for turning one's back on denominational differences. The implications were revolutionary, a step toward secular societies in which religion tends to be seen as one compartment of life rather than its essence.

(James Anderson, Man and Mason, in Freemasonry on both sides of the Atlantic: Essays concerning the Craft in the British Isles, Europe, the United States and Mexico, ed. R. William Weisberger, New York, Columbia University Press, 2002).

Amid the modernising came a transformation of masonic understanding of 'God' and 'Religion'. Here are the words of the first charge of Anderson's *Constitutions* of 1723:

A Mason is oblig'd, by his Tenure, to obey the moral Law; and if he rightly understands the Art, he will never be a stupid Atheist, nor an irreligious Libertine. But though in ancient Times Masons were charg'd in every Country to be of the Religion of that Country or Nation, whatever it was, yet 'tis now thought more expedient only to oblige them to that Religion in which all Men agree, leaving their particular Opinions to themselves; that is, to be good Men and true, or Men of Honour and Honesty, by whatever Denominations or Persuasions they may be distinguish'd; whereby Masonry becomes the Center of Union, and the Means of conciliating true Friendship among Persons that must have remain'd at a perpetual Distance.

Further elucidation was given in the sixth charge of the 1738 *Constitutions*:

The next thing that I shall remember you of is to avoid Politics and Religion ... any association with them as a Society [in conversation in lodges], for... our Politics is merely to be honest and our

Religion the Law of Nature and to love God above all
things, and our Neighbour as our self; this is the true,
primitive, catholic and universal Religion, agreed to
be so in all times and Ages.

That 'this was the true, primitive, catholic and universal
Religion' was some claim! It might have been 'agreed to be so in
all times and Ages' by those that agreed with it, but however
exalted the simplicity of the conception – a claim after all to an
archetypal religion – it shows strongly Anderson's tendency to
take on the mantle of arbiter of religious debate.

Of course, if you examine the statement carefully, it says
nothing more than that the mason tries his best to follow God's
laws (by which Nature works) and accepts the ethical obligation
to love God above all things, and to love our neighbour as our
self. It might be said that only an atheist would object to the
fullness of this itinerary – and atheists cannot be masons
because they do not love God above all things. The style of the
charge, however, has led some scholars to consider that what
was being proposed was a kind of 'masonic religion', or that the
words echoed the vogue for 'Natural Religion' as opposed to
revealed religion. According to Matthew Tindal's *Christianity as
old as the Creation or the Gospel a Republication of the Religion of
Nature*, Natural Religion consisted simply of:

i)   Belief in God;
ii)   Worship of God;
iii) Doing what is good for one's own good or happiness
      and
iv)   Promoting the common happiness.

Natural Religion of this type was flatly opposed by William
Law and, later, by another great disciple of Böhme, William
Blake (*There is no Natural Religion*, 1794). Nevertheless, as a
result of the central notion implicit in the geometrical
paradigm, that God's revelation is discernible in Nature, the
idea of 'Natural Religion' and of its sister idea, deism, has

frequently been stuck to the edifice of Freemasonry. This may be a result of many thinkers finding Voltaire and Rousseau easier to digest than Böhme. Masonic scholar Robert Peter explains why 'Natural Religion' appears to co-inhere with the latitudinarian views of Anderson's *Charge Concerning Religion*:

> Natural religion is completely transparent to human reason: nothing can be a truth of natural religion if it is mysterious or not demonstrable. It is fit to stand as the common truth (and perhaps common origin) behind all religions ... Mystery is also rejected by John Locke because it has no empirical basis.
>
> (*Freemasonry and Natural Religion*, in
> *Freemasonry Today*,
> issue 12, pp.40-42.)

There can be little doubt that masons who shared this outlook might find Masonry congenial, but that is not the same as suggesting that that was what the 'Charge concerning God and Religion' had in mind. Ambiguity has also lain the charge open to the imputation of deism with its external 'watchmaker'-like deity.

In the deist image, the deity-mechanician makes the machine and watches it tick harmoniously on, indifferent to the scrapes and triumphs of humankind. He makes the universe according to his laws – and that's it: no miracles, no special graces, no spirituality. As romantic philosopher Samuel Taylor Coleridge would counter later in the century, the deist conception was religion 'cut and dried to suit the intellect' and inaccessible to the heart. But Anderson was not a deist.

Careful study reveals perhaps a simpler picture. First, the charge is perhaps very clever in being so 'non-specific' about such great issues; this was wise. Second, the 'catholic and universal religion' may echo Hermetic and 'Noachian'/Patriarchal conceptions of the universe – a universe free of theological conflict, a wise and loving creator; human beings who can by rising from their lower nature enjoy *gnosis* of Him and themselves (before the 'Flood' of time and space).

The 'catholic and universal religion' may also be compared to Stukeley's motives for joining the craft referred to earlier: to find the uncorrupted patriarchal religion common to Adam and to Noah, before the deluge (the 'Great Flood' that only Seth's, or Hermes's, pillars of knowledge – and the Ark itself – could withstand).

This idea of there being a 'catholic and universal religion' (not identified with Roman orthodoxy) was in vogue. Unpublished notes reveal Isaac Newton's thoughts on what he called 'the essential part of religion', binding on all nations. This essential part was 'of an immutable nature because grounded upon immutable reason'. Love of God and neighbours were the essentials, so 'This religion may therefore be called the Moral Law of all nations.'

Free Mason Robert Samber (or 'Eugenius Philalethes Junior') echoes the idea in *The Long Livers*, published the year before Anderson's *Constitutions* and from which well of wisdom Anderson may well have drawn:

> ...the Religion we profess...is the best that ever was, or will or can be...for it is the Law of Nature, which is the Law of God, for God is Nature. It is to love God above all things, and our Neighbour as our self; this is the true, primitive, Catholic and universal Religion, agreed to be so in all times, and confirmed by our Lord and Master Jesus Christ.

Third, the *Constitutions'* charge concerning God and religion sits comfortably with the Old Testament and therefore with the beliefs of Jews who had been active in London since they had been permitted to re-enter Britain in the 1650s.

Fourth, loving one's neighbour as oneself echoes the great moral commandment of Christ.

Fifth, the charge permits harmony among people from different sects, denominations, churches and even religions (the 1738 Charge explicitly adds the word 'religions': good men and true are welcome by whatever 'Names, religions, or Persuasions they may be distinguished'; p.143).

Sixth, taken at face value, the clear implication is 'that religion on which all men can agree' cannot and perhaps should not be defined so as to divide men and nations. And, in a common sense way, this religion is everything you were taught was good without everything that has ever been cause of dispute. The very clever thing here is that in no way whatsoever does the charge deny any point of doctrine on which men might disagree; it recommends people hold to what is good, true and honourable.

The charge implies that in the *Society of Free-Masons*, no thing that causes disagreement outside of Freemasonry (so long as it is not contrary to the moral law) need cause dissension within it. The lodge is to be ruled by harmonious geometrical simplicity, as is man's conduct. Here lies the allegory of the operative craft: the mason is to measure himself, be ruled by principles of what is 'true' – straight, square, of good use and in harmony with the geometry inherent in God's creation.

The stone he works on is himself: his ultimate aim is profound (not superficial) self-knowledge; knowledge of what he is truly made of – whence he comes, what he is made for, and whither he goes. This process may be characterised by struggle, but bearable so long as the end is kept in sight. Life is a third degree and it requires will and courage.

Anderson now makes a special claim for the status and civilising value of the ideal lodge, shaping ideal masons. We need to look carefully at the last section of the charge.

If masons are good men and true, regardless of the religions and denominations that might have divided them, then 'Masonry becomes the Center of Union, and the Means of conciliating true Friendship among Persons that must have remain'd at a perpetual Distance'. Let's hear that again: *Masonry becomes the Center of Union, and the Means of conciliating true Friendship among Persons that must have remain'd at a perpetual Distance.*

This conclusion is revolutionary. Seen clearly in its early 18th century context, the charge establishes a new principle of union in the world, not a utopia, but a living society. Now we can understand Chevalier Ramsay's excitement as evinced in his *Oration* of 1736. The model of the lodge has the potential to be a raising leaven in the dough of humankind. If what has formerly divided men may be transcended by the masonic principle of tolerance and archetypal harmony, then the world may indeed be on the road to becoming a humane republic in which evey nation finds its home as a family.

Such an harmonious, global republic must have seemed a glorious vision to many in the year 1736. This was the year in which Russia, on seeing France seeking the help of Turkey in the war of the Polish Succession, invaded Turkey. Russia was repelled and forced back to the Balkans with heavy losses. One dynastic conflict: four countries at each other's throats.

The charge concerning religion lays the foundation for the view that Free Masonry may serve as a renewal principle for all of humankind; it needed one. In a world divided between protestant and catholic, catholic and catholic, protestant and protestant, Frenchman and Englishman, Scotsman and Englishman, what the charge quietly proposed was nothing less than a new 'Centre of Union', and that *Centre of Union* was Masonry. Freemasonry will become 'the Means of conciliating true Friendship among Persons that must have remain'd at a perpetual Distance'.

Masonry preceded Babel, the nations and the religions. *Alleluia!* This charge is a visionary statement, albeit expressed in a relaxed manner, as if it were a commonplace of common sense. It may have been unconscious, a kind of gambit its author lacked the vision to control. On the other hand, its true author may have been Desaguliers, seeking a way of applying Newtonian principles to the business of masonic polity.

In 1730, a famous 'exposure' of Freemasonry was published, purporting to contain the secret words of the Freemasons' degrees. Since we know so little about what constituted the ceremonies of Freemasons in this period, Samuel Prichard's exposure is sometimes employed as a guide in discerning elements of the pre-1813 rituals.

In the 1730 exposure of the entered apprentice degree, the master asks the candidate: 'How many principles are there in Masonry?' The answer is given thus: 'Point, line, superficies and solid. Question: Explain them. Answer: Point the centre (round which the Master cannot err) Line. Length without breadth, superficies length and breadth, Solid comprehends the whole.'

Similar words are to be found in contemporary masonic catechisms. The master mason who concentrates on the centre of the circle 'cannot err'. This centre is within the being of the master mason. The charge tells us that Masonry will become the centre of union. Among masons, the leading principle is to be found within the being of the mason. 'In the centre of the circle, the Master Mason cannot err'. While this is highly suggestive to those recognising the mystical principle of the craft, we do not know if Desaguliers wrote these words; his papers – as we have observed – have disappeared.

Nevertheless, the couplets within the degrees as revealed by Prichard are very much in the poetic or versifying style of Desaguliers as demonstrated in his allegorical poem, the *Newtonian System of the World*:

> When all the Powers of the throne we see,
> Exerted, to maintain our Liberty:
> When Ministers within their orbits move,
> Honour their King, and shew each other Love,
> When all Distinctions cease, except it be,
> Who shall the most excell in Loyalty:
> Comets from far, now gladly wou'd return,
> And pardon'd, with more faithful Ardour burn,
> ATTRACTION now in all the Realm is seen,
> To bless the Reign of George and Caroline.

In answer to the prosaic question 'What do you come here to do?' the candidate in Prichard's entered apprentice degree must alight into verse:

> Not to do my proper Will
> But to subdue my Passion still;
> The rules of Masonry in hand to take,
> And daily Progress therein make.

> But boldly let thy perfect Model be,
> Newton's (the only true) Philosophy: ...

The last two lines are *Desaguliers's*. But would you have known?

Desaguliers was seriously interested in establishing a form of science that was also a form of enlightened social organisation. He wanted to make the link between Newton and sound government, between Newton and society, or science and society. This drive may have informed his contribution both to masonic reorganisation, and to the establishment of those principles in the *Constitutions*.

Desaguliers and Anderson present us with an understated, calming vision of a scientific and mystical principle joining itself to a political one. Rebellion is self-interest and the cause of Man's Fall. To find the centre, the self must be transcended, that is one interpretation applicable to the symbolic death of the candidate in the master mason's degree.

According to the outlook of Desaguliers and Anderson, the enthusiasms of Jacobitism and rebelliousness must be forgone; they belong to the infancy of society. They must not rule the future as they have the past. England and Scotland are now joined in common destiny. No longer will the country's history be dominated by old hatreds of catholicism and protestantism. There is a new monarchy, with new liberties and wealth for all who seize the new opportunities. There is a great wide world out there that needs to be brought into its true and fundamental order. Think not, they say, that this is novel! Why! This is a return to antediluvian order – a divine blessing: man, nature and reason combined, refreshed and forward-looking. Join the winners! Hail the Enlightenment!

What would older members make of all this novelty? For example, the first charge tells us that in ancient times masons were charged in every country to be of the religion of that country or nation. But *Grand Lodge MS. No 1* (1583) states, 'That ye shall be true men to God and Holy Church, and you shall use no error or heresy by your understanding or discretion but ye be discreet men or wise men in each thing.'

All copies of the *Old Charges* except the *Regius* MS. begin with an invocation to the trinity. In Anderson there are no saints and there is no trinity. A mason is obliged to follow the moral law and, if he 'rightly understands the Art', that understanding, not the sacraments, should serve to keep him from atheism and loose living. Anderson, himself a presbyterian, could hardly have disapproved of regulations that eased the path for some dissenters and all those who hated political and religious arguments, and who longed for harmony and unity.

It is probable that the wording concerning religion in Anderson's second (1738) edition was changed to allay some of the above concerns. Regarding Christ, it is now asserted that in him the Word was made flesh. He was, according to pages 41–2 of the 1738 edition, the Lord Jesus Christ Immanuel, great architect or grand master of the Christian Church. He was crucified; he rose from the dead, for the justification 'of all that believe in him'.

That last phrase seems to be a caveat. Belief is not compelled and 'Immanuel' – God with us – is not an essentially trinitarian term. Stevenson has observed that the 1723 assertion that in ancient times masons were charged 'to be of the religion' of the country they were in might be taken as implying that Christian masons in non-Christian countries were bound to conform to other religions.

The 1738 Charge is reworded so that past Christian masons were charged to 'comply with the Christian usages' of countries in which they travelled or worked. However, now that Masonry was to be found in all countries 'even of divers Religions', brethren were now only obliged to the religion on which all men agree. This was a recognition of the growing place of the world beyond Britain and Europe. This was a recognition of a potential common empire of humanity.

One can almost hear the melancholy strains of John Lennon's wistful *Imagine*. But the new masonic vision is most definitely to be played in the major key: *E major* to be precise, the key of heaven. There's not a 'major seventh' in earshot, and that, perhaps, encapsulates the essential difference between Anderson's time and ours.

Christianity's unique place in Masonry might appear to belong to the past. That is not to say that there is any incompatibility. Many have argued that you cannot have your cake and eat it. Masonry holds that if it is true then it is true for everybody. Many Christians would say the same, but then, Masonry is not a religion, but a place where religious people may meet, only religious on those principles where all agree, the which principles are not open for discussion since Masonry celebrates only that which unites men, not divides them. This was and is still a remarkable formula. And it can be shown to work. Worldwide Freemasonry proves in practice what many today still only espouse in theory. Religion, race and politics do not have to lead men into conflict; there is a higher polity and a deeper human identity.

Anderson may not have considered himself revolutionary in this respect. For example, his work shows a special interest in the lodge wherein Elias Ashmole was made a Free Mason in October 1646. Within it were supporters of king and supporters of king and parliament, adherents of the catholic faith of Rome and the catholic faith of England. Opponents divided in matters outside the lodge could yet meet on the universal basis, for the lodge is a universe and deals with the centre of man, not the accretions.

Page 23 of the 1738 *Constitutions* contains another remarkable phrase: *Liberty of Conscience.* This is now a mainstay of human rights legislation. It could be argued that the term is a misnomer. Having a conscience means being conscious of a moral law. That is what the conscience is conscious of. If you adhere to a moral law, you have no liberty in the matter, since the law is a compulsion to itself, not a liberation from itself. However, if we mean, the right to worship as conscience dictates, then I think we are close to what Anderson was getting at, when he writes:

> They [the Zoroastrians] are here mention'd, not for
> their Religious Rites that are not the subject of this
> Book: for we leave every Brother to Liberty of
> Conscience; but strictly charge him to maintain the
> Cement of the Lodge, and the 3 Articles of Noah.

Here, Anderson is beginning to get on difficult ground. Liberty of conscience outside of the lodge may well mean conflict, since moral laws of which people are conscious may be, and frequently are, different. However, this need not upset the members of a lodge, for there, the consciences of the members are circumscribed by an alleged universal principle, common, it is hoped, to all consciences. This principle is probably meant to be a synthesis of geometry, science, natural law or the creative *logos* or divine Word, but it has to be given a kind of religious authority. What Anderson comes up with is ingenious. The 1738 History has stumbled upon 'the Noachidae': 'the first name of Masons, according to some old traditions', offers Anderson. Stevenson thinks these *Noachidae* have been invented for the occasion. I do not think so, though 'they' may have been manipulated for Anderson's purpose.

Stukeley mentions the Noachian era and connects it with the pristine, patriarchal knowledge before the Flood swept it away. The original columns of knowledge, preserved by father Hermes, according to the *Old Charges*, which survived the Flood, were the basis of perpetual Masonry. And so the argument comes full circle. That which provides liberty of conscience in the lodge is Masonry, seen in the context of that religion on which all men can agree, which must be the uncorrupted religion surviving in all hearts and in all religions. So brethren: *Know Thyself.*

So, Were Anderson's Constitutions Heretical or Revolutionary?

It seems to have been an unspoken or unconscious intention of the *Constitutions* to obliterate the very concept of heresy; this, it may be argued, is one of the truly revolutionary things about them. The papal inquisition, we should remember, was still in business. Being England, Desaguliers's (suspected) vision of Masonry was never completed, if indeed it was intended. But he and Anderson left a system in some respects more capable of evolution (at the outset at least) than that of their predecessors.

Arguably, the abduction of Acception Masonry (even if only in name) from the trade was detrimental both to the trade and to symbolic Free Masonry. The process added a high level of pretentiousness to the 'Grand Lodge' phenomenon. From the time of the *Constitutions* onwards we see a luxuriant growth of hierarchy and regulation, largely for the maintenance of authority, rather than, as in former days, the good of the trade: the old meeting place of art, science and money.

Were the *Constitutions* heretical or revolutionary?

Well, if you like the new model Free and Accepted Masonry, then Anderson's *Constitutions* are brave and revolutionary. If, however, you suspect the authentic society of Accepted Free Masons was preferable, then the new *Constitutions* were the work of an unwitting, or unrepentant, heretic.

There is another way of looking at the question. The *Constitutions* themselves offer us an unwitting choice in the form of an aesthetic competition. Anderson is wont to call the work of the great 'Gothick' architects 'rubbish'. The word 'Gothic' of course means 'barbarous'. (One thinks of Blake's defence of the old architecture of Europe: 'Gothic form is living form', an observation that so inspired the Pre-Raphaelites and some Victorian architects.) Anderson seemed to think a return to the 'Augustan' classical style marked a new beginning in civilised construction (coinciding with the 'revival' of 'real' Masonry). This view seems to have positively taken off throughout the century. Everywhere, once-marvellous Jacobean houses were given the 'classical' treatment, not always happily. Every country manor or civic building began to resemble a limestone parthenon; aristocrats began wearing togas. Napoleon wasn't satisfied with being a king; he had to be an emperor.

Do you favour the 'Augustan' or the 'Gothick'? Or, politically, do you favour the Whig or the Jacobite? Many in the 18th century could (reluctantly) see that while there was a political and economic benefit to be had from the Whigs and their pragmatic support of the Hanoverians, they could also see that there was a spiritual loss. (Dr Johnson felt it keenly.) We can glimpse this private agony in the apparent contradiction of anglican churchmen in the late 18th and 19th centuries solemnly celebrating the martyrdom of King Charles Stuart on the one hand, while being grateful for the defeat of Bonnie Prince Charlie Stuart (and popery) on the other. This dichotomy haunts the English psyche to this day. It is deeply enshrined in the complexities of choice between 'liberal', 'conservative' and 'labour'. Politics and religion are truly unhappy bedfellows; they cannot make love even if they want to. In this context, retreat to the non-political, non-partisan lodge might seem a welcome solace indeed.

In June 1723, the Jacobite Duke of Wharton stormed out of Grand Lodge, never to return. But he left a gauntlet of challenge behind him.

That challenge is still with us.

Interlude Two
Edward Jenner

Our second interlude concerns Dr Edward Jenner, a member of the lodge known as the Royal Berkeley Lodge of Faith and Friendship, No 449, in the 'Masonic Province of Gloucestershire'. Jenner is now world famous as the father of vaccination. He discovered the principle whereby vaccination with the harmless cowpox gave protection to people from the deadly smallpox.

Jenner's pioneering work on vaccination, published in 1798, has led to the saving of millions of lives. This is not a common claim. During Jenner's lifetime, smallpox was bringing misery and death to the tribes of Native Americans beyond and within the then frontiers of the United States and Canada. Hearing of the Red Indians' terrible plight, Jenner sent the cowpox virus and a book of instructions to the Five Nations of North America. The Native American chiefs, overwhelmed by the benefits that Jenner had imparted to their people and their posterity, gave the Englishman a special wampum belt. With it, the chiefs dispatched a message, that 'they would teach their children to lisp the name Jenner in blessing until the Great Spirit should gather all their generations to Himself'.

Every regular Freemason is expected to believe in a spiritual, creative principle – a supreme being. It would be perfectly acceptable to Freemasons to refer to this being as 'the Great Spirit'. Freemasons do not presume to define the supreme being that English-speakers are taught to call 'God'.

On receipt of the wampum and its message, Jenner was deeply moved. He valued the wampum as highly as his fellowship of the Royal Society and wore the belt over his masonic apron at lodge meetings. It must have looked very fine and rather odd at the same time, like many new things.

Through Jenner's encouragement, the Berkeley lodge functioned as a local learned society. A monthly paper on a scientific subject was presented to non-masons, before the lodge was opened for masonic work.

Jenner himself became master of the lodge in 1812 at the age of 63.

This little story, modestly secreted in the copious – and little known – annals of masonic history, tells us something special about the substance and legacy of Freemasonry. We hear about the benevolent charitableness of Freemasons, a powerful characteristic of masonic activities in Jenner's day and in ours.

Freemasons in England, for example, raise more money every year for charities than the BBCs famous annual *Children in Need* campaign, a campaign that undoubtedly benefits from a mass media support system unavailable to the craft.

From the story of the Berkeley scientific gatherings, open to non-masons, we also learn that Freemasonry, while keeping some of its business private, did not – at least in Jenner's day – strive to keep either its existence, or its benefits, secret.

Lodges were not simply for masons alone. When the anti-slavery movement sought – against all opposition – venues in London to speak publicly of the justice of their cause, the premier Grand Lodge of England provided premises.

Looking again at the little science meetings, we may note the serious interest among Freemasons in what the second degree of masonic development calls the 'hidden mysteries of Nature and Science'. Education, as well as charity, has been a highly significant masonic principle. Knowledge for its own sake is to be valued by Freemasons. The laws of the universe cannot be properly adhered to, if they are unknown.

Freemasons are expected to be a leaven in the dough of human society, harbingers of peace and goodwill to all men. This is the 'secret plan' of Freemasonry. We may also note the global reach and extensive geographical interest of Freemasons, even as long ago as the 1790s when a trip to market was the longest journey the majority of human beings could expect to undergo in a lifetime. Such a trans-national interest is another instance of that universality dear to serious Freemasons.

Chapter Twelve
Made in Britain for Export

Evidence suggests that the third degree, in its distinctly Hiramic form, was a late development, a form of the ceremony originating in the 1720s. The first minute of the working of the third degree comes not from a lodge but from the minute book of the *Philo Musicae et Architecturae Societas Apoloni*, the Apollonian Society for the Lover of Music and Architecture.

All of the members of this society were Freemasons. Interestingly, architecture and music were seen and heard as kindred arts. On 12 May 1725 Brother Charles Cotton Esq. and Brother Papillion Ball 'were regularly passed Masters'. Cotton had already been initiated and passed to the second degree in a regular lodge at the Queen's Head Tavern, Hollis Street in the Strand. The Duke of Richmond was master of that lodge, as well as being grand master of the premier grand lodge of England. According to John Hamill (*The Craft*, 1986), 'The proceedings of the *Philo Musicae* were, of course, completely irregular and they were strongly reprimanded by the Grand Secretary.'

From 1726, references begin to appear to show lodges working all three degrees. For example, on 5 March 1737, at Kew, an occasional lodge was held at the palace of Frederick Lewis, Prince of Wales, eldest son and heir to George II, presided over by Dr Desaguliers, ever keen for royal patronage and greater masonic authority and influence. The Prince of Wales was made entered apprentice and fellow craft on the same evening.

The lodge was reconvened at a later date to pass the Prince of Wales a master mason. In 1738, the prince became master of a lodge. With three degrees established as customary (though the third was often reserved for lodge masters within the premier grand lodge of England until the end of the century) – and with the blessing of members of the royal house and British aristocracy – Freemasonry was ready for export.

The Spread of Freemasonry

In spite of the fact that by 1730 Grand Lodge had established itself as a governing body in London, the spread of Freemasonry around the known world would soon encounter problems of competing authorities. Nevertheless, the existence of the grand lodge model as a basis for authority ensured that a standard of order had been created to which competitors could refer. After 1723, the Grand Lodge began to extend its authority into provincial England, and by issuing 'deputations' it encouraged the export of the craft abroad, constituting lodges in Spain and India. Provincial grand masters appear, as does the 'Central Charity Fund', abundant charitable giving being a central pillar of masonic activity from that time to this. Brotherly love and truth are held to be diminished principles without the corresponding practice of 'Relief' or charity. By 1730, the number of affiliated lodges had grown to seventy, according to John Hamill (*The Craft*, 1986, p.44), 'by existing independent lodges agreeing to come under the control of Grand Lodge and by the constituting of new lodges by authority of the Grand Master'.

As in the case of Scotland, we have the phenomenon of lodges 'appearing' when compelled to create records by an external authority. Initially, in the provinces of England, Grand Lodge was (for existing lodges) an external authority. Knowing nothing of lodges' pre-existence (there are exceptions), records give the impression that, in the main, lodges in England came into existence after the founding of Grand Lodge. This can be misleading, as has been shown in the case of Yorkshire Masonry in Rev Neville Barker Cryer's recent book *York Mysteries Revealed* (2006).

York possesses records relevant to fraternities of masons going back to early medieval times. Grand Lodge introduced the concept of recognised and unrecognised lodges. Masons were forbidden to enter unrecognised lodges characterised by 'irregular' practices. As grand lodges developed in other countries, this issue of recognition would come, every so often, to plague the administration of grand lodge-style jurisdictions everywhere.

A foreign grand lodge may be recognised as being in amity with the Grand Lodge of England, but if Grand Lodge decides something has been done that it considers contrary to the 'landmarks of the craft', recognition can be withdrawn. Rival grand lodges may be recognised by the Grand Lodge of England instead.

Issues of recognition become particularly acute when rival jurisdictions are seen as operating in the territory of another. By and large, the United Grand Lodge of England will recognise only a single grand lodge in any given area, even if the constitution of the other grand lodge is regular. However, the Grand Lodge of England does not adopt the strict principle more familiar in the United States where state grand lodges have adopted postures of authority over territory, rather than over members.

Masons who once met in fraternal goodwill are encouraged earnestly to desist from masonic contact, should the brother belong to an unrecognised masonic sodality. Common sense might suggest that such a situation must degenerate on occasion into farce, and this has sometimes been the case. Much of this situation may be traced back to the enormous masonic influence of the Anderson *Constitutions* in its various editions. The earliest Irish constitutions were modelled on Anderson's. The Americans, in 1735, reprinted Anderson word for word, while the English original, sometimes in pirated editions, went all over the world 'transmitting the principles and tenets of Freemasonry and in encouraging Brethren to found lodges on the English pattern'. (Bernard E. Jones, *Freemasons Guide and Compendium*, 1956, p.184).

In spite of attempts made by the Grand Lodge of England to establish jurisdiction, the Grand Lodge of Ireland was founded on St John's Day, 24 June 1725. It covered the whole of Ireland, north and south, as it does today. As far as Freemasonry is concerned, Ireland has never been divided.

There were 'time immemorial' lodges active before Ireland's grand lodge was established. The earliest lodges were established around the southern seaports, from Dublin to Limerick and Galway. A very strong link with maritime Bristol ensures that lodges in Munster still use the famous 'Bristol Working'.

Scottish Masonry has an enviable recorded pedigree, with lodge minutes going back to the very end of the 16th century, as we have seen. Scotland has not yielded evidence for 'Acceptions', however. Ties between symbolic Masonry and lodges of stonemasons are stronger in Scotland. Non trade-working gentlemen were initiated directly into the tradesmen's lodges; Accepted Masonry appears to be an English phenomenon. The usual term for the trade in Scotland was 'mason', rather than the English common usage of 'freemason'.

In spite of the Act of Union between England and Scotland, Scottish masons demanded their own grand lodge and it was duly consecrated in Edinburgh in November 1736.

Some of that mystique generated in the 18th and 19th centuries around Scottish Freemasonry has gathered about *The Royal Order of Scotland*, whose origins are obscure. Certain lodges were functioning in London in 1741. The Royal Order now works two degrees: *The Royal Order of the Heredom of Kilwinning* and the *Knight of the Rosy Cross*. (The word 'Heredom' is generally considered to derive from the Hebrew 'harodim', for *overseers* supervising temple construction.)

Freemasonry heads for the Continent

The 'modern' Freemasonry of Anderson and Desaguliers reached Italy around 1729 when Charles Sackville, Duke of Middlesex, founded a lodge in Florence together with some Englishmen living there, such as Henry Mann, along with Tommaso Crudeli, the first 'martyr' of Italian Freemasonry.

Italy saw the phenomenon of Jacobite lodges, lodges established to further the cause of the Old and Young Pretenders, lodges regarded as highly irregular in London and subject to British intelligence activity. This confluence of secret lodges and foreign intelligence activity appears to have been behind the first papal bull against Freemasonry in 1738. The bull *In Eminenti Apostolatus Specula* iterated Pope Clement XII's prohibition of any masonic assembly, forbidding any involvement by catholics in Freemasonry on pain of excommunication. Many catholics ignored the prohibition. Anti-masonic papal bulls issued in 1738 and 1751 went unheeded in independent Venice. In 1729, Thomas Howard, 8th Duke of Norfolk and a prominent mason visited Venice and Florence. Members of the Florence lodge also included Antonio Cocchi, personal physician to Teophilus Hastings, Earl of Huntingdon, and the Abbot Antonio Niccolini, erudite patron of art and literature. Niccolini was on friendly terms with the Prince of Wales and Horace Walpole (fourth son of Sir Robert Walpole, Earl of Orford).

In Venice, Paduan Antonio Conti was an active Freemason. He had met Newton and Desaguliers in England, as well as the Duke of Montagu and the Chevalier Ramsay who was at this time showing Venice to Montesquieu (later initiated at the Horn lodge, Westminster, by Desaguliers).

Francesco Algarotti and Scipione Maffei were two other prominent citizens of the republic of Venice who were in contact with the Royal Society in London and the masonic circles of England and France. According to Montesquieu (*Freemasonry in the Serene Republic of Venice*, Alessandro Bonelli, *FMT*, issue 10, 1999), Maffei was one of the founders of a lodge in Verona. 'It can be assumed then that a Venetian Freemasonry existed as early as 1730' (Bonelli). From the 1730s English craft Masonry was introduced into Belgium, Denmark, France, Germany, Gibraltar (1728; British troops were at war with Spain), Holland, Malta, Minorca, Russia, Switzerland and Turkey.

Provincial grand lodges flourished in Hamburg between 1737 and 1811; in Frankfurt 1767–1823; Hanover 1746–1828; Holland 1756–70, when the Grand Lodge of England signed a treaty recognising the sovereignty of the 'Grand East of the Netherlands' in its jurisdiction.

The first provincial grand master of Russia was appointed in 1731, though the provincial grand lodge did not come into existence until 1772 (it was banned in 1794 under orders from Catherine the Great, alerted by the Russian Orthodox Church which sensed a spiritual rival).

A provincial grand lodge existed in Minorca between 1792 and 1794; there were also district grand lodges in Gibraltar and Cyprus. The movements of the army and navy were significant in spreading Freemasonry round the world, often taking with them the customs of the 'Antients' after that grand lodge's establishment in 1751.

English Freemasonry was introduced into North America by the appointment of Daniel Cox as provincial grand master of New York, New Jersey and Pennsylvania in 1730. Henry Price was made provincial grand master for New England in 1733. Between 1730 and 1776, the premier Grand Lodge of England (as opposed to the 'Antients') appointed twenty-three provincial grand masters for parts of what is now the USA (Hamill, *The Craft*).

In 1729, Captain Ralph Farr Winter was made provincial grand master of the East Indies. There were provincial grand lodges established in Bengal (1729), Bombay (1764) and Madras (1767).

The first native Indian recorded to have been initiated into the craft was Omdat ul-Omrah, Nabob of the Carnatic, in 1775. The first lodge in China was Amity Lodge in Canton in 1767. A provincial grand master for Sumatra was appointed in 1796 with two lodges under its charge.

In 1730, Randolph Took was made provincial grand master for South America; something of a task one might think. There were provincial grand masters appointed for Antigua (1738), Barbados (1740), and a lodge at Jamaica in 1739. There were three provincial grand masters appointed in 1736 for Gambia, the Cape Coast and 'the Coast of Africa and the British Islands in America'.

A great deal seems to have come from an alleged meeting at the *Apple Tree* tavern in 1716.

Freemasonry in France

While the largest number of Freemasons to be found anywhere in the world today are in the United States of America, the case of France is the most important to understand when trying to disentangle the many strands involved in the global proliferation of masonic rites.

French aristocrats, gentry and learned people took to Freemasonry like the proverbial ducks to water when it became established in that country after 1725. However, the peculiar French talent for innovation, stylistic individuality, philosophy and sentimental artistry quickly went to work on the masonic inheritance and led within forty years to an extraordinary variety of masonic ritual inventions, several of a distinctly bizarre kind.

French successes in colonisation and empire-building ensured that French forms of Freemasonry would find their way around the world where French-originated traditions may still be found in many parts, often in dominant positions – though that is not the case with regard to the stranger kinds of 'fringe' rites. French models of Freemasonry may be categorised as belonging to the following streams:

1. Freemasonry broadly in line with that ratified by the Grand Lodge of England (currently represented by the National Grand Lodge of France).
2. Chivalric-influenced masonic orders, such as the 'Ancient & Accepted Rite' or 'Scottish Rite' with its thirty-three degrees – enormously influential in the Americas.

3. 'Grand Orient' Freemasonry. Traditionally run by a small body of masonic oligarchs, Grand Orient Freemasonry has pursued a more or less independent path of masonic development. On account of its removing references to religion from its constitutions, it has stood as an unrecognised body from the point of view of the British grand lodges. There has also been a countenancing of politically oriented philosophising within the Grand Orient that has also been deemed a deviation from the 'landmarks' respected by British Freemasonry.

4. Freemasonry of the 'Scottish Rectified' type. This kind of Freemasonry has a considerably more developed mystical, magical and philosophical side than 'craft' Freemasonry. It has been linked to the development of a number of strands of continental esoteric thought and development. While its orders are not recognised by the British grand lodges, it has been influential on the history of thought, but is often confused with mainstream Freemasonry in a manner that has been used to prejudice consideration of the mainstream movement.

5. 19th century 'fringe' Freemasonry arising out of the appearance of the Theosophical Society in 1875. This movement includes 'Co-Masonry', today represented by *Le Droit Humain*, an order that permits men and women to meet in masonic amity to pursue a philosophically and mystically oriented fraternal emphasis. Disagreements between English and French-based Co-Masonic authorities have occasionally punctuated its existence. It is difficult to insist on 'recognised' masonic landmarks when the order has itself deviated from the 'recognised'

masonic model. Inter-necine bickering and personality inflammation has been a characteristic element of this category of masonic activity, though such does not characterise all of its members.

Established in France between 1725 and 1730, Freemasonry grew rapidly, partly due to a fashionable interest in English institutions among the French educated classes. While the Parisian grand lodge dominated French Masonry in the 1730s, more exotic forms of Freemasonry began to proliferate across the nation.

In 1737 the *Journal de l'Avocat Barbier* referred to courtiers making up a Masonry different from the English and using such expressions as 'chevalier', 'chevalerie' and 'chapître'. Chivalric and specifically Christian concepts of Freemasonry appear however to go back to its first appearance in France. It should be noted that Anderson's *Constitutions* effectively de-Christianised the craft, and the loss was felt acutely, especially, in the first instance, on the continent. Orders involving Christian knighthood thus appealed in a dual way, being both more 'classy' and more religiously traditional.

Astronomer Joseph Jerome Lefrançais de Lalande was responsible for the earliest written history of the origins of Freemasonry in France. Writing in 1773 he informs us that the first lodges appeared in Paris in 1725. The astronomer named the Jacobite Charles Radclyffe, later Earl of Derwentwater, as the founder. Radclyffe's elder brother James had been executed for his part in the 1715 Jacobite Rebellion. Unfortunately there is no corroborative evidence for de Lalande's assertion.

Chevallier's *Histoire de la franc-maçonnerie française* (Paris, 1974, vol.i, p.7) states that the first grand master of France was appointed in 1728. He was none other than Philip, Duke of Wharton. Wharton had walked out of London's grand lodge – of which he had also been grand master – in disgust, five years earlier.

A Jacobite enclave seems to have developed in Paris between the Rue de Boucy, which ran into the square before St Germain des Prés, and another road off the square, the Rue des Boucheries where the lodge allegedly founded by Radclyffe was located. An important associate of Charles Radclyffe, notable for his encouragement to chivalric and mystical Masonry, was Andrew Michael Ramsay.

Born in the 1680s, Ramsay joined English Jacob Böhme enthusiasts, the Philadelphians, when a young man. A friend of philosopher David Hume, Ramsay later associated with Desaguliers.

In 1710, Ramsay was in Cambrai studying with his 'mentor' François Fénelon, the French idealist philosopher who defended the Jansenists and the mystic Madame Guyon. On Fénelon's death in 1715, Ramsay went to Paris, becoming intimate with the French Regent, Philippe d'Orléans. The Regent inducted Ramsay into the neo-chivalric Order of St Lazarus. This elevation seems to have alerted Ramsay to the values of chivalry and he liked thenceforth to be known as the Chevalier Ramsay.

By 1720, Ramsay had himself become affiliated to the Jacobite cause and tutored Charles Edward Stuart, the 'Young Pretender'. Notwithstanding his Jacobite sympathies on the French side of the Channel, he was, in 1729, admitted to both the Royal Society and the Gentlemen's Club of Spalding whose members included the Duke of Montagu, the Earl of Dalkeith, Rev Dr Desaguliers, Alexander Pope, Isaac Newton and François de Lorraine.

On 26 December 1736, the day on which Ramsay's associate Charles Radclyffe assumed grand mastership of French Freemasonry, Ramsay gave his famous *Oration* at a Parisian restaurant in the Rue du Paon. Chevalier Andrew Michael Ramsay delighted the assembly with his view that the order's great aim was to unite all virtuous, enlightened minds with a love of the fine arts, science and religion to the end that 'the interests of the Fraternity shall become those of the whole human race'. This was a great hope and was apparently based on the great claim of the first charge of Anderson's and, it is supposed, Desaguliers's, *Constitutions*.

The *Oration* was modified and re-presented to the public on 20 March 1737. In a statement plundered from the works of Fénelon, Ramsay declared that 'The world is nothing but a huge republic of which every nation is a family, and every individual a child.' These words would have a tremendous influence on 18th century radical thought. As if this were not enough, Ramsay accused London's grand lodge of being 'heretical, apostate and republican' (Chevallier, vol.i, p.18). This language sounds like the echo of a tirade from the Duke of Wharton; Ramsay seems to have been having his masonic cake, and eating it.

According to Baigent and Leigh (*The Temple and the Lodge*, Cape, 1989), the *Oration* was part of a plan to dissuade French chief minister de Fleury from antipathy to Freemasonry and the Jacobite cause by associating its pedigree with royalty and nobility; Ramsay hoped to initiate Louis XV.

Ramsay wrote of how 'at the time of the Crusades in Palestine, many princes, lords and citizens associated themselves, and moved to restore the Temple of the Christians in the Holy Land, and to employ themselves in bringing back their architecture to its first institution'. (Gould's *History of Freemasonry*, vol.v, pp. 84–9).

While this kind of language would doubtless inspire later creators of chivalric orders with a vein of profound symbolism, the statement could also be read as an allegory for the return of the Stuarts to Britain. De Fleury wanted to keep his king away from further conflict with England.

On 2 August 1737, Freemasonry was interdicted in France (the police report said the craft was indifferent to religions) and the grand secretary was arrested. Freemasonry was certainly active again in Paris by 1742, for that was the time when Baron Gotthelf von Hund claimed to have been initiated into an order of the Temple in Paris, in the presence of a man he thought to be the Young Pretender, Charles Edward Stuart. The date is interesting because it occurs only a year after the first record of lodges of the Royal Order of Scotland, in London. We do not know if this order was connected to von Hund's alleged initiation.

The question of the identity of von Hund's alleged initiator, 'the Knight of the Red Feather' (as von Hund called him) and the issue of Scottish aristocratic traditions in connection with this account is discussed in Baigent and Leigh's popular work, *The Temple and the Lodge*. *The Temple and the Lodge* represents a speculative hypothesis regarding Scottish masonic origins and development involving legends of the Knights Templar.

From the 1730s onwards, it seems to have become a current thought in France and elsewhere that behind the Freemasonry of London's Grand Lodge, stood an older Masonry. In principle, such was indeed the case. However, the typifying of this 'older Masonry' was built, in the established masonic tradition, on myth, legend, romance and propaganda. The French needed little encouragement to entertain a benign view of 'Scottish' or *Écossais* Masonry, (allegedly) more ancient, more mysterious, more noble – even somehow connected with a mystery of the Rose Cross. Surely, many surmised, there was more to this story than the legends of stonemasons. France and Scotland had enjoyed amicable political relations for centuries.

This concoction made for a heady brew and for many, then as well as now, was irresistible. Von Hund said that he was commanded and empowered by his 'Unknown Superiors' (a concept that will become very strong in mystical and occult continental Freemasonry of the Martinist genus) to develop a new rite.

In 1754, Baron von Hund launched his Strict Observance Rite on a long and colourful career. A central legend of the rite contained an account of how the last martyred grand master of the Knights Templar (dissolved in 1312) had yet been succeeded as grand master by Pierre d'Aumont, the Templar Prior of Auvergne who took the order (and its secrets) to Scotland. Thence the order continued in an unbroken line of grand masters who kept their identities secret. These men were the 'Unknown Superiors'. The 'Superiors' could, potentially, show up anywhere; they become the 'Men in Black' of quasi-masonic legend.

The presence of Scots nobles in France in the early 18th century on a 'mission from God', if readers will pardon the expression, must have made the legend come curiously alive.

Scots nobles, secrets, initiations, condemnation (1738) by the Pope, French king, a suppressed message of liberation...

Like the imaginary and invisible *Rose Croix* Brothers who had haunted the imagination of Parisians in 1623, the Templars appeared to be making a 'come-back' with knowledge from the east (preserved) in the mists of distant Scotland. The trouble was that no sooner had 'they' appeared, than they disappeared again! *How very like the Rosicrucians...*

The *Strict Observance Rite* is supposed to have ceased in 1776 (David V. Barrett, *Secret Societies*, Blandford, 1999) on account of a pressing inability to identify the 'Unknown Superiors' of the order. However, as Baigent and Leigh point out (*The Temple and the Lodge* p.282ff.), 'It is hardly surprising that Hund's 'Unknown Superiors' who were all prominent Jacobites, never contacted him again. Most of them were dead, in prison, in exile or lying very low.'

Von Hund had been initiated in 1742 when Jacobite currency was still good. Three years later, the disastrous '45 Rebellion, with its sorrowful *dénouement* at the battle of Culloden, ended any realistic hope that the Stuarts would be restored. Charles Radclyffe was captured in a French ship off Dogger Bank and executed for his part in the rebellion. The executions of leading Scottish noblemen (such as the Earl of Kilmarnock, executed at the Tower on 18 August 1746) did not of course make the symbolism of Scottish Masonry any the less attractive. It might be supposed that such might become a substitute for the absence of political reality. That which had begun as a romance might yet become a cult.

Many of von Hund's ideas were picked up by the *Rite of the Philalèthes* at Lyons, founded by Savalette de Langes, keeper of the royal treasury, in 1775. These were adapted into a rite a form of which is still practised today by the Grand Priory of Helvetia.

The 'Grand Priory of the Rectified Scottish Rite', also known as the *Chevaliers Bienfaisants de la Cité Sainte* (Beneficent Knights of the Holy City, or CBCS for short), is in effect a modification of the 'Old Rite' of Strict Observance of Baron von Hund and is today regarded by many masons as an exalted pinnacle of the craft.

The order of *Chevaliers Bienfaisants de la Cité Sainte* was founded by Jean-Baptiste Willermoz. We shall hear more of him in the next chapter. (Entry in England is restricted to a small number of the 'Great Priory of the Temple' – masonic Knights Templar).

If the 'Unknown Superiors' cannot be found, one had, perhaps, better make some, only, this time they could be known – to a few, at least. In the next chapter we shall encounter the 'Unknown Philosopher' who wrote quite tangible books on intangible subjects.

What is the point, one might ask, of knowing an unknown superior? Surely then they would no longer be *unknown* superiors and, one may suppose, they would not be quite so superior any more either. It seems the knowable superiors might yet need some 'Unknown Superiors' to back them up. In fringe Freemasonry, 'Unknown Superiors' are not unknown. Trying to locate the lost 'Unknown Superiors' would become a staple activity of forms of Freemasonry that developed on the continent in the middle to late 18th century, all with a distinctly Hermetic and alchemical tinge: though gold was, as ever, hard to come by.

It should be noted that if you have decided that your fraternity owes its spiritual cause to 'lost' Rose Cross Brothers, 'lost' Knights Templar, or simply the 'lost word' of Hiram Abif, you are logically bound to suppose some kind of existence of 'Unknown' or at least invisible superiors. This logical trap would encase a great deal of western esoteric thought down to the present day, where any number of self-proclaimed hierophants have claimed or still claim to receive their 'authority' from other-worldly beings or – since the era of alleged 'flying saucer' sightings – 'extra-terrestrials'.

'Extra-terrestrials' occupy all of the psychological aspects once reserved for august spirit entities and remote Himalayan *mahatmas* ('great souls'). This must show the influence of technological science, as demonstrated at Hiroshima and Nagasaki. It is no accident that James Hilton called his highly successful novel about westerners saved by the agency of 'Shangri-La', *Lost Horizon*. It was, of course, invisible. The plane of western technology would have to crash before its survivors could see the alleged superior wisdom.

Such seems to be an analogous hope of certain unspoken strands involved in the current 'global' Green movement. Man will always be the 'other-worldly being' when he insists on re-inventing himself as a god. As Kipling realised, we all share in *The Man who would be King*. According to the theory, we may all aspire to be 'Unknown Superiors' – that part of our being that is unknown to ourselves. Wouldn't it be stranger than fiction if all this strangeness had come about simply because Baron von Hund couldn't recognise Bonnie Prince Charlie, or his stand-in, when he 'saw' him. But then again, perhaps von Hund was blindfolded: a useful tool when in the company of unknown superiors.

The truth was soon lost in Scotch mist.

Chapter Thirteen

Hermetic Freemasonry in Europe

Like the Royal Order of Scotland, the 4th degree of the Holy Order of the Knights Beneficent of the Holy City makes it clear that it prefers Christianity (*pace*, Anderson, 1723ff.) as it seeks to interpret the temple of Solomon as the mystical temple that is the 'Body of Christ'.

In the degree of 'Perfect Master of St Andrew', the candidate is shown the allegorical personality of the master builder revealed as the risen Christ. Or, put another way, the knight is identified as being in union with Hiram Abif, and in this rite, the knight sees Hiram rise to new life.

The Scottish Master

It is worth familiarising readers with some of the words and concepts used today in the rite of making a 4th degree Scottish Master of St Andrew (we do not know to what extent the words of the rite have been altered in detail since the 18th century).

> When the wise man studies the history of the human race in the light of every individual, he does not follow on the footsteps of the vulgar man who sees and seeks only things that are apparent. He directs his gaze beyond the sensible sphere; he knows that above him there is an Intelligent, Active, Eternal, and Almighty Cause which is the secret council of its will, tends always to its ends by the must useful and the wisest means; bringing good out of evil; utilising

even the vices and passions of man to accomplish its
designs and to lead the race at large to the happy end
which it has proposed to itself.

(from the deputy master's First Discourse, 1992:
Directoire Écossais de Belgique. As promulgated at the
General Convocation of Wilhelmsbad, Anno Lucis
5782 [1782AD], The Perfect Ceremonies of Reception
to the degree of a Scottish Master of St Andrew –
convened by the Grand Priory of Belgium. Régime
Ecossais Rectifié au Convent des Gaules, 1778, Vlle
Province. The English translation was made by the
historian of occultism, A. E. Waite for the Rectified
Scottish Rite of Helvetia and compared with that of
the Sovereign Directory of Burgundy.)

The candidate is informed how to interpret the story
of Solomon's temple:

> The destruction of the first Temple – which is
> depicted for the candidate by means of an illustration
> – gives the idea of a great loss, which must be
> repaired. The destruction was within God's
> judgement, for breaking faith and going astray from
> his will. The Temple symbolises the candidate's
> natural, unenlightened tendency and of humanity in
> general. The Temple must be rebuilt: the essential job
> of the Master, and the divine will for human beings
> accomplished. You have come amidst us today as
> came of old to Jerusalem the dispersed masons of the
> primal Temple, and you seek to co-operate at the
> building of that Sanctuary which we raise to Virtue
> and Beneficence.

The candidate is asked to reflect on how suffering and adversity,
unavoidable on the path of life are yet necessary. They quicken
the soul to strive for the source of comfort: the pleasing
knowledge that there is life beyond the gloom and destruction,

the 'prospect of futurity' as the third degree of craft Freemasonry has it. Fortitude is a great masonic virtue.

> It was thus with the Masonic Fraternity. Pursued in France, Spain, Germany and England, it found refuge in Scotland and there *In silentio et in spe* it laboured at the restoration of its destroyed Temple.

The *Third Discourse* takes the craft's image of Hiram to a new level:

> The ancient and most secret word of the Master was concealed in this place of rest [he means the grave]. Like the grain sown in the earth, it germinated in its time, and here you behold Hiram rising from the dead, freeing himself from the cerements and issuing gloriously re-born to a new life. He reappears surrounded by the four Masonic virtues... the significance of the names Hiram Abif and Adon Hiram, contains the seed of truths of an exalted order which primitive peoples interpreted in their primal language and in their hieroglyphs by the typical words – Supreme King of the World. In the Aramaic dialect Adon Hiram signified literally, the Father glorified by death; and Abif, the envoy of one who is greater.
>
> The Word of the Grade is HIRAM.

The candidate is asked to reflect on the heavenly Jerusalem as described by St John the Divine in his Apocalypse:

> In the midst of the Temple you behold the mysterious lamb raising the standard of victory. It is the symbol of the triumph of the true light in the heart of humanity, regenerated by that fraternal love which unites all men.

The Knight must 'cultivate with care that which is spiritual within us; to strive towards the attainment of absolute perfection...'

Employing the 16th century Christian Cabala of Reuchlin (*de verbo mirifico*, 1494), the deputy master unites humanity with the divine: 'On adding of the [Hebrew] letter Shin to Hé who subsists by Himself, Who was, Who is, and Who will be becomes JEHOSHUA – JESHUA or Jesus. Liberator, Saviour, Redeemer.'

> The time has come, my Brother, to announce that our Order is Christian, though in the largest and highest sense of the term. It calls as such, and seeks to unite in its labours, all those, whatever their creed or belief, who aspire without mental reservation to the fulfilment of the chief Christian maxim, 'Glory be to God in the Highest, and on Earth, peace, goodwill toward men!

From the catechism:

> Are you a Scottish Master?
> I am. I have beheld the glory of the restored Temple.
>   ...
> Why are Masons of the 4th grade denominated Scottish Masters?
> Because the Scottish rites were conserved in a distant part of the Isles of Scotland and spread elsewhere from that point.

It may be observed that there is an implicit contradiction in 18th century continental Masonry, and this contradiction contains within it the dynamic for two broad masonic currents. The contradiction lies in the fact that while on the one hand all men are brothers, united as a species under the 'Great Architect', on the other hand, secret wisdom embodied in symbols is revealed exclusively to privileged initiates.

Depending on the extent to which the concept of 'brotherhood' might reach, masons can 'go either way': towards the movement of Enlightenment, with its broad social itinerary, or towards more esoteric and personal masonic expressions. It is also possible to combine the two.

It has long been observed that man needs a sense of the past, of his ancestral roots, of his essential beliefs. Mythologies of knighthood help to bring forth precisely this sense. Romanticism is a great motivator, necessarily ill at ease with rationalism and logic chopping; man cannot live on bread alone.

The Elect Cohens

Interacting and overlapping with the world of 18th century French Freemasonry were a number of organised esoteric and mystical currents.

In 1754, Martines de Pasqually, a man said to have travelled the east in search of wisdom (the Rosenkreuz archetype) set up an order called the Scottish Judges in Montpellier. Six years later, in Bordeaux, he established the Order of Elect Cohens, of which order Pasqually was 'Grand Sovereign'. The Elect Cohens practised a form of ceremonial magic: a combination of the catholic mass with the works of Renaissance occultists such as Henry Cornelius Agrippa.

Pasqually claimed to be in contact with unearthly beings. He held an animist conception of the universe, a universe pulsating with life on many planes or in ulterior dimensions to those experienced by human beings ordinarily. His ceremonies were regulated by astrological considerations. According to Pasqually, 'The bodies of the universe are all vital organs of eternal life.' (Auguste Viatte, *Les sources occultes du romantisme*, ch.2; 2 vols., Paris, Champion, 1928). The moon and the sun figured prominently in his system. Equinoxes were chosen as propitious times for important rituals, to encourage the operation of good spirits.

There was a daily invocation wherein the Elect Cohen would trace a circle on the floor, at the centre of which was inscribed the letter W below a candle. The Cohen then stood in the circle and, holding a light to read the invocation would begin: 'O Kadoz, O Kadoz, who will enable one to become as I was originally when a spark of divine creation? Who will enable me to return in virtue and eternal spiritual power?' (René le Forestier, *La Franc-maçonnerie occultiste au XVIIIe siècle et l'ordre des Elus Coëns;* Paris, Dorbon, 1928).

The purpose of the invocations and evocations was ultimately to open communication with what Pasqually described as the 'Active and Intelligent Cause' (a phrase we may have noticed in the Scottish Rectified Rite). In 1772, Pasqually sailed to Santo Domingo in the Caribbean, leaving the *Assemblée* in the hands of his followers Bacon and Jean-Baptiste Willermoz. Pasqually never returned, dying in Port-au-Prince in 1774.

Bacon then joined the Grand Orient, the mainstream French masonic order (founded in 1772), while Willermoz (1730–1824) not only joined Baron von Hund's *Strict Observance Rite* but also founded several influential orders of his own. The high degree masonic order of *Chevaliers Bienfaisants de la Cité Sainte*, also known as the *Rite Écossais Rectifié*, encountered in the previous chapter. Meanwhile, the *Chevaliers de l'Aigle Noir et Rose-Croix* performed a rite containing strong alchemical and neo-Rosicrucian themes.

The fecund pen of Jean-Baptiste Willermoz is also credited with the creation of one of the most influential set of 'higher' masonic orders. That is, the *Ancient & Accepted Rite*, and in particular, that which was to later become its 18th degree, Knight of the Rose Cross and the Pelican, or as it is more generally known, simply *Rose Croix*.

Rose Croix

According to A. C. F. Jackson's study, *Rose Croix, A History of the Ancient and Accepted Rite for England and Wales* (Lewis Masonic, 1980), it was in the year 1761 that mention first appears of the 'Sovereign Prince Rose-Croix'. The dignity was applied to the holders of the degree of Knight of the Eagle. According to Jackson, it was possibly in the year 1765 that Willermoz completed a *Rose-Croix* ritual, which apparently forms the basis of that practised today as the 18th degree of the Ancient & Accepted Rite. Four years earlier, in 1761, a French creole named Estienne Morin (d.1771) received a patent from the Grand Lodge of France, naming him as 'Inspector General' with duties to spread Masonry across the Atlantic.

Unfortunately, Jackson does not make it clear whether Morin headed to the West Indies (arriving in 1763) with a *Rose-Croix* ritual, least of all the one 'possibly' completed by Willermoz two years later! Nevertheless, a year after this 'possible' completion, Morin seems to have begun the '1762' (backdated) *Constitutions*, which the Ancient & Accepted Rite of today regards as important foundation documents. One would like to know something of Morin's relationship (if there was one) with Willermoz and all those occult-minded masons back in Bordeaux and Lyons.

According to Jackson (*Rose Croix*, p.25):

> The modern Rose-Croix degree seems to have originated from one that was mainly of German origin and associated with the Rite of Strict Observance, which in its turn, was influenced by Rosicrucianism. The correspondence of the masons at Lyons of this period is in the archives of that city, and has been studied by Madame Alice Joly who subsequently wrote *Un Mystique Lyonnais et les Secrets de la Franc-Maçonnerie, 1730-1824*, in 1938. Her researches show that the Rose-Croix degree was developed by a Frenchman, Jean-Baptiste Willermoz, a leading local mason. He was the moving force behind a group of Lyons masons forming a new rite of 25 degrees about 1761, the last of which was Knight of the Eagle, of the Pelican, Knight of St Andrew or Mason of Heredom. Most of these

degrees were little more than names until Willermoz developed them. In 1761, he was corresponding with a Master of one of the Metz lodges, an important Mason named Meunier de Précourt, who was in touch with a number of nearby German lodges. De Précourt knew little about the Rose-Croix degree, except that it existed in some form in Germany, and it is not known where he got his information. A plausible theory is that the information came from the Baron de Tschoudy who wrote the work, apparently written about 1769, though not appearing until 1781, giving the first ritual of the Kadosh or Knights Templar degree. It is known under the title of *G.I.G.E.* [Grand Inspector General Écosse] *Chevalier Kados, connu sous les titres de Chevalier élu* [elect], *du Chevalier de l'aigle noir*. De Tschoudy lived in Metz from 1756 to 1765, presumably busy writing his book, *l'Etoile Flamboyante*, a long and critical letter from 'an old Masonic friend':

> I make out a similar case [of approval] for the Rose-Croix, not that of the inextinguishable lamp [presumably some earlier degree of the same name] but the Rose-Croix properly called or 'Mason of Heredom' though in truth it is no more than a new type of Masonry or the Catholic religion put in a degree.

Whatever the contacts were, de Précourt wrote to Willermoz in 1762 that the German Rosicrucians knew of the 'Order of the Temple' and that they were in possession of 'a thousand marvellous secrets'. These secrets he apparently passed to Willermoz, and Naudon's suggestion is that they were the basis upon which Willermoz completed the Rose-Croix ritual about 1765. Willermoz's degree, if he was in fact the author, did not come entirely from German sources. A degree of Knight of the Eagle is also thought to have been in existence at least as early as 1761, with recipients using the title of Sovereign Prince Rose-Croix. The degree may have been a name only but it is possible that Willermoz knew about it and included extracts in those parts of his degree, which dealt with the Knight of the Eagle. A curious feature of these events is that, within months of Willermoz completing his degree, the printed book of ceremonies, *Les Plus Secrets Mystères*, was published and this had a degree 'The Knights of the Sword and of the Rose-Croix' which was totally unlike the Willermoz version.

(*Rose Croix*, pp.25-26)

The working became very popular and there were attempts made by the French grand master, the Comte de Clermont, in 1766–1767 to restrict its use. Despite this, in Paris in 1768, a body calling itself the 'First Sovereign Chapter Rose Croix' issued statutes and regulations in June 1769.

'It is almost certain,' writes Jackson (*op. cit.* p.28), 'that it was from members of this chapter or other high degree organisations in France that the 18th degree spread to Britain where, like in France, it claimed to be the most important or *ne plus ultra* degree'.

Ne plus ultra means that 'there is nothing more beyond it'. This phrase has also been used of the third degree – and the 'degree' (or is it 'order'?) of the Royal Arch. Masonry is not always sure of where to stop, or even if it should.

From *c.*1775, the *Rose Croix* degree was worked as such in most English masonic Knights Templar 'Encampments'. The first mention of masonic Knights Templar in England comes from 1772. A reference in a Bristol newspaper records a Knight Templar degree being conferred in *Phoenix* lodge No 257 in Portsmouth.

1766 is a possible date, according to Jackson, when Morin began his '1762 Constitutions' and supporting documents. In the following year, 1767, Morin's deputy, Francken, formed the 'Lodge of Perfection and Council of Princes of Jerusalem' at Albany, New York – the same year in which France's grand master, the Comte de Clermont, expressed his wish that *Rose-Croix* degrees be restricted to a few masons of high rank. And so, after (a somewhat disgraced) Morin's death in 1771, a 'Lodge of Perfection' was opened at Charleston in 1783: a key date for today's 'Supreme Council, Southern Masonic Jurisdiction' (USA).

In 1813, the 'Supreme Council, Northern Masonic Jurisdiction' USA was founded. In 1845, England's 'Junior Grand Deacon' Dr Crucefix (1797–1850) received a patent from the Supreme Council, Northern Masonic Jurisdiction, and thus became England's 'Most Puissant Grand Commander', with Dr George Oliver DD (1782–1867) as his lieutenant 'Grand Commander'.

In 1911, England and Wales' Supreme Council moved to 10 Duke Street SW1, its current headquarters. The *Rose Croix* ritual as currently practised in England is a trinitarian Christian ritual which places the aspirant symbolically among the events of the 'Easter weekend' after a long journey, during which he has learnt the value of faith, hope and love. He turns up in Jerusalem to hear that the 'cubic stone' (a masonic/alchemical image for Christ – the 'lost Word') is pouring forth blood for the redemption of mankind.

As 'Knight of the East and West', the candidate arrives at Jerusalem, or rather he faces a black curtain. From beyond he hears the following (according to the version of the ritual in current use):

> The earth quakes, the rocks are rent, the veil of the Temple is rent in twain; darkness overspreads the earth, and the true Light has departed from us. Our altars are thrown down, the Cubic Stone pours forth blood and water, the Blazing Star is eclipsed, our Shepherd is smitten, the Word is lost, and despair and tribulation sit heavily upon us.

By the end of the 'Perfection' ceremony, however, the *Word* is found, the cubic stone changed into the mysterious *Rose*, the blazing star shines in all its splendour, altars are renewed, and the temple is rebuilt. The true light is restored, darkness is dispersed and the new commandment to love one another is heard. Truly it has become (as the *Order of the Red Cross of Constantine* puts it) 'the hour of a Perfect Knight-Mason'.

As we have learned in chapter nine, the true origin of this peculiar being, the 'knight mason', is to be found in the confusion and obfuscation regarding two begging letters from Scottish stonemasons to the lairds of Roslin sent in the first quarter of the 17th century.

Nevertheless, the symbolism of the rite is potent and not without beauty, when properly enacted. The aspirant learns that life is a ladder to perfection symbolised in part by the fragrance of roses and vouchsafed by deep thought on the meaning of the cross, and held in balance by the triple virtues of faith, hope and love. Effectively, the 'slain master' of the craft degrees is identified with Christ and to 'die in Him' is to be reborn in the spirit. As usual in masonic ceremonies there are some signs communicated to recognise those similarly perfected 'Princes Rose Croix'.

After the conferring of knighthood, the newly made knight of today participates in the 'Third Point' (he has already experienced the first two) where the 'Chapter' is addressed as follows:

> Princes, we have now arrived at the perfection of Masonry, let us then unite in forming the Living Circle as an emblem of Eternity.

The assembly drinks wine from a common cup. Seen from another perspective, that of neo-Rosicrucian alchemy, the candidate is participating in a dramatic abstraction of an alchemical operation, in which a mystical union with Christ – the lost Word – is strongly inferred. It is about as close as one might get to being treated as a transformable substance in an alchemical vase. This latter interpretation was seized upon by the late 19th century occult investigator and author, A. E.

Waite, the creator of a Christian offshoot of the Hermetic Order of the Golden Dawn. In his *Brotherhood of the Rosy Cross*, Waite writes of how,

> I am personally convinced that the whole arrangement of the Rose-Croix Grade, its clothing, its jewel, its entire mise en scène, the chambers in which it is worked, are reminiscent of the older order [he means a Rosicrucian order stemming from the 17th century]. The three points are in crude correspondence with the Hermetic working in Alchemy – blackness, death and finally resurrection into the red or perfect state. ...I could carry these intimations much further... exhibiting parallels drawn from Rosicrucian and Hermetic texts on the Cubic Stone, the seven mystical circles, the Rose of Sharon, the Lily of the Valley, the Eagle... The bond of kinship lies upon the surface and those that have eyes can scarcely fail to see it.
>
> Quoted in A. C. F Jackson, *Rose Croix*, p.30)

The Unknown Philosopher

Apart from Jean-Baptiste Willermoz, another significant follower of Pasqually at Bordeaux was Louis Claude de St Martin (1743–1803), initiated into the Elect Cohens in 1768. St Martin was known as *le Philosophe Inconnu*, the 'Unknown Philosopher' – for what reason is not exactly clear – but an unknown philosopher would go very well with an invisible fraternity.

In 1774, the year of Pasqually's death, St Martin began writing his very influential work *Des Érreures et de la Verite* (published in 1775), the book which, together with Eckartshausen's *Cloud upon the Sanctuary*, would make a great impact on Tsar Alexander I and which was read widely across Europe.

St Martin's greatest influence was the ubiquitous Jacob Böhme (*Correspondence*; see A. E. Waite, *The Life of Louis*

Claude de Saint-Martin). St Martin called Böhme 'The greatest light that has appeared on earth since One who is the light itself'. St Martin also had a great social dream: a 'natural and spiritual theocracy' governed by men chosen by God, men with demonstrable divine consciousness.

St Martin's dualistic outlook is reminiscent of Gnosticism. In spite of the advantage of Reason man cannot, according to St Martin (echoing the words of the modern third degree charge), by his own faculties light the torch to guide him in the darkness. Physical existence is a state of continual suffering (whether one is immediately conscious of it or not). In his misery, man is cut off 'from the one source of light and the only aid for living beings'. *(Des Erreures et de la Vérite,* 'Edinbourg' [Lyon] 1782 edition pp.1–31, quoted in Christopher McIntosh, *Rose Cross and the Age of Reason,* Leiden, 1992, p.41)

According to St Martin (the ultimate founder of what today is called 'Martinism'), the system of the materialists 'reduces human-beings to a lower level than the beasts.' *(op.cit. Des Erreures et de la Vérite* p.44) In the view of the 'Unknown Philosopher', theocratic monarchy offers the only solution capable of bringing into the temporal world 'the functions of a true and infinite Being' *(op.cit.* p.287).

Eighteenth century France was a very fruitful field from the point of view of gnostic advocates. On 13 February 1716 Antoine-Joseph Pernety was born, the founder of the *Illuminés d'Avignon,* often confused with the *Illuminati,* with which phenomenon Pernety's order had practically nothing in common. In 1732, Pernety became a Benedictine monk with unusual interests. He became fascinated by alchemy when he read *L'Histoire de la philosophie hermétique* by the Abbé Longlet-Dufresnoy (1741).

In 1765, he dropped the habit but was still referred to as Dom Pernety. He went to Avignon and became a Freemason. He wrote his own rite, the *rite hermétique,* based on alchemical principles, which was adopted by the lodge *Les Séctateurs de la Vertu.* The rite had six degrees:

1. Vrai Maçon.
2. Vrai Maçon de la Voie Droite.
3. Chevalier de la Clef d'Or.
4. Chevalier de l'Iris.
5. Chevalier des Argonautes.
6. Chevalier de la Toison d'Or.

The Dom later added the grade *Chevalier du Soleil* whose ritual, he claimed, contained a complete course in Hermetism and *gnosis* (Christopher McIntosh, *Eliphas Lévi and the French Occult Revival*, Rider, 1972, p.28). In 1738, escaping from a papal bull against Freemasonry, the Dom went to see Frederick the Great. The Prussian king made Pernety a member of the Royal Academy of Berlin with the post of curator of the Royal Library. Pernety contacted Berlin occultists. He was, he said, guided by the angel 'Assadai'. Assadai helped him in the accomplishment of the Great [alchemical] Work: the transformation of the soul.

In November 1783, Pernety left Berlin, as instructed by the angel 'Holy Word', to return to Avignon. At the estate of Bédarrides near Avignon he formed a new people-of-God community (as predicted by 'Holy Word' in Berlin) called the *Illuminés d'Avignon*. All members were masons.

The order had two grades: *novice* and *illuminé majeur*. The leader was simply called *mage*. There was a temple there, and alchemy was practised.

French revolutionaries persecuted illuminist sects. In 1793, Pernety was arrested. Later released, he died in Avignon in 1796, aged eighty, guided to the end by the angel 'Holy Word'.

By 1800, the *Illuminés* had declined to only fifteen circles. (After Pernety's death, his *Chevalier du Soleil* grade was turned into the 27th and 28th grade of the Ancient & Accepted Scottish Rite).

As stated earlier, the *Rite of the Philalèthes* ('Lovers of Truth') founded by the Keeper of the Royal Treasury, Savalette de Langes, in 1775, also contributed to the Ancient & Accepted Rite. This rite combined ideas from Emanuel Swedenborg and Pasqually. There were twelve degrees. The ninth degree,

'Unknown Philosopher', was the name of a spirit familiar to Pasqually's rituals and this is perhaps whence S.Martin's pseudonym derived.

In the years before the French Revolution, all kinds of Masonry flourished. One of the most exotic forms was that of the Sicilian, Alessandro, Count Cagliostro (Joseph Balsamo 1743–1795), founder of the so-called *Egyptian Rite* of Freemasonry, purportedly dating back to the times of ancient Egyptian hierophants from whose descendants Cagliostro claimed initiation.

Cagliostro gathered devotees from all over Europe, claiming to be in possession of miraculous occult powers. He certainly appears to have been not only adept in the art of fascination but no mean hand at numerology as well. His brilliance in selecting winning numbers for the royal lottery of France made him a darling of Parisian society, for a time. In 1785, he founded the Temple of Isis, in the Rue de la Sondière in Paris which, notably, admitted women. He was later falsely implicated by his enemies in the scandal of Marie Antoinette's diamond necklace and thoroughly and quite unfairly disgraced. He later went to Rome where he was arrested by the Inquisition and died alone in prison.

By 1789, there were some 629 lodges in France with something like 30,000 members. Many lodges were explicitly political, while a number had been infiltrated by the followers of Adam Weishaupt, leader of a subversive secret political organisation known (somewhat tongue in cheek) as the *Illuminati*: a group often (and mistakenly) confused with Freemasonry by the movement's enemies. Many masons helped to create the conditions and the desirability for some kind of social revolution in France: the philosophical rationale. Members of the Grand Orient of France, for example, included Voltaire, Bailly, Danton and Helvetius. At the great masonic congress at Wilhelmsbad (1782), the rationalist and revolutionary masons, led by Bode, were defeated by the moderates.

Bode and his followers allied themselves with the Bavarian *Illuminati*. Some masonic lodges in France had the definite knack of turning philosophical principles into political action. When in the critical year 1789 Louis XVI summoned the States General to meet the impending crisis, the coherence of the *cahiers de doléances*, the list of grievances, which were submitted for redress to the King, showed a high level of organisation for liberty and equality.

As things turned out, Freemasons were unable to check the storm that overtook the country. Esotericists rarely acquit themselves well in politics, being concerned with fundamental, timeless principles ('My kingdom is not of this world').

In the wake of France's suppression of the Catholic Church, strange if not absurd revolutionary cults developed. One of the most famous was that of the cult of the goddess 'Reason' erected as an aesthetic abomination in Nôtre Dame de Paris. Worshippers at Reason's throne were greeted by a girl, dolled up in red, white and blue and surrounded by young nymphs performing a spot of ballet.

The main propagator of this cult, Anaxagoras Chaumette, succumbed to the logical chop of the guillotine in 1794. The cult of Reason was swiftly followed by Robespierre's cult of the 'Supreme Being and the Immortality of the Soul', again observed with theatrical rites. These cults have often been linked in observers' minds with the idea of a masonic deism, prevalent in the minds of some reformers (especially in France) during the 18th century. As we have seen, deism is an approach to religion, and as such is emphatically not masonic, Freemasonry being made up of men holding different approaches to religion.

The order is not constitutionally capable of favouring any approach in particular, nor does it by any means discount those approaches. Judgements of theology or primacy (or otherwise) of religion are beyond the competence of Masonry to make, and are not made by Freemasons as Freemasons.

Once and for all, there is no 'Masonic God'. For example, if a certain Freemason's religion happens to be Islam, his God is Allah and his 'volume of the sacred law' is the Koran.

Freemasonry represents an ideal of human fraternity within the specific context of lodges, under the eye of the creator of the universe. Clearly, certain political reformers in France, America and elsewhere who were Freemasons were keen to see something of this ideal active in society as a whole. If one has 'seen the light', it is difficult to keep it to oneself!

However, the image of a body of benevolent reformers meeting in secret to promote political and social improvement – however good or noble the intention – has disturbed the sense of security of those who have not fully understood that Freemasonry explicitly forbids political or religious partisanship within its bounds. It is a notable feature of the Roman Catholic Barruel's famous attack on the role of Freemasonry in the French Revolution that he is explicit on the fact that political involvement was a feature only of extremist masons in France, and was definitely not a feature of British Freemasonry. Such an admission by a vociferous anti-revolutionary Jesuit priest residing in a protestant country must carry some weight!

Neo-Rosicrucian Orders

As we have seen, following the consolidation of the grand lodges in Britain – including the 'Antients' grand lodge founded by Irishman Laurence Dermott in 1751, in defiance of the Grand Lodge of England – lodges became established throughout the world. Originally chartered by these national grand lodges, and by mavericks such as the 'Mother Lodge' of Kilwinning, Freemasonry spread.

French Freemasonry added great impetus to the extent and diversity of the movement. But as Freemasonry expanded steadily on the continent, masonic lodges found themselves in growing philosophical relationship with analogous movements of ideal fraternity, and with philosophical movements stemming from the impact of Renaissance philosophies of man.

Of these movements, the most significant for continental Freemasonry was that of neo-Rosicrucianism. In Germany, Poland and Russia, for example, masons found themselves attracted by the existence of fraternities of *Gold und Rosenkreuzers*. This order appeared obscurely in the early 18th century as a kind of private ideal of men who sought a union of alchemical ideas and practice with a kind of recrudescence of the ideal 'Rosy Cross fraternity', together with a philosophical and Godly Freemasonry. What began among mystically minded men (often illuminated by the thought of Jacob Böhme) as a 'paper ideal' seems to have been further inspired by the appearance of organised masonic lodges. Masonry provided a new model that, paradoxically perhaps, appealed to conservative-minded men who wished to stem some of the anti-spiritual implications of the more ultra-rationalist proponents of 'Aufklärung' or European Englightenment.

For many dismayed at the possibility of extreme atheism or deism in religion, and of materialism in science, the *Gold und Rosenkreuz* movement had much to commend it. Its members formed themselves into sodalities with quasi-masonic, adapted structures. Their history is fascinating and their legacy has been influential on esoteric thought, as well as broadening the capacity of western Europeans to engage with eastern philosophies. Readers wishing to know more about the neo-Rosicrucians and how their membership crossed over with Freemasonry may consult my book *Gnostic Philosophy* (Inner Traditions, 2005) which contains an account of their influence within the context of the development of European gnostic or neo-gnostic movements.

Freemasonry in Germany

The first masonic lodge in Germany was established under English influence in Hamburg in 1737, providing a base for what later became the English 'Provincial Grand Lodge for Hamburg and Lower Saxony'. In 1731, Francis, Duke of Lorraine, later to be Holy Roman Emperor, was made a mason in Den Haag. This event doubtless gave impetus to the acceptance of Freemasonry on German soil.

In 1738, the Crown Prince of Prussia, later Frederick the Great, was initiated at Hanover. In 1744, a lodge was established for Braunschweig (Brunswick), followed by a steady growth of lodges throughout Germany. Between 1761 and 1780, during the great period of German masonic expansion, about 265 lodges were founded in the north and about 28 in the (overwhelmingly catholic) south. By 1800, there were in existence about 490 lodges in the north and about 67 lodges in the south. (Statistics from Michael Voges, *Aufklärung und Geheimnis*, Tübingen, Max Niemeyer, 1987, pp.64ff.)

The so-called higher degrees were the most popular, promising occult as well as moral mysteries. In the 1780s, there were between 20,000 and 30,000 active masons in Germany.

The lodges provided welcome homes for exponents of the Enlightenment, due to Masonry's universalist and egalitarian principles, as well as offering the simple opportunity to meet men of like mind and to discuss ideals and beliefs in a tolerant surrounding. The lodges were conducive to moral, intellectual and artistic progress.

Masonry undoubtedly influenced Frederick the Great of Prussia's tolerant social beliefs and encouragement of new science and thought. In Austria, the composers Haydn and Mozart were masons. (Mozart's character Sarastro in his *Magic Flute* was based on fellow mason Ignaz von Born.) The great legal reformer Joseph von Sonnenfels was a mason. Masonry brought in a whole spectrum of thought, from spiritual idealists to exceptionally radical social and intellectual revolutionaries. Some wanted the best of both worlds: radical progressive thinking and a privily guarded *gnosis*: men such as Adolf, Freiherr von Knigge who was to become Adam Weishaupt's (founder of the radical *Illuminati*) chief collaborator but who, unlike Weishaupt, retained his spiritual and esoteric interests.

Furthermore, the figure of the knight sallying forth against oppressive thought and rule represented a vital moral contribution to the culture, effecting a rebirth of an idea of chivalry which had perished in the Thirty Years War if not long before. Now, and significantly, the middle classes could be drafted into knighthood, through Masonry.

Templar Masonry answered a pressing social need: an idealist standard of conduct in a milieu of intellectual adventuring which for some threatened the basis of morality. Masonry suggested, for some of its adherents, the existence of a higher religion, offering a privileged oversight above the countless religious and ideological divisions that had sundered Europe into armed camps. Masonry could be a liberating influence.

In the 1760s, the Strict Observance Rite of Karl Gotthelf, Baron Hund (1722–1776), made great progress in establishing the mythology of a Knights Templar origin for Freemasonry, and neo-Templarism 'caught on' in lodges across Europe. Rival to the Strict Observance Rite was that of the 'Clerks Templar', founded by Johann August Starck (1741–1816) who claimed that it was the *clerk* and not the *knight* Templar who was the guardian of masonic secrets. The clerk, lacking the archetypal power of the knight, was not as successful a mythology for attracting new masonic adherents. The Braunschweig lodge *Zu den drei Weltkugeln*, adopted the Strict Observance and later became a nerve-centre for the *Gold und Rosenkreuz*.

Masonic Rosicrucians in Poland

Poland contained an idiosyncratic co-mingling of Enlightenment, counter-Enlightenment, rationalist, mystical, humanist and theosophical strains of Freemasonry.

The last Polish monarch was a mason, the enlightened King Stanislas Augustus Poniatowski (1732–98). In 1777, he joined the German-affiliated masonic lodge *Karl zu den drei Helmen*, led by Reichsgraf Aloïs von Bruhl (McIntosh, *Rose Cross and the Age of Reason*, p.148). The king took an interest in high-grade masonry, was promoted to *Chevalier Rose-Croix*, brother of the 21º and became a Rosicrucian, but of what denomination is unknown. He may have become an adherent of the *Bon Pasteur* ('Good Shepherd') system that co-existed in Poland with the *Gold und Rosenkreuz*.

It is possible that the king's friend, Toux de Salverte founded the *Bon Pasteur* system in about 1750. There were lodges of this system in Warsaw and in Wilna (Lennhoff and Posner,

Internationales Freimaurer-Lexicon, p.207ff.). They operated an idiosyncratic mystico-qabalistic system of twelve degrees, which were confined to Poland. Since to be a member it was first necessary to have gone through the three craft degrees, as well as the rite of 'Scottish Master', the *Bon Pasteur* degrees begin at:

5. Chevalier du Soleil.
6. Chevalier de la Rose-Croix.
7. Prince Chevalier de la Croix d'Or.
8. Maître Intérieure du Temple.
9. Erhabener Philosoph.
10. Ordre des Chevaliers Hospitaliers de Christ et du Temple de Salomon (sic).
11. Architect Souverain ou Philosophe du premier Ordre.
12. Frater Operator.

The religious outlook of the Bon Pasteur system expressed a pietistic and gnostic-dualist sensibility. An extract from the *Instruction to Candidates* asserts that 'the light must rise out of the darkness, and our souls, having received and recognised the true light, must allow themselves to be led by the heavenly spirit... Thus the fruits of the spirit are life and purity, while the fruits of the body are earthly death and destruction.'

The system was not anti-Enlightenment. Reason was credited with bringing man out of darkness and superstition, but reason needed to be divinely enlightened. The lodges featured the familiar masonic pillars of Jachin and Boaz and these were interpreted kabbalistically as the twin opposites that (as in Böhme) make the All possible. The order regulations were almost certainly based on those of Sincerus Renatus (Samuel Richter) made for a Rosicrucian order (real or ideal), published in 1710 at Breslau, Silesia, or else the two share a common source as yet unknown. We do not yet know what became of the *Bon Pasteur* lodges.

Russia

Freemasonry reached Russia in 1731, its growth proceeding initially from out of the English provincial grand lodge, based in St Petersburg. In 1775, the philanthropic journalist and publisher Nikolai Ivanovich Novikov (1744–1818) was initiated, so beginning a great masonic-Rosicrucian career.

Novikov was a supporter of the Enlightenment in Russia and worked tirelessly against bureaucratic corruption and the oppression of the serfs in Russia's feudal economy. Martinism (followers of Louis Claude de St Martin) also flourished in Russia, as did Jean-Baptiste Willermoz's *Chevaliers Bienfaisants de la Cité Sainte* or 'Lyons system'. Novikov also became an initiate of Willermoz's 'Beneficent Knights of the Holy City' (Antoine Faivre, *Eckartshausen et la théosophie chrétienne*; Paris, Lincksieck, 1969, p.620; note 329).

After the Wilhelmsbad Masonic Congress of 1782, Russia became the seventh province (of masonic jurisdiction), with Novikov as president and fellow-mason Johann Georg Schwarz (*c.*1751–1784), a Transylvanian German friend of Novikov, as chancellor. (Georg von Rauch, *Georg Schwarz und die Freimaurer in Moskau*, in *Beförder Aufklärung in Mittel-und Osteuropa*, edited by Eva H. Balázs, Ludwig Hammermayer, Hans Wagner and Jerzy Wojtowicz; Berlin, Ulrich Camen, p.213, 216–7.)

It also appears that Schwarz was the head of the *Gold und Rosenkreuz* in Russia. He persuaded Strict Observance members of the superiority of the Rosicrucian system. Schwarz also gave Sunday lectures in Moscow on such doctrines as the emanations of God and the spiritual hierarchy. His greatest influences were Thomas à Kempis's *Imitation of Christ*, German pietist Joannes Arndt, the poet Angelus Silesius and Jacob Böhme. His spirited promotion of German literature contributed greatly to Russia's receptivity to the romantic movement: a movement that was to bear astounding artistic fruit.

Schwarz died at the home of his patron, Prince Trubetskoi at Ochakovo in February 1784. He was thirty-three. Novikov meanwhile echoed Pico della Mirandola's seminal treatise, the

Oration on the Dignity of Man (1486) in his article *On the Dignity of Man in his Relations to God and the World*, published in his own journal, the *Morning Light*.

Novikov advanced the Hermetic view of man as 'lord of the universe', the link between matter and spirit. On the basis of this vision he argued that all human beings deserved respect, regardless of origin or social status. Every individual should work for the common good as an individual, and joyfully so.

Novikov next took the step of forming a highly significant publishing syndicate along with other publishers such as I. P. Turgenev and the Rosicrucian I. V. Lopuchin: the 'Typographical Society'. The society published works by Böhme, Silesius, John Pordage, the mystic Madame Guyon (1648–1717, whose works so pleased William Law), St Martin's incredibly influential work *Des Erreures et de la Vérite*, ('Of Errors and Truth') as well as works of Paracelsian alchemy and works of Rosicrucian provenance. Novikov himself favoured Hermetic and alchemical works, while Lopuchin's publishing-house preferred mystical and pietistic works, proving that men of different preferences can work together to a common aim.

Through the efforts of the Typographical Society, the (reading) Russian public was introduced to a whole range of mystical and esoteric writings. The society, amazingly, produced 893 titles between 1779 and 1792 – that is more than 30% of all works printed in Russia in that period. This was a most remarkable achievement.

The society also involved itself in charitable activities, establishing both a hospital and an apothecary shop for the poor. During the famine of 1787, Novikov and fellow Rosicrucians were out on the streets, active in poor relief. The great heyday of Rosicrucian lodges in Russia ended when the commander-in-chief of the Moscow militia, Yakov Bruce, took advantage of an impending state visit of Catherine II to declare that the Moscow lodges were subservient to Berlin, a not uncharacteristic attack of xenophobia from the perennially suspicious militaristic brain.

Inspections and false-witness led to the closure of all Rosicrucian lodges at the beginning of 1786. In 1792, Novikov was condemned without trial to fifteen years in prison. He was released, happily, four years later when Paul I came to the throne, a man friendly to Novikov and appreciative of some of his ideas. Russian Rosicrucians continued their work in loose association and exerted a liberalising influence on the *weltanschauung*: an influence that touched both Paul I (d.1801) and his successor Tsar Alexander I.

Paul I liked the theocratic ideas brought by the Martinists and Rosicrucians. The conception of the 'Holy Tsar', mediator between heaven and earth, was promoted by Novikov. He believed that the prince should be a mystical initiate drawing on spiritual and supernatural virtues and sanctified by the 'Inner Church' (a conception voiced roundly by the 16th century radical reformers Sebastian Franck and David Joris, influential on the young Johann Valentin Andreae). Novikov's 1783 novel *Chrysomander* featured a magus-king, Hyperion, who used alchemy to relieve the hardship of his subjects (Antoine Faivre, *Eckartshausen et la théosophie chrétienne*, pp.623–4).

After Bonaparte's retreat from Moscow (1812), Tsar Alexander I – who regarded the retreat as an act of divine grace – turned to the writings of Böhme, Swedenborg, St Martin and the works of Karl von Eckartshausen (which had been appearing since 1793). Alexander I was particularly impressed by Eckarthausen's *Die Wolke über dem Heligtum* (*The Cloud upon the Sanctuary*, 1802), published in Russia in 1804, the year in which William Blake released his beautiful poetic prophecy *Jerusalem* to an uncomprehending English public.

Eckartshausen's work is an eloquent treatment of the theme of the invisible body that perpetuates the true, esoteric Christian message. It was presented to Tsar Alexander in 1812, probably stimulating his interest – along with the influence of Baroness Julie von Krüdener who helped the Tsar to understand Eckartshausen's work – in the political realisation of the Holy Alliance. The alliance was promulgated in September 1815 (three months after Waterloo) in an attempt to realise the dream of a Christian theocratic order in Europe.

It was not to be. The Russian Orthodox Church, like the Roman Catholic Church in its intolerance to competition, worked hard against the mystical influence. In 1824 the Archimandrite Photius declared the 'new religion' of illuminism was that of the Antichrist, and a stirrer of revolution. Alexander moved back to orthodox conservatism and a significant masonic-Rosicrucian dream died.

Had the dream been encouraged, then – who knows? – there might never have been a Russian Revolution, and we should all be living very different lives.

A Fecund Marriage

As marriages go, the many-twined relationship between Freemasonry and Rosicrucianism in the 18th century seems positively incestuous. It is frequently impossible to tell where the Masonry begins and the Rosicrucianism ends. For many of those people we have encountered in this chapter, the relationship was less of a marriage than a complete fusion. The fusion, of course, did create a very different conception of 'Rosicrucianism' to that envisioned by the creator of the original mythology, Johann Valentin Andreae in the early 17th century.

High grade (so-called) Freemasonry was also a very different conception of the craft to that envisaged by the members of four lodges who may have gathered to plan a midsummer feast at the Apple Tree tavern in the year 1716.

Nevertheless, the basic ideas struck chords with the creative imaginations of many people who felt for a variety of reasons that the 'wicked world' was running away with them and that humankind needed more than ordinary intelligence to avoid being swallowed up in the chaos. The opening chords soon became a full-blown symphony and while it may have generated not a little misguided frenzy – and some peculiar tunelessness – this marriage nevertheless produced some rather extraordinary children. These were, as the alchemists would put it, philosophical children who would go on to promote some extraordinary movements. Among these movements we can name the 'French Occult Revival' with its impact on art and esoteric philosophy and the combination of the two.

Stemming in part from France, we have the revival of Hermetic studies in late 19th century London that coalesces in the ill-fated Order of the Golden Dawn, with all its literary, philosophical and artistic influences.

The explosion of Theosophy from 1875 has been very influential on many strains of culture, perhaps most notably upon the still-thriving 'Anthroposophy' movement of Rudolf Steiner.

The descendants of the fecund marriage also account for much early 20th century social experimentation, the openness to Indian and Chinese philosophies that we now take for granted. We have also made some (hopefully not temporary) moves towards some social and religious toleration. We should not forget Sir Steven Runciman's words: 'Tolerance is a social, not a religious virtue.'

Perhaps the greatest art is charity, for it enables so many to see. And it has enabled so much art and constructive activity, much of it unseen by those who consider themselves 'self-made'. The philosophical children have been responsible for much charity and imaginative stimulus, undertaken and generated by any number of the various masonic and masonic-influenced movements active in the freer world.

This is a timely moment to explore a little of some of the activities of masonic groups around the world today – groups that should not have existed without much that we have related in this and the foregoing chapters.

The legacy lives on.

Chapter Fourteen

Freemasons around the World

Masons say that the sun is always at its meridian with respect to the craft. That means, globally speaking, there is Freemasonry *24/7*. How then could any book contain the true and total history of Freemasonry? Its compass is vast. Every day the busy bees gather fresh store, largely unnoticed in the world.

So let us assume the appearance of a busy – and unusually well endowed – bee and make our way around the planet, gathering pollen from just a few of the blooms of contemporary Masonry. The aim, for those of less poetic countenance, is to render an impression of the extent and sources of global Masonry, as well as something of its activities during the last twenty years or so.

Undoubtedly, the part of the world that has changed the most during those years is that portion of the world's tragedy once known as the 'Eastern Bloc' – though there was abundant Soviet communist tyranny in the north as well.

On 27 September 1998, the then deputy district grand master (Estonia Division) of the Grand Lodge of Free and Accepted Masons of Finland, 'Right Worshipful Brother' Arno Köörna, with representatives of four lodges in that division, met in Mustpeade Maja Fraternity Hall in Tallinn. There they decided to establish the Grand Lodge of Estonia, petitioning the Grand Lodge of Finland to be mother lodge and to carry out the consecration and installation ceremony.

The ceremony eventually took place on Tuesday 18 May 1999, in the White Hall of the magnificent Gothic Blackheads building (built in 1538), at a consecration led by Ilkka Runokangas, grand master of Finland. More than one hundred brethren attended from the four Estonian lodges.

Finland had established the first lodge in Estonia after independence from the Soviet Union in 1991, but that was not the *first* lodge to be established in the country. While the Tsars held sway over all the Russias, Isis Lodge was constituted in Tallinn on October 12, 1773. The mother lodge was Harpocrat Lodge, St Petersburg (Russia would ban Freemasonry in 1822 due principally to the implacable opposition of her Orthodox Church).

Across the Baltic, in freer lands, Sweden played host to the tri-annual international conference of Great Priories of the Knights Templar in October 1997. Tim Lewis, grand secretary in charge of Mark Masons' Hall, London, joined grand masters and grand vice chancellors of 'Priories' from Australia, Canada, Denmark, Norway, England, France (Scottish Rectified Rite), Germany, Greece, Ireland, Iceland, Portugal, Scotland, Helvetia and Sweden for the Stockholm conference.

Representatives of the Beneficent Knights of the Holy City (CBCS) were also present at the waterfront hotel, with a lodge at its rear, that hosted discussions on many charitable topics, including the priories' maintenance of the ophthalmic hospital in East Jerusalem – most of whose patients are Palestinians.

Members had the opportunity to visit the stunning lodge rooms that characterise Sweden's unique masonic jurisdiction of eleven degrees (including the three craft degrees), under the protection of the King of Sweden. When asked by *Freemasonry Today* magazine why members should bother to keep the 18th and 19th century chivalric orders going in a cynical era, grand secretary Tim Lewis, replied: 'I think it's because people like it. They're getting across a pretty powerful moral teaching in a lot of these orders in a very powerful way.'

The Swedish system has not entirely kept itself within the boundaries of that great country. Hamburg, for example, in Germany, is home to forty recognised 'St John's' lodges, belonging to four different grand lodges. The 'Freemasonic

Order' follows the Swedish system. The 'Ancient, Free and Accepted Masons of Germany' is similar to the English constitution. The *Three Globes* is an old established Prussian Grand Lodge, while the 'Grand Lodge of British Freemasons' in Germany is represented by the Anglo-Hanseatic Lodge.

Belgium

On 27 March 1999, the Regular Grand Lodge of Belgium celebrated its twentieth anniversary at a hotel close to the grand lodge building. A delegation from twenty-five grand lodges included representatives from eight African jurisdictions, as well as the grand masters of Ireland, France, Holland, Germany, Switzerland, England, Luxembourg, the United States, Spain and elsewhere.

Delegates enjoyed a re-creation of an 18th century ceremony, as well as an exhibition of paintings and sculptures by the grand lodge's 'masonic artist'.

Belgian independence from the Netherlands in 1830 led to a re-organisation of lodges under the title, 'Grand East of Belgium'. The *Grand East* developed 'under the Protection of His Majesty King Leopold I'. However, becoming more and more politicised, getting itself involved in disputes with the Catholic Church, the Grand East became isolated from the regular masonic world.

In 1959, four lodges seceded to form the Grand Lodge of Beligum. This was reorganised (and recognised by the United Grand Lodge of England) in 1974, but drifted into irregular practices of visiting unrecognised bodies. Matters were resolved when the Regular Grand Lodge of Belgium was established in June 1979, in conformity with standards of regularity held by the United Grand Lodge of England.

There are some 37 lodges and about 1,500 members. It takes some courage to join this grand lodge. As a result of a past reputation in Belgium for anti-clericalism and political activity, masons have been known to lose their jobs or contact with family members, especially where religious resistance to the idea of a secular society is strong. The situation in Belgium reflects the well-established divergence between the strict policies regarding religion and politics held by the United Grand Lodge of England and the variant approach of 'Grand Orient' Masonry, which sees its principles as necessitating an active political responsibility for the betterment of the human condition.

Eastern Europe

The old rivalry has manifested itself in those parts of the former Soviet Union that have taken an interest in reviving Masonry after many years of suppression and persecution. Where Grand Orient Masonry has not achieved total masonic jurisdiction in a territory, the United Grand Lodge of England has been glad to extend recognition to newly established, regular grand lodges.

The 'Symbolic Grand Lodge of Hungary', for example, was formed in 1989 with the fall of the Berlin Wall. It was recognised in 1990; in 1997, it had five lodges and about 150 members. The Grand Lodge of Czechoslovakia, originally recognised in 1930, was forced to close by the Nazis in 1939. It revived again in 1947 but was forced to close again by the communists in 1951. It was revived once more in 1990, recognised in 1991, and in 1997 had established four lodges with about 140 members.

Standing for Masonry in these territories has created hundreds of stories of sacrifice and heroism. Masonic membership could put you in a concentration camp or a Soviet gulag. While the Grand Lodge of Austria formed three lodges in Croatia (at the same time as the United Grand Lodges of Germany founded a lodge in Lithuania) in 1997, the situation in Serbia has shown little sign of recovery. According to Serbian masonic researcher Zoran Petrov (*Freemasonry Today*, Autumn 1999, p.18), the devolution of Freemasonry in Serbia began more than 50 years ago and continues.

In January 1919, three lodges of the Symbolic Grand Lodge of Hungary approved a provisional Grand Lodge of Yugoslavia. Lodges involved then joined three lodges released from the Supreme Council of the Kingdom of Serbia (Scottish Rite) to form the Grand Lodge of Serbs, Croats and Slovenians *Yugoslavia*.

The Supreme Council of the Kingdom of Serbia operated the first eighteen of the thirty-three degrees, derived from the Supreme Council of Rumania, and the nineteen to thirty-three degrees were chartered from the Supreme Council of Greece. The Grand Lodge *Yugoslavia* was recognised by the United Grand Lodge of England in 1930. In 1938, the grand lodge was subjected to investigation by the Nazi Secret Service, as a result of (it was claimed) English influence, and the existence of the Association for Slav Immigrants (ASI). This association was founded in Belgrade in 1937 by prominent Freemasons, and helped several thousand refugees to transfer to third countries.

After World War Two, according to Petrov, Yugoslav premier Tito was given *carte blanche* by the western powers and attacked Serbs favourable to Serbian monarchy. Serb Freemasons acquainted the west with information as to the true situation in Yugoslavia regarding persecution and summary execution. Freemasons were watched closely by the secret service, the UDB. Gathering only in flats and restaurants, Freemasons were declared an illegal organisation by the state.

After 1990, with the help of the United Grand Lodges of Germany, Grand Lodge *Yugoslavia* was re-established. Recognition was withdrawn in 1994 and given to the newly formed Regular Grand Lodge *Yugoslavia*, also recognised by the Regular Grand Lodge of Portugal and the Grand Orient of Italy. Ex-members of Grand Lodge *Yugoslavia* then founded the Grand Orient of Serbia.

Petrov refers to Masonry in Serbia as 'the broken square'.

The Grand Lodge of Croatia was formed in 1997 by three lodges in Zagreb, formerly working under the Grand Lodge of Austria. It was recognised by the United Grand Lodge of England.

In Vienna, meanwhile, the *Sarastro* lodge (named after the magician in Mozart's masonic-influenced *Magic Flute*), formed in 1969 for visiting businessmen, diplomats and civil servants, after having experienced a near fatal decline, enjoyed something of a revival around the year 2000. Working the English Emulation Ritual, it now attracts masonic visitors from all over the world.

In November 2001, artworks by Czech artist and Freemason Alphonse Mucha (1860-1939) were shown in London's Canonbury Masonic Research Centre after being unearthed by a Czech family who had hidden them through the Nazi and communist regimes. The cache included paintings and jewels for lodge use. Mucha, committed to the foundation of Czecho-slovakia after the break-up of the Austro-Hungarian empire also helped to found the first Czech lodge in that new country. He also created stained glass for Prague's cathedral as well as the country's first stamps and banknotes. He died in despair in 1939 after the fall of his country to the Nazis.

In 2002, the terrible floods that hit central Europe that year severely damaged the headquarters of the Czech Republic's grand lodge. The office, library and archives were inundated with mud and water. Declared unstable, the building had housed now-damaged records of Freemasonry during the Nazi and communist periods.

In January 2003, the National Grand Lodge of Rumania under its grand master, Gheorghe Comanescu, celebrated the first ten years of post-communist masonic freedom. On 24 January, the national grand lodge was re-constituted with the aid of the Grand Orient of Italy and the Grand Lodge of California. The movement has now attracted several thousand Rumanian members. The Rumanian grand master asserted that, 'The Masons practise a kind of art by interpreting the mystery of life and by conveying a noble sense to human existence.'

The vitality and necessity of that 'noble sense to human existence' perhaps explains in part the very great, positive interest shown in Freemasonry by newly liberated former Soviet territories. The Grand Lodge of Russia was recognised by the

United Grand Lodge of England on 10 December 1997. It was formed from four lodges sponsored by the *Grande Loge Nationale Française* (GLNF). Registered with the Russian government, the grand lodge had at the time about 140 members in seven lodges, meeting in Moscow, St Petersburg, Voronezh, Arkhangelsk and Zvenigorod.

In June 1997, in the Republic of Moldova, Professor Giuliano di Bernardo, then grand master of the Regular Grand Lodge of Italy, consecrated the *Alliance* lodge in Chisinau. On 7 February of the following year, di Bernardo consecrated *Hiram* lodge in Odessa, in the Ukraine. Returning to Moldova, the Italian grand master formed the masonic districts of Moldova and the Ukraine on 10 October 1998. He then visited Chisinau in Moldova and consecrated five lodges to work Emulation Ritual.

On 15 October 1999, the grand lodges of Moldova and the Ukraine were formed in a ceremony at Chisinau. The grand master of the Grand Lodge of the Ukraine, Velery N. Saporozhan, and Professor Giuliano di Bernardo were interviewed for Russian broadcast media, while di Bernardo was awarded academic honours at Odessa University.

The grand masters of the two new grand lodges decided to found the 'Federation of Grand Lodges of Eastern Europe' as a governing body to create lodges in Armenia, Georgia and Azerbaijan.

In Bulgaria in April 2001, articles of union were signed by the former rival grand masters of the Ancient Free and Accepted Masons of Bulgaria and the Grand Lodge of Bulgaria (Yanko Bonev). The resulting body, the 'Grand Lodge of Ancient Free and Accepted Masons of Bulgaria' was recognised by the United Grand Lodge of England in 2004, adopting Emulation Ritual in 2006.

In AD 2000, Freemasonry returned to the far east of Russia. The 'Alaska-Russia Relations Committee', established by John Grainger, past grand master of the Grand Lodge of Alaska had begun his plans for two new masonic lodges in eastern Russia in 1993. Constituted in 2000 in the presence of the grand master of Russia, *Pacific Rim* lodge No 12 in Vladivostok is 8,700km from Moscow.

By the end of 2001, the Grand Lodge of Russia was still small, having about 250 members in seven lodges. Notwithstanding, it brought a photographic exhibition on its history to Freemasons' Hall, Istanbul, held after the general assembly of the Grand Lodge of Turkey, in December 2001. The headquarters of the Grand Lodge of Turkey are in Nuru Ziya Street, Beyoglu, Istanbul.

The grand secretary of the Grand Lodge of Turkey, Ahmet Örs, opened the exhibition in the presence of Russian grand master, George Dergachev, and Andrey Serkov, author of a 3000-word masonic dictionary in Russian.

Turkey

The following month, Turkish Freemasons expected completion of a sports building, a vital addition to the school whose foundation stone was laid at Derince in the devastated region of Izmit in September 2000. This was in response to a ruinous earthquake. Financed by Freemasons, the new school has seventeen classrooms, five laboratories and a kindergarten. It was handed over to the Turkish ministry of education in April 2001, to the benefit of 1200 students. The kindergarten was funded by the 'White Gloves Society', a society for Turkish masons' wives. English masons also contributed to the earthquake relief fund.

Freemasonry in Turkey goes back a long way. A London newspaper mentioned a lodge meeting in Smyrna as far back as 1738. Ten years later, Ottoman Sultan Mahmut I forbade all masonic activity, but Masonry survived clandestinely until the time of the French Revolution in 1789 when it re-emerged. However, in 1826, Sultan Mahmut II (1808–1839) closed all masonic lodges.

Masonry came out of the shell again after the Crimean War. The French Grand Orient was the most active. It warranted eleven lodges, one being established in Ottoman Egypt. Not to be outdone, the United Grand Lodge of England warranted fourteen (eight in Izmir), the Grand Lodge of Scotland, six, and the Grand Lodge of Ireland, one. Another seventeen were warranted from Germany, Italy, Spain and Belgium.

A Supreme Council of the Ancient & Accepted (Scottish) Rite was established in 1861. Freemasonry was reconstituted in Turkey in 1909, two years after the initiation of modern Turkey's founding father, Mustapha Kemal 'Ataturk', at lodge *Veritas* in Salonica (Grand Orient constitution). The constitution of the Grand Lodge of Turkey was signed at Noradukyan Plaza, Galata, Istanbul, on 13 July 1909. Prince Aziz Hasan Pasha was the Supreme Council representative. Mehmet Talat Sait Pasha, minister of the interior, and later grand vizier of Turkey, was elected grand master.

Mehmet Reshat V and many other senior Turkish politicians joined the new grand lodge.

When the founder of modern Turkey, Ataturk, landed at Samsun on 19 May 1919 to begin the struggle for a new Turkish constitution and nation, six of seven of his senior military staff were Freemasons.

Freemasonry is a controversial subject in Turkey. Home to 70 million people, there are only about 14,000 masons. However, Turkey has regularly experienced what small numbers of well-organised people can do. For those who virulently oppose the secular Turkish state, that state can be imagined as a product of a kind of masonic-influenced *coup*. Before 1909, Turkey was ruled by a sultan who ran a Muslim caliphate. Removing him from the throne, the so-called 'Young Turks' began a process that within two decades would lead to the secularisation of Turkish state institutions.

Supported mainly by educated people in the cities, it was, above all, supported by the army. Masonic ideas such as liberty of conscience and education seemed progressive and reassuringly European, a way out of the 'bad old days' when a sultan could have a man put to death at a whim. Out of the 'Young Turks' Committee of Union and Progress', emerged Mustapha Kemal, who would call himself *Ataturk* – father of the Turks.

Part of the opposition to the old Sultan Abdul Hamid was formulated from Italian Grand Orient lodges in Thessalonica, spied upon by the sultan's agents. Most of the members of the Committee of Union and Progress were Freemasons, initiated into Grand Orient Freemasonry. Grand Orient Freemasonry has shaped perceptions of masonic priorities among opponents in Turkey, because the Grand Orient has been associated with political movements and does not require its members to believe in God – at least, in the unequivocal manner advocated in the English constitution. Thus, there is an Islamist argument that Freemasonry is atheistic and materialistic, and in Turkey's case, that Freemasonry motivated the split between state and faith.

Ataturk himself tried to avoid the issue of Turkey's semi-theocratic past by promoting the idea of an heroic pre-Islamic Turkish identity. However, Freemasonry in Turkey has changed a great deal since the days of the Young Turks. On 9 October 1935, under pressure from Stalin, Hitler and Mussolini, Ataturk himself closed the lodges because of widespread fears of foreign interference. But after World War Two, masons met in their old buildings, though unofficially. Lodges were officially re-opened in the 1960s and operated in a national association.

In 1965, this Grand Lodge of Turkey split and some of its members founded the now larger Grand Temple of Free and Accepted Masons of Turkey, recognised in London and conforming to the English masonic pattern. Belief in God is essential. Confusion of Masonry with politics is forbidden and an openness policy is advocated.

Such distinctions of regularity did not prevent the bombing of one of its lodges in Kartal District, Istanbul, by anti-semitic jihadists, in March 2004.

Turkey also provides a home for the Liberal Grand Lodge of the Freemasons of Turkey. The Liberal Grand Lodge is in amity with the Grand Orient of France. It does not require any religious statement from its members. Such a requirement, it asserts, would hinder what it considers the universality of the aims of Freemasonry.

The Turkish masonic scene brings us to the issue of the status of Freemasonry in some other countries where the dominant religion is that of Islam.

The Middle East

During World War Two, the middle and near east were rained upon by sheet on sheet of fascist propaganda – in particular, the fantasy of a masonic-Jewish conspiracy, as told in the ubiquitous book *The Protocols of the Learned Elders of Zion*. This short book – purporting to be the deliberations of a 'Zionist Congress' held in Switzerland in the late 19th century – was a fraud perpetrated by the Russian Tsarist secret service to link Jews and communists to the concept of secret global subversion, exercised under masonic-style secrecy.

Since Freemasonry was routinely attacked by the Church in Russia, the idea of a Freemasonry subverted by Jews to effect world domination was an easy link to make in the service of populist, vulgar propaganda. How could the small number of Jewish people subvert the world? Answer: by cleverly subverting Freemasonry's global organisation.

All this might have been forgotten had it not been for consequences arising from the establishment of the state of Israel, so soon after the war's end. The Arab nations' relationship with Israel declined sharply. Meanwhile, Freemasonry had flourished in some predominantly Arab countries. Indeed, the craft provided a philosophical framework for some of Arab politics' most inspiring representatives, such as Jamal al-Din al Afghani (d.1897), founder of Islamic modernism and the Free National Party in Egypt. Afghani's student, Sheikh Mohammed Abduh, campaigned for Islamic scientific renaissance, as well as colonial liberation. Another Egyptian Freemason, Saad Zaghloul Pasha, was a leader of Egyptian independence, becoming, after the Egyptian elections of 1924, the first prime minister of Egypt.

After the war, however, Freemasonry came to be regarded as a 'tool of Zionism'. If western powers supported Israel, it was, claimed Masonry's enemies, because a secret body of anti-

Islamic Freemasons wanted it that way. The old propaganda was given a remix for a new occasion.

Meanwhile, a new minority strain of anti-western opinion was embracing an utterly uncompromising and literalist form of Islam as an antidote to the perceived immorality of western materialist civilisation and as an alternative to atheist communism or any other regime that would not submit to favoured teachers of religion. Muslims who had tolerant or peaceful views began to be seen as weak, even corrupt agents of the 'Enemy'. As communism as a liberating creed declined, it may be seen that an extreme fundamentalist Islam rose to fill the ideological vacuum.

Freemasonry was a soft target. It was outlawed in Iraq in 1958, in Egypt in 1964 and in Syria and Lebanon in 1965.

On 17 July 1968, the Ba'ath socialist party seized power in Iraq. In 1975, the 'Revolutionary Command Council' of that party amended Article 201 of the Iraqi penal code. The article now reads as follows: 'Whoever promotes or incites Zionist principles, including Freemasonry, or belongs to any one of its institutions, or helps them materially or morally, or works in any form for achieving its purposes, shall be executed.'

After toppling the Shah of Iran's regime in 1979, the Islamic Republic executed more than 200 Freemasons. That number included Iran's former prime minister, Amir Abbas Hoveyda. The Palestinian 'Hamas Covenant' of 1988 claimed that Zionism recognised no bounds to its activities. *The Protocols of the Learned Elders of Zion* was cited as evidence for this. Articles 17 and 22 of Hamas's Covenant mentions Freemasonry, along with organisations like Rotary and the Lions as sources of financial power for Hamas's 'enemies', that is, 'Zionist' Israel.

In 1998, Sheikh Abdul Aziz bin Baz died, after 30 years as Grand Mufti of Saudi Arabia. He dubbed Freemasons 'a very evil and dark fraternity' as well as being 'Zionist'. The venerable Sheikh chaired the World Muslim League. The League is a channel for government funds to Islamic causes worldwide.

One of the very sad developments that has taken place in recent years is the proliferation of a large number of 'conspiracy books', blending some fact and much fiction. These works also find Freemasonry a 'soft target'. Perhaps the authors should consider that by creating the miasma of myth about what is in fact a serious subject, they themselves contribute to an atmosphere of conspiracy.

This atmosphere and its mythologies are in turn seized upon by those who are quick both to swallow and to disseminate gross untruths about Freemasonry and who use these myths to work harm upon the innocent. While Freemasonry is not perfect – nor to everyone's taste – at least it advocates a respect for perfection, leaving the highest knowledge to the one God and creator of the universe. Men and women who sincerely do their best in His service of peace and goodwill to humankind deserve respect. When we depart from the truth, even for purposes of entertainment or propaganda, we become the servants of lies. This is not a vocation for true men and women. The case of Freemasonry in Palestine and Israel ought to be sufficient to destroy extremist myths promulgated about the craft and its place in middle-eastern societies.

The first verifiable masonic meeting in Palestine was a 'Secret Monitor' ceremony (see Chapter Fifteen), held by the American Robert Morris, past grand master of the Grand Lodge of Kentucky. The meeting took place on 13 May 1868 in 'Zedekiah's cavern', a cave stretching under Jerusalem. Also present was Freemason Captain Charles Warren of the Palestine Exploration Society. Warren would become master of the 'premier lodge of masonic research', *Quatuor Coronati* No 2076, London.

It is little recognised how significant Freemasonry has been in encouraging the field of archaeology, much of which could be seen as a long-term 'fact-finding' mission instigated after reading the historical sections of Anderson's *Constitutions*!

Morris found only five other masons in Palestine, one being the Turkish governor of Jaffa, Noureddin Effendi 29th degree (*Knight of the Sun*) of the Ancient & Accepted *Amitié Clementi* lodge, Paris. After rejection by US grand lodges (possibly due to his support for the women's 'Eastern Star' order), Morris finally convinced the grand master of the Grand Lodge of Ontario, Canada, that a lodge in Palestine was a good idea.

The Canadians granted a charter to the Royal Solomon Mother Lodge No 283 'of Jerusalem and surroundings'. On 17 February 1873, it met in the Howard Hotel in Jaffa. It was extinct by 1907.

In about 1890, Arab and Jewish Freemasons petitioned the 'Misraim Rite', a fringe masonic society based in Paris. The lodge *Le Port du Temple de Roi Salomon* appeared, but changed affiliation to the more mainstream (if from the English point-of-view, irregular) Grand Orient, in 1906. The lodge was eventually integrated into the Grand Lodge of the State of Israel.

English, Scots, German, Egyptian and Grand Orient of France all founded lodges in the 20th century. On 3 January 1933, the National Grand Lodge of Palestine united French and Egyptian jurisdictions. English-speaking jurisdictions did not join until 1953. That occasion was marked by an impressive ceremony led by the Earl of Elgin and Kincardine, past grand master of the Grand Lodge of Scotland.

Lodges display three volumes of the sacred law: the Hebrew Tanach (the 'Old Testament'), the New Testament, and the Koran. Discussion of politics and religion within the lodge is of course forbidden; that traditional masonic restraint having especial resonance in the region.

From 1981 to 1982, an Arab lawyer, Jamil Shalhoub, was elected grand master of the Grand Lodge of Israel.

In Jerusalem, or rather under it, those enclosed stone spaces sometimes called King Solomon's Quarries host masonic meetings several times a year. Here, Muslims, Christians and Jews meet in amity and respect for their own and for each other's religion under the eternal eye of the 'Great Architect of the Universe' who made man – not 'Jewish man' or 'Muslim man' or 'Christian man' or 'Hindu man' or 'Buddhist man', but *man*.

Some masons may believe the craft began in Jerusalem, but it certainly did not stop there. Our busy bee alights in India, where Arthur Gilbert, district grand master of the masonic district of Bombay and Northern India is giving sixteen hearing aids for the Indian Red Cross Society's school for the deaf. The school is run for very poor families, and Indian masons, in this year of 1997, give as they can, and have done since the craft arrived in India over 200 years before.

On 13 March 1999, the 'Grand Chapter' (Royal Arch) of Bombay and Northern India, will mark their centenary with a fine festive board and collections for charity.

The Far East

Our bee flies east, then south to the masonic district of the Eastern Archipelago, whose headquarters are in Kuala Lumpur and in Singapore. The district covers Singapore and Malaysia – peninsular Malaysia and eastern Malaysia (Sabah in the former British North Borneo).

Sarawak in Borneo is a member of the district of the middle east, (Scottish constitution), and has close ties with Sabah. The lodge Kota Kinabalu is in Sabah. There is an 'annual communication' in Kuala Lumpur and a half-yearly communication in Penang.

Elopura lodge No 2106 was warranted in 1885, but never consecrated. In 1893, the Borneo Lodge of Masonry No 2403 was consecrated. Lodge *Kinabalu* No 7047 (English constitution) was consecrated in 1951 in Jesselton, later renamed Kota Kinabalu, on the northwest coast of Borneo. At a distance of 1000 miles from Kuala Lumpur, the lodge is the most easterly lodge in the district.

Under a corrugated iron roof, the lodge met at the former All Saints' church, where some of its members were once married and confirmed! On 16 April 2000, Lord Northampton, 'Pro Grand Master' of the United Grand Lodge of England laid the foundation stone for a fine new lodge at Kota Kinabalu. Lord Northampton returned to dedicate this faraway lodge on 24 May 2004.

In 1998, masons from all over New Zealand gathered to celebrate in thanksgiving for the 150th anniversary of the settlement of March 1848. Twelve years after the settlement, in 1860, Lodge of Otago No 844 (English constitution) was formed. Today, four constitutions work in harmony in New Zealand: English, Irish, Scots and (from 1890) the Grand Lodge of New Zealand.

Freemasonry thrives in Australia. In June 2002, the Grand Lodge of Victoria lowered the admission age to the craft from twenty-one to eighteen: a privilege formerly only granted to a 'lewis', that is, a mason's son. The first initiate and beneficiary of the new rule was 19-year-old Peter Noonan, initiated by grand master of the Grand Lodge of Victoria, John Wilson.

South America

Our bee heads east again, across the vast Pacific to South America and the Netherlands Antilles in the north of that continent.

Curaçao is one of only a handful of unattached lodges meeting under the English constitution. Founded in 1855, *Igualdad* lodge No 653 meets in the colourful, Dutch-influenced city of Willemstadt. In 1997, the lodge established a committee to foster an openness campaign to alert people as to the true nature of Freemasonry.

To the southwest of Curaçao, the Grand Orient of Brazil was formed in 1882 and now has over 100,000 members in some 1,828 lodges. Recognised by England's grand lodge for over a century, a breakaway group ruptured the jurisdiction's unity, however. This was healed by a treaty of mutual recognition between the Grand Orient of Brazil and the Grand Lodge of the State of Sao Paulo. The treaty opened the door to the United Grand Lodge of England's recognising both bodies in 2000. Every state of Brazil has its own grand lodge.

On 5 February 2003, at a meeting of the 'Supreme Grand Chapter of England' (Royal Arch) held in Rio de Janeiro, Lord Northampton and other senior 'Companions' (as members of the Royal Arch degree are called), constituted a 'Supreme Grand Chapter of Brazil'.

South America is extraordinarily rich in masonic activity, especially of the specifically Christian type (Ancient & Accepted Rite). It is frequently the case that the rituals of the first three (craft) degrees are worked in accordance with the wording of the first three degrees of the thirty-three degree system.

Almost certainly composed in France by the year 1770, admirers believe the language of these degrees to be of an especial beauty. The first grand lodge to be established in South America was the Grand Lodge of Free and Accepted Masons of Argentina (1857). The first lodge in Argentina is believed to date from 1795, and belonged to the Grand Orient of France's constitution. The Grand Lodge of Bolivia was established in 1929, that of Chile (descended from France) in 1862.

The Most Revered National Grand Lodge of Columbia was established in 1918. Two years later, the Most Serene National Grand Lodge of Columbia (at Cartagena) was formed. There are five other grand lodges working the 'Scottish Craft Rite' in Columbia, founded in 1922, 1935, 1945, 1972 and 1984 respectively.

Ecuador's grand lodge was founded in 1921. French Guiana (formerly a penal colony) has no grand lodges, but the *Grande Loge Nationale Française* has warranted three lodges.

Guyana has district grand lodges of the English and Scottish constitutions. The 'Symbolic Grand Lodge of Paraguay' was established in 1869, then refounded in 1895. Peru's grand lodge was founded in 1882.

One of the oldest extant lodges in South America is the first Dutch lodge of Suriname. *Concordia* No 10 at Paramaribo was founded in 1761. Today's members might like to know that the first appointed secretary of Suriname was none other than Accepted Free Mason Elias Ashmole (February 1661) from the time shortly after the 1650s when Lord Willoughby sent out settlers from Barbados. Suriname was ceded to Holland after the Treaty of Breda (the Dutch had invaded in 1667).

The Grand Orient of Uruguay was founded in 1856. The Grand Lodge of the Republic of Venezuela was formed in 1824, working the Scottish (craft) rite, and the north American 'York Rite'. The Scottish (craft) rite and York Rite are also worked by the grand lodges of Costa Rica (formed in 1899), El Salvador (1912) and Guatemala (1903), which also works the German 'Schroeder Rite'.

Nicaragua (1907) works the Scottish (craft) rite, as does Haiti with its surprisingly large masonic membership (6000 masons in forty lodges). The Grand Lodge of Honduras (Scottish craft rite), by contrast, has only thirteen lodges, with a membership of about 350 brethren.

Panama, formed in 1916 and working the (US) *Webb* ritual is also small in masonic membership by comparison with other South American countries. Panama has some fourteen lodges with a collective membership of about 400 masons.

Puerto Rico was formed in 1885. Its seventy-three lodges provide a centre for some 3443 Freemasons.

The Caribbean

The British Virgin Islands is in the masonic jurisdiction of the district of Barbados and the eastern Caribbean. The district stretches from St Thomas in the US Virgin Islands in the north to Grenada, 600 sea miles to the south. At least eleven of the islands have at least one English constitution lodge, so there is plenty of work for the district grand master who must travel to every installation of lodge officers!

In February 1986, after a taxing fundraising effort by members, the foundation stone was laid for *St Ursula* lodge No 8952 (English constitution) in the British Virgin Islands. In the presence of the governor of the islands, the event was also shared by Hollywood star Miss Maureen O'Hara whose cousin is a mason. This was not the first lodge in Road Town, Tortola.

Tortola and Virgin Islands lodges were established by the Antients in 1760 and 1763, and by the Grand Lodge of England in 1765. Nobody knew at the time of the laying of St

Ursula's foundations that they were being laid on land originally owned by the senior warden of lodge No 351, Tortola and Beef Island, plantation owner James Pasea, 200 years before. Rare masonic pipe bowls of the period were discovered in the vicinity.

Freemasonry is well regarded by the people of Jamaica, and the island supports English, Irish and Scottish masonic constitutions. Most lodges are to be found in Kingston and in Spanish Town, but masons also assemble at lodges in Montego Bay, Mandeville, St Anne's Bay, Port Maria, Linstead and on the Cayman Islands. The 1990s saw a surge in membership. The Grand Lodge of Ireland has been particularly active. Jamaica is now a province of that grand lodge, with seven lodges consecrated by 2001. The Scottish constitution can boast 17 lodges, the English, 23.

The Scottish bailiwick of the Bahamas is notable among brethren for its hugely charitable character and complete absence of racism. In Jamaica, the Cayman Islands and the Bahamas, members of the Scottish constitution number some 4,500 members.

Life in the Caribbean can be rough. A volcano eruption in Montserrat in 2000 destroyed *St Anthony's* lodge No 4684 (English constitution) in the masonic district of Barbados and the eastern Caribbean. A fund to rebuild the masonic hall was launched. The first known lodge in Montserrat came after the Grand Lodge of England issued a patent to one James Watson in 1734.

Freemasonry has been active in Trinidad and Tobago since a lodge in St Lucia called *Les Frères Unis* received a charter from the Grand Orient of France in 1787. This lodge received recognition from the Grand Lodge of Scotland in 1812, and was called the *Lodge of United Brothers*, No 251 (Scottish constitution), making it the second oldest lodge out of Scotland under that constitution. There are today ten Scottish constitution lodges in Trinidad and one in Tobago. The English constitution governs seven lodges. In 1958, the district grand lodge of Trinidad and Tobago (Scottish constitution) was formed; in 1968, the district grand lodge of Trinidad (English constitution). The 'Prince Hall' Grand Lodge of Massachusetts (recognised by the United Grand Lodge of England in 1996) provides the constitution for four lodges in Trinidad and Tobago. Cross-membership flourishes in Trinidad and Tobago, which, as we shall see, is a significant fact; Prince Hall Freemasonry is the Freemasonry of the black-skinned man. It is important to understand the vital role played by the Prince Hall grand lodges, both in the Caribbean and, most particularly, in north America.

Prince Hall

It is one of the saddest reflections of American and European colonial history in general that during the 18th century, with traffic in black slaves to the Caribbean and the Americas a big business, equality of consideration to men and women of black skin was virtually unknown. As a result of prejudice and mutual fear built up for some two centuries, those black men who were free in the Americas did not feel able to join lodges of Freemasons run by white colonists. Nor, we may surmise, would they have been welcome.

Deep prejudice was not the absolute rule, but it was practically impossible for persons engaged in the economic system of the time to see a 'negro' and think of him as a 'free man', an essential requirement for candidacy in Freemasonry. The fact of slavery robbed the African American of this first principle of membership. Division of lodge followed division of church membership. It is a matter that prompts profound misgiving that aspects of this long ingrained situation still exist in the United States of America. What was once necessity has now become custom and is taken for granted; great strides have been made both forwards and backwards.

One should like to have thought that Freemasonry would have found a way forward where other institutions have stumbled on this very difficult issue. It is an understandable attitude to be found among black Americans that they often feel most secure when among people of their own background, looking to each other for advancement and dignity. This latter fact provides the context for understanding one of the most significant phenomena of Freemasonry in the United States, the founding of Prince Hall grand lodges.

In about 1780, a group of black skinned, free men in Boston, Massachusetts, attempted to form a lodge in that city under the jurisdiction of the state grand lodge of Massachusetts. A charter was not granted. However, Prince Hall, a Barbadian man of character and determination, looked to England for support with his scheme. It is to the Grand Lodge of England's credit (given the nature of the times) that in 1784 it granted a warrant to Prince Hall. *African Lodge* No 459 thus appeared on the English register of lodges.

However, by 1802, contact between the lodge and England appeared to have been lost, perhaps as a result of disrupted maritime traffic in the Napoleonic wars. In fact, the Prince Hall lodge was doing very well, but, contrary to its warrant, had chartered other groups of African men to meet in lodges. From this activity came lodge No 459B, Philadelphia. This lodge was instrumental in forming the Prince Hall Grand Lodge of Pennsylvania in 1815. In 1827, the Grand Lodge of Massachusetts again refused to recognise Prince Hall lodges. Prince Hall masons declared themselves an independent grand lodge, the *African Grand Lodge of Massachusetts*, from which all the Prince Hall grand lodges derive.

Prince Hall grand lodges were founded in Alabama (1870), Alaska (1969), Arizona (1920), Arkansas (1873), California (including Hawaii, 1855), Colorado (1876) and Connecticut (1873).

In Connecticut, in October 1989, the Prince Hall grand lodge and the state grand lodge (descended from England and Scotland) voted to extend fraternal recognition and visiting rights mutually. Other US state grand lodges followed.

Prince Hall masons have led the way in exchanging recognition with mainstream grand lodges in the US, Canada, England, Europe, South America and Australia. The Prince

Hall Grand Lodge of Delaware was formed in 1849, the District of Columbia in 1848, Florida (including Belize) in 1870, Georgia in 1870. In Idaho, two lodges of Prince Hall affiliation meet in Oddfellows' Hall at Mountain Home. Other Prince Hall grand lodges are to be found in Illinois (1867), Indiana (1856), Iowa (1881), Kansas (1867), Kentucky (1866), Louisiana (1863).

In Maine, *North Star* lodge No 22, chartered by the Prince Hall Grand Lodge of Massachusetts (1791), meets at Bangor. Maryland established its Prince Hall grand lodge in 1845, Michigan in 1866, Minnesota in 1894, Missouri in 1865.

While Montana appears to have no Prince Hall lodges, the 'Most Worshipful Stringer Grand Lodge of Free and Accepted Masons' (Prince Hall affiliated) established its jurisdiction in Mississippi in 1875. Nebraska's Prince Hall grand lodge dates from 1919, Nevada's from 1980, New Jersey's from 1848, New Mexico's from 1921. There are Prince Hall grand lodges in New York (1845), North Carolina (1870), Ohio (1849), Oklahoma (1893), Oregon (1960), Pennsylvania (1815), Rhode Island (1858), South Carolina (1867–1872), Tennessee (1870), Texas (1875), Virginia (1865), Washington (1903), West Virginia (1877) and Wisconsin (1925).

In New Hampshire, there are a number of affiliated Prince Hall lodges at Portsmouth. In North Dakota, there are two Prince Hall affiliated lodges for members of the military, linked to Minnesota, while in South Dakota, *North Star* lodge No 114 was chartered by the Prince Hall Grand Lodge of Kansas, meeting at Box Elder.

In Utah, there are Prince Hall affiliated lodges meeting at Salt Lake City and Mount Ogden. Similarly, Wyoming has Prince Hall affiliated lodges at Cheyenne and Caspar. Vermont appears to have no Prince Hall lodges. Recognition of Prince Hall lodges has dramatically increased since the 1980s. In 1997, for example, the United Grand Lodge of England recognised the Prince Hall grand lodges of Colorado, Washington State, Wisconsin, and Oregon (descended from the Prince Hall Grand Lodge of Ohio). In September 1998, Indiana joined the list of Prince Hall grand lodges recognised in England.

There are some 4,740 Prince Hall lodges in the United States with a combined membership of approximately 220,500 (I am indebted to Kent Henderson and Tony Pope's superb *Freemasonry Universal – A New Guide to the Masonic World*, Vol.1, Global Masonic Publications, Victoria, 1998, for these figures.)

Meanwhile, back in Trinidad and Tobago, May 1998 saw the three constitutions of the islands get together in the persons of their senior representatives for the first time. At the invitation of the district deputy grand master of the four Prince Hall lodges of the eighth masonic district of Trinidad and Tobago, Courtney W. T. Browne, the district grand masters of the English and Scottish constitutions joined him to witness a first degree ceremony.

The invitation was made in response to an invitation extended to Courtney W. T. Browne to the annual communication of the District Grand Lodge of Trinidad and Tobago in March 1998.

The public procession of Prince Hall masons, the district grand master wearing a top hat, flanked by motorcycle escorts and fronted by a brass band, on their way to a St John's day celebration at an Anglican church, must have been a sight to see!

Another impressive sight was witnessed on 8 July 1997, when a group of Freemasons from Iowa visited a lodge in Moseley, in England's West Midlands, to demonstrate the first and second parts of Iowa's customary third degree.

Like the deputy grand master of the Prince Hall masons of Trinidad and Tobago, 'Most Worshipful Brother' D. Dean Johnson, Grand Master of Iowa, also wore a striking top hat for the duration of the ceremony. The ceremony itself came as a real surprise to English masons. The drama of the murder of Hiram Abif and subsequent hunt for his killers was dramatised in a quite literal way, reminiscent perhaps of the old mystery plays that masons used to enact in the middle ages at religious festivals.

English Masons are now of course used to a more restrained approach; Iowa Masons are not. According to the grand master of Iowa, 'Our third degree ritual came, I believe, out of Ohio and Missouri, from the pioneering days. It was passed on by word of mouth.' When asked about the issue of retention of members, Johnson was realistic: 'Well, we're ageing. We lost a generation to the hippy crowd. Now we're beginning to get it back.'

The United States of America

Freemasonry in America may be going through a reduction in numbers after a post-war high, bolstered by thousands of returning servicemen, but it is still a mighty edifice of masonic commitment. In terms of scale, there is nothing like it in the world. It would indeed be surprising if an institution that arrived in America (in the heart of at least one person) only sixty years after the 'Pilgrim Fathers', should lose its iconic place in the fabric of American society.

A look at the number of lodges in the United States, and the numbers of members a decade ago, is instructive in itself:

State	Lodges	Members
Alabama (1821)	358	46,000
Alaska (1981)	5	170
Arizona (1882)	71	11,820
Arkansas (1838)	328	28,152
California (1850)	419	110,227
Colorado (1861)	147	19,162
Connecticut (1789)	114	22,091
Delaware (1806)	29	6,736
District of Columbia (1811)	32	6,032
Florida (1830)	311	64,984
Georgia (1735)	440	62,000

Solomon's Lodge, with a warrant from the Grand Lodge of England, met in Savannah, Georgia, in 1735.

Idaho (1867)	73	6,629
Illinois (1840)	619	94,335
Indiana (1818)	485	98,256
Iowa (1844)	354	35,127
Kansas (1856)	290	43,810
Kentucky (1800)	441	65,161
Louisiana (1812)	272	27,637

Louisiana's masonic history has been characterised by great disharmony, chiefly as a result of the French Grand Orient-inspired struggle between craft and 'Scottish Rite' Masonry.

Maine (1820)	193	28,447
Maryland (1787)	118	25,154
Massachusetts (1733)	296	52,000
Michigan (1826)	406	66,313
Minnesota (1853	196	23,920
Mississippi (1818)	280	29,998
Missouri (1821)	442	59,000
Montana (1866)	104	9,400
Nebraska (1857)	174	19,505
Nevada (1865)	43	5,844
New Hampshire (1789)	77	9,710
New Jersey (1786)	159	42,125
New Mexico (1877)	66	8,204

New Mexico's grand lodge grew out of two military lodges established during the American-Mexican War.

New York (1781)	677	85,563

The Grand Lodge of England appointed Daniel Cox as provincial grand master of north America, based at New York in the 1730s. *St John's* lodge, New York, was warranted in 1757.

North Carolina (1787)	384	60,500
North Dakota (1889)	72	4,947
Ohio (1808)	608	154,638
Oklahoma (1874)	264	37,337

Oregon (1851)	152	16,877
Pennsylvania (1731)	487	153,755

The first records of Masonry in Pennsylvania appear in an article in Benjamin Franklin's *Philadelphia Gazette* in 1730. Franklin joined the *Tun Tavern* lodge between January and June 1731. After the War of Independence, the 'Moderns' (Grand Lodge of England) lodges expired, with only the Antients remaining. In 1786, the Antients provincial grand lodge declared independence from England: 13 lodges met and erected the Grand Lodge of Pennsylvania.

Rhode Island (1791)	39	6,989
South Carolina (1737)	329	56,051
		(descended from England)
South Dakota (1875)	105	8,292
Tennessee (1813)	367	72,397
Texas (1837)	907	144,884
Utah (1872)	32	2,714
Vermont (1794)	89	8,870
	(Descended from Massachusetts, England *via* Canada	
		and Connecticut).
Virginia (1778)	336	50,720
Washington (1858)	224	26,802
West Virginia (1865)	149	30,083
Wisconsin (1843)	222	22,141
Wyoming (1874)	50	6,500

The first known Freemason to settle in America is believed to have been one John Skene of Newtyle, England, born in about 1649. Skene arrived *via* the Delaware River with his family aboard *The Golden Lion* in 1682. He settled at Mount Holly, New Jersey, at a plantation named Peachland. He became deputy governor of the Jersey colony and died in 1690.

The first Freemason born in America is a distinction usually given to Andrew Belcher, son of Jonathan Belcher, who, in spite of an unfortunate name, was a former governor of Massachusetts and New Hampshire. Jonathan Belcher had been made a mason in England in 1704; son Andrew was admitted in 1733.

The first regular warrant was presented to Henry Price on 30 July 1733. Meeting in the Bunch of Grapes tavern, Price's lodge claimed the title of 'first lodge in Boston' and named it *St John's Grand Lodge*. Not wishing to miss the masonic boat, the Grand Lodge of Scotland granted a rival dispensation to that of the English on 30 November 1752. The result was *St Andrew's* lodge, No 82. Joseph Warren became grand master of the province. Relations between the rival grand lodges were bad for many years.

The 'Scottish Rite' is, unlike in England, a major part of Freemasonry in the USA. The 'Scottish' or Ancient & Accepted Rite is administered by northern and southern jurisdictions, through which jurisdictions thousands of American men experience the first three craft degrees. Masons who follow the Scottish Rite are used to the thirty-three degrees being divided up as follows.

The 4th to the 14th degrees constitute the 'Lodges of Perfection'; the 17th and 18th degrees constitute the 'Chapters Rose Croix'; the 19th to the 32nd degrees are called 'the Consistory', while the few who attain the 33rd degree represent the 'Supreme Council'.

The second human being to walk on the moon, 'Buzz' Aldrin, is a 33rd degree mason. Its ritual emphasises courage in the face of death, the necessity for self-sacrifice and its concomitant, spiritual rebirth, and, above all, the absolute necessity of benevolence and exaltation to serve the human race – qualities and ideals as useful here on earth as in outer space, one might think. The degree is held in high esteem by American masons, and is only granted to men who have given especial service according to the high ideals of the degree.

Scottish Rite temples are like large theatres with lighting, sound systems and props. Often, groups of candidates watch as the ritual is performed before them to an individual 'ideal' candidate. Costs doubtless dictate the nature of the practice. One Scottish Rite temple may serve a 'Valley' (membership unit) of as many as 30,000 or more. One in five of these masons will hold the 32nd degree.

Another important system in America is called the York Rite. The rite covers nine, ten or eleven degrees or orders, all worked in full. The degrees conferred in a Royal Arch Chapter are the 'Mark Master' degree, the (virtual) 'Past Master' degree, the 'Most Excellent Master' degree, and the degree of Royal Arch mason. These four are known as the 'Capitular Rite'.

Conferred in a 'Council of Royal and Select Masters' are the 'Royal Master' degree, the 'Select Master' degree and the 'Super Excellent Master' degree (optional) together forming the 'Cryptic Rite' (because they refer to the symbol of a crypt beneath Solomon's Temple).

Conferred in a Knight Templar 'Commandery' are the 'Order of the Red Cross', the 'Order of Malta', and the 'Order of the Temple'. These three orders form the 'Chivalric Rite'.

Another important aspect of the craft in America is the organisation known as 'The Shriners'. While the United Grand Lodge does not recognise the Shriners, since it is a truly non-masonic order, it nonetheless consists of Freemasons, admitting only the holders of the 32nd degree or Knights Templar of the York Rite.

The Shriners are properly named the 'Ancient Arabic Order, Nobles of the Mystic Shrine', membership of which – despite its sounding like something from the musical *Kismet* – is yet considered by many American masons as the summation of masonic achievement. Shriners raise huge sums for charitable causes along with a joyous emphasis on social activities. The Prince Hall masons have their own version of the order, called the 'Ancient Egyptian Arabic Order, Nobles of the Mystic Shrine'.

Other rituals are worked in America. Many Americans' first acquaintance with the first three degrees is through rituals of the 'Webb' type. In the late 1790s, Thomas Smith Webb attempted to produce a standardised ritual a few years before the United Grand Lodge of England formalised Emulation Ritual (after 1813).

Webb used the English *Antients'* ritual as a basis, thus ensuring that details of the older ritual forms would be worked in America after the Grand Lodge of England had dispensed with them or synthesised them into the new Emulation Ritual. In fact, different grand lodges have different versions of the 'Webb-form', often having been passed down by word of mouth and adapted over time. These differences offer a great deal of charm to the life of masons who enjoy the surprise of familiar themes in variant settings, as we saw in the case of the Iowa masons who performed in England in 1997.

One of the very rare customs of Freemasonry, more familiar to Americans than to Europeans is the 'making of a Mason at sight', a privilege claimed by some grand masters. It lends itself to an extrovert nature such as is not unknown in the United States.

In 2003, the governor of New York State, George E. Pataki, accepted the offer of grand master Carl J. Fitje to become a master mason. The grand master said that governor Pataki had 'displayed the kind of leadership and quality in a man that our organisation looks for'. Fitje was referring to Pataki's committed handling of state resources after the tragic devastation of 9/11.

Canada

In November 1997, a new grand lodge was formed in Newfoundland and Labrador, thus separating the territories from the United Grand Lodge of England's masonic governance. Twenty-seven of the thirty former United Grand Lodge of England lodges agreed to the move to independence, as did those lodges belonging to the District Grand Lodge of Scotland. Independence from English and Scottish grand lodge control began in Canada with the formation of the Grand Lodge of Ontario in 1855. Ontario was followed by Nova Scotia (1866), New Brunswick (1867) and Quebec (1869).

In spite of the fact that Quebec is today predominantly French speaking, by the time of the English Union of 1813, Quebec possessed seven military lodges and thirteen stationary lodges, working in English under predominantly Antients masonic control.

With the amalgamation of the Antients and the premier Grand Lodge of England in 1813, much of Canada's masonic life came under the aegis of the United Grand Lodge of England. British Columbia achieved independent grand lodge status in 1871, Manitoba in 1875, Prince Edward Island also in 1875, Alberta in 1905 and Saskatchewan in 1906.

In the North West Territories, *Yellowstone* lodge No 162 meets under warrant from the Grand Lodge of Alberta, while in the Yukon Territory, three lodges are warranted from the Grand Lodge of British Columbia.

Our imaginary, and uniquely equipped, time-travelling busy bee now negotiates the coldness of the north Atlantic, and, succumbing to pains of cold, decides to buzz down south to warmer climes and tasty pollen. Before doing so, however, he just has time to take a listen to the Icelandic Freemasons' Choir performing for their new CD, *Braedralög*, in 1997.

The phenomenon of masons raising their voices in song is not uncommon in the masonic world. In 1995, a new organ was constructed for Reykjavik's masonic hall, two years after the Icelandic Freemasons Choir received a charter from their grand master to enhance the brotherhood of all song-loving masons.

Spain

Such brotherhood has been very difficult to establish in Spain. In December 1997, Barcelona's Sants Hotel hosted the eighth international symposium on Freemasonry. This event was organised by the 'Centre for the Study of Spanish Masonry', whose president is Professor José Ferrer Benemelli. Benemelli began his studies of Freemasonry in the 1960s and organised the institute after Franco's death in 1975. The offices were firebombed by rightwing extremists in the 1970s.

The 1997 conference brought over 100 delegates from universities as far afield as Cuba. The then president of the government of Catalonia, Jordi Pujol, was honorary patron.

During the 19th century Freemasonry championed the cause of liberty in Spain, upsetting the rigorous doctrinal authority of the Roman Catholic Church in the process. Seven Spanish prime ministers were masons.

The Grand Orient of Spain was the most important masonic institution to survive the Spanish Civil War, but the Ancient & Accepted Rite also drew significant masonic support. Freemasonry in Spain is now, however, a very small presence indeed, on account of General Franco's obsession with the mythology of masonic-Jewish-communist conspiracy.

English mason Matthew Scanlan's research into the subject, made possible by the work of Benemelli's institute, has brought to life the true nature of the fascist hatred for Freemasonry and everything it stood for, and was falsely accused of standing for. Blaming Freemasons for everything that was wrong (in his opinion) with Spain during the Spanish Civil War, Franco's invective against the movement did not abate with his victory over the republicans. According to Scanlan (*Freemasonry Today*, Autumn 2004, pp.32ff.), 'In March 1940, he [Franco] issued a decree banning Fremasonry and Communism. All Masonic assets were to be 'confiscated immediately' and anyone deemed to be a Mason would be subject to a minimum twelve-year gaol sentence. Masons of the 18th degree [*Rose Croix*] and above were deemed guilty of 'Aggravated Circumstances', and usually faced the death penalty. The former Catalan president and organiser of the Workers' Party (POUM), Luis Companys, was arrested by the Gestapo in northern France and sent back to Spain where he faced a firing squad.'.

After World War Two, Franco continued his deadly rant with speeches, books and articles written by himself, accusing anything that happened in the United Nations or in the United States perceived as prejudicial to his regime as a result of the masonic membership of statesmen and diplomats. In 1950, he accused the BBC of being run by masons. The obsessive attack on masonic-communist plots continued until the last month of his life when he told the Spanish people that the two evils facing his country were communism and

Freemasonry. The EEC, he told the Spanish people, was the work of left-wing Freemasons.

Today, Spanish people are free to make up their own minds on these issues, and are free to practise and learn the truth about Freemasonry if they wish to. The United Grand Lodge of England recognised the Grand Lodge of Spain in 1987. On 3 March 2001, the grand lodge officially merged in amity with the larger Spanish Grand Orient: a peaceful end to a long, dark tunnel of paranoia and murderous hatred.

Portugal and Greece

The Regular Grand Lodge of Portugal was formed in June 1991. In the year 2002, Portugese Freemasons celebrated the 200th anniversary of the original charter granted to the first regular Portuguese grand lodge by English Freemasons in 1802.

An English delegation, headed by Pro Grand Master, the Marquess of Northampton, flew to Portugal to attend the celebrations. Delegations also arrived from the *Grande Loge Nationale Française* (GLNF) and from the Grand Orient of Brazil. The president of the Portuguese parliament, Mota Amaral, received the delegations, along with the prime minister of Portugal, Durrão Barroso, and Lisbon's mayor, Santana Lopes. The president of the republic of Portugal, who was unable to attend, sent a message stressing the important values of regular Freemasonry.

Our bee now heads across the warm waves of the Mediterranean, passing over Greece. In June 2000, the Grand Lodge of Greece was recognised after seven years of isolation. The Grand Lodge of Greece was first recognised in 1875. The Grand Lodge of England withdrew recognition in 1993, however, on account of the Greek grand lodge's engagement in political discussion. In 1999, neither it nor its rival the 'National Grand Lodge of Greece' was recognised. This made visiting impossible for many masons. Recognition was finally granted when the Grand Lodge of Greece satisfied the United Grand Lodge of England as to its regularity, and in consideration of the nine regular English constitution lodges under its jurisdiction.

Sadly, our bee has no time for visiting. He is buzzing off to…

Africa

In the autumn of 1998, district grand master of East Africa, Sir Jayantilal Keshavji Chande KBE, known affectionately as Sir 'Andy' Chande, is helping the children of breadwinners killed in the devastating embassy bomb explosions wrought by supporters of Al Qa'eda on 7 August 1998.

Freemasons have contributed 1.7 million Kenyan shillings to the initial fund.

On 22 August 1998, the 'District Grand Lodge of East Africa' met in a non-masonic building for the first time since the district was formed on 15 October 1926. 146 members met beneath a thatched roof to deliberate plans for the district's future organisation and to honour the high moral standing and generosity of East Africa's Freemasons, under the awe-inspiring, energetic leadership of Chande. Chande quoted the phrase from the Bible that unless a man be born again, he cannot find the kingdom of heaven, and compared the essential idea to the masonic third degree ceremony. He said that the burying of the past, together with the raising of new life, was a lesson in spiritual rebirth.

From three lodges under the *Grande Loge Nationale Français*, a new grand lodge of Madagascar was formed in March 1997, now recognised by the United Grand Lodge of England. To the west, 14 July 2001 saw the birth of a new masonic hall in the suburb of Arusha, in northern Tanzania. The foundation stone was laid by grand master, J. K. Chande, for the use of *Mount Meru* lodge No 7504 (English constitution) and other orders.

The first *Mount Meru* lodge was warranted in 1932. The present lodge was consecrated in 1957 at another lodge building near Mount Kilimanjaro (*Kilimanjaro* lodge No 5111).

The west coast of Africa has not had the blessing of J. K. Chande's inspirational leadership. Times have been very hard there for Freemasons, especially in Liberia and Ghana. Liberia became an independent republic in 1847, encouraged by the United States as a place where black Americans might find a home. Consequently, many of the republic's founders were Prince Hall Freemasons. The Liberian Grand Lodge of Free and Accepted Masons was established in 1867, with Thomas Amos as its first grand master.

In 1980, a *coup d'état* led to Freemasons coming under attack; the grand master was murdered. Since the late 1980s the conflict has led to many masons seeking refuge in Liberia's outback. The first lodge to be founded in Ghana – then known as the Gold Coast – was the aptly named *Torridzonian* lodge No 621, in 1810.

In 1931, the United Grand Lodge of England created a masonic district, and in 1949, the *Travellers Lodge* No 6758 broke the mould of separate lodges for Africans and Europeans and Masonry developed happily enough. This process ended in 1984 when Jerry Rawlings took over the Ghanaian state; Freemasonry was banned. Normality was restored in 1985. Freemasonry is slowly picking up.

There is no doubt that the world can be a dangerous place for Freemasons and for all the beliefs they share with spiritually optimistic people everywhere. What happens, for example, when a formerly benign government is superseded by a government intent on curbing existing liberties? Masons can quickly become isolated. Such happily has not been the case in Hong Kong, now a part of China's mammoth economy.

China

On 30 January 2000, the 50th anniversary of Zetland Hall was celebrated by Hong Kong's Freemasons. This masonic hall had been the centre of Hong Kong's masonic districts under English, Irish and Scottish constitutions.

The dedication ceremony embraced all major religions with passages from the Japanese Mahayana Buddhist tradition (Freemasonry thrives in Japan too), the Muslim tradition, the Hindu tradition and the Christian tradition. All of these traditions met in harmony in the masonic temple. A most interesting sermon was given by the Rev John Chinchen, from which I should like to quote the following:

> These robes preserve my identity as an Anglican priest. However, this morning, with great humility, I feel privileged to have stepped outside the confines of my own tradition of faith… outside the perimeter of denominations to stand here as a Christian cleric in a wider, all-embracing sense. And further, beyond, to share this act of worship with all of you who believe in, and love, the Great Architect and Creator of the Universe. I join hands with those that worship the Hindi deity, and follow the path of Buddha, with our brothers and sisters in Islam, with the Jewish people from whom we Christians come, and those of other persuasions too numerous to mention individually.

It is difficult to avoid thinking of the famous ancient Bible prophecy that one day all people from all over the world would converge to respect God in His temple. In Freemasonry, in a unique sense – and perhaps even as a vague pattern of the future – they can, and do. Of course, as we shall discuss in chapter sixteen, such a vision, profoundly liberating as it may be, is unable to satisfy the conflicting ambitions of the world's organised religious governments. *So mote it be?*

Our bee must now buzz back to his old hive in Britain where he was born. There he, like many Freemasons, faces a bewildering choice of orders and degrees. All of these orders are based on the three degrees discussed in chapter one of this book, but they may well look and sound as if they came from another planet!

It is time to examine, in brief, other significant aspects of British Freemasonry. These aspects also represent a return journey of Freemasonry to Britain's shores. For, as we have observed in the global spread of Freemasonry from its original hive, the movement has by no means been all one-way. The inspiration for much of Britain's additional (falsely called 'higher') degree systems, has come from the European continent and from America, developed by those who received the British inheritance and then worked on it themselves. During the late 18th and 19th centuries, many of these additional masonic orders found their way, sometimes uncomfortably, back to the place of their ultimate source, before, on occasion, being exported again around the honeyed world.

Chapter Fifteen
Additional Degrees
of Freemasonry

It cannot be stated strongly enough that the existence of other degree systems, together with the increase in the numerical weight of degrees, does not mean that Freemasonry is a kind of Mithraic or ancient Gnostic graded system of progressive steps promising ever greater esoteric knowledge or occult power. If this were so, we might suppose that a thirty-third degree mason of the Ancient & Accepted Rite would be ruling the world as a result of having acquired a supernal wisdom of incalculable power!

There is no holy grail at the 'top' of Freemasonry. There is no great alchemical secret by which common lead might become solid gold. If there were, its leading exponents would be locked up in Fort Knox or some other government institution. A 33rd degree mason – or, indeed, a third degree master mason (there is no essential or necessary difference in the man according to masonic rank) – should find the wisdom to rule *his* world, not yours!

It is of the nature of delusionary psychologies that the would-be dictator really does think he has mastered the universe of his imagining. A course in real Freemasonry might – were it not for the typical psychosis attendant on such perennial types – persuade the deluded egomaniac that he had not yet learned to govern himself, never mind a corner-shop or great country.

Perhaps, incidentally, this may in part explain the extraordinary hostility shown to Masonry by the world's dictators or would-be dictators. Mussolini, Franco, Hitler, Stalin, Saddam Hussein, Mao Zedong all hated Freemasonry. Perhaps, this so-called secret society really got under their skin. Maybe it exposed the scotoma before their own warped vision of life. Who knows? Perhaps it was all a result of the fake *Protocols of the Learned Elders of Zion*, still doing their dirty work on the minds of the vulnerable, the paranoid and the arrogant conspiracy-obsessed. Now, the *Protocols* really were a product of a real secret society – the old Russian Secret Service.

The psychology of the archetypal 'fascist' is basically that of the elemental 'pagan' type. He likes things at the earth-level, blood and soil. He is, as Becker brilliantly described him in *The Birth & Death of Meaning*, the driven, mostly unconscious, 'anal sadist' who wants to sodomise mystery out of existence. His idea of architecture is, when not heavy granite, basically stolen, second-hand, tasteless, gaudy, preferably plundered on the cheap from elsewhere. His artistic taste is either banal or affected. Low art appeals because it keeps man low. This type does not want to be raised, unless it is to the top of a heap he recognises as only fit for dumping on. He is not nearly so rare a type as the 'liberal' of today may imagine.

Physical and degrading punishments please him, the subjugation of women in any posture pleases him, the blind obedience of children pleases him; guns and explosions are delights. Sheer animal, unconscious power, thoughtless will: all of these things appeal to him. Imagine then his reaction on catching a glimpse of Freemasonry: seven liberal arts, moral development, self-mastery, charity, tolerance, joyous fellowship, universality. He is sent into a state of virtual apoplexy. Whatever happened to the animal order of things? He rages, he spits, he hates, he kills. Do not fear him; fear that you might, inadvertently, support this beast. For he is in you and me. Our inner failure is the secret quarry from which he builds our prison. In the light of this analysis, made with such science as is present in the discipline of modern psychology, we can understand that the aping of Freemasonry will appeal to the so-called 'fascist' type (the type goes back much, much further than that!).

Fake chivalric orders with grotesque costumes, gold and silver braid, initiation rites, gaudy hangings, flags, medals, uniforms, mass assemblies, ersatz occultism, cod mysticism – all to the glorification of the animal *id* that loves destruction and revels in defecation. One thinks, of course, of the SS, but that was only one instance, though sufficient, one would hope, to get us thinking. It is a sad thing that Freemasonry is so often confused in popular fiction with its blind but deadly ape – the secret 'order' hell-bent on global domination, the *SPECTRES* of our dreams and nightmares.

Have we gone far enough? We have forgotten something.

Above all, the type we have been describing hates Jews, that race that has been burdened with the almost unbearable weight of God's peculiar interest, never let off the hook of His expectation and judgement: a people raised to please Him, as they believe. How awful a destiny is that! How tempting for the blind outsider to stick the boot in, or more commonly, encourage others to do so. Who has the courage to stand with the Jews? And then, what do we find in Freemasonry, including, and perhaps especially, in the additional degrees? We find a fabulous glorification and adaptation of episodes from the Hebrew Bible. We find attempt after attempt to try to get inside the soul of some of these ancient stories. Legends they may be, but the essence of their moral and spiritual force may be made real.

The story of the Flood and Noah's Ark is important (Royal Ark Mariners). The loving friendship between David and Jonathan is important (Order of the Secret Monitor). The encampment of the Hebrews by Sinai is important (Ancient & Accepted Rite). The raising of the serpent in the wilderness is important (Ancient & Accepted Rite). The struggle for the Promised Land is important (the third degree). The building of the temple is paramount (in a sense, in all the degrees!). The return of the Jews from exile is important (the Royal Arch).

All of these Bible stories are enlivened in a quite unique manner in many of the degrees of modern Freemasonry. It is hardly surprising that movie director and impresario Cecil B. de Mille was a Freemason. The additional degrees of Freemasonry are often played out on an epic scale, and yet, like cinema, confined to a chamber.

But, let it be understood, all of the additional degrees are in some way or manner a kind of commentary or expanded discourse on some element or other already present in the first three degrees. So, for example, the principle of fellowship is important in the first and second degrees; this principle is expanded in the Order of the Secret Monitor to show how important the principle of fellowship can really be.

So, the idea of a lost word or substituted secret word is important in the third degree; in the 'Supreme Degree' of the 'Holy Royal Arch', the essential meaning of this lost *Word* is revealed. So, in the third degree, the idea of a slain master is important; in the 18th degree of the Ancient & Accepted Rite this idea is used to illuminate the Easter events sacred in memory and heart to Christians.

So, the idea of a journey towards the 'Holy of Holies' is implied in the three craft degrees; in the Knights Templar degrees, the idea of a long, hard slog to Jerusalem – and the virtues necessary to undertake that symbolic pilgrimage – are illustrated and symbolically enacted.

The additional degrees are symbolic. One might well understand the symbolism of the holy grail better after participating in a number of ceremonies, true. One may well come to see that it is the lead of man's lower consciousness that must be raised to the golden spirit of divine love, that is the real, accessible point encoded within the stories of alchemy that have touched the world of Freemasonry. Symbolic realisations can of course be very powerful, should they come alive within the right soil. No degree can make the soil! And no symbol will come alive if the mind is closed to its light.

So let us begin this necessarily brief excursion with perhaps the most important and masonically significant degree that has been added to the three craft degrees – because this degree is, in a sense, all about bringing something precious out of the darkness and into the light. That is really what Freemasonry is all about, and perhaps for this reason, the Royal Arch degree has been called 'the climax of Freemasonry'.

And please, note that there is a very great difference between reading about a degree, and actually participating in one. Shakespeare reads very well indeed, but it's better to hear his words uttered from the tongue of a master. The only things we need are masters, which is why bad boys miss school so much; good boys learn to be masters themselves.

The Royal Arch

The Royal Arch has had a colourful history. The first reference to something like it comes from an account of a public procession in Ireland in 1743. Two characters called 'Excellents' were observed carrying an arch. This arch was referred to as 'Royal', perhaps a reference to a biblical King: Solomon or Hiram of Tyre.

The word 'Excellent' is now used as an honorific in the degree. Members are called 'Companions', having been 'exalted'. There are 'Excellent Companions' resplendent in vivid blues, greys and reds, and the word 'excellent' has found its way into a number of other additional degrees, sometimes with additional superlatives, such as 'Super Excellent'. As we have seen during the 18th century, the boat was always being pushed that bit further out as time went on. It seems many masons couldn't resist the urge to get 'higher and higher'.

In the same year as the Irish procession was observed, a writer called Dr Dassigny referred to a charlatan in York who was admitting Irishmen into an order of the Royal Arch of which he claimed to have been a master. Dassigny referred to the Royal Arch as this 'excellent piece of masonry'. The charlatan was unmasked by a brother who had attained the degree in London.

The degree seems to be strongly connected with Ireland; it may have been formed there, perhaps as an alternative to, or addition to, the third. Possibly, it is older. We have no idea of its original components, as with so much in Masonry.

The Royal Arch certainly proved to be very popular with the Antients Grand Lodge, formed in 1751 by Irishman Laurence Dermott. Most of the original members of the Antients were Irishmen working in London. For them, the Royal Arch was a veritable 4th degree and the 'root, heart and marrow of Masonry'.

The oldest lodge minute referring to it comes from Ireland in 1752. The first record of a brother 'raised to the degree of the Holy Royal Arch' is recorded as having taken place at a lodge in Fredericksburg, Virginia, on 22 December 1757. All offices in the Antients Grand Lodge were elected; this doubtless added to its appeal both in the armed services and in the colonies. The Royal Arch was something the Antients had that was denied to many lodges under the arms of the premier Grand Lodge of England.

This situation became intolerable for senior members of the older grand lodge, as one might expect. But how could they admit another degree? How could they admit that the upstart rival might be right? They were losing potential members to the Antients, many attracted by the lure of a 'more ancient Masonry'. Did the Grand Lodge of England know everything there was to know of the secrets of the ancient craft? In July 1766, a 'Charter of Compact' was signed. This document created the 'Grand and Royal Chapter of the Royal Arch of Jerusalem', parent of today's 'Supreme Grand Chapter of the Holy Royal Arch', the administrative body governing the order. It meant that a small number of grand lodge masons could join the Royal Arch, but only as something separate to the three ancient craft degrees.

But is the Royal Arch really an 'order' or is it a degree? Obviously, the premier grand lodge did not feel comfortable with either. After all, it was the order of Free and Accepted Masons, and three were its regular degrees. But times had moved on. Lots of degrees were being bought and sold on the wicked continent; some of the material was coming back. Some masons really liked the 'new stuff'.

The tide of change was surging, while every day the Antients cocked a snook at the premier Grand Lodge of England. The union of the Antients and the premier Grand Lodge of England required the latter to give more weight to the Royal Arch than had formerly been the case. The articles of union accepted the Royal Arch as part of 'pure Ancient Masonry' (a great admission), but insisted it be worked in separate chapters. However, these chapters would be affiliated to craft lodges, and would carry the craft lodges' number. This was one of those great British compromises that enabled the Act of Union to declare, with a straight face, that pure ancient Freemasonry consisted of the degrees of entered apprentice, fellow craft and master mason, including the 'Supreme Order of the Holy Royal Arch'. Again, we have the confusion of 'degree' and 'order'.

The Supreme Grand Chapter, formed in 1817, describes the 'Order of Royal Arch Masons'. During the degree's 'Exaltation' ceremony, the 'Most Excellent Zerubbabel' informs the candidate that he has not taken a 4th degree, but that this is the *third completed*. Zerubbabel then goes on to say that he will explain the mystical portion of this 'Supreme Degree'!

During the Exaltation, the Royal Arch is seven times described as an order, and eleven times as a degree. The wording suggests some kind of psychology of denial, like a man who can't quite admit that his wife has left him.

The Royal Arch seems to be content to be both. As Zerubbabel says, '…as you seek preferment in our Order, and have been entrusted with the Passwords leading to this Supreme Degree'.

Obviously, the confusion stems from the awkwardness of the premier grand lodge's position. It wants to be seen to be maintaining the pure ancient landmarks of the order, while having to admit the sheer fact that masons like, and are ready to practise degrees that it can't easily bring itself to approve of. This understandable reticence marks out the whole history of relations between the Grand Lodge of England and the additional degrees. Furthermore, it is also the case that members of some of the additional degrees have been, and still are, maybe even in spite of themselves, inclined to look down on the plain, 'blue' Masonry now administered from Freemasons' Hall, Great Queen Street.

The Royal Arch is, nevertheless, unique in British Masonry since it is effectively an additional degree, but has become woven into the fabric of craft Freemasonry. Perhaps that explains part of its continued appeal. In fact, so great was its appeal that original rules demanding that candidates had to be, or have been, installed masters of lodges was changed by another awkward addition to custom. That is, the creation of the 'installed Master' whereby a man who had never been master of a lodge could, by 'passing the Chair' become a virtual past master, or 'Installed Master', in order to join the Royal Arch. In 1823, the admission requirement was lowered again to that of requiring a man to have been a master mason of one year's standing.

In 1893, this stipulation was reduced to just four weeks. Nowadays, it is normal in the UK that the newly raised master mason is very soon approached to consider 'completing his third' by entering a Royal Arch chapter.

Much of the appeal of the Royal Arch is that it claims to offer what has only been hinted at in the third. While the third offers 'substituted secrets' – the originals having somehow gone with Hiram Abif to his grave – the Holy Royal Arch offers its explanation of the lost mason's word. In doing so, the Exaltation ceremony, re-creates a most fascinating legend around the idea of the reconstruction of the temple of Jerusalem, along with a crystalline teaching about the nature of God that you might be hard pressed to find expressed quite so well in a modern church.

It should be stated that there is nothing in the degree that suggests that some secret of religion may be obtained in the Royal Arch ceremony that cannot be found in the whole body of Jewish or Christian tradition. The teaching of the degree is illuminated in relation to the stories of masons that occur in the Bible.

Since much of the spirit, and indeed the content, of the Royal Arch Exaltation ceremony permeates the worlds of the other additional degrees, it is worth going into some detail as regards its dramatic components.

The main characters in the Royal Arch ceremony are as follows: Zerubbabel, a prince of the returning Jewish exiles from Babylon; Haggai the prophet; and Joshua, a high priest. These three are called 'Principals'. Then there is the 'Scribe Ezra' (secretary) and 'Scribe Nehemiah'. The action is completed by the 'Sojourner' and his two assistants.

The sojourners are so called because they have experienced the long 'sojourn' in Babylonian captivity after the destruction of the temple and the laying waste of Jerusalem in 587BC. The events take place after the Edict of Cyrus in 538BC allowing the return of Jews to their homeland to rebuild their temple.

The idea of sojourn may also refer to the 'pilgrimage' implied from entered apprentice to the brink of the holy of holies in the third degree. The sojourners wear craft aprons because they are masons set to work on clearing the foundations of the proposed new temple. In the process of clearing the foundations, the masons make a momentous discovery. Now, anyone who thinks the Royal Arch is simply a presentation of the Bible stories concerning the return of the captive Jews to their homeland is quite mistaken. It is perfectly clear to anyone familiar with the relevant sections of the Bible – and the para-literature available to Freemasons after the 17th century – that the Royal Arch 'events' are very cleverly compounded from a number of sources, each conveying different but strangely complementary ideas. The story is not intended to be taken literally.

This fact becomes immediately apparent when one realises that in America, for example, the Royal Arch events are not set in the times of governor Zerubbabel, but in the reign of King Josiah (640–609BC). The reason for this seems clear enough.

A scripture-read individual has probably looked at the British Royal Arch story, with its discovery of the *Word*, during the rebuilding of the temple and has said: 'Dear me! Don't these fellows know their Bible? The discovery of the Word is plainly recorded as having taken place in the Bible in the reign of King Josiah!'

Well, however clever this person may have thought they were, they have not understood the composite nature of the Arch legend, nor have they understood the peculiar character of Freemasonry. Freemasonry is not a literal celebration of the Bible stories; it is a symbolic reflection of meanings inherent within those stories. In this sense, its treatment of the Bible is close to the kabbalistic Jewish mystical tradition that seldom takes a biblical text at 'face-value'. However, such Kabbalah as appears in masonic traditions tends to be of a fairly rough and ready kind; the Hebrew is very often 'cod' and the lineaments not infrequently derive from non-conformist 18th century dabbling in Hebrew. We may recall how 'harodim' becomes the mountain of 'heredom', to take just one example.

However, as we shall see, there may be traces of Christian Cabala, a peculiar branch of the art that developed in the minds of Florentine Neoplatonist Christian philosophers such, notably, as Pico della Mirandola whose *Oration on the Dignity of Man* we have quoted from earlier. I suspect that the Royal Arch ritual contains elements of Christian Cabala, though I am aware that this conception will not please some masons. It would help perhaps if the 'rulers of the craft' were theologically trained.

However, to return first to the Josiah account. Josiah orders repairs to be made to the temple of Solomon. In the course of clearing out the temple treasury, a 'book of the law' is discovered. In II *Chronicles*, the book is described as being authored by

Moses. This has led some commentators to believe that the book found was the basis of what is now called the Book of *Deuteronomy* – or the second book of law. Josiah reads the book, rents his clothes in astonishment, and launches a massive religious reform programme, tearing down the pillars dedicated to the goddess of popular worship, and clearing away the 'sacred groves':

> And Hilkiah the high priest said unto Shaphan the scribe, I have found the book of the law in the house of the LORD. And Hilkiah gave the book to Shaphan, and he read it.
>
> (II *Kings* XXII.8)

> Go ye [says Josiah], inquire of the LORD for me, and for the people, and for all Judah, concerning the words of this book that is found: for great is the wrath of the LORD that is kindled against us, because our fathers have not hearkened unto the words of this book, to do according unto all that which is written concerning us.'
>
> (II *Kings* XXII.13; a similar account is found in II *Chronicles* XXXIV.8ff.)

Clearly in the non-British version of the temple discovery legend, the 'Word' has been taken in its protestant emphasis as meaning biblical texts. This emphasis makes it very difficult for those of a protestant religious background to get a clear idea of the variant meanings of the word 'Word' when used in a religious, and particularly masonic, context.

When *John* I.1 says, 'In the beginning was the Word', for example; it does not mean 'in the beginning was the Bible'. Likewise, when that chapter refers to the Word becoming flesh and dwelling amongst us; it does not mean that the Bible was made man, since the passage referring to the event had not been written at the time of the incarnation.

However, one can understand how the conflation of the 'book of the law' and the Word discovered in the Royal Arch was easily made. We can be reasonably sure that the 'Masons' Word' of the old freemasons was a secret word of recognition coined from within the imaginative world of the craftsmen. It is likely that the linkage between this word and the religious concept of the 'Word' was a later (post-1550) development; how much later or earlier cannot be determined. The old masons were aware of their special place in religious stories, although the work of Neville Barker Cryer regarding the masons' contribution to medieval mystery plays shows no particularly esoteric interests that masons chose to dramatise or make public. That there is esoteric meaning in the Bible is plain to those that know it well, though the concept of the 'esoteric' has changed since ancient times, and especially since the Renaissance.

For whatever reason, the composer of the Royal Arch ritual decided to make explicit the idea that the lost word of the master had a profoundly religious meaning. However, those persons familiar with today's ritual will be aware that the 'word' itself is not secret. It is, however, secreted, in a vault. This secret vault, presumably arched over by an arch of King Solomon's original structure, does not appear in the text that is apparently the source of the British Royal Arch ceremony. Its value is symbolic. The relevant biblical texts for this ceremony occur chiefly in the book of *Ezra*:

> Then stood up Jesh-u-a the son of Jozadac, and his brethren the priests, an Zerubbabel the son of Shealtiel and his brethren, and builded the altar of the God of Israel, to offer burnt offerings thereon, as it is written in the law of Moses the man of God.
>
> (*Ezra* III.2)

> But the foundation of the temple of the LORD was not yet laid. They gave money also unto the masons, and to the carpenters, and meat, and drink, and oil, unto them of Zidon, and to them of Tyre, to bring cedar trees from Lebanon to the sea of Joppa, according to the grant that they had of Cyrus King of Persia.
>
> (*Ezra*, III.6–7)

The setting is there. We have the reconstruction, the proposed laying of the foundation of God's house. This story has been conflated with the story of a discovery of lost law (in the reign of Josiah) and then conflated again with what looks very much like a masonic re-working of the account of the vault of Christian Rosenkreuz as described in the *Fama Fraternitatis* (first published in 1614).

In the Rosenkreuz legend, an architect, 'Brother NN', is doing repairs to his house when he uncovers a nail in a wall. Pulling the nail out removes sufficient stonework to reveal the presence of a hidden vault. Inside the secret vault of seven sides are geometrical shapes and inscriptions relating to the constitution of the universe. Beside the sarcophagus of Father C.R. himself, there stands a round altar, on which is a brass plate with figures and inscriptions, one of which is 'The whole Glory of God'. The books of the order are placed in chests or arcas by each side of the wall. The whole is lit by an 'inner sun' self-powered in the ceiling of the vault.

We now come to the legend of the Royal Arch itself. During the clearing of the site of the temple, three masons are working on the site of what was the Holy of Holies. They have three tools, the pickaxe, the crowbar and the shovel, to aid them. In the course of labour, they break through the masonry beneath their feet and find a hole. Gazing through it, they find a vault beneath the site of the Holy of Holies, where the Ark used to be. The masons go and report the discovery to the Principals who recommend exploring further into the mystery.

The 'Principal Sojourner' is lowered down by a rope into the vault to discover there a white marble altar, made of a double cube (the double cube being an established model for the body of a temple). Upon the altar is a round plate (of gold). Upon the plate are inscriptions, including a triangle and a circle (like the plate in the Rosenkreuz legend). The name on the circle is made of the English letters JEHOVAH. This is an old English transliteration of the original Name of God – the Word:

יהוה

Reading from right to left, that is the letters *Yod, Hé, Vau, Hé*. YHVH or JHVH. The Hebrew letter *vau* can also be transliterated as a 'w'. To pronounce this word in English, it is usual to insert a vowel between the first and second and third and fourth letters, producing the word/name Yahweh (or Jahveh) familiar enough to divinity students. This is God's name in its authentic language. The universe embodies its creative expression or extension. An interpretation of the meaning of this word is given to the candidate as part of his Exaltation.

He is informed that the word is constituted from the past, present and future tenses of the verb *to be*. God's name is 'I am that I am'. He is the Most High, True and Living God: 'The name on the circle is that great, awful, tremendous and incomprehensible Name of the Most High. It signifies 'I am that I am', the Alpha and Omega, the beginning and the end, the first, and the last, who was, and is, and is to come; the Almighty. It is the sacred and mysterious Name of the actual, future, eternal, unchangeable and all-sufficient God who alone has His being in and from Himself and gives to all others their being; so that He is what He was, was what He is, and will remain both what He was and what He is, from everlasting to everlasting, all creatures being dependent on His mighty will and power.'

The candidate is informed of the essence of his Exaltation: 'It has virtue for its aim, the glory of God for its object, and the eternal welfare of man is considered in every part, point or letter of its ineffable mysteries.'

The recovery of the name is presumably considered synonymous with the finding of the master's lost word. This all sounds well and good, as far as it goes. But it hides a hidden history. The current English use of the word 'Jehovah' is in fact a replacement for a word that had been cobbled together from Hebrew sources, '*Jabulon*', some time in the 19th century. Enemies of the craft reckoned that 'Jahbulon' denoted some composite 'Masonic god' made of Jahveh, Baal and Osiris, for example. It was in no wise intended that way.

As far as we can tell, the word 'Jabulon' had been put in as a secret word – or yet another substituted secret – for another word that for some reason had to be removed. According to John

Hamill, during the 1830s, a special committee of the grand chapter was set up to reshape the Royal Arch ceremonies: 'The Special Committee also completed the removal of all overtly Christian references in the Royal Arch' (*The Craft*, p.108).

The ridiculous word 'Jabulon' covered a former word. I should like to advance a theory as to what the original word may have been when the ritual was first formulated. Otherwise, it is extremely difficult to see why the Royal Arch should be seen as the root, marrow and heart of Freemasonry.

Discovering a name for God that used to be on the lips of every Victorian Sunday school child – *Jehovah* – can hardly constitute a major masonic breakthrough, however beautiful the exposition of the meaning of God's name. One has to try to put oneself in the position of a thinking Freemason in the early 18th century. Great claims have been made for the antiquity of Free Masonry, and the profound nature of its secrets. Finding out that the old masons' word was 'Mahabyn' for example, must have come as a great disappointment to those thinking that there must be more to this Freemasonry than some old stonemasons' customs!

Someone in the line of thought followed by Robert Samber (a neo-Rosicrucian line of thought) would not have been at any loss to come up with a good idea of what the amazing masons' word may have been. Well, anyone familiar with John's Gospel would have been acquainted with the idea that the Word that was 'in the beginning' was afterward made flesh as Jesus Christ. They would also know of passages in Paul's letters and the gospels wherein Jesus is associated with the foundation and the cornerstone of the new spiritual temple that must replace the one destroyed in 70AD.

Destroy this temple – said Jesus – 'and in three days I will raise it up'. Three days; three degrees. But what happens on the third day – does the mason just get a stonemason's codeword, meaning he's OK to build with fellow masons? Does he not gain access to the Holy of Holies?

What if the Word is literally the Word of *THE* Master Mason: the one who can rebuild the destroyed temple in three days ('He spoke of the temple of his body').

This line may explain why the Royal Arch derived from

Ireland. It would have been well known that the Free Masonry practised before Anderson's time was Christian, even mystically Christian. Anderson's first de-Christianising of the craft must have caused upset, even if the cause was in principle perhaps a good one. Religious sensibilities may have been touched differently in Ireland. Why should they accept the word of a Scot, or an English mason for the established truth? After 1813, we see a second major attempt to de-Christianise the craft. They had to change, or universalise, the meaning of the Lost Word: the slain Word, at whose death the veil of the temple was rent in twain, like the garments of Josiah on beholding the lost book of the law. So, where does the man look for his lost word? He looks to the original word for the *Word*.

The Wonder Working Word

In 1494, the brilliant German humanist scholar, expert in Hebrew and Greek, Johannes Reuchlin (1455–1522) published a book called *De verbo mirifico*. It means the 'wonder working word'. (We have already heard of this work with reference to the 'Scottish Master' in chapter thirteen.)

Reuchlin had visited Florence and met Pico della Mirandola, who he commended enthusiastically as one bringing ancient truth to light. Pico's work inspired Reuchlin.

In his *Magical Conclusions* (1486), Pico had emphasised that the art of *Magia* – the art of the Magi – must always be associated with Cabala, to render it pure and holy, powerful and safe. An important aspect of Cabala meant looking at Hebrew words, assessing their numerical – and by implication mathematical value – and finding through the study of those words and letters secret messages from God to man. If mathematics was the key to understanding the universe, it was because numbers were deeply part of the creative Word of God.

God's self expression in the universe could be read as the Hebrew Word-made-Universe. And another 'word' for the creative *Word* was *Hokmah* – Greek: *Sophia*; English: *Wisdom*. Thus, the universe is the *House of Wisdom*.

The word lost in the world of man is Wisdom, whom we slay

in ignorance. The Bible had a superficial meaning and a hidden meaning; the universe also. When Pico tried to recommend to the learned men of his time the vital importance of Cabala – in association with *magia* and with mathematics – for realising the hidden potential of man, one of the best arguments at his disposal was to assert that Cabala proved the divinity of Christ.

This argument had even convinced Jews of a kabbalistic inclination that there was indeed a 'Christian' mystery within the Hebrew kabbalah worth taking seriously; some were converted.

Pico and Reuchlin listened hard to what the Jewish kabbalist teachers had to say. Pico strained with all his being for the universal – for universal concepts to unify man and all knowledge. Reuchlin was similarly inspired, and in his book, *Concerning the Wonder Working Word*, Reuchlin shot dynamite into the minds of the learned of his day. Reuchlin made kabbalah – or Christian Cabala – not only important, but vital to the thinkers of his era. What was the 'wonder working word' and how did it work?

'Jesus' is the name we know for the messiah. But what is the original name? Why do Christians sing that, 'At the NAME of Jesus, every knee shall bow'? In short, the Hebrew name of 'Jesus' is the holy name of the LORD, *Jahveh* or *Yahweh*, with an 'S' (Hebrew *Schin* or *Shin*) lowered into its centre.

It goes like this:

יהוה   – JHVH

וה   יה

ש   – add *Shin*

וה   יה

יהשוה   – YHShWH

YHShWH, or JHShVH, is the name we can transliterate as Yeheshuah, Yeshuah, Joshua.

It is Jesus' name.

The Greek *Iesous* is the Greek attempt to transliterate it; we get our English 'Jesus' from the Greek.

So why was this letter *shin* so significant?

According to Reuchlin, the sound of *shin* – *Shh*... – makes the silent letters of the name JHVH audible. It is like the sound of rushing wind, or breath, or spirit, and yet, paradoxically, a sound made when one wills *Peace*.

Look carefully at the Hebrew letter *shin*. It has three components. To a Christian, that suggests the triune majesty of God, the three days in which the temple of the spirit is raised – that is the temple of the Christ body (*New Adam*). The letter also looks like flames, like the flames seen on the heads of the apostles when the spirit came to them at Pentecost.

But above all, as stated before, the addition of the fifth element transforms a word that could never be uttered into a manifest reality (the Jewish scriptures use the word 'Adonai' the LORD when God is referred to; not taking the Lord's Name in vain). Thus Yeheshuah means God manifest, God incarnate as Word.

His Word was miraculous. This then would be the 'wonder working word' of the true and highest level of the master mason. The Word is God made flesh, made real to the senses of man; the Word is the creative power that builds the universe. And the Word is God made audible. We can now literally HEAR THE WORD! If we will.

To the powers of the world, the Word is silent, His Nature unseen. We slay the Word, the source of the secret, because 'we know not what we do'. So, it doth seem most likely true and consistent with the entire *corpus* of masonic symbolism that this Royal Arch ritual originally referred to the one who was Himself the Royal Arch.

That is to say, the figure called by John Dee, 'Our Heavenly Arch-Master'. The one called 'King of the Jews', the rejected stone. The Arch completes the divided pillars: the Lost Word, the missing keystone of that arching glory or, if you like, rainbow over the Ark.

Now, it may be that the original word of the Royal Arch ritual was the wonder working word, even YHShWH, only to be found in the process of rebuilding the fallen temple. But, it was known after 1723 that Freemasonry was intended for all men who adhered to 'that religion on which all men can agree'.

I should like humbly to suggest that at some time a very brilliant stroke was pulled in relation to the resistance to de-Christianising the craft. Look again at those three tools of the sojourners. The crowbar, the pickaxe and the shovel are hardly the normal masons' tools! Not much use for fine carving, and hardly the kit for an architect. Nor do we find them in the craft traditions. However, if we think again of our wonder-working letter – a working letter mind – that brings the Word into dynamic life, what do we find?

Cannot this letter be made of a pickaxe – the long curve with a handle, the crowbar and a little shovel? If these 'tools' are lowered into the hidden 'Word' below, into the dark vault of the earth – lowered and joined in will (the circle and the triangle) to the creative word of God – do we not find therein not only a potent image of the incarnation, but also the vital lesson of the potential of Masonry? That is, namely, to incarnate the highest in the lowest, from the high heavens to the labour of the head and heart and hand.

Then we can perhaps understand better those words of the ritual, wherein it is stated that 'the eternal welfare of man is considered in every part, point or letter of its ineffable mysteries' – *every part, point or letter*.

Observant masons and non-masons may think of the significance of other masonic objects: keystones for example, without which, the two halves of the 'arch' – or beginning – cannot be balanced on earth. *Alpha* and *Omega*, twin pillars: the same before, the same after. Perhaps now we can see why Laurence Dermott and his Antient brethren considered the Royal Arch to be the 'root and heart and marrow' of Masonry.

Mark Masons' Hall

While the Royal Arch has been very close to the life of craft lodges of the English constitution for nearly two centuries, by far the largest number of additional degrees have found their collective administrative home in the splendid Mark Masons' Hall.

Mark Masons Hall, (originally the home of 'Mark' Masons), is situated at 86 St James's Street, across The Mall from St James's Palace, London.

In fact, craft, and assemblies for other degrees, are not really so far apart. Many craft members also enjoy one or several of the additional degrees. The bright and airy interior of Mark Masons' Hall provides beautifully appointed rented facilities for over 300 craft lodges, as well as administrative backup for some 120,000 members of additional degrees. Among the most popular orders are the Mark and the Knights Templar.

Many of the additional orders really only make sense if the mason is familiar with the Royal Arch. That is because the legends of the additional degrees often build on the Royal Arch story and set their stories before and after the rediscovery of the Word at the time of the rebuilding of the second temple. The use of temple symbolism is all pervading in most of the additional degrees. The temple as a symbolic *locus* brings together masons – builders – and religious virtues. Many of the orders are primarily concerned with the cultivation and celebration of moral virtues and spiritual strength. Admittedly, many members simply enjoy the colourful ceremonies and the warm fellowship that masonic orders encourage. You don't have to be a practising Christian to be moved by a cathedral.

This seems an odd thing today, that grown men should spend time and money (regalia can be quite expensive) working (and learning) their way through ceremonies designed to ram home the lessons that former generations used to acquire in church, chapel or Sunday school. But the orders' ceremonies are not just sermons where some authority speaks down to a silent congregation. The emphasis is on participation. The members build the moral lessons, like erecting states of mind receptive to the spiritual core that often lies hidden in a virtue such as fortitude, patience, endurance, trustworthiness or courage. Mark Masons' Hall is home to the following additional orders:

> The Grand Lodge of Mark Master Masons
> The Ancient and Honourable Fraternity of Royal Ark Mariners
> The Grand Conclave of the Order of the Secret Monitor or Brotherhood of David and Jonathan in the British Isles and Territories Overseas
> The Grand Council of the Order of Royal & Select Masters of England and Wales and its Districts and Councils Overseas
> The Grand Council of the Order of the Allied Masonic Degrees (St Lawrence the Martyr; Knight of Constantinople; Grand Tilers of Solomon; Red Cross of Babylon; Grand High Priest)
> The Grand Imperial Conclave for England, Wales and Territories Overseas of the Masonic and Military Order of the Red Cross of Constantine & the Orders of the Holy Sepulchre & of St John the Evangelist
> The Great Priory of the United Religious, Military and Masonic Orders of the Temple and of St John of Jerusalem, Palestine, Rhodes and Malta of England and Wales and Provinces Overseas.

The titles do sound very grand. They come from times when human history seemed to stretch out endlessly, like great northern skies. There was no conception of nuclear war or the other potential 'apocalypses', real or imagined, that stalk the post-20th century mind. These orders are, in a way, survivals of the great romantic reaction to the logic-chopping conceit and dry rationalism of the 18th century. Many sound distinctly medieval, and one may justifiably think of the aesthetics that shaped the Gothic revival in the 19th century, as well as the Pre-Raphaelites, and the Oxford Movement.

They come from a time when it was feared (with reason) that excessive recourse to reason would cut men off from their heart – their most precious sepulchre.

The heart is that organ by which and through which we become conscious of love and care, through which we arc moved to embrace beauty and eschew our darker, more primitive and selfish instincts. These are orders more for the heart than the head and, unlike movies, which also appeal to our longings for romance and mystery and meaning, they have the advantage of actually taking men out of their seats and getting them to 'act out' the ideas therein.

There is nothing particularly esoteric about the orders' teachings. The secrets are the secrets we once felt, but through the effect of modern living, have forgotten about or never explored. It should be said that some of the orders' ceremonies do occasionally contain the most surprisingly radiant expositions of what one can only call 'the beauty of morality' and the 'beauty of truth'. The writers often seem overcome by vast visions of goodness. One can only hope that repetition does not dull, but serve to deepen these survivals of vanished times.

One also finds in the rituals wonderful little titbits of history, legend and theological nuance. Who else today, for example, over the age of twelve, takes a look at the meaning of Noah's Ark and the rainbow covenant (Royal Ark Mariners), or finds the idea of 'Melchizedek' – the 'King of Righteousness from the City of Peace' whom Abraham encounters in *Genesis* – a source of illumination?

If I was a bishop, I think I would ask some of these orders to perform their ceremonies in the nave of my church for the edification of all that would care to witness them, including myself. But this raises questions that must wait until chapter sixteen of this book.

It is worth saying a little more about the orders, but a little knowledge is a dangerous thing, and if one really wants to know about them, perhaps one might consider contacting a member of such an order through the administrative department of Mark Masons' Hall, or through your local masonic lodge.

The Grand Lodge of Mark Master Masons

Mark Masonry, according to Keith Jackson, (*Beyond the Craft*, Lewis Masonic, 1994) first appeared at Portsmouth in 1769. It was excluded in 1813 with the union of Antients and Moderns, but enthusiasts for it founded their own Grand Mark Lodge in 1856 with Lord Leigh as grand master. A 'concordat' with the 'Grand Chapter of Scotland' secured its authority and its future. Its place in masonic development is usually thought to follow fellow craft and is based on the old practice of a mason being accorded his own 'mark' so that his work might be recognised and judged.

The candidate 'advances' from *Mark Man* to *Mark Master Mason*. The ritual sets itself in the context of the building of the temple, and the moral is plain and strong: fraud can never succeed, while labour's reward is education, thus emphasising lessons inherent in the first and second degrees.

The Ancient and Honourable Fraternity of Royal Ark Mariners

This order appeared in records kept at Bath, Somerset, in 1790. Surviving with difficulty under the wing of the mark master masons after 1816, the mother lodge of Royal Ark Mariners No 1 began its first working under new constitutions in 1872. There are today over 830 lodges working under this constitution.

The graces of God's providence and mercy are celebrated in the degree with specific reference to the Ark that saved the patriarchal religious inheritance from the global flood of God's judgement. In the course of the lecture on the Royal Ark Mariner tracing board, the candidate is shown a stone, a perfect ashlar that the mason is encouraged to raise:

> 'In the centre of the Stone is a Triangle within a Circle. The Triangle is the emblem of this Degree and is also symbolic of the Deity; the Circle represents Eternity. Their conjunction teaches you the fundamental truth that Deity pervades Eternity, and as this combined symbol also relates to the Royal Arch Degree, you are again reminded that there is still greater knowledge to which you may yet attain.'
> (*Lecture on the Tracing Board*, The Grand Master's Royal Ark Council, 1995)

The Grand Conclave of the Order of the Secret Monitor or Brotherhood of David and Jonathan in the British Isles and Territories Overseas

Originating in the Netherlands, Dr I. Zacharie brought the degree from America after the Civil War in 1875, forming a Grand Council in 1887 out of what had been a side degree administered by anyone who had received it. Disputes with the 'Grand Council of Allied Masonic Degrees' soon ensued and continued until 1931, when a variant version was removed from the list of allied degrees. A lesson in friendship and fidelity is taught in the first degree of Secret Monitor. The second degree ('Prince') builds on the story of Saul's jealousy over David and how Saul's murderous intent was thwarted. A third degree ('Supreme Ruler') deals with Installation; the 'Supreme Ruler' is a reference to King David.

The Grand Council of the Order of Royal & Select Masters of England and Wales and its Districts and Councils Overseas

Formally constituted in New York in 1873, the order's degrees are sometimes referred to as 'Cryptic Degrees' because they deal with the imaginary 'crypt' beneath the Holy of Holies first encountered in the Royal Arch. In this sense, they may be said to provide a link between master mason and Royal Arch Mason. The degree of 'Select Master' begins in the crypt at the stage of its building; its secrets are hidden in the arches. While the grand masters Hiram Abif, King Hiram and King Solomon meet, along with twenty-four *Menatschin* (the 'Council of 27') the meeting is intruded upon by a mason. For failing to secure the vault, another mason is executed and the intruder set free. After a time, the council is neglected and knowledge of the vault fades away.

References to tunnelling under the temple may explain why some today hold that Knights Templar tunnelled under the Temple Mount in the many, oft-repeated (but unsubstantiated) myths linking Templars to Masonry.

The second degree of 'Royal Master' includes a striking discourse on the subject of death as a fellow craft asks Hiram Abif as to when he may become a master: 'My hope, Companion Adoniram, rests in that Higher Lodge to which I am advancing...'

The degree shows how the secrets were deposited in the crypt.

The degree of 'Most Excellent Master' describes the lodging of the Ark of the Covenant in the Holy of Holies and celebrates the temple's completion.

The degree of 'Super-Excellent Master' deals with the eventual fall of the temple with the attack of Nebuchadnezzar from Babylon, after the rebellion of Zedekiah.

The reception ceremony advises the candidate: 'The object of this Degree is to inculcate true devotion to the Most High, to strive to enlighten our minds and purify our hearts, that they may become wiser and better, shining more and more unto the perfect day.' (*Ritual No 1*, Mark Masons' Hall, 1995)

The Grand Council of the Order of the Allied Masonic Degrees
(St Lawrence the Martyr; Knight of Constantinople; Grand Tilers of Solomon; Red Cross of Babylon; Grand High Priest)

The 'Grand Council' came about in 1879 as a result of trying to bind under its wing a number of otherwise loose orders that might stand a better chance of survival under common administrative fellowship.

Fortitude is the lesson drawn from the example of the legend of St Lawrence the Martyr who was roasted over a gridiron. It is thought to come from an old 'operative' ritual of Lancashire over 200 years ago to distinguish between the old craft and the purely symbolic mason. Justice, universal equality and humility are emphasised in the degree of 'Knight of Constantinople'; it was worked in America in 1831. The degree tries to link Masonry with the first Roman emperor to encourage Christianity, Constantine.

Like the story of the select master, the degree of 'Grand Tilers of Solomon' deals with intrusion into the secret crypt. It dates back to America in 1893.

The Red Cross of Babylon is a very old degree, associated with the Royal Arch, in which the candidate assumes the name of Zerubbabel. Zerubbabel must pass a bridge over a river before entering a debate whose theme (taken from *Esdras*) is the greatness and power of truth. Scotland calls it 'The Babylonish Pass'; America has joined it to the Templar grades and shares the Irish name of the 'Order of Knight Masons'.

The degree of 'Grand High Priest' was worked in France and Germany as two separate degrees respectively, in the mid-18th century. It was an honorary degree for the first 'Principal' of a Royal Arch Chapter. The president plays the part of Melchizedek, King of Salem (Peace).

The blessing of Abraham and the consecration of the priesthood of Aaron is referred to.

Usually subtitled, the 'Plymouth Working', the degree of 'Knights of Constantinople' acquired the appellation after a 'Council of Knights' was formed at Devonport, Plymouth, in 1865. Humility and equality are taught through its ceremonial.

The Grand Imperial Conclave for England, Wales and Territories Overseas of the Masonic and Military Order of the Red Cross of Constantine & the Orders of the Holy Sepulchre & of St John the Evangelist

Dating from the early 19th century, or possibly the late 18th, an early ritual was developed into an order by Robert Wentworth Little.

Robert Little was one of the founders (1865) of the *Societas Rosicruciana in Anglia*, a group of masons enthusiastic about the Rosicrucian tradition, and out of which the notorious and remarkable Hermetic Order of the Golden Dawn was founded in 1888. The *'Soc. Ros. in Anglia'* (as it is known) is still going strong from its offices in Blackheath, while a number of spin-offs and revival versions of the Golden Dawn's system of magic exist in Britain, Europe and America.

Wentworth Little was an inventive soul. Jackson calls the order of the *Red Cross of Constantine* 'delightful'. Its first degree of knighthood asserts that Constantine's victory over rival imperial claimant Maxentius led to the founding of the first order of Christian knighthood. Much is made of Constantine's highly charged banner, the *Labarum*, which serves as the basis for inculcating a secret doctrine.

Faith, unity and zeal are the watchwords of the order. The 'Traditional Oration' describes Godfrey de Bouillon unfurling the ancient banner before 'expelling the invaders' from the vicinity of the holy sepulchre.

The holy sepulchre, its defence and service, is the theme of the second chivalric degree, said to be derived from Helena, the Christian mother of Constantine who went to Jerusalem to adore the 'True Cross'.

The third degree joined to those preceding concerns a discovery made in the ruins of the Jerusalem temple leading to the foundation of the Knights of St John. It attempts to explain the craft degrees and Royal Arch in a Christian sense ('the mysteries of the craft are the mysteries of religion' *Ritual No 2*, 1996). This is the kind of 'traditional history' that unfortunately has been woven into the fateful 'para-history' of modern templar-grail-masonry myths, now dressed as 'secret history'.

> Dearly beloved Knight, your initiation of toil and blood is now finished, and there is no longer any temple, because the light of the Lord is universally diffused, and the world has become one holy house of wisdom. The hour cometh, and now is, when the true worshippers shall worship the Father in Spirit and in truth.
>
> (*Ritual No2*, 1996, p.57)

The Great Priory of the United Religious, Military and Masonic Orders of the Temple and of St John of Jerusalem, Palestine, Rhodes and Malta of England and Wales and Provinces Overseas

I once knew a mason who, having joined the masonic Templars, experienced some disappointment to find that he would not be permitted to carry a mighty broadsword, nor clothe his features in chain mail. The masonic Templars derive from Freemasonry. Their first appearance can be dated not to Scotland in the middle ages but to Portsmouth in 1777.

A 'Grand Conclave' was formed in 1791 but little progress was made until after the death of grand master, HRH the Duke of Sussex (1773–1843) who had 'sat on' the 'Encampments' after the earlier years of dynamic leadership under Thomas Dunckerley, grand master from 1791.

After that period, the order went from strength to strength, benefiting hugely no doubt from the medievalism that coloured the life of middle and upper class Victorians while the lower orders filled the colourless manufactories.

There are now over 490 'Preceptories' on the 'Great Priory' of England's Roll. Needless to say perhaps, but there is absolutely no historical link whatsoever between the Knights Templar and Knights of Malta (the two orders were united) and the orders of knights who fought bloody battles in 12th century Palestine. The overriding idea is one of Christian pilgrimage, from which incurable fantasists might draw the historical truth that it was pilgrims that the authentic knights were first enjoined to protect.

Meditation and penance are part of the knightly vows before the candidate may become a 'Knight of the Temple'. Courage in battle, fighting for truth, humility before God – all of these virtues may find a place in the modern world. Chivalry is not dead; humility requires that it be seldom spoken of.

Understandably, the order appeals to persons engaged or formerly engaged in Her Majesty's armed services, from whence the most extraordinary patience may be expected in the face of political pressures at home.

A second degree of 'Knight of St Paul' or 'Mediterranean Pass' is built around the necessity for a pass degree to the third degree of 'Knight of St John of Jerusalem, Palestine, Rhodes and Malta'. Mystical resurrection is a theme of the legend of the degree, which recounts the journeying from Jerusalem before reaching a base on the island of Malta, after a long struggle against the enemies of Christ.

Last Orders

We have already looked into the origins of the Supreme Council of the Ancient & Accepted Rite (chapter seven). The English headquarters of that rite are in Duke Street, St James's, London, a short walk from Mark Masons' Hall, and quite a long one (philosophically speaking) from the epicentre of craft Freemasonry in Great Queen Street.

The rite consists of thirty-three degrees, as we saw in our section on the United States. No masons of whom I am aware employ the first three degrees of the *Ancient & Accepted Rite* in Britain (as is often the case in South America). The supreme interest of British masons in the so-called 'Scottish Rite' lies in the 18th degree, 'Knight of the Rose Croix and the Pelican'.

Rose Croix is much respected in Britain, though it is in many ways difficult to see why. It has a very peculiar atmosphere, quite alien to any mainstream religious tradition, and yet it is loaded with New Testament references and quotations. The British generally do not wear either their hearts, or their religion, on their sleeves, at least that was the case before the funeral of Princess Diana. But in the *Rose Croix*, one can wear it on one's collar, and magnificently too. The embroidered pelican feeding its young on its own blood in silken pink and gold is quite beautiful by many people's standards, though the even more stunning *Rose Croix* apron is no longer worn in England, except as part of the 'Baldwyn Rite' enacted in Bristol. There should be little doubt in the mind of the candidate 'perfected' in a chapter of the *Rose Croix* as to the true identity of the Lost Word of Masonry.

If YHShWH *was* removed from the Royal Arch at some stage (though the *Name* is still present in the figure of 'Joshua' the high priest), He is nonetheless triumphantly present as the spiritual goal of the *Rose Croix*. Faith, and hope and love lead the 'Prince Mason' to-be to the summit of the degree, after hearing of the cubic stone who pours his blood in the darkness of Jerusalem for the redemption of humankind.

Very few masons in England receive either the 30th, 31st or 32nd degrees of the rite, unlike in America. Like the 33rd, they are reserved for 'Princes' who have been perceived to be of great service to Freemasonry.

Those wishing to know more about the first 32 degrees of the Ancient & Accepted Rite may obtain a copy of the famous, and highly compendious, *Morals and Dogma* (1871), by American self-educated Freemason, Albert Pike. Pike was a man of physical courage and great adventurousness whose mind was extraordinarily hungry, impatiently so. Unfortunately, this impatience seems to have been directed at potential readers. The book is hard work, but contains much moral depth and lashings of out-of-the-way knowledge of an intermittently and determinedly gnostic kind.

Another degree system of great extent in terms of numbers (though, like the Ancient & Accepted Rite, seldom worked) culminates in the degree of 'Holy Royal Arch Knight Templar Priest'. From the extraordinary title of this unusual degree, one might think the recipients were either pulling one's leg or having one's cake and eating it. But no, in spite of regalia consisting largely of a tunic bearing a large red cross (and a mitre that could compete with an archbishop's), the members of this order are perfectly serious.

Now administered from Castlegate House, Castlegate, York, the degree appears to have its origin in Ireland, in the last twenty years of the 18th century. Keith Jackson has also observed that it was found as the 41st degree ('white Mason') in the Irish Early Grand Rite, a most obscure rite for sure.

The conferral of the degree seems to have come from 'Union Bands' derived from the temporary union of craft lodges with Royal Arch Masons combined with masonic Templars where the presiding officer would be designated a 'High Priest' for the purpose. I can only presume what you have here is some kind of conflation of the priestly figure of the Royal Arch (Jewish) combined with the priestly requirements of medieval knights (Christian).

Anyhow, this ritual was taken to Scotland in 1798 and spread south from York to Bath. Throughout the 19th century there were administrative problems as it was taken into the basket of the 'Allied Masonic Degrees', yet required Knights Templar membership, which the Allied Masonic Degrees could not confer. Relinquishing control in October 1922, a 'Grand College' for administering the degrees (over thirty of them) was incorporated in Newcastle upon Tyne in May 1924.

There is much reading from the Old Testament (especially Hosea) and the New. The candidate is conducted to seven pillars, laid out in the form of a triangle. A 'Pillar Officer' sits at each pillar. The officers have a word refering to the attributes of the book of *Revelation*'s Lamb of God who opened the seven seals, revealing the various spirits of God. Quite a mix.

Keith Jackson, an expert in the world of additional masonic degrees, is of the opinion that this degree is of special interest to experienced and thoughtful Freemasons. There must be quite a lot of these, as there are now over 220 consecrated 'Tabernacles' divided into forty-five districts in fifteen countries. One presumes these occasional priests are entitled to marry.

Women's Freemasonry

You do not have to be a man to be a Freemason, though most women Freemasons call each other 'Brothers', which might make things interesting for the Seven Brides.

It is perhaps fitting that the main masonic bodies that admit women in Britain today stem from the tireless work of Annie Besant. Her stirring speeches, made at the turn of the 20th century, now seem prescient of the heyday of feminist protest and outrage of the 1970s and 80s.

In 1879, the first 'Co-Masonic Order' (admitting men and women), the *Grande Loge Symbolique Écossais Mixte de France,* was founded. Its first lodge was called *Le Droit Humain* (Human Right), a name that now covers Co-Masonry's contemporary descendant. It worked only craft Masonry to begin with, but in 1902, a 'Supreme Council' of thirty-three degrees was established. Mademoiselle Marie Deraismes was elected first *Grande Maitresse* and president of the Supreme Council.

A Co-Masonic lodge was consecrated on 26 September 1902 in London. Uncompromising light of the Theosophical Society and political freethinker Annie Besant took the helm of lodge *Human Duty* No 6, giving the movement in England an esoteric outlook and emphasis from the start.

The contemporary *Droit Humain* Federation in England is administered from Hexagon House, Surbiton, near London. In 2000, Helen Boutall was 'Most Puissant Grand Commander' of the order in England. There are consecrated lodges throughout England, as well as in Australia, the USA, Australia, New Zealand, South Africa and India.

As Annie Besant was initiated into all of the craft and 'higher' degrees (in irregular lodges), there is no separation between these aspects of Freemasonry in the federation structure. The grand commander is responsible for a 'Grand Council' of the 33rd degree, a 'Consistory Council', twenty-three craft lodges, four Mark lodges, three Holy Royal Arch chapters, seven *Rose Croix* chapters, one 'Knights Kadosh' of the 30th degree, one Knights Templar preceptory and priory, as well as the 31st, 32nd and 33rd degrees.

The International Federation *Le Droit Humain* adopts the system of Masonry of the country in which it finds itself. In France, it has adopted the Grand Orient constitution – irregular in the eyes of the United Grand Lodge of England. Of course, from the point-of-view of England's grand lodge, all female or mixed Masonry is irregular, though attitudes, at least, have softened considerably in the last twenty years: softened, but not melted.

The conception of Freemasonry in the (sexually) mixed order of Co-Masonry is essentially focused on the individual, providing access to a set of ideals that are intended to support the inner growth of the adept; self-knowledge is the essential purpose of participation.

Two other women's orders flourish in England stemming from the first arrival from France at the turn of the 20th century of Co-Masonry. Both have chosen to take an all-women's road to masonic practice. In 1908, three lodges established by the Co-Masons called themselves the 'Free Masonic Association of Men and Women'. On 6 March 1908, the 'Ancient Masonic Union' split off from this association. In 1913 members from lodge *Stability* No 5 seceded and became the 'Honourable Fraternity of Antient Masonry' (they wanted to work the Royal Arch).

Since 1958, the order has been known as the *Order of Women Freemasons*. Its temple is based in Penkridge Gardens, Notting Hill, London, and its grand master in 2000 was 'Most Worshipful Brother' Brenda I. Fleming-Taylor, who in that year presided over 349 lodges.

Another splinter group from the Co-Masonry crisis of 1908 was the 'Honourable Fraternity of Ancient Freemasons', a women's order now based at 68 Great Cumberland Place, Marble Arch, London. They had three lodges. In 1935, they took the title *The Order of Women Freemasons*, but have since returned to their old name (HFAF).

The order now has more than 350 women's lodges in the UK, Canada, Gibraltar, and Australia (see Enid L. Scott's *Women and Freemasonry*, 1992).

In 1999, the order's grand master was Eileen Grey CBE who stated quite plainly in that year that 'Freemasonry is a way of life as applicable to a woman as it is to a man!' If more people knew of the opportunity for women's Freemasonry, I dare say it should prove even more popular than it is already. But then, the women's orders do not aim at popularity; they aim at Freemasonry.

Seven Pillars of Wisdom

Our third and last interlude may seem a trifle peculiar. Perhaps that is because it is one I have found for myself. Many readers will, I'm sure, have seen David Lean's masterpiece of cinematic adventure, *Lawrence of Arabia*. Those who remember the original movie posters will have noted that the film was based on Colonel T. E. Lawrence's revered account of the Arab Revolt that took place during World War One. Lawrence's book was called *Seven Pillars of Wisdom* and many readers have doubtless enjoyed or heard of the book. How many have been intrigued by its stirring title?

Reference to the 'seven pillar'd house' also occurs in *Seven Pillars of Wisdom*'s opening poem, dedicated 'To S. A.' In that poem, the seven pillar'd house in which Wisdom dwells seems to be equated with *freedom*, the gift that Lawrence desired to bring to 'S. A.'

Where did this image of the seven pillars of wisdom come from? It comes from the book of *Proverbs*, chapter nine, verse one following:

> WISDOM hath builded her house, she hath hewn out her seven pillars:
> She hath killed her beasts; she hath mingled her wine; she hath also furnished her table. She hath sent forth her maidens: she crieth upon the highest places in the city, Whoso is simple, let him turn in hither: as for him that wanteth understanding, she saith to him, Come, eat of my bread, and drink of the wine

which I have mingled. Forsake the foolish and live;
and go in the way of understanding.

Wisdom lays out a feast to be enjoyed, an offering of herself.
Who is this *Wisdom* and what are those 'seven pillars'?

> The LORD possessed me in the beginning of his
> way, before his works of old. I was set up from
> everlasting, from the beginning or ever the earth
> was. When there were no depths, I was brought
> forth; when there were no fountains abounding
> with water. Before the mountains were settled,
> before the hills was I brought forth: While as yet he
> had not made the earth, nor the fields, nor the
> highest part of the dust of the world. When he
> prepared the heavens, I was there: when he set a
> compass upon the face of the depth: When he
> established the clouds above: when he strengthened
> the fountains of the deep: When he gave to the sea
> his decree, that the waters should not pass his
> commandment: when he appointed the
> foundations of the earth: Then I was by him, as one
> brought up with him: and I was daily his delight,
> rejoicing always before him; Rejoicing in the
> habitable part of his earth; and my delights were
> with the sons of men.
>
> (*Proverbs* VIII.22–31)

Wisdom was with the Lord in the work of creation; she was at
the foundations and she was with the work of God's compass.
Wisdom is in the works of God, 'For whoso findeth me findeth
life, and shall obtain favour of the Lord.'

Why do we call Wisdom 'she'? The Greek version of the Old
Testament uses the feminine noun *sophia* for wisdom, and she
has long been regarded as a feminine power. Wisdom's attributes
in the book of *Proverbs* seem to owe a great deal to Egyptian
goddesses, in particular Maat and Nut (pronounced 'Noot').

Maat was goddess of truth and justice. She was a favourite of the high gods of Egypt and they would rather be offered an image of her than any other offering. This chimes in well with the famous proverb, 'For wisdom is better than rubies; and all the things that may be desired are not to be compared with it.' (*Proverbs* VIII.11). Wisdom is inseparable from truth and justice.

The other goddess, Nut, gives us perhaps some insight into Wisdom's seven pillar'd house. Nut is the goddess of the starry night sky. In one myth she is a cow who lifts Ra (the sun) so high that she becomes dizzy, and each of her legs receives a god so that they become pillars to hold up the heavens. In another Egyptian story she has five children – the number of the planets known to the ancients. Nut's body is the night sky, the stellar vista dwelt upon by the minds of the wise people of ancient times and in whom they found divine signs and divine guidance. Nut's body is outer space, whose starlight is reflected on earth.

Once we understand something of these images and their meaning, we can quickly discern the likelihood that when the Book of *Proverbs* tells us that 'WISDOM hath builded her house, she hath hewn out her seven pillars', we are meant to see the universe as the *body* of Wisdom. The seven pillars may then be seen as the sun, the moon and five planets we know as Mercury, Venus, Mars, Jupiter and Saturn. Wisdom's house is the universe. The universe runs according to the laws of God, exhibiting wisdom, truth and justice.

Study the laws of the universe and you will live aright and benefit: 'I wisdom dwell with prudence, and find out knowledge of witty inventions.' (*Proverbs* VIII.12)

The man who fails to heed the counsels of wisdom 'wrongeth his own soul: all that hate me love death.' (*Proverbs* VIII.36)

Perhaps now we can see why in a famous masonic catechism still surviving from the 17th century, in answer to the question, 'How high is your lodge?' the answer is returned by the candidate: 'Without foots, yards or inches, it reaches to heaven.'

The lodge reaches to heaven. Properly understood, it not only reaches, or extends, heavenwards, but is also coterminous with the universe. The lodge of the Freemason is understood as a body of wisdom, of truth and justice.

When a person first enters a lodge as a candidate, his journey within is attended by seven principal officers. Do they represent the five planets along with the sun and the moon? Were not these figures once considered the luminaries greeting the soul as it descended from its source into the world fashioned for its sojourn and education?

The masonic candidate may see two pillars, sometimes supporting an arch on which stars (or planets) appear. Above images of the pillars (forming the entrance to the temple) we may see a sign for the sun and a sign for the moon. These twin pillars are sometimes identified with pillars believed to grace the entrance to Solomon's temple in Jerusalem. Insightful persons may also come to the conclusion that these pillars represent the fundamental dualism that makes the manifest universe possible: light and darkness, good and evil, and all the contraries of nature and mind.

The temple of the Freemason is the universe herself; his principles are those on which the universe was constructed. Otherwise, how could the wise builder build aright?

> Now therefore hearken to me, O ye children:
> for blessed are they that keep my ways.
> (*Proverbs* VIII.32)

From this story of seven pillars of wisdom we can begin to understand what one writer on Freemasonry (William Preston) meant when he defined the craft as 'a peculiar system of morality, veiled in allegory and illustrated by symbols'.

Images have a deeper meaning. Deeper acquaintance with these images takes us deeper into the body of wisdom. Perhaps this emphasis on the universe has something to do with the universality of Freemasonry. 'Where do we come from? Why are we here? Where are we going?' These are universal questions, asked by all thoughtful persons at some time or another.

If we take the idea that Freemasonry is 'veiled in allegory', it would be unwise to imagine that if we simply tear off the veil, then we shall find the 'hidden truth', or 'secret' or, *God forbid* 'The Answer'! This hasty action would, and does, prove as unprofitable as to imagine that if we think we can 'explain' the meaning of a symbol, we can dispense with the symbol and live with its wordy explanation.

It was the apostle Paul who wrote that 'spiritual things are spiritually discerned'. We have eyes, and we have *inner eyes*. We see, and we are seen.

Wisdom is not prosaic, though it might appear plain. Wisdom is not superficial; it has depth, breadth, height, indeed, infinite extension. Wisdom is a body. And that is an allegory. An allegory is a story where the key elements stand for definite things or ideas, things or ideas that are best seen when viewed through the interpretative process of allegory. Symbols enclose deeper meanings in images, where mere words might be misleading. Wise people have chosen to speak in parables; philosophers have chosen to explain them.

Truthful principles are true in a myriad of contexts, so that universality may be best grasped in terms of stories. It is said that there are only seven basic stories, but there are hundreds of thousands of tales, as there were once thought to be seven principal heavenly bodies and hundreds of thousands of stars. One story or myth may be as true today as it was when first uttered thousands of years ago. Silent movies, like great buildings, were once a great universal language, before the Babel of sound. Sound particularised the image in terms of an exclusive language. A good ritual is like a silent movie; you should be able to understand the core of its meaning even without hearing the words.

Freemasonry contains many symbols and has generated many allegories. What they mean for the initiate depends on how far he or she has travelled into the body of wisdom. As William Blake wrote, 'A fool sees not the same tree a wise man sees.'

One image of central significance to Freemasonry is that of the 'house', understood as a structure (something constructed) in which something lives. An ark is also a house. If a divine power dwells in a house, or is worshipped in a house, that house is called a temple and as such becomes the centre of a devout person's life. At the centre of a person there may also be room for a house, or temple, if the debris of human waste is first cleared.

St Paul speaks of a house made without hands, a house made in the heavens: a spiritual house. Many traditions have spoken of an inner temple, a home for a soul or spirit, a true centre. Freemasonry is famous for making much allegorical use of the story of the building of Solomon's temple in Jerusalem. It should be noted that the use made of this story is allegorical and symbolic, however interesting any supposed history connected with the story might be.

Along with the use of the image of construction undertaken in a noble and holy purpose, is the use of the symbolism of stone. Stone may be rough, wild, unfinished or unperfected, or it may be smooth, square, or otherwise moulded and shaped through art and science for high purposes. Like a man. Masonic traditions speak of 'living stones'.

Unlike man, stone has a permanence that outlives him. Stone is a record of our striving for eternity. These are all images of our mysterious acquaintance with the body of the universe. The link between the outer universe – the body, or house, of Wisdom – and the inner universe is the province of traditions, which we call 'esoteric'. 'Esoteric' is an adjective meaning knowledge or information to do with the innermost nature of things, the deeper things; dark only perhaps for those unused to the light.

Freemasonry contains esoteric content for those who see it. The relationship between the inner life and the outer world is for most people mysterious, baffling. Esoteric insight, first glimpsed 'in the spirit' and reflected in the inner house or soul, and usually gained over long periods of experience and study, helps us to understand something of this mystery. The whole experience makes for wisdom, whose price is far above rubies, for no amount of money can buy wisdom. The one who has lost it cannot buy it back again, not for all the money and power available in the world. The one who finds wisdom has true wealth; this is a challenge to the world, for the wise man stands with the universe. The deeper we go, the higher we fly. The lodge reaches to the heavens.

It will be noted in all of this discussion the central significance to Freemasonry of the Bible, the collection of sacred books considered in the past to contain the greater part of the history of the world and, indeed, the universe. Freemasons call the Bible, 'The Volume of the Sacred Law', and the 'VOSL' is taken as one of the three 'Great Lights of Freemasonry'. Calling the volume by this name has enabled the light to be seen as issuing from the works held sacred by people of other religions. Lodges of Muslims may contain the Koran; lodges of Hindus, the Bhagavad Gita, for example. The key issue is that the 'Volume of the Sacred Law' is the work in which the wisdom of the creator is found by those who would live in conformity with that wisdom. Wisdom is universal; it is of the universe and the universe is of Wisdom. She has spoken in many tongues and her temple is hewn both without and, significantly, within. Her delights are, we are told, with the sons of men. Wisdom will lead her children to ultimate truth.

In the beginning was the word, and the 'word' (*logos*), according to 1st century Jewish philosopher Philo of Alexandria, may be identified with Wisdom (*Sophia*). If readers wish to know in more detail of the true benefits of Freemasonry, I should lead them to the Book of *Proverbs* in the Old Testament or Jewish scriptures, and to the Book *Ecclesiasticus* in the *Apocrypha*. This is not an exclusive choice, but would serve as an excellent start, for those who labour on the building site should know their reward.

Freemasonry is nothing less, and nothing more, than the pursuit of Wisdom.

> Treasures of wickedness profit nothing:
> But righteousness delivereth from death.
> (*Proverbs* X.2, attributed to Solomon)

Chapter Sixteen

Freemasonry and Religion

In a British poll of 2006, 62 per cent of young adult Muslims believed that the British government was subject to a Jewish-masonic conspiracy. In March 2004, a masonic lodge in Istanbul narrowly escaped complete destruction when extreme fundamentalist anti-semitic suicide bombers attacked the premises armed with pipe bombs. A recent pronouncement by an anglican authority in Australia declared that membership of Freemasonry was incompatible with membership of the anglican communion.

The relationship between Freemasonry and religion has seldom appeared more significant, or more complex. Conspiracy scenarios both familiar and deadly derive directly from the relationship between Freemasonry and religion. Routinely attacked by Roman Catholics, methodists, evangelicals of every stamp as well as Islamic preachers and pundits, it is difficult for those whose concept of Freemasonry is *not* embedded in a landscape of conspiracy to understand what the problem with Freemasonry for organised religion actually is.

As we have seen, much of Freemasonry is broadly religious but absolutely non-denominational in nature (in so far as self-knowledge or wisdom is the aim). Members are encouraged to honour their commitments to their particular religious tradition. Masonry claims no authority or special competence whatsoever in matters of theology or dogma.

In fact, so positively non-dogmatic is Freemasonry's religious content that a very great number of members are genuinely surprised to think that the religious content has any essential significance to their joining at all. For a great many members of the craft, Freemasonry is simply a secular society that has some traditional prayers, like Boy Scouts or 'Boys Brigade' meetings or the school assemblies of their childhood. Most people joining Freemasonry in search of some kind of religious satisfaction or knowledge are almost certain to experience great disappointment. Many masons would simply say to such people: if you want spiritual understanding, go to church, not to Freemasonry; we don't discuss religion or politics here, dear.

While interesting questions may be asked about the additional degrees (many of which require sympathy with Christian beliefs or even committed trinitarian belief), the three craft degrees encourage a secular fraternity while honouring the almighty God common to all members.

As far as Freemasonry knows – and as most people recognise – the God of the Jews is the same God as the Christians who is the same God of the Muslims. If there's one God, then there can only be one God. That's as far as Freemasonry goes. Freemasons respect the books in which the one God is believed to have revealed Himself. It does not offer any other competing book, or offer advice as to interpretation. Freemasonry looks to the common good. This conception seems not at all far away from what HRH Prince Charles seemed to be getting at when he stated that he would like the monarch to be seen as a 'defender of faith', rather than a defender of 'the' or one particular faith.

Are opponents of Freemasonry simply misinformed? Whose interest would such misinformation serve and why? How has Freemasonry come to be the object of suspicion and hatred by orthodox religious critics? And, conversely, why is it that knowledge of Freemasonry has become a staple ingredient in the education of those seeking esoteric spiritual understanding?

Are these two questions connected? Is the fear or accusation of masonic conspiracy itself a conspiracy against Freemasonry? In this hall of mirrors, clear understanding of the issues is vital; lives and livelihoods are at stake. Tensions between Freemasonry and some religious groups date back at least as far as the papal bull against Masonry of 1738; sundry petty tensions with the state are recorded as far back as the 15th century.

Freemasonry's place in the world of conspiracy derives directly from its conflicts with organised religion. Is Freemasonry a rival to organised religion? Is Freemasonry, in fact, a religion? While some masons may treat it as such, Freemasonry makes no claim to independent or privileged revelation. It claims no unique source of doctrine or ethics; it has no prophet, liturgy or its own sacred book. It does not proselytise nor utter divine sanctions. Freemasonry does not offer salvation or redress from sin. It absolutely forbids any kind of religious bickering among its members. It has no special understanding of God, and yet some opponents of the craft still speak of a 'Masonic God', identified by a small minority of anti-masonic Muslims today with the satanic 'Dajjal'.

This is a profoundly false identification constructed entirely of the imaginations of anti-masonic speculators, confounded with false or deliberately distorted information. The roots of the propaganda go back to the anti-Jewish activities of the old Russian secret service in the years before the 1917 revolution.

Wicked forgeries regarding alleged Jewish internationalist intentions were then picked up as part of the racist policies of European fascist leaders and disseminated around the world. There is no Jewish-masonic conspiracy. Masonry stands for an ideal brotherhood beyond racial and religious boundaries. Politically, masons come in many shades and share no political viewpoints as Freemasons. Politics and religious conflict disturb harmony and serve to split asunder in mutual suspicion and hatred those who might otherwise find fellowship and charity under the God of humankind.

Those who wish to erect or maintain or reinforce such boundaries perceive Freemasonry as an enemy and use religious texts combined with political propaganda to attack something that has always been a friend to religious tolerance and mature religious understanding. True master masons are adults, not hotheads desperate to burn their names in history's pages for the kind of quick-glory attractive to young men in search of a cause and self-justification. *O youth! half in love with easeful death* ... Such persons make their minds up on massive issues that tax the greatest minds of our species before they have even had time to live or acquire, through long and challenging experience, the all-necessary wisdom to live in peace with their fellows. Hatred is no foundation for a better world.

Masons have been subject to the ridicule of the ignorant. Masons espouse three principles: brotherly love, charity, and truth. Are these not essential foundations for a better world? Are those who espouse them, and endeavour to live by them, worthy of ridicule, or of respect? If one dare speak in darkly fashionable terms of 'covert intentions', Freemasonry has no covert plan for mankind. Its record openly declares that its adherents raise their sights to a 'plan' (well known to the prophets of all religions) whose end is glory to God, peace on earth and goodwill to all men. This is perhaps 'that religion on which all men (except, according to Anderson, the atheist or libertine) can agree'.

Freemasonry specifically tolerates religious traditions and encourages its members to be loyal to their personal faith. The exception to this rule is the 'Grand Orient' European tradition. Grand Orient Masons extend their fraternal embrace to those who do not believe in a personal God, as well as those who do.

Freemasonry's relationship with religion has been a persistent feature of its own internal history, as the previous statement suggests. Observers of Masonry have called it a 'lowest common denominator' of religion, or even a rational foundation of all religion. Grand Lodge Freemasonry's most detailed early *Constitutions* (Anderson; 1723, 1738) may have been influenced by ideas of 'natural religion' – that is, that the cosmos furnishes, of itself, sufficient evidence for belief in God and ethical conduct – without the requirement of supernatural revelation.

The issue of masonic 'deism' (arguably the 'religion of the Enlightenment') is still debated within the world of masonic scholarship, though it is plain that on closer inspection Anderson's book of *Constitutions* is not deistic in outlook, though it might have appeared so to a committed deist.

Freemasonry's own relationship with religion has passed through a number of distinct phases. For example, Freemasons' charges dating from the 15th century invoke the authority of the Catholic Church as the sole religious guide to members and specifically condemn heresy.

By 1730, all monotheists of sound morals were eligible. Specifically Christian orders (such as masonic symbolic Templars and the Ancient & Accepted Rite) may have developed in part as a reaction to the weakening of traditional Christian spiritual content in masonic practice.

Esotericism – the suppressed spiritual component of all organised religions – has, arguably, enjoyed a persistent relationship with Freemasonry, though not by any means with all its members. Freemasonry has its own special emphases and preferred images; it is, after all 'a peculiar system of morality veiled in allegory and illustrated by symbols'. The dominant images all derive from a broadly spiritual vision of life on earth. These images, tied to no orthodox or required interpretation, may be listed as follows:

The Great Architect – Euclidean and Pythagorean Geometry
Traditions of Christian Charity and fraternal love
The Cornerstone
The Pillars
The Holy Royal Arch
The Jewish Bible – including the Sethian and Hiramic craft tradition
The Temple
The Gospel of John (and Saints John the Baptist and John the Evangelist)
Chivalry
The Hermetic tradition – including Astrology
Alchemical traditions
 Rosicrucian traditions
 Various Near Eastern mythological traditions

For many masons, Freemasonry does offer a powerful message for sincere religious believers: namely, that it *is* practically possible for people of different religious traditions to meet in amity and warm respect without compromising religious affiliation. In Jerusalem today, there is a working lodge with

Jewish, Islamic and Christian members, offering charitable assistance to afflicted persons, regardless of ethnicity. Is it Freemasonry's ability to transcend ethnic and religious differences that has earned it the vilification of those whose interest is to emphasise and exploit difference?

The widespread publication of the faked *Protocols of the Learned Elders of Zion* in the middle east has done much to persuade some Muslims – and others – that Freemasonry is locked in conspiratorial embrace with zionist Judaism. But does the *real* hostility to Masonry derive from a sneaking perception that traditions of Freemasonry represent a survival of an ancient, antediluvian 'proto' or 'first religion': a pure religion and science of divine knowledge that later became corrupted and divided? In other words, does Freemasonry have a secret capacity to enlighten the religions organised subsequent to the division of mankind after Babel, and the subsequent division of monotheist religions?

How can we explain the persistent link between Freemasonry and esoteric traditions, however much some masons might disapprove of such connections? It was the belief of the earliest known freemasons that their fraternity went back to the patriarchs of human civilization: the 'Noachidae' and Sethian traditions. Are these masonic traditions to be dismissed as mythology, with no religious significance? Is there a pristine 'para-religion' fragmented within masonic traditions for those 'with the eyes to see'?

Such questions, being both fascinating and speculative for open-minded people, are not exactly encouraged by the United Grand Lodge of England. This is understandable. The prime task of the institution is to protect itself and its members from the attacks of those who seek its downfall. It must therefore engage point for point with the thrust of attacks made against it; first, by politicians who could, in theory, suppress it completely, and second, attacks made by well-known religious authorities that seek to discourage 'their' believers from joining it.

It is, of course, practically impossible to deal rationally with the attacks of the fundamentalist kind, since fundamentalists always believe they are unarguably right, and where reason suggests otherwise, reason itself is deemed inadequate. At the heart of the fundamentalist critique of Freemasonry, there is nearly always some kind of political agenda as well as a profound incapacity to come to terms with the idea of the 'esoteric'. Nevertheless, their criticism of Freemasonry needs to be addressed. People are entitled to hold such beliefs as they may, so long as they mean no harm to other people and similarly respect the like entitlement in others. That is a principle of western democratic society; it has served well. The problem for Freemasonry is when partisan agendas become embroiled in politics. It was painful to see how the chair of the parliamentary committee investigating Freemasonry in the judiciary in 1997 and 1998, Chris Mullin MP, admitted that his main source of information on the subject was a book called *Inside the Brotherhood* – a book hostile to the craft. Let us look at the main thrust of ecclesiastical attacks on Freemasonry, and how the United Grand Lodge of England has addressed those attacks.

The Roman Catholic Church

It was Pope Clement XII who issued the first bull against Freemasonry. *In Eminenti Apostolatus Specula* appeared on 28 April 1738, at a time when Freemasonry had arrived in Italy. Jacobite Freemasons were being spied upon by the British government in Florence and elsewhere.

At this time, the Vatican ruled a substantial portion of Italy as a state. Its interests were not entirely theological. In this bull, Masonry was attacked because masons were men of every religion; because masons manifested as men of upright morals; because masons made oaths to support one another; because oaths were made on the Bible and advocated punishment for the breakers of oaths contrary to law; because Freemasonry has been banned in other states as being contrary to the state's welfare; because of other 'just and reasonable motives known to us' (the pope).

The main motive behind the bull seems to have been a political one. The pope simply did not want what appeared to be a new sect involving catholics active and secretly influencing politics outside of his knowledge. The theological reasons were, and are, related to the status of the Catholic Church as it perceives itself to be.

The Roman Catholic Church, regarding itself as the sole path to salvation, will not tolerate being put on a par with other religions, or accepting that its absolute claims may be made relative claims in the interests of tolerance. As Sir Steven Runciman has said, tolerance is a social, not a religious virtue; hence wars of religion.

The Church did not want to be 'tolerated' by protestants or other kinds of religion. The idea that a catholic might have to help a heretic by virtue of an oath was simply anathema. Furthermore, we have the interesting irony of the Church attacking the idea that a man can appear to be morally good and acceptable to God by adjusting his behaviour to a moral ideal. The Catholic Church is here advocating the doctrine of original sin.

People cannot be judged as being good – or fundamentally improve themselves morally – so long as they are open to sin by their very nature. Without the sacraments, their efforts on the path to holiness are void and fundamentally fraudulent. Their thoughts, if not their acts, condemn them. Acceptability, justification (acquittal before divine trial) and forgiveness are acts purely of grace administered by the Church and its sacraments. Genuine (holy) goodness is not an ideal possible to a secular society.

The Freemasons were accused of setting up a rival 'good', a humanistic one. The irony is that this theological argument centres to some extent around the old Reformation theological contest between 'good works' and 'justification by faith alone'. Luther had attacked Rome for suggesting (through 'indulgences' paid for by acts of financial giving to the Church) that good works could secure forgiveness of sins, granted by the pope. Luther stressed the Pauline doctrine that since man was sinful in the core of his being, while good works were expected of Christians, they could not secure special graces in themselves.

In the final judgement, it was not man's goodness that would secure salvation from hell, but faith in Christ alone that would acquit the sinner. God demanded perfection, not the self-assured man who thinks, and is proud, that he has done the right thing. God knows that man sins; God wishes to see man at his ultimate, desperate state of truth to himself, admitting sin but throwing himself utterly on the mercy of God through faith in Christ and corresponding obedience to His Church.

Only when the sinful self has cast itself utterly under the power of, and in submission to, the love of God (manifest in the grace of the Church) can a man hope seriously for salvation. The Catholic Church regarded Luther's challenge as impious at the least, arguing that good works as adumbrated in the *Epistle of James* particularly, were important with regard to the matter of God's judgement of a man. Ultimately, Luther's doctrine could undermine the whole doctrine of charity in the Church: charity that kept the monastic and related orders alive.

In short, the Catholic Church sensed in Freemasonry a new kind of rival in its midst; more particularly so because it could not sense any specific doctrinal heresy to pin its condemnation on. The problem with the condemnation (and the bull was absolute) was that it seemed to treat Freemasonry as if it were some kind of claimant to a religious authority. If a heretic was about to fall out of a window, was a catholic morally compelled to save him if he could? In countries where the bull was published, a catholic could be excommunicated (after inquisitorial trial), putting him under the civil penalties that existed for such persons in countries like Spain and Portugal.

Relations between the Catholic Church and Freemasonry got worse through the next two centuries, all as an indirect result, no doubt, of Anderson's revolutionary view that Freemasonry could stand as a 'centre of union' regardless of the particular religious affiliation of its members. What was good in England and Scotland, encountered severe problems in catholic or orthodox countries, or in areas where religious tolerance was (and is) regarded with contempt.

The essence of that first bull's condemnation stands today, though the idea that Freemasonry necessarily poses a challenge to the security of states has been modified since World War II. Also, the conscience of the individual catholic plays a larger part in deliberations than it did in 1738, or in the later bull of Pope Benedict XIV (*Providas...*) in 1751. Nevertheless, the crux of the argument still hinges on the idea of what kind of society Freemasonry really is. Is it a religious society or a social religion? These questions have been taken up by anglicans, and by the methodists, notably, it should be stated, after two and a half centuries of anti-masonic catholic propaganda.

On 12 June 1985, cognisant of problems in the methodist conference and the fact that the general synod of the Church of England intended to investigate Freemasonry's relations with the Church, the United Grand Lodge of England issued a statement. This is the opening clause:

> Freemasonry is not a religion, nor is it a substitute for religion. It demands of its members belief in a Supreme Being, but provides no system of faith of its own. Its rituals include prayers, but these relate only to the matter instantly in hand and do not amount to the practice of a religion. Freemasonry is open to men of any faith, but religion may not be discussed at its meetings.
>
> (*Freemasonry and Religion – The English View*,
> John Hamill,
> The Canonbury Papers, vol.iii, CMRC, London
> 2006, p.1ff.)

According to the best judgement of the United Grand Lodge of England's 'Board of General Purposes', Freemasonry could not be a religion since it lacked what it considered to be the 'basic elements of a religion':

> it has no dogma or theology (and by forbidding the discussion of religion at its meetings will not allow a Masonic dogma to develop)
> it offers no sacraments
> it does not claim to lead to salvation, by works, secret

knowledge or any other means (the secrets of freemasonry are concerned with modes of recognition, not with salvation).

The old wisdom of the United Grand Lodge of England in keeping institutionally separate from the additional degrees was an advantage in being able to make these statements so unequivocally. It is almost touching to see in its assertion of innocence of the charge another kind of innocence, or naivety, made in its defence. What was a pious Christian to make of a society that forbade the discussion of religion in its midst? This is tantamount to forbidding the word of God being uttered in the very place where the blessing of the Great Architect of the Universe is invoked on the allegedly just proceedings.

This difficulty comes as a direct result of Anderson's special plea in the 1723 *Constitutions*. While the *Charge Concerning God and Religion* was perhaps a brilliant stroke in dealing with the challenge of getting catholics, anglicans and presbyterians into common society; as a principle, in the face of a full religious inquisition of its implications, it will always look somewhat ragged, having been contrived.

Anderson's contrivance for producing his 'centre of union' is not a revelation; it is a utilitarian formula: a political solution. The masons claim no special revelation; therefore, under what authority do they feel able to prohibit the utterance of the word of God? The only real defence of the United Grand Lodge of England's position (with regard to organised religious criticism) in the modern world is that it is essentially a secular society. As such, its moral teaching extends only to the dimension of man's relations with man, not man's relations with God. Within the lodge, religious men of their own free will and in good conscience choose to restrict their religious enthusiasms out of consideration for the feelings of others – a principle that is normally held in other social relations. For example, an Easter Day parade of Christians would not walk into a mosque carrying a cross. That is to say, the criticisms of the Catholic Church only can apply where the Catholic Church is the undisputed catholic religious authority.

Of course, the standing doctrine of the Catholic Church is that its authority was given by Christ to be extended, in due course, all over the world. Furthermore, a teaching of the Church is *de facto* true all over the world, even if rejected. The issue of the limits, or otherwise, of religious authority is one of the burning questions of our time, and the masonic aspect of the question is really only a tiny footnote to a far greater debate that the world must face.

What the Catholic Church fundamentally objects to is the existence of a secular society, of a space where the will and judgement of God and His Church is not held to be the paramount concern of life. Perhaps the Catholic Church early on sensed, in the practice of the masons, the beginnings of secular society – a conception that no church or religion can ever be truly at home with. This is because churches speak continually in the realm of the absolute. Science, on the other hand, speaks of relatively true or possibly true 'truths', always open to change subject to new knowledge. The bodily resurrection of Christ is not a religious hypothesis for the Church; it is a fundamental truth.

Masonry has always had a special interest in the world of science and technology: twin threats to absolute religion. Freemasonry is, frankly, part of the modern world. It could be argued that it practically invented the secular ideal and the concept of full religious tolerance. By the time of the American revolution, such ideas (soon to become 'rights') had come to appear to some as to all intents and purposes 'inalienable': mankind has an innate freedom that is dignified and of his deepest and best nature, unstained by the doctrine of original sin. This is Pico's neo-Neoplatonist doctrine and America knows it; Europe is not so sure. Masonry is, if you like, a cat that got out of the bag of the Renaissance and has just kept running. He's found more mice to play with in America than he has anywhere else. In America, note, Tom never kills Jerry.

In this debate of relative absolutes, it is not surprising that Masonry has assumed a place larger than its real presence in the world can justify. The manifestation of Freemasonry is in some respects a marker of the appearance of a modern world.

Absolute religion belongs to the world before its manifestation. However, optimistic reformers are foolish to think mankind is ready to let go of its past, just because his favourite old haunts have been replaced by concrete blocks and glass towers.

Something in people still hankers after the old 'certainties', and religious leaders of all the faiths know it only too well. 'Freedom' is hard to justify as a good in itself when it threatens things that many hold dear. It is interesting that in John Hamill's admirably clear exposition of the craft's position in relation to religion (*op.cit. The English view*) he refers to the days of the 18th century when almost nobody thought of Freemasonry as anything more than a 'social organisation that tried to do some good in the community' (p.2). This is touching, but in the 18th century, the 'modern world' had yet to tear away the veils of religion and expose her to the scrutiny of reason and scientific methodology.

Until the 'testimony of the rocks' and the Darwinian challenge to *Genesis* in the mid-19th century there was a general acceptance that religion had its proper sphere and claim to authority and should be solemnly respected.

Kant had shown that reason justified the existence of moral absolutes. Since Freemasonry respected religion, then it could do as it thought best within the law. Science, however, brought reason firmly into the sphere of revealed truth. That is to say that truth could be revealed by reason where religion had been either dumb or inaccurate (how old is the earth?).

The significance of religion as not principally a rational belief but rather, requiring faith in a revealed belief became, and has become ever sharper. Freemasonry's constitutions were formulated at a time when religion and reason were still entwined: 'Reason surveys the Lodge and makes us one', as Anderson's *Constitutions* put it. One could say that the theological and philosophical underpinning of Freemasonry today comes from a now vanished era, however admirable its principles appear to its devotees. The once revolutionary and bright beliefs of the early Enlightenment now sound rather quaint and delightfully old-fashioned. Masonry, it could be argued, is very much stuck in the past. Does it have the potential to recast itself into a new era? Readers must judge for themselves.

Freemasonry's unwillingness to enter into the debate of revealed absolutes leaves it vulnerable to charges by religious bodies that in its apparent indifference to such things, it could be prejudicial to the religious development of their members. Unfortunately, for catholic, methodist or anglican arguments, they have simply been unable to prove such a thing. Where are the damaged believers? Where are the believers whose beliefs have been affected adversely by regular Freemasonry?

This all leads us neatly into the whole 'New Age' problem. All of the mainstream churches today have bodies within them who fulminate against what they call 'New Age' alternatives to the traditional faith. Unfortunately, the mythologies of Freemasonry have been taken up and distorted by writers who advocate various kinds of free-for-all 'spirituality'. The institutions of Freemasonry are helpless in the face of an open culture that publishes what will sell. In any case, religious critics of the craft are so often shown to be influenced by the conceptions of the very books they seek to condemn!

The United Grand Lodge of England is rather in the position now of many old institutions. It carefully puts its case forward in clear language – and practically no one (but themselves) reads the defence. The myth is simply more magnetically attractive. People have approached TV stations with ideas for documentary series about the history of the Freemasons, only to be rebuffed when the programme commissioners find there's no 'dirt' in the story. The only right of the Freemason is to be a bogeyman in modern media-dominated society. In this sense, perhaps, the Vatican and the grand lodges have much in common. *The Da Vinci Code* accused the catholic *Opus Dei* of the very kind of things catholic extremists have accused Freemasonry of since the time of the French Revolution! Perhaps they could find common cause in this, but one doubts such a happy consummation. As poet and singer Jim Morrison challenged his listeners nearly 40 years ago: 'Do you know we are ruled by TV?'

Freemasonry is a survival from the past. Is it fair to judge it according to conceptions that were irrelevant at the time of its era of consolidation and transformation? Fairness has little to do with arguments about religion. That is not always the case. The position of the Roman Catholic Church has thawed somewhat since the 'Second Vatican Council' showed that the Church was not simply prepared to turn its back on the wicked, liberal, free-thinking, humanistic modern world. It looked for the activity of the holy spirit in all that was happening. The world had changed strangely since Hiroshima, Nagasaki and the discovery of the pit of human foulness at Belsen and Auschwitz. God's will might be yet discernible in a world where soon a man would walk on the moon 'in peace for all mankind' and young people imagined something like the holy paraclete had activated the Beatles to rid the world of 'Blue Meanies' through love and peace.

In 1974, the then 'Pro Grand Master' of the United Grand Lodge of England, the late Earl Cadogan, wrote to Cardinal Heenan, Archbishop of Westminster, to obtain clarification as to the Church's position on its members being Freemasons. The cardinal's secretary replied (the cardinal was in hospital):

> Earlier this year a statement went out to all Presidents of Hierarchy Conferences from the Sacred Congregation for the Doctrine of the Faith. This document made it clear that the particular Canon in the Code of Canon Law which forbids Catholics under pain of excommunication to become members of Masonic societies or other societies of the same kind could be interpreted in a restricted sense. The restricted sense in this case would mean that the prohibition and censure applied only to societies which in fact 'plot against the Church'.

It appeared that the Catholic Church still found the Grand Orient of France offensive because of its reputation for anti-clericalism and political involvement, but that the English constitution, so long as it had nothing to do with the Grand Orient, might not be held in like manner, so long as it effectively submitted to the Church's understanding of what might constitute a Masonry free of censure.

Canon 2335 forbidding catholics to join Freemasonry was still to remain unchanged 'until the revision of the whole Canon Law'. However, the 'Sacred Congregation for the Doctrine of the Faith' ruled that the canon (law) no longer automatically barred a catholic from masonic membership, so long as the 'policy and actions of the Freemasons in his area' were not 'known to be hostile to the Church.' (statement of the Catholic Bishops of England and Wales appended to the letter of Monsignor Miles to the Earl Cadogan.)

According to John Hamill (*The English View*, p.4), 'The 1974 advice was welcomed and circulated to all lodges. Its central message that a man's religion must come first accorded with the principles of Freemasonry, in particular that a man's first duty is to God, however he worships Him.' Hamill refers to the canon law reform of 1981 that, notably, did not mention Freemasonry, but omits in his treatment to mention the most recent authoritative act on the subject. This is the *Declaratio* on Freemasonry by Cardinal J. Ratzinger, 'Prefect' of the Congregation of the Doctrine of the Faith (now Pope Benedict XVI), issued in latin on 6 November 1983:

> Declaration on Freemasonry: The question has been asked whether the judgement of the Church has changed at all with regard to Freemasonry since it is not expressly mentioned in the new Code of Canon Law as it was in the earlier Code.
>
> This Congregation is able to respond that this circumstance is due to an editorial criterion followed for other associations equally not mentioned, since they are included in wider categories.
>
> Therefore the negative judgement of the Church is unchanged with regard to Masonic societies, because their principles have always been considered

incompatible with the doctrine of the Church and thus adherence to it is still prohibited. The faithful who belong to Masonic societies are in a grave state of sin and may not take Holy Communion.

It is not up to the local Church authorities to pass any judgement on the nature of Masonic societies which might imply any form of revocation of what has been established above; this is in accord with the Declaration of this Holy Congregation of 17 February 1981.

> (*Freemasonry and its Image of Man*,
> Giuliano di Bernardo, Freestone, 1989, p.122)

Ratzinger clearly did not approve of the catholic bishops of England and Wales' relaxation of discipline in the matter of catholics entering masonic societies. That the matter is still, arguably, in the position of a not fully and canonically expressed legal loophole, is by far the most positive position one might take on the subject of catholic toleration of Freemasonry. In the meantime, catholic writers still oppose what they consider to be the religious drawbacks of masonic 'philosophy'.

Technically, a heresy may be regarded as a perversion of catholic doctrine; the problem of Freemasonry (for catholic authority) is that it may be perceived as an alternative to, or qualification of, catholic authority.

The Methodists

A methodist report was published in the 'Agenda & Reports' for the methodist annual conference that took place at Blackpool, England, in 1985. It revealed a rare sensitivity to public misconceptions of the craft. Admitting that the craft did not claim to offer salvation, secret salvific knowledge or impart spiritual light, it was very concerned about masons acting in secret in the secular world of business and law. It did not bar methodists from joining but asked them to examine their consciences.

Methodist Freemasons were deeply offended by the content and tone of the report. As far as they knew, Masonry had supported the ideals of their religious life. An 'Association of Methodist Freemasons' was formed. Refused an exhibition stand at the annual conference, they approached the masonic hall in the town where the conference of methodists was gathering and installed a stand, inviting anyone who wished to inspect it. The methodist conference remains suspicious of Freemasonry, though not as suspicious (it was stated in 1996) as it had been in the 1980s. Masonry had apparently done much to dispel the accusations of its opponents.

At the very least, the sticking point appears to be the idea of a rival system of moral advancement and the idea that prayers can be said to God in totally exclusive settings, that is, that do not permit any person to participate in those prayers. This kind of objection goes back to the earlier point about whether the word of God should ever be closed or restricted. However, it should be stated that Jesus himself advocated the primacy of private prayer. He was extremely critical of public manifestations of piety. People who made a great show of their religious credentials he called 'hypocrites' which means 'actors', not showing their true selves to God, but being content with the good feelings to be obtained from public display.

Jesus also seems to have supported the idea of exclusive revelation to those fit to hear it. To those 'that are outside' all things are done in parables, he said. The exclusive brotherhood of disciples was privy to the 'mysteries of the kingdom of God'. The contemporary churches believe themselves to be in full possession of all necessary mysteries. Many of their members do not seem to share this confidence. I do not wish to compare masons to the apostolate by any means, merely to point out a certain inconsistency of doctrine as regards the principle of the claim of the churches to preach 'what is open and declared'.

It is interesting how democratic experience has affected people's perception of what constitutes religious propriety. The public demands a 'right to know'; masons demand a right to privacy. Are church congregations to be admitted to our bedtime prayers? In a communist society, there is no right to privacy from the eyes of the state. Must it be likewise in Christian or liberal-secular societies?

Jesus expressly forbade the making of religious judgements; God knows. The conception of what a masonic lodge truly is just does not seem to be accessible to certain kinds of mind. Simply by virtue of a lodge being a separate meeting place, it is subconsciously perceived as a kind of rival commitment. This, paradoxically, could never have been the case under the old catholic hegemony of Christendom. Methodists might note that the Roman Catholic Church claims to judge methodist assemblies in the same light.

The Anglican Church

Relations between Freemasonry and the Anglican Church – if we should use this word 'between' – have not always gone well since the 1950s. The Anglican Church is, of course, a broad church – a *via media* between extremes – and different styles of voice are heard from its ranks from time to time. There was a time, not so long ago, when many a bishop and priest was a proud mason, perhaps belonging also to one of the trinitarian Christian additional orders that can offer vivid insight into Christian and Jewish ethical priorities. Those days seem to have been over for some time, though there are exceptions. Anglicans read popular books like everyone else, and many books have appeared over the last 50 years that have presented Masonry in either an unsavoury light, or in a mythical and perhaps heretical light. The subject does look very muddy to those who do not specialise in it.

Of course, that is the main motive for writing this book: to present the subject in the light, as far as possible. It should not have been necessary, but as we have learned, masons themselves are often very much in the dark as to the meaning of what they enjoy saying and doing. Before the churchman cries, 'Ah! That's the problem. Masons should be taught better!' – though it is probably true – he should consider the incredible ignorance over matters of religion often to be found in believers of very longstanding.

Perhaps we have got a bit further than the Rev Dumbbell who, in the 16th century, believed that 'Our Father' referred to Henry VIII, but many believers are still in great confusion over many matters concerning the Bible's extraordinary range of contents. Religion is a minority interest when taken to its specialist level. Many would say that there is not much religion one needs to know. *Love thy neighbour as thyself, honour God and keep His commandments*, would seem to be accessible pronouncements to guide one's spiritual life. Does one need to know whether St Paul wrote the *Epistle to the Hebrews*? Who can say? But it seems you don't need to know much about Freemasonry in the Church today to make all kinds of pronouncements against it.

The *Independent* newspaper of Friday 15 November 2002 carried a highly inaccurate report that the appointed Archbishop of Canterbury, Dr Rowan Williams thought Freemasonry was a satanic sect and was unacceptable. The United Grand Lodge of England sought clarification. Dr Williams said that he had never believed any such thing, that his father was a mason, so he knew something of it, but that he did have misgivings about clergy being involved. This may be because of Freemasonry's claim on a person's time and personal commitments, though he did not say this was the reason for his misgivings.

The general synod of the Church of England – which is supposed to represent 'the voice' of the laity in the Church – has been far more outspoken. Dr Margaret Hewitt's 'contribution to discussion' arising out of an anglican 'Working Party' appointed by the synod in 1985, doubted whether Freemasonry and Christianity were compatible. Gnosticism, pelagianism, syncretism, indifferentism were mentioned, while the Royal Arch was considered as possibly blasphemous. Grave offence was caused to anglican masons by this 'contribution to discussion' which was formally acknowledged as fit for discussion at York's general synod in 1986. Masons joined the ensuing debate in the Church, quite properly referring to the enormous contribution that Masonry has made, and still makes, to the life of the Church in the form of both religious commitment and substantial donations.

According to John Hamill, 'Today, except in relation to the

evangelical wing of the Church, relations are much happier and freemasons – individually and as a group – are again welcome in the Anglican Church.' One side effect of all this controversy is that as a result of so much time and money spent at Grand Lodge dealing with these attacks, could Grand Lodge administration become somewhat less tolerant of 'creative tendencies' within its own fold? This can happen when maintaining the *status quo* is seen as a priority. The needs of the institution may stifle the creative life of the body of the institution. It is generally impossible to prove this kind of effect, but it is nonetheless a general rule that an institution under attack is most likely to find solace and security in greater conservatism. It can become more alarmed at its own membership than at its external opponents. The history of the Roman Catholic Church demonstrates the principle to some extent. Persecution from the outside created heresy hunting within it. After a while, it can become more important what the opponent thinks of the institution than what people under its protection think. Creative dynamism is essential to the life of an institution if it is to be more than a preservative jar.

Strict orthodoxy is the result of persecution. The institution defines itself in response to attacks from outside. This process may be glimpsed in the direct manner in which the United Grand Lodge of England has dealt with the theological nature of attacks made against it. Whenever it rebuts a charge, it creates a definition. Thus, in answer to the charge that Freemasonry corrupts religion, the response is that Freemasonry is not a religion. From that point, we swiftly move to re-emphasising the forbidding of religious discussion in lodges (an old stipulation for sure).

Does this masonic 'fatwa' include discussing the building of Solomon's temple? We then slide to the view that religion and Freemasonry are barely even connected, that religious forms are really only traditional and incidental to the practice of social amity and conviviality. Even the hint of denial of an institution's essential nature under pressure of conformist tendencies is somewhat unnerving, especially in an institution that has done so much to foster tolerance and understanding.

A little booklet published by the United Grand Lodge of England in November 2001, *Your Questions Answered*, gives in answer to the question, 'What is Freemasonry?' the following:

> Freemasonry is the UK's largest secular, fraternal and charitable organisation. It teaches moral lessons and self-knowledge through participation in a progression of allegorical two-part plays.

Ritual has become 'play', theatre. Freemasonry is secular; it is outside of religious qualification. In fact, the statement is curious. 'Freemasonry' is not the largest secular, fraternal . . . &c. *The United Grand Lodge of England* is. Freemasonry covers a globally located philosophy, history and society, or number of societies, philosophies and histories. It is clear to this author that the moment the United Grand Lodge of England tries to define or re-define itself in relation to the question of religion, it starts to get itself into a curious mess, however clear, crisp and military-like its responses seem, or strive, to be. On p.9, we have a striking case: 'Freemasonry', we are instructed, 'deals in relations between men; religion deals in a man's relationship with his God.' This statement is flatly contrary to a great deal of religious teaching. Relations between men are, according to the biblical prophets, precisely what God is concerned with, far more so than with the observation of primarily religious duties (feasts, dedications, sacrifices). I shall not weary the reader with copious quotations.

No religious person can make a division between relations between men and, as it puts it, 'a man's relationship with his God.' This sounds like the old adieu of comedian Dave Allen, 'May your God go with you.' This is not the product of a religious mind; this is a secular distinction. How can it come from a body that says all its members owe their first allegiance to their religious commitments? While the statement is false with regard to religion, it is equally false with regard to 'Freemasonry'.

The third degree is quite explicit that the veil of darkness cannot be penetrated without the aid of 'that light which is from above'. Freemasons are informed that they may expect to be judged by the 'Great Architect' for their conduct.

Here is a case where attempting to save the institution from calumny leads to a quite unnecessary distinction between religion and Freemasonry. Freemasonry has every right to be 'as religious' as its members perceive it to be. Its roots, let it be repeated, are to be found entwined in the now lost world of medieval religious confraternities. Perhaps the reason defenders of the craft cannot say simply that Freemasonry is not an individual or independent belief system is because, to an extent, it is, although (and this is truly important) the belief-content is brought to the system *from outside* by its members. That is what is so unique about masonic systems.

The craft is a formula (nothing more) for religious and social tolerance, made possible by a common devotion to divine wisdom, held universally (it is hoped) as being diffused throughout the universe. All volumes of sacred law refer to the universe that God created. (The fact that the universe is held to be created by the 'Most High God' is just one reason why the accusation of heretical Gnosticism to Freemasonry is simply absurd; the most radical Gnostics believed the Most High God was separate from the universe's 'Great Architect', or *demiurge*/creator.) Freemasonry is entirely orthodox on this issue of the creator of heaven and earth.

The beliefs brought to the masonic system from outside join the beliefs that are built *in* to the masonic system. For example, David McCready (*The Theology of Craft Rritual as Demonstrated in Emulation Working*, The Canonbury Papers, vol.iii, CMRC, p.112) has found the following teachings within Emulation ritual:

  i).   God exists;
  ii). He created the world;
  iii). He watches over it in love;
  iv). He has revealed Himself in Scripture;
  v).   He will judge us after this life.

It is not at all clear what the word 'religion' means in the protective mode of discourse employed by the United Grand Lodge of England in its engagement with critics. The word 'religion' is not defined. Which 'religion'? All religions have things in common, but they are not common in all things.

A 'religion' is by etymological definition, a 'binding together' of beliefs in a system. It is also something to which the 'religious' person is bound, as in an oath or sacred declaration. The ancient definition of a 'religious' or 'pious' person was someone who kept strictly to an obligation. In practice, this involves acts of devotion. What is called 'religion' today was 'science' thousands of years ago. To keep the sun going, its motion required the fuel of sacrifice: an act of religion. (Today, people are sacrificing their air travel out of devotion to the 'Green Planet'; 'science' demands it.)

A 'religion' does not require sacraments or even a principle of 'salvation'. Paganism may involve simply an accepting of the perceived facts of life and a willingness to be part of those facts. If the gods want to eat one, then so be it. It is a plain fact that any body of beliefs that becomes sacred to a person may function effectively as a religion or life of devotion. Art may function for some as a religion. Freemasonry, for some, may function as a religion. In Brazil, for example, football is the formula that brings the panoply of religion and spiritual belief to its otherwise 'secular' field. 'Brotherly love, Relief and Truth' are, collectively, a morally compelling trinity. Add to that the oaths of obligation made upon the 'Volume of the Sacred Law' and you have the makings of what may justly be called 'a religion', if you wish so to do.

Nevertheless, expressed as 'a religion' (it does not have to be) Freemasonry is extremely and definitively peculiar. It itself says that it is a 'peculiar system of morality', where 'peculiar' means different, special or unique. This is so. Unlike the three main monotheist religions, there is no sense of competitiveness of the 'my religion is better than yours' school. This peculiar characteristic, in a world too often darkened by religious hatreds and mutual suspicions, is surely something in which to express pride, even wonder. Masonry deserves a more confident defence. In the end, I suspect Freemasonry will be defended best by those who do not themselves feel to be under attack.

Perhaps the essential problem with the statements of the United Grand Lodge of England with regard to religion is that they continually identify the word 'Freemasonry' with the institution. Therefore, if the institution has decided that it is in no way a religion, and does not wish to be considered a religion, or be seen as a religion, then 'Freemasonry' is not a religion because Freemasonry is synonymous with the United Grand Lodge of England. This is sublimely ironic. For we see an analogous institutional assumption made by the Roman Catholic Church with regard to 'Christianity'.

Really, the United Grand Lodge is functioning rather like the Vatican; its senior members, often called rather grandly 'the rulers of the craft' or even 'the high rulers', function as emissaries of masonic orthodoxy – defenders of the masonic system. It would be a tragedy – even if an amusingly ironic one – if a system in part designed to eradicate the conception of 'heresy' yet became the latest institution to sign up to the 'solution' of inquisition, however benign in operation.

What would happen, the reader might wonder, to the Freemason who contacts his local TV station (without seeking prior approval) to declare that Freemasonry has become his religion? Under current provincial grand lodge regulations, he will come under severe reprimand, since it is a rule upheld in some of those grand lodges to forbid any mason talking to the media about Freemasonry without first acquiring the formal approval and guidance of the 'Provincial Grand Secretary'. We should, I dare say, expect a similar measure of control to be enacted over members of any large business corporation or government department. What Christianity is to the Roman Catholic Church, Freemasonry is to the United Grand Lodge of England.

This is arguably all very sad. But the principle is sound. When a belief system is threatened, the governing institution expands its discourse of definition. Attacking Freemasonry does cause pain for at least some of its members, even if that pain is in due course passed on from masonic 'higher-ups'. Having said that, it should be stated as a matter of demonstrable fact that the United Grand Lodge of England's communications department spends most of its time not in rebutting the negative attacks of opponents, but in trumpeting the joys and healing benefits of the craft. These benefits largely concern the massive amount of human welfare stemming from the craft's extensive charitable operations to both masonic and non-masonic causes. The charities embrace the good causes of disaster relief, education, health care and any number of initiatives for children, the poor, the infirm and the bereaved throughout the world. On the balance sheet of good works, Freemasonry passes with flying colours.

English newspapers and TV media persistently ignore the masons' extraordinary charitable work (of which they are regularly informed), revealing a deep prejudice against a currently unfashionable institution. It could well be argued that if the craft was indeed 'a religion', then its religion would be charity, followed by brotherly love and truth. Just for the record, churches (all of them) receive money from their members; Freemasons dig into their own pockets. Masons have never had to offer indulgences or commutations of time spent being purged in purgatory in order to build their temples to the wisdom of the Great Architect.

The Freemasons paddle their own canoe and mind their own business.

Chapter Seventeen
The Mysteries of Freemasonry

The medieval word 'mistery' in relation to freemasons simply meant knowledge and practice of the craft in its organisation. However, there can be little doubt that men in search of religious mysteries and mystical initiation have been attracted to the symbolic form of the craft. This cannot be entirely accidental. In the thought of men such as John Yarker (1833–1913; *Arcane Schools*, 1909) freemasons inherited, by some obscure process, some basic forms derived from what Yarker saw as ancient 'art' mysteries. These 'art' mysteries had, he believed, once served as governance of 'craft' mysteries, and involved a higher philosophy than the practical knowledge of the crafts themselves.

Specifically, the art mysteries involved the stock-in-trade of the great agricultural mysteries of the ancient world, such as those of Eleusis, but focused entirely on the individual's spiritual destiny. Art mysteries, according to Yarker, involved symbolic death rituals, of dying to one's former self and being reborn in a new spirit. Freemasonry had inherited fundamental forms of mystical initiation. Thus, if we take the Yarker model, the reason why mystical influences flooded in to Masonry in the 18th century (especially on the continent) was because the basic form of the 'lodge' had once held the lineaments of such a mystical initiation school. The mystical content simply recognised its proper 'shape' or 'cup' and rejoined, or flowed easily into, its archetypal form, to go on as 'speculative Freemasonry'.

Yarker did not seem to have recognised a predominant feature of Europe before and after the French Revolution, namely, the need for rationalists of the Enlightenment to find some kind of authentic or personal outlet for an incipient spirituality no longer content with organised religion.

It was difficult for free-thinkers, particularly after the revolution, to live lives of faith in the Church; there had to be some authentic personal initiatory and rationalisable experience, that nonetheless guaranteed man's identity as a spiritual being with a greater destiny than mere citizenship.

Freemasonry seemed to promise a fulfilment of just this need.

The character of Pierre Bezuhov in Tolstoy's *War and Peace* exemplifies the struggle that men waged in themselves in Napoleonic times between orthodox and traditional religion and the promise (eventually rejected by Tolstoy's character) of a masonic alternative. Tolstoy would not have encountered this problem in England, where Masonry promised no religious or spiritual substitute to traditional church membership.

Moreover, Yarker's view has little historical validity because he made the methodological error of putting back in remote time what he knew of a present form. We do not know what precisely constituted a 'lodge' before the very end of the 16th century, and what scraps of knowledge we have to work with regarding the following century is still in important respects, obscure. Nevertheless, the question remains, if Freemasonry had only incidental religious content, why did the form so attract neo-Rosicrucians, occultists, theosophists and 'illuminists' of various kinds? Why did Stukeley, even before any neo-Rosicrucian or alchemical/Hermetic penetration of the craft, seek in Masonry for the 'wisdom of the Ancients'?

We can never be sure, of course. But the mythology of the *Old Charges* already contained a predisposition to regarding Masonry as a repository of ancient learning and wisdom, associated with the mystic-mathematician Pythagoras and the holy *genius* Hermes Trismegistus of late antique lore. Masonry dated itself back to an era of antediluvian, sacred wisdom. The full linkage of mysticism with technological science was available to the middle ages in works translated into Arabic (and later Latin) from the Sabian schools of Harran and Baghdad between the end of the eighth century AD and AD 1050. (see my book, *The Golden Builders, Alchemists, Rosicrucians and the First Free Masons*, part one, Weiser, 2005).

All of this was, we may suppose, fine under the old catholic order in Europe. Before the Reformation, the 'Church' was not somewhere you might visit on a Sunday; the 'Church' was the Body of Christ extended universally. That there were unbelievers in various parts of the world simply showed rebelliousness against, or ignorance of, God's purposes that would 'some time soon' be dealt with. The 'Church' was God's self-expression, not a particular place. Thus, churches and abbeys had confraternities attached to them. Religious lore blended with civic life in a more or less unbroken pattern. There were lay orders attached to dedicated monks, canons and so on. The Church could never have argued that a confraternity dedicated to a particular saint, with its own special rituals and legendary religious stories extolling its favourite virtues, was encroaching on the Church's territory.

The Holy Cross guild of Nantwich, Cheshire, for example, was run by lay persons, but employed a number of chaplains, and was responsible for the foundation of the St Nicholas Hospice in that town – part of the Church's mission of charity or relief. That accusation – that confraternities encroached on the Church's preserve – could only be made after the Reformation divided Europe up into competing churches, sects and conventicles. Re-emerging as a defined and distinct body after the Reformation, Freemasonry could only appear to the eyes of the Church – in catholic countries at any rate – as another *arriviste* sect. The political situation in Britain meant that Freemasons could never make any avowal of their former dedication to 'Holy Church', nor the avowal to abjure heresy as conceived in the 15th century *Cooke* MS. From the point of view of Rome, the Church of England was now in doctrine heretical and in polity apostate.

Freemasonry looked protestant, yet it seemed to have mysteries, secrets and oaths of attachment. The response of the Roman ecclesiastical body was thus predetermined: Freemasonry was encroaching on the Church's territory as magicians had been accused of trespassing on the Church's preserve by invoking angels or evoking demons.

Furthermore, everything about this 'new' masonic animal

suggested the establishment of an independent system of authority outside the Church (traditional states were similarly concerned by this independent system of authority). The Church felt the cool whiff of something dangerously new; 'Mother Church' was being relativised. If this was allowed to continue, catholicism might become that awful, liberal thing, that dead nothing and disgrace to conscience: a mere point-of-view.

In the late 19th and early 20th century, the Catholic Church would follow Cardinal John Henry Newman's lead, to some extent, and act as if Newman's words were true, namely, that liberalism was the halfway house to atheism. Surrender to the world now; pay with your life and soul later.

Territorial instinct is one of the most basic instincts in a person, and it is fundamental to institutions as well. This 'basic instinct', strong in a religious institution, crosses all the sectarian divides, so that protestants also accuse Freemasonry of being involved with things that are not in its competence – as protestants are tacitly accused of likewise invading sacred precincts by catholic doctrinal authorities. In response, the masonic institution agrees; Masonry is not concerned with the special territory of religious dispensations. The Churches are temporarily mollified. Freemasonry has responded in an almost obedient manner, respecting the preserve of religion.

But those mysteries remain. We have seen how the United Grand Lodge of England de-Christianised aspects of its inheritance after 1813 and it continues to keep the more overtly religious Christian masonic orders institutionally apart. This distinction has now reached a stage where it is not unusual for members of additional orders to regard craft Masonry as lacking the more sublime 'secrets' inherent in the craft story, however mistakenly.

Stone Theology

I was minded of the significance of religious mysteries being secreted in masonic lore when analysing the Royal Arch degree (or order) in chapter fifteen. It occurred to me that Christians or Jews perhaps might resent the idea that the 'Word', or name of the Lord, Jehovah (JHVH) or Jahveh, had been hidden away in a vault, unseen. While the story itself suggests that this loss occurred only between the ruin of the temple in 586BC and the return of Zerubbabel from Babylon after 538BC, it might yet seem surprising to believers that, as far as the Royal Arch candidate was concerned, this lost word was, as it were, being discovered and revealed 'for the first time' for the benefit of his exaltation' to the Holy Royal Arch.

Literally speaking, if the lost word had been found 500 years before Christ, why make so much of it? If the lost word had been found, why didn't everyone now know it?

But everyone does know it. If, that is, the lost word is indeed 'Jehovah'. And since everybody does know the word 'Jehovah', why make its revelation a matter of secrecy, and of initiation – or 'exaltation'? It didn't really make a lot of sense, especially as all this Royal Arch legend was intended to be the 'third degree completed'. And then, following further study of the problem, I came upon the solution (or a solution) right in front of my eyes. Within the pages of the book *Freemasonry and Religion* (The Canonbury Papers, vol.iii, p.127ff.) can be found a fascinating study by Henrik Bogdan of the theology department of the University of Gothenburg, Sweden. It is called *Kabbalistic Influence on the Early Development of the Master Mason Degree in Freemasonry*.

What was even more extraordinary to this author was that what Professor Bogdan sought in the *Third*, I thought I had possibly been the first to find in the context of the 'Fourth' degree (as the Antients considered the Royal Arch). Bogdan had also called on the works of Reuchlin and of Pico della Mirandola with respect to the 'wonder working word' (see the section on the Royal Arch in chapter fifteen).

To recap, some readers may have concluded that the idea of the word being hidden in a vault (not mentioned in the Bible) was just a plain masonic fantasy. Was this simply a case of Freemasonry perhaps encroaching on the preserve of the Church: a specious case of playing clever games with sound theology? In rebuttal to the charge, the United Grand Lodge of

England could assert that this business of the 'Name 'was a detail of the Royal Arch (and not the three craft degrees). Defenders of craft Masonry could still insist that the three degrees contain no religious mysteries.

However, Bogdan was of the opinion that the lore regarding the lost word – and of its being connected to the *tetragrammaton* was pertinent to the 'substituted secrets' of the third degree.

The *tetragrammaton* means the four Hebrew letters of God's Name. Bogdan also was aware that this word became audible when the letter *shin* was added between the twin letters either side of the centre. It then became YHShWH: the Hebrew name of Jesus. The letter *shin* stands for fire (it resembles flames), or for spirit in the lore of the Christian cabalist. Readers may recall that it is this author's theory that this letter represents the keystone that completes the Royal Arch: the word made flesh: John chapter one, verse one. *In the beginning was the Word.*

The 'completion' represents the reconciliation or 'recapitulation' of God's relations with humankind: the new covenant – a second rainbow to signal a new world cleansed. The twin orders of matter and spirit are brought back into fresh harmony.

Bogdan takes the view that the essential initiation of the third degree requires a mystical union with God at the 'death' of self-centredness. Now, one might think that this would delight all Christian believers – the secret word of the Holy Royal Arch may have been the realisation of the divine becoming manifest. However, one suspects that religious authorities would not take kindly to being informed of such things by Freemasonry, allegedly a transgressive activity.

Pursuing his enquiries further, Bogdan then looked into the work of the leading Dutch masonic historian Jan Snoek. Bogdan became aware of a Zoharic kabbalist tradition concerning a significant loss with respect to the holy divine name. The 'Zohar' is a massive work of kabbalistic commentary on the Hebrew Bible, thought by scholars to have been composed by a Jewish mystic during the 13th century in Spain.

Bogdan was amazed to see a Zoharic tradition that did not speak so much of the word of God's proper name being lost, but that the knowledge of *how to pronounce it* being lost. The idea behind this story is quite simple. Many of us have been taught not to take the Lord's name in vain. This is specific to the actual name of God: JHVH or YHWH.

'God' is a generic term; it is not the one God's actual name. This word in the Bible seldom appears (Royal Arch masons are enjoined to put their finger to their lips if they ever think of saying the word). The word usually used in the Bible is *Adonai*, the LORD. Because no one knows the original pronunciation, the letters JHVH took vowels from *Adonai*, to make a rough pronunciation. The English (poor) transliteration of this combination is the well-known 'Jehovah'. The only person in ancient time who was supposed to say the true word was the high priest at the temple in Jerusalem, and that, only once a year, when he entered the Holy of Holies.

According to the Zoharic story, when the temple was destroyed and the Jewish leaders went into captivity in Babylon, the knowledge of how to pronounce the word was lost, because the high priest could not enter the Holy of Holies, where the secret of pronunciation was kept. Thence was derived the conception that the pronunciation (or word or letter) that made God's name audible had been encrypted, or en-vaulted. So, while an actual secret vault is not recorded in the Bible, the idea of an encryption became part of Jewish mystical tradition.

Bogdan was convinced that this helps knowledge us to understand what the secret of the third degree 'Lost Word' was in some original form, now lost. He only had one problem. At the end of his paper, he could not work out how the lost word of God had never appeared in any form connected with the master's word or the third degree.

It seems to me that it is in the *Royal Arch* story that the lost word was hidden, and that this degree held not only the secret of the lost word, but more particularly, the secret letter by which the 'true' pronunciation of the master's word could be made.

As Reuchlin and Pico affirmed, the problem of the *tetragrammaton* was how to make it audible, how to pronounce the word. How to, as it were, make the word flesh, or bring it into the world with breath. This problem is satisfactorily solved with the addition of a fifth letter, *shin*. In the beginning was the Word. And the Word was made flesh. That is to say, it entered the world and, now vibrating, could be heard ever thereafter (by those with the ears to hear). Jesus (JHShVH) picked the ears on the sabbath, and was condemned for it.

There is a great deal in the New Testament to suggest that some kind of stone symbolism or 'stone theology' was known either to Jesus or to the sources employed by the gospel writers. Jesus quotes the psalmist, that 'the stone the builders rejected has become the head of the corner'. He applies this psalm to himself; *He* is the rejected stone. He says he will rebuild the temple in three days. He says that he who trips upon the stone shall be broken (the blind do not see it) but he on whom the stone falls shall be winnowed, that is, separated, blown through with air or spirit. There was something missing from the old temple dispensation; that this was perceived to be so we know amply from the words of the gospels and from some documents in the 'Dead Sea Scrolls'. Jesus redefined the temple, and this re-definition is at the heart of Freemasonry.

It may be that Christian theologians have something to learn from the curious lore preserved in the traditions, albeit fragmented, of Freemasonry. It may be that the churches and the Freemasons do, after all, need one another.

Chapter Eighteen

Freemasonry Tomorrow

Ishould state at the beginning of this chapter, that since I am putting myself somewhat in the position of a seer (I know nothing certain of the future), its content will be of a less objective nature than the previous seventeen chapters. What is stated in this chapter is based upon the personal experience of the author. I have observed many things in my lifetime and some of those observations may be of use in determining something of the 'shape of things to come' or, at least, what one might aim for. The future remains, of course, a convenient place to store our dreams.

Admittedly, seers are proved time and time again to be wrong – generally less so than politicians, who also trade on the 'never happened yet'. Matthew Arnold bewailed the imminent end both of British power and of civilisation at the end of the 1830s on the very cusp of the moment when the nation entered upon its period of greatest expansion and never-to-be-seen-again wealth. Every prophet has something of 'wishful-thinking' in his quiver of darts.

Nevertheless, tomorrow is something that we are all concerned with, and its seeds have been planted in our own present, and, indeed, long before. Every gardener has at least some idea of what is likely to rise in spring, even if he has forgotten what was there ten years ago.

The Image and Status of Freemasonry

The status of Freemasonry is perceived very differently in different countries and places around the world. In parts of eastern Europe, for example, it is seen as something modern and progressive, a new force for moral order, even as a return to the civilised traditions that existed before Soviet communism fell like a sledgehammer upon the world.

In America, its reputation is generally quite high, except in those minds where it is seen as a challenge to fundamentalist Christianity. In Germany it still has difficulty in being perceived as a genuinely rational order; Germany is often afraid of 'irrational' or mystical orders because Germans were told after the war that Hitler's rise was a product of irrationality; scientific reason will, they believe, keep them on the straight and narrow.

In France, people mind their own business. In Spain, as we have seen, Freemasonry is extremely small in extent and the legacy of Franco's wrath against it goes on under the surface of new money and new opportunities.

In Ireland, Freemasonry's reputation is fairly sound. National hero Daniel O'Connell was a Freemason (he reluctantly resigned from the craft on advice from the Catholic Church). In Scotland, people see Freemasonry in many different ways. There is the common British concern that Freemasons are supposed strong in the police force and in the judiciary, and some people feel that people with public duties should not have secrets in private. (So unpleasant has public service become in Britain, that we may doubt whether the best people will be attracted to it in the future).

In the Caribbean, as we have seen, Freemasonry is generally considered a good thing. In South America, it is all part of the very rich mix of cultures and colourful traditions that characterise the societies of that continent. Apart from the middle east, where propaganda and state persecution has made it practically impossible for lodges to operate in most parts, the country which has shown the most virulence towards Freemasons in recent times is, perhaps surprisingly, England, the true birthplace of the modern movement.

In 1997, Tony Blair came to power with a 'New Labour' formula that had as part of its less trumpeted agenda the desire to isolate and belittle what Blair called 'the forces of conservatism'. Most people thought he was just talking about the Conservative Party. This is perhaps comforting, but the evidence suggests otherwise. It is a well-attested ultimate aim of socialism (regardless of what 'brand' it currently operates under) to eradicate the social class system altogether; all that smells of rank, distinction or hierarchy in the old sense must go, eventually. The 'Party' must be the sole donator of social privileges. Only the party may claim to represent the forward-marching *uni-class* (my expression), which, today, is likely to be a kind of dumbed-down amorphous (mortgaged) lower middle middle-class, with no speech distinctions, except where regional accents suggest working-class ethnicity. These may pass in time as the country is reduced piecemeal into an administrative consistency, and state education, state health, state TV, and state transport make it progressively more difficult to avoid paid-up participation in the socialist utopia that the indefinite future must, theoretically, bring. Utopia is invariably the last stop before the train crunches to a halt in hell.

It has never been clear which parts of the socialist programme Tony Blair chose to favour; doubtless, 'much work remains to be done', if the public can be persuaded of the righteousness of the general cause. The ultimate cause is never named specifically, for the sake of maintaining votes. 'Social justice' is the usual, all-purpose cry; lawyers specialising in social issues do well.

However, two curious targets were set very early on in the administration. One involved the rural norms of the upper middle and higher classes (though not exclusively): a ban on fox hunting with dogs was proposed and fought over for a considerably long time. This measure has been revealed as being motivated by a determination to show the upper classes that Britain had 'changed'. There could be no escape from the will of the 'people' (or rather, the party) in the imagined rural retreats of the upper classes.

Tens of thousands of 'the people' persistently demonstrated against this interference in old custom, but being presented as representative of the 'forces of conservatism', their democratic action did not count. The self-appointed righteous always know best. Such is the class-suspicion that still regrettably exists in modern Britain that the illiberal measure received just sufficient support to carry it through.

The media never got the hang of the essence of the debate. Without a class-issue to rant about, the 'Left' would be at a loss for rhetoric. Perhaps abolition of class-consciousness is really not in the Left's (or centre-left's) long-term interest. Where the urgency without the alleged bogeyman?

The second target was extremely subtle and interesting, and gives us some idea of the political challenges for Freemasonry in the future. A parliamentary select committee, led by campaigning MP, Chris Mullin (Labour), had read Martin Short's anti-masonic book, *Inside the Brotherhood*. Here he found alleged 'evidence' for favouritism in the police force and the judiciary in Britain.

In spite of extensive and painful sessions, the committee could find not a single case of corruption to bring to the bar of justice. (The United Grand Lodge of England has never denied that it occasionally finds 'bad apples' in the barrel; they are expelled.) Notwithstanding, a measure was enacted making it compulsory for those engaged in management positions of public service to be presented with the question of whether or not they were Freemasons. So, if you were a member of the public and thought you had witnessed a case of covert corruption, you could check this list of state-declared 'suspects' and find the 'evidence' you could be looking for. The masons were effectively charged with membership of a questionable organisation without trial or proof. How was this possible?

Again, in spite of many objections, the Labour MP had chosen a target that could be humiliated with very little mainstream resistance. As fox hunters were generally perceived as 'toffs' indulging in cruel sports redolent of gothic novels, so Freemasons were perceived as a shady bunch of dark suited men engaged in 'looking after their own' and subverting government to their own malevolent ends. These stereotypes were of a not dissimilar order to the kind encouraged by fascist groups in attacking Jews and other perceived enemies. Interestingly, letters to the broadsheets objecting to the measures frequently came from Jewish people with experience of 'creeping' states casting the shadow of prohibition over past liberties – the liberty to be what you are, for instance. The measures did not affect the people's pay packets; there was no revolt.

Socialism seems to have a problem with Freemasonry, at least in Britain. Can we find out why? Is it to do with the class system? The point about an upwardly mobile class system (as we have in much of the western world) is that you can move higher if you choose to and possess the requisite talents (even HM The Queen looks up to the Almighty).

In the polished socialist state (we're not there yet), the lid is permanently on; there is nowhere to go, no higher principle to appeal to. The state makes the laws and the laws are gods. To go against 'the will of the people' is the deepest heresy, and requires public shaming, repentance and punishment. The individual is not significant, except as a willing and manipulable part of the system.

Every dictator loves being photographed with children: innocents led by hand to the social and spiritual slaughterhouse. But Freemasons come from all classes and observe equal respect for one another as masonic brethren. If not the class system, is there then a problem with the individualism inherent in masonic development?

Social critics of a past era recognised that 'social democracy' was nothing more than a potential instrument of new tyranny: the rule of 'King Demos'. So long as people are subsumed into a defined group ('indexed, stamped and numbered') governed by a group who 'act in their name', their existence is relativised to that which serves the interest of the smaller, allegedly 'representative', group.

'King Demos' is ultimately ruled by his ministers, or rather, masters. He is soon no more than a puppet for the oligarchy. The soul of man labours under this burden with little hope of release in this world; men and women in the old 'Eastern Bloc' realised they had a soul when their practical freedom was removed. Apparently, Tony Blair, New Labour's once essential spokesperson, learned from 'Christianity' that individuals should find their essential meaning and identity through 'membership of society'. Individualism (as allegedly advocated by Margaret Thatcher) is basically sinful because it might lead to 'social injustice'.

Such 'injustice' is defined by the ideals and prejudices of politicians, backed up by legal rights legislation. Were not the hungry fed, the prisoners visited, the sick healed, the naked clothed, and the thirsty satisfied under the previous Conservative administration?

The New Testament is not as strong on legal or 'human rights' as 'Christian socialists' might imagine. I once made a study of all the parables in the New Testament and found to my surprise that the vast majority promised very little more than destruction for the sinful human race; they are not very nice at all. Perhaps Christian socialism sees itself as executing this judgement on sinful humanity, slowly and painfully. It could explain quite a lot.

Jesus was not a socialist and had no interest in democracy. In the Bible, the majority is always wrong; David slays Goliath.

Speaking as a theologian (with an Oxford training), there is absolutely nothing in the New Testament to support the principle that the Christian believer in any sense 'belongs to society'. Christ found himself against 'the People'. The People wanted Barabbas; and they still do. The 'Body of Christ' that the Christian is baptised into is a wholly mystical conception of fellowship in the spirit of God, a heavenly society, that is 'not of this world'. 'Narrow is the way and few be they that find it.' To any wise man or woman, the notion that large numbers of people know anything better than small numbers of people is palpable nonsense. Hitler was voted in by popular vote in 1933.

The genius of mankind has always had to struggle with the ignorance of his so-called fellows. Democracy as a defence against tyranny is one thing; used in the interests of tyranny, it is itself tyrannical. Charity for the poor is the duty of the gentleman and the conviction of the lady; it has never been a priority of 'society' as a whole. Welfare is an insurance system, not an act of loving charity. Legal measures were required to care for the disabled and unemployable only after the monasteries, the guilds and the confraternities were smashed during the Reformation. The Church does not engage in charity for the sake of 'society' but because it is seen as the sign of Christian love expected by the Saviour from his 'sheep'. Christian socialism blurs this vital distinction. The state cannot function as a religious society; history demonstrates this time and time again.

As Freemasonry has advocated, religion and politics neither enjoy the same bed, nor are they matters which, when arrayed as for-or-against options, promote harmony. If politicians wish to invoke the word of the saints, they should renounce all their worldly goods and ambitions and follow the 'Way, the Truth and the Life' for its own sake. The fact is that politicians want power, and that power invariably comes from outside of themselves. People give it to them as an act of insurance.

The people, it is argued, can hardly complain of the consequences, when they are so ready to abrogate so much responsibility at the ballot box. In this sense, politics is a sign of human weakness, usually accompanied by folly.

The principle of the *sovereignty of the individual* is the only defence against creeping state tyranny. Freemasonry declares it. The 'brotherhood' (fraternal love, not legal obligation) serves the self-knowledge of the individual. The administration of the order should have no other primary aim. From this aim, the virtues spring.

To the great credit of the United Grand Lodge of England, the institution did not become hysterical in denouncing its government opponents but rather developed its existing programme of openness into a veritable national fest of masonic open-days and information opportunities. The press covered some of these events, and thoughtful people saw the benefits. However, the effect of the administrative adjustments were nonetheless registered overseas where, in Kenya for example, the press argued the case that there *must* be something wrong with Freemasonry, or else the British government would not have ordered a registration of its members should they be involved in public service. The reputation of Freemasonry was besmirched. This must reflect on Britain's membership of the craft, numbering some 275,000 loyal subjects of the Crown.

The government has expressed no interest in maintaining the dignity of Freemasons. To say that King Edward VII, King Edward VIII, George VI and Winston Churchill were Freemasons would most likely earn a smirk of derision. In the opinion of the author, the fundamental objection to Freemasonry by leading members of the Labour Party (who know just a little more about it than the vulgar public image) is because, according to the underlying 'progressive' theory of socialism, Freemasonry is simply an embarrassing survival of history. According to the *credo* (or what is left of it) of socialism, socialism itself has rendered the *need* for Freemasonry void. (This was the argument against Christianity offered by the old Soviet Union.) Freemasonry now represents 'reactionary' forces, and is part of the web (perceived) of 'forces of conservatism' that must be neutered by progressive laws and punitive assaults on its reputation.

It is recognised by socialists that in the past, Freemasonry had some revolutionary potential: that it established charitable schools and hospitals, resisted tyrannical philosophies of government (in France and South America for example) and bound men together in song and by oath for the betterment of mankind. (This model is rather Grand Orient in flavour.) It is recognised that class-distinctions were nullified (in lodge) in its cry of brotherhood and masonic equality. Early trades unions modelled themselves on masonic fraternities. Nevertheless, according to the socialist viewpoint, the need for such things has now passed. All of the 'good' benefits of Freemasonry are now encompassed by the re-named form of socialism, that is, 'Social Democracy'.

Freemasonry has no justification for existence, other than a 'silly' game with rolled-up trouser legs and handshakes for curious, and socially unacceptable, men. Social democracy is endowed, apparently, with a higher knowledge. Just add the word 'liberal' to this concoction, and you have the proposed future of Britain in Europe. Forces of conservatism, such as Freemasonry,– shall not prevail against this 'manifest truth'. The poor public, battered by twenty-four hour media news-assault, never has time to think about what is happening before its overworked eyes.

According to the picture I have painted, the future of Freemasonry in Britain may appear rather bleak. Potential new members are doubtless put off by the prevailing winds of anti-Masonry. If you go for a job in the public service, you might be asked if you are a Freemason; membership could affect your job prospects – and you might never know the reason why. Labour-controlled public services and membership of so-called 'secret societies' are not compatible. You may not even be able to get ordained as a minister of religion for the same reason.

Freemasonry is being slowly muscled out of the British social picture. This will, in turn, affect the morale of Freemasonry worldwide. Those who thought the fall of the Berlin Wall represented the final end of socialism were misinformed or over-optimistic. As a modified formula, social democracy marches on . . . but where to? The future is indeed a convenient place to store our dreams. When (or if) we get there, we may find that we have already exhausted them.

Another Freemasonry There I See

Shortly before the great psychologist's death, John Freeman interviewed the Swiss genius Carl Jung for the interrogatory-style TV programme, *Face to Face*. Perhaps Freeman had been reading the curious mysticist works of Teilhard de Chardin, I don't know. Freeman posited a future where every member of society somehow mulched their individuality – each one's individual self (or soul?) – into a greater social whole. The satisfaction of the collective many would be the joy of the selfless individual component. Such a social model seemed to have somehow attracted Freeman as being a kind of synthesis of intellectual socialism and a kind of ego or humanity destroying mysticism.

Turn off the mind; go with the flow. What bliss!

This quasi-spiritual theory is basically a socialised, this-worldly abstraction of Buddhist '*anatta*' (or no-soul) theory. Nothing is real; nothing is bliss. This view, coupled with 'logical-positivism' in fitful, if sterile, embrace was still quite current among intellectual circles at the BBC when I worked there twenty odd years ago.

Carl Jung saw through the proposed prospect immediately. This was, I think, rather to the surprise of the interviewer, John Freeman. Jung asserted his belief that there would always be something in the individual that simply would not accept being reduced to a kind of nothingness by a greater number of human beings, whatever transitory bliss might accompany the soul's slide into the whirlpool of collective being (and nothingness).

Human beings do not find their absolute fulfilment in the group, contrary to the basic doctrine of socialism (deriving from Hegel *via* Ludwig Feuerbach and Karl Marx). The group is invariably a corrosive and eroding force on the self. Willing barter of skills to common ends is all very well, and necessary, arrayed as we are against the mighty forces of Nature. But there is something in the individual that does not accept the sovereignty of the many. And why should he? Crowd psychology is always low psychology. The majority is very often wrong. Democracy is not an oracle. Individuals have their own principles of action, there to be found, through acquiring wisdom and self-knowledge, not self-annihilation. Pasternak's *Dr Zhivago* is full of this awareness. Interestingly, the 1960s socialist did not recognise the principle and thought David Lean's movie of the book old-fashioned. Few could hear the message coming from the Soviet gulags in that era of false, dismembered optimisms.

Here, I think, lies the future of Freemasonry. The one thing that is truly positive that can be heard in the western world, faltering and misguided as it may often be, is the cry for *self-knowledge*. The socialist, of course, resents what he or she considers this alleged *retreat* into the self – the very luxury of individuality. They sneer; they look the other way. They say it is all 'at the expense of others', though most individuals carry more 'expenses' today on their shoulders than ever before in history. But what else is this rag-tag of new ageisms, if not the cry of the individual against the mass that Jung voiced so prophetically just before the Beatles released their first single – a plea for love and love-action? *Love me Do…*

People want to know. What an opportunity for Freemasonry!

However, if the craft is to find a refreshed role in the world, worthy of its past, and fully able to do more than defend itself, I think it will have to re-generate its entire structure. At the moment, it resembles a besieged castle.

So, from the luxury of the yacht christened 'Personal

'Opinion', I should like to lob some bottles of messages towards the shores of Masonry, in the hope that perhaps one of them might be picked up and appreciated.

Meanwhile, inside the besieged castle, the structure of modern English Freemasonry rather resembles *Upstairs Downstairs*, for those who recall the programme of Edwardian stratified household management.

At the top is the frequently absent Grand Master (of the house), HRH the Duke of Kent. His job is mostly symbolic. He is consulted but does not initiate administrative ideas. When the grand master is not about, the Marquess of Northampton, as 'Pro Grand Master', stands in. The Marquess of Northampton is deeply involved in the running of the craft and gives Freemasonry a great deal of his time, thought and personal resources. Below him, there is a grand secretary, in charge of the overall administration of the craft in England and Wales. He has a large, dedicated team to help him, based at Great Queen Street, London. The current grand secretary is Nigel Brown, an ex-Guards officer and 'Deputy Grand Director of Ceremonies' 32° (Ancient & Accepted Rite), with a business and management background.

In autumn 2006, the responsibilities of the office of grand secretary were divided. A new office – 'Grand Chancellor' – was created. This office, currently held by Alan Englefield, who has also served as secretary general of the Supreme Council 33° (Ancient & Accepted Rite), is concerned with external relations with grand lodges on the continent and overseas.

The presence of two senior officers from the trinitarian Ancient & Accepted Rite running grand lodge activities is a relatively novel development that seems to have begun in 1999 with the appointment of James Daniel – also from the Supreme Council's base in Duke Street, St James's – as grand secretary. Soon after, the size and power of the old 'Board of General Purposes' was significantly slimmed down to reduce bureaucracy and promote organisational effectiveness.

A mason critic might be concerned at the presence of senior members of a non-craft Christian order having such senior roles in masonic governance.

The government of the craft (the three degrees) in England is perceived as being more autocratic than it was in the 1990s when the Board of General Purposes took carefully selected members from the masonic provinces and functioned as a kind of collectively responsible 'cabinet'. However, a proliferation of unnecessary committees and sub-committees rendered the board, as it was, rather unwieldy and somewhat out of touch. All this was brought into relief with the government's attack on Freemasonry that exposed the old system's weaknesses. The rank and file wondered what the administration was really doing to defend their interests. 'Provincial Grand Masters' (PGMs) were not, astonishingly, allowed to know what was discussed on the Board of General Purposes.

Critics of this position would rebuff this view by saying that the net effect of reorganisation has been to strengthen the direct will of the 'rulers of the Craft'. Freemasonry is an order, not an elective democracy. The question remains as to how much governance masons really need. Perhaps the real secrets of Freemasonry today relate to administrative decisions made ostensibly on behalf of the members who pay their fees. An overall impression is one of near-Draconian authority weighing heavily on members, reinforced by lodge and provincial attitudes of a quasi-military kind ('Masonic obedience' and 'Masonic discipline' is all). This is in spite of the fact that the Pro Grand Master has stated openly that the *purpose* of the administration is essentially to maintain the practice of the craft degrees for the benefit of the individual mason's search for truth in self-knowledge. Lord Northampton has inherited an old system, akin to a government civil service of the 1930s, highly resistant to fundamental development, initiative and change.

It is not unheard-of to hear masons say that what they like about Freemasonry is that, unlike the rest of the painful world, Freemasonry does not change – and must not change. Is this the cry of the dodo? On the other hand, the central administration is very much involved with international relations with other masonic bodies, ensuring masonic regularity and granting or withdrawing recognition. Given the potential of Freemasonry to go off the rails (like anything else), an established concept of regularity coupled with the will to enforce it is, arguably, a vital role and benefit to world Masonry. But it could also be argued that what we have here, in practice, is London dictating to the world.

Most masons have very little idea of what is really involved in these dimensions of administrative discipline, however; ordinary masons are often treated like children. Intelligent and educated members can find this exasperating, and many leave soon after initiation or after experiencing the three degrees. The experience of falling numbers (and fees) dominates the current administrative crisis. The craft has become old, perhaps a gerontocracy. Young men with responsible positions are often made to feel like office juniors, good for making the tea. Their first experience of masonic office is to wait at table. Old members are quick to defend this, of course. Most members who have attained high office and rank in the system truly believe they know what there is to know about Freemasonry. My experience has often been that this is a false and self-serving assumption, often of an embarrassing and spiritually unpleasant nature. Sometimes it's a bit like a train-spotter, covered with badges with a book filled with meaningless numbers thinking he could build a train and run a railway.

As in the middle ages and beyond, a true master mason needs no higher appellation to dignify his work and character.

Great Queen Street is also the focus of provincial grand lodges, with their provincial grand masters, provincial grand secretaries, and other administrative staff. The provincial grand lodges ensure that what is decided in Great Queen Street is practised in the masonic provinces – though PGMs and their senior staff often like to think they have great independent powers. Many ordinary members soon acquire embarrassing habits of deference to these figures. The individual lodges do not have much of a say in how things are run, unless perhaps one or several of their members have sufficient rank in the hierarchy. Here we have one of the great problems of modern Freemasonry, in England, at least.

The magnet of upward-tending masonic interest is the rank system – not that there is any desire to exclude masons. A mason is expected to take an interest in working his way through the lodge-officer roles, up to being installed master of a lodge, and, if possible, beyond. Rewards for consistent masonic service (mostly engaged in organising stipulated charity work) are given in the form of medals, promotion and accompanying access to 'higher levels' of the masonic system. Where there is no actual job to be done, members are given 'past' rank status. Thus, a mason may be a 'Past Provincial Grand Sword Bearer', or 'Past Provincial Grand Deacon', and so on. These titles refer to places held in provincial grand lodge assemblies; they sound cumbersome, but are highly prized.

If you like this sort of thing – and let's not mistake, many do (and why not?) – there's plenty to occupy the time of the mason as he works through his masonic life, learning more rituals by rote and, hopefully, fulfilling the various ranks available. However, for those who come for a course in self-knowledge, returns can be distinctly disappointing.

The craft must make up its mind firmly as to what its primary aim is. The complexity of the situation, however, and the many justifiable arguments on all sides of the debate tend to mean that any discussion of this type ends with the 'well, that's your opinion' flannel and the movement trudges on regardless – which is, admittedly, what old institutions tend to do.

Perhaps the fundamental problem is that those in the position to recognise the overall need for reform and renewal have themselves the most to lose from serious structural amendment. Nobody likes to give up a status long sought and striven for, and no one cherishes the thought of causing such pains either. It would take rare acts of sacrifice for the rulers to identify more closely with the ruled. Such acts would seem unlikely – after all, what or who would take their place?

Bad governors take the place of potentially good ones who are not hungry enough to chase the prize of power and status, however ultimately illusionary. Does not this explain the perpetual misery of dull, uninspiring government?

It is not all bad, however. The openness campaign has in the past decade given birth to a number of promising initiatives and movements in and out of the lodges of the nation. A 'Cornerstone Society' was formed in 1999 with a special emphasis on seeing and articulating the *meaning*, often unnoticed or brushed aside, in the oft-repeated craft rituals. Meetings are well attended and younger members are keen. The Marquess of Northampton himself has financed the establishment of the 'Canonbury Masonic Research Centre' (CMRC), which now holds an annual international conference, organised by curator, Carol McGilvery, which brings in the cream of academic talent from around the world in the growing research discipline of Freemasonry and Western Esotericism.

Sheffield University, since 2001, now has its own 'Centre for Research into Freemasonry' together with an endowed chair, held until 2007 by Professor Andrew Prescott.

The Department of Humanities and Social Sciences of the University of Exeter now runs an MA course in Western Esotericism, which includes modules on Freemasonry and Rosicrucianism, leading to greater academic awareness of these fascinating subjects. The director of the course is Professor Nicholas Goodrick-Clarke.

The Library and Museum of Freemasons' Hall, London, is open to the public in Great Queen Street, and is ably administered by museum director, Diane Clements. The museum organises frequent exhibitions and imaginative displays on many subjects related to the craft.

It is good to see so much that has long lain largely invisible at last coming into the light. The international journal *Freemasonry Today*, a colourful quarterly, again brings the best talent on the subject into a magazine that has set high standards of reporting, photography and presentation. The magazine has brought masons from around the world to a greater understanding of what it is they have joined and what they have in common, and of issues relevant to members and the world at large. It shows that Masonry is not a boring subject, but one that fascinates people well beyond the restrictions of membership.

This is all to the good. The further away we can get from the notion of Freemasonry as some kind of exclusive club, trading on mere social conviviality and a hearty meal, the better and more enjoyable Freemasonry may be for everyone, involved directly in the order or not. The rank system can appear somewhat tacky or base to those mindful of the higher ideals of the craft, and it does diminish the idea of all masons being in a common pursuit of wisdom and goodness. Those who like the system will obviously disagree, but they should recognise that the rank system has grown up over time, and like many a familiar branch of ivy, may need pruning, for the simple reason that it is obscuring something of greater significance beneath it.

It seems to me that attainment in any system should be entirely related to a significant achievement. Since the second degree, for example, is adamant that the mason should acquire knowledge of the seven liberal arts, then it would make sense for the 'rank system' to be concerned with such attainments. On the continent, it is not unknown for initiates to have to write an essay about what the craft means to them, their reasons for joining and so on. I don't see why the craft cannot generate a long-term course at a number of levels concerning the seven liberal arts.

The longterm future of the craft will be assured when the system functions as what it is: a system of attainment of relevance to all human intellectual and technological endeavours. The craft is certainly a part of English, and indeed global, heritage. Its survival and development has been remarkable. It has earned its place in the honourable polity of the world. It must go on earning that position through the labour of its members and sympathisers.

Truly civilised governments ought to recognise that Freemasons are a benefit to a country. A devoted, disciplined system of high morality and spiritual idealism will maintain the inner fabric of a land – and, as for Freemasonry's internationalism, no country today can afford to act as if it were entirely separate of all its neighbours. This was a masonic principle; it has now become a global principle. As Chevalier Ramsay gleaned from the works of his French mentor Fénelon in 1736, the world has become something of a republic, and every nation is a kind of family within it. Families argue; wisdom is required: the light of wisdom from above.

There are innumerable benefits to all countries that may be obtained from a clear application of time-honoured masons' principles. The world is currently threatened by extremist religious zealots who are convinced that their idea of the good supersedes any other nation's idea of the good, and that opponents can be scared into submission through violent acts and incessant and unreasoning propaganda. How can the religions of the world find common purpose; what means can be found to concentrate on the common good, even where there are significant differences of belief? Who or what can hold the ring when each side believes its interpretation of religion is a paramount truth?

Surely the long experience of Freemasonry has something important to offer our bewildered world in this regard. Notably, it has been long observed, by sages and seekers after truth, that the esoteric aspects of the great religious traditions find themselves in essential agreement one with the other. Authentic spiritual experience of life is, in principle, universally accessible. Spiritual experience, purified of false accretions, brings us to a universal awareness. Prophets have always declared that God is the same for all and every one, but that we see Him according to our limitations: limitations of consciousness that make the object of our desire appear different. Everything we think is constrained by the limitations of our consciousness.

As the psalmist says: 'None is righteous, no, not one.'

When we have the courage to encounter the genuine spiritual experience of another, we often have the wonderful sense of having met a traveller on the same road. Like Sir Robert Moray in the 17th century, we need to see the truth beyond appearance, the radiant star within, whose light is our light.

Christian *gnosis* (not necessarily of the radical and often misinterpreted kind), Islamic Sufism, Jewish Kabbalah, so-called 'pagan' Hermetism and Neoplatonism, the wisdom of the Hindu *Upanishads*, much ancient Chinese wisdom – all of these traditions (and many more) have brought humankind into 'man's deepest knowledge of himself'. Through following the homeward path, that which is most universal in man realises that at his deepest root, he partakes of the essence of the divine: the light which is from above and for which words are inadequate.

This spiritual knowledge is not an automatic or even instinctive natural consciousness, but something that can be approached through esoteric paths, honest searching or through grace and grace-full *acceptance*. It can be argued that a profound respect for these spiritual traditions will lead to greater understanding, not only of the religion or spiritual belief of individuals, but also of the religious traditions of others.

Freemasonry may yet be vindicated in its ancient tradition (not peculiar to itself) that there was once a unity between man and God, a world of pristine consciousness before humankind and religion were both divided by all-too-human superficiality, materialism, folly, greed, impatience and ignorance.

We do not need 'one world religion' (it is all too likely to have one monster running it), but we do perhaps need to know, as individuals, the *One* in all religions. From the experience, or search for the One, we may learn thereby how to transcend our differences, while yet celebrating the things we love in what we have come to know best. The One has spoken through many tongues in many books, but the voice itself is higher still. Who can honestly say that they have heard the full range of that voice? Every person can embark on the search that masonic tradition calls a search for 'the lost secrets'.

According to masonic allegory, the loss of knowledge came as a result of tragedy and folly. Indeed, a succession of tragedies, with their accompanying loss, have both distanced us from the essential knowledge, and, at the same time, made the need for the search that much more pressing and urgent. The temple falls; the temple is rebuilt. The secrets may seem distant, but the loss is close to our hearts. In our search, we tread where others have trod before us. This search does not find its end on earth, though there is a ladder in the desert that extends from here, if we can find it.

The Future Calls

Freemasonry cannot be forever associated with the secret society syndrome. It is not a secret society, though when persecuted it has been sensible to be discreet. But a healthy society will promote greater openness and understanding for all. It is not good for Freemasonry to hide itself; it has no more trade secrets to defend. The principles of Freemasonry, if they are good for Freemasons, are good for all people. Initiation is a very important principle in psychological development. There is no harm at all in having a degree of theatrical secrecy in the process of initiation. Many of the criminals who haunt the streets and crime statistics of developed and undeveloped nations, would rather go to prison than give up their special membership of gangs, membership earned through processes of initiation. If initiation to bad ways is often so attractive, should there not continue to be initiation into good ways?

Surely, our education systems could be well modelled on the conception of progressive initiation of the body and the mind. Fanciful or absurd as this may sound to some minds, the masonic tri-gradal system offers an excellent principle or model on which to reform education: to make our young people strong in mind and body, not just helpless exam-passers, tossed on to the dung-heap if they don't make the prescribed 'grade'. Life is an initiation.

The word education comes from the Latin, educare. The idea is to draw forth from the person what is there; not stuff them with information as if they were involved in the rites of some intellectual taxidermy. Masonry has a vital educational principle to offer the world. The entered apprentice learns his social place in the world, his responsibility to others, his need for pass-knowledge, to respect himself and to seek greater enlightenment. He learns to hold himself in an upright manner, befitting our species. The second degree enlightens the mind and brings the person to deeper levels of fellowship. The third degree brings wisdom, purpose, enlightenment and spiritual meaning to the person. From then on, he knows that life is a quest for self-knowledge. He has been given and has taken into himself that which is most natural to him: equilibrium, balance, tolerance, responsibility – and acception.

No sensible government would do anything to truncate the development of such wisdom. And let us be clear, Freemasonry stands in need of development and adaption, like all living things. The future of Freemasonry, declared the prophetic Ramsay all those years ago, will become the future of the world. This is not to say that – God forbid – Masonry will 'take over the world', as if some dread secret order were gnashing its teeth in secret readiness to grab the pinions of all that lives on this planet. The true 'Masonry' is inscribed, as Anderson wrote, on every human heart. *Everyone* is a secret mason! We just haven't realised it yet. We are all capable of playing our part in building and creating a better world, in conformity with the laws known, and unknown, of the universe. The sky is not the limit; the true lodge is as high as the heavens and as great and magnificent and beautiful as our extraordinary planet.

In the words of Alexander Pope, 'the proper study of man is man', and in a sense, Masonry only involves man's truest knowledge of himself; this explains its universality – and the hostility of partial or narrow visions of the hidden and manifest nature of humankind.

The future of the race is now an issue. This was the first challenge in the old legends of Freemasonry. How will the knowledge survive?

Seth had his pillars of knowledge built to survive fire and flood – the ancient catastrophe brought about, according to the Bible, by man's blindness, ignorance, stupidity and selfishness. Not only knowledge was preserved; Noah in his great Ark, his marvellous nave of life that only found rest on the earth's highest mountain – like our hungry souls – Noah preserved the very life of earth, the animals and family of men and women. While Noah built his ship, the commoners laughed. Would they join his 'lodge'? No, they wouldn't. Why build a ship on land while the sun is shining? A lesson for our times and all times. Masons have borne this message within their private *arca* of legends and declared privately that this man Noah was a true Master Mason. Now this message concerns the whole world.

There is also in the traditions of Masonry meat for the theologians and religious pundits who so often talk as if they have it all. Seek and ye shall find, said Jesus. There's no need to seek, if you know it all already. Now they too may look for the missing *shin* – the letter of fire and spirit – the fifth element that makes a living universe, and a new universe. He who trips on that stone will be broken, but he on whom the stone falls shall be winnowed.

This will be the message of Freemasonry Tomorrow.

Bibliography

Agrippa, Henry Cornelius, *Three Books of Occult Philosophy*, Moule, 1651

Anderson, Rev James, *The Constitutions of Free-Masons, Containing the History, Charges, Regulations &c. of that Most Ancient and Worshipful Fraternity*, London, 1723

The New Book of Constitutions of the Ancient and Honourable Fraternity of Free and Accepted Masons, published by Caesar Ward and Richard Chandler, London, 1738

Andreae, Johann Valentin (auth. susp.) *Fama Fraternitatis*, English translation: *The Fame and Confession of the Fraternity of R:C: Commonly, of the Rosie Cross*, Eugenius Philalethes [Thomas Vaughan] Printed by J. M. for Giles Calvert, 1652

ARS QUATUOR CORONATORUM, No 2076,

Transactions of the Quatuor Coronati Lodge (*AQC*): An invaluable collection of research papers into all aspects of Freemasonry published since the inception of the lodge in 1888. The current volume and some past transactions can be obtained from QCCC Ltd, Great Queen Street, London, WC2B 5AZ. Website for correspondence circle: www.qccc.co.uk. Papers consulted as follows:

Conder, Edward, *The Masons' Company*, paper in *AQC*, vol.9, 1896

Coulthurst, S. L. and Lawson, P. L., *The Lodge of Randle Holme at Chester*, paper in *AQC*, vol.45, 1932

Knoop, Douglas, & Jones, G. P., *Freemasonry and the Idea of Natural Religion*, AQC vol.56, 1943

Rogers, Norman, *The Lodge of Elias Ashmole*, paper in *AQC*, vol. 65, 1952

Williams, W. J., *The Use of the Word 'Freemason' before 1717*, paper in *AQC*, vol.48, 1935 (re Richard Ellom 'Freemason' of Lymm, Cheshire)

Ashmole, Elias, *Theatrum Chemicum Britannicum*, 1652

Baigent, Michael, & Leigh, Richard, *The Temple and the Lodge*, Cape, 1989

Barker Cryer, Rev Neville, *York Mysteries Revealed*, York, 2006

Barker Cryer, Rev Neville, *The Arch and the Rainbow*, Lewis Masonic, 1996

Béresniak, Daniel, *Symbols of Freemasonry*, Editions Assouline, Paris, 1997

Bullock, Stephen C, *Revolutionary Brotherhood: Freemasonry and the Transformation of the American Social Order, 1730-1840*, Chapel Hill, North Carolina, University of North Carolina Press, 1996

Cassirer, Ernst, ed., *The Renaissance Philosophy of Man*, University of Chicago Press, 1948

Churton, Tobias, *The Golden Builders, Alchemists, Rosicrucians and the First Free Masons*, Red Wheel-Weiser, 2005

Churton, Tobias, *Gnostic Philosophy*, Inner Traditions, Vermont, 2005

Churton, Tobias, *The Magus of Freemasonry*, Inner Traditions, Vermont, 2006

Clulee, Nicholas, *John Dee's Natural Philosophy*, RKP, 1988

Di Bernardo, Giuliano, *Freemasonry and its Image of Man*, Freestone, 1989

Dyer, Colin, *Symbolism in Craft Freemasonry*, Ian Allan Regalia, 1991

Emulation Ritual, Lewis Masonic, London, 1991

FREEMASONRY TODAY, Summer 1997-Winter 2005/06, (Quarterly journal, ed. Churton, Tobias, 1997-2000; Baigent, Michael, 2001-)

Gimpel, Jean, *The Cathedral Builders*, Michael Russell, 1983

Gilly, Carlos, *The Theophrastia Sancta – Paracelsianism in Conflict with the Established Churches,* In de Pelikaan, Amsterdam, 1994

Gould, Robert Freke, *The Quatuor Coronati & the Four Crowned Or Four Holy Martyrs*, Kessinger, 2005

Gould, Robert Freke, *The History of Freemasonry, its Antiquities, Symbols, Constitutions, Customs, etc*. London, Thomas C. Jack, 1884-1887

Hamill, John, *The Craft, A History of English Freemasonry*, Crucible, 1986

Henderson, Kent, & Pope, Tony, *Freemasonry Universal, Vol 1, The Americas*, Global Masonic Publications, Victoria, 1998

Hirst, Desirée, *Hidden Riches,* Eyre & Spottiswoode, 1964

Jackson, Keith B., *Beyond the Craft*, Lewis Masonic, 1994

Jacob, Prof Margaret, *The Radical Enlightenment: Pantheists, Freemasons and Republicans*, George Allen & Unwin, 1981

Jeffers, H. Paul, *Freemasons – Inside the World's Oldest Secret Society*, Citadel Press, 2005

Katz, Jacob, *Jews and Freemasons in Europe 1723-1939*, Cambridge, Mass., Harvard University Press, 1970

Knoop, Douglas, & Jones, G. P., *London Mason in the 17th Century*, Manchester University Press, 1935

Knoop, Douglas, *Genesis of Speculative Masonry*, Kessinger, 2005

Knoop, Douglas, & Jones, G. P., *Handlist of Masonic Documents*, Manchester University Press, 1942

Knoop, Douglas, & Jones, G. P., & Hamer, Douglas, *The Early Masonic Catechisms*, Manchester University Press, 1943

Early Masonic Pamphlets, Manchester University Press, 1945

Jackson, A. C. F., *Rose Croix*, Lewis Masonic, 1980

McArthur, J. E., *The Lodge of Edinburgh (Mary's Chapel) No 1, Quatercentenary of Minutes 1599-1999*, Edinburgh, 1999

McIntosh, Christopher, *The Rose Cross and the Age of Reason*, E. J. Brill, Leiden, 1992

McIntosh, Christopher, *Eliphas Lévi and the French Occult Revival*, Rider, 1972

Piatigorsky, Alexander, *Who's Afraid of Freemasons? The Phenomenon of Freemasonry*, London, Harvill Press, 1997

Roberts, John M., *Freemasonry: Possibilities of a Neglected Topic* in English Historical Review, 84, pp.323-335, 1969

Sadler, Henry, *Masonic Facts and Fiction*, London, 1887

Scanlan, Matthew, *The Mystery of the Acception, 1630-1723: A Fatal Flaw*, paper in *Heredom*, The Transactions of the Scottish Rite Research Society, ed. S. Brent Morris, Washington, D. C., vol.11, 2003. Also published as a paper in *Freemasonry on both sides of the Atlantic: Essays concerning the Craft in the British Isles, Europe, the United States and Mexico*, ed. R. William Weisberger, Columbia University Press, New York, 2002

Operative versus Speculative, paper in *Ars Macionica*, 5 June 2004, Brussels

Scanlan, Matthew, ed., *The Social Impact of Freemasonry on the Modern Western World*, London, CMRC, 2002, (A collection of ten essays)

Scholem, Gershom, *Major Trends in Jewish Mysticism*, Schocken Books, New York, 1947

Stevenson, David, *The Origins of Freemasonry, Scotland's Century, 1590-1710*, Cambridge University Press, 1988

Stevenson, David, *The First Freemasons*, Aberdeen University Press, 1988

Stevenson, David, *James Anderson, Man and Mason*, paper in
Freemasonry on both sides of the Atlantic: Essays concerning the Craft in the British Isles, Europe, the United States and Mexico, ed. R. William Weisberger, Columbia University Press, New York, 2002

Stewart, Trevor, ed., *Freemasonry and Religion, Many Faiths, One Brotherhood*, Canonbury Transactions, CMRC, 2006 (collection of papers read at Canonbury International Conference on Freemasonry, 2004)

Stoudt, John Joseph, *Sunrise to Eternity, A Study of Jacob Boehme's Life and Thought*, 1957

Ward, G. & Langcake, T. (ed.), *The Supersensual Life*, from *The Works of Jacob Behmen*, translated by William Law, London, 1764-81, 4 vols

Yarker, John, *Arcane Schools*, Belfast, 1909

Yates, Frances, *The Occult Philosophy in the Elizabethan Age*, RKP, 1979

Yates, Frances, *Giordano Bruno and the Hermetic Tradition*, RKP, 1964

Some useful websites

Adam Mclean's Alchemy website: www.levity.com/alchemy/home.html

Amsterdam Chair in Esoterica: www.amsterdamhermetica.nl

British Library – public catalogue: http://blpc.bl.uk

Freemasonry Today: www.freemasonrytoday.co.uk

Heredom – Scottish Rite Research Journal (has edited samples of past papers): www.srmason-sj.org/web/heredom.htm

Lane's Masonic Records online search:
freemasonry.london.museum/Lane_v3/ui/frame.htm

Library and Museum of Freemasonry (Grand Lodge Library's new title):
www.freemasonry.london.museum/catalogue.htm

Joost Ritman's Bibliotheca Philosophica Hermetica, Amsterdam:
www.ritmanlibrary.nl

Sheffield University – Centre for Research into Freemasonry
www.shef.ac.uk/~crf/

Warburg Library and Institute of Historical Research online search:
http://lib.sas.ac.uk/search/

Index